Marx and Social Justice

Historical Materialism Book Series

The Historical Materialism Book Series is a major publishing initiative of the radical left. The capitalist crisis of the twenty-first century has been met by a resurgence of interest in critical Marxist theory. At the same time, the publishing institutions committed to Marxism have contracted markedly since the high point of the 1970s. The Historical Materialism Book Series is dedicated to addressing this situation by making available important works of Marxist theory. The aim of the series is to publish important theoretical contributions as the basis for vigorous intellectual debate and exchange on the left.

The peer-reviewed series publishes original monographs, translated texts, and reprints of classics across the bounds of academic disciplinary agendas and across the divisions of the left. The series is particularly concerned to encourage the internationalization of Marxist debate and aims to translate significant studies from beyond the English-speaking world.

For a full list of titles in the Historical Materialism Book Series available in paperback from Haymarket Books, visit:
https://www.haymarketbooks.org/series_collections/1-historical-materialism

*For my grandchildren
Eliana Danielle
&
Warren Scott
and my sister
Rusty McCarthy, M.D.*

The self-confidence of the human being, freedom, has first of all to be aroused again in the hearts of these people [philistines]. Only this feeling, which vanished from the world with the Greeks, and under Christianity disappeared into the blue mist of the heavens, can again transform society into a community of human beings united for their highest aims, into a democratic state.

– KARL MARX, letter to Arnold Ruge, May 1843

Contents

Acknowledgements XIII

Introduction: The Ethical Archaeology of Justice in Marx 1

PART 1
Dialectic between the Ancients and the Moderns: Natural Law and Natural Rights

1 Natural Law and Natural Rights in Locke: Indifference and Incoherence of Liberalism 27
   Thomas Hobbes and the State of Nature and War 28
   Richard Hooker and the Laws of Nature and Ecclesiastical Polity 31
   Locke on Natural Rights and Natural Law 34
   Ethics and Structure in Natural Law 36
   Natural Law Limits to Natural Rights in the Original State of Nature 42
   Eclipse of Natural Law and Social Justice in the Second State of Nature 45
   Irrelevance of Natural Law, Incoherence of Liberalism, and the Return to Hobbes 51

2 Justice Beyond Liberalism: Natural Law and the Ethical Community in Hegel 72
   Early Theological Writings and Dreams of Classical Antiquity in Hegel 75
   Hegel's Natural Law and Critique of Liberalism and Natural Rights 80
   Social Ethics and Integration of Natural Law and Natural Rights 89
   Hegel's Philosophy of Right, Law, and the State as Objective Spirit 95
   Formation of the Ethical Life in the Family, Civil Society, and the State 100
   Marx's Critique of Hegel and the Revival of Classical Democracy in Spinoza and Rousseau 106

PART 2
Ethics, Virtue, and Natural Law in Marx

3 Civil and Legal Justice: Integrating Natural Rights and Natural Law   129
    Religious Prejudice, Judaism, and Civil Rights   130
    Natural Rights as Ideology and Alienation   138
    Transition of Politics from Pure Ideology to Human Rights and Emancipation   141
    Critique of Liberal Democracy and Contradictions between Economic and Political Rights   143
    Marx's Theory of Emancipation and Human Rights   148
    Natural Rights of Free Press and Universal Suffrage   150

4 Workplace Justice: Ethics, Virtue, and Human Freedom   163
    Alienation and the Virtue of Work and Self-Determination   165
    Work as Productive Life and Creative Beauty   170
    Ethics, Human Needs, and Natural Law   175
    Virtue and Late Medieval Thomistic Natural Law   180

5 Ecological Justice: Historical Materialism and the Dialectic of Nature and Society   192
    Alienation of Production, Labour, and Nature   195
    Dialectic of Nature and the Alienation of Consciousness   201
    Natural Science as the Objectification and Social Praxis of Species Being   204
    Science as Objectivity and Alienation   206
    Social Metabolism, Contradictions, and Ecological Crises   210
    Social Justice and the Natural Laws of Ethics and Ecology   216

PART 3
Structures of Democracy, Economy, and Social Justice in Marx

6 Distributive Justice: Justice of Consumption, Economic Redistribution, and Social Reciprocity   235
    Labour, Nature, and Society in the *Gotha Program*   236
    Equality, Fair Distribution, and the Public Expenses of Production   239
    Distribution, Fairness, and the Means of Social Consumption   241
    Socialism, Self-Realisation, and Human Need   247

Critique of Reformist and Vulgar Socialism – Happiness without Meaning   255

7 Political Justice: Ethics and the Good Life of Democratic Socialism   272
    Franco-Prussian War and the Formation of the Paris Commune of 1871   273
    Dismantling the Old State and Rise of Political Democracy in the Commune   278
    Organisation of Labour and Economic Democracy   282
    'Declaration to the French People' and the Social Programmes of the Commune   285
    Marx, Lincoln, and the Human Emancipation from Racial and Wage Slavery   291

8 Economic Justice: Ethics, Production, and the Critique of Chrematistics and Political Economy   309
    Commodities, Exchange, and the Labour Theory of Value   314
    Labour Power, Surplus Value, and the Alienation of Chrematistic Production   322
    Natural Law of Contradictions, Crises, and Capital   327
    Natural Law of Justice and Natural Law of Value   338

Bibliography   363
Index   386

Acknowledgements

There is too little time and too little space to thank all those individuals who have played an important role in helping to create this book. I am always reluctant to mention particular individuals for fear of leaving someone out. However, I would like to thank my many students at Kenyon College who have enthusiastically participated in classroom discussions that have helped me reformulate complex ideas into analytically clear thoughts and theories. My courses in classical and contemporary social theory, German social theory, and social justice have been instrumental in producing this work. With the help of these wonderful students, I have had the opportunity to teach my books first before their actual publication. Thanks to my son, Devin, for his aesthetically beautiful and inspiring artwork that appears as the frontispiece; he has captured the heart and soul of this book in his painting of Dike, the Greek goddess, balancing the possibilities of justice in the integration of the Ancients and the Moderns. I would be remiss if I did not mention my old friend and colleague Royal Rhodes for his continued intellectual encouragement and spiritual support. I would also like to thank Hays Stone for her friendship and editorial dedication in helping to make this a better work. Finally, I would like to express my appreciation to Michael Thompson for publishing my essay 'Last of the Schoolmen' in his edited anthology *Constructing Marxist Ethics: Critique, Normativity, Praxis* (Leiden: Brill, 2015). It was this piece that precipitated in my mind the need to write a much longer work on Marx's theory of social justice; it also provided the starting point and foundation for the ideas and pages that follow.

INTRODUCTION

The Ethical Archaeology of Justice in Marx

In the 1970s and 80s in the United States there was a brief renaissance in Marxian scholarship which focused on whether or not Karl Marx had a theory of justice in his writings. Part of the inquiry by Analytical Marxists became known as the Tucker-Wood thesis. It was an important contribution to the rediscovery of Marx's discussion on issues of justice and morality in the context of his overall critique of political economy. Within this debate there were three distinct strands of thought: there were the followers of Robert Tucker and Allen Wood who maintained that because of his theory of moral ideology and historical materialism, Marx eschewed grounding his critical social thought in any moral philosophy or theory of justice; there were those who like Ziyad Husami and Gary Young argued for a distinctive theory of juridical justice in Marx's early and later writings based on legal rights and economic distribution; and, finally, there was a third group of authors who agreed with the fundamental thesis of Tucker and Wood, thus rejecting any consideration of justice in Marx, but who also claimed that he did develop a moral philosophy based on the principles of freedom, self-determination, self-realisation, well-being, and human dignity.[1] Much of this discussion hinges on the interpretation of a limited number of texts in Marx's writings, emphasising the *German Ideology*, *Manifesto of the Communist Party*, the first volume of *Capital*, and the *Critique of the Gotha Program*.

This manuscript outlining Marx's theory of social justice takes a different approach from those mentioned above. Rather than continuing to examine the same texts from a different perspective, it may be useful to approach the issue from an entirely different vantage point by providing a broader and more comprehensive theoretical context to the texts, thereby mapping out the internal dynamics and structure of Marx's overall theory of political economy. That is, by a textual mapping of the overall outline and structure of Marx's early and later writings, we begin to see an interesting internal coherence and logic that closely mirrors Aristotle's ethics, politics, and physics. The specific comparisons between the two authors have already been examined in detail elsewhere by a number of scholars and it is not the goal of this work to repeat these earlier writings. In this work, however, we will examine the deep archaeological layers of Marx's works and map out his overall design that mirrors Aristotle's formal definition of justice as it develops throughout his intellectual and political career. We will see that Marx's definition of justice fits the overall design of

Aristotle's writings and provides it with an organisation and coherence that at first does not surface using traditional methods of exegesis. A major difficulty with the thesis developed by Tucker and Wood is that it begins with a definition of justice that is simply not a reflection of Marx's own understanding of the issues.[2]

The Tucker-Wood thesis is based on a two-part definition of justice that highlights the law, rights, wage contracts, and the economic distribution of benefits and income. The whole focus of this tradition is directed at Marx's criticisms of the natural rights of man in the French *Declaration of the Rights of Man and of the Citizen* (1793) and the fair and equitable distribution of income in the wage contract between capital and labour. Both features of justice – rights and distribution – are grounded in a labour theory of value and the capitalist defence of the rights of property and the labour market that have clearly been rejected by Marx as the basis for a future democratic and socialist society. The ideals of equality and fairness at the heart of this definition of bourgeois legal and civil justice rest upon a historically limited ideal of individual freedom that is tied to the materialism and utilitarianism of capitalist production and a market economy. According to Tucker and Wood, with a revolutionary transformation of industry, capital, and class within this historical economy, its corresponding ideals of justice will also disappear. It is Marx's theory of historical materialism and the social relations between the economic base and political/cultural superstructure that provide the insight that politics under capitalism is an unnecessary mystification and juridical illusion designed to conceal the exploitation and domination rampant in a class society. For these reasons, revolution will dissolve the economic foundation of society along with its political ideals of liberal justice. Tucker recognises that the application of justice to the wage contract in the workplace has some 'superficial plausibility', but that results from an inability to understand the nature of work, subsistence wages, and the wage contract in a capitalist economy, along with an inability to appreciate how moral principles are derived from and are expressions of the prevailing economic relations of civil society. Tucker summarises his analysis of *Capital* on this position when he writes: 'It [wage agreement] is nowise an injustice because the subsistence wage is precisely what the commodity labour power, sold by the worker to the employer, is worth according to the laws of commodity production'.[3]

The wage relationship and the creation of surplus value may be a form of exploitation, but it is not unjust according to the labour contract and market standards applied. The capitalist purchases a commodity and the worker receives a wage to recompense and replace the loss of labour power; this is the law of equivalency exchange between the commodity of labour power and the wages contracted in the workplace. By the standards of the wage agreement, the capitalist has a right to the property, production, and surplus value created in production and consumption. The amount of subsistence wages reflects the full value of labour power sold on the market and the capitalist has the right to any surplus or profits created by this mode of production. Distribution is determined by exchange value and the laws of market production. Capitalists have paid a fair price on the open market for the labour power of the worker for a full day; work and commodities produced over and above that necessary for the sustenance of the labourer belong to the capitalist as legitimate profits. This is the standard of justice and rights inherent in the law of commodity exchange and thus the only liberal standard capable of being used by Marx.[4] There are no transcending values in the Tucker-Wood perspective that could judge the economic system as unjust since, as Marx has clearly stated in *The German Ideology* (1845), the ethical and political values are tied to the mode of production of each historical period.

> The production of ideas, of conceptions, of consciousness, is at first directly interwoven with the material activity and the material intercourse of men, the language of real life ... The same applies to mental production as expressed in the language of politics, laws, morality, religion, metaphysics of a people. Men are the producers of their concepts, ideas, etc. – real, active men, as they are conditioned by a definite development of their productive forces and of the intercourse corresponding to these, up to its furthest forms.[5]

Tucker further argues that any attempt to impose external and autonomous standards or moral principles on the workplace is 'crass, vulgar, superficial, and simply wrongheaded'.[6] By the standards of commodity production and market exchange, no injustice has occurred. He writes: 'Each mode of production has its own mode of distribution and its own form of equity, and it is meaningless to pass judgment on it from some other point of view. Thus, capitalism, for Marx and Engels, is evil but not inequitable'.[7]

Tucker then quickly turns his focus from rights to distribution in his analysis of the *Gotha Program* of 1875: 'It should be clear in the light of all this that a fair distribution of the proceeds of labour is not the moral goal of Marx. The ideal of distributive justice is a complete stranger in the mental universe of Marxism'.[8] And since there are no higher principles or ideals to which we might appeal, we have to recognise that the workplace contract is, in fact, an expression of bourgeois justice. According to Tucker's reading of Marx on the issue of fair distribution, justice can never be an expression of a higher goal, but is, instead, an articulation of the values of a specific mode of production to which it is bound.[9] Wood continues to develop Tucker's ideas and expands upon them: Although Marx does not reject capitalism because it is an unjust social system, Wood recognises that Marx is critical of the social system because of the social evils of human misery, alienation, slavery, and the 'grinding poverty, the degradation and emptiness of their mode of life, the precariousness of their very existence' created by an intolerable class society.[10] Wood clearly states his position in the following: 'As I read him, Marx bases his critique of capitalism on the claim that it frustrates many important *nonmoral* goods: self-actualization, security, physical health, comfort, community, freedom ... But Marx never claims that these goods ought to be provided to people because they have a *right* to them, or because *justice* (or some other moral norm) demands it'.[11]

Wood seems to be reducing Marx to a non-moral utilitarian interested in revolutionising the economy for the material well-being of its citizens. However, there is no moral rejection of capitalism since, by Wood's definition, this would require relying on the ethical principles of rights and justice which can only reaffirm capitalist production. These values are only forms of ideology used to confuse, oppress, and justify the existing social relations of production. Marx is caught in a theoretical dilemma between his critical science and historical materialism. He cannot use ethics to undermine the normative foundations of the social system since they themselves are only a product of the material conditions of human life. Ethical principles have no validity outside the society that gave birth to them; they can never be used to reject the system which created them in the first place. And, thus, there are no legitimate moral values outside the system capable of challenging it. Since all morals are bourgeois prejudices and ideological interests, the purpose of morals and justice is to legitimate the social system, ensure social stability, and promote and protect class interests.[12] Wood never explains why self-realisation, freedom, liberation, and prosperity are not moral categories. Nor are there any legitimate concepts of justice beyond the limits established by liberalism. Wood is bounded on one side by his views of moral ideology and legal apologetics in historical materialism, and on the other by the limitation of justice to liberal categories only capable of justifying the existing economic reality (empiricism). Justice is an empty category of pure liberal prejudice and mystification and, therefore, cannot be used for human emancipation. It is this complex relationship among ethics, critique, and science that will be a central theme in the work that follows.

According to Wood, Marx rejected the ethical ideals of Pierre-Joseph Proudhon and Ferdinand Lassalle, who viewed socialism 'as a means of securing justice, equality, and the rights of man'.[13] Marx could not rely on justice as the standard for the critique of capitalism because justice was a formal, legal category. In order to validate his position, Wood, referring to Engels's 'The Housing Question' (1872), contends that justice is 'fundamentally a juridical or legal (*rechtlich*) concept, a concept related to the law (*Recht*) and to the rights (*Rechte*) men have under it. The concepts of right and justice are for them the highest rational standards by which laws, social institutions, and human actions may be judged from a juridical point of view'.[14] Although Wood argues that this juridical concept of justice is the foundation of Western society all the way back to Plato, as well as being 'the highest measure of all social things',[15] he maintains that it is the standard that Marx will ultimately reject as the basis for the social evaluation of society since it is too narrow – it is an 'essentially one-sided' and 'distorted concept of that reality'.[16] Wood is also critical of idealising or romanticising the Greek world in order to obtain the horizons from which to make an ethical critique of capitalism. He interprets Marx as rejecting the theoretical project of both Jean-Jacques Rousseau and G.W.F. Hegel 'to idealize the political life of the ancient world and to long for its restoration or to conceive of the modern state as a principle of social unity to be imposed on the fragmented world of capitalism'.[17] The main thesis of this book will be that Marx's inspiration for his critique of modernity lies in the very appropriation of the ethical and political ideals of antiquity in the works of Aristotle through Rousseau and Hegel.

Wood continues to argue against a Marxian concept of justice by emphasising the historical foundation of all principles of justice within a historically relative mode of production. Thus there can be no universal principles of natural law or philosophy which can be the basis for social critique. Wood claims that 'abstracted from a concrete historical context, all formal philosophical principles of justice are empty and distorting, since they encourage us to treat the concrete context of an act or institution as accidental, inessential, a mere occasion for the pure rational form to manifest itself'.[18] From this perspective, Marx's real critique of capitalism rests not upon a theory of justice, but upon a theory of economic and historical reality – that is, upon his theory of value, exchange, and the rising organic composition of capital which produces poverty, class inequality, and economic crises. Wood also mentions that by emphasising issues of law and rights, some Marxist thinkers have inadvertently switched their emphasis in the study of economic exploitation and alienation from production to distribution and the law. With any self-conscious revolution, a change in the nature of distribution and the formal structure of the law will not advance a truly revolutionary transformation but will miss the heart of Marx's critique of industrial society. Finally, a post-capitalist theory of justice and rights is inapplicable as the basis of critique and social change 'since any such standards would not be rationally applicable to capitalism at all, any such condemnation would be mistaken, confused, and without foundation'.[19] A legal or social ideal of an 'eternal juridical structure' cannot be critically applied to the social reality because of Marx's theory of historical materialism; ideals are reflections and expressions of the mode of production (materialism), they are not the essence of capitalism (idealism). Wood pushes this mechanical and deterministic argument to its logical conclusion by arguing that the state, rights, and justice will not be necessary in a truly free, classless society since there will be an abundance of material wealth for all.

Wood appears legitimately fearful that by measuring modernity by forms of justice, social criticism will be reduced to abstract moralising, while social change will become another kind of moral therapy or political reformism. Nothing substantive or essential will result from moral protest that does not understand the nature of industry, production, and class structure. Revolution would be reduced to correcting ethical abuses in the social system while leaving its oppressive structures intact. The transformation of human consciousness is not the final goal of social change. It is for these very reasons that Wood argues that Marx rejects an emphasis on moral ideology and the useless and mystified trivia which focuses upon issues of rights, equality, and fair distribution; they are not the underlying causes of the mode of production nor can they be the basis for social change.[20] Neither a simple transformation of distribution enforcing the equalisation of income and wealth nor the expansion of natural rights to liberty and property to a broader population would change the alienation and exploitation of the mode of production. Using Marx's theory of historical materialism and revolution, Wood emphasises that moral and political ideals cannot be the basis for his critique and transformation of the structural foundations of the technical forces and social relations of capitalist production.

Tucker and Wood present many interesting and valuable ideas for our consideration, as do the other two distinct groups of critics of their main thesis within Analytical Marxism. Whether they view Marx's social critique as grounded in science and historical positivism (Tucker, Wood, Derek Allen, Allen Buchanan, Andrew Collier, and Anthony Skillen), legal and distributive justice (Husami, Young, Norman Geras, G.A. Cohen, Jon Elster, William Shaw, Nancy Holmstrom, and Donald van de Veer), or an alternative ethical theory (Allen Brenkert, Richard Miller, Stephen Lukes, and Douglas Kellner), all three groups accept the narrow judicial and political definition of justice as the basis for further discussion. This is the case whether or not they agree with the original Tucker-Wood thesis or whether they believe that Marx had a theory of justice. However, it is this very definition of justice in Analytical Marxism that is most problematic and the subject of the following inquiry. In fact, Marx does have a theory of social justice, but it is uncovered not only by a close exegesis of his enormous theoretical output but also by a critical and hermeneutical mapping of his whole work in relationship to Greek philosophy. In spite of the fact that Marx infrequently used the term 'justice' and never formally developed it in his writings, the whole of his critique of political economy is framed within the context of Aristotle's theory of ethics, politics, and social justice.[21] In his contribution to this discussion, Gary Young, in 'Doing Marx Justice', methodically traces Marx's references to robbery, theft, exploitation, plunder, and greed throughout his writings as he maintains that these ideas are the vocabulary of justice. Young is also in agreement with Husami that the 'ruling ideas of an age do not exhaust the meaning or content of value expressions. It is possible to criticise a society using the same words its supporters invoke to defend it'.[22] At this point I would simply add to the above comment by Young that the ruling ideas are dialectically part of a much broader tradition that goes back to classical antiquity that must also be considered. This is not to say that Aristotle was the only influence on his theory of justice, just that he was central to his intellectual development. There were a number of other traditions that affected Marx's theory. The following treatise will emphasise the visionary imagination and political wisdom of the Hellenic community in Athens.

The overall outline and logic of Marx's analysis of capitalist production is organised around Aristotle's *Nicomachean Ethics* and *Politics* – that is, from his earliest to his later writings, Marx designs a theory of justice reflecting the formal structure of Aristotle's theory of virtue, politics, and social justice. In more Hegelian terminology, he integrates moral philosophy (Kant) and social ethics (Hegel) through his critical historical science based on a radical appropriation of classical nineteenth-century economics. The final exercise of this introduction is to create an interpretive design of the contours and forms of justice in both Aristotle and Marx. Once this is accomplished, there will be no need to compare the two authors, but simply to proceed to examine in more detail the various forms of justice in Marx in each of the following chapters. What we will see is that Marx never accepts the limited juridical view of justice in the fashion presented by Tucker and Wood except as a tentative beginning to an immanent critique of capitalism – measuring the justification and contradictions of capitalism by its own legal standards of rights and distribution. He, instead, appropriates the history of the Western tradition of natural law from ancient Greek philosophy to medieval Christianity in the form of Aristotelian social ethics. Unlike the dualism found in the Tucker-Wood thesis between science (historical materialism) and ethics (moral values), Marx integrates ethics, politics, science, and history into his overall social theory.

The various chapters on Marx's theory of social justice parallel in interesting and unexpected ways the logic and formal design of justice found in Aristotle's writings. According to Aristotle, justice is a social virtue concerned mainly with institutional issues of legal, political, and economic equality, fairness, and the appropriate allocation of the common goods of the household and polity within a moral economy. There are three distinct forms of particular justice: rectificatory or corrective justice which focuses on equality and the rebalancing of legal transgressions and unjust actions in civil and criminal cases; reciprocal or commutative justice which deals with the natural fairness in economic exchanges among farmers, workers, artisans, and foreigners based on the ethical principles of proportional need, grace, friendship, and kindness; and distributive justice which stresses the proper distribution of public property, social wealth, and political offices in the polis. Finally, universal or political justice deals with 'the friendship of brothers' or love of one's fellow citizens (*philia*) in political participation, public discourse, and the development of practical wisdom and a virtuous character in an ideal democratic community based on an organic relationship with nature. Within political justice Aristotle examines issues of the ideal, best, and correct political constitutions.

Aristotle	Marx
Ethics, Virtue and Natural Law	
1 Rectificatory Justice, Law, and Politics	Civil and Legal Justice
2 Ethics, Virtue, and Practical Wisdom	Virtue and Workplace Justice
3 Physics and Metaphysics of Organic Nature	Ecological Justice
Politics, Economy, and Democracy	
4 Particular Justice, Reciprocity, and Oikonomike	Distributive Justice
5 Universal Justice, Politics, and Democracy	Political Justice
6 Chrematistike and Critique	Economic Justice[23]

All those areas in Analytical Marxism and Enlightenment philosophy that were not considered part of justice or moral philosophy more broadly – species being, self-realisation, community, human dignity, etc. – have now been incorporated into a comprehensive and critical theory of social ethics (*Sittlichkeit*) that reintegrates legal, workplace, ecological, distributive, political, and economic justice. The Greek view of justice is holistic as it presents the totality of society, its social institutions, and the integrative functions of laws, customs, and traditions. Aristotle's theory of justice then is a 'state of character which makes people disposed to do what is just and makes them act justly and wish for what is just'.[24] Justice refers to the manner in which individual citizens develop their main function or purpose in life towards the full realisation of their character, moral and intellectual virtues, and reason in a polity based on economic sharing and grace, equality, friendship, and political participation. Aristotle's view incorporates issues of economic and political justice, along with other private and public issues of virtue, happiness, knowledge, practical wisdom, citizenship, and the household economy.[25] And it is this very breadth of understanding that influences Marx's framing of his own definition of justice. According to Aristotle, justice involves living the virtuous and rational life of the soul within a political and economic system that encourages self-realisation, freedom, and political self-determination. This approach to justice requires the integration of ethics (character, virtue, and reason) and politics (economics, constitutions, and deliberative democracy) that has been lost since the Enlightenment.[26]

Because the law is not separated from society, the individual from the community, politics from economics, morality from ethics, or virtue from politics, Aristotle's theory of justice encompasses the whole social system. The liberal and Enlightenment view of justice, limited as it is to issues of individual rights and fair distribution, was not the standard of social critique used by Marx. Rather he rewrote Aristotle's ethics and politics for the modern era, expanded the notion of practical activity (*praxis*) to include creative work and political understanding, and rejected capitalism using the standards of the Western ideal of natural law from the ancient Greeks, medieval Christians, and modern Idealists. Following in these traditions, justice is the good and virtuous life within a free society. It is this view that will cement the classical horizons of Marx's own theory of social justice. In Aristotle, there are particular chapters in his works on ethics and politics devoted not only to a discussion of universal and particular justice, but also to a broader range of classical issues on virtue and happiness, knowledge and practical wisdom, economic reciprocity and human need, and political participation and public deliberation in a democratic polity.[27] Marx, drawing upon this tradition, views justice as a form of ethical community based on beneficence, equality, and freedom which nurtures and enhances the function or end of humanity towards (1) the self-realisation and self-determination of its species being; (2) physical well-being and spiritual enlightenment; (3) human creativity, virtue, and happiness in the workplace; (4) a symbiotic balance between humanity and nature; (5) the communal fulfilment of economic reciprocity and need; and, finally, (6) the industrial democracy of producers' co-operatives and workers' communes, as well as the political democracy of human rights and emancipation. Marx redesigns these issues in terms of natural law based on human nature (species being), human needs (self-realisation and self-determination), the natural environment, and democracy (equality, freedom, and participation).

In conclusion, Marx's theory of justice is not defined by the rights of man to life, liberty, and property or the fair distribution of commodities, exchange value, and wage labour, but rather is defined by the institutions, structures, and cultural values that promote virtue, reason, creative productivity, and caring friendship in the private (ethics) and public (politics) spheres. Justice refers to the institutional actualisation of full human potentiality as species and moral beings who create their own lives, values, and history according to the laws of beauty. Although there will be substantive differences between Aristotle and Marx about what some of these categories mean, their overall forms and mapping of justice correspond in striking ways. This book will begin with John Locke and an analysis of his initial attempts in the *Second Treatise of Government* (1690) to integrate the ancient natural law of love, compassion, fellowship, dignity, and equality with the modern natural rights to life, liberty, health, and property into his seventeenth-century theory of the state and civil society. Hegel, in turn, attempts to accomplish the same ends in the nineteenth century by constructing a modern liberal state according to the Greek ideals of an integrated and ethical community. In his early writings, as he moves from an examination of religion, reason, and the spirit to his later writings on law, rights, and the state, he creates a synthesis of liberalism and individualism with the communal good and general will. Although both attempts failed, they provided Marx with the inspiration and vision that opened an alternative ethical path to the future.[28]

As Marx took a different turn from either Locke or Hegel, he created the conditions for a substantive and objective break with both modern liberalism and capitalism by redefining the nature of social justice and classical democracy from the dreams and ideals of the ancients. This book is organised around the different elements or forms of his theory of justice starting with:

1. Legal and Civil Justice: Human and Political Rights
2. Workplace Justice: Virtue, Species Being, and Social Praxis
3. Ecological Justice: Consciousness, Nature, and Moral Ecology
4. Distributive Justice: Grace, Reciprocity, and Human Needs

5. Political Justice: Democracy and Workers' Co-operatives in the Commune
6. Economic Justice: Critique of Chrematistics and Unnatural Political Economy and Wealth Acquisition

And it is this view of justice and natural law based on virtue, law, species being, nature, and participatory democracy that will form the groundwork for his integration of the ancients and moderns in a new theory of political community and social ethics beyond liberalism. Finally, in his later writings Marx will integrate his theory of the natural law of ethics and social justice with his economic theory of the historical natural law of value and capitalist production expressed in the overproduction of capital, tendential fall in the rate of profit, high unemployment, and economic crises. Although they are quite distinct understandings of natural law, it is the natural law of capital which makes the classical natural law impossible in modernity. By integrating the two forms of natural law, Marx succeeds in rejoining ethics and economics into his comprehensive critical social theory; his theory of justice represents an integral part of his critique and science of political economy.

Notes

1   *The Tucker-Wood Thesis and its Critics*: Some of the key works representative of this thesis include: Robert Tucker, *Philosophy and Myth in Karl Marx* (Cambridge, UK: Cambridge University Press, 1961) and *The Marxian Revolutionary Idea* (New York, NY: W.W. Norton and Company, 1969) and Allen Wood, 'The Marxian Critique of Justice', in *Marx, Justice, and History*, ed. Marshall Cohen, Thomas Nagel, and Thomas Scanlon (Princeton, NJ: Princeton University Press, 1980), pp. 3–41, 'Marx on Right and Justice: A Reply to Husami', *Philosophy & Public Affairs* 8, 3 (1979): 267–95 and in *Marx, Justice, and History*, pp. 106–34, and *Karl Marx* (London: Routledge and Kegan Paul, 1981). The thesis was criticised and rejected by a number of theorists including: Ziyad Husami, 'Marx on Distributive Justice', *Philosophy & Public Affairs* 8, 1 (Autumn 1978): 27–64 and Kai Nielsen, 'Marx on Justice: The Tucker-Wood Thesis Revisited', in *Marxism and the Moral Point of View: Morality, Ideology, and Historical Materialism* (Boulder, CO: Westview Press, 1989), pp. 155–92. An overview and summary of this debate may be found in Norman Geras, 'The Controversy about Marx and Justice', *New Left Review*, I, 150 (March–April 1985): 47–85 and 'Bringing Marx to Justice: An Addendum and Rejoinder', *New Left Review*, I, 195 (September–October 1992); Steven Lukes, *Marxism and Morality* (Oxford: Clarendon Press, 1985), pp. 48–70; Kai Nielsen, 'Marx, Engels and Lenin on Justice: The Critique of the Gotha Program', *Studies in Soviet Thought*, 32, 2 (1986): 59–60; R.G. Peffer, *Marxism, Morality, and Social Justice* (Princeton, NJ: Princeton University Press, 1990), pp. 169–211; Thomas Mayer, *Analytical Marxism* (Thousand Oaks, CA: Sage Publications, 1994); Robert Sweet, *Marx, Morality and the Virtue of Beneficence* (Lanham, MD: University Press of America, 2002); and Haroon

Rashid, 'Making Sense of Marxian Concept of Justice', *Indian Philosophical Journal*, 24, 4 (October 2002): 445–69.

Both Nielsen and Peffer view the Tucker-Wood thesis mainly as a debate within Analytical Marxism over the issues of moralism and anti-moralism in Marx, that is, over whether or not Marx has a theory of justice. There are three fundamental approaches to these issues: (1) the anti-moralist position, which stresses issues of scientific socialism, positivism, historical materialism, technological determinism, economic predictions, and the rejection of moralism or idealism, is represented by Robert Tucker, Allen Wood, Derek Allen, Andrew Collier, Allen Buchanan, and Anthony Skillen; (2) the second perspective, which stresses Marx's theory of juridical and civil justice, is represented by Ziyad Husami, Gary Young, Norman Geras, G.A. Cohen, Jon Elster, William Shaw, Nancy Holmstrom, and Donald van den Veer; and (3) the third school of thought, which contends that Marx did have an ethical theory grounded in his ideas of alienation, distribution, moral philosophy, social ethics, fairness, equality, and freedom, but not one based on a theory of justice, includes Allen Brenkert, Richard Miller, Stephen Lukes, and Douglas Kellner.

Taking a different position, Geras examines the same literature but from a narrower perspective of whether Marx condemns capitalism from the principles of justice or from another normative position. Geras contends that as Marxists they all agree that Marx offered a moral condemnation of capitalism. (Geras, 'The Controversy over Marx and Justice', pp. 1–2). Others who are outside of this debate within analytic philosophy and positivist science and who have taken a moral, ethical, or Hegelian view of Marx's social theory include Eugene Kamenka, Shlomo Avineri, and Philip Kain. For more recent writings on Marx and ethics, see the essays in Michael Thompson, ed., *Constructing Marxist Ethics: Critique, Normativity, Praxis* (Leiden: Brill, 2015).

Summarising the Tucker-Wood thesis, Nielsen in his Introduction to *Marx and Morality*, ed. Kai Nielsen and Steven Patten, *Canadian Journal of Philosophy*, supplementary volume 7 (1981) writes: 'For Marx and Engels, as Tucker and Wood read them, justice is not and cannot be an abstract general standard by which human reason, in or out of reflective equilibrium, assesses social practices, institutions, whole socio-economic formulations such as capitalism or socialism or ways of life ... Marx does, of course, condemn capitalism for its exploitation of people, its economic instability, its creating and sustaining of servitude and for its failure ... to satisfy as fully as possible human wants and needs. But he does not, Tucker and Wood paradoxically claim, condemn it morally or condemn it on the basis of even some implicit normative ethical theory' (1981, p. 8).

2   One could argue that the key representatives of the Tucker-Wood thesis use a liberal and Rawlsian definition of justice: In his work *Defining Environmental Justice* (Oxford: Oxford University Press, 2007), David Schlosberg writes regarding the followers of John Rawls's theory of justice: 'They focused on a conception of justice defined solely as the distribution of goods in a society and the best principles by which to distribute those goods' (p. 3). Schlosberg goes on to say that this view articulated in Rawls's *A Theory of Justice* is inadequate because there are 'a number of additional ways of understanding the processes of justice and injustice' (pp. 4, 11–12). Schlosberg wishes to open the discussion with a broader theory of justice based on ideas of recognition and capacities (functions)

initiated by authors such as Iris Young, Nancy Fraser, Axel Honneth, Amartya Sen, and Martha Nussbaum.

There is a philosophical irony in this whole discussion within analytic philosophy since the existence or non-existence of a Marxian theory of justice in the debates surrounding the Tucker-Wood thesis revolve fundamentally around a liberal standard of justice; a Marxian theory of justice is rejected because it ultimately does not conform to the standards established by liberalism or historical materialism. This latter position has been held by Marxist theorists who have separated the science of historical materialism from ethics. Ronald Meek has written: 'The labour theory was a scientific tool for the analysis of capitalist reality, and to suggest that it embodied a particular ethical or political viewpoint was simply to mix up economics and morality' (Ronald Meek, *Studies in the Labour Theory of Value* [New York, NY: International Publishers, 1956], p. 128).

3   Tucker, *Philosophy and Myth in Karl Marx*, p. 19.

4   Nielsen, 'Introduction', to *Marx and Morality*, p. 9. The form of justice accepted in a capitalist society is that defined, 'conditioned', and 'determined' by capitalist production. Because justice can only be tied to a particular mode of production within Marx's theory of historical materialism, the central ethical finding is 'that this standard of justice is the only standard applicable to the mode of production' (ibid.). Taking Marx's historical materialism and using it as the foundation for a theory of justice is the key to the Tucker-Wood thesis. There are no other possible theories of justice applicable to a capitalist society since the only legitimate ones are those produced by that society itself. Since all moral values are a product of a particular type of society, there can be no moral values that transcend the social system and criticise it from the outside. The function of bourgeois law is legitimation, not critique. The central question remains: Is this the only moral standard by which capitalism can be evaluated? The second question that one finds in Wood's analysis is that of moral dualism: Is there a distinction between moral and nonmoral values that constitutes our understanding of justice? The Tucker-Wood thesis reduces moral values to rights and distribution. (See endnote 11). These two arguments are viciously circular in nature and mean that Marx could only apply the liberal standards of justice or none at all. Historical materialism has been used in a reductionist and naturalistic fashion to inhibit the grounding of a critique of political economy in ethics and justice, thereby reinforcing a mechanical, predictive, and positivist view of science in Marx. Knowledge as a practical (ethical) and critical (contradictions and crises) science is lost as the broad range of critical, historical, and dialectical analyses is replaced by liberal justice and Enlightenment science. Marx's writings are stripped of any ties to the ancient Greek world or to the modern world of German idealism. According to Tucker and Wood, Marx 'does not condemn it [capitalism] morally or condemn it on the basis of even some implicit normative ethical theory' (p. 8).

5   Karl Marx, *The German Ideology* (New York, NY: International Publishers, 1965), pp. 13–14; *Karl Marx/Friedrich Engels Werke* (*MEW*), Band 3 (Berlin: Dietz Verlag, 1978), pp. 13–14. *Historical Materialism and Moral Values*: In the preface to *A Contribution to the Critique of Political Economy* (New York, NY: International Publishers, 1970), Marx again outlines the basic features of historical materialism: 'The totality of these relations of production constitutes the economic structure of society, the real foundations on which arises a legal and

political superstructure and to which correspond definite forms of social consciousness. The mode of production of material life conditions the general process of social, political, and intellectual life' (20–1; *Karl Marx/Friedrich Engels Werke* [*MEW*], Band 13 [Berlin: Dietz Verlag, 1961], pp. 8–9). The theory of historical materialism expresses how our social institutions, culture, and values are products of the mode of production and the underlying material basis of human life. However, it is not a mechanical relationship here; ideas are not simply determined by the economic foundations of society. There are a number of critical voices and calls for social change within the present system: (1) human emancipation, human rights, and the rights of the citizen arise out of a liberal society. Politics, just as morals, are not simply forms of false ideals and ideology; (2) socialist and communist theories of distribution based on equality and human need arise out of capitalism and become the basis for a rejection of equivalency exchange of commodities; and (3) Marx is capable of rejecting market exchange and industrial production on the basis of their internal contradictions and crises. This would not be possible if all thoughts and principles were reduced to those of a capitalist society. There has been relative agreement that the judicial concepts of justice and law reflect the values of liberalism, but this does not also mean that a society is incapable of self-consciously imagining or creating democratic alternatives or that ideas are mechanically bound to the economy and thus cannot express ideals that transcend capitalism.

6 Tucker, *The Marxian Revolutionary Idea*, p. 50. Nielsen, in his essay 'Marx on Justice: The Tucker-Wood Thesis Revisited', *The University of Toronto Law Journal*, 38, 1 (Winter, 1988), outlines Wood's observation that, if the juridical concept of justice is not accepted as the only legitimate form of justice, one is forced to rely on subjectivity and intuition which can only lead to relativism or historicism. Morality cannot be imposed from the outside of society in the manner of a socialist theory of justice (p. 35). An implication of this position is that not only has historical materialism accepted the legal definition of justice, but that ethics cannot rationally ground or morally legitimate an alternative view; historical materialism has been interpreted in a naturalistic and deterministic manner whereby the forms of distribution, rights, and law are reduced to being reflections of the established mode of production (p. 36). According to the Tucker-Wood thesis, historical materialism or dialectical science is tied to a labour theory of value, exchange value, and surplus value, but not to a moral theory of values.

7 Tucker, *The Marxian Revolutionary Idea*, p. 46.

8 Tucker, *Philosophy and Myth in Karl Marx*, pp. 19 and 20. Tucker states that he is reading Marx's texts through Karl Popper's *The Open Society and its Enemies*. Morality is unnecessary when the revolution is 'historically inevitable' (p. 21). Tucker continues this position in *The Marxian Revolutionary Idea*: 'The fundamental passion of the founders of Marxism was not a passion for justice. Their condemnation of capitalism was not predicated upon a protest against injustice, and they did not envisage the future communist society as a kingdom of justice' (pp. 36–7). A few lines later Tucker reveals that Marx's actual inspiration for his social critique came from Henri de Saint-Simon, Charles Fourier, Louis Blanc, and Pierre-Joseph Proudhon, who saw 'the moral basis for socialism was not the ideal of justice but rather the ideal of the human brotherhood or love' (p. 37). Tucker emphasises his central point from his reading of Marx's marginal notes on the Gotha Program that

concepts such as 'fair distribution', 'equal right', and 'undiminished proceeds of labour' are 'obsolete verbal rubbish'. Tucker concludes his analysis of Marx and justice with the idea that Marx 'showed contempt for socialists who attempted to ground a critique of capitalist society on the principle of justice' since 'the principle of distributive justice is alien to the mental world of Marxism' (p. 41). Finally, Tucker sees that any theory of justice is antithetical to Marx's interpretation of history and society (historical materialism). However, despite the forcefulness of Tucker's position, it remains an open question whether Marx is critical of all forms of justice or just liberal and utopian justice. Marx even refers to Proudhon's theory as 'bourgeois or conservative socialism'. What would a critical theory of social justice look like? Justice and historical materialism are not antithetical concepts, but are dialectically interrelated. More on this idea later. Tucker concludes his critique of a Marxian theory of distributive justice by remarking that political ideals and justice are irrelevant since the emphasis should be on the mode of production, not the mode of distribution (p. 52).

9   This is Tucker's interpretation of the famous line from Marx's *Critique of the Gotha Program* where he states that 'right can never be higher than the economic structure of society and its cultural development conditioned thereby' (*Philosophy and Myth in Karl Marx*, p. 19). The two main places in Marx's writings that have been the central point of contention for Tucker and Wood are *Capital: A Critique of Political Economy*, vol. 1: *The Process of Capitalist Production* (New York, NY: International Publishers, 1968), pp. 193–8 (wage contract and surplus value); *Karl Marx/Friedrich Engels Werke* (*MEW*), Band 23 (Berlin: Dietz Verlag, 1962), pp. 207–13; and the *Critique of the Gotha Program*, *Marx and Engels: Basic Writings on Politics and Philosophy*, ed. Lewis Feuer (Garden City, NY: Anchor Books, 1959), p. 119 (distributive justice); *Karl Marx/Friedrich Engels Werke* (*MEW*), Band 19 (Berlin: Dietz Verlag, 1987), p. 21.

10 Wood, *Karl Marx*, p. 125.

11 Ibid., p. 127. This distinction between moral and nonmoral goods is derived from Wood's reading of Immanuel Kant and John Stuart Mill (p. 129).

12 This idea that justice is simply a juridical notion which reflects and rationalises the social system assumes there can be no transcending moral values in the concept. But is this Marx's view? In both *On the Jewish Question* and *Critique of the Gotha Program*, there are indications that the concept of justice defined as rights and distribution does transcend the historical moment as it looks to the future in the 'rights of the citizen' and human emancipation and distributive justice based on human need, respectively. According to Marx, the principle of right can never be higher than the economic structure. Recognising the validity of this idea, Tucker concludes in *The Marxian Revolutionary Idea*: 'In short, the only applicable norm of what is right and just is the one inherent in the existing economic system' (p. 46). On the other hand, a theory of justice can reside in the technical and social potential of the social relations of production that transcend the historical moment.

13 Allen Wood, 'The Marxian Critique of Justice', p. 244.

14 Ibid., p. 246. Wood's definition of legal justice stresses the skill, technique, regulation, and administration of law, behaviour, and practices in the state. It is less a political and public process and more an issue of purposive rational action and the application of legal and

political technology guaranteed by natural rights to maintain social order and technical rules of behaviour.

15 Ibid. There are a number of issues in Wood's analysis that must be more critically examined in detail: (1) Is his analysis of the juridical concept of justice and the state an adequate reflection of the ancient philosophy of Plato and Aristotle or is it more a product of eighteenth- and nineteenth-century political economy? (2) In criticising the ethical principles underlying legal and civil rights, is this a rejection or a transcendence (*Aufhebung*) of human rights? And finally, (3) does Aristotle offer an entirely different view of justice from simply juridical concepts of law and rights? The term 'eclipse of justice' resulting from moral positivism may be appropriate here since the Tucker-Wood thesis represents a hollowing out of the historical context within which Marx considers these ideas. See also the analysis of Alasdair MacIntyre's theory of ethics and the Enlightenment in *After Virtue: A Study in Moral Theory* (Notre Dame, IN: University of Notre Dame Press, 1981) found in endnote 24.

16 Wood, 'The Marxian Critique of Justice', p. 255.
17 Ibid., p. 254.
18 Ibid., p. 257.
19 Ibid., p. 270.
20 Ibid., pp. 271–3; and Tucker, *The Marxian Revolutionary Idea*, pp. 48–52. Wood concludes this essay by saying that capitalism is a social form of physical, intellectual, and moral impoverishment, servitude, exploitation, and instability, but not injustice.
21 *Forms of Immanent Critique of Political Economy: Liberal and Socialist Justice*: The Tucker-Wood thesis is to some extent a false debate grounded upon an inadequate understanding of the nature of both justice and science. It may be argued that the thesis is provisionally correct in that the bourgeois view of justice is limited to juridical categories of rights and fairness. Relying on this limited view of justice, Marx is able, thereby, to undertake an immanent critique of capitalism by showing that its own standards of justice, as they have evolved out of the capitalist mode of production – market exchange, the wage contract, and fair distribution based on equal exchange – do not reflect and are contradictory to the actual structural reality of capitalism based on the exploitation of labour, labour power, and surplus value, dehumanisation of human creativity and potentiality, and the alienation of species being, nature, and the community. Marx moves beyond this narrow and limited view of justice as he returns to the classical Greek tradition and incorporates its vision into a critique of the unnatural political economy. This represents his external or substantive critique of capitalism which is grounded in the values of Western society in its totality of natural law – justice, self-consciousness, self-determination, freedom, and so forth. Justice cannot be limited by the accepted law, judicial realism, moral positivism, or historical materialism, but is an expression of the very possibilities inherent in species being, human reason, and the democratic imagination. The distinguishing characteristic of humans is that they create their own histories and societies. These values are immanent to the Western traditions and the transcendence of human reason. The validation for this second form of critique Marx borrows from Rousseau and Hegel; its justification lies in the power of the practical will and objective spirit for self-determination and freedom. Ernst Cassirer makes an

interesting and relevant observation about Rousseau's theory of the original goodness of humankind in *The Question of Jean-Jacques Rousseau*, trans. and ed. Peter Gay (New York, NY: Columbia University Press, 1954): 'This goodness [of man] is grounded not in some instinctive inclination of sympathy but in man's capacity for self-determination ... He does not tarry in his original condition but strives beyond it; he is not content with the range and kind of existence which are the original gifts of nature nor does he stop, until he has devised for himself a new form of existence that is his own' (pp. 104–5). The same may be said about Marx. The justification for his second critique and natural law lies in the human capacity for evolution, self-determination, and self-creation of objective social reality in history. Morality and justice are not simply mechanical and deterministic expressions of a historically specific mode of production but are capable of transcending those social and technical relationships.

Nielsen in 'Marx on Justice' argues that 'Marx is not telling us that our moral understanding, our understanding of right and wrong, can never transcend the relations of production we are immersed in' (p. 63). Historical materialism helps historically locate justice and its possible ideological distortion of the social reality, but ideals, self-consciousness, and human potentialities also direct human action beyond the present social system. If justice, morals, and ideas were simply products of class production and property relationships, then there would be no hope, no future, and no socialism. To agree with Tucker and Wood that the juridical and bourgeois definition of justice is a product of capitalism is not the end of the discussion. Justice, as with other moral values of self-determination, freedom, dignity, brotherhood of man, etc., is not limited to the empirically given. Change is not directed by political realism or scientific inevitability, but by the power of the human imagination to recognise and realise alternatives in human life. Justice has a long history in the Western tradition that incorporates ancient, medieval, and the modern experience and their potential that may not be presently used as the normative standard by which to judge human action. There may be unrealised possibilities inherent in the Western concept of justice beyond liberalism. The questions not raised by the Analytical Marxists are: Why should we judge modernity only by the standards of liberalism and not the broader standards of the traditions of Western society (or for that matter non-Western society)? Why should the standards of justice be employed which only favour the oppressing and exploiting class to the detriment of those who suffer at their hands? And why do Marxists limit themselves to liberal justice and not incorporate Marx's own theory of natural law?

Ziyad Husami, in 'Marx on Distributive Justice', argues that, according to Marx, the moral values of any society are determined by the given mode of production and by class interests, opening the possibility that moral values of the oppressed class could develop that were in conflict with the values of the bourgeois ruling class. With their opposing class interests, concepts of equality, freedom, and liberty could vary widely. Although moral norms are historically grounded, 'the Marxian sociology of morals does not state or imply that a norm arising in, or pertaining to, one mode of production cannot be validly used in the *evaluation* of another mode' (p. 34). Husami maintains that Tucker and Wood misunderstand Marx's sociology of morals and historical materialism, leading to their conclusion that ideas and norms of the legal system can only reflect the particular mode of production of a given society. Husami states that they can also oppose the standards and institutions of that society because of conflicting class interests. Thus, within Marx's historical materialism there is a distinction between the explanatory method of the legal system (science) and the evaluative method of social critique (ethics) (p. 61). The former emphasises historical materialism and the determination of the superstructure by the economic base; the latter emphasises the dialectical independence of class consciousness and critical ideals to evaluate and judge the social system by standards other than natural rights and liberalism. Husami accuses the defenders of the Tucker-Wood thesis of 'moral positivism', because they utilise the standards of the existing economic system to explain and judge that system (p. 36). Because of their position, they are unable to criticise capitalism on the basis of other moral principles and a theory of justice. He concludes with the sentence: 'The Marxian norms of self-realization, humanism, community, freedom, equality, and justice are not reduced to insignificance merely because the institutional framework they require is absent under capitalism' (p. 39). Moral norms thus serve conflicting social functions for Marx – ideology and critique. The weakness of Husami's position is that it is not radical enough; it does not connect these ethical and political values to classical antiquity and the theory of justice of Aristotle.

22   Gary Young, 'Doing Marx Justice' in *Marx and Morality*, ed. Kai Nielsen and Steven Patten (Guelf, Ontario: Canadian Association for Publishing in Philosophy, 1981), p. 268. It should be noted that Greek philosophy, history, and society are extremely complex and fraught with difficulties. The same may be said of Marx's theory of capitalism and social justice. The power of Marx's imagination is that he abstracted from the Greek experience to help him dream of the future possibilities of humanity in a classless and industrialised world. Toward that end he integrated the Greeks into French and German romanticism and idealism, radical socialism, and his critique of classical political economy. This book will emphasise the formal Greek influence on Marx to the exclusion of the other philosophical traditions. For more on the substantive and philosophical connections between Marx and Aristotle, see George E. McCarthy, *Marx and the Ancients: Classical Ethics, Social Justice, and Nineteenth-Century Political Economy* (Savage, MD: Rowman & Littlefield Publishers, 1990), n. 2, pp. 303–4; George E. McCarthy (ed.), *Marx and Aristotle: Nineteenth Century German Social Theory and Classical Antiquity* (Savage, MD: Rowman and Littlefield Publishers, 1992); and Martha Nussbaum, 'Aristotelian Social Democracy', in *Liberalism and the Good Life*, ed. R. Bruce Douglas, Gerald Mara, and Henry Richardson (New York, NY: Routledge, 1990), pp. 203–52.

23   The correspondence between Marx and Aristotle can be fine-tuned even more:

(1) *Civil and Legal Justice*: natural rights, law, political emancipation, liberal freedom, citizenship, and democracy **** *Rectificatory Justice, Ethics, and Politics*: civil and legal justice (*diorthotikos*) in the Athenian polity and the distortions of virtue, reason, and democracy in a market economy.

(2) *Workplace Justice*: virtue, freedom, self-determination, species being, praxis, goodness, and alienation **** *Ethics, Virtue, and Practical Wisdom*: moral and intellectual virtue, function of man, happiness, and reason.

(3) *Ecological Justice*: nature and humanity in a moral ecology and social praxis ****

Physics and Metaphysics: nature as a living, organic whole with reciprocity to ethics and humanity, causality, and teleology.
(4) *Distributive Justice*: fair distribution, reciprocity, grace, and human needs **** *Reciprocal or Particular Justice, Politics, and Oikonomike*: distributive (*dianemetikos*) and reciprocal (*antipeponthos*) justice in a moral economy based on merit and needs (*chreia*).
(5) *Political Justice*: popular sovereignty, self-determination, and self-government in democratic socialism of the Paris Commune of 1871 **** *Political or Universal Justice and Democracy*: democratic polity, citizenship, practical wisdom (*phronesis*), political deliberation (*bouleusis*), practical action (*praxis*), freedom, equality, popular sovereignty, the best political constitutions of monarchy, aristocracy, and democratic polity, and the ideal of a middle-class democracy.
(6) *Economic Justice*: ethics and critique of political economy, chrematistics and exploitation, structural contradictions, economic crises, and the history and logic of capital and surplus value production **** *Chrematistike and Critique*: rejection of competition, self-interest, class property, and inequality in a market economy that is destructive of democracy, virtue, human reason, and the function and telos of humanity. These ideas were taken from George E. McCarthy, 'Last of the Schoolmen: Natural Law and Social Justice in Karl Marx', in *Constructing Marxist Ethics*, ed. Thompson, n. 37, pp. 220–1.

Marx's theory of human nature and species being in his early writings on ethics and virtue and his theory of human needs in his later writings on politics and institutions ground his appropriation of Aristotle's idea of the potentiality of human development and self-realisation. They also provide Marx with the substantive content (2 and 4) to his formal and procedural analysis of democracy and political justice (5). For an overview of the discussion about Marx's view of human nature, see Norman Geras, *Marx and Human Nature: Refutation of a Legend* (London, UK: Verso Books, 1983). Other scholars who develop this line of thought about human nature, especially in relation to the alienation of nature, include Erich Fromm, Eugene Kamenka, István Mészáros, Bertell Ollman, and Philip Kain. Nature and need will be integrated in Marx's later writings as he fuses the ideals of ethics and politics, the *zóon politikon* (polis being) and the *Gattungswesen* (species being).

There have been a number of criticisms of both Rousseau and Hegel for providing only the procedural outlines or forms of the general will and objective spirit as the realisation of self-determination and freedom, but no specific analysis of what would constitute the content of freedom, good and virtuous actions, and just political decisions. This is a more contemporary version of Hegel's own criticisms of Kant's abstract and transcendental moral philosophy and practical reason as inherently a form of moral positivism and relativism (nihilism). The contentless abstractions and empty formalisms of Rousseau and Kant, according to Hegel, led to the tyranny and terror of the Jacobins during the French Revolution. The universalism and formal rationality of the general will and categorical imperative could and did lead to violence. How are the rational decisions of democratic socialism and workers' collectives to be judged as good or bad? Both Aristotle and Marx have offered a substantive analysis of the relationship between the virtuous character and democratic polity, ethics and politics, and human nature and needs and the structures of economics and politics. The former offer corrections to the possible abuses of the latter; the former offer an objective moral standard – ethics and virtue – by which to measure and evaluate the rationality of the latter – democracy. The principles of natural law (human nature and needs) offer a dialectical and substantive balance to the formal institutions of democratic socialism and a solution to the extremism of the French Revolution. On this issue for Hegel, see Joachim Ritter, *Hegel and the French Revolution: Essays on the Philosophy of Right*, trans. Richard Dien Winfield (Cambridge, MA: MIT Press, 1984), p. 5 and Steven Smith, *Hegel's Critique of Liberalism: Rights in Context* (Chicago, IL: University of Chicago Press, 1989), pp. 13, 27–9, 55–6, 75, 87–94, 130, 221–2, and 225.

24 Aristotle, *Nicomachean Ethics* (New York, NY: The Modern Library, 1947), book v, chapter 1, 1129a8–9, p. 397. According to Aristotle, the function or end of man is an 'activity of soul which follows or implies a rational principle … [H]uman good turns out to be activity of soul in accordance with virtue', and the most important virtues are wisdom, friendship, and justice (book 1, chapter 7, 1098a7–8, p. 318 and 1098a16, p. 319). Ethics is grounded in both morality (virtuous action of moderation, courage, nobility, honour, political wisdom, friendship, and justice) and social structure (economy, state laws and constitution, and political community).

25 For a substantive and more detailed analysis of Aristotle's theory of legal (rectificatory), economic (distributive and reciprocal), and political (universal) justice, see George E. McCarthy, 'Aristotle on the Constitution of Social Justice', *Dreams in Exile: Rediscovering Science and Ethics in Nineteenth-Century Social Theory* (Albany, NY: State University of New York Press, 2009), pp. 19–77. What is very interesting is that the formal breadth of Marx's theory of justice throughout his writings closely conforms to Aristotle's theory of economic and political justice at the same time that he rejects the liberal view of justice based on property contract, fair wages, labour contribution, and market distribution.

26 Both Alasdair MacIntyre, *After Virtue*, pp. 52–62, 152–64, 172, 195, and 258–9 and *A Short History of Ethics* (New York, NY: The Macmillan Company, 1966), pp. 199–214, and Agnes Heller, *Beyond Justice* (Oxford: Basil Blackwell, 1987), pp. 74–115 recognise that with the birth of modern Enlightenment liberalism and individualism, moral philosophy and its questions of virtue, character, intelligence, and morality have been separated from traditional socio-political justice and its concerns for the nature of the law, friendship, political community, and moral economy; ethics has been separated from social and political theory; modern individualism from the virtuous good life; and, finally, moral philosophy from sociology and social justice (p. 23). These forms of separation are expressions of the theoretical incoherence and prejudice of liberalism. Kant, too, had unintentionally expressed this underlying contradiction of modern moral philosophy in his separation of practical reason and justice (law). The objective spirit or substance of morality has been lost to practical reason and conscience. According to Heller, the tradition of Hegel and Marx sought to end this ethical dualism: 'Modernity threw itself back into antiquity to keep the ethico-political concept of justice intact for and against modernity' (p. 92). Thus, Marx's theory of social justice must be examined within its historical and theoretical context and should not be viewed through the prism of Enlightenment moral philosophy. MacIntyre sees this conflict between the Ancients and the Moderns best represented as a conflict between

Aristotle and Nietzsche – moral universals and moral nihilism. The Analytical Marxists followed this Enlightenment tradition by continuing to separate ethics from moral philosophy (character, virtue, and practical reason), political economy (value production and crisis theory), and science (historical materialism).

Rejecting the Enlightenment dualism between ethics and politics, as well as ethics and science, Marx defines justice as the interrelationship between ethics and structures, morals and institutions, and virtue and politics in the tradition of Aristotle. The *Nicomachean Ethics* is organised around the following main themes of Virtue, Justice, Knowledge, and Friendship in books: (1) virtue, happiness, and goodness; (2) moral and intellectual virtues; (3) passions and voluntary action, rational deliberation, the right rule of reason, and courage and temperance; (4) ideal man and character, goodness, nobility, and honour; (5) theories of particular or economic justice: distributive justice, rectificatory justice, and reciprocal justice, and universal or political justice: reason, deliberation, and judgement, and the nature of knowledge, prudence, and truth; (6) intellectual virtues and forms of knowledge: technical knowledge of the artisan (*techne*), practical wisdom of the citizen (*phronesis*), and universal knowledge of the philosopher (*episteme*); the details of practical wisdom as reason – demonstration, deliberation, understanding, and judgement; and, finally, the integration of moral goodness and political and legislative wisdom; (7) impossibility of practical wisdom: knowledge and action, noble pleasures vs. the negative moral states of vice, incontinence, and brutishness, and the self-indulgent man as a non-repentant utilitarian seeking bodily pleasure; (8) civic and personal friendship, citizenship, goodness, friendship, love, and justice, and the friendship of brothers; (9) friendship and the good man, good will, unanimity, benefactors, self-love, and friendship as a human need sharing in discussion and thought, reason and deliberation; and (10) virtue and happiness and the best constitution.

The Politics continues to develop the social and political dimensions of ethics with the questions of Virtue, Economy, Politics, the Right and Best Constitutions, and Democracy in books: (1) natural exchange of simple commodities (C-C and C-M-C) and unnatural exchange of commerce and banking for money and profits (M-C-M' and M-M'), critique of political economy and chrematistics; (2) best constitution and ideal states in Phaleas (distributive justice and human need), Hippodamus, and Spartan constitutions; (3) citizenship, defence of democracy as ideal constitution (virtue, political participation, deliberation, collective wisdom, contribution, and the common good); (4) ideal constitution in theory and practice, right constitutions: monarchy, aristocracy, and democratic polity, and deviant constitutions: tyranny (rule by one), oligarchy (rule by wealth), and democracy (rule by poor); best constitution: democratic polity because of its moderation, deliberation, middle class, social stability, and structures and functions of the state: Assembly (*Ekklesia*), council (*Boule*), and judiciary (courts of law); (5) equality, justice, and social revolutions, avoiding factionalism, class conflict, and tyrannies, and the role of education in social stability; (6) function of the state and constitutions, principles and structures of democracy, and best democracy; (7) integration of individual and community, virtue and citizenship, happiness and the relation between virtue and prosperity, the good life, virtue and dignity, property and virtue, and education and citizenship; and (8) the nature and purpose of education and the state.

As we have seen, the concept of 'justice' in Marx has received a number of different definitions thereby precipitating broad debates within the academic community. Justice refers to issues of the moral character and development of the individual toward a life of virtue, happiness, and rationality and also refers to the macro-structures of society in the economy and polity which nurture and encourage such a life. This integration of ethics and moral virtue reflects the position taken by Aristotle in the *Nicomachean Ethics* and *The Politics*, and is also found in German Idealism and the movement from Kantian morality to Hegelian social ethics or *Moralität* to *Sittlichkeit* (Charles Taylor, *Hegel and Modern Society* [Cambridge, UK: Cambridge University Press, 1979], pp. 84–95). Thus the key to understanding the nature of justice in these traditions is to appreciate the interrelationships between ethics and politics.

Morals, Virtue, and Justice: One can only be impressed by the range of questions Aristotle discusses under the nature of a good and just society: the function of man or human nature, ethics, moral virtues (courage, moderation, truthfulness, nobility, honour, friendship, and justice) and intellectual virtues (technical knowledge, universal knowledge, and practical wisdom), distributive justice (fair distribution of public and private wealth and power), reciprocal justice (reciprocity of grace and fairness, proportionality, friendship, mutual sharing, and human need [*chreia*] in economic exchange), restitutive justice (repairing damages created by economic and legal transgressions), political or universal justice (political participation, practical wisdom [*phronesis*], deliberative rationality and discursive judgement), best constitutions (kingship, aristocracy, and polity), ideal polity (democratic polity, equality, freedom, and popular sovereignty), rationality as political participation and rational discourse, and a just economy based on household management and a moral economy (*oikonomike*) as opposed to the distortions of virtue and democracy in a market economy (*chrematistike*). The very nature of Aristotle's description of individual virtue and happiness binds the citizen to the constitution, law, economy, and polity since virtue and happiness are ultimately political categories and cannot be realised in an isolated social vacuum. Marx's theory closely resembles Aristotle's in that he, too, views justice from the perspective of individual freedom, equality, self-realisation, and rationality of the species being, friendship, and citizenship realised through political rights and participation, human emancipation, economic democracy, the ideal polity and the best constitution of democratic socialism in the Paris Commune, and macro-political economy and critique of chrematistics or a market economy in the *Grundrisse* and *Capital*.

From this perspective the three variations within Analytical Marxism found in endnote 1 are to some extent all true: The defenders of the Tucker-Wood thesis are correct in that Marx did not have a formalistic or legalistic definition of the rights of man or an ideal of distributive justice based on the equivalency of commodity exchange; the critics of this thesis are also correct in that they argued that Marx had a different view of human rights and fair distribution based on political emancipation and human needs, respectively; and the third group, in perhaps the most interesting and useful variation of all, held that Marx did not base his criticisms of capital production on a judicial concept of justice, but did ground his rejection of it on moral principles, such as human dignity, freedom, community, and self-realisation. The problem with the third group is that they did not see that these moral values were part of a more comprehensive theory of justice following in the path first laid out by Aristotle. Endnote 24 may provide answers as to why they overlooked this approach and held a form of moral dualism keeping ethics and politics, ethics and science (historical materialism and positivism), separate; Analytical Marxism seems to have been caught in the Enlightenment understanding of moral philosophy. For Marx, his theory of social justice incorporated all three variations in that he, too, rejected a judicial and liberal theory of justice; did incorporate post-capitalist political rights and distributive justice into his theory; and did broaden his theory of social justice to include a wider range of moral values and natural law principles in the tradition of the ancients.

PART 1

Dialectic between the Ancients and the Moderns: Natural Law and Natural Rights

∴

CHAPTER 1

Natural Law and Natural Rights in Locke: Indifference and Incoherence of Liberalism

At the end of the seventeenth century, John Locke penned his major work *The Second Treatise of Government* (1690) in which he greeted the last echoes of the Scholastic period with the beginnings of modern liberalism. Caught between the two worlds of the ancients and moderns, he attempted to justify the new economic and political system created by the rise of British agricultural and commercial capitalism. However, the ideas he was introducing were so new and revolutionary that he needed to create a moral justification which rested upon traditionally accepted values and which would provide the legitimate foundation for this new social system. Thus he set himself the task of introducing the natural rights tradition with its unique defence of individual equality and liberty with the natural law ethical principles of community, public good, compassion, and love. At first glance, it might appear that these two sets of principles would be antithetical to each other. But, building on the model established by Thomas Hobbes in the *Leviathan* (1651) with his theory of the state of nature, Locke created a whole new world with an emphasis on individualism, liberty, property, and self-preservation. The truths of liberalism (rights and civil society) and capitalism (property and a market economy) first had to be placed within a broader and older philosophical and theological tradition of natural law and social justice which traced its origins back to ancient Greece and medieval Christianity. The natural rights of the individual were rooted initially within the ethical principles and economic structures of natural law of the medieval and late medieval Scholastic tradition of Thomas Aquinas.[1]

Hobbes used his theory of the state of nature to justify the psychology and passions of human nature which produced a picture of human beings as rational, self-interested and self-moving, calculating machines, motivated by primordial egoism, aggression, and violence. It was this negative image of anomic humans without a broader commitment to God or the community which ultimately framed individual freedom and equality in a world Hobbes characterised as 'solitary, poor, nasty, brutish, and short'.[2] Locke challenged this orientation by creating an alternative to Hobbes which began with a more sophisticated anthropology and philosophy of humanity grounded in the Anglican theology of the late English Renaissance of Richard Hooker's path breaking work, *Of the Laws of Ecclesiastical Polity* (1594). According to

Hooker in the first book of his work, God, through the act of his eternal will, is the first and final cause of all things; he is the rational order and purpose of the universe. Through the divine will, he has created nature or reality as the common inheritance of humanity and thereby has provided the basic moral principles, rules of behaviour, and ethical laws that guide rational human will and activity. It is the divine author of the world who has created good and evil.[3] 'Wherefore to return to our former intent of discovering the natural way, whereby rules have been found out concerning the goodness wherewith the Will of man ought to be moved in human actions'.[4] The moral principles that guide human activity have been created by God, and through the powers of right reason are open to human understanding. 'For that which all men have at all times learned, Nature herself must needs have taught; and God being the author of Nature, her voice is but his instrument'.[5] By examining nature, the holy scriptures, and religious and Church traditions, humans are capable of knowing the eternal moral truths and principles of God that should guide human activity in the social world.

Locke, building upon Hobbes's political theory, while also relying on Hooker's theory of the natural moral order of human life, attempts a grand synthesis in the state of nature of the principles and institutions of the modern economic realm with the divine moral realm. According to Locke, it is natural law which ultimately grounds and frames the natural rights tradition because it is the former which morally justifies and supports the values and institutions of the latter. The key question considered in this chapter is whether the two traditions are compatible at any level. The traditions provide the basis for the political and legal writings of both Locke and Marx as they take quite different responses to them, thereby helping to clarify the social philosophy of both theorists. The difference between natural rights and natural law, a market economy and a moral economy, will frame Locke's theory of property and legal rights, as well as Marx's later theory of civil and legal justice.

Thomas Hobbes and the State of Nature and War

The state of nature in Hobbes's *Leviathan* is a hypothetical construct whose main purpose is to examine human nature and interaction before the creation of a social contract and organised civil society in the form of governments, laws, constitutions, rules of behaviour, etc. Knowing empirical human nature would provide the basis for questions about individual rights and freedom before civil society was formed. Questions may then be asked: Stripped of our legal, moral, and religious codes, what is the essential nature of humanity;

how would we act unencumbered by the restraints of God and community? Hobbes's response was not very reassuring as he described humans as living barely tolerable and isolated lives in a 'time of war' in which there is no security, industry, culture, knowledge, or economic exchange; there is no economy, state, or system of laws. It is a life of intense anxiety, struggle for survival, fear of violent death, and minimal amenities and quality of existence without any sense of a natural community or moral obligation to others. Law is a later artificial social construct, not a prior condition or product of human reason. Hobbes describes it as a state of war of all against all – *bellum omnium contra omnes* – in which everyone is governed by their own reason and prudential opportunities.[6] It is a world of utility and materialism run amok in which individuals strive for unlimited power. In this barbaric and violent state, there is an equality of hope and success in accomplishing goals and an equality of ability in mind (prudence) and body (strength) since everyone has the ability to kill one another or form temporary alliances to accomplish specific ends; it is a state of existence in which there are no morals or principles of justice since every action undertaken by an individual is without social restraint; and, finally, it is a state where there is an equality of fear, insecurity, and ability.

There is no common bond or common restraint uniting individuals together for a universal ethical purpose or social ideal. There is only a continuous and unrelenting opposition of interests, rights, and power in which everyone opposes and is opposed by everyone else. Unlike the ancient Greeks, who held that humans were social and political by nature, held together by the virtuous life of the citizen for the common good and protection of the community, Hobbes represents the modern liberal view of the isolation, competition, distrust, and insecurity of human existence. Power and isolation are the defining characteristics in this seventeenth-century view of humanity framed during the English Civil War. Under the conditions of the state of nature, force and fraud are the only rational forms of existence since humans have the right of self-preservation and a right of liberty to act in any way expedient to the real life situation and exigencies of the moment to protect themselves and ensure their survival. Even under these barbaric conditions, there are 'natural laws', discoverable by reason, which are universally binding on all individuals. The first fundamental law of nature is a universal condition of war that 'every man has a right to every thing' and a right to the use of everyone else who will benefit his survival and life.[7] Limitless domination, control, and power over nature and humanity is the fundamental right of the state of nature. Hobbes's theory of natural rights as a right to everything (nature) and everyone (others) is based upon his underlying understanding of the human sciences of physiology and psychology – humans as self-moving systems of matter and self-interested calculating machines. Comparing his view of this world to that of classical natural law, one can conclude that with the rise of liberalism, death replaces telos, despair replaces hope, instincts replace politics, and naked self-interest and passion replace reason and the universal moral order. Because of the fear of violent death, constant anxiety created by these extraordinary conditions, and desire for a good, industrious, and pleasurable life, Hobbes states there is a second law of nature that 'every man ought to endeavour peace' and this, in turn, leads to the third and final law of nature – justice and the creation of social contracts and artificial covenants for the maintenance of social peace and individual rights. Natural law recognises the universal violence of everyday life, while the natural rights turn it into a virtue. With the formation of civil society, the first law of nature, along with its corresponding right to control and use everything and everyone for one's own benefit and survival, is transferred to the political commonwealth or the Leviathan state.[8] Terror and violence are now recognised as the chief means by which the artificial state functions to insure the maintenance of social order, peace, and harmony.

Locke will develop his particular theory of liberalism, individualism, freedom, and the state of nature in a critical reaction to Hobbes. He does this by expanding natural rights to include life, liberty, health, and property and by returning to the more ancient and medieval concept of natural law. He will use a theology of moral law to ground his economic theory of natural rights in a divine ethical order created by God, but open to the light of reason and understanding. Locke's view of the state of nature and the human condition is certainly more moderate and modulated than Hobbes. In fact, the former holds that this original state was characterised by reason, tolerance, moderation, and a market economy, and not the brutality, competition, and violence of Hobbes's view. Thus a harmony among God, nature, and the economy already exists in the state of nature. The liberal principles of economic rights within a market economy are deeply imbedded in and balanced by ancient philosophy and medieval theology. The ethical and economic theory of natural law frames the legitimacy and possibility of the rights of liberalism. That is, natural law morally justifies the new social system at the same time that it makes the system possible by providing not only its values and ideals but also the structures and institutions that nurture and protect them. It is in this context that Locke begins the *Second Treatise* by arguing that the law of nature is balanced between natural law and natural rights and governed by the principles of equality and freedom.

The relationship among individuals in the state of nature is characterised as a 'state of perfect freedom to order their actions and dispose of their possessions and persons as they think fit, within the bounds of nature, without asking leave or depending upon the will of any other man'.[9] Within this state, there is no subordination or unequal distribution of power. All individuals are equal and each has the freedom to act in any way they deem fit, limited only by the 'bounds of nature', that is, by the moral principles of the law of nature whose main imperative is not to harm others. Unlike in Hobbes's writings, the state of nature is governed not by self-interest, but rather by the laws of God and reason. As humans are made in God's own image after his own likeness and bearing the perfection of nature, human reason is capable of discovering these laws, along with scripture and the Christian tradition, which are broken down into natural rights, ethical principles, and economic restraints on action. According to Locke, individuals, because they are equal and free, possess a right to life, health, liberty, and possessions, which cannot be infringed upon or harmed except when they transgress the more fundamental laws of nature. These natural rights and moral laws are universal and absolute because they are the creation of the 'one omnipotent and infinitely wise Maker' and 'sovereign master'. In this original state there is an initial harmony and balance between the individual and community, between natural rights and natural law, and between freedom and social responsibility.

Richard Hooker and the Laws of Nature and Ecclesiastical Polity

Early in his treatise on civil society and government, Locke introduces into the state of nature his theory of ancient natural law whose ultimate moral imperative is not to harm others or the community. For an articulation of these fundamental moral insights, Locke, in paragraphs 5 and 15 of his work, turns to the theological writings of Hooker for inspiration, especially book one, sections 7–10, of his *Of the Laws of Ecclesiastical Polity*. Hooker, who is known as the 'father of Anglicanism' and the 'last great representative of the medieval natural-law school'[10] attempted to mediate a tolerant and judicious middle road (*via media*) or theological compromise between the theologies of Calvinism and Catholicism by relying on biblical revelation, the church tradition of the early Church Fathers and Aristotelian Scholasticism, and human reason in his search for the truth. Scripture, tradition, and reason became the building blocks for his moral philosophy and political theology. Alexander Rosenthal has identified some of the main influences of Hooker on Locke's moral and political theory, which are as extensive as they are profound, including: (1) Locke's rejection of the monarchical views of Robert Filmer during the seventeenth century, including the latter's identification of absolute paternal and regal authority, paternal and political powers, defence of patriarchalism and absolute monarchy, rejection of the principle of natural liberty, and Filmer's defence of the state of absolute and natural subjection to the will of another in the *First Treatise of Government*; (2) his theory of the state of nature or the pre-political conditions of man based on Hooker's theory of natural law, equality, liberty, and sociality; (3) theory of the sovereignty of the whole community and mutual, voluntary agreement as the basis for political obligation, government, and human laws for the purpose of security and possessions in civil society; and (4) the limits of government and political society in natural law and the eternal moral order.[11] It is also from Hooker that Locke develops his understanding of right reason and free will as the true soul and perfection of man whereby natural law, as the voice of God, becomes the guide of virtuous action and moral duty.[12] Hooker writes, 'His meaning is, that by force of the light of Reason, wherewith God illuminateth every one which cometh into the world, men being enabled to know truth from falsehood, good from evil, do thereby learn in many things what the will of God is'.[13] Reason, as the 'rule of divine operation', is the determination of the providence and wisdom of God known to humans in an immediate and apparent way through clear principles and self-evident truths. And it is the constant longing and love of humans to emulate his law and goodness through the development of their character and virtuous life. It is a desire for perfection of goodness and virtue that lies in the nature and end of humanity itself; this is the object and inclination of the human will and practical reason. The ultimate end of life is the seeking of the final perfection of the good, true, and beautiful discovered by reason and producing joy and delight.[14] And this end is accomplished by achieving a righteous life and reaching the kingdom of God. Recapitulating Aristotle's and Aquinas's theory of moral and intellectual virtues, Hooker writes that humans by nature desire a life of happiness, virtue, wisdom, nobility, courage, and friendship.[15] 'All men desire to lead in this world a happy life. That life is led most happily, wherein all virtue is exercised without impediment or let'.[16] And it is natural law which forms the conscience and heart of every human being, guiding them in their everyday life.

Just as the first and main moral commandment of Christianity is to love God with one's whole heart, soul, and mind, the second principle is to love thy neighbour as thyself. Hooker then quotes from Plato, Aristotle, and Augustine to show how reason, too, has unearthed these primary moral imperatives. Locke later incorporates the principles of mutual love, nobility, righteousness, charity, and social justice among equals into the foundations of the moral soul in his state of nature. Drawing upon the texts of the Old and New Testament and natural reason, both Hooker and Locke contend that by natural inclination men have a life's desire and duty to love one another as equals, to develop a life of human dignity and mutual respect, and to seek the good and virtuous, all of which require a natural measure of fellowship and community, moderation and tolerance.[17] Reason is essential for the perfection of humanity through the realisation of its moral and political potential. Hooker summarises this imperative by stating that it is the duty of all men to love others as themselves. 'My desire therefore to be loved of my equals in nature as much as possible may be, imposeth upon me a natural duty of bearing to them-ward fully the like affection'.[18] This is the natural law of reason and human nature which universally and absolutely defines what is good and how humans must act; it cannot be rejected by anyone. Hooker states, 'This Law, I say, comprehendeth all those things which men by the light of their natural understanding evidently know, or at leastwise may know, to be beseeming or unbeseeming, virtuous or vicious, good or evil for them to do'.[19]

Finally, Hooker argues that governments are formed by general agreement because humans have a natural inclination for fellowship and the common good. There is also an implication here that men have a 'natural right' to form their government because no one family or person has the rightful authority over another; this could also be accomplished by the 'immediate appointment of God'.[20] The law of nature precedes the formation of the body politic or law of the commonwealth. Hooker, in book 1, chapter x, maintains that a 'righteous life presupposeth life; inasmuch as to live virtuously it is impossible except we live; therefore the first impediment, which naturally we endeavour to remove, is penury and want of things without which we cannot live'.[21] The creation of civil or public society (state) is another necessary precondition for a life based on the moral principles of the law of nature and reason.[22] It is also a necessary precondition for nurturing righteous persons and living the good life. Anticipating Hobbes's theory of the state of nature, Hooker maintains that before civil society individuals lived an indifferent, corrupted, solitary life where there was no institutional fellowship or binding agreement about politics and civil laws among them, but only a life of envy, strife, and violence; Hooker finds this a pitiful, miserable, and brutish state of a wild beast.[23] By implication this early, imperfect, and defective stage of nature is a world without dignity and virtue; the economic, ethical, and political preconditions necessary for human striving – the perfection of virtue and self-realisation – did not exist. 'In nature they are as indifferent one as the other'.[24]

Although natural law existed, it was necessary that it be institutionalised through a common agreement to be made real. This distinction between morals and politics (ethical life) will later be developed through Hegel's critique of Kant's theory of *a priori* morals and practical reason. Hooker writes that this period before civil society was a time of wickedness, malice, and evil, a time of endless strife and troubles in which there were no more than eight righteous persons in the world.[25] By not having communities, nature is also characterised as not providing the basic economic foundations for a life of dignity and virtue, a life of pleasure, tranquillity, and happiness. This will require individuals uniting together to form political societies. For his understanding of nature before society, Hooker relies on the biblical writings of *Genesis* and the *Letters of Peter* and the *Rhetoric* of Aristotle to make his case. The creation of natural and civil law, as well as the maintenance of the virtuous life of the soul and reason within a political community, requires a quality of life (bk. 1, ch. x, sec. 2) and a developed system of agriculture and commerce. 'To take away all such mutual grievances, injuries, and wrongs, there was no way but only by growing unto composition and agreement amongst themselves, by ordaining some kind of government public, and by yielding themselves subject thereunto'.[26]

Hooker continues that only by means of creating civil society and public law is it possible to form a life of peace and tranquillity; without law there would only be 'inconveniences' and 'troubles and strife'. Civic polity (bk. 1, ch. x, 1) and a developed economy (bk. 1, ch. x, 2) are the two necessary structural preconditions for the realisation of natural law and the moral principles of reason. Thus men have a 'natural right' through the law of nature to govern themselves by mutual consent and universal agreement; it is this mutual consent that provides the laws with their legitimacy and force. Through wise deliberation, consultation, and practical experience men form positive or human laws and governments because of this inherent corruption of humanity. These laws will constrain and educate the citizens, reward virtue and punish vice. The actual form and structure of government created by these laws will vary as there is no one ideal form of polity. But to avoid discontent and internal divisions dangerous to the stability of society, public offices at the lowest level should be filled by lot, while for those requiring wisdom and character, the appropriate method of choice should be public elections. Hooker is critical of an oligarchy since rule by wealth and power only produces resentment and hatred by the people.

Locke on Natural Rights and Natural Law

Locke borrows these ideas of natural law and places them in the state of nature along with the individual's rights to life, liberty, and property. By combining the modern rights of liberalism with the more ancient ideals of community, social responsibility, and fellowship, Locke has provided political theory its radical distinctiveness in the seventeenth century. Whereas Hobbes emphasised the brutality and competitive self-interest of liberalism as the basis for natural rights and the fear and terror of the primitive state of nature as the justification for the modern state, Locke takes an entirely different approach. He recapitulates, with the help of Hooker, the history of Western thought from the ancient Hebrews, Hellenes, and Hellenists through the medieval theologians, almost anticipating Hegel, as he makes ancient moral law part of the modern legal and political experience.

According to Hooker, the end or final cause of human existence is the good and happy life of virtue, wisdom, and fellowship under equality that requires a developed economy and state to succeed. Locke, as we will presently see, reorders the relationship among these social components of natural law, civil society, and an advanced economy in order to redefine the end of man and the ultimate purpose of civil society to protect natural rights, private property, and a market economy. Although he builds his whole intellectual edifice on Hooker's political theology, he ultimately inverts the relationships between natural law and natural rights. Natural law is viewed as an expression of the divine order and the guiding moral principles and laws in human life. However, Locke uses natural law less as the final cause of human existence and more as a moral restraint on economic life. Thus, the concept of perfect freedom in the state of nature is a very modern notion since it represents only a rejection of external authoritarian power over the individual. This is what has come to be known as a 'freedom from' arbitrary rule and authority, while the ancient Greek and medieval Christian view expressed a 'freedom to' some preconceived end, such as happiness and virtue. In the former view of freedom, there is no hierarchy, division, or superiority, but there is also no final end or purpose to human existence other than the preservation and protection of that very existence. Natural law is not the telos of human beings but simply acts as a set of moral and structural restraints on an individual's natural rights to life, action, and possessions. Locke has taken the ancient philosophers and theologians and stripped them of their metaphysics while maintaining their ethics. As a result, natural law becomes simply a restraint on economic activity and economic rights. Although we have a right to self-preservation (life), the choices and actions that maintain our continued preservation (liberty), and the products of human labour (private property), these rights are limited by the sacred imperative not to harm others.[27] Natural law has become fully incorporated into modern liberalism and the economic theory of natural rights. A problem remains: Although Aristotle and Aquinas seem to frame Locke's view of the world, he has thoroughly changed the meaning of their ethics and metaphysics to fit the needs of a modern economy and propertied individualism.

The state of nature in Locke is not that state characterised by either Hooker or Hobbes. It is a state of calm reason and conscience, flexibility and wisdom; a state of perfect freedom and equality wherein no man has jurisdiction over another; and a state of proportionality reflecting the broader needs of the community for common equity and common security expressed in natural law. Locke is very clear that although this is a state of freedom, it is not a state of personal licence since actions are bound by the moral restraints of natural reason. Although there is no public state with its legal rules and civil regulations, natural law serves the function of maintaining peace and security. When these rules are transgressed, individuals have the right to individually punish offenders and seek reparations from them based on the 'rule of right reason' to ensure self-preservation. However, due to individual prejudices and passions, along with the general difficulties attached to carrying out punishment and reparations, Locke argues for the creation of civil government to regulate these transgressions. 'I easily grant that civil government is the proper remedy for the inconveniences of the state of nature, which must certainly be great where men may be judges in their own case'.[28]

When these inconveniences and crimes become more serious and thus rise to the level of fear for one's personal safety and security, that is, when we are in danger of death or slavery, we have reached a stage Locke refers to as a 'state of war'. This is a stage going beyond simple inconvenience to a real threat to natural rights and to the danger of absolute, arbitrary power over individual wills and the subsequent loss of perfect equality and freedom. This is the most serious reason to leave the state of nature by general agreement. The only legitimate restraint on human will and action in the state of nature is natural law, and for both convenience and protection a civil government is necessary to ensure the continued exercise of this natural law.[29] At this point in his analysis, Locke seems to use the term natural law to include both natural economic rights and natural moral law which restrains these rights.

Ethics and Structure in Natural Law

Upon a closer review of Locke's main ideas about the state of nature, things appear more difficult and complex. Locke's state of nature thesis is a way of articulating the principles of divine natural law and natural rights and, in turn, justifying his defence of particular rights to personal freedom and private property before the creation of civil society. But his argument is complicated by the fact that there are two distinct and contradictory theories of the state of nature in his work. There is the original state of nature in chapter 2 and the second state of nature in chapter 5: The former is grounded in the natural moral order of God, nature, and reason in chapters ii, iii, iv, and v, sections 4–35, whereas the latter is grounded in the unlimited and unrestrained accumulation of private property, capitalist institutions, self-interest, and class struggle in chapter v, sections 36–50. In each state, property is justified in two distinct ways: common property as the material foundation of human life and health in the original state of a moral economy and private property as the product of human labour in both the original and second state of nature. Although private property is introduced in the first state, there are clear ethical (love, compassion, and friendship) and structural (spoilage, labour, and sufficiency) limitations placed on its acquisition and use. Although there is private property in this original state, it is bounded by both moral principles and ethical structures.

These natural law limits are dropped in the second state as property and rights become independent of all moral obligations and limitations. In the original state of nature, natural rights to life, liberty, health, and property are the material foundations of natural law, human life, and the community, whereas in the second state, natural rights are the ends of human existence. At first, rights to property and health are means to achieve life and liberty; in the second state property becomes the supreme right. The argument to be made in this chapter is that, in the second state of nature, rights become merely theoretical justifications and mystifications for class power and domination; natural rights ironically now undermine true human freedom, equality, and life choices.

Rights require a moral or natural law that protects, ensures, and enhances human life, self-preservation, and the quality of life (health, freedom, and equality) by means of access to the material conditions and structural prerequisites of life through common property, labour, and nature. Rights require a common ground in universal health care and property to exist and to protect the universal rights to life and liberty; rights cannot independently stand on their own or be used to abuse or harm others; rights are essential for the existence of a moral economy. This leads to a broader observation about natural rights: Without natural law and common property for all, there can be no real rights to property and without common property, there can be no rights to life and liberty. Although property is central to the issues of rights, it is not well understood. It is generally viewed as an unquestioned and independent right superseding all the others. However, in the original state of nature, property is central only because it provides the material foundations for self-preservation, individual freedom, and social equality. There must be common property available to everyone in order for the other rights to exist, including the right to private property. Rights are only an expression of communal and private property for all. All this radically changes with the reconsideration of the role of private property in the second state of nature.

As briefly mentioned above, Locke selectively borrows his theory of natural law and social justice from the writings of Hooker, thereby relying on the history of Western thought. This theory of law in the original state of nature may be broken down into two major areas: moral philosophy (ethics) and economic theory (structures). Shortly after beginning *The Second Treatise*, Locke offers the reader a long quotation from Hooker that outlines the major principles of the latter's theory of the law of nature, as well as his intellectual indebtedness to Aristotle and Aquinas. If natural rights are limited in their application by the moral principles and laws of natural reason not to harm others, it is Locke's appropriation of Hooker's moral and economic theory which will ultimately justify the particular rights of nature. Along with law, rights are part of God's creation and therein lies their ultimate justification; they are not created by society, legislature, or positive law, but by the divine will of God in nature.

It will be natural law which establishes the foundations and legitimation of modern liberalism. The new liberal system of individual freedom, market self-interest, and economic competition will be grounded in the will of God, nature, and the Christian scriptures and traditions. Without natural law, the legitimacy of liberalism and capitalism become impossible. The moral principles of Locke are the same as those shared by Aristotle, Aquinas, and Hooker: the moral and intellectual virtues of reason, wisdom, judgement, dignity, love of others (*philia*), community, and friendship. The economic structures in the state of nature which constrain possible abuses of natural rights include the limits of spoilage (sec. 31), labour (secs. 32–36), and sufficiency (secs. 33–34). It is the relationship between natural law and natural rights in Locke which will define his relationship to both Hooker and Hobbes, classical philosophy and theology and modern political theory. The central question for our understanding of Locke, and more importantly for our understanding of Marx in the next few chapters, is whether the former creatively integrates the ancients and moderns or, rather, repudiates the ancients and natural law as incompatible with the ideals of liberalism.

The introduction of natural rights and the original state of nature in *The Second Treatise* is bounded by two long quotations from Hooker.

> The like natural inducement hath brought men to know that it is no less their duty to love others than themselves; for seeing those things which are equal must needs all have one measure ... my desire therefore to be loved of my equals in nature, as much as possibly may be, imposeth upon me a natural duty of bearing to them-ward fully the like affection; from which relation of equality between ourselves and them that are as

ourselves, what several rules and cannons natural reason hath drawn, for direction of life, no man is ignorant.
Eccl. Pol., book 1, ch. 8, sec. 7

The laws which have been hitherto mentioned (i.e., the laws of nature) do bind men absolutely ... but forasmuch as we are not by ourselves sufficient to furnish ourselves with competent stores of things needful for such a life as our nature doth desire, a life fit for the dignity of man; therefore to supply those defects and imperfections which are in us, as living singly and solely by ourselves, we are naturally induced to seek communion and fellowship with others. This is the cause of men's uniting themselves at first in politic societies.[30]
Eccl. Pol., book 1, ch. 10, sec. 1

According to Locke, the exercise of natural rights to self-preservation and self-determination – the liberty to organise and define our personal lives and everyday decisions in any way we wish within a state of natural equality and freedom – requires that this be accomplished in an environment that respects human dignity and needs based on mutual love and obligation and that encourages and protects community and fellowship. Thus, there is a balance between the freedom to prioritise and order our individual lives and a broader moral duty to the community to respect the rights of others. Individual liberty and equality are only possible because of this prior natural law and moral imperative to others. What is interesting is that this relationship between the individual and community is one that occurs within the state of nature prior to the formation of civil society. Locke is clearly emphasising that this is both a reflection of human nature and of the perfection of God. Responsibility to ourselves is reflected in our responsibility to others. The two elements of rights and law are inextricably bound together for a life of dignity. The modern defence of individual liberty and rights is balanced by the classical recognition that humans are social and political animals, a position lost in Hobbes's view of the state of nature but rediscovered by Locke through Hooker.

These communal bonds in the state of nature are not simply abstract moral principles but require structural constraints to give them concrete institutional support. Just as this state of liberty is not a state of arbitrary licence, just as individual free choice cannot lead to suicide and self-destruction, and just as individual self-determination cannot eliminate the moral obligation to the community, natural rights are bound by a fundamental responsibility to the community since it is through the community that natural rights, self-determination, and freedom – a life of human dignity – are made possible. Law and rights are inextricable partners in the state of nature because the community provides the moral and structural possibilities for natural rights. Rights without law are ideals without actuality since natural law provides the religious, moral, and economic foundations for individual freedom and equality. Some have argued that because this theory of natural rights is so different and new, Locke first had to establish their theological, ethical, and economic validation in the classical norms and canons of natural law before they could be generally accepted as valid by a modern audience in the seventeenth century.

Locke begins chapter five with the statement that natural reason informs us 'that men, being once born, have a right to their preservation, and consequently to meat and drink and such other things as nature affords for their subsistence'.[31] He is also aware that for rights to be possible there must also be material subsistence available to everyone; there must also exist the structural or economic conditions that make rights real and relevant. As mentioned above, reason is not the only source for the justification of rights. Locke continues in the same sentence to say that scriptures, as the word of God, are another source of knowledge about individual rights when, quoting David in *Psalm* 115 and then later *Timothy* 6 and *Genesis* 26, he states that it is clear that God has given the earth to Adam and his children as their common possession and inheritance. But it is the next step in his argument that is even more interesting. Locke continues by stating that although humankind initially received the earth as common property, it later developed into private property: 'God, who has given the world to men in common, has also given them reason to make use of it to the best advantage of life and convenience. The earth and all that is therein is given to men for the support and comfort of their being'.[32] Originally in the natural state of things, all the crops and animals belonged to the common stock of goods for human consumption as they were the product of a spontaneous and beneficent nature created by God. And although God, as the 'one omnipotent and infinitely wise Maker', created nature that was bountiful and generous in its goods that were to be held in common for all, he also gave humans, as the products of his workmanship, the ability to reason and develop alternative means to appropriate nature 'for the support and comfort of their being'. That is, nature, which was given to humanity in common for individual consumption and, thus, for the self-preservation of human life, was also given the potential to develop more effective and rational ways of utilising the physical environment for its 'best advantage and convenience'. Being industrious and hard working, as well as developing the mechanical arts and inventions with new forms of production, are ways of accomplishing this task. God created nature to develop the moral and physical potential of human beings that would evolve over time. Locke introduces the example of American Indians who, he maintains, had no concept of enclosure or private ownership of property but of necessity consumed the fruit and venison that was available from the commons through individual appropriation and action. The very act of picking fruit and acorns gives each a right to them.

Property itself is held in common for everyone by the will and wisdom of God. However, the means of subsistence and of sustaining human life is private, that is, it is maintained through the personal appropriation of nature. Locke concludes with perhaps his most important statement: 'Though the earth and all inferior creatures be common to all men, yet every man has a property in his own person. This nobody has any right to but himself. The labour of his body and the work of his hands, we may say, are properly his'.[33] In the state of nature, human labour provides the continuance of material bounty and human life through the time, effort, and productive labour of the worker. Removing the material goods and products of physical labour produced through agriculture and husbandry from the common stock in this original state produces the right to ownership of property. Since humans own their own body – they have a right to life – they thereby also own the products of their own body and have taken these products onto their own.

Private property is created by the continuous act of human labour whereby the goods and products of nature are taken from the common stock and turned into private property for personal consumption and the continuance of life. Since property is absolutely essential to the maintenance of human life, it, too, must be a natural right. 'God gave the world to men in common, but since he gave it them for their benefit and the greatest conveniences of life they were capable to draw from it, it cannot be supposed he meant it should always remain common and uncultivated'.[34] In this way, Locke legitimates the right to private property from the common state and in the process excludes other men from making similar claims to this property. By expanding natural rights in this way, Locke defines life, liberty, and property as sovereign expressions of the ownership of the self, labour, and the products of labour. Life and liberty are now defined less in terms of natural human development and potentiality that we find in the classical tradition, and more as a manifestations of labour and property. C.B. MacPherson has termed this view of human action and natural rights 'possessive individualism'.[35] This will have profound implications for how individuals define the meaning and purpose of human life, equality, and freedom.

It is human labour that gives value to work and turns common property into private property, however, within certain ethical and structural limitations. 'For this labour being the unquestionable property of the labourer, no man but he can have a right to what that is once joined to, at least where there is enough and as good left in common for others'.[36] The natural law imperative not to harm others is still operative in the state of nature even with these economic developments and justification of private property. The labour theory of value and natural rights do not negate the moral foundations of the state of nature. One easily recognises that, although only a few pages into this political treatise, Locke is already expressing a tension between rights and law that will take interesting turns before he is finished. This takes us to a consideration of the natural law limits to natural rights and property ownership.

Natural Law Limits to Natural Rights in the Original State of Nature

We now turn to the economic and structural constraints on the natural rights to liberty and property and ask if these rights are in any way antithetical to the social principles of equality and freedom, on the one hand, and the moral principles of reason, virtue, friendship, and justice, on the other. How profound and deep are the tensions between rights and law? Locke clarifies the issue when he states that it is natural law which has given us private property, but it has also provided a moral restriction on its accumulation in order to live a healthy and happy life. In perhaps the most important line of the work, Locke writes, 'The same law of nature that does by this means give us property does also bound property too'.[37] This is the clearest statement by him that natural law bookends natural rights and frames the later discussion in his treatise. It is God in the beginning of creation and the state of nature who has given humans both common and private property, the latter justified through their wisdom, judgement, technology, and hard work, and it is God who, on the other end of rights, has provided for the moral limits to its accumulation. Both the justification and limitations of natural rights lie in the hands of God. It is natural law which comes first and, thereby, provides for the foundation and later the limits to natural rights for 'the support and comfort of their being'.[38] The three limitations to the accumulation of private property are the spoilage, labour, and sufficiency limitations. They are the basic ethical principles of distributive justice in Locke's political philosophy. Property is not an absolute right but must serve a social function for the common good.[39]

The first structural limitation to the accumulation of private property rests in the spoilage limitation and the law of nature which states that property is given by God for human enjoyment. But then immediately thereafter Locke contends: 'As much as any one can make use of to any advantage of life before it spoils, so much he may by his labour fix a property in; whatever is beyond this is more than his share and belongs to others'.[40] The ownership of property by individuals is a right of nature that has been given to humanity before the formation of civil society and regulated rules of political and legal behaviour. Given by God, it cannot be taken away by arbitrary power or by the positive laws of the legislature. It is an inalienable and essential part of human nature; it cannot be bought or sold, won or lost, given away or surrendered, negotiated or merited. Where natural law is absolute, rights are not. There is no absolute right since there are limits placed on the acquisition and accumulation of property. One cannot accumulate so much land, animals, and agricultural produce that some of it eventually spoils because it is well beyond what an individual or family can consume and enjoy. The basic satisfaction of human need and material sustenance is the central moral imperative of this limitation. After a certain point in time, further accumulation beyond need can only result in waste, useless production, and the destruction of nature. 'Nothing was made by God for man to spoil or destroy'.[41] Labour justifies property but spoilage nullifies that absolute right of nature. Production and property beyond a certain point must be returned to the community and the commonly owned shares of nature as a moral obligation not to harm others. Private property should never act as a prejudice to others, nor should it be an occasion for 'quarrels or contentions'. Nothing should disturb the harmony and happiness of the community or the moral order established by God. The privatisation of property always has the possibility of establishing internal divisions and particularised self-interests within the community that would undermine the natural order of things. The concern for the appropriate and natural distribution of the fruits of the earth rests in a moral concern for natural waste and social strife within the state of nature.

The second structural restraint to the accumulation of private property is the labour limitation. The actual amount of energy and production of human labour justifies the appropriation of the fruits of nature. Beyond a certain point, however, that accumulation becomes unnatural and immoral. The individual has a right to any property acquired but with the provision: 'As much land as a man tills, plants, improves, cultivates, and can use the product of, so much is his property. He by his labour does, as it were, enclose it from the common'.[42] Referring to *Genesis* and the act of creation of nature and humanity, Locke recalls that in the moment God created the earth and gave humanity the world in common to it, he also commanded humans to work and cultivate the land in order to move beyond their pitiful state of penury by subduing nature and improving their living conditions. This labour commanded by God (and his reason) is what justifies the taking of property for one's own personal use and consumption for the betterment of human life.[43] With a slight adjustment in his original argument, Locke is now saying that although labour is a central element in the justification of the private use of property, it is also the result of a direct command of God to cultivate and subdue the earth. It is a direct command to apply human labour to nature for the benefit and improvement of life expressed in higher material standards and a more comfortable physical existence. Labour provides the justification for the personal use of property for one's own benefit, so long as it does no injury to others from whom it is taken.

The third structural restraint on the private appropriation of property is the sufficiency limitation. This economic condition assures that whatever property and material goods are removed from common ownership and general consumption do not leave other individuals at a distinct disadvantage. By improving and perfecting nature and humanity, by being industrious and productive, no one is harmed in the process. There is no prejudice done to others since 'there was still enough and as good left, and more than the yet unprovided could use'.[44] Enclosing land for greater efficiency and production did not produce any negative side effects on those who continued to draw upon the material goods of the commons. Their collective well-being was intact because there was more than enough land for everyone. Locke continues to reinforce his argument by saying: 'There was never the less left for others because of his enclosure for himself; for he that leaves as much as another can make use of does as good as take nothing at all'.[45] Turning the commons into private property has no negative consequences since there is always sufficient land remaining that can be cultivated for the betterment of humanity. No one is at a disadvantage under these changing circumstances. Although the method of production and distribution of the material wealth of society changes, this leads to the improvement of all.

The introduction of private possessions by God's commandment to work and appropriate the material resources in land, crops, animals, and buildings – the commandment to subdue, dominate, and cultivate the land – does not infringe upon the rights of others to do the same and leaves enough property for the good of one's neighbour either to continue to live off the common land or begin themselves to privately appropriate land on their own. God, in the 'first ages of the world', has provided more than enough land and space for everyone. Even after the later population expansion of the human race and the building of cities, there were still opportunities to access unused wasteland in Europe or even virgin land in the Americas. No one is harmed materially and everyone is enriched by this appropriation of land. Equality and freedom are maintained as the fundamental ethical principles at the foundation of society in the state of nature. Everything is done in moderate proportion for the enjoyment and conveniences of life within the boundless space of the wilderness and the moral limits of human labour and the natural order established by God.

If Locke had stopped his argument for private property at this point with its delicate embrace and balance of natural rights and the ethical and structural limitations of natural law, he would have provided a firm foundation for a modern view of individual freedom and liberty. Unfortunately, Locke did not stop there, but continued his argument past the point of moderation, coherence, and tolerance. His first theory of the state of nature is replaced by a second theory that introduces the institutions and values of a developed capitalist society which then, in turn, must renegotiate the relationship between law and rights, the ancients and the moderns, to the detriment of the former. The dynamic between natural law and rights created in the first five chapters of *The Second Treatise of Government* has been radically altered by the end of chapter v, section 36, and with it Locke's classical understanding of God, creation, and natural law. The elegant synthesis of the ancients and moderns, the sensitive integration of classical philosophy, medieval scholasticism, and modern Anglican theology has been irreconcilably broken, and with it the moral foundations of property and production have been irretrievably lost – and with it the very legitimacy of liberalism itself. At the very moment Locke was expounding on the virtues of hard work on uncultivated and unexplored lands, he introduced a new concept to his discussion that changed his whole argument. This was the mercantilist concept of 'money' in the form of gold, commerce, banking, wages, and profits.

Eclipse of Natural Law and Social Justice in the Second State of Nature

Locke had just finished articulating in detail the ethical and economic limitations on the private possessions placed on humanity by the wisdom of God, when new social institutions seemed to be arbitrarily introduced into the discussion, transforming Locke's theory of natural law and rights in the first part of his work. His vision takes him in an entirely different direction. He now sees that the moral rule of property to be bounded by labour, sufficiency, and spoilage would have remained intact 'had not the invention of money and the tacit agreement of men to put a value on it introduced – by consent – larger possessions and a right to them'.[46] The social circumstances of property ownership have changed.

Moving beyond the moral conditions of human life for the common good in the original state of nature, Locke proceeds to outline the revised material conditions for economic life, thereby placing unlimited private property, profit accumulation, and an advanced market economy in the state of nature. Thus, there is a fully developed capitalist society in the second state of nature before the creation of a constitutional state. Instead of building upon the distinctions between *oikonomike* and *chrematistike*, between a household or moral economy based on natural law and a market economy based on unnatural wealth acquisition as found in the first book of Aristotle's *Politics*, Locke simply asserts that the economic structure necessary for a dignified life based on natural reason lies in a market economy embedded in the institutions of commerce (secs. 45, 47–48, and 50), banking, private property, and wage labour (secs. 28, 50, and 85). Deviating from the classical Greek and medieval worldview, Locke locates a capitalist economy in the heart of his new theory of law and nature. The revised relationship between natural law and natural rights, along with the distinctive features of the economy are best highlighted in Locke's chapter v on property.

The world has been turned upside down as we no longer live in a moral universe created and ruled by God, natural law, and the principles of social justice but a new universe constructed by humankind where natural rights are absolved of any connection to and restrictions by natural law and the rule of right reason. We have now moved imperceptibly into a second state of nature where the logic and morality of the market economy defines the boundaries of human reason and action. The market has replaced morality and social ethics as the foundation of natural rights and private property. The moral imperatives and rules of the state of nature have now been superseded by the logic of the commercial market. Hooker has been replaced by Hobbes.

Sufficiency of material goods in land, food, and animals for the community is a key ethical imperative for Locke. The sufficiency limitation – stating that enough land and material goods must be left for the good of the community after property is privately appropriated from the commons – has been negated by the efficiency of the market toward greater productivity. 'To which let me add that he who appropriates land to himself by his labour does not lessen but increase the common stock of mankind; for the provision serving to the support of human life produced by one acre of enclosed and cultivated land are – to speak much within compass – ten times more than those which are yielded by an acre of land of an equal richness lying waste in common'.[47] Other than quoting from the biblical account in *Genesis*, Locke does not provide any evidence that with a growing population, expanding urban centres, and proliferating industry, the increased productivity of private land over public or unassisted/waste land results in greater prosperity and 'an increase in the common stock'. Locke only asserts that the new form of production and distribution benefits the common good or, at least, does not negatively affect it. The case is simply assumed that the value of labour with its greater productivity and efficiency will benefit the other members of the community. Leo Strauss, in agreement with Locke, summarises the latter's position on this point when he writes that the emancipation of acquisitiveness is conducive to the common good, happiness, and public prosperity. Strauss continues, 'The day labourer of England has no natural right even to complain about the loss of his natural right to appropriate land and other things by his labour: the exercise of all the rights and privileges of the state of nature would give him less wealth than he gets by receiving "subsistence" wages for his work'.[48]

Labour, as the second limitation to property rights, is discussed in other parts of Locke's analysis. He argues that if the common land is not utilised for tillage or grazing, but is allowed to lie fallow, the standard of living will itself remain fallow. It is only through the exercise of labour that humans add value to the land and their products. He offers the example of the American Indians who symbolise for Locke economic underdevelopment and a wasteful life of the commons. They own vast tracts of land but live a primitive life of material comfort that is surpassed by even the lowest of labourers in England. Private property is more valuable than the commons since it is a product of human industry and labour. 'It is labour, then, which puts the greatest part of the value upon land, without which it would scarcely be worth anything'.[49] It is labour which distinguishes between the production of bread, wine, and cloth from the production of acorns, water, and animal skins; the latter are objects found immediately available on the commons, while the former are products of human reason and labour. The improvement in the material and consumer conditions of life result from the effort and engineering of human labour to create 'commodities'. Over time, these new property relationships are formalised into positive laws. As population and production are expanded, money and markets grown, nations and states formed, common land became more rare, which invited even more compacts and agreements in the legal and political forms of civil society. Private, county, and national boundaries were created that helped regulate this transformation of society.

Spoilage is the third structural limitation on property rights that Locke examines. An individual has the right to all that his property, labour, and invention can produce so long as it does not spoil. With the intervention of money in a commodity economy, perishable goods that spoil over time can be bartered for other needed essentials or more durable products that are then consumed or exchanged for money in the form of gold and diamonds. There are now no limits to an individual's accumulation of products and wealth since the limits to production lie in spoilage which has been overcome; through commerce, industry, and banking, the moral limits are dissolved. 'The exceeding of the bounds of his just property not lying in the largeness of his possession, but the perishing of anything uselessly in it'.[50] Larger possession of land does not result in theft from the commons and injury to others. No one is disadvantaged by the expansion of agricultural production and the creation of a robust commercial economy based on it. According to Locke, the rights of others to life, liberty, and property are not infringed upon by expanding estates and production. Locke is critical of the waste of the common lands going unused and the waste of the overproduction of perishable items. When these issues are resolved through the restructuring of the market – through labour in the former case and money and capital in the latter, the moral and economic restraints on property and wealth are eliminated. While common property is a finite resource that ensures the protection and well-being of the community, money is infinite and does not admit of ethical restrictions.

Locke has reached the point where the traditional natural law restrictions on property and economic activity have been dissolved. Concerns about issues of spoilage, labour, and sufficiency have been overcome by privatisation, efficiency, and productivity. There is no longer spoilage in the profits and savings of mercantilism and banking, no longer limits on labour when workers can be hired for a wage, and no longer concerns about the good of others when technical development and productivity have increased so dramatically for the benefit of all. Economic growth and industry in a market economy have solved all the moral issues and economic limits initially put in place by Locke. The market has outgrown the moral limits of natural law making them irrelevant for the economy and polity. The issue now is what are the implications of this irrelevancy of natural law for Locke's ethical and political theory?

After having outlined the ethical and structural limits to property and their absorption into the economy, Locke concludes his analysis with the remarkable comment that a new social arrangement has evolved in the state of nature since 'it is plain that men have agreed to a disproportionate and unequal possession of the earth ...'.[51] Economic expansion of profits and capital, creation of large estates, hiring of wage workers at subsistence levels, and growing inequality and social divisions have all been accomplished, according to Locke, through mutual consent and without prejudice or injury to anyone. Only later with the dissolution of the state of nature are these new economic relations formalised in the social contract and civil law for the regulation of property. Labour has given individuals the right to property, industry has expanded agriculture and commerce, and the consent of men has redefined the issues of equality, freedom, and rights. In the original stages of nature, these categories had broader moral implications tied to Hooker's view of intellectual and moral virtues, and social justice. Now their meaning has been depleted of moral and ethical content; they have been reduced to purely monetary categories as natural rights have displaced natural law.[52] Equality and freedom are no longer connected to classical and medieval natural law with their dreams of a moral economy and a humane world. The end result is that with a market economy there is no longer a state of freedom where individuals 'order their actions and dispose of their possessions and persons as they think fit' or a state of equality 'wherein all the power and jurisdiction is reciprocal, no one having more than another'.[53] With the loss of natural law in the second state of nature, there is also a loss of true freedom and equality. All that is left is the defence of the right to private property. C.B. Macpherson has critically summarised this transition in his book, *The Political Theory of Possessive Individualism*.

> For on this view his [Locke's] insistence that a man's labour was his own – which was the essential novelty of Locke's doctrine of property – has almost the opposite significance from that more generally attributed to it in recent years; it proves a moral foundation for bourgeois appropriation. With the removal of the two initial limitations which Locke had explicitly recognised, the whole theory of property is a justification of the natural right not only to unequal property but to unlimited individual appropriation ... The traditional view that property and labour were social functions, and that ownership of property involved social obligations, is thereby undermined ... He also justifies, as natural, a class differential in rights and in rationality, and by doing so provides a positive moral basis for capitalist society.[54]

The profound implication of this revised position is that Locke views capitalist production and exchange as a social form of justice.[55] Justice is now no longer associated with law but rights. From this perspective, there is no longer a positive view of the future since everything is reduced to a justification of property rights. Freedom and liberty are defined by what is, not what could be or should be. For example, in chapter vi, Locke defines liberty as 'to be free from restraint and violence from others' and 'to dispose and order as he lists his person, actions, possessions and his whole property'.[56] However, if both equality and freedom are reduced to economic categories and redefined in terms of property – equality as a right to property and freedom as a right to dispose of it without interference from external, arbitrary powers – the majority of wage workers in the second state of nature are without property and without access to the common stock, and, thus, are by definition no longer persons, no longer equal, and no longer free. This evolved state of nature which Locke characterises as the 'disproportionate and unequal possession of the earth' and as the 'inequality of private possessions' is no longer a state of freedom and equality of the original state of nature, but is instead a capitalist state of alienation, servitude, and unequal rights.[57]

To maintain the integrity of the new economic system and to adjust to the inconveniences and uncertainties of economic transgressions, the corruption of men, and the irrationalities of war in the state of nature, civil society is created by the consent of the majority of others 'for their comfortable, safe, and peaceable living one amongst another'.[58] And the key to this new social form is the constitution and legislature through which new positive laws are created to ensure the continued protection of natural rights and property. Locke offers as examples of the transition from the state of nature to civil society a group of Spartans under the leadership of Phalantus who founded a new polity in Tarentum, Italy, kings of Indian nations in America, and the judges and kings in ancient Israel. Unlike the purpose of the Greek polity or medieval Christian town, civil society or a government of laws is formed ultimately for the mutual preservation of property and security against those who do not have it. Without natural law to give horizons and breadth to human life within the community, the new social contract or body politic is based on the utilitarian and materialist principle of the self-preservation of human life. Unfortunately, life has no other purpose in this society than the continued existence of the person and property. There is no goal of salvation, no profound purpose of virtue, wisdom, and goodness, and no community of friends living a life of higher purpose whether divine or human. Liberty, equality, and freedom are simply reductionist categories of this new economy. There are no moral duties or social obligations restraining liberalism; there are no moral ideals or hopes restraining utilitarian nihilism.[59] Enclosure and incorporation have no transcending rational values other than the protection of the unlimited accumulation of property in a market economy 'for the preservation of property being the end of government and that for which men enter into society'.[60]

A few pages later Locke will, in more dramatic fashion, reemphasise that the government 'has no other end' than the preservation of property.[61] He continues to refer to the privileges of perfect freedom, uncontrolled enjoyment, equality, and natural rights in the state of nature. In chapter vii, 'Of Political or Civil Society', the purpose of the state of nature and civil government is to protect property broadly understood as life, liberty, and estate. However, there is no longer any mention of the moral principles and ethical ideals of natural law that would provide humanity with some transcending goal or meaning in life. The state becomes the indifferent arbiter or neutral umpire of legal interpretations and disagreements regarding these rights while having the legislative, judicative, and executive power of making, interpreting, and enforcing the laws; it has no higher function or final end. In turn, the citizens of the new commonwealth have given up the right of self-enforcement of natural rights and punishment of transgressions within the state of nature to the civil judge. This power and consent of the majority to constitute a new political community or change an old polity through revolution is part of the law of nature and reason.[62] Once constituted, the new government with the prerogatives and powers to ensure the public good and property is based on the trust of the governed. Trust, majority consent of the governed, and the separation of powers within the government among the legislative, executive, and federative (international action) powers are important aspects of Locke's theory which will have an impact on later generations. But at this point in his analysis the question must be raised: What could natural law and reason possibly mean at this point after Locke has already disassembled and dissembled the principles and structures of natural law in the state of nature?

Irrelevance of Natural Law, Incoherence of Liberalism, and the Return to Hobbes

Although Locke continues to quote extensively from Richard Hooker and frequently mentions the law of nature throughout this work well after his analysis of the second state of nature in chapter v, especially when referring to the family and the creation of the political community and legislature, he does so without ever reviving the lost elements discussed earlier from natural law. He either does not appear to recognise the problems and lack of consistency connected with having eliminated the intimate connection between natural law and natural rights, or he has other reasons for maintaining the concept without the content. But there is one more surprise that Locke offers the reader. In the eleventh chapter on legislative power, he provides a profound but unrealisable insight given his earlier arguments on property and unlimited accumulation in chapter v. 'For the preservation of property being the end of government and that for which men enter into society, it necessarily *supposes and requires* (italics added) that the people should have property; without which they must be supposed to lose that, by entering into society, which was the end for which they entered into it'.[63] A startling revelation given his earlier treatment of wage workers and servitude, along with the inequality of economic distribution, capital formation, and profit accumulation; in a commercial market economy, inequality and class would become extensive with many individuals not having access to private property. In the original state of nature Locke admits that for there to be a natural right to property, there must also be real institutions of common and private property available within the community; otherwise there would be real harm done to others. Rights must be protected and ensured by natural law and social institutions. This was exactly the purpose, clearly articulated by Locke himself, for the existence of the commons and the moral and economic restrictions on property accumulation in the original state of nature. But the whole edifice of natural law, moral principles, and ethical/structural restraints has already been dismantled by civil society and the liberal state.

The commons and the original structural limitations not to harm others were specifically instituted to assure the right to property for all those with the wisdom and industry to accomplish their task of forging a pleasurable and secure life for themselves. According to Locke, the right to property 'supposes and requires people should have property'. There must be institutions in both the state of nature and civil society which ensure, by the will of God, or by moral persuasion of rational and moderate individuals, or by legislative action in positive laws, the actuality of property. This was the very nature and main purpose of natural law.[64] Rights not only justify and legitimate, they also protect and secure property; they presuppose, support, and require property. Rights provide a dual role in the modern commonwealth – ethics and structure, legitimation and support. They provide legitimation at the same time they supply the structural basis for material welfare. Without property or the real possibility of attaining property, rights in the state of nature and civil society are meaningless. Property is not a gift or merit of hard work; it is the universal and necessary precondition or law of nature to natural rights. Natural law provided both the divine and moral foundation of natural rights, but also the economic foundations in its structural limits to property acquisition. God and community give meaning and limits to economic endeavours; they provide its legitimation, ultimate goal, and economic possibility – its potentiality and its possibility; metaphysics and economy were foundations upon which the state of nature and civil society rested.[65] Finally, just in case the reader had missed the point that Locke was emphasising, he continues to focus on the implications of his own position by stating that not to have property but to possess only the right to property is 'too gross an absurdity for any man to own'.[66] The right to property does not imply a possibility lying in a future which, under certain fortuitous conditions of hard work and economic opportunity, will become real. This is why rights are universal, innate, and inalienable. Property or the technical and economic conditions for human life must first exist through natural law before there can be rights.[67]

In the original state of nature the right to property is a product of positive law that is acceptable only as long as it does not supersede or violate the right of freemen to access the common stock of property. Liberty is always endangered by property, especially if that property becomes unrestrained by the law of God, nature, and reason. In this sense the natural rights to life and liberty should have primacy even over property.[68] Rights by their very nature make an ethical demand upon society that the means for their actualisation also be part of natural law and natural rights; the social contract is just the realisation and protection of these rights and law. The implications of this are rather startling: Without natural law, there are no natural rights – no legitimation and no possibility; without social justice, there is no individual equality and freedom. Natural law and a moral economy provide the basic material sustenance, property, and communal welfare for self-preservation, health, and material security. These latter values cannot rest on a market economy with its indifference to economic inequality, class divisions, and the unequal power of private property and wage labour. To use terms such as freedom, liberty, and equality, without society providing the basic material means of support and satisfaction of fundamental human needs for the realisation of these needs, leaves the individual unprotected and vulnerable before the irrationalities and vagaries of a market economy. Rights must be compatible with needs; rights presuppose and support property. But the divine and ethical foundations of human relationships disappear in the second state of nature and later civil society.

The contradictions between moral law and market law, between the natural law of God and the economic law of the market manifest the basic incoherence of liberalism; without a moral economy, there is no happiness, enjoyment, or virtue. The irony of Locke's work is that the institutions of liberalism are incompatible with its own understanding of natural rights because it reduces the latter to the values of effort, hard work, and merit, while at the same time disposes of the institutional limits of spoilage, labour, and sufficiency necessary for their actualisation. For these reasons both natural law and natural rights are incompatible within a capitalist economy based on inequality, self-interest, market competition, and unequal distribution of profits and property. With the dissolution of natural law in a market economy in the revised natural state, Locke has moved away from Aristotle, Aquinas, and Hooker while returning to the political theory of Hobbes and the greed, self-interest, and barbarism of infinite wants, unlimited property, and an unfettered market war of all against all.[69] Heinrich Rommen nicely captures this insight when he writes concerning Locke's theory of civil authority and government: 'The *status civilis* is thus not the objective result of man's social nature itself; it is not a realization, through man's moral actions, of the natural order in the universe. The state is the utilitarian product of individual self-interest, cloaked in the solemn and venerable language of the traditional philosophy of natural law'.[70] Rommen refers to Locke's reliance on natural law as 'useless' and 'degenerative', whose only purpose was to vindicate the 'Glorious Revolution' of 1688–9 and provide the legal foundations of bourgeois society.[71] Natural law is just an ideological facade hiding the underlying empty utilitarianism and materialism of Locke's political philosophy in order to justify natural rights. (Marx will make a similar argument in his comparison of political emancipation and civil society, on the one hand, and the French 'rights of man' and the 'rights of the citizen' on the other in his work *On the Jewish Question*, 1843). Community, compassion, mutual love, and social justice have been replaced by economic rights, property, and the values of market ideology. There are no longer social restraints on market expansion (secs. 28, 36, 43–50, and 85–87).

Locke's theory of the political commonwealth ends in a variation of moral positivism – rights simply reflect and justify the structures of market liberalism; there are no transcending moral principles involved whether grounded in God, nature, or reason.[72] There is only a hollowing out of liberalism. The unfortunate irony of Locke's philosophy is that not only do natural rights undermine natural law, but natural rights in the end undermine individual equality and freedom – the very things they were intended to legally protect. What began as a relatively egalitarian and free society for the general welfare of the community and protection of individual rights to own their own life, actions, and means to material survival ends with a hierarchical class system based on large estates, commodity circulation, and the wage labour characteristic of modern liberalism. There is no longer an objective moral standard over social organisations and economic behaviour by which to measure economic activity.[73] Rights are no longer given to freemen by God but adhere to particular persons on the basis of their economic power and class interests; rights are conferred by the market, economic opportunities and successes, education, wealth, and merit. Without complete equality and common property for the benefit of all citizens, there are no universal natural rights. A similar argument can be made about the right of humans to fly. Without wings underneath their arms, humans have no inherent or inalienable right to fly. There are no moral or structural reasons to fly established by God, nature, or reason. Rights require a moral natural law that protects and supports human survival, liberty of action, health and well-being, and material comfort and an enjoyable and happy life. Rights require some form of socialism (equality and common property) to be made real; otherwise, rights are political forms of pure mysticism and ideology. All we have now is the *bellum omnium contra omnes* of liberalism with its class inequality, private property, and market self-interest.

After chapter v, natural law, God, and moral rules of economics are no longer relevant. There are no longer moral grounds to natural rights. Rights are now grounded on a growing market that produces more and more goods for more and more people. Economic productivity and human labour are the ultimate justifications for the new economic system. The Achilles heel of Locke's theory is that natural law was never the end of being as it was for Aristotle, Aquinas, and Hooker, and as it will be for Marx; Locke had very early on in his treatise separated metaphysics from ethics, law from rights. Natural law was only an initial means or restriction on the application of rights. When those limitations were dissolved by commerce and profit accumulation, there was no purpose left to human existence other than production, consumption, and exchange. The right to property had overwhelmed the rights to life and liberty, freedom and equality. In the end, natural rights are simply rights to alienation – the alienation and market exchange of one's life and liberty for greater material wealth. Rights have morphed into the rights to private property, inequality, and class power, just as God and nature have become irrelevant.[74] With the rise of modern science and mechanical reason in the eighteenth century, the Enlightenment did a forensic autopsy on the corpse of classical natural law and questions about the philosophical and theological meaning and purpose of human life; with the rise of existentialism in the nineteenth and twentieth centuries, theorists simply recognised the obvious and buried the remains.

It is at this point that these arguments about natural rights and natural law are joined by G.W.F. Hegel and Karl Marx; and it is at this point that many of the problems faced by Locke in his integration of the ancients and moderns, natural law and natural rights, resurface in interesting ways.[75] Locke inadvertently showed how liberalism and natural rights, on the one hand, and the classical ideals of justice and natural law, on the other, were incompatible philosophical traditions. Hegel, too, will attempt to join these traditions together in his early and later writings, but will ultimately fail because he could not integrate rights, property, and civil society with the ethical state. In the nineteenth century, it will be Marx's turn to focus on these same issues as he rejects the natural rights of personhood, self-preservation, and property along with the law of value and capitalist production. Instead he returns to the tradition of love, friendship, and citizenship and unites it with universal political rights, human emancipation, and socialist democracy. This requires Marx to rethink the whole foundation of social justice and human rights at the same time as it requires him to integrate the ethics (social justice) of his early writings with a critical and dialectical science searching for the historical laws of the motion of modern society from commodity production and money to commerce and capital.

Notes

1 Natural law consists of a set of moral principles and social institutions, ethical obligations and rules of social conduct, legal and political philosophy, political economy, and practical rationality and action created by God and articulated in the Old and New Testament, divine revelation and providence, early Church Fathers and medieval Christian traditions, and the rule of right or natural reason. Natural law is the moral wisdom of God found in scripture, tradition, and reason. It is a reflection of the divine order of the universe (metaphysics), eternal truths of nature (physics), and universal moral principles (ethics). As examined in this chapter, natural law represents the universal and absolute moral, legal, and political principles that guide human action in our everyday life. The ancient natural law tradition rests on Roman Stoicism (Cicero and Seneca) and the Early Church Fathers of the fourth and fifth centuries (Cyprian of Carthage, Basil of Caesarea, Ambrose of Milan, Clermont of Alexandria, John Chrysostom, and Isidore of Seville) to medieval Schoolmen (Anselm of Canterbury, Peter Abelard, Alexander of Hales, Albertus Magnus, Duns Scotus, William of Ockham, John Bonaventure, and Thomas Aquinas).

The natural law theologians of the Middle Ages may be grouped around four broad headings: (1) Platonists (9th–12th century) who included John Scotus Erigena, Anselm of Canterbury, and Peter Abélard; (2) Aristotelians or Golden Age of Scholasticism (13th–14th century) Albertus Magnus, Thomas Aquinas, John Bonaventure, and John Duns Scotus; (3) the Nominalists (14th–17th century) William of Occam, John Buridan, and Francisco Suárez (School of Salamanca); and (4) the Late Medieval Scholastics (16th–17th century) Robert Bellarmine and Gabriel Vásquez, and members of the School of Salamanca: Francisco de Vitoria, Francisco Suárez, and Domingo de Soto, and the Anglican Thomist Richard Hooker. Mention should be made of the Cathedral School of Chartres (11th–12th century) which was the centre of classical renewal and renaissance in Europe and included Bishop Fulbert, Bernard Sylvester, William of Conches, and John of Salisbury, and the Victorines or Augustinian School of St. Victor (part of University of Paris, 11th–12th century) whose members included William of Champeaux, Hugh of St. Victor, Richard of St. Victor, Walter of St. Victor, Godfrey of St. Victor, and Thomas Gallus. Whereas medieval scholasticism attempted the integration of classical Greek philosophy and medieval Christian theology, late scholasticism also attempted an integration of medieval Thomist theology but with Franciscan Scotism (voluntarism and free will) and the contemporary theology of the Jesuit Ignatius Loyola. Late scholasticism reaffirmed the primacy of divine reason in creating natural law, along with the primacy of the intellect over the will. Heinrich Rommen, *The Natural Law: A Study in Legal and Social History and Philosophy*, trans. Thomas Hanley (Indianapolis, IN: Liberty Fund, 1998), pp. 53–8. Locke, with the aid of Richard Hooker, integrates the ideas of Aristotle and Aquinas in his theory of natural law and natural rights as the foundation of modern liberalism. The Early Church Fathers and Aquinas were critical of private property as an expression of greed, sin, and the Fall from grace in the Garden of Eden.

2 Thomas Hobbes, *Leviathan: Or the Matter, Forme and Power of a Commonwealth Ecclesiasticall and Civil*, ed. Michael Oakeshott, intro. Richard Peters (New York, NY: Collier Books, 1977), p. 100.

3   Richard Hooker, *Of the Laws of Ecclesiastical Polity*, in *The Works of that Learned and Judicious Devine, Mr. Richard Hooker* (Oxford: Oxford University Press, 1845), book 1, chapter 2, secs. 2–6, pp. 148–52 and chapter 3, secs. 1–2, pp. 152–4.
4   Ibid., book 1, chapter viii, sec. 1, p. 170.
5   Ibid., book 1, chapter viii, sec. 3, p. 172.
6   Hobbes, *Leviathan*, p. 101.
7   Ibid., p. 103.
8   Ibid., p. 130.
9   Locke, *The Second Treatise of Government*, ed. and intro. Thomas Peardon (Indianapolis, IN: The Liberal Arts Press, 1955), chapter ii, sec. 4, p. 4. This political and economic treatise may be broken down into the following distinct areas: natural law and natural rights (chapter ii), economy (v), family (vi), state (vii–ix), forms and powers of government (x–xiv), and deviant politics and revolution (xv–xix). Where Aristotle made the connections between the self-sufficient family and the broader economy of the polis, Locke uses the governance of the family as a transition to an understanding of the body politic.
10 Peter Munz, *The Place of Hooker in the History of Thought* (Westport, CT: Greenwood Press, 1971), pp. 206–8. Munz develops the argument that the economic and political weaknesses of the Vatican in the sixteenth century paved the way for the Reformation (pp. 11–12). Intellectually, this path had been paved by the nominalism of Duns Scotus and predestination of William of Occam (pp. 51 and 125) along with the revival of Augustinian theology of the free will, salvation, personal emotion and purity, human wickedness, and renunciation of the world (pp. 25–6). Finally, in the seventeenth century, Grotius pushes the foundation of natural law beyond God to human nature. The origins of ethics, politics, and law, of the universal moral law that guides human action, lie within rational human nature or the rule of right reason, and not God (p. 208). This latter point is central to the evolution of natural law since Marx, too, will ground his theory of social justice in a secular natural law based on human nature and the institutions of democracy.
11 Alexander Rosenthal, *Crown under Law: Richard Hooker, John Locke, and the Ascent of Modern Constitutionalism* (Lanham, MD: Lexington Books, 2008), pp. 210–35. Hooker is cited sixteen times in *The Second Treatise of Government*. Rosenthal even mentions that Locke's use of Hooker, as representative of the orthodox Anglican Church, may have had political and theological motives in order for Locke to attack the Tory position at the same time as he was rejecting Filmer's defence of absolute monarchy (p. 211). Also Locke's theory of the state of nature has its origins in Hooker, but this too could be traced back to the late scholasticism of Francisco Suárez and Francisco de Vitoria (p. 218). Both Hooker and Locke are in agreement with the Aristotelian and Scholastic traditions which saw the nature of human beings as social and communal and subject to the natural moral order and the laws of reason and the divine. In this pre-political state of Hooker and Locke, there was initially liberty and equality. See also Quentin Skinner, *The Foundations of Modern Political Thought*, vol. 2 (Cambridge: Cambridge University Press, 1978), p. 158.

As a summary of Hooker's theory of constitutionalism and defence of Elizabethan England, Rosenthal writes: 'Hooker's purpose was essentially traditional – perceiving a Puritan attack on the foundations of civil and ecclesiastical life, he wishes to demonstrate the sound foundations of the English constitution by showing that its characteristic institutions of Crown, Parliament, and common law are grounded in consent, tradition, and natural law' (p. 233). It is interesting to note that although Hooker bounds political society by natural law, there is no mention of natural law in Locke as having a strong egalitarian moral foundation. This aspect of natural law has disappeared from the political conversation, even among contemporary political theorists.

12 Hooker, *Of the Laws of Ecclesiastical Polity*, book 1, chapter vii, sec. 1–4, pp. 165–8 and book 1, chapter viii, sec. 4, p. 173. Hooker defines natural law as 'any kind of rule or canon, whereby actions are framed, a law' (book 1, chapter ii, sec. 6, p. 152); 'wherefore to come to the law of nature: albeit thereby we sometimes mean that manner of working which God hath set for each created thing to keep' (book 1, chapter iii, sec. 2, p. 153); 'the law whereby man is in his actions directed to the imitation of God' (book 1, chapter iv, sec. 3, p. 161); and 'a rule therefore generally taken, is a directive rule unto goodness of operation. The rule of divine operations outward, is the definitive appointment of God's own wisdom set down within himself' (book 1, chapter viii, sec. 4, p. 173).

13 Ibid., book 1, chapter viii, sec. 3, pp. 172–3 and book 1, chapter x, sec. 2, p. 185.

14 Ibid., book v, chapter v, secs. 2–3, pp. 162–3 and chapter vi, sec. 3, p. 164.

15 For an interesting analysis of the relationship between Hooker and Thomas Jefferson, see Edward Furton, 'Richard Hooker as Source of the Founding Principles of American Natural Law', in *The Failure of Modernism: The Cartesian Legacy and Contemporary Pluralism*, ed. Brendan Sweetman (American Maritain Association Publication and distributed by the Catholic University of America Press, Washington, D.C., 1999), pp. 101–9. Furton's thesis is that Richard Hooker is the crucial mediator between Aquinas on the one hand, and Locke and Jefferson on the other. Hooker's political theory, according to Furton, is that the final end of human existence is happiness expressed as the natural good and perfection of human nature through moral and intellectual virtues.

16 Hooker, *Of the Laws of Ecclesiastical Polity*, book 1, chapter x, sec. 2., p. 185.

17 Locke, *The Second Treatise of Government*, chapter ii, sec. 5, p. 5 and chapter ii, sec. 15, pp. 10–11.

18 Hooker, *Of the Laws of Ecclesiastical Polity*, book 1, chapter viii, sec. 7, pp. 176–7.

19 Ibid., book 1, chapter viii, sec. 9, p. 179.

20 Ibid., book 1, chapter x, secs. 3–4, pp. 186–7.

21 Ibid., book 1, chapter x, sec. 2, p. 185.

22 Ibid., book 1, chapter viii, sec. 9, p. 179.

23 Ibid., book 1, chapter x, sec. 1, p. 184, chapter x, sec. 3, p. 186, and chapter x, sec. 4, pp. 187–8. There seems to be an inconsistency here since Hooker distinguishes the natural inclination of humans for fellowship and communion at the same time that he argues for an original imperfect nature of solitary and indifferent brutishness in bk. 10, ch. x, sec. 1. Hooker never resolves this difference between human nature and nature.

24 Ibid., book 1, chapter x, sec. 1, p. 184. Aquinas had used the term 'state of nature' but in an entirely different context than Hobbes or Locke. For him, as for Aristotle, it referred to the political community itself.

25 Ibid., book x, chapter x, secs. 3–4, pp. 186–7.

26 Ibid., book 1, chapter x, sec. 4, pp. 186–7. Locke will later amend this position of Hooker that natural law requires human law and civil society to fully develop the moral and

legal potential of natural law in human activity. Locke expands this by adding that in the state of nature, natural rights within a market economy require the ethic and structure of natural law. As viewed by Hooker, without civil society and a developed economy, the full actualisation of natural law is impossible; however, without natural law, civil society and natural rights, too, become impossible for Locke, at least in the second chapter.

27 Michael Zuckert in *Natural Rights and the New Republicanism* (Princeton, NJ: Princeton University Press, 1994) provides a further clarification of the rights and obligations in the state of nature that pushes Locke closer to Hobbes's thought on the state of nature. Zuckert reminds the reader that Locke held 'the no-harm principle' in the state of nature but also provided individuals with the natural executive power to use violence to protect their lives and property and punish offenders. The right of preservation entails the executive power principle in the state of nature which could entail violence and a state of war. 'Contrary to the initial impression, there will be much violence in the state of nature, much, perhaps most, of it morally allowable under the law of nature. Given all the force used in the state of nature, it is not so clear how different Locke's version of the natural condition is from Hobbes's' (p. 236). Hobbes and Locke differ over the nature of government, with the former favouring an absolute monarchy and the latter a limited constitutional government. However, according to Leo Strauss, both see government as a 'mighty leviathan' and the social contract as a 'contract of subjection'. For this insight, Zuckert is relying on the work of Robert Goodwin, 'John Locke', in *A History of Political Philosophy*, ed. Leo Strauss and Joseph Cropsey (Chicago, IL: University of Chicago Press, 1987), pp. 479–80. In their analysis of the closer relationship between Locke and Hobbes, Zuckert and Goodwin are critical of the work of Geraint Parry, *John Locke* (London: Allen and Unwin, 1978), pp. 59 and 111, who takes the opposite account of their relationship. Zuckert is restrained from making full use of this connection between Hobbes and Locke, because he recognises that Locke also moves in the direction of classical (Aquinas and Hooker) and modern natural law (Pufendorf and Grotius). Following a similar path, Thomas L. Pangle, in his *The Spirit of Modern Republicanism: The Moral Vision of the American Founders and the Philosophy of Locke* (Chicago, IL: The University of Chicago Press, 1988), writes: 'Tacitly following Hobbes, Locke breaks with the tradition which he traces to Aristotle's *Ethics* and sharply distinguishes "natural right" from "natural law"' (p. 187). For another critical review of the Straussian interpretation of the relationship between Hobbes and Locke, see John Yolton, 'Locke on the Law of Nature', in *John Locke: Critical Assessments*, ed. Richard Ashcraft (New York, NY: Routledge, 1991), p. 78; Francis Oakley, 'Locke, Natural Law and God-again', *History of Political Thought*, 18 (1997): 625; and Alexander Rosenthal's analysis of whether Locke is a disciple of Hobbes in *Crown under Law*, pp. 221 and 282–5.

28 Locke, *The Second Treatise of Government*, chapter 2, sec. 13, p. 9.
29 Ibid., chapter iv, sec. 22, p. 15.
30 Ibid., chapter ii, sec. 5, p. 5 and chapter iv, sec. 15, pp. 10–11.
31 Ibid., chapter v, sec. 25, p. 16. Locke wants to use the 'right rule of reason' to acquire the 'principles of human nature' (chapter ii, sec. 10, p. 7).
32 Ibid., chapter v, sec. 26, p. 17. Hooker writes that the will does not desire, nor reason instruct us toward the good, without this goal being possible of realisation (book 1, chapter vii, sec. 5, p. 168). The will of man desires 'the utmost good and greatest perfection whereby

Nature hath made it capable' (book 1, chapter viii, sec. 1, p. 170). Locke develops this idea with his argument that for rights to be real, they too must be made possible through natural law. Hooker maintains that in 'nature', we came into the world empty and naked, multiplied and expanded the population under conditions of envy and violence leading to an economy that was incapable of sustaining a life of dignity for mankind. Humans were also given reason and courage by God. Due to these 'defects and imperfections' of a solitary economy, humans were 'induced to seek communion and fellowship with others' (book 1, chapter x, sec. 1, p. 184) and to create a government and law of the commonwealth. Locke will take a similar position to argue that in the state of nature originally there was common property but the need for greater productivity forced humans to create not only a new political and legal system, but a new economy ostensibly grounded in natural law.

33 Ibid. chapter v, sec. 27, p. 17.
34 Ibid., chapter v, sec. 31, p. 20.
35 C.B. MacPherson, *The Political Theory of Possessive Individualism: Hobbes to Locke* (London: Oxford University Press, 1970), pp. 3 and 263–71.
36 Locke, *The Second Treatise of Government*, chapter v, sec. 27, p. 17.
37 Ibid., chapter v, sec. 31, p. 19. This is the clearest statement on the relationship between natural law and natural rights.
38 For an analysis of the moral limits to property, production, and commerce in ancient Greece, see Aristotle, *Nicomachean Ethics*, in *Introduction to Aristotle*, ed. and intro. Richard McKeon (New York, NY: Random House: 1947), book 5, chapter v, 1133a–1134a, pp. 408–10 and *Politics*, trans. T.A. Sinclair, revised Trevor Saunders (London: Penguin, 1981), book I, chapter ix, 1256b40–1258a14, pp. 81–5. Aristotle saw the natural limits of the household economy resting in self-sufficiency, which is the natural means to happiness within the polis. There were other limits established in a moral economy based on household production, including grace and reciprocity among households, friends, and citizens; the law and tradition of a just price; and human need. Ethics and structure are central to Locke's theory of natural limits which derive from classical and medieval philosophy: From Aristotle, he borrows the ideas of need (spoilage) and sufficiency (of *oikos* and *polis*) and from Aquinas, John Calvin, Hugo Grotius, and Samuel Pufendorf, he relies on the importance of human labour in the creation of value. See Emil Kauder, 'The Retarded Acceptance of the Marginal Utility Theory', *Quarterly Journal of Economics* 67 (November 1953): 564–75; James Tully, *A Discourse on Property: John Locke and his Adversaries* (Cambridge: Cambridge University Press, 1980), pp. 111–16; and Peter Dooley, *The Labour Theory of Value* (London: Routledge, 2005), p. 1. Kauder speculated that it was the Calvinist training of Locke that led to the labour theory of value and his rejection of Grotius and Pufendorf.
39 Tully, *A Discourse on Property*, pp. 102–4. Tully in chapters 4 and 5 provides an interesting analysis of the seventeenth-century context of Locke's discussion of natural property in the state of nature and conventional property in civil society as the latter responds to the ideas of Robert Filmer, Pufendorf, and Grotius. Tully takes the position that Locke never held that private property is natural; rather property in a political society is not private but a convention created by natural law to fulfill a social function to preserve life and mankind (p. 99). The central point here is that much of the debate among scholars

as to the nature of property after the state of nature rests upon their understanding of the political community and the role, if any, of natural law. It is certainly true that Locke mentions natural law a number of times after chapter five and especially when referring to the formation and powers of the civil state. The real question is whether the concept has any validity or effectiveness after its power was dismantled in the second state of nature. Tully simply assumes that the natural law in the state of nature is the same as the natural law after the introduction of money and government. What is not in doubt is that Locke develops a theory of property quite different from Grotius and Pufendorf. For more on Locke's theory of natural law and property, see John Locke, *Essays on the Law of Nature*, ed. W. Von Leyden (Oxford: Clarendon Press, 1988). For a further analysis of the natural law and communal limitations to natural rights and the ownership of private property, see MacPherson, *The Political Theory of Possessive Individualism*, pp. 199–220. MacPherson argues that natural law disappears with the movement out of the state of nature into civil society and the state. I would argue that natural law disappears earlier in the second state of nature.

40   Locke, *The Second Treatise of Government*, chapter v, sec. 31, p. 19.
41   Ibid., chapter v, sec. 31, p. 19.
42   Ibid., chapter v, sec. 32, p. 20.
43   Ibid., chapter v, sec. 35, p. 21. 'So that God, by commanding to subdue, gave authority so far to appropriate; and the condition of human life which requires labour and material to work on necessarily introduces private possessions'. God gave humanity land in common for 'their benefit and the greatest convenience of life'; he gave it to the 'industrious and rational'. But Locke also emphasises that 'it cannot be supposed he [God] meant it should always remain common and uncultivated' (chapter v, sec. 34, p. 20).
44   Ibid., chapter v, sec. 33, p. 20.
45   Ibid.
46   Ibid., chapter v, sec. 36, p. 22. *Natural Law and Structural Limits to Private Property in the Original State of Nature*: The economic and structural limitations to the legitimate ownership of private property are stated in chapter v: spoilage (secs. 31 and 37–8), labour (28–30, 32, 36, 39–41, and 51), and sufficiency (33–4). *Dissolving Natural Law and the Limits to Property in the Second State of Nature*: With the early transformation of the modern economic system and the invention of money, commerce, and banking, these limits are dissolved: spoilage (46–8 and 50), labour (41–4, 50, and 85), and sufficiency (37).
47   Ibid., chapter v, sec. 37, pp. 22–3.
48   Leo Strauss, *Natural Right and History* (Chicago, IL: University of Chicago Press, 1965), p. 242.
49   Locke, *The Second Treatise of Government*, chapter v, sec. 43, p. 26.
50   Ibid., chapter v, sec. 46, p. 28.
51   Ibid., chapter v, sec. 50, p. 29.
52   MacPherson, *The Political Theory of Possessive Individualism*, p. 199. The chapter on property is the crucial chapter, for it begins with a natural law justification for natural rights but ends in the elimination of natural law. Natural law and the moral order were replaced by labour and property. MacPherson writes: 'But in fact the chapter on property does something much more important: it removes "the bounds of the Law of Nature" from the

natural property right of the individual. Locke's astonishing achievement was to base the property right on natural right and natural law, and then to remove all the natural law limits from the property right' (ibid.).

53   Locke, *The Second Treatise of Government*, chapter ii, sec. 4, p. 4.
54   MacPherson, *The Political Theory of Possessive Individualism*, pp. 220–1. Strauss, in agreement with MacPherson on this point, states that the end of government is the protection of property and plenty. To emphasise his point about Locke, he quotes from the Federalist James Madison on this issue, 'The protection of [different and unequal faculties of *acquiring* property] is the first object of government' (*Natural Right and History*, p. 245).

From another perspective, Tully, in *A Discourse on Property*, criticises MacPherson for treating Locke as a philosophical defender of seventeenth-century capitalism before the actual development of capitalist society in the late eighteenth century. Tully uses Marxist historians to make his point, including the works of Maurice Dobb, Harry Braverman, Karl Polanyi, and even Marx himself. His thesis is that Locke was not supportive of these changes, but was, on the contrary, very critical of the invention of money and the growing inequality and violence created by conventional private property in the state of nature: 'The acceptance of money brings with it the fall of man. Prior to its appearance men were motivated by need and convenience; now they are driven by the most corrupt of human motives: the desire for more than one needs' (p. 150). Natural law has been contravened. It was because of this, Tully argues, that Locke supported the peaceful transition to civil society ruled by the consent of the majority and natural law so that a just society could be created. Although Tully's argument is interesting, MacPherson is not saying that Locke is ideologically supporting an advanced capitalist society (pp. 140–3 and 149).

Tully continues to argue based on these historical analyses that the social division of labour up to the end of the eighteenth century in England was a non-capitalist mode of production, presumably based on masters and journeymen in the remnants of the medieval artisan guild system. If one were to use just these critical sources, an argument could be made that Locke had misunderstood the nature of the commons, agricultural production, guild workshops, and distributive justice at this time.

Rather, Locke's work is an accurate articulation of the earliest stages of commercial capitalism in England and points to future developments in the economy. Locke is not anticipating the much later rise of industrial capitalism which is the focus of the above mentioned Marxist historians. He is more in tune with the earlier commercial market established by the Medici in Tuscany, the Strozzi in Florence, and the Sforza in Milan. To support his critique of MacPherson, Tully relied on the following authors: John Dunn, *The Political Thought of John Locke* (Cambridge: Cambridge University Press, 1969); Edward Hundert, 'The Making of Homo Faber: John Locke Between Ideology and History', *Journal of the History of Ideas*, 33, 1 (1972): 3–22 and 'Market Society and Meaning in Locke's Political Philosophy', *Journal of the History of Philosophy*, 15 (1977): 33–44; and Alan Ryan, 'Locke and the Dictatorship of the Bourgeoisie', *Political Studies* 13, 2 (1965): 219–30. Their arguments are that Locke is not trying to establish a justification for liberalism in his political philosophy. It might have been helpful to supplement these authors with the alternative positions of Henri Pirenne, *Economic and Social History of Medieval Europe*, trans. I.E. Clegg (New York, NY: Harvest Book, 1937) and *Medieval Cities: Their Origins and the Rival of Trade*, trans. Frank Halsey (Garden City, NY: Doubleday Anchor Books, 1956); S.T. Bindoff, *Tudor England* (Baltimore: MD: Penguin Books, 1966); and Max Weber, *The City*, ed. and trans. Don Martindale and Gertrud Neuwirth (New York, NY: The Free Press, 1966) for their analyses of the rise of commercial capitalism in fifteenth- and sixteenth-century Europe.

Tully continues to reject MacPherson's thesis throughout his work. Perhaps most importantly, he criticises the latter's argument that with the invention of money natural law is no longer operative in the state of nature. (It should be noted that, for Tully, money is not capital or a medium of exchange but hoarded, non-perishable goods [p. 149]). This then justifies unlimited accumulation and a capitalist inspired economy. Tully rejects this thesis. He maintains that Locke's position is that new moral restraints on property must be put in place based on conventional rules and freemen consent. Tully writes, 'It seems to me remarkable to suppose that Locke should attempt to dismantle the Thomistic framework of positive natural law which constitutes the basis of his theory. For he clearly could not do away with this without destroying exclusive rights as well' (p. 153). Rights and law are naturally interlinked. Tully is certainly correct that this is the heart of the matter. Whether he has correctly evaluated Locke's position is something entirely different.

But what is the revised relationship between natural law and property after the invention of money? According to Tully, the debate hinges on the connection between sections 34 and 35 or between the early times of the natural appropriation of the commons without consent and the later times after the invention of money with a conventional appropriation which now requires consent of the commoners to enclose land (pp. 153–4). Conventional appropriation now requires a government constituted in natural law. It is in the very last sections of his book that he outlines his most provocative and radical ideas about Locke. He unequivocally says that as we enter into the public contract fleeing the state of nature, all property reverts back to the general ownership of the community. 'All the possessions a man has in the state of nature, or shall acquire in his commonwealth, become the possession of the community' (p. 164). Thus the legislative powers of the government have the duty to enforce natural law principles on a just and fair distribution of this common property and define the limits to property (pp. 163–70). By entering in a commonwealth, land reverts back to common property over which the government now has jurisdiction defined by natural law (Locke, *The Second Treatise of Government*, ch. xii, sec. 143, p. 82). Natural rights and natural possessions are exchanged for conventional ones. Tully notes that the enclosure laws requested by wealthy landowners for the expansion of their personal property were introduced in the House of Commons in 1664, 1661, and 1668 and defeated. He rejects the arguments by Filmer and MacPherson that only landowners could be citizens possessing legal rights. Now a consideration of the moral limits to property and the centrality of natural law lies not in the economy but in the newly formed government with its regulation of property based on trust and the natural principles of justice (p. 154).

The power to enforce the rights of equality, liberty, and executive power of the state of nature are now surrendered and entrusted to the legislative power by common consent to the constitution and government for the preservation of mankind and political society.

Distributive justice and property rights are no longer tied to natural law of the state of nature but to the rules and regulations of civil society. In section 135, Locke states that natural law does not end in society; positive laws only reinforce the eternal law of God, just as civil rights reinforce natural rights. Tully emphasises that distributive justice has taken on a new face: civil rights are distributed to the citizens. There is no longer any discussion of the particular moral and structural limits to property although toward the end of his book, he contends each person 'has the civil right and duty to work and the civil right to his share of the community's possessions for support and comfort' (pp. 166–7). But what does it mean to have a civil right to the community's possessions? Tully also declares that Locke is firmly in the tradition of John Lilburne and Richard Overton. However much Tully claims that there are obligations to God in the way property is created and distributed, there is no articulation by Locke of these issues as there was in chapter 5 of his work. If property is still held in common by the state and redistributed on the basic principle of labour and distributive justice for a good and secure life, there is no indication either of the specific natural law or the structural economic enforcement in the market of its moral principles. In the original state of nature, individuals not only had the right to labour and property, but there was a broader obligation for nature to provide the material foundations of life in the common land and animals used for personal and family consumption. In the second half of his treatise on politics (chapters viii–xix), Locke integrates natural law with the political community but provides no structural analysis of political economy to institutionally support the preservation and sustenance of the dispossessed without property. It is natural law and distributive justice without economics. Not having done this means that natural law, too, is dispossessed.

Contrary to Tully's claim, with the formation of political society, there are civil rights without natural law – a right without enforcement or prior moral obligation or structured restraint and support to provide the basic means of sustenance and self-preservation similar to that which existed in the original state of nature. Natural law is used as a legitimation of state government but ultimately has lost its meaning within the classical and medieval traditions. The question remains why was Locke so precise about the nature of the moral limits to property, plenty, and prosperity in the state of nature, while so unclear and imprecise about these restrictions in civil society unless, in fact, natural law was dissolved?

55 MacPherson, *The Political Theory of Possessive Individualism*, p. 217.
56 Locke, *The Second Treatise of Government*, chapter vi, sec. 57, pp. 32–3.
57 Ibid., chapter vii, sec. 85, p. 47. See also, MacPherson, *The Political Theory of Possessive Individualism*, p. 231.
58 Locke, *The Second Treatise of Government*, chapter viii, sec. 95, p. 54.
59 MacPherson, *The Political Theory of Possessive Individualism*, pp. 203–20; and Michael Zuckert, *Natural Rights and the New Republicanism*, pp. 234–40 and 252–72 and *Launching Liberalism: On Lockean Political Philosophy* (Lawrence, KS: University of Kansas Press, 2002), pp. 192–3. It is easy to see at this point in the early stages of liberalism the beginnings of moral nihilism and an existential crisis. See Erich Fromm, *Marx's Concept of Man* (New York, NY: Frederick Ungar Publishing Company, 1961), pp. 61–79.
60 *Property, Civil Society, and the End of Government*: Locke, *The Second Treatise of Govern-*

ment, chapter vii, sec. 85, p. 48, chapter vii, sec. 87, p. 48, and chapter vii, sec. 90, p. 50; chapter viii, sec. 95, p. 54; chapter ix, secs. 123–4, pp. 70–71; and chapter xi, sec. 138, p. 79.

61 Ibid., chapter vii, sec. 94, pp. 53–4.
62 Ibid., chapter viii, sec. 96, p. 55.
63 Ibid., chapter xi, sec. 138, p. 79.
64 Aristotle, Jean-Jacques Rousseau, Marx, and J.S. Mill, and a number of eighteenth-century radical Protestants (James Burgh, Richard Price, Joseph Priestly, John Wilkes, John Cartwright, Granville Sharp, Catharine Macaulay, and Thomas Paine) agreed that social ethics requires political economy, that is, a society based on justice, virtue, natural rights, freedom, and/or happiness requires the fulfilment of basic material human needs as a social and structural prerequisite. Natural rights require natural law for their existence and perpetuation. These ethical and political principles are meaningless in a society with rampant poverty, class inequality, and abuse of power; class destroys the possibility of rights, freedom, and justice. Thomas Jefferson in the *Declaration of Independence* drops property as an inalienable right and replaces it with the 'pursuit of happiness' because of his fear that property could undermine life and liberty. He, too, was concerned about the violation of equality and liberty by the abuse of property rights and wanted to limit property acquisition through progressive taxation, tax remittance for the poor, redistribution of wealth, and extension of common property.

The authors who argued that property is not a natural right include Hugo Grotius, the Levellers John Lilburne and Richard Overton, Rousseau, Paine, Jefferson, Benjamin Franklin, Joseph Priestly, Daniel Raymond, J.S. Mill, William Godwin, and Henry David Thoreau. The seventeenth-century Levellers accepted Locke's labour theory of value as they argued for a 'dismantling of economic privileges and the equalisation of property'; they fought for the radical egalitarianism of rights and social reality along with political democracy. On the other side of the debate, Alexis de Tocqueville in the eighteenth century, while defending democracy, sought to protect property against equality and the tyranny of the majority. (Richard Schlatter, *Private Property: The History of an Idea* [New York, NY: Russell & Russell, 1973], pp. 132–4, 195–9, and 236–7).

65 The issue of ethics and structure, rights and law remains at the heart of Locke's theory of natural law, at least in the beginning of his work. The relationship between metaphysics and ethics, metaphysics and politics is central because it expresses the Aristotelian ideas of causality, action, and becoming. There must be a union of form and matter, essence and potency (possibility) before an individual substance is to develop. According to Aristotle, the form is both the efficient and final (end) cause of the object. If the final goal of humanity is the virtuous and good life (Aristotle) or the preservation of property and humanity (Locke), there must be a material or real possibility in the form of both a moral and structural end – a political community – to realise these ideals. This is why Aristotle's ethics and politics are so intimately connected in his writings. For the virtuous life to be made real, there must be a balance between ethics and structure, that is, citizens must have an ethics of virtue, practical wisdom, and public participation along with reciprocal (commutative), distributive, legal, and political justice. Equality, citizenship, and community require the political institutions which make these values relevant and possible – synthesis of form and matter. Natural law contains both its moral form or

essence and its legal and legislative possibility, since the legislature and positive law must embody this law and bring it to life. Hypothetically, if a society views education as a natural right, there must be schools, teachers, books, classrooms, etc. for this right to be made real; without the structures, the right is worthless. There must be a material foundation to realise the right as the essence of citizenship. See Rommen, *The Natural Law*, p. 15.

66   Locke, *The Second Treatise of Government*, chapter xi, sec. 138, p. 79.

67   Regarding this issue of inalienable natural rights, human needs, and economic structures, Staunton Lynd, in his work *Intellectual Origins of American Radicalism* (1969), tells the story of Langdon Byllesby, a Philadelphia printer and socialist best known for his work *Observations on the Sources and Effects of Unequal Wealth* (1826). Writing about the *Declaration of Independence*, Byllesby wrote: 'To speak of inalienable rights of life and liberty without providing the material means to sustain them would be like saying that "an ox has an inalienable right to fly, or a fish to walk"' (p. 89). Without providing wings or feet to these animals – or without providing sufficient material means to sustain human life – these rights are useless and absurd. Even Locke saw this very point clearly. Without an egalitarian society and communal property, there are no rights to life, liberty, and security (pp. 83–4). Later Hegel will retranslate this discussion by arguing that without *Sittlichkeit*, there is no *Moralität*. Rights easily turn into political abstractions and ideologies without meaning. Having no wings, oxen have no 'right to fly' and having no material security and welfare in a class society, human beings have no 'right to life and liberty'. Since these rights are inalienable, they cannot be dissolved or displaced by other rights or ethical principles, such as meritocracy, effort, wealth, or class. The right to property entails the existence of common property and natural law of the community from which the individual makes it private by his labour. Property is the universal and necessary condition for the assurance of the natural rights to personhood, life, liberty, and security. Without property and universal health care, there are no natural rights and, without natural law, common property, and universal health for all, there is no property or personhood. The irony of Locke's position is that both natural law and natural rights become impossible in a class society under capitalism.

68   Richard Schlatter, *Private Property: The History of an Idea* (New York, NY: Russell & Russell Publishers, 1951). Thomas Jefferson was part of the eighteenth-century agrarian movement along with Thomas Spence, William Ogilvie, and Thomas Paine who used the right of property against its unnatural accumulation by English landholders. Private appropriation of land by labour is justified in a state of plentitude of common land. However, by the eighteenth century this dream of Locke's state of nature was no longer visible or possible. Ogilvie continued to defend the principle of labour but with the provision that property be equally distributed when the supply is limited. On the other hand, Spence and Paine rejected the principle of labour as legitimating property and maintained that 'land itself always remains common' (p. 174). These arguments go back to the radicals of the seventeenth century with the Levellers John Lilburne and Richard Overton who called for a radical egalitarianism, economic redistribution, and equal property; during this period there were also the Diggers, who like Gerrard Winstanley, sought economic equality and the end to private property. Jefferson, an 'agrarian apostle of equality' and critic of concentrated land wealth, was aware that equality, life, and liberty could not survive in a class

system based on inequality of property ownership. For this reason, he defended popular sovereignty, economic equality, and economic redistribution, and even discussed with Paine in 1789 the possibility of state control over private property (pp. 198–9).

69 As we have seen in endnote 27, Strauss in *Natural Right and History* has also interpreted Locke as having a political theory and state of nature similar to Hobbes. His approach, however, is quite different. According to Strauss, Locke held that the state of nature was violent and corrupt and that the natural right to property precedes natural law in the state of nature since the priority is on self-preservation. Strauss's argument has other serious limitations as he: (1) ignores the central importance of natural law in state of nature and civil society; (2) drops labour and sufficiency limitations as being of central importance to Locke; (3) contends that self-interest and self-preservation are the bases for human labour; (4) overlooks Hooker and the moral and economic restraints on property acquisition in the state of nature; (5) holds civil society at first formed through democratic rule but later tended to be the rule of the wise and wealthy elite; (6) argues that upon entering civil society, citizens would surrender their natural rights to life and liberty; and (7) does not view natural law as too different from natural right – this is also indicated in the title of his book and his use of natural right to characterise the classical Greek period of Socrates, Plato, and Aristotle. The result is that Strauss views the supposedly reasonable and tolerant Locke as much closer to the ideas of Hobbes than had been previously thought by scholars.

According to Strauss, Locke initially characterised the original time of the state of nature as 'a state of peace, good-will, mutual assistance, and preservation' with relative material plenty – as 'a golden age ruled by God or good demons' (p. 224). But shortly thereafter, Locke 'demolishes it as his argument proceeds' and turns the state of nature into a continuous violent conflict with little concern for the well-being of others; in this state 'the law of nature ... would be ineffectual' (p. 224). Self-preservation was the primary imperative of social action, and this led to violence, material scarcity, and conflict in a world of 'corruption and viciousness of degenerative men', a world of 'mutual grievances, injuries, and wrongs' (ibid.). For Strauss, since the state of nature is based on competition over scarce resources for self-preservation, it was a time of wretchedness, poverty, habitual war, and social anarchy.

To make matters even worse, the state of nature is without universal and absolute natural law or moral principles to guide or restrain individual action; if it were under natural law, it would be a state of peace and good will (p. 225). Since it is an age of innocence and penury, there is no time to study or learn the law of nature. A few pages later Strauss qualifies this point by stating that 'the original natural law' and its economic restriction of waste did exist in the very early stage of the state of nature at the beginning of the world, when there was material plenty and a sparse population (p. 238). But the state of nature changed with the loss of natural abundance and material well-being for everyone. Strauss briefly mentions labour but does develop it along with sufficiency as a moral restriction on the rights of property and self-preservation. The principle of no harm to others is left behind in the first stage of human evolution in 'the first ages'. In fact, he even adjusts the moral principles of natural law in the state of nature to include the duty to appropriate nature through labour and prevent waste, but 'permitted unconcern for the need of other human beings' (p. 239). Strauss continues, 'Appropriation without concern for the need of others is simply justified because it is justified regardless of whether men lived in a state of plenty or a state of penury'. In the footnote at the bottom of the page, he continues, 'man must have the natural right to appropriate by his labour what he needs for his self-preservation, regardless of whether or not there is enough left for others' (ibid.). Strauss's interpretation of Locke's theory of the state of nature as a state of violence and destruction – a state of war – confuses the original and second state of nature. The thesis presented in this book is that violence and war started after the disappearance and loss of natural law, common possessions, and the ethical and economic restraints on property acquisition that resulted from the invention of money, unlimited private property, and a market economy in the second stage of the state of nature.

Nothing remains of natural law in Strauss's reading of Locke. The former develops an unusual and idiosyncratic characterisation of Locke's state of nature as a state of war which could only be remedied by the peace and prosperity of civil society. Later, however, Strauss maintains that 'property is an institution of natural law' (p. 234) but continues with the comment that 'natural law regarding property ceases to be valid' (p. 235). Property is no longer burdened by the obstruction of natural law limits to the economy and becomes the spirit of capitalism (p. 246). So, natural law does not exist in the state of nature or in civil society; natural law is just not an essential element in Strauss's understanding of Locke's ethical, economic, and political theory. Justice has been reduced to market categories of unlimited acquisition of money and wealth. Strauss maintains that since the nineteenth century, scholars have had difficulties understanding why and how Locke used the idea of the state of nature. Later scholars no longer believed in natural law since they understood that Locke himself did not believe in the moral principle and did not accept the idea that unlimited capital formation was unjust (ibid.). Strauss writes that civil society must be grounded in the desire for self-preservation, self-interest, and private vices; these desires result in the common good and greater public benefits. Ideals and hopes are not the basis of human life and civil society; vices are their foundation and inspiration. The end result is a society built on natural drives and moral nihilism (p. 250); the end result is a return to Hobbes. For Strauss this represents the beginning of his turn to Friedrich Nietzsche, Martin Heidegger, and Carl Schmitt.

Where Locke and Hobbes differ is in the form of government that will be created in civil society. For Hobbes it is an absolute government, whereas for Locke it is a limited constitutional government, although both view the creation of civil society as an expression of self-preservation. Strauss even refers to Locke's theory of government as 'a mighty leviathan where citizens give up their natural rights and power to the civil government' (p. 233). Strauss distinguishes between the power of the majority to protect the right to self-preservation against tyrannical governments and the ideal government which protects property 'against the demands of the indigent, that is, protects the industrious and rational against the lazy and quarrelsome. This is essential to public happiness or the common good' (p. 234). Thus, for Strauss, violence is part of Locke's view of the state of nature and civil society, while for MacPherson, violence is part of Locke's view of unnatural wealth acquisition resulting from a runaway economy.

For a critical review of Strauss's interpretation of Locke as 'imposing an apriori structure on the history of ideas' (p. 270) that creates static ahistorical categories of ancient and modern objective natural law and subjective natural rights; that does not see the theological and philosophical continuity between the ancients and moderns; and that fails to trace the origins of natural rights theory to the late medieval legal scholarship of William of Ockham, Jean Gerson, and Hugo Grotius, see Brian Tierney, *The Idea of Natural Rights: Studies on Natural Rights, Natural Law and Church Law 1150–1625* (Atlanta, GA: Scholar's Press, 1997); Annabel Brett, *Liberty, Right and Nature: Individual Rights in Later Scholastic Thought* (Cambridge: Cambridge University Press, 1997); and Rosenthal, *Crown under Law*, pp. 267–306.

70   Rommen, *The Natural Law*, p. 79. Rommen continues: 'Locke substitutes for the traditional idea of the natural law as an order of human affairs, as a moral reflex of the metaphysical order of the universe revealed to human reason in the creation of God's will, the conception of natural law as a rather nominalistic symbol for a catalogue or bundle of individual rights that stem from individual self-interest' (ibid.). Locke's theory of a universal common good is simply a nominalist summary of particular natural rights and self-interests without a more comprehensive foundation in the ethical and economic features of natural law. Natural law has been reduced to common consent, the formation of civil government, self-interest, and the preservation of property. Natural law no longer has metaphysical and ethical primacy over natural rights but has become indistinguishable from natural rights; natural rights are now prior to natural law in Locke's political theory and have become the actual content of law itself. There is no transcendent or universal moral order which underlies rights and civil governance. In his brief overview of Locke in his work, Rommen makes the interesting observation that, besides Locke's political and ideological interests, it is his own epistemology that would undermine his political theory. His empiricism, nominalism (legacy of the Franciscan theologians William of Ockham and Duns Scotus), relativism, and metaphysical skepticism 'undermined the philosophical bases of the natural law', just as his own legal theory would undermine its political foundations. Rommen concludes that Locke, in fact, had prepared the way for the later criticism of natural law found in the skepticism of David Hume and the utilitarianism of Jeremy Bentham (pp. 97–108). Rommen contends that in the classical period natural law served as the moral basis for human law that found its realisation in positive laws; it is the essence of man and the very foundation of justice (pp. 4–29 and 182). Playing off the distinction between morality (relations with self) and ethics (relations with others), Rommen nicely summarises the distinction between the two in the sentence: 'Politics is and remains a part of the moral universe ... for a more perfect realisation of the good life ... at the same time the common good under the rule of law' (p. 235). Locke, following in the path of Hobbes, who was a nominalist, ended his political theory by denying natural law or by reducing it to the law of the self-preservation of person and property.

71   Ibid., p. 80.

72   Richard Tawney, *Religion and the Rise of Capitalism: A Historical Study* (New York, NY: Harcourt, Brace and Company, 1926), pp. 175–93. A similar position is held by George Bull in 'What Did Locke Borrow from Hooker?', *Thought* 1 (1932): 'Hooker makes society arise, by consent. So does Locke, but it is a consent which transfers individual powers, not a consent which actuates a moral obligation from the Natural Law, to live in a society whose prerogatives, rights, and duties come not from individuals but from the same Law

of Nature' (pp. 134–5). Bull concludes his essay by excoriating the fact that Locke used Hooker's Anglican theology against himself, Filmer, and other clerical defenders of the divine right of kings.

73   Tawney, *Religion and the Rise of Capitalism*, p. 179. 'The process by which natural justice, imperfectly embedded in positive law, was replaced as the source of authority by positive law ... had its analogy in the rejection by social theory of the whole conception of an objective standard of economic equity. The law of nature had been invoked by medieval writers as a moral restraint upon economic self-interest'. By the seventeenth century, natural law had been replaced by natural appetites and the psychology of self-interest and self-preservation. Natural law became a moral extension and justification of the secular public policy of the state but in the process lost its own economic ethic (p. 165). Economics and politics were branches of ethics throughout the classical and medieval period but were reduced to issues of technical utility and economic expediency in the sixteenth and seventeenth centuries. Tawney refers to this as the 'secularization of political theory' (pp. 6 and 278–9).

74   There have been a number of different critical interpretations of Locke's political theory used in this chapter, including the following: (1) the incoherence and contradictions of liberalism; (2) the evolution within the state of nature from a self-sufficient family or moral economy (*oikonomike*) to a competitive market economy or unnatural wealth acquisition (*chrematistike*); (3) the dissolution and disappearance of natural law, social justice, and the moral justification of capitalism through natural rights to property (MacPherson); (4) natural law as the justification and legitimation of natural rights, on the one hand, and as the structural possibility for natural rights, on the other; (5) natural law as providing the ideological or exoteric facade for a defence of modern natural rights and liberalism against the denunciation of Locke as a heretic (Strauss); (6) natural rights as justifying a return to Hobbes's state of nature and the 'war of all against all' (Zuckert); and (7) natural rights reduced to a defence of property in terms of persons, liberty, and estates.

75   In the seventeenth century, four major natural law theorists were born in the same year, 1632: Samuel Pufendorf, John Locke, Richard Cumberland, and Benedict Spinoza. Interestingly, they all read Hugo Grotius's writings. See Aaron Garrett, 'Was Spinoza a Natural Lawyer?', *Cardozo Law Review* 25, 2 (December 2003): 627–41. Natural law theory contends that through the rule or light of reason we are capable of knowing the laws of nature (metaphysics and physics) and the laws of humanity (ethics and politics) as a product of God's creation (ancients and Scholastics) or the creation of nature itself (modern natural law). Lloyd Weinreb in his work *Natural Law and Justice* (Cambridge, MA: Harvard University Press, 1987) argues that the objective conditions and moral foundations of natural law lie in 'the bare human nature, or the purpose of a divine Creator, or the general will' (p. 89). In the history of the Western tradition, nature (Aristotle), God (Aquinas), or the community (Aristotle and Rousseau) has provided the moral foundation of nature law and the objective normative order of justice (pp. 248–51). Weinreb applies this view of natural law to his understanding of neo-Aristotelian communalism, specifically Alasdair MacIntyre, Michael Sandel, and Michael Walzer. But Marx, following Aristotle, has also based his natural law and social justice principles on human nature and the community (democracy).

Weinreb writes: 'the main significance that Locke drew from the idea of natural law is not that reason leads us to God but that reason enables us to order our affairs correctly'. This transformation of natural law is developed in Jürgen Habermas, *Theory and Practice*, trans. John Viertel (Boston, MA: Beacon Press, 1973), pp. 41–81. Habermas contends that the Aristotelian notion of practical wisdom or *phronesis* had been replaced by liberalism with the concept of *techne* or technical knowledge. Knowledge becomes the technical engineering of the correct social order of the state based on natural rights rather than the search for social ethics and the justice of natural law. Deliberative rationality, virtue, prudence, and political discourse are replaced by a science of domination (*Herrschaftswissen*) based on the universal principles of the correct order of society: political wisdom is replaced by political technology, natural law by science and natural rights; social ethics by the physics of human nature; *praxis* by *techne*; and the public sphere by civil society. Habermas writes: 'The engineers of the correct order can disregard the categories of ethical social intercourse and confine themselves to the construction of conditions under which human beings, just like objects within nature, will necessarily behave in a calculable manner. This separation of politics from morality replaces instruction in leading a good and just life with making possible a life of well-being within a correctly instituted order' (p. 43).

CHAPTER 2

Justice Beyond Liberalism: Natural Law and the Ethical Community in Hegel

There is another philosophical tradition that parallels that of liberalism and possessive individualism in the modern world which emphasises the community, common good, and general welfare. Rather than defending natural rights and a utilitarian individualism with all its encompassing defence of private property and a market economy, Karl Marx will turn to natural law with its roots in the ancient and medieval traditions of communal responsibility, social identity, and self-worth. For him, individuals are defined not by their rights or ownership of property, but by their participation within an ethical community and their commitment to self-determination and self-realisation within a working democracy. In fact, Marx will take the older natural law tradition and replace its spiritual and metaphysical foundation in God with an ethical foundation in *praxis* (reason, will, and work) and politics (economic and political democracy). As in the case of Aristotle and Hegel, ethics is not a private or metaphysical affair between individuals and their conscience or God; rather, ethics is social and must be embedded in the economic and political institutions of society to be made real and relevant. Social institutions are the rational and objective manifestation of individual freedom; without them, freedom is purely subjective, arbitrary, and, thus, irrelevant. As he follows in the path of Immanuel Kant and Jean-Jacques Rousseau, Hegel will make a break with the early natural rights tradition of Hobbes and Locke which emphasised, as we have already seen, individual liberty, security of life, and protection of property. He will base his theory of natural law on the rational will and its own universal moral law. This chapter will examine the intellectual heritage so influential on Marx which drew its inspiration from the natural law tradition of Aristotle, Aquinas, Hooker, and Hegel.

There is a tension in the work of Georg Wilhelm Friedrich Hegel between classical natural law and modern natural rights, between communalism and liberalism, and between the ethical community and competitive egoism. His earliest theological writings were attempts to make real the ancient ideal of the community in *The Positivity of the Christian Religion* (1795–6) and *The Spirit of Christianity and its Fate* (1798–9), *On the Scientific Ways of Treating Natural Law* (1802–3), *System of Ethical Life* (1802–3), *First Philosophy of the* Spirit (1803–4), *German Constitution* (1802), and the *Jenaer Realphilosophie* (*Philosophy of*

Spirit, lectures at the University of Jena from 1803 to 1806).[1] By the time of the *Phenomenology of Spirit* (1807) and the *Philosophy of Right* (1821), he was making adjustments to his early philosophy by attempting to integrate the two opposing traditions.

Hegel's early writings were an ode to the ancient Greeks and their commitment to unity and harmony and the essential responsibility to the ethical life of the community (*Sittlichkeit*) within the polity. But in the *Phenomenology* things begin to change. First, the book begins with an analysis of Consciousness, Self-Consciousness, and Reason, but then something very interesting transpires at the beginning of the next section on the Spirit. Hegel opens with an analysis of the true spirit and ethical order of the Greeks but falls immediately thereafter into a discussion of the Enlightenment, alienation, corrupted reason, Kantian philosophy, and the French Terror. This is followed by the Absolute Spirit which attempts to heal the wounds created by the Enlightenment, Kant, and Robespierre; it provides for the modern version of the unhappy consciousness where human reason creates a harmony of the mind at a time when it cannot exist in the reality of social institutions – when Roman philosophy and Christianity offered a mental and metaphysical escape from the reality of the master-slave relationship of the Roman Empire. According to Hegel in the *Philosophy of Right*, resolution of the conflict between natural law and natural rights is accomplished with the rise of the liberal state, which provides the mechanism for integrating the family, economy, and polity into an ethical unity. In Hegel's works, natural rights of the economy and civil society are integrated with the natural law and moral order of the modern state in an idealist fashion that will later become unacceptable to Marx.

Hegel's later writings attempt to modify his earlier aspirations and dreams by making them compatible with the modern view of subjectivity, natural rights, individual liberty, and private property. Locke had attempted this synthesis of the ancients and moderns but failed. Hegel also never resolves this tension between the ancients and the moderns, but he does frame the issue in a certain way that is helpful for later theorists, in particular, Marx. Initially, he is very critical of natural rights as he turns to Kant and Rousseau for his rejection of the materialism and empiricism of Thomas Hobbes and John Locke. Kant provides Hegel with a theory of justice and virtue that Hegel develops into a theory of social ethics. Following in the tradition of Aristotle, he sees that moral philosophy lacked a social and political dimension. That is, Kant's theory of the categorical imperative with its emphasis on moral autonomy, human freedom, and practical reason rested on an abstract individual will and subjective moral values that abstracted from the values, laws, and institutions of society. As in the case of Aristotle, who connected ethics and politics into one comprehensive social theory, Hegel would build his ethics and social theory on the basis of the Objective Spirit and ethical life of the community. To be made concrete and practical, moral values have to be made real in the living spirit of the social institutions, thus reuniting ethics and politics back into the community.

For Hegel, natural law, as the rational and moral principles that guide human action, is not justified on the basis of some metaphysical or abstract principle of God, human psychology, or the state of nature. Rather, Hegel's natural law is a social and historical phenomenon grounded in the self-conscious spirit of humanity as it builds its social, economic, political, and legal institutions (Objective Spirit) and its cultural forms of art, religion, and philosophy (Absolute Spirit). Unlike Kant, Hegel believes that moral values and action, to be made real, must be embedded in concrete social institutions; values and ideals, to be real, must be externalised and moved beyond an internal self-consciousness into the objective institutions of the state, constitution, and laws, that is, 'the rational social order'. As the Enlightenment and modern liberalism progressed, and with it a theory of natural rights and possessive individualism, there occurred an increasing social competition, self-interest, and community fragmentation produced by the logic of the market and civil society. The state as it developed in the seventeenth and eighteenth centuries became a technical intermediary to protect the social contract, positive law, and the abstract rights of the individual. Writing about this issue, Abel Garza Jr. states: 'Classical Athens offered an ideal that Hegel wished to regain in the modern world of social fragmentation and mutually competing individuals ... In the idealized version of ancient Greek politics the essence of the human condition was embodied in politics where the Greek citizens were inseparable from political activity and shared a common ethics'.[2] With the rise of liberalism, there was an eclipse of the community, that is, a loss of a real sense of political commitment in which individuals defined their very being and identity. Rather, it was in their private and public lives, in their family associations and citizenship, that individuals were inextricably bound together in the ethical life of the community. And with this loss of social unity and a concern for the common good, the ideal of an integrated and harmonious polity was becoming a more and more remote possibility to Hegel. However, he never surrendered the dream which he attempted to reconstruct in his *Philosophy of Right* by integrating the Greek ideal with a broader understanding of modern subjectivity, moral autonomy, and self-conscious reason.

We have seen in the previous chapter that faced with a similar dilemma of the natural law and natural rights dichotomy, Locke used natural law to justify rights, property, and a market economy with unlimited accumulation. Hegel, on the other hand, in his later writings sees the problem and attempts to integrate the two opposing traditions into the modern liberal state. Hegel does not attempt to abandon the classical ideal, but to incorporate it into its living spirit. Marx, in turn, will ultimately have to deal with these contradictory traditions by rejecting the natural rights of liberalism and capitalism and expanding the modern natural law tradition of Rousseau, Benedict Spinoza, and Kant with their emphasis on freedom, action, and politics. Whereas Hegel utilised the modern liberal state as the mechanism for the reconciliation and integration of natural law and natural rights in the moral life of the community, Marx will use the memory of the ancient polity (Aristotle) as the means to accomplish this end. For Marx, natural law will be based on a view of human nature and needs bound to the economic and political democracy of decentralised workers' associations.[3]

Early Theological Writings and Dreams of Classical Antiquity in Hegel

In one of Hegel's earlier essays, *The Positivity of the Christian Religion* (1795), written while a tutor in Berne, Switzerland, he outlines the relationship between religion and politics as he compares the folk religion of ancient Greece and Rome to that of early Christianity. Religion is an expression of the underlying ideals and moral principles of the political community. He contends that the Greek and Roman religions were the product of free peoples that satisfied their basic human needs. When society changes its mode of politics, the religious consciousness also changes. At one point in the essay he outlines the specific character of classical antiquity:

> As free men the Greeks and Romans obeyed laws laid down by themselves, obeyed men whom they had themselves appointed to office, waged wars on which they had themselves decided, gave their property, exhausted their passions, and sacrificed their lives by thousands for an end which was their own. They neither learned nor taught [a moral system] but evinced by their actions the moral maxims which they could call their very own. In public as in private and domestic life, every individual was a free man, one who lived by his own laws. The idea (*Idee*) of his country or of his state was the invisible and higher reality for which he strove, which impelled him to effort; it was the final end of his world or in his eyes the final end of the world, an end which he found manifested in the realities of his daily life or which he himself co-operated in manifesting and maintaining.[4]

This is a powerful and beautiful vision of the Greek and Roman ideal projected by Hegel. Their moral values were neither metaphysical nor scholastic, but a living embodiment of their personal and social lives. The beginnings of Hegel's theory of natural law lie in the blending of classical antiquity with a renewed Kantian philosophy; the moral maxims which guided humans during this ancient period were self-directed and self-created. In both the public and private spheres, individuals were free. The antagonisms that are distinctive characteristics of the eighteenth and nineteenth centuries, that is, the contradictions between the public and the private spheres, the state and civil society, did not exist in this idealised vision of Hegel's philosophy. The purpose and meaning of human life became expressed in the moral life of the community. It is in his return to this world that Hegel found a solution to the problems of modernity. The abstract moral imperatives and transcendent ideals of Christianity and the antagonistic drives of possessive individualism and natural rights were tearing apart the fabric of society.[5] The ancients offered Hegel insights into an alternative in which the goals of the individual and community were no longer at odds; the ancients offered Hegel the possibility of thinking beyond the present into the future by using the vision and ideals of classical antiquity. The dedication to the ideals of the Greek polity and Roman republic became the driving force that reintegrated the human spirit and the self-conscious will. This will be the driving intellectual force throughout Hegel's life.[6]

The ancient Greeks and Romans were content in the political enjoyment of this life and did not need an escape into some eternal realm of absolute truth or personal salvation. Humans constructed the world through perception and participation, through knowledge and activity. There was no division between the individual and community, for individual morality found its highest expression in political action. And there was certainly no thought of an eternal afterlife that gave meaning to a corrupted human life, for that meaning was achieved among the ancients by their self-determination and construction of their own social and political reality. Meaning came from human activity within the bonds of an ethical community. The Christian God and afterlife were necessary constructions only after this moral life with its social harmony and rational coherence broke down with the rise of the Roman Empire and Christian theology. The new religion was not something that arose from the inner strength and values of the moral and political community, but was an external imposition that attempted to provide existential comfort in a world that had lost its purpose and meaning.

According to Hegel, 'the Greek and Roman gods held sway in the realm of nature and over everything which could bring grief or happiness to men'.[7] They were asked for their wisdom, gifts, advice, and their blessings. The gods were, in fact, manifestations of humanity's own self-awareness and freedom. In an interesting twist to a sociology of knowledge, Hegel views the Greek and Roman gods as the religious expression of a democratic or republican society. The gods could be implored to help with the fortuitous circumstances of everyday life, but they could not impose a metaphysical or moral system on human beings. Moral laws were not the product of divine commands, but, rather, the product of a self-conscious free will. At this point in the essay, Hegel moves from the ancients to the moderns and the moral philosophy of Kant to develop the implications of his theory of subjectivity and natural law. Hegel defines humanity not by its pregiven nature or psychological predispositions to act in certain ways, but by its rationality and free will. Natural law is defined by its own moral order and set of moral principles. Individuals have a duty or obligation to act based on the good while respecting others and treating them as ends in themselves. Each must respect the freedom, will, and purposes of the other. Hegel states that 'they did not set up and impose on others any moral system, whether one that was divine or one manufactured or abstracted [from experience] by themselves'.[8] In the same breath, Hegel integrates Aristotle's theory of the Athenian polity with Kant's theory of practical reason. This synthetic harmony of ethics (virtue and politics) and morality (reason and will) represents the best of both the ancients and the moderns. Freedom is to be understood as political liberty, equality, and self-conscious rational action; these are the prerequisites to a virtuous and happy life. In both cases, freedom refers to political freedom to create the constitution and laws of a free society and to the self-determination and moral autonomy of a kingdom of ends. Natural law is the natural social order of human reason created by free individuals within the moral life of the community. This is a view of natural law and individual freedom that is quite at odds with the values of liberalism and the Enlightenment view of natural rights, equality, and economic freedom.

With the breakdown of the old moral economy and social ethics of antiquity, a new social system evolved based on a class aristocracy, market economy, and a military empire. The state became less and less an expression of the moral community and more and more the private property of the nobility. With the rise of the Roman Empire and Christianity, something profound is lost in the human experience. Turning to Baron de Montesquieu, Hegel deeply bemoans the loss of a political life of virtue and freedom in which the collective interests of the public have priority over self-interest, private ambitions, and personal avarice. People now lived in a society ruled by oppressive, despotic political and religious authorities who based their authority on wealth, rank, and privileged power: 'The picture of the state as a product of his own energies disappeared from the citizen's soul'.[9] And with it disappeared the passionate love of the laws of one's country, equality, moderation, reciprocity, honesty, political participation, and republican virtue; with it disappeared an ethical concern for the other as a citizen of the state. With the decline of the Roman republic, power rested on the shoulders of the one or the few. The state was no longer a public sphere for the expression of the virtuous and happy life, but now became, according to Hegel, a lifeless machine whose 'great end' was to maintain political order, stability, and utility for the aristocracy. The result of these transformations was a new type of society where 'all activity and every purpose now had a bearing on something individual; activity was no longer for the sake of a whole or an ideal. All political freedom vanished also; the citizen's right gave him only a right to the security of that property which now filled his entire world'.[10] Political freedom disappeared with the ancient polity and republic, to be replaced by the insufficient and ignominious materialism of liberty and security of property. The very concept of freedom was depleted of all ethical and political substance and eclipsed by a crude utilitarianism. Hegel seemed to be transplanting a critique of modern liberalism back into the Christian world of the Roman Empire where he envisages the rise of individualism and materialism. The replacement of the Christian God for the ancient polity was by any standard an insufficient and inadequate trade that was unfortunately not noticed by later Enlightenment and liberal political philosophers. Only those who, like Hegel, still remembered critical elements of the ancients were able to recollect a natural law still burning in their hearts (reason and morality) and spirit (politics).

The right of the citizen to freedom and virtue in the public sphere is replaced by the abstract right to self-interest, private property, and security in civil society; self-determination and self-realisation in politics are replaced by the maximisation of gain and profits in the economy. At this point in his analysis, Hegel makes a very interesting observation that with the end of the spirit of laws and virtue, death becomes more terrifying because there is nothing that lives beyond human mortality – there is no universal polity or republic that continues the citizen's soul and in which the dreams and aspirations of the individual continue to live on. The universal classical ideals are dead, producing an existential crisis that can be repaired only by the creation of a 'positivity' or objective religion grounded in an abstract heaven, external moral norms, and a transcendent deity. Religion becomes an oppressive manifestation of the underlying political conditions of slavery which create abstract individuals no longer intimately bound to a higher communal ideal. Christianity is an objective religion of political failure. Individuals are alone and isolated and seek solace in some metaphysical system that is no longer 'self-subsistent within their own hearts'.[11]

Duty to one's own rational will and moral law is replaced by blind obedience to the external moral authority of an unhappy consciousness in a Christian church.

Religion was no longer a self-expression of the community, but something that was passively awaited and rested on hope. Religion became the consciousness of the despised, impotent, and the weak founded upon a metaphysical system of emotional consolation; human self-creativity and self-determination became a sin that had to be extirpated and condemned. In the end, 'men looked to him [Christian God] for every good impulse, every better purpose and decision'.[12] The most noble graces and potentiality of humanity now became its greatest weaknesses since moral freedom and creativity became subservient to moral obedience in a corrupted and sinful world. Nature was corrupted and all human happiness and pleasure was to be avoided. A saddened Hegel wistfully remarks:

> Thus the despotism of the Roman emperors has chased the human spirit from the earth and spread a misery which compelled men to seek and expect happiness in heaven: robbed of freedom, their spirit, their eternal and absolute element, was forced to take flight to the deity. [The doctrine of] God's divinity is a counterpart to the corruption of the slavery of man.[13]

The happiness of political participation and community life, the creation of moral laws, and a social life defined by human reason are lost with the advent of Christianity, and with them the spirit of virtue and law, moral freedom, and a true natural law. The harmony between the individual and society, humanity and nature, also disappeared and what remained was a fragmented, lonely, and disenchanted world whose purpose now had to be supplied by an alien and transcendent deity imposed upon humanity. This was a religion that represented in Hegel's view the 'perversion of the maxims of morality'.[14] From this perspective of the positivity of Christianity, morality would disappear and would have to wait for another time when Aristotle and Kant, virtue and morality, and politics and reason would be reintegrated into a new morality of social ethics.

A couple of years later, Hegel writes another of his famous early theological writings entitled *The Spirit of Christianity and its Fate* (1798–9), but with an entirely different approach to both Christianity and Kantian philosophy. Previously, in the middle of the decade, Hegel attempted to integrate the ancient political ideal with Kantian moral reason in order to better understand the nature of the ethical life (*Sittlichkeit*) and the union of the community and individual. Christianity was viewed as a form of cultural alienation. With this new essay, there is a decided shift in Hegel's orientation with his fusion of the Greek spirit and beauty with Kantian reason to form a higher unity in the charity and love of the Christian gospel. Religion has replaced politics as the central spiritual and unifying force in human life. Christianity, now no longer a form of external positivity, has transformed into a religion of the heart and love; it is no longer juxtaposed to ancient folk religion and modern moral reason as an alienating experience, but has become their highest expression. Love becomes the means by which the community (Aristotle) and the individual (Kant) are integrated through a reconciliation of opposites into a living, harmonious social totality – the unity of ethical life. His goal was to unite nature, ethics, and politics: 'The need to unite subject and object, to unite feeling and feeling's demand for objects, with the intellect, to unite them in something beautiful, in a god, by means of fancy, is the supreme need of the human spirit and the urge to religion'.[15] Hegel's classical goal was the same as before, but now Christianity became the means to reconcile moral and metaphysical differences.

Hegel's Natural Law and Critique of Liberalism and Natural Rights

In 1802 and 1803, Hegel's essay *On the Scientific Ways of Treating Natural Law* was published in the *Kritisches Journal der Philosophie* edited by him and his close friend and former fellow student at the theological college in Tübingen, Friedrich Wilhelm Schelling. This was Hegel's first formal inquiry into the nature of natural law but with a language that today makes it nearly impenetrable because it drew so much from the technical vocabulary of the logic and metaphysics of Schelling, Fichte, and Kant.[16] Also during this time, Hegel writes *The System of Ethical Life* and a year later his *First Philosophy of Spirit* (1803–4). The essay *Natural Law* is important because it introduces Hegel's treatment of his moral and ethical theory of law and rights. He divides 'modern natural law' or natural rights theory into two distinct schools of thought – the disconnected and fragmented empiricism of Hobbes and Locke, and the *a priori* and empty formalism of Kant and Rousseau.[17] What is lacking in both approaches is an organic unity or social totality in the multiplicity of moral relations (essence); natural rights theory has been plagued by a diversity of principles and laws or by an abstract and idealised unity. What is missing in both traditions is the moral and legal unity produced by an ethical community or polity. In both traditions the state is an artificial invention constructed to insure the protection of the rights to life and property or to give the appearance of a unified political whole through formal and abstract principles. In effect, both schools of modern natural law (natural rights) are caught in the Enlightenment and modern liberalism, and have lost the ideals of the classical tradition of ancient natural law.

By developing a critical theory of both schools of thought, Hegel introduces the very beginnings of his political theory of the ethical life of the community (*Sittlichkeit*) that will find final expression only years later in his *Philosophy of Right* (1821).[18] In this essay he rejects key elements of both branches of modern natural law since they only reproduce the given moral values of society and do not understand the logical conflict between the ideal and the real, the potential and the actual, and reason and perception. Modern natural law and moral philosophy are still tied to particular individuals and human nature (empiricism) or to a particular system of moral values (formal rationalism) that no longer offer a critical perspective of the rational or absolute whole of the ethical principles of the community. Hegel is here applying his insights into the classical ideal of the Greek polity from his early theological writings to a critique of modern natural rights theory.[19] The outlines of his argument have not really been formed, and it is only the very beginnings of his later critique of natural rights and liberalism. But it is an important first step.

According to Hegel, 'for pure empiricism, everything has equal rights with everything else; one characteristic is as real as another, and none has precedence'.[20] These diverse elements are mechanically posited within an abstract unity of the state of nature held together by an underlying psychological predisposition to act in certain ways. These psychological capacities of a mechanical human nature become the fate and destiny of humanity upon which is built a technological state of law or civil society to ensure its rational functioning. In this tradition the state of nature and the state of law of Hobbes and Locke are illusory and arbitrary categories that have no inherent or rational connection to the real world. Reason attempts to make sense of all the moral and legal principles, laws, duties, and rights and to place these 'disconnected characteristics' of modern society into a coherent unity. But empiricism can only grasp the individual and diverse elements of society without understanding how they fit together in a complex society.

Continuing his criticism of empiricism, Hegel writes: 'This proof of their nullity is present most convincingly by showing the unreal basis and ground from which they grow, and whose flavor and nature they absorb'.[21] Since there is no inherent unity in the object of scientific inquiry of natural law – a form of moral positivism – this unity is created by smuggling into the analysis formal and *a priori* categories which give an arbitrary coherence to moral and political philosophy – theory of the state of nature. 'Formalism can extend its consistency so far as is generally made possible by the emptiness of its principle, or by a content which it has smuggled in'.[22] Political theory based on empiricism abstracts from history, tradition, cultural values, political principles, and the modern state. Hegel sees natural rights theory as a mechanical fiction used to justify a specific set of transitory and arbitrary characteristics of the individual and the state. This explains why natural rights stress different accidental elements of society at different times: self-preservation (Hobbes), life and property (Locke), and pleasure (Jeremy Bentham and James Mill). As an empirical science of politics collects an enormous amount of data, it arbitrarily highlights temporary aspects of this multiplicity of information. When examining the content of natural law, the scientific data from the simple experience of objects and their qualities remains a multiplicity of unconnected, indifferent, and isolated objects until the theorist arbitrarily focuses on distinct, particular aspects of the object of inquiry.

To help explain the Hobbesian and Lockean theories about the consensus formation of civil society from the chaos of the state of nature, Hegel argues that certain principles and characteristics from the multiplicity of society are abstracted and displaced to the original state of nature. A defence of liberalism and its privileges and rights can be attained by the abstraction of certain 'capricious and accidental' characteristics from civil society that are then projected backwards by the imagination into the fictitious state of nature. This latter state is then grounded in an empirical psychology that emphasises certain temporary characteristics and capacities of human beings in society. Human nature becomes natural destiny; the transitory and historical particulars become the transhistorical; and the arbitrary and contingent become the absolute and the essential. '[B]y separating out everything capricious and accidental from the confused picture of the *state of law* (*Rechtszustand*), it must after this abstraction be left directly with the absolutely necessary'.[23] According to Hegel, the concept of the state of nature is thereby derived from particular and indifferent characteristics of the existing civil society. This is counter to the stated position of the natural rights theorists who argue the exact opposite – civil society is derived from the inherent *a priori* principles and logic of the state of nature. Hegel reverses the causal relationship in order to show that the exact opposite is true, that is, the state of nature is a derivation from the particular characteristics of civil society. Rationalism is claimed as the preferred method of inquiry while empiricism is the actual approach. The essential and absolute (formalism) is, in fact, derived not from some initial rationalist principles of human nature in an original and primitive state, but rather from the empirical world itself. In the logical presentation of the derivation of civil society and positive law from the state of nature – the values, principles, and ideals of the state of nature are ensured and protected by the modern state in civil society – Hegel criticises the natural rights tradition for actually deriving the state of nature from the state of law. The state of nature is constructed from an abstraction from the isolated social and historical particulars of the jumbled multiplicity of experiences in order to create the universal or essential potentialities of humanity contained in the state of nature. This is an arbitrary abstraction from the empirical linking the multiplicity of human experience together by the artificial unity of a political theory. The theory itself does not capture the essential characteristics of humanity which Hegel still views from the perspective of the classical ideal of the Greek polity. This is not the universal of a historical self-conscious being creating its own moral and political law. Rather, it is an abstraction from the values and institutions of a liberal state and chrematistic economy. Contained in these early writings is the foundation for Marx's later theory of historical materialism and the relationship between the ideal and real.

Empiricism lacks the ability to develop a moral and political theory that is capable of distinguishing between what is essential and what is mere appearance in a theory of natural law; that is, it is incapable of distinguishing between the multiplicity of objects and their inherent unity. This is important because, without this ability, humans would not be capable of overcoming the fragmentation of their social worlds and building a humane and moral community. Without reason to act as a guide, the *bellum omnium contra omnes* would represent the guiding principle of liberal society. For Hegel, concepts such as the state of nature, human nature, and law are derived as abstractions from immediate experience and not from their essential characteristics derived from human reason. As Hegel says so succinctly, if not obscurely:

> The governing principle for this *a priori* is the *a posteriori*. If something in the idea of the state of law is to be justified, all that is required ... is to transfer into the chaos [state of nature] an appropriate quality or capacity and ... to make, for the purposes of so-called explanation of reality, hypotheses in which this reality is posited in the same determinate character, though only in a formal-ideal shape as force, matter, capacity, etc.[24]

The key elements necessary to understand and justify aspects of the liberal state are projected back into the state of nature to create a seemingly coherent and logical argument justifying a radical and indifferent individualism and natural rights.[25] The argument appears irrefutable because the conclusions are already included in the initial premises. The state of nature is not the beginning of the argument, but its end. What appears as the *a priori* part of the argument – the concepts of human nature, freedom, equality, and abstract rights, which will later justify the social contract and formation of the modern state – is actually the end of the argument that began with the basic empirical assumptions of civil society and liberalism. These political concepts are empty abstractions whose sole purpose is to justify the appearances of an existing social system; they are 'baseless features drawn from common experience'.[26]

The concept of the state of nature is not an *a priori* rational construct, but the product 'contaminated' by empirical abstractions from the existing social reality. There is no inner necessity created among the integrated social whole, traditions, laws, culture, etc. The original unity of the state of nature and the absolute unity of the liberal state are incompatible and push each other to 'mutual destruction'. Hegel's conclusion regarding the empiricism of the political philosophy of Hobbes and Locke is that it is logically and theoretically incoherent and contradictory. These ideas are only indifferent human constructs held together by an externally imposed and historically specific set of ideas about modern society and human nature. They do not reflect the essence of natural law or the telos of society. Rather, they reflect the actual appearances of the values, laws, duties, and principles of that society; they reflect not what could or should be, but what is. This natural rights theory is the mirror of nature as presented in its immediate empirical state of affairs. Natural law and social theory are creations of empirical science and not the absolute ethical community itself; they are the result of experience and not reason.

Hegel next turns to the moral philosophy of formalism or rationalism. In order to expand the parameters of his critique of modern natural law, Hegel examines Kant and his formal principles of natural law and moral autonomy. Kant had internalised and formalised natural law in practical reason and the categorical imperative. Reason would no longer have to search for the universal moral guides to human action which now lie *a priori* in human subjectivity or consciousness itself. The principles of practical reason are now the universal values of natural law; reason does not just discover these principles in nature, revelation, or scripture, but creates the law itself through self-reflection and practical action. The empirical situation precipitates a need for a course of action about issues of moral right and wrong. A situation has arisen which demands a moral response that something is right or wrong. The individual now searches for answers to the appropriate course of action no longer based on the word of God or tradition, but on the moral commands of human reason itself. The objective necessity of practical action is appropriately defined through a formal and logical process grounded in the principles of non-contradiction and universalisation. Morality is not to be based on private inclinations or personal interests, but on universal reason and the practical will. Reason creates the objective and universal laws that become a subjective duty to follow by moral individuals – the categorical imperative of practical reason. No action to be morally legitimate can be undertaken which is in violation of the principles of reason and the universal law of nature. Taking this position, Kant rejects both the *a priori* rationalism of the state of nature argument and the empiricism of contingent and arbitrary circumstances of momentary desires and pleasures. In his *Fundamental Principles of the Metaphysic of Morals* (1785), he remarks: '[T]he basis of obligation must not be sought in the nature of man, or in the circumstances in the world in which he is placed, but *a priori* simply in the conceptions of pure reason'.[27] According to Hegel, both *a priori* rationalism and utilitarian empiricism are based on arbitrary and non-universal principles that cannot be the guide to moral action. Law has now been internalised into subjectivity, thereby producing new meanings and horizons for the Western concepts of the individual, freedom, and equality.

According to Kant, natural law lies in the integration and unity of the form (*a priori*) and the content (action) of practical reason. By this method, he is integrating the strengths of both rationalism and empiricism into his version of subjective idealism. But, it is Hegel who sees in Kant's practical reason a continued separation between form (ideal) and content (real), duty and inclinations, and possibility and actuality. As with his criticism and rejection of empiricism as the foundation of natural law, Hegel here, too, dismisses formalism as indifferent moral relationships. Neither tradition has been able to uncover the ethical unity of individual moral life which lies neither in human nature, the empirically contingent, or in an isolated and indifferent human reason. These moral traditions of empiricism, rationalism, and formalism (subjective idealism) cannot ground moral law in the ethical unity of the community, but are lost in the isolated contingency of the Enlightenment view of egoism, self-interest, and utility. This accounts for Hegel's deeply critical response to these attempts to establish the modern tradition of natural law. They are all forms of what Hegel calls the 'unity of indifference and relation' which creates an artificial and mechanical unity of indifferent individuals in civil society, the state, and the market economy. Looking for that one ideal, that cohesive and integrated unity in a moral order, takes a perverse turn during the Enlightenment which is unable to solve the dilemma of the unity of the others. How one can turn the indifferent other into a moral subject and then into a rational citizen is the central issue – and dilemma – facing Hegel during this period of his intellectual life.

Hegel is critical of formalism as a school of natural law which is grounded in an *a priori* universal law of human reason since it confuses and combines the form and content of that law. It is based on the moral principle of practical reason to act in such a way 'that a maxim of thy will shall count at the same time as a principle of universal legislation'.[28] Hegel is here quoting from Kant's *Critique of Practical Reason* (1788). In approaching the choice in any moral situation, each individual must first ask if the action undertaken could itself become the basis for a universal moral law. Thus the law must be universally and formally applicable in every similar situation – questions of whether I may lie, steal, kill, commit suicide, etc. must first pass the rigorous test of universal and non-contradictory logic. Although the form of the law is determined by the universal maxim and logical principle itself, the central question for Hegel remains: What determines the particular content of the law upon which the universal maxim is grounded? There appears to be a contradiction between the universal form and particular content of Kant's philosophy of moral law. Practical reason supplies the form to the content of natural law. Kant has spent all his time justifying the logical nature of the law in the principles of non-contradiction and universalisation. That is, the law cannot contradict itself and must be universally applicable in all situations and to all persons. But he did not reflect on the actual content of the law itself unless the content is also supplied by the form, which makes the maxim self-contradictory and tautological. As Hegel reflects, it is an analytical statement in which the object of the sentence is already contained in the subject. Hegel concludes: 'But the essence of pure will and pure practical reason is to be abstracted from all content. Thus it is a self-contradiction to seek in this absolute practical reason a moral legislation which would have to have a content, since the essence of this reason is to have none'.[29] Practical reason imposes its abstract universal maxim and analytic form on the moral will (*Wille*) by abstracting from all specific content. But in the process of creating a formal and abstract universal, the result is to establish an arbitrary content of the will (*Willkür*). Reason abstracts from all content of the will (particulars) in order to impose its own arbitrary content (universal) on the will. Hegel argues that it is a logical contradiction to search for the content of moral action in the moral law itself because 'anything specific can be made into a duty'.[30]

Added to this problem of the self-contradictory nature of Kant's theory of moral legislation, Hegel argues that Kant's natural law is also incoherent. This incoherence is another problem in his moral philosophy since any content can be made into a universal natural law. Any and every particular moral situation or legislative action can become the basis of a moral law; every particular can be made into a universal. As Hegel succinctly states: 'There is nothing whatever which cannot in this way be made into a moral law'.[31] Even opposites, if they abide by the formal and logical principles of application of the moral law and the categorical imperative, can provide the particular content of the law itself. It is universal legislation that defines the legitimacy of practical reason, not the specific content. In fact, practical reason itself through its powers of self-legislation defines the particular content of a moral law.[32] For example, if practical reason posits property as the content of a moral law, then the sentence 'property is property' is a logical tautology. Any moral action that infringes upon this content, such as theft, fraud, redistribution of property, and so forth, cannot be a legitimate form of moral action.

However, if the content is defined as 'no property is no property' then the application of a universal moral law takes on a completely different content and moral maxim. If property is not assumed from the beginning as the legitimate moral content of natural law, then its opposite could easily replace it and still be consistently and universally applied. Both property and its negation of non-property may be universalised into a moral law. (This also works with issues of killing, suicide, and lying). There is no contradiction in the statement rejecting property as the moral foundation of practical reason if the content and form in an analytic sentence are the same – property is property, or its negation, no property is no property. If under the assumption that theft, murder, and suicide are acceptable acts of human behaviour, or there are no moral or legal prohibitions against them, then there is no formal or logical reason why they cannot be committed using Kant's definitions of the categorical imperative and practical reason. In the cases of property or non-property discussed by Hegel, we have an empty and formal tautology that says nothing and reflects no moral judgement, but it does reflect Kant's logical principles of non-contradiction and universalisation. Either property or non-property may be made the basis of the practical will and moral action. Beginning with the negative premise of 'no property' means that any illicit activity, such as theft, may itself be the basis for natural law.[33] If the opposite of property is accepted as the universal foundation of practical reason then the ideals of liberalism and natural rights collapse. Louis Dupré summarises Hegel's argument nicely when he says: 'In fact, no action can be excluded by pure reason alone, for any action, no matter how criminal, can be made into a principle of universal law without becoming an intrinsic contradiction'.[34] But in Kant's writings on practical action the determination of the content of moral action is not arbitrary but reflects the underlying values of liberalism itself. For Dupré the philosophical implication of this dilemma is that the 'transcendental idealism [of Kant] ultimately turns into some sort of moral empiricism'.[35] The actual content of the moral law is always the unarticulated and unconscious values of the existing society itself.

The legislation of practical reason can only define the empty form of moral action, not its particular content, and the latter can never be universal and absolute. The application of the universal form to any content turns the latter into a categorical imperative and moral duty, while the choice of a particular content is, according to Hegel, arbitrary and illegitimate, absurd and immoral; the content is always predetermined and presupposed, and is simply assumed as valid by practical reason; and, finally, the content is simply the empirical and contingent multiplicity which makes it immoral. Thus Kant's theory of practical reason is not only inconsistent and incoherent, it is now labelled by Hegel as immoral because anything may be turned into an absolute and universal standard of duty and law if it can be applied consistently and universally in an analytic moral maxim. And most important of all, there is no logical method in Kant's philosophy for defining or justifying the content of any moral law. Hegel summarises his position on Kant: 'But pure reason demands that this [determining content] shall have been done beforehand, and that one of the opposed specific things shall be presupposed, and only then can reason perform its now superfluous legislation'.[36] Reason can only universalise the already chosen moral content and decide practical action on the basis of universal logical principles. It can universalise the content, but cannot decide the substance; logically, the content is arbitrary, but, as a practical matter, it is society's own values that are assumed or smuggled into practical reason. 'But by confusing absolute form with conditioned matter, the absoluteness of the form is imperceptibly smuggled into the unreal and conditioned character of the content; and in this perversion and trickery lies the nerve of pure reason's practical legislation'.[37] This is simply another way of saying that Kant's natural law formalism is in reality a variation of empiricism, for the *a priori* logic of the law ultimately rests upon the *a posteriori* grounds of the empirically given concrete experience of everyday life. Although Kant has a different view of subjectivity, freedom, human creativity, and the natural law, his moral philosophy is fundamentally grounded in an 'empirical multiplicity' and the 'force of perception and presentness', that is, it is grounded in liberalism, the acceptance of the empiricism of the British natural rights tradition, and the values of civil society and a market economy with their emphasis on life, liberty, and property.[38] According to Hegel, the difference between empiricism and formalism in the philosophical tradition of natural law has disappeared since both traditions of moral liberalism are contradictory and incoherent. This only leads to the next question: What is Hegel's theory of natural law and the ethical life?

Social Ethics and Integration of Natural Law and Natural Rights

In Hegel's next work, his first major surviving work on social theory, *System of Ethical Life*, written about the same time as *Natural Law*, he undertakes to move beyond modern natural rights and subjective idealism, empiricism and formalism, and human nature and reason as the basis for the moral order. Hegel now looks to the spirit of the law and the ethical community (*Sittlichkeit*) – the modern liberal state – as providing the foundation for the moral (individual) and ethical (polity) life of society. Hegel returns to the ancient Greek ideal of the classical polity and joins it with Kant's theory of the individual as self-legislating practical reason. Although critical of Kant's formalism and method for determining moral laws, Hegel nevertheless turns to Kant's theory of individual freedom, equality, moral autonomy, and creativity as the foundation for a new natural law. This turn in natural law anticipates Marx's early economic and philosophical writings, where he too will join together ethics and virtue with politics and democracy to form the beginnings of a comprehensive theory of social justice. Toward the end of *Natural Law*, Hegel makes the turn to the Greeks quite clear when articulating his break with liberal natural law. He maintains that the absolute ethical life is essential in order to structurally and functionally integrate all the elements of society into a living totality. The ethical life unites both morality and natural law, the individual and the social into this living whole of the absolute; it becomes the essence of being. To stress the correctness of his argument, Hegel quotes from Aristotle's *Politics*:

> The state comes by nature before the individual; if the individual in isolation is not anything self-sufficient, he must be related to the whole state in one unity, just as other parts are to their whole. But a man incapable of communal life, or who is so self-sufficing that he does not need it, is no part of the state and must be either a beast or a god.[39]

The modern state, on the other hand, overcomes the multiplicity and indifference of market competition, class power, and natural rights as it integrates the norms, values, ideals, and laws, as well as the structures, functions, and institutions of society into a universal or absolute spirit that permeates the consciousness and soul of each of its members. This ethical spirit expresses itself at all levels of class and society, including the family and education, civil society and the system of needs, and the state, constitution, and the law. This means that the moral virtues of courage, moderation, wisdom, and justice are intimately bound to the life and potentiality of the individual; virtue and natural law are living parts of the same polity. As does Plato, Hegel equates social classes with specific types of virtues: nobility with honour and courage in war; bourgeoisie with mastery of nature, gain, intellectual labour, honesty, and prosperity; and peasantry with intuitive natural virtue, labour, and trust in the military nobility. With these component parts of the total social system, what Hegel refers to as 'the different rights of the system', there is a need for strong coordination by 'an organic central authority' whose purpose is to preserve the constitution.[40] This is the duty of the society's elders who have the wisdom and experience to pull together their different class interests and the structural imperatives that might pull society apart. And the role of the legislature is similar, since it, too, must ensure the solidarity of virtues and stability of class and structure: 'Above all it has to decide in every case where different rights of the systems [i.e. the class structures] come into collision and the present situation makes it impossible to maintain them in their positive stability'.[41] The absolute right of the government to ensure against disharmony lies in its classless power and aged wisdom. It is above all classes and conflicts; it is the absolute ideal or universal authority which mediates among the various conflicting interests within society. The central function of the modern state is to maintain the continuous harmony among class, virtue, and social structure, and, by so doing, Hegel believes that he is keeping the Greek ideal alive within the modern liberal society. 'This absolute maintenance of all the classes must be the supreme government and, in accordance with its concept, this maintenance can strictly accrue to no class, because it is the indifference of all'.[42] The role of the government is to provide for a system of need and justice, that is, protect the civil society to ensure its economic well-being and to instil a sense of responsibility and justice in the community. There is no longer any antagonism between its citizens, nor is there any antagonism between the individual and community because there is now a universal *ethos*: 'Conversely, the essence of the ethical life of the individual is the real and therefore universal absolute ethical life; the ethical life of the individual is one pulse beat of the whole system and is itself the whole system'.[43] The organic life of the community permeates every living individual and guides their moral activities to form the living substance of the polity.

A virtuous, ethical life envisioned by Aristotle and Hegel is impossible in the purely private consciousness of isolated individuals protecting their natural rights but indifferent to the community and responsibility for the common good. The opposition and indifference of natural rights, liberalism, and civil society are transcended by this new ethical life and the common being of the citizen; the individual through civic education and political participation integrates the particular and universal into the common being of humanity. All this is accomplished without changing society's institutions and structures. The Greek polity is integrated with the modern economy and civil society.

Natural law is no longer external to human beings or imposed from above by God, nature, or practical reason; it is no longer deduced from *a priori* practical reason or inductively abstracted from experience itself. The universal moral imperative of right and wrong is not an accidental and contingent thought or experience, but instead, is part of the common essence and living identity of objective ethical principles, laws, and the spirit of the community.[44] The universal laws of the state infuse the particular and subjective by making the community part of one common integrated whole. For Hegel, the actual bourgeois state based on the principles and institutions of liberalism is a form of barbarism. Possessive individualism and *Moralität* are replaced by *Sittlichkeit* and the *Volk* (people) as morality is reborn as law and politics. Hegel argues that the synthesis of individual morality and politics does not result in coercion by these social and legal limits to human freedom, but expands the horizons of public freedom to include a cultural and political widening of a common heritage and human potentiality beyond the limits of pure consciousness and the immediate will.[45] Freedom is not the liberty to act on abstract rights or the imperatives of rational duty – thus it is not a 'freedom from coercion', but rather a freedom towards a goal (telos) and a freedom with others (ethical community). Ethics now is defined as the virtuous life within the organic polity. Natural law is not the product of an abstract right or subjective consciousness, but the living moral principles and spirit of the political community that pervades all aspects of the nation and the individual. It is their true being and universal truth, and no longer an abstract and external positivity of laws and morals. The values, ideals, rights, and law are not external to each individual residing in an alien state, but have become internalised as part of their very existence and being through trust and respect. Virtue and morality are made possible by ethics and social institutions; the former without the latter are not real and the latter without the former are empty and meaningless.

In the *Natural Law*, Hegel announces the nature of the ethical life and its clear difference from individual morality, whereas in the *System of Ethical Life* he begins to outline a theory of the forms of virtue and the forms of government. Hegel, following Aristotle, distinguishes among the best laws and constitution – monarchy, aristocracy, and democracy – as the external and institutional manifestation of the ethical community. These are, in turn, juxtaposed to their correspondingly worst forms of constitutions in despotism, oligarchy, and ochlocracy, respectively. The best forms of free government are based on the principles outlined by Aristotle of the rule by the one, the few, or the many. The state makes virtue and morality possible because it provides the public space within which humans can realise their potential as social beings. The focus of

Hegel's attention in ethics and natural law has now shifted to an analysis of the structures of the state and the creation and facilitation of a virtuous life. Here again there is a strong Platonic dimension in his analysis of the forms of virtues of the various classes and their functional importance for maintaining the organic unity of the state in the form of the institutions of the family, economy, abstract rights, civil justice, military, and the government. The purpose of the state is to organically link these classes and estates into a coherent ethical whole through the process of the 'separation of powers', a healthy balance among various natural classes, maintenance of social solidarity, and popular elections for the legislature. That is, the chief cultural function of the state is to maintain the spirit of virtue, constitution, and law that permeates all aspects of society and gives voice to individual freedom and liberty; its chief economic and legal functions are to ensure material needs of society, class and estate differences, economic stability, regulation of supply, prices, and demand of the market, protection against massive poverty and inequality, and ensure education, training, war preparedness, and justice.

On the economic and technical side, the function of the state is to create a stable system of need in the labour, production, and property of civil society in the form of government taxation, distributive justice, balancing the natural inequality of wealth and estates, ensuring society against 'the bestiality of contempt for all the higher things' in life and the barbarism of too much wealth, inequality, and poverty, as well as the mechanisation and division of labour in the factories.[46] Redistribution of excessive wealth along with a more general participation of the people in the material well-being of the economy are suggested in these passages in order to protect the universality of law and the communal trust. The living unity and relations of the community become impossible when the people are reduced to a mechanical and quantitative mass burdened by economic poverty and barbarism. The government must replace this 'unconscious and blind' alien power of the system of need (market economy) based on an infinite number of private interactions by indifferent and unrelated producers creating their own surplus, commodities, and property. The result of this cacophony of labour and the irrationality and indifference of the market is the structural requirement to replace it with the conscious and rational decisions of the government based on the universal needs of society as a whole. The equilibrium and balance of the market must be maintained by the state; private interests cannot outweigh the universal interests of society. The government must ensure a stable price system and guard against the irrational oscillation in prices, supply, and demand: Too low prices threaten the economic viability of the producers, while too high prices threaten the population as a whole. Too much disequilibrium in the market produces a risk of instability of trust and confidence in the society and its system of needs, as well as threatens the livelihood, values, and happiness of sections of the population. The role of the state is thus to ensure the economic equilibrium and system stability of the ethical totality by protecting the proper functioning of the market, profits, property, and possessions by balancing scarcity and surplus, as well as by protecting the general interest and material needs of the ethical community.

Taxation should be based on the principle of contribution according to the amount of landed and industrial property. Hegel is quite aware that taxation is a way for the government to influence various parts of the economy. In the end, the government must protect against chaos and radical changes to market value, prices, and the class system. The danger lies in a state unable to perform these functions, which will result in the dissolution of the ethical principle and natural law binding the community into a coherent whole. 'The government has to work as hard as possible against this inequality, and the destruction of private and public life wrought by it'.[47] Disproportionate wealth undermines the authority of the state and unravels the ethical bond of community members. It creates disruptive divisions and false allegiances based on economic and class dependence. This type of social relationship takes us back to the lordship and bondage relations of previous times. Hegel refers to this as a 'mechanical universality' where society is held together no longer by the spirit of law but by the dependence of the economic bondage of labour. This is the 'unmitigated extreme of barbarism'. It is this type of social system based on the unrestrained market economy and growing class inequality that produces the Hobbesian principle of the war of all against all: 'The mass of wealth, the pure universal, the absence of wisdom, is the heart of the matter (*das An-sich*). The absolute bond of the people, namely ethical principle, has vanished, and the people dissolved'.[48] The government has the responsibility of intervening into these structural changes to avert massive inequality by limiting the amount of profit and gain and even dismembering parts of the wealthy class and turning them into factory labourers. The key is to change the inner values and orientation of the wealthy class, to strengthen the ethical bonds and living relations within the moral society so that these social divisions and economic disequilibrium do not happen in the future. The natural law, which is the living spirit of the ethical whole and remains the universal that binds the disparate and particular parts of society together, is not the result of economic and mechanical dependencies based on market relations, profits, or property.

Hegel is quite aware that the modern liberal economy has the real potential to destroy the ethical community and universal state, and therefore the market mechanism and the system of need must be controlled. As Hegel clearly reminds the reader, the universal lives in the individual; it is not imposed by a false economic dependency of mechanical laws and technical behaviour. The government must provide for the material well-being of the nobility, protect the stability of the economy, and ensure the public welfare in the form of maintenance of churches, streets, and public facilities. And the chief means of accomplishing these structural and functional duties of the government is through the power of taxation. The other two main functions of the state are the system of justice and the system of discipline. The former includes the administration of justice, civil and criminal law, and the rights of life and property, while the latter includes education for talents, inventions, and science, training (*Bildung*) for self-development and deliberation, disciplining of a people for war, and, finally, colonisation.

The harmonious balance within the state is also maintained by the delicate balance between the different structures and functions of the state: economic policy and commerce, judicial and military policy, and education and colonisation. Extremes of any kind are detrimental to the organic unity of the ethical community, and thus social ethics must also take into consideration potentially disruptive issues of class structure, market crises, and economic policy that have the potential to undermine solidarity, trust, civic virtue, and, ultimately, social and political stability. Virtue and ethics now require a detailed economic and social theory. Hegel is aware that private rights and market liberties are potentially at odds with a stable and harmonious polity. Class and structure become two key categories in his political philosophy because of his concern with the need for a liberal state that pulls together any social antagonisms into an organic ethical unity. 'The people as an organic totality is the absolute identity of all the specific characteristics of practical and ethical life'.[49] It is the people, the state, this ethical totality which make practical reason, moral action, and a virtuous life possible. The universal and the particular are brought together in a living whole, not as a discrete and indifferent people, but as one people united in the spirit of virtue, law, and the constitution (objectivity) that pervades the consciousness and being of its citizens (subjectivity). '[T]he individual subsumes absolute ethical life under himself and it appears to him as individuality ... Like everyone of its moments, it is supreme freedom and beauty, for the real being and configuration of the eternal is its beauty'.[50] According to Hegel, the ethical life is not imposed on the individual consciousness as an abstract and formal moral duty or natural law as found in Kantian formalism, but is part of the very essence of subjectivity itself cultivated through the process of education (*Bildung*). The opposition between subjectivity and objectivity is cancelled as they are joined together in an organic polity through the life and love for one's country and law integrating the ancient and the modern traditions of natural law. Human potentiality, or the essence or telos of human life, now infuses individual consciousness and freedom, cancelling all the Kantian antinomies of subject and object, inclination and duty, individual and society, and particular and universal. Actually, how the state accomplishes this feat of synthesising the ancients and the moderns, or synthesising the classes and structures into a harmonious totality, is not clear in Hegel's early work.

Hegel's Philosophy of Right, Law, and the State as Objective Spirit

These ethical and political concepts in both his early writings on social theory, *Natural Law* and *System of Ethical Life*, will evolve over time so that by his later writings of the *Phenomenology of Spirit* and the *Philosophy of Right* the idea of ethical life will be more fully developed.[51] The *Phenomenology* traces the development of modern self-consciousness and social institutions in the formation of the culture and spirit of modernity. The massive work begins with an analysis of Consciousness (sensation, perception, and the understanding), Self-Consciousness (classical lordship and bondage, stoicism, scepticism, and the unhappy consciousness of Christianity), and Reason (modern practical reason, morality, hedonism, romanticism, virtue, and law), and then proceeds to an examination of the Objective Spirit of the ethical community, alienation, culture, the Enlightenment, terror of the French Revolution, and Kantian morality and law. It ends with a study of the Absolute Spirit of religion, art, and philosophy. What is of striking interest now is that Hegel begins his examination of the Objective Spirit of the ancients, but drops it quickly to proceed to an examination of its complete breakdown in modern culture, revolution, and morality – the Enlightenment, French Revolution, and Kantian moral philosophy.[52] Over a decade later, Hegel will produce his *Philosophy of Right*, which is a work in ethical and political theory designed to recreate the social bond and solidarity of the ethical community lost by the Enlightenment and Revolution. It was also an attempt to reintegrate the ancients and the moderns within the modern liberal state and complete the project of his early political writings.

The later Hegel appears less critical of the market economy, industrial production, and the mechanisation and fragmentation of the division of labour than in his early writings. The central emphasis of the latter on the spirit of law and constitution, the organic totality, and the ethical community is also missing, as Hegel, responding to the problems created by liberalism, exchange, and the individualism of the Enlightenment, Terror, and Kantian philosophy, attempts to reconcile these differences not by challenging their normative and ethical validity, but by arranging the structures of the state to accommodate a reconciliation and integration of these conflicting parts of the social system. The notion of transcendence or *Aufhebung* becomes the key concept here. This explains his emphasis on the Estates, civil service, and the government in overcoming any divisions within industry and the market in the *Philosophy of Right*. The state, being able to transcend all internal social divisions of class, inequality, and power that divide the community, will resolve any antagonisms and problems introduced by the burgher class and the economy. Marx will see the same world as Hegel but forcefully argue that no resolution of the inner contradictions of society is possible within its present structure. Marx, too, will be mesmerised by the power of the classical Greeks, but that vision will transform his aesthetic and political horizons and be partially responsible for forcing a break with liberalism and capitalism. Hegel succeeds in his philosophy of law only at the expense of his early vision of the ethical life and his hopes for a society created by free, rational, and self-conscious human beings. To accomplish his end, Hegel wants to subdue the Hobbesian dimension of liberalism, but not eliminate it, for this is the economic foundation of his system of needs and material well-being. Hegel's vision of antiquity is no longer a political ideal or hope to move beyond modernity; his goal now is to modify and integrate it.

The *Philosophy of Right* provides us with the missing elements of the Objective Spirit from the *Phenomenology of Spirit* since it begins with the foundations of the ethical community in the abstract self-consciousness of the person, law, and rights and develops toward its completion in the state and ethical spirit. It represents a return to and completion of chapter six of the *Phenomenology* which begins the move from practical reason and morality to social ethics. However, this phenomenal development of the human spirit is historically derailed by the rise of the alienation, social fragmentation, and modern individualism of the Enlightenment and bourgeois zoo.[53] Only the theological, philosophical, and aesthetic abstractions of the modern form of 'unhappy consciousness' in religion, art, and philosophy temporarily hold together the values of the social totality until a time when the objective spirit of the law and state can make them real and concrete again. The absolute spirit reflects the alienation of reason and spirit, as well as the utopian impulse toward unity, harmony, and meaning – it is only a dream of unity or absolute hope. The purpose of the *Philosophy of Right* is to regain the direction lost by modernity toward absolute freedom and self-consciousness in an ethical community. Following Aristotle and Rousseau, Hegel agrees that the real essence and substance of humanity is its social being as manifested in the Greek polis and its participation in the ethical community and the common experience of politics and the good life. This spiritual experience has been lost with the rise of bourgeois culture and the chrematistic economy which separates the public and private, community and individual, thereby reducing citizenship to the common antagonisms of market self-interest and egoistic competition. The objective spirit makes morality, freedom, and individual self-determination possible because it provides the objective normative rules and the institutional space within which practical reason and true individuality realise themselves. Without culture and social institutions, morality is a purely theoretical or scholastic exercise without real, practical implications and has no objective meaning or purpose. Self-consciousness, reason, and morality evolve only through the creation of the ethical community in the modern state. That is, political participation creates the condition of real knowledge, truth, and freedom. Rights of modern natural law and duties of Kantian morality become possible only through participation in social institutions.[54] And this is why the *Philosophy of Right* begins with the initial stages of self-awareness and mutual support at its most basic level in the recognition of personhood, property, and abstract rights.

Hegel commences the *Philosophy of Right* with an analysis of the abstract self-conscious will and human freedom. The latter is defined not as private caprice, arbitrariness, or natural impulses, but rather as self-awareness by the individual of its own freedom and unified identity. He is quick to point out that this is only the initial stage of subjective freedom and self-consciousness because it remains unconnected to any objective or institutional content of right, law, ethical life, and the state. Free will is defined as a formal, natural, self-determining activity initially devoid of any social content; it first expresses itself as a crude impulse and later as a reflective duty toward social and civil institutions. This is the early Kantian stage of the phenomenal development of law and ethics before rights and morality have been integrated into society and politics. Hegel refers to this process as 'self-determining universality' when the object of reflection is the will itself as social institutions. Practical reason and free will evolve into their own potentiality; they become actual because they are no longer expressions of abstract impulses, but have been embedded into the living soul or universal mind (*Geist*) of society itself; reason has become objectified into law. Only then is the true essence or concept of free will realised in the objective spirit of the constitution, laws, and government of the state. Hegel writes about this transformation:

> When the will's potentialities have become fully explicit, then it has for its object the will itself as such ... it is only as thinking intelligence that the will is genuinely a will and free. This self-consciousness which apprehends itself through thinking as essentially human, and thereby frees itself from the contingent and the false, is the principle of right, morality, and all ethical life.[55]

> The absolute goal ... of free mind is to make its freedom its object, i.e., to make freedom objective as much in the sense that freedom shall be the rational system of the mind, as in the sense that this system shall be the world of immediate actuality ... The will's activity consists in annulling the contradiction between subjectivity and objectivity and giving its aims an objective instead of a subjective character, while at the same time remaining by itself even in objectivity.[56]

When these conditions are met, reflection is no longer abstract and philosophical, but becomes ethical and political; this represents the transformation from philosophy to politics. When writing about morality, moral autonomy, and human freedom, along with his critique of liberal natural rights theory and Kantian moral formalism, Hegel was forced to reintegrate philosophy, political economy, and social theory returning to the natural law tradition of the ancients. Hegel is aware that those who hold the modern liberal view of natural liberty, self-interest, and self-will see the ethical community and state as an unnatural and external imposition on individual freedom and self-expression. The state is viewed as a protector of individual rights to possessions and property, not as the spirit of law and reason.[57] The very notion of freedom is so different in these conflicting traditions: One emphasises private inclinations in a market economy to free economic and social choices, whereas the other stresses the essential rationality of the ethical community. According to Hegel, right is the highest expression or concept of self-conscious reason and freedom,[58] and manifests itself in a variety of social forms:

> Morality, ethical life, the interest of the state, each of these is a right of a special character because each of them is a specific form and embodiment of freedom ... To consider a thing rationally means ... to find the object is rational on its own account: here it is mind in its freedom, the culmination of self-conscious reason, which gives itself actuality and engenders itself as an existing world.[59]

Hegel has undertaken a phenomenology of will and right as he explores the various parts of the objective spirit of society as abstract right (personality, possessions, and property), morality (subjectivity of purpose, intentions and the good), and the ethical life (family, civil society, and the state).

The *Philosophy of Right* begins with the most abstract and immediate forms of ego and free will expressed in the distinct individual personality who is recognised and respected by others as having rights, owning property, and capable of engaging in binding legal contracts. This is the most immediate form of freedom because it is the freedom of a particular individual. It is part of the broader development of objective freedom expressed in the ethical community and the state. Critical of the abstract individualism of natural rights theory, Hegel emphasises that 'a person must translate his freedom into an external sphere in order to exist as Idea [as real]'.[60] Because there is no state of nature or inherent human nature, human beings create their own freedom through their mastery and appropriation of nature and through their creation of legal and economic institutions. (This theme of the creation of reason [epistemology] and law [politics] that runs throughout the writings of Kant and Hegel will become essential to Marx's theory of social justice and his theory of social praxis). Through the actions of free will and the appropriation of objects in the physical world, things become possessions, including one's own self-consciousness. The will of a person becomes an external object of reflection through the creation and ownership of property and recognises itself as such; objects become my possessions. Through this means individuals see themselves as distinct and free when they take possession of their own body and mind as their own distinctive property. This is thus the first primitive stage of the phenomenal development of human freedom and self-identity and does not stop until humanity is free in all its institutions, that is, until it reaches its culmination in the Idea of freedom, 'until we recognise that the Idea of freedom is genuinely actual only as the state'.[61] And between property and the state, between the earliest stages of freedom and personality and its completion in the state, there are the intermediate stages of practical reason and morality, family, love, trust, care and mutual sharing, and civil society and a market economy. These are the essential elements in the formation of the classical ethical community in modern times.

Morality is the next stage of the determinate existence of consciousness or subjectivity. At first, the individual sees itself as a free being legally recognised by others in property and contract relations. Now moving beyond the reflection of others to self-reflection, the individual sees itself as a moral being who is not just a person or legal entity, but a subject – a free, self-conscious being having freedom. The determination of the individual has moved from the external legal world to the inner life of free will and moral action, from legal reason to practical reason. Hegel's view of freedom and reason has moved from Locke's defence of labour and property to Kant's critique of pure and practical reason. In both cases, humans constitute the external world they inhabit through technical and practical activity, that is, through legal and subjective freedom.[62] Morality remains a form of subjective freedom and must move beyond this level to freedom being expressed in concrete social institutions. This stage of development of the free will is important for Hegel because 'the right of subjective freedom is the pivot and centre of the difference between antiquity and modern times'.[63] Hegel is here following the path already traced in the *Phenomenology of Spirit* where he outlines the development of this right of subjective reason from Christianity, love, romanticism, and salvation to the categorical imperative and moral duty. The good, conscience, and duty remain tied to pure theological, philosophical, and practical subjectivity. Reason has evolved from the time of the breakup of classical Greece to the contradictions and hypocrisy inherent in the logic of Kantian moral philosophy of the eighteenth century that dialectically challenge self-consciousness to move beyond subjectivity and reason to self-consciousness and spirit – the objectivity and spirit of the ethical life, law, and the state. As Hegel puts it, the subject becomes substance as the concept or essence of freedom is actualised in the real world of economics and politics; subjectivity expands into objectivity. The external institutions bear witness to and nurture the freedom and self-consciousness of the individual to the point where the ethical life becomes 'the actual living soul of self-consciousness'.[64] As reason evolves into spirit, 'the ethical life is the concept of freedom developed into the existing world and the nature of self-consciousness'.[65] The free will moves beyond pure subjectivity and abstraction to the intersubjectivity and institutions of modern society where it can express itself within the ethical life of the community. Hegel refers to this process as the ethical order becoming objective substance, that is, morality, goodness, and freedom have become actual principles living in social institutions and not simply occupying the mind of individuals. They are the essence of the mind made actual and concrete: 'As substantive in character, these laws and institutions are duties binding on the will of the individual'.[66]

Formation of the Ethical Life in the Family, Civil Society, and the State

In the *Philosophy of Right*, Hegel argues that the first and most basic form of ethical life appears in the family, which is bound together in a common unity of marriage, love, and mutual obligation and sharing. By renouncing their personal desires and contingent feelings, they are joined together in a common substance, thereby expanding their self-consciousness and freedom. Ethical life does not restrict free will, but deepens it. This bond is the first stage of the movement from morality to ethics, of self-consciousness through another. Individual egoism or selfishness 'is here transformed into something ethical, into labour and care for a common possession'.[67] Hegel recognises the close relationship between marriage and property rights, since the latter only strengthens the bonds of unity. Although it is the early stage of an ethical bond, the family remains a limited, immediate, and contingent one, since it is based on inner feelings and subjective commitments of recognition and trust of the other. It is expanded with the love and the moral education of children. The movement from the inward feelings and subjective commitments of marriage to more objective commitments to civil society and the state begins the process whereby the ethical life is made more substantive and concrete. In this way, individual freedom is made more real and actual.

With the creation of civil society and a system of needs, institutions are formed to satisfy the needs and desires of each person. Although not as critical of civil society as he was in his work *Natural Law*, Hegel is still aware of the antagonism created by a market economy. Try as he might, he cannot distance himself completely from Aristotle. In civil society and market exchange, there is a further bond of recognition and self-awareness created by an economic system in which individuals are related to other individuals as means to the satisfaction of their physical needs. Unfortunately, Hegel does not develop Aristotle's economic theory of needs, grace, and reciprocity but appears to be more influenced here by classical political economy. Human needs are satisfied through other human beings creating the economic foundations of the ethical community. This is an interesting variation of Bernard Mandeville's *Fable of the Bees* (1714) and Adam Smith's *The Wealth of Nations* (1776) notion that seeking private interests in a market economy benefits the public good. Hegel dialectically pushes this argument to form the basis of the ethical life in which selfishness in civil society helps to form 'a system of complete interdependence, wherein the livelihood, happiness, and legal status of one man is interwoven with the livelihood, happiness, and rights of all'.[68]

Whereas Aristotle saw the market economy (*chrematistike*) as potentially dangerous to the Athenian polis and a life of virtue and happiness, Hegel inverts the classical world of antiquity to place the market in the heart of his new ethical system. Smith's invisible hand of private needs replaces Aristotle's reciprocity of social needs; the market has replaced social justice. The intellectual and moral virtues and public happiness and rational deliberation of Greek citizens standing on the Pnyx is now replaced by self-interested competition, wealth creation, and the mechanical division of labour of the factory. Hegel's early critique of liberalism has been modified to fit the market and industrial needs of modern production and the liberal state. In spite of this, Hegel does recognise that this economy 'is accidental because it breeds new desires without end, is in thoroughgoing dependence on caprice and eternal accident, and is held in check by the power of universality [state]. In these contrasts and their complexity, civil society affords a spectacle of extravagance and want as well as of the physical and ethical degeneration common to them both'.[69] Hegel also realises that this 'ethical corruption' was the cause of the breakdown of classical Greece. But just as he approaches Aristotle's critique of a chrematistic economy, Hegel backs away from its implications and instead argues that the rise of a new self-conscious individualism is necessary for the full development of the ethical life of the modern state and therefore, the full realisation of human self-consciousness and freedom. Modernity is slowly overwhelming and displacing the classical horizons of his early writings.

According to Hegel, civil society consists of three components: a system of needs and work, the administration of justice and property, and the protection of particular interests through the police and corporations. With civil society, Hegel's view of freedom and the individual has evolved from the person and subject to the burgher as craftsman, manufacturer, and merchant. Civil society provides the economic framework within which reciprocal needs are satisfied, rather than, as for Aristotle, where reciprocal justice is manifested. Aristotle attempts to ground justice in needs, whereas Hegel attempts to justify an equality of reciprocal dependence within a market economy. According to Hegel, it is work that confers value and utility upon the products of human labour. The modern conditions of work result in the subdivision of the means of production, the division and deskilling of labour, inequality of skills and resources, greater efficiency and productivity, interdependency and reciprocity of needs, production and exchange, mechanisation and automation of work, the production of the public good, and the modern class system of agriculture, business, and the civil servant.[70] The public policy role of the modern state as outlined in *Natural Law* to stabilise the economy because of the shortcomings and irrationalities of the market has now been replaced by the invisible hand where private interests are magically turned into the public good.

Hegel borrows the rationality and logic of the market economy from classical political economy at the same time as he incorporates Plato's theory of classes and inequality into the political mix. This inequality has a rational foundation in the inequality of skills and resources. In the end, civil society is that part of the ethical life which recognises the institutionalisation of property rights and power relations based on social positions and class differences. Because the structure of the social system is inherently rational, grounded as it is in property, law, and rights, it only reaffirms the truth and universality of freedom being expressed in its objective spirit. Right and justice are no longer simply abstract philosophical categories of consciousness, but are now determinate and embedded in the lifeblood of the ethical community and civil society; they have become actualised. Right and reason are no longer abstract thoughts, but are now part of the structure and law of society recognised by everyone. With the development of civil society, the main role of the legal system is to stabilise and strengthen the laws protecting and ensuring private property.[71] Although this is automatically done by the market, sometimes external political bodies are necessary to accomplish this task. This is quite different from his early writings.

Besides the system of needs in the market and the court of justice in law, civil society also consists of corporations or public authorities which are voluntary associations based on professional and occupational interests, business and trade guilds, religious associations, educational groups, municipalities, etc. whose goal is to oversee and regulate production, distribution, and consumption within the economy. They were formed almost as an extension of the family unit to protect the private and public sphere against the negative side effects of the market, that is, to ensure the interests of the common good and public welfare in law and the interests of producers and consumers against fraud and consumer abuse, to fix prices when necessary for the public good, to protect public rights against clashing private interests, to ensure a good public education, and to protect the welfare of the poor during difficult times. The corporations act as 'public regulatory and welfare authorities' within civil society to protect the public good.[72]

Finally, civil society must deal with increasing poverty as the economy expands. Here private charity and public almsgiving are enormously helpful. However, at this later stage of his writings, Hegel subscribes to the idea of the inner workings of the law of supply and demand, growing productivity and profits, and the resulting overproduction of consumer goods. With growing poverty, an increasing delegitimation of society and the law, and the loss of self-respect and personal honesty, Hegel reaches for an economic solution from within classical political economy. The solution cannot be the artificial creation of work and employment by the state because the real problem is that of the overproduction of commodities – an excess of wealth. Hegel concludes that 'it hence becomes apparent that despite an excess of wealth civil society is not rich enough, i.e. its own resources are insufficient to check excessive poverty and the creation of a penurious rabble'.[73] Hegel seems to be suggesting that, in times of economic crisis of overproduction, when the corporations in civil society are no longer capable of maintaining peace and stability, the best remedy is to permit the mechanical laws of the market to decide the fate of the poor, as was the case in Britain and Scotland. Nothing more can be done except economic expansion, creation of new international markets to absorb its overproduction, and colonisation by transplanting its poor and surplus population to other lands. In effect, the market is capable of solving its own internal economic crises by exporting its production, population, and crises overseas. The public welfare is ensured by the efficient laws of the market.

The state pulls together the various component parts of the ethical community into a coherent whole. As Hegel says: 'The state is the actuality of the ethical Idea ... and the actuality of concrete freedom'.[74] The state is the collective mind of the people which embeds itself in the constitution, laws, institutions, character, and consciousness of its citizens. It is the realisation of self-consciousness and rationality in objective social institutions and substantive freedom – or in Hegel's terminology, the union of subjective freedom and objective freedom, the union of form and content as the subjective will is bonded with the general will of the state.[75] Natural law no longer resides in God, tradition, scriptures, the state of nature, human nature, or natural reason. Rather, it is now realised in the ethical life of politics and the state.[76] Hegel turns to an investigation of the various functions and division of power of the rational state which, for him, is represented by a constitutional monarchy.[77] He proceeds to divide it into three substantive political areas: the legislature which determines universal laws, the executive (civil servants and advisors) which applies the laws to particular situations, and the crown (monarchy) which has the power of ultimate decision-making and self-determination as it integrates the two other divisions. The sovereignty and self-determination of the state lies in its ability to integrate these component parts and functions of the political organism into a coherent whole. It is the practical will, that is now expressed as the practical will of the state in the form of the sovereign monarch, that differentiates Hegel's ethics from Kant's morality.

In order to carry out the monarch's will and official universal duties of the maintenance of the laws, regulations, and organisation of the various state functions, as well as the security of the state against private caprice and the abuse of power, he is aided by the executive advisory body or public bureaucracy of civil servants, high advisors, and public officials. Since these are universal responsibilities, the executive bureaucrats must be above the particular interests of those in civil society and must represent the universal ends of the state. Hegel notes that these positions are usually held by members of the middle class.

> What the service of the state really requires is that men shall forgo the self and capricious satisfaction of their subjective ends; by this very sacrifice, they acquire the right to find their satisfaction in, but only in, the dutiful discharge of their public functions. In this fact, so far as public business is concerned, there lies the link between universal and particular interests which constitutes both the concept of the state and its inner stability.[78]

The third division of the state is the legislature, whose purpose, along with the other political institutions of the monarchy, state bureaucracy, and judiciary, is mainly to ensure the general welfare and public happiness of its citizens and the protection of their private rights and freedoms through the creation of universal legislation and determinate laws. According to Hegel, the role of the legislature, which consists of members from two social classes – the agricultural (landed gentry) and business classes or estates (*Stände*) – is to provide a middle ground between the isolation of the monarchy and the private interests of individuals and corporations in civil society. This assembly of the estates or parliament is divided between an upper and lower house and mediates between the universal interests of the monarchy and the private interests of civil society through public deliberation and decision-making regarding public business. Rights have developed beyond the private opinions and desires of particular individuals to the public opinion and public communication of the collective assembly of the estates. In the union of these various political institutions of the state lies the ethical ideal of the organic political community and the highest development of substantive human freedom.

The purpose of the state is to maintain stability in the face of conflicting private and class interests in the economy and government. Taking a position quite different from the modern natural rights theorists, Hegel argues that the state is not an artificial political mechanism for the maintenance of property and power, but an ethical community that integrates opposing interests and inclinations into an organic whole. Although in the *Philosophy of Right* he appears to return to the ethical ideal of the ancient Greeks found in his earlier writings, he is now simply using Aristotle as a political cover for the rediscovery of Hobbes and Locke. In the previous chapter, we saw how Locke used natural law as a justification and rationalisation for natural rights. Now Hegel is making a similar argument by using natural law and the state to justify abstract rights, law, and civil society of private interests and property. Hegel uses a different approach to arrive at similar conclusions. Whereas Locke in the state of nature accepted natural law as the justification for natural rights and then dropped natural law, Hegel proceeds from the opposite direction as he begins with abstract rights and incorporates them into natural law or the ethical life of the state. However, in both cases the state winds up endorsing natural rights at the expense of the integrity of the ethical community. Although Hegel attempts to bring together elements of both ancient political theory and modern political economy, there remains an unresolved tension in his theory of the state. Although neither Aristotle nor Marx desired to join together a chrematistic economy of liberalism with classical political ideals of the Greek polity, Hegel attempts the project but fails. If he was critical that modern society in the late nineteenth century ended in the French terror and Kantian formalism with its unconscious defence of natural rights, he does not finally recognise that his own view of the state ultimately supports the 'unmitigated extreme of barbarism' of civil society. The philosophical project of integrating natural law and natural rights by both Locke and Hegel ultimately failed.

Marx's Critique of Hegel and the Revival of Classical Democracy in Spinoza and Rousseau

Marx's critique of Hegel's theory of the state in the *Contribution to the Critique of Hegel's Philosophy of Law* (1843) was one of his first major early writings and central to laying the foundations for his own theory of social justice. Marx objects to Hegel's use of phenomenological logic and the dialectical method in this work, as well as his acceptance of the structural antagonisms between civil society and state. Although Hegel recognises that the family and civil society are part of the ethical community, he understands their relationship as the determinate and objective development of the concept as it evolves from its early stages to its full realisation in the state. Hegel is not doing a historical and empirical analysis of the state but, rather, tracing the concept (*Begriff*) and logic of the state as it develops toward its own telos or end in the mind (*Idee*) or spirit (*Geist*) of a nation. The key point for Marx is that 'empirical actuality is thus accepted as it is. It is also expressed as rational, but it is not rational on account of its own reason, but because the empirical fact in its empirical existence has a different significance from it itself'.[79] Marx states that it is never explained how the family and civil society are related to the political constitution and the state. Nor are the various structures and functions of the state examined in any detail. The ideas about the ethical life of the family, economy, and government are simply subsumed into the phenomenal evolution of the concept of the modern liberal state on the basis of some mystical principle. The state evolves logically from its earlier component parts into a universal and ethical whole (the Absolute or Idea) that integrates them into a coherent living political organism. But Hegel never explains how this is done.

According to Marx, Hegel never examines the nature of the modern state in liberal society, but only analyses the concept or essence of the state as it actualises itself in consciousness and as it is idealised in the mind. The state manifests and realises its own essence or perfection as Idea in history as an objective reality (objectivity) through human self-consciousness and the freedom of the will (subjectivity) within an ethical community.[80] History and social reality are reduced to the logical unfolding of an ethical Idea. By tracing the development of this Idea of the state, Hegel has inverted the real relationship between the real (existence) and ideal (essence), as well as between the economy and polity; his theory of the state is based on an abstract logic and metaphysics and not on history and empirical analysis. He, too, has committed the transgression which he originally attributed to Kantian logic and moral formalism. This is why he can refer to the state using terms such as self-conscious, sovereign, freedom, and rational. The terms are never justified or explained; they are simply assumed into the logic and theory of the state. Marx summarises his criticisms in the following: 'He [Hegel] does not develop his thinking from the object [state], but expounds the object in accordance with a thinking that is cut and dried – already formed and fixed in the abstract sphere of logic'.[81] Marx refers to this as 'a manifest piece of mystification ... The soul of objects, in this case of the state is cut and dried, predestined, prior to its body, which is really mere appearance'.[82] The heart of the state is the mind knowing itself in abstract thought as it develops dialectically in time; the component parts and functions of the state are determined by the logic of Hegel's analysis and not by their empirical interactions within society. The state integrates all conflicting parts of the family, class antagonisms, market economy, and law through a predetermined logic and not through any social transformation. There is no analysis of the actual structures and functions of the modern state, the actual role of the executive and legislature, or how they relate to broader considerations of class, power, and legal and political authority. Hegel only examines the idealised state of logic and mind (*Geist*) and not the actual state of civil society and law (materialism); he never moves beyond abstract and speculative philosophy to a critical social theory and historical science.

According to Marx, Hegel does see the profound contradictions between civil and political society but 'is wrong, however, to be content with the appearance of this resolution and to pretend it is the substance'.[83] By integrating the class elements of civil society into the various functions of the state, Hegel assumes that he has overcome these antagonisms in the unity and harmony of the state. He does not adequately appreciate the class nature of society nor the actual structures and functions of the liberal state in civil society. He fails to realise that 'the political constitution at its highest point is therefore the *constitution of private property*'.[84] The essence of the state is not the ethical life of the community that raises its citizens to the highest development of human potentiality in common traditions, institutions, and political ideals. Rather, it is, in fact, simply the political appearance and facade of its underlying reality – property, possessions, and class. Underlying Hegel's concept of the state is the reality of Locke's state of nature and law. Marx asks:

> What then is the power of the political state over private property? The *power of private property itself*, its essence brought into existence. What remains for the political state in contrast with this essence? The *illusion* that the state determines, when it is being determined. It does, indeed, break the *will of the family and society*, but only as to give existence to the *will of private property without family and society* and to acknowledge this existence as the supreme existence of the political state, as the supreme existence of *ethical life*.[85]

Marx contends that the final purpose of the state is to protect abstract rights, the private person, and private property. The very notion of freedom has become synonymous with liberty as the former loses its political implications and reconnects with possessive individualism and the goals of civil society. This is the hidden secret of the political state: '"Real private property" is then, not only the "pillar of the constitution" but the *"constitution itself"*'.[86] Politics is simply a theological facade that hides the real function and goal of the state – its goal is not to realise the ethical ideal of the ancients, but instead, to ensure the wealth and property of the bourgeois class.

Two central political philosophers in Hegel's development of the relationship between natural law and the state are Spinoza and Rousseau, who will help motivate Marx toward his general discussion of the modern state, virtue, and democracy as the new foundation of natural law in his writings. Rousseau in the *Social Contract* (1762) will be essential in helping Marx ground his theory of democracy and human rights with the former's distinctions between the rights of man (economic rights to property) and the rights of the citizen (political rights to assembly and deliberative participation), critique of private property, and theory of the general will and participatory democracy.[87] Spinoza, too, will provide Marx with the necessary grounding of his theory of the state in his theory of democracy, sovereignty, reason, freedom, and the general welfare of the citizens in chapter 16 of the *Tractatus Theologico-Politicus* (1670).[88]

Faced with the same dilemma of conflicting traditions, Hegel and Marx will both turn to Spinoza and Rousseau to provide inspiration and resolution to the conflicting traditions of law and rights expressed by Locke.[89] How they accomplish this end will help us better understand the differences between liberalism and socialism in modernity. Marx will use his early writings *Contribution to the Critique of Hegel's Philosophy of Right* (1843) and *On the Jewish Question* (1843) to reject both Hegel's political idealism and the Hobbesian and Lockean theory of liberalism and natural rights as he begins to develop the outline of his own theory of social justice. In his nuanced critique of natural rights and political emancipation, Marx will reject the economic rights of man and property, while accepting the political rights of the citizen to public discourse and participation in the liberal state as the start of the movement toward a broader and more comprehensive view of human emancipation and human rights. With the aid of Spinoza, Rousseau, and Hegel, the natural law tradition will evolve from philosophy (nature, virtue, and politics of Aristotle), religion (scholasticism of Aquinas), and political theory (natural rights of Locke) to a critical social theory (social ethics of Hegel). As we have seen, in the Middle Ages natural law was grounded in the trinity of God, reason, and nature, but is now replaced by political reason and economic democracy in Marx – social justice. In *On the Jewish Question*, he will reappropriate the ancient natural law tradition at the same time that he rejects most of natural rights as he creates a new social ethics and theory of justice. He will accomplish this by rewriting the ethics, economics, and politics of Aristotle to fit the new contours of modern capitalism. Hegel did not fully appreciate that the realisation of his Kantian dream of individual freedom and moral autonomy required the strengthening and not the weakening of his classical Greek ideals. The two were intimately bound together, but were held apart by civil society and liberalism. Marx does not make this mistake.

Although Marx is very critical of Hegel's theory of the state, there are clear indications in his analysis that he appreciates Hegel's attempt to see the state as the ethical community or true being of humanity. Both will use the same term – *Gemeinwesen* – to describe these goals. Marx rejects Hegel's logic, method, and theory, but not the inspiration for his work on the philosophy of law. The ethical spirit that unites citizens behind the species being of humanity is not the liberal state, but socialism and democracy.[90] And it is this view of democracy that Marx will use as the foundation for his theory of natural law and social justice. Democracy is the truth of all other constitutions since it represents the realisation of the ethical ideals implicit in human nature and human needs as a species being; it represents the ethical goals of practical will, self-consciousness, self-determination, freedom, and human rights (rights of the citizen). While Hegel thought these ideals resided in the concept or essence of the modern state, Marx will show in his next writings that the state must be a democracy to be ethical.

> Democracy is the solved *riddle* of all constitutions. Here, not merely *implicitly* and in essence but *existing* in reality, the constitution is constantly brought back to its actual basis, the *actual human being*, the *actual people*, and established as the people's *own* work. The constitution appears as what it is, a free product of man ... Just as it is not religion, which creates man but man who creates religion, so it is not the constitution which cre-

ates the people but the people which creates the constitution ... In democracy the constitution, the law, the state itself, insofar as it is a political constitution, is only the self-determination of the people, and a particular content of the people.[91]

Democracy and self-determination now become the basis for the ethical community and the return to classical antiquity. Although Hegel had the spirit of the ancients as his legal guide, he lost it in the abstractions of his theory of law and rights and his inability to examine the content of his abstract idealism. Marx took a different turn, and in the process, created the conditions for a substantive and objective break with modernity by redefining the nature of social justice and classical democracy from the dreams of the ancient Greek ideals. The foundations of natural rights in the British tradition of Hobbes and Locke rested upon human nature and the natural desires and passions of the individual to get what they wanted in order to ensure private life and self-preservation (naturalism). In Locke, this was supplemented by his reliance on the natural law given by God and accessible to human reason, as the voice of God, and the Christian tradition and scriptures. This British tradition separated the rights of man from the community and citizenship as well as from natural law and also confirmed the separation of civil society from the state. The French and German traditions, on the other hand, ground natural law and political theory (justice) in reason as articulated and actualised by the general will (Rousseau), practical reason and the universal categorical imperative (Kant), the ethical community, self-consciousness, and the liberal state (Hegel), and workers' co-operatives and participatory democracy of labour (Marx). With Rousseau, Hegel, and Marx, natural law and reason are ultimately justified by the freedom, collective wisdom, and public discourse of the political community as it creates the good, happy, and virtuous life through self-legislation as *praxis* (practical action) and *phronesis* (practical wisdom).

It should also be noted that Marx in his early writings will also develop an anthropological theory of ethics and virtue based on human nature as free, creative producers of their own experience, history, and social institutions. This more Aristotelian approach to ethics, as the self-realisation of human nature and potentiality through practice and politics, becomes the core of Marx's critical social theory. Natural law evolved from the medieval tradition based on God, nature, and reason to the modern tradition of nature, reason, and democracy.[92] With a growing alienation and homelessness in an increasingly foreign world of new institutions and values; with a growing inability to justify the meaning and morals of individual existence in a Christian metaphysic; and with a new political economy changing the fabric of modern society, these theorists attempted to lay the foundation for a new ethic of natural law in reason and politics. Finally, Marx used the first juridical definition of justice developed by Locke with its emphasis of natural rights and legal justice as the basis for his immanent critique in *Capital*, while using the voices of continental philosophy on social justice as the basis for his substantive critique of capital throughout his writings.[93]

Marx's overall theory of social justice will be outlined in the following chapters. He undertakes to redefine and reintegrate Hegel's theory of the ethical community (ancients) and individual moral sovereignty (moderns) into a democratic, moral economy by transforming the latter's idealism into a materialist view of history, freedom, and self-consciousness. He does this by organising his critical social theory into two main parts closely paralleling the writings of Aristotle: ethics and social institutions. Under Ethics, he investigates the moral values used to reject modern liberalism and capitalism – human nature as creative species being, human needs as self-realisation, self-determination, and economic freedom, and natural law as the synthesis of nature (virtue) and needs (institutions); under Institutions, he applies his distinctive method of analysis based on history, critique, and dialectics. Marx broadens his social theory by using a variety of critical methods: (1) a historical and empirical analysis of the rise of commodity and commodity exchange, money and commerce, and capital and production; (2) an immanent critique and comparison of the political ideals of liberalism and the historical and economic reality of capitalism; and (3) a dialectical investigation into the logical and structural contradictions of the capitalist organisation of production based on the economic rifts between use value and exchange value, material production and class distribution, market realisation and capital production, and the conflict between the productive and technological forces and the social relations of production resulting in profound economic and ecological crises. In the end, these institutional relationships of capital make the realisation of a virtuous, free, and happy (*eudaimonia*) life impossible.

Notes

1 These early writings of Hegel on social and political theory while at Berne (1793–6, *The Positivity of the Christian Religion*), at Frankfurt (1797–1801, *The Spirit of Christianity and its Fate*), and at Jena (1801–7, *Natural Law, System der Sittlichkeit, Realphilosophie I and II*, and *Phenomenology of Spirit*) will set the philosophical space for his later works in the field at Berlin (1818–31), especially the *Philosophy of Right* (1821, actually appeared in October 1820). Neither the *System der Sittlichkeit* (1802–3) nor the Jena lectures of the *Real-*

philosophie I and II were published during Hegel's lifetime. The former was published in 1913 and the latter in the 1930s. For an introduction to the importance of Hegel's early to his later writings, see Herbert Marcuse, *Reason and Revolution: Hegel and the Rise of Social Theory* (Boston, MA: Beacon Press, 1960); Shlomo Avineri, *Hegel's Theory of the Modern State* (Cambridge: Cambridge University Press, 1972); Georg Lukács, *The Young Hegel: Studies in the Relation Between Dialectics and Economics*, trans. Rodney Livingstone (Cambridge, MA: MIT Press, 1976); and Axel Honneth, *The Struggle for Recognition: The Moral Grammar of Social Conflicts*, trans. Joel Anderson (Cambridge, MA: Polity Press, 1995).

2   Abel Garza Jr., 'Hegel's Critique of Liberalism and Natural Law: Reconstructing Ethical Life', *Law and Philosophy* 9 (1990–1): 376–8.

3   *Integrating Natural Rights and Natural Law*: Just as Aristotle attempted to integrate ethics and politics into a democratic polity, Locke ethical principles and economic structures in the state of nature, and Hegel virtue and justice in social ethics, Marx created a practical science by pulling together human creativity and self-realisation (social praxis) and a critique of political economy into a comprehensive theory of social justice. Locke, Hegel, and Marx framed much of their political theory around the integration of natural law and natural rights for the ultimate purpose of justifying natural rights and a market economy (Locke), freedom within the ethical community of the liberal state (Hegel), and the virtuous life within an economic democracy (Marx).

4   Georg Wilhelm Friedrich Hegel, 'The Positivity of the Christian Religion', in *On Christianity: Early Theological Writings*, trans. T.M. Knox (New York, NY: Harper Torchbooks, 1961), p. 154; 'Die Positivität der christlichen Religion', in *Frühe Schriften*, Werke 1 (Frankfurt/Main: Suhrkamp Taschenbuch Verlag, 1971), pp. 204–5. Although written in the eighteenth century, this work was not published until the twentieth century.

5   Alasdair MacIntyre, *A Short History of Ethics: A History of Moral Philosophy from the Homeric Age to the Twentieth Century* (New York, NY: Macmillan Company, 1971), p. 199. MacIntyre begins his analysis of Hegel with the statement that it was Christianity which separated theology and politics, universal morality and public citizenship. MacIntyre writes: 'Yet if Hegel's vision of Greek harmony is exaggerated it provides him with clues for the direction of individualism, and with clues of a historical kind' (ibid.).

6   *Dreams of Classical Antiquity in Hegel*: There are a number of secondary sources which have made similar arguments about Hegel's idealising of ancient Greece as an important part of his moral and political philosophy, including E.M. Butler, *The Tyranny of Greece over Germany* (Cambridge: Cambridge University Press, 1935); J. Glenn Gray, *Hegel's Hellenic Ideal: The Mystical Element in Hegel's Early Theological Writings* (New York, NY: King's Crown Press, 1941); Judith Shklar, 'Hegel's Phenomenology: An Elegy for Hellas', in *Hegel's Political Philosophy: Problems and Perspectives*, ed. Z.A. Pelczynski (Cambridge: Cambridge University Press, 1971), pp. 73–89 and *Freedom and Independence: A Study of the Political Ideas of Hegel's 'Phenomenology of Mind'* (Cambridge: Cambridge University Press, 1978); Avineri, *Hegel's Theory of the Modern State*; Lukács, *The Young Hegel*; George Kelly, *Hegel's Retreat from Eleusis: Studies in Political Thought* (Princeton, NJ: Princeton University Press, 1978) and *Idealism, Politics and History: Sources of Hegelian Thought* (Cambridge: Cambridge University Press, 1978); Charles Taylor, *Hegel and Modern Society* (Cambridge: Cambridge University Press, 1979); Raymond Plant, *Hegel, An Introduction* (London: Basil

Blackwell, 1983); Manfred Riedel, *Between Tradition and Revolution: The Hegelian Transformation of Political Philosophy*, trans. Walter Wright (Cambridge: Cambridge University Press, 1984); Joachim Ritter, *Hegel and the French Revolution*, trans. Richard Winfield (Cambridge, MA: MIT Press, 1984); Z.A. Pelczynski, 'Political Community and Individual Freedom in Hegel's Philosophy of State', *The State and Civil Society: Studies in Hegel's Political Philosophy*, ed. Z.A. Pelczynski (Cambridge: Cambridge University Press, 1984), pp. 55–76; M. Inwood, 'Hegel, Plato and Greek Sittlichkeit', in *The State and Civil Society*, ed. Z.A. Pelczynski, pp. 40–54; Lewis Hinchman, *Hegel's Critique of the Enlightenment* (Tampa, FL: University Presses of Florida, 1984); Steven Smith, *Hegel's Critique of Liberalism: Rights in Context* (Chicago, IL: University of Chicago Press, 1989); Garza, Jr., 'Hegel's Critique of Liberalism and Natural Law', pp. 371–98; Alfredo Ferrarin, *Hegel and Aristotle* (Cambridge: Cambridge University Press, 2001); and Gary Pendlebury, *Action and Ethics in Aristotle and Hegel: Escaping the Malign Influences of Kant* (Farnham: Ashgate, 2005).

7   Hegel, 'The Positivity of the Christian Religion', p. 155; *Frühe Schriften*, p. 205.
8   Ibid.
9   Ibid., p. 156; *Frühe Schriften*, p. 206. It is interesting that Émile Durkheim will begin his intellectual career by turning to Montesquieu's *The Spirit of the Laws* (1748) in his first dissertation in Latin, entitled *Montesquieu's Contribution to the Rise of Social Science*. At this early stage he also produced a manuscript and a series of lectures on Rousseau's *Social Contract*. See *Montesquieu and Rousseau: Forerunners of Sociology*, trans. Ralph Manheim (Ann Arbor, MI: Ann Arbor Paperback, 1975). He, too, was interested in the relationships among Aristotle, Montesquieu, and Rousseau.
10 Hegel, 'The Positivity of the Christian Religion', pp. 156–7; *Frühe Schriften*, p. 206.
11 Ibid., p. 157; *Frühe Schriften*, p. 207.
12 Ibid., p. 160; *Frühe Schriften*, p. 209. At this point in his analysis of Christianity, Hegel seems to be anticipating Max Weber's summary of the Protestant ethic and the powerless and corrupted view of human nature caught in the 'unceasing machinations and cunning of an evil spirit' that penetrated deep into nature and the mind. The result of these social and religious transformations was a 'hopeless triviality' or moral nihilism held in check by a despotic God viewed as the highest expression of perfection, divinity, and moral sanctity. Human nature was reduced to the passions and pride as God occupied a position of dignity, worth, and power. In this scholastic and theological transformation of folk religion into a metaphysical doctrine concerned with origins, creation, and causality, the very notion of human morality and action was perverted and lost. Hegel offered a warning that 'such a perversion of nature could only entail a most frightful revenge' (p. 162; *Frühe Schriften*, p. 211).
13 Ibid.
14 Ibid., p. 163; *Frühe Schriften*, p. 212.
15 Georg Wilhelm Friedrich Hegel, 'The Spirit of Christianity and its Fate', in *On Christianity: Early Theological Writings*, trans. T.M. Knox (New York, NY: Harper Torchbooks, 1961), p. 289; 'Der Geist des Christentums und sein Schicksal', in *Frühe Schriften*, Werke 1 (Frankfurt/Main: Suhrkamp Taschenbuch Verlag, 1971), p. 406.
16 At about the same time as the appearance of this essay on natural law by Hegel in 1802–3, a number of other works important to Hegel also appeared, including Schelling's *New*

Deduction of Natural Law (1796) and *System of Transcendental Idealism* (1800), Fichte's *The Foundations of Natural Law* (1796), and Kant's *Metaphysics of Morals* (1797). In his 'Introduction' to the English publication of Hegel's *Natural Law: The Scientific Ways of Treating Natural* Law, trans. T.M. Knox (Philadelphia, PA: University of Pennsylvania Press, 1975) (referred to throughout this book as simply *Natural Law*), H.B. Action writes that Schelling in his *System of Transcendental Idealism* referred to a possible league of nations as 'a universal Areopagus of the peoples' tying the ancients back into modernity (p. 41). A more detailed exposition of this work would require placing it in its broader philosophical context.

17 For a critical summary of Hegel's critique of the epistemological foundations of natural rights in unreflective empiricism and empty formalism, see Smith, *Hegel's Critique of Liberalism*, pp. 57–97. Smith's main thesis is that Hegel attempted to integrate the ancient view of education, culture, and polity of Aristotle with the modern insights into life, liberty, individual rights, freedom, and reason from Kant, thereby creating a stronger form of liberalism and the liberal state (*Rechtsstaat*) than either generated by empiricism or formalism (pp. 6–8). Connecting epistemology with social theory, Smith takes an interesting perspective on Hegel's theory of truth by arguing that 'truth is, then, less a matter of objectivity than of agreement; less a matter of correspondence than consensus ... The community becomes the standard for all values, including truth ... Agreement in judgments cannot be legitimately produced by force or fraud but must be the outcome of discussion, persuasion, and dialogue' (pp. 221–2). He clearly places Hegel within the tradition of classical dialogue and collective consensus of Hans-Georg Gadamer and Jürgen Habermas (p. 222). The Absolute Spirit is the actualisation of the ethical universal in the traditions, laws, and institutions of the liberal state. The ideals of freedom and self-realisation that once were ancient Greece have now been realised in the German spirit. For the Hegelian integration of Aristotle and Kant, see Taylor, *Hegel and Modern Society*, pp. 82–95; Robert Solomon, *In the Spirit of Hegel: A Study of G.W.F. Hegel's 'Phenomenology of Spirit'* (New York, NY: Oxford University Press, 1983), p. 523; and Ferrarin, *Hegel and Aristotle*, p. 330.

18 Action, in his 'Introduction', mentions that Hegel offered 'Natural Law and Political Science in Outline' as a possible alternative title to his *Philosophy of Right* of 1821 (p. 16). See also Solomon's *In the Spirit of Hegel*, where he describes Hegel's early understanding of *Sittlichkeit* in the following manner: '*Sittlichkeit* consists mainly of community practices, rituals, unspoken as well as explicit rules and roles into which every community member is born and in terms of which he or she defines not only self-identity but the seemingly absolute order of the world' (p. 484). Later, it begins to refer to objective institutions of the constitution, right, law, and the state which make morality, community, and political freedom possible.

19 It should also be mentioned at this point that Hegel's other seminary roommate in Tübingen besides Schelling was Friedrich Hölderlin, the famous German poet who, along with Friedrich Schiller, was also influential in forming Hegel's (and Marx's) early vision of the Greek ideal. See George E. McCarthy, *Marx and the Ancients: Classical Ethics, Social Justice, and Nineteenth-Century Political Economy* (Savage, MD: Rowman & Littlefield Publishers, 1990), pp. 141–3.

20 Hegel, *Natural Law*, p. 62; 'Über die wissenschaftlichen Behandlungsarten des Naturrechts, seine Stelle in der praktischen Philosophie und sein Verhältnis zu den positiven Rechtswissenschaften', *Jenaer Schriften 1801–1807*, Werke 2 (Frankfurt/Main: Suhrkamp Taschenbuch Verlag, 1970), p. 444. This characterisation of the moral and political philosophy of empiricism is also characteristic of its disunity of multiple and diverse objects in epistemology.

21 Ibid., p. 61; *Jenaer Schriften*, p. 442.

22 Ibid., p. 62; *Jenaer Schriften*, p. 443. It is interesting that Hegel, in his analysis of empiricism and natural rights theory, introduces an examination of *a priori* formalism (rationalism) as a way of explaining the formation of moral and political theory from the diversity and multiplicity of the empirical data collected. When examining Kant's moral philosophy and the continental tradition of natural law, he will argue that Kantian rationalism will also introduce empiricism to explain his theory of the categorical imperative and practical reason. In both cases British and continental natural rights traditions are grounded in the arbitrary selection of particular elements of experience and reason as the foundational principles of their philosophy. The consistency and 'completeness of the picture' that is attempted by the natural rights theorists remains negative, formal, and empty (ibid.; *Jenaer Schriften*, p. 443). Hegel views both traditions as ultimately arbitrary in the manner in which they attempt to give coherence and meaning to the social whole – the ethical life.

Another way of looking at Hegel is that he is arguably the first modern social theorist to articulate the need for a critical sociology that gives an account of the underlying social totality within society that ultimately gives coherence to its various parts, laws, principles, culture, and social (self-conscious) relationships. This is what Hegel refers to as the essence or absolute unity that holds society together. This will be Hegel's greatest gift to Marx's theory of historical, structural, and functional materialism.

23 Ibid., p. 63; *Jenaer Schriften*, p. 445.

24 Ibid., p. 64; *Jenaer Schriften*, pp. 445–6.

25 Hegel contends that these natural rights theorists create an artificial unity of the state bringing a semblance of coherence to the multiplicity of individual inclinations and desires for liberty and property (Locke). Hegel sees the connection here to nineteenth-century physics with its theory of isolated atoms (original unity) and entities (absolute unity), quantitative multiplicity of parts and relations, and a temporary unity in physical objects or the ethical state (ibid., p. 65; *Jenaer Schriften*, p. 447). Even God as the creator of heaven, earth, and natural law remains formal and external to this multiplicity.

26 Ibid., p. 68; *Jenaer Schriften*, p. 451.

27 Immanuel Kant, *Fundamental Principles of the Metaphysic of Morals*, trans. Thomas Abbott (Indianapolis, IN: Bobbs-Merrill Company, 1949), p. 5; *Grundlegung zur Metaphysik der Sitten, Kants Werke*, Band IV (Berlin: Walter de Gruyter & Company, 1968), p. 389. Action, in his introductory essay to *Natural Law*, mentions that in his work on the life of Hegel in 1844, Johann Karl Friedrich Rosenkranz reminded his readers that Hegel had written a commentary on the *Metaphysic of Morals* in 1798 (p. 22). The terms rationalism and empiricism have slightly different meanings in Kant than in Hegel's *Natural Law*. It is interesting to note that Hegel recognises that the Enlightenment natural rights theorists

equate freedom with indifference (*Natural Law*, p. 73; *Jenaer Schriften*, p. 457). The free society is built not on the ethical community or on the moral life, but on an artificial and contingent unity of diversity and indifference. Kant will refer to the empiricist's view of freedom as natural liberty in civil society, while reserving the notion of freedom for self-conscious actions of practical reason. Hegel will build upon this latter view of freedom while recognising its limitations. It is only when Hegel connects Kant with Aristotle that we have the beginnings of a social theory of ethics and justice.

28 Hegel, *Natural Law*, p. 76; *Jenaer Schriften*, p. 461. This quotation was taken from Kant's *Critique of Pure Reason*, book I, chapter 1, para. 7.
29 Ibid.; *Jenaer Schriften*, p. 461.
30 Ibid., p. 79; *Jenaer Schriften*, p. 464.
31 Ibid., p. 77; *Jenaer Schriften*, p. 461.
32 Ferrarin, *Hegel and Aristotle*. Regarding Hegel's notion of self-legislation, Ferrarin writes: 'This shows that Hegel conflates under the heading of spirit's self-realisation, not just Aristotelian practice and production, but also both Kantian hypothetical and categorical imperatives. Reason is by itself practical; it necessarily actualizes itself ... To actualize ends is to subject oneself to reason's autonomous rule; but to do so is only possible on the basis of man's self-understanding within a world of relations to be shaped by him' (p. 330).
33 This same logical dilemma reappears years later in Hegel's *Philosophy of Right* (1821), trans T.M. Knox (London: Oxford University Press, 1967), when he makes the following argument: 'The absence of property contains in itself just as little contradiction as the non-existence of this or that nation, family, etc. or the death of the whole human race. But if it is already established on other grounds and presupposed that property and human life are to exist and be respected, then indeed it is a contradiction to commit theft or murder; a contradiction must be a contradiction of something, i.e. of some content presupposed from the start as a fixed principle' (para. 135, p. 90); *Die Grundlinien der Philosophie des Rechts oder Naturrecht und Staatswissenschaft im Grundrisse* (Frankfurt/Main: Suhrkamp Verlag, 1970), p. 253.
34 Louis Dupré, *The Philosophical Foundations of Marxism* (New York, NY: Harcourt, Brace & World, 1966), p. 20.
35 Ibid., p. 21. On this point of the moral empiricism of Kant's categorical imperative and practical reason, see also Alasdair MacIntyre, *A Short History of Ethics*, pp. 197–8. Steven Smith has argued that the failures of the French Revolution could be traced to the inadequate theory and principles of natural rights that had a variety of problems including faulty theories of the self, the common good, and civic virtue. Patrick Murray, *Marx's Theory of Scientific Knowledge* (Atlantic Highlands, NJ: Humanities Press International, 1988), pp. 37–8 and 206; Smith, 'Hegel and the French Revolution: An Epitaph for Republicanism', *Social Research*, 56, 1 (Spring 1989), pp. 243–53 and *Hegel's Critique of Liberalism*, pp. 55 and 85–97; and Robert Solomon, *In the Spirit of Hegel*, pp. 561–2. Smith maintains that it was an empty and faulty conception of rights which undermined the republican community during the French Revolution. The French had the democratic procedures in place without any substantive and objective knowledge of the public good and virtuous action by which to restrain its citizens during the years of the Terror (p. 91).
36 Hegel, *Natural Law*, p. 78; *Jenaer Schriften*, p. 463. By combining the subject and object

(analytic sentence) and the content and universal in a formal unity of pure reason, the essence of reason and morality is undermined, resulting in a form of morality that is contingent and arbitrary, that is, based on the immediacy of the empirically given. Hegel writes at the end of his analysis of Kant that this approach 'makes the morally necessary into something contingent ...; however, contingency, which coincides with the empirically necessary, is immoral' (p. 81; *Jenaer Schriften*, p. 467).

37   Ibid., p. 79; *Jenaer Schriften*, p. 464.
38   *Hegel's Critique of Kant's Critique of Practical Reason*: Marcuse, *Reason and Revolution*; Dupré, *The Philosophical Foundations of Marxism*, pp. 19–21; MacIntyre, *A Short History of Ethics*; W.H. Walsh, *Hegelian Ethics* (New York, NY: St. Martin's Press, 1969); Georg Lukács, *History and Class Consciousness: Studies in Marxist Dialectics*, trans. Rodney Livingstone (Cambridge, MA: MIT Press, 1971); Leo Kofler, *Geschichte und Dialektik* (Darmstadt: Luchterhand Verlag, 1972); Taylor, *Hegel and Modern Society*; and Smith, *Hegel's Critique of Liberalism*. When articulating his moral philosophy in the *Fundamental Principles of the Metaphysic of Morals*, Kant relies on the values of life, promise, human capacities, and the common good as unquestioned normative values and moral content that are presupposed before the actual application of the categorical imperative. From Hegel's perspective, these are the values of the empirically given and indifferent multiplicity.
39   Hegel, *Natural Law*, p. 113; *Jenaer Schriften*, p. 505.
40   G.W.F. Hegel, *System of Ethical Life* in *System of Ethical Life (1802–3) and First Philosophy of Spirit (1803–4)* (New York, NY: State University of New York Press, 1979), p. 161; *System der Sittlichkeit*, hrsg. Georg Lasson (Hamburg: Verlag von Felix Meiner, 1967), p. 74.
41   Ibid.; *System der Sittlichkeit*, p. 74. Hegel writes: 'The government is absolute power for all the classes because it is above them. Its might whereby it is a power is not something external whereby it would be something particular against another particular ... On the contrary, it is absolutely and solely universality against the particular; and as this Absolute, this Ideal, this Universal, in contrast with which everything else is a particular' (p. 163; *System der Sittlichkeit*, p. 75).
42   Ibid., p. 158; *System der Sittlichkeit*, p. 71.
43   *Natural Law*, p. 112; *Jenaer Schriften*, p. 504.
44   Hegel gives Montesquieu and his 'immortal work' on the individual and the nation credit for his rejection of both empiricism and rationalism (formalism), common experience and reason as the foundation of moral and civil laws (ibid., pp. 128–9; *Jenaer Schriften*, pp. 524–5). Hegel makes an important reservation to this integration of the individual and society when he writes: 'But if the whole does not advance in step with the growth of the individual, law and *ethos* separate; the living unity binding the members together is weakened and there is no longer any absolute cohesion and necessity in the present life to the whole' (p. 129; *Jenaer Schriften*, p. 526). Hegel reconnects the Kantian subject and individual freedom with the ideal of the Greek polity. The individual exists in and through the ethical totality of the law, customs, and the nation. There is always an ethical dialectic and intimate bond between the particular and the universal, individual and state that creates the free self-conscious individual within the 'living bond and inner unity' of the absolute totality, that is, the total social system held together by natural law and virtue – the ends of society (p. 131; *Jenaer Schriften*, p. 527). Just as parts of the human

body cannot maintain their vitality without the functioning of a total healthy body, so too a moral and virtuous individual cannot exist with just simply reason and experience but must also have a total ethical life in the family, civil society, and the state. Hegel argues that virtues are potentialities of individual morality and are made possible and practical because of the law and state; the content of morality lies in the spirit of natural and positive law organically living in society's culture, character, and institutions. The essence of humanity is politics and thus our true public freedom can only be found in the ethical totality of the social system. In a playful juxtaposition of ideas, Hegel writes: 'Natural law is to construct how ethical nature attains its true right'. He rejects the possibility that the social abstractions of a league of nations, world republic, or the rights of man can satisfy the requirement for an ethical life which lies in the local community (p. 132; *Jenaer Schriften*, p. 530). At this stage in the development of his ideas, the absolute spirit is the living community of natural law which creates 'the purest and freest individuality' (ibid., p. 133; *Jenaer Schriften*, p. 530).

45 Ibid., p. 116; *Jenaer Schriften*, pp. 508–9. Action, in his 'Introduction', *Natural Law*, summarises Hegel's position in relation to Kant when he writes: 'Rationality, according to Hegel, is more than logical consistency, and is exhibited by each individual through the unity of life rather than by the mere logical consistency of the maxims he adopts. Reason shows itself in society through "the spirit" of its laws and policies rather than in any single aim pursued by all its members' (pp. 25–6).

46 Hegel, *System of Ethical Life*, p. 171; *System der Sittlichkeit*, p. 84. Rosenkranz and Lukács contend that Hegel's view of civil society and the market economy was influenced by James Steuart's *Inquiry into the Principles of Political Economy* (1767). H.S. Harris, in his introductory comments to this work of Hegel, entitled 'Hegel's System of Ethical Life', also argues that Adam Smith's *Wealth of Nations* played an important role in this theory of the state and economy (ibid., pp. 74–5).

47 Ibid., p. 171; *System der Sittlichkeit*, p. 84. Toward the end of the manuscript there are cryptic comments borrowed from Aristotle about the nature of freedom, the identity of ruler and ruled, and citizenship and equity, but they are not developed by Hegel.

48 Ibid.

49 Ibid., p. 145; *System der Sittlichkeit*, p. 56. In the language of Hegel, this synthesis in the ethical totality integrates the empirical consciousness with the absolute consciousness (concept or essence) of the state; for moral consciousness to be made actual, the ethical values and virtues must be objectified and institutionalised in the political and social institutions of the family, civil society, and the state. They must be given life (institutional life) beyond the abstract subjectivity of pure consciousness. The subject is integrated into the object. *Moralität* is made possible by *Sittlichkeit*. To state this in another way, it is Aristotle who makes Kant possible; only within a free polity is the self-determination and moral autonomy of practical reason realised. The polity must first exist before a virtuous life of courage, honour, and wisdom can be made real. Beginning the section of this manuscript on the 'ethical life', Hegel writes: 'Thus in the ethical life the individual exists in an eternal mode: his empirical being and doing is something downright universal; for it is not his individual aspect which acts but the universal absolute spirit in him' (p. 143; *System der Sittlichkeit*, p. 53).

50 Ibid., pp. 146–7; *System der Sittlichkeit*, pp. 56–7.
51 Over the years there has been a vigorous debate in Hegelian scholarship about the central importance of the Greek ideal in Hegel's later writings of the *Phenomenology of Spirit* and the *Philosophy of Right*. Scholars who argue that the Greek polity continued to exert a strong hold over Hegel include Rudolph Haym, Charles Taylor, Z.A. Pelczynski, Judith Shklar, H.S. Harris, and Joachim Ritter. Others who argue that the Greek influence waned toward the end of his writing career include Philip Kain, George Kelly, Bernard Cullen, Shlomo Avineri, and Manfred Riedel. For more information, see McCarthy, *Marx and the Ancients*, n. 58, p. 313.
52 See Robert Solomon, 'The Phenomenology of Spirit: Its Structure', *In the Spirit of Hegel: A Study of G.W.F. Hegel's 'Phenomenology of Spirit'* (New York, NY: Oxford University Press, 1983), pp. 211–36.
53 This critique of liberalism and the Enlightenment begins with Hegel's analysis of culture, alienation, and individualism in chapter six of the *Phenomenology of Spirit* and develops in the writings of Nietzsche on idolatry and the last man in the preface to *Thus Spoke Zarathustra* and the *Twilight of the Idols*, Max Weber's theory of the last man and the iron cage in 'Science as a Vocation', and Max Horkheimer's theory of positivism and the Holocaust in the *Eclipse of Reason*. These same themes of the fragmentation of the economy, classes, and the bourgeois zoo were also discussed in Hegel's *Jenenser Realphilosophie. Vorlesungen von 1803/04*, ed. Johannes Hoffmeister (Leipzig: F. Meiner, 1932). Solomon summarises this section of the *Phenomenology* on Reason (chapter five) and the rise of the modern individual and the good life in individual hedonism and pleasure, heart and romantic feeling, virtue and asceticism, philosophical stoicism and skepticism, religion and metaphysics, and Kantian moral autonomy with the statement: 'It [individual self] is an artificially conceived atom in isolation from society and culture which alone can give it meaning. They all prove to be not what they seem, not a conception of self or the good life, but a kind of confused abstraction from concrete social life or *Sittlichkeit* which will not bear critical examination' (p. 523). This search for the good life and communal happiness in the various historical forms of radical individualism – utilitarianism, romanticism, asceticism, stoicism, and moral action – ultimately leads to alienation, despair, and terror. And Kant's practical reason is its highest philosophical manifestation in the fragmented isolation, abstract formalism, and moral empiricism of the categorical imperative and human reason. For more on the relationship between Kant and Robespierre, practical reason and the terror, see endnote 35 on the dialectical relationship between empiricism and rationalism and its totalitarian implications in the abstract individual.
54 Hegel has introduced sociology into the heart of modern philosophy since without the former the latter is made impossible. This is the wisdom of the ancients applied to modernity. Without the shared norms, values, and ideals, as well as social, economic, and political institutions, human self-consciousness remains an unrealised and unhappy consciousness.
55 Hegel, *Philosophy of Right*, para. 21, pp. 29–30; *Grundlinien der Philosophie des Rechts*, p. 72.
56 Ibid., para. 27, p. 32; *Grundlinien der Philosophie des Rechts*, p. 79.
57 This issue about the nature of reason and the state has developed into a question of

whether Hegel holds a theory of the state that is totalitarian or liberal. For a discussion of the former position, see Karl Popper, *The Open Society and its Enemies*, vol. 2: *The High Tide of Prophecy: Hegel, Marx, and the Aftermath* (Princeton, NJ: Princeton University Press, 1971). The latter position has been taken up by Marcuse, *Reason and Revolution*; Walter Kaufmann, 'The Hegel Myth and its Method', in *Hegel: A Collection of Critical Essays*, ed. Alasdair MacIntyre (Notre Dame, IN: University of Notre Dame Press, 1976) and Dante Germino, *Machiavelli to Marx: Modern Western Political Thought* (Chicago, IL: Chicago University Press, 1979).

58   There is some difficulty at this early stage in Hegel's *Philosophy of Right*. He wishes to combine the best of the ancients and moderns by integrating Kant's self-conscious practical reason with Aristotle's ethical community – *Moralität* and *Sittlichkeit*. The problem is that as he integrates these two features, he will also incorporate abstract law, contract, and property of natural rights, the market economy of civil society, and the model of representative government of liberalism. The key theoretical question is whether the synthesis is successful. For Marx's response, see *Contribution to the Critique of Hegel's Philosophy of Law, Karl Marx/Frederick Engels Collected Works*, vol. 3 (New York, NY: International Publishers, 1975); *Kritik des Hegelschen Staatsrechts, Karl Marx/Friedrich Engels Werke* (*MEW*), Band 1 (Berlin: Dietz Verlag, 1961).

59   Hegel, *Philosophy of Right*, para. 30, p. 34; *Grundlinien der Philosophie des Rechts*, p. 83.
60   Ibid., para. 41, p. 40; *Grundlinien der Philosophie des Rechts*, p. 102.
61   Ibid., para. 57, p. 48; *Grundlinien der Philosophie des Rechts*, p. 124.
62   It is objectification or work which produces value and gives a person the right to own private property. This idea was taken from Locke's *Second Treatise of Government* (New York, NY: Liberal Arts Press, 1952), para. 27, p. 17 and 39–40, pp. 24–5 (54). The determinate characteristics of the individual have evolved from abstract rights, property, and contacts to an immediate form of self-conscious reflection involving questions of right and wrong. The individual has developed a new understanding of self that moves beyond the legal to the moral self. The subject will define and determine itself through practical reason and moral action, and not simply through property ownership.
63   Hegel, *Philosophy of Right*, para. 124, p. 84; *Grundlinien der Philosophie des Rechts*, p. 233. Hegel is here following the path already traced in the *Phenomenology of Spirit* where he outlines the development of this right of subjective reason from Christianity, love, romanticism, and salvation to the categorical imperative and moral duty. Reason has evolved from the time of the breakup of classical Greece to the contradictions inherent in the logic of Kantian moral philosophy of the eighteenth century that dialectically force self-consciousness beyond subjectivity and reason to self-consciousness and spirit. Later, Hegel writes that subjectivity is the foundation for freedom. From this perspective Kant was correct. However, Hegel continues: 'At the level of morality, subjectivity is still distinct from freedom, the concept [essence] of subjectivity; but at the level of ethical life it is the realization of the concept in a way adequate to the concept itself. The right of individuals to be subjectively destined to freedom is fulfilled when they belong to an actual ethical order ...' (paras. 152–3, p. 109; *Grundlinien der Philosophie des Rechts*, p. 303). This objective ethical order is the manifestation of the realised essence and universality of subjectivity. The individual and the social, the particular and the universal have been

joined together in a living ethical community where happiness, goodness, and freedom are made possible.

64   Ibid., para. 147, p. 106; *Grundlinien der Philosophie des Rechts*, p. 295. True freedom represents the liberation from abstract consciousness and indeterminate subjectivity – subjectivity abstracted from the social reality. It is a liberation from both natural inclinations (empiricism) and the self-enclosed consciousness of practical reason (rationalism); it is a movement toward substantive freedom where the values, ideals, and moral principles are integrated into an ethical system of social institutions. The dialectical relationship between subjectivity and objectivity, between the individual and society, creates the conditions for substantive freedom and true self-consciousness in the realm of social ethics.

65   Ibid., para. 142, p. 105; *Grundlinien der Philosophie des Rechts*, p. 292.

66   Ibid., para. 148, p. 106; *Grundlinien der Philosophie des Rechts*, pp. 296–7.

67   Ibid., para. 170, p. 116; *Grundlinien der Philosophie des Rechts*, p. 323.

68   Ibid., para. 183, p. 123 and para. 199, pp. 129–30; *Grundlinien der Philosophie des Rechts*, pp. 339–40 and 353.

69   Ibid., para. 185, p. 123; *Grundlinien der Philosophie des Rechts*, p. 341. Hegel in an interesting observation remarks that in the *Republic* Plato had outlined the ideal ethical life in which the self-subsistent individual and subjective or individual freedom of the personality expressed in terms of the ownership of property, family life, and the subjective will were excluded from his ideal state (para. 185, p. 124; *Grundlinien der Philosophie des Rechts*, p. 342). The theory of needs of Aristotle and Hegel are diametrically opposed to each other and presuppose entirely different views of ethical life. For Aristotle, the family provided for the satisfaction and self-sufficiency of human needs, and upon this ethical system rested reciprocal and distributive justice of the economy. For Hegel, needs are simply physical requirements and material desires that are satisfied by market production and exchange; for him, needs justify the market, whereas for Aristotle, needs provided the basis for a self-sufficient family and economy, virtuous life, and social justice. The reciprocity of needs and production in civil society replaces the reciprocity of needs and exchange in the Greek polis. The former leads to the liberal class system, whereas the latter leads to the happiness of ethics and politics. The public good is reached by greed, self-interest, and market competition in one tradition and virtue, political deliberation, and classical democracy in the other. It seems that the spirit of the Greek ideal has been overwhelmed by the spirit and institutions of capitalism. The latter might not lead to salvation but it surely will replace justice with utility and expedience. Whether intended or not, Hegel has committed the same contradiction as Kant. By laying out the formal requirements of the categorical imperative and the ethical life, Kant and Hegel, respectively, have substituted for the principle of non-contraction and universalism, as well as the principle of substantive and objective reason, the same moral or ethical empiricism. In both cases the principles and values of liberalism form the rational foundation for the will of practical reason and the ethics of objective reason, for morality and social ethics, and for subjectivity and the ethical life; in both cases the philosophical foundations of natural law collapsed. The idealism of both Kant and Hegel have reproduced the epistemology of moral empiricism.

70   Ibid., para. 198, p. 129; *Grundlinien der Philosophie des Rechts*, pp. 352–3. With his analysis of industry and production, Hegel appears to anticipate the critique of political economy of

Karl Marx. But just when the reader thinks that Hegel will undertake a critique of civil society, he dialectically changes the logic of his position since 'subjective self-seeking turns into a contribution to the satisfaction of the needs of everyone else' (para. 199, p. 129; *Grundlinien der Philosophie des Rechts*, p. 353). A market economy ultimately produces general capital for the common good. This is the accepted position of classical political economy and not classical political philosophy; the former comes to the rescue of capitalist production as Hegel turns away from Aristotle's critique of chrematistics toward the economic theory of Mandeville, Steuart, and Smith.

71   Ibid., para. 218, p. 140; *Grundlinien der Philosophie des Rechts*, pp. 371–2. Hegel succinctly summarises these points when writing: 'By taking the form of law, right steps into a determinate mode of being. It is then something on its own account, and in contrast with particular willing and opining of the right, it is self-subsistent and has to vindicate itself as something universal' (para. 219, p. 140; *Grundlinien der Philosophie des Rechts*, p. 372). Instead of an injury to conscience and free will, a moral transgression is now a legal infringement and requires the intervention of the court of justice and the state.

72   Pelczynski, 'Political Community and Individual Freedom in Hegel's Philosophy of State', p. 61. Pelczynski's contribution is to emphasise the importance of Hegel's theory of the modern state, its structure and function, as well as the mechanism of civil society, as a means of providing an 'ethical, social and political context' to Rousseau's view of the '"abstract" freedom of the individual' (p. 62). By integrating the individual will (abstract right), civil society (system of needs), and the ethical community (*Sittlichkeit*) in the modern state, Rousseau's abstract individual is made 'concrete' and real by Hegel. The danger in Rousseau's political theory, according to Pelczynski, lay in his emphasis on the free will, personal conscience, and individual virtue to the exclusion of any 'external, objective, rational principle to guide our will'. The result was action directed by the individual will that was 'arbitrary and amoral' and unguided by the ethical community or any universal standard of morality or truth – the Idea (p. 59). The danger is that freedom would morph into nihilism. This led to the excesses of the French Revolution. This is a similar critique leveled by both Hegel and Marx against the dualism within Kant between practical will and the state. See Hegel, *Philosophy of Right*, para. 258, pp. 156–7; *Grundlinien der Philosophie des Rechts*, pp. 399–400. Freedom then for Hegel can only be defined as the moral autonomy and self-determination of the individual within the rational state. Marx will quickly reject Hegel's theory of the state as a form of political mysticism and abstractionism that conceals the oppression of civil society in *On the Jewish Question* and eventually argue that freedom, self-determination, and self-realisation can only occur within a transformed political economy that does not accept capitalism as empirically given. Just as the individual and state cannot be separated but are essential to freedom, so too must a democratic state and economy become part of the community life or species being of the individual. Marx is just redefining the social context for a grand incorporation of the ideals of Aristotle, Rousseau, Kant, and Hegel into modernity.

73   Hegel, *Philosophy of Right*, para. 245, p. 150; *Grundlinien der Philosophie des Rechts*, p. 390.

74   Ibid., para. 257, p. 155 and para. 260, p. 160; *Grundlinien der Philosophie des Rechts*, pp. 398 and 406.

75   Hegel's integration of the subjective will of Kant and the general will of Rousseau is central

to the development of his modern theory of the state. Hegel mentions this connection in para. 258, pp. 156–7; *Grundlinien der Philosophie des Rechts*, p. 400.

76   Regarding the nature of the government, Hegel reflects: 'The constitution is rational in so far as the state inwardly differentiates and determines its activity in accordance with the nature of the concept' (ibid., para. 272, p. 174; *Grundlinien der Philosophie des Rechts*, p. 432). In his understanding of reason, the logic of the concept has replaced the logic of the categorical imperative. Here again Hegel in his critique of objective reason seems to be committing the same epistemological error of empiricism as Kant in his critique of practical reason. Just as the content of practical reason and the categorical imperative was unconsciously determined by the formal and logical principles of non-contradiction and formalism, thereby reproducing moral empiricism and the content of the natural rights of life, liberty, and property, Hegel, too, assumes the rationality of the ethical life of the state without further rational justification than the institutionalisation of abstract right, morality, family, and civil society. Whereas the content of morality lay in natural rights, the content of ethics, law, and the state lies in the same tradition of rights, individualism, and property. Kant's categorical imperative and Hegel's state occupy the same theoretical ground and justify the same chrematistical economy. See endnotes 31, 32, and 35. According to Hegel, 'political virtue is the willing of the absolute end in terms of thought' (ibid., para 257, p. 155; *Grundlinien der Philosophie des Rechts*, p. 398). It is not political participation and self-determination in the political arena; nor is it related to the development of a particular character grounded in moral and intellectual virtues. It should be noted that Hegel himself would reject this interpretation of reducing the ethical substance and objective freedom of the state to simply a defence of abstract rights, property, and possessions. See para. 324, p. 209; *Grundlinien der Philosophie des Rechts*, p. 492, where he writes: 'An utterly distorted account of the demand for this sacrifice results from regarding the state as a mere civil society and from regarding its final end as only the security of individual life and property'.

77   Hegel is critical of democracy as an ideal and rational form of the state since it is ruled by the sentiment of virtue. Quoting from Montesquieu's *The Spirit of the Laws* in paragraph 273, page 177 (*Grundlinien der Philosophie des Rechts*, pp. 437–8), and his analysis of the three forms of government – monarchy, aristocracy, and democracy – Hegel follows him into a rejection of democracy as a political ideal since the republic is without virtue as its leaders have devolved into a politics of licence, ambition, and greed. Aristocracy is also not an ideal form of government because of its tendency, as shown by Roman history, to transform itself into feudal privilege, tyranny, or anarchy. Democracy is held together by feelings and sentiment and an aristocracy by ideas and opinions. Democracy and the idea of the 'sovereignty of the people' is a confused idea since the people 'is a formless mass and no longer a state. It lacks every one of those determinate characteristics – sovereignty, government, judges, magistrates, class-divisions, etc. – which are to be found only in a whole which is inwardly organised' (Hegel, *Philosophy of Right*, para. 279, p. 183; *Grundlinien der Philosophie des Rechts*, p. 447).

78   Ibid., para. 294, p. 191; *Grundlinien der Philosophie des Rechts*, p. 462.

79   Marx, *Contribution to the Critique of Hegel's Philosophy of Law*, p. 9; *MEW* 1, pp. 207–8. The content of the phenomena is the uncritically examined immediate present subsumed

under the metaphysics of the state. 'The actual becomes a phenomenon, but the idea has no other content than this phenomenon' (ibid.; *MEW* 1, p. 208).

80 In his work *The Philosophical Foundations of Marxism*, Dupré writes about Marx's critique of Hegel's methodology and theory of the state: 'He [Hegel] abstracts some determinations from empirical reality, transposes them into a logical universe, and brings them back to life in an empirical subject, directly deduced from the logical Idea. Thus the State of 1820 receives a mystical, ideal necessity, and the various political institutions within it seem to be derived directly from the Idea' (p. 91). What is interesting here is that this is Hegel's own critique of the natural rights theory of empiricism and rationalism from his early writings. Dupré completes his analysis by stating that in the end the 'highest ethical reality' in Hegel's political theory is not the state, but private property (pp. 104–5). For Marx, Hegel's state is an illusion, that is, it is a form of false consciousness and alienation that exists by only integrating itself with civil society without recognising the fundamental contradictions of this process. The state rationalises and represses the social and class conflict of civil society. See also Shlomo Avineri, *The Social and Political Thought of Karl Marx* (Cambridge: Cambridge University Press, 1968), p. 25.

81 Marx, *Contribution to the Critique of Hegel's Philosophy of Law*, p. 14; *MEW* 1, p. 213.

82 Ibid., pp. 14 and 15; *MEW 1*, p. 213.

83 Ibid., p. 75; *MEW 1*, p. 279.

84 Ibid., p. 98; *MEW* 1, p. 303.

85 Ibid., p. 100; *MEW* 1, pp. 304–5.

86 Ibid., p. 107; *MEW* 1, p. 312.

87 Jean-Jacques Rousseau, *The Social Contract or Principles of Political Right*, in *The Social Contract and Discourses*, trans. and intro. G.D.H. Cole (New York, NY: E.P. Dutton and Company, 1950), pp. 3–141. *Rousseau and Marx on Property, Rights, and Democracy*: For an analysis of Rousseau's critique of private property, theory of participatory democracy, distinction between the rights of the bourgeois man and the citizen, and the relationship between Rousseau and Marx, see Nathan Rotenstreich, 'Between Rousseau and Marx', *Philosophy and Phenomenological Research* 9, 4 (1949): 717–19; Irving Fetscher, 'Rousseau's Concepts of Freedom in the Light of his Philosophy of History', in *Liberty*, ed. Carl Friedrich (Piscataway, NJ: Transaction Publishers, 1962) and *Rousseaus politische Philosophie: Zur Geschichte des demokratischen Freiheitsbegriffs* (Frankfurt/Main: Suhrkamp, 1975); Lucio Colletti, *From Rousseau to Lenin* (New York, NY: Monthly Review Press, 1972); Stephen Ellenburg, *Rousseau's Political Philosophy: An Interpretation from Within* (Ithaca, NY: Cornell University Press, 1976), pp. 159–64; Ramon Lemos, *Rousseau Political Philosophy: An Exposition and Interpretation* (Atlanta, GA: University of Georgia Press, 1977), pp. 164–91, 212–26, and 240; Galvan della Volpe, *Rousseau and Marx*, trans. John Fraser (Atlantic Highlands, NJ: Humanities Press, 1979), pp. 138–58; Norman Fischer, 'Marx's Early Concept of Democracy and the Ethical Bases of Socialism', in *Marxism and the Good Society*, ed. John Burke, Lawrence Crocker, and Lyman Legters (Cambridge: Cambridge University Press, 1981), pp. 59–83; Helmut Bloehbaum, *Strukturen moderner Dialektik. Am Beispiel Naturzustand und Herr- und Knecht-Verhältnis bei Rousseau, Hegel und Marx* (Frankfurt/Main: Peter Lang, 1988); Andrew Levine, *The General Will: Rousseau, Marx, and Communism* (Cambridge, MA: Cambridge University Press, 1993),

pp. 75–100; Jason Andrew Neidleman, *The General Will is Citizenship: Inquiries into French Political Thought* (Lanham, MD: Rowman & Littlefield Publishers, 2000); James Swenson, *On Jean-Jacques Rousseau: Considered as One of the First Authors of the Revolution* (Stanford, CA: Stanford University Press, 2000); David Held, *Models of Democracy* (Stanford, CA: Stanford University Press, 2006); Louis Althusser, *Politics and History: Montesquieu, Rousseau, Marx*, trans. Ben Brewster (London: Verso, 2007); Andrew Levine, *The General Will: Rousseau, Marx, Communism* (Cambridge: Cambridge University Press, 2008); and Sally Campbell, *Rousseau and the Paradox of Alienation* (Lanham, MD: Lexington Books, 2012).

88   Benedict Spinoza, *Theological-Political Treatise*, trans. Samuel Shirley (Indianapolis, IN: Hackett Publishing Company, 1998), chapter 16, pp. 173–84. *Spinoza and Marx on Democracy*: For an analysis of Spinoza's theory of democracy and the relationship between Spinoza and Marx, see Maximilien Rubel, 'Notes on Marx's Conception of Democracy', *New Politics* (1962): 81–2; Pierre-François Moreau, *Marx und Spinoza* (Hamburg: VSA Verlag, 1978); Ronald Commers, 'Marx's Concept of Justice and the Two Traditions in European Political Thought', *Philosophica* 33 (1984): 113–14; Fred Schrader, *Substanz und Begriff: Zur Spinoza-Rezeption Marxens* (Leiden: Brill, 1985); Joel Schwartz, 'Liberalism and the Jewish Connection: A Study of Spinoza and the Young Marx', *Political Theory* (February 1985): 58–84; Shlomo Avineri, *Moses Hess: Prophet of Communism and Zionism* (New York, NY: New York University Press, 1985), ch. 2 and pp. 210–14; Sigmund Krancberg, 'Karl Marx and Democracy', *Studies in Soviet Thought*, 24 (July 1982): 27–8; Allan Arkush, 'Judaism as Egoism: From Spinoza to Feuerbach and Marx', *Modern Judaism*, 11 (1991): 211–23; Stephen Smith, 'Spinoza's Democratic Turn: Chapter 16 of the Theologico-Political Treatise', *The Review of Metaphysics* 48, 2 (December 1994): 359–88; Eugene Holland, 'Spinoza and Marx', *Cultural Logic*, 2, 1 (Fall 1998); Lee Ward, 'Benedict Spinoza on the Naturalness of Democracy', *Canadian Political Science Review*, 5, 1 (2011): 55–73; Andre Campos, *Spinoza's Revolutions in Natural Law* (London: Palgrave Macmillan, 2012); and Daniel Chernilo, *The Natural Law Foundations of Modern Social Theory: A Quest for Universalism* (Cambridge: Cambridge University Press, 2013). For further readings of Spinoza within the critical tradition, see Etienne Balibar, *Spinoza and Politics*, trans. Peter Snowdon (London: Verso, 1998), Warren Montag, *Bodies, Masses, Power: Spinoza and His Contemporaries* (London: Verso, 1999), Antonio Negri, *The Savage Anomaly*, trans. Michael Hardt (Minneapolis, MN: University of Minnesota Press, 2000), Filippo Del Lucchese, *Conflict, Power, and Multitude in Machiavelli and Spinoza* (London: Continuum, 2009), and Hasana Sharp, *Spinoza and the Politics of Renaturalization* (Chicago, IL: University of Chicago Press, 2011).

89   Locke used natural law to justify and protect natural rights, property, and the market economy within a constitutional monarchy; Hegel uses the modern natural law tradition of Rousseau and Kant to protect and ensure subjectivity, moral autonomy, and individual freedom within a liberal state; and Marx uses the natural law tradition of Aristotle to encourage individual freedom, moral action, and political participation within a socialist state. With Locke natural law is a means to ensure the final end of abstract rights; with Hegel, the liberal state will ensure the moral life of the ethical community; and with Marx, natural law is realised in and nurtures democracy.

90   Miguel Abensour examines the four main characteristics of a 'true democracy' in Marx's

social and political theory in *Democracy Against the State: Marx and the Machiavellian Movement*, trans. Max Blechman and Martin Breaugh (Cambridge: Polity, 2011), pp. 47–72.

91 Marx, *Contribution to the Critique of Hegel's Philosophy of Law*, pp. 29 and 31; *MEW* 1, pp. 231 and 232.

92 With David Hume's inability to justify the nature of substance (objectivity), causality (science), and self (psychology) through empiricism or rationalism in his work *An Inquiry Concerning Human Understanding* (1748) in *The Empiricists* (Garden City, NY: Dolphin Books, 1961), sec. iv, pp. 323–33 and sec. xii, pp. 419–22 and with Kant's theory of representations and moral truths contingent upon human creativity of the understanding and categorical imperative (transcendental subjectivity), in the critiques of pure and practical reason, the notion of truth lying outside of subjectivity is abandoned by Hegel. Truth becomes for him the recognition that the objects of experience and morality are human constructions of self-consciousness and the ethical community. Reason is a form of epistemological and ethical self-legislation. Both Hume and Kant reintroduce the 'dilemma of double affection', which begins with the recognition that there is no objectivity of reality or method; they are both critical of realism and false objectivity. There is no autonomous objective reality (objectivism and realism) in Hume's skepticism or Kant's subjective idealism and, thus, no basis for comparison or verification to an original reality (thing-in-itself). There are only impressions or representations of reality as mental constructs that cannot ultimately be compared. Thus reason as Enlightenment science based on empiricism (empirical facts) or rationalism (mathematics) cannot be the basis for the justification of natural law. Reason can only create through self-determination and self-legislation the foundation for reality and ethics within an ethical community and moral economy. The idea that objectivity is a construct forms the heart of Hegel's logical and ethical systems – reason and morality are forms of self-determination and freedom in which self-consciousness recognises itself in the world of experience and the understanding, as well as in the community of ethical life of abstract rights, property, and contracts, family, civil society (system of needs), and the state and constitution (Crown, Executive, and Legislature), that is, in the world of its own creation of institutions and culture. For an overview of themes in Hegel's analysis of economics and civil society, see *Hegel on Economics and Freedom*, ed. William Maker (Macon, GA: Mercer University Press, 1987).

93 For a discussion of the types of critique utilised by Marx – immanent, dialectical, substantive, ethical, and economic critique – see George E. McCarthy, *Dreams in Exile: Rediscovering Science and Ethics in Nineteenth-Century Social Theory* (Albany, NY: State University Press of New York, 2009), n. 2, p. 334.

PART 2

Ethics, Virtue, and Natural Law in Marx

CHAPTER 3

Civil and Legal Justice: Integrating Natural Rights and Natural Law

Later political scholars who examined John Locke's ideas of property and civil society with the intent of unpacking his view of liberal justice stressed his theories of natural rights and distributive justice within the framework of the Aristotelian-Thomist tradition. As we have already seen in the first chapter, however, as much as he wanted to integrate the classical and medieval traditions with modern liberalism, he was unable to do so because of the incompatibility and incoherence between natural law and individual rights. In the end, Christian theology and utilitarian materialism did not mix well. This is why Locke begins *The Second Treatise of Government* with the moral and ethical principles of natural law presumably to justify natural rights, only to drop the former as human beings enter the second state of nature and civil society. He was unable to successfully synthesise natural ethics with liberal economics into a coherent social and political theory. To integrate individual freedom and creativity – labour as value and workmanship – with the broader concerns for fairness and social justice would require a rethinking of the relevance of the natural law tradition to modern social institutions. Natural law may have been irreconcilable to civil and political rights for Locke, but for Marx, it was not incompatible with the ethics and institutions of socialism. Unlike those who view Marx as detailing a natural law of positivism and science – production and prediction – he was, in fact, rewriting social theory to make classical natural law relevant for modernity and social change. This was a key purpose behind his writings.[1]

Toward the end of reconfiguring modern economic and political theories in order to make them compatible with classical ethics and politics, Marx had to rethink and expand the issues of social justice beyond the horizons of liberalism. To accomplish this task, he had to broaden the theoretical framework within which issues of economic and political justice were considered; to accomplish this he returned to the natural law tradition of Aristotle. This inheritance will be explored over the next six chapters. Justice in this critical tradition involves a consideration of the totality of society and not simply questions of individual rights and fair distribution of material goods. There has to be a moral balance among the state, society, ethics, and the deep structures of political economy. In this chapter, we will examine the very beginnings of

Marx's theory of social justice found in his earliest writings on civil and legal rights in 'Debates on Freedom of the Press' (1842), 'Debates on the Law on Thefts of Wood' (1842), *Contribution to the Critique of Hegel's Philosophy of Right* (1843), and *On the Jewish Question* (1843). In these writings he explores different forms of rights, including the rights of free speech and a free press, the rights of the common and poor to fallen wood in a forest, right as the legal foundation of society, and the economic (natural) and political (civil) rights of the French Revolution in the late eighteenth century.

Religious Prejudice, Judaism, and Civil Rights

In 1843, Bruno Bauer, a Left-Hegelian who taught at the University of Bonn, published a work, *The Jewish Question*.[2] Marx responded quickly the same year with his own essay, *On the Jewish Question*. Marx's essay is rarely read today but contains an important response to Bauer, and even more importantly, a critical response to the defenders of natural rights theory. Ostensibly beginning with a question about the nature of Judaism and Christianity, religion and religious prejudice, and voting and civil rights, Marx's work quickly moves to issues of the economy and state, economic and political rights, and political emancipation and human emancipation. That is, what begins as a defence of Jewish equality, freedom, civil rights, and political liberties in Germany evolves into a general critique of bourgeois rights, liberal democracy, and the modern state in France and the United States.[3] Although it is only an exploratory and preliminary piece, and it will take many years for Marx to develop the full implications of his own analysis, the essay does provide us with the beginnings of a framework to analyse the failed connections in Locke between the natural rights of modern liberalism and the natural law of classical philosophy and medieval theology. As noted in the first chapter, Heinrich Rommen criticised Locke's political theory for having depleted natural law of its moral and metaphysical heart found in Scholasticism (Thomas Aquinas and Richard Hooker). Leaving only an empty concept to justify his theory of government, Locke replaced it with a mechanical and nominalistic listing of the rights to life, liberty, and property which was simply an extension of Hobbes's theory of self-preservation.[4] In criticising the natural rights tradition, in particular the French Revolution document *The Declaration of the Rights of Man and of the Citizen* of 1793, Marx will in a very unconventional manner provide a deeper moral foundation to human rights in his political philosophy of human emancipation.

Marx begins his essay with a summary of Bauer's observation that German Jews wished to be politically emancipated and provided the civil rights to citizenship, religious freedom, voting, and holding public office. Bauer's response is that members of the Jewish community are asking for political and civil rights that the average German does not have, since all Germans are politically oppressed. In addition, they are asking for equal rights within a Christian state, which may be even more problematic. Bauer appears disappointed that Jews are not more critical of either the limits of civil rights themselves or the nature of political and religious oppression by the Christian state. Marx returns to Bauer, who redirects the question of rights back upon those seeking emancipation: 'Why should the Germans be interested in the liberation of the Jew, if the Jew is not interested in the liberation of the German'.[5] Providing the Jewish members of society with civil rights does not eliminate the right of 'religious prejudice' of the Christian state and the Jewish community. Both have rights which the other does not share. By asking for incorporation into the Christian state, is not the Jew asking for Christian rights at the same time as maintaining their own distinctive rights to practice Judaism? In the end civil emancipation requires Christians to forego their exclusive control over the state while members of the Jewish community retain their religious prejudice.

Bauer asks on what grounds Jews demand civil emancipation and rights of the broader Christian community. The Jews are separated by political ostracism, religious prejudice, and the general political oppression of the German populace. Since no one is free in German society, what legitimate claim do the Jews have for civil rights at the same time as they demand that which others do not have? Moreover they do this, according to Bauer, while still maintaining their religious separation from Christianity. Bauer's response to this complex issue is to redefine the issue and ask the question again. The answer, according to Bauer, is to redirect our understanding of the nature of emancipation to incorporate both the legal and religious aspects of it. This means that all religious groups must be liberated before the Jews can be liberated. Working within the boundaries of the old question only leaves us with our religious prejudices and differences intact; the issue of emancipation can never be resolved. The only answer is to think outside the box and broaden our conception of emancipation and freedom to include all members of civil society by the abolition of all religious bonds, differences, and prejudices, that is, by abolishing religion itself. The central issue in Bauer's response, according to Marx, is the contradiction between religious prejudice and political emancipation.

The Germans have to free themselves before they can free others. Bauer sees that the solution to this problem of the Jewish question lies in rethinking the nature of religion and human prejudice. His solution is very Hegelian, involving simply seeing religion as a historical and phenomenal form of consciousness whose time has come and passed. Neither political nor religious repression should be barriers to the attainment of citizenship and legal rights. Bauer's solution is twofold: universalise rights to incorporate the Jewish community into the broader fabric of the German state and at the same time recognise that Enlightenment rationality and science have replaced the public face of religion as the foundation of truth and human relationships. Christianity and Judaism will be forms of private conviction and personal conscience but will not serve as public barriers of religious prejudice. Religion will be turned into a private form of consciousness and no longer act as a political wall between the Christian and Jewish communities. Bauer's solution is clearly political – expand political emancipation and get rid of religious prejudice. The state will expand citizenship and rights at the same time as it emancipates itself from religion. Bauer's response is for Germans to universalise politics and particularise religion – universalise the natural rights of life, liberty, and property at the same time as religion is depoliticised into the private sphere. The monopoly and privilege of Christianity is dismantled; the Sabbath and Sunday are made irrelevant to political participation. Religion now becomes a matter of personal conscience that does not disenfranchise any member of German society for political or religious reasons. Religion is no longer an entrance or barrier to politics; it becomes irrelevant to the protection of citizenship and rights. The abolition of religion represents the end of slavery for the Jews and the beginning of their political freedom. Bauer accomplishes his task of unification by rethinking the nature of politics and freedom in the broader society. Marx summarises Bauer's position on the Jewish question in the following: 'Thus Bauer demands, on the one hand, that the Jew should renounce Judaism, and in general that man should renounce religion, in order to be emancipated as a citizen'.[6]

Although this summary of Bauer's position occupies only a brief four pages, it seems interminably longer. There is an apparent reason for this which is to clearly frame the question of political emancipation within the theoretical boundaries of the desired liberal state. Marx's response is that Bauer considered who should do the emancipation and who should be emancipated, but he fails to reflect on the more important philosophical question – what is the nature of emancipation itself? Marx's solution to the Jewish question is to critically re-examine Bauer's political theory. The fact is that Bauer does not question the nature of rights, freedom, and equality within the tradition of liberal political thought, especially French political thought. And this is the direction towards which Marx directs his reflective energies. It is at this point that many of the problems in Locke's theory of natural rights and natural law will resurface. This essay on the Jews is no longer a dialogue between Marx and Bauer about the nature of religious emancipation and the political expansion of liberal values to include more individuals. Rather, it has been transformed into a confrontation between Marx and Locke about the very nature of modern politics itself. The Jewish question of political emancipation has expanded first into the liberal question of political rights, and then, secondly and more broadly, into the issue of human rights and emancipation. Marx is, in effect, asking the Jewish community to rethink and redefine the concept of emancipation beyond the limits set by the liberal political theory of natural rights. Is liberalism the answer to the Jewish question and is the Jewish community willing to accept such a limited dream of freedom?

Bauer was interested in the question of whether Jews should be given civil rights, whereas Marx turns the question around to expose the moral and structural weaknesses of the liberal state while asking more important questions about the nature of religion, politics, and rights. Bauer's question about religious prejudice and political emancipation turns into a question about equality, political rights, and human emancipation. At first, Marx asks what appears to be an obvious and mundane question: 'Why does he [the Jew] want rights which he does not have but which the Christians enjoy?'[7] What begins as a question about incorporating Jews into the political community of the Christian state turns into a question about rights and the modern state. For Bauer, political emancipation was inherently a good thing. For Marx at the very beginning of his intellectual career, it was the starting point of a more profound series of questions about the nature of rights and political freedom. Marx is asking the more fundamental question: If Jews become citizens, does that really change their situation of religious and political oppression? Does the political abolition of religious slavery change anything about the political and religious oppression in Germany? Both Bauer and Marx when discussing the politics of the state refer to the French constitution and its underlying political theory as a more advanced statement on political emancipation than its German counterpart. Bauer is concerned with a technology of politics since he focuses upon the extent of citizenship in Germany; the abolition of religion leaves the existing structures of oppression intact. Marx, on the other hand, questions the underlying moral philosophy that justifies politics itself. He is interested in the Jewish question and beyond. He raises the central issue – whether Jews should be given citizenship in the German state – but his response is very nuanced since he believes that the question itself is inadequate because the anticipated liberal state does not represent true emancipation.

It is at this point in his essay that Marx reopens and engages Locke's political theory and his theory of natural rights. Marx does this by beginning to unpack the values and assumptions of Bauer's political theory with a more detailed analysis of the theory of the modern state and natural rights that underlies Bauer's response to the Jewish question. The issue of civil rights for the members of the Jewish community loses its central importance for Marx. He appears to use this initial question raised by Bauer merely as his starting point, but then proceeds with his own analysis of the nature of political emancipation to uncover the relationship between politics and religion, private property, civil society, and natural rights. More specifically, he undertakes an examination of the following: politics and religion as ideology, the contradictions between the state (public political interests) and civil society (private economic interests), the alienation of the species being of humanity and the community, religious alienation, the differences between the rights of man (natural or economic rights) and the rights of the citizen (political rights) in the French declarations of 1791 and 1793, and ends with a brief statement beyond the limits of political freedom on the 'authentic man', political life of the citizen, and human emancipation.

It is not that Marx is no longer interested in Jewish civil rights and liberation; he has not turned away from the Jewish community and their political needs, but turns instead to the more comprehensive question of the liberation of humanity in general. He recognises that the emancipation of the Jews involves a broader human emancipation along with the complete transformation of German society itself. It is no longer a question of rights for a particular group of individuals and their legal incorporation into the already existing structure of civil society. Nor is it simply a question of applying Bauer's political theory of emancipation and civil rights to a new situation or to a particular group of people. The Jewish question, as initially raised by Bauer, permits Marx to inquire into the very nature of modern bourgeois society and the liberal state. Marx has dramatically changed the original question from Jewish rights to natural rights, political emancipation to human emancipation. Is the liberal state adequate to the task of providing religious and legal rights; can it liberate the Jewish community; and what are legal and civil rights and their relationship to a new democratic state? What began as a focused and limited question of Jewish rights and freedom within Germany has developed into a question about the nature of universal rights and freedom; what began as a question about religious tolerance and freedom becomes a question about the modern state. For Marx, this is 'the general question of the age'. In this essay, he fully engages, in a preliminary and admittedly underdeveloped form, the new question of the moral foundations of the state, natural rights, and civil society as he looks ahead to a new emancipation of humanity while looking back to older ethical traditions. This new question is, in fact, not new at all, but one raised by classical and medieval natural law theorists. Richard Tawney, who in *Religion and the Rise of Capitalism* had referred to Marx as 'the last of the Schoolmen', has written extensively on the revival of Thomism and natural law among Catholics and Protestants in the sixteenth and seventeenth centuries, between the Reformation and the Restoration.[8] His comment about this late-medieval revival of natural law is also applicable to Marx: 'It is to summon the living, not to invoke a corpse, and to see from a new angle the problems of our own age, by widening the experience brought to their consideration'.[9] More on this issue in Chapter 4.

It is in this spirit that Marx turns to a more detailed examination of Bauer's theory of the Christian state and political rights in Germany. The question is now what constitutes political emancipation and what is the nature of the modern state? Marx criticises Bauer for not examining the issue of the state and rights in more depth. He simply accepts the social institutions as they presently exist while trying uncritically to incorporate Jews into them. He does not go beyond the established institutions and traditional definition of natural rights; he never questions the nature or adequacy of political emancipation and, thus, can never resolve the issue behind the Jewish question. Finally, Bauer never develops a comprehensive political theory but ventures instead into the realm of theology and the relationship between Christianity and Judaism. Marx believes that Bauer has missed the central point at stake and thus never really answers the Jewish question. To put it bluntly, it was never about the Jews to begin with. It was about the nature of political oppression in Germany as a whole. The Jews were just one group, perhaps the most visible group, of people caught in the web of the state's oppressive mechanism and limited rights. This, according to Marx, leaves Bauer open to the criticism that he does not consider the relation between political emancipation and human emancipation. He never moves beyond what is to what could be, or to what should be.

Since there is no real state in Germany at this time, only separate provinces and principalities, the dispute over Jewish incorporation into the state is a purely theoretical or theological question about the nature of Christianity and Judaism. In France, on the other hand, which does have a constitutional state, the question continues to have relevancy because of the lack of full incorporation of Jews into the political community. In America, Marx sees the issue as a real and secular concern because it is truly about politics, government, laws, and rights. It is in France and America that the issue is politically relevant and historically real. Since there is no constitutional government in Germany, the issue remains a discussion at the level of speculative and abstract theology, and not politics and the law. Because Bauer was caught up in the Jewish question within German society, he never realised that it was always a political question about the nature of the constitution and political rights and never about the nature of religious differences and prejudices. Bauer confused the precipitating question with the final issue. He was unable to approach the real question; he could never move beyond religion to politics. Marx's goal is to 'turn theological questions into secular ones'.[10] There appears to be two reasons for this long prolegomena to political metaphysics: on the one hand, Marx is rejecting Bauer's idealism and Hegelian philosophy that leads him to approach questions in such an abstract and metaphysical fashion and, on the other hand, Marx is playing with this very concept of theology as a way of introducing his radical critique of the liberal state and the natural rights to life, liberty, and property. The concept of theology is used to introduce and criticise Bauer but also to introduce and criticise bourgeois political theory. Liberal politics is just another form of political theology. The two issues are interrelated because this critique of Hegel acts as a preliminary to a confrontation with Locke and, at the same time, to Marx's argument that Locke's principles of rights are truly theological in character and application.

At this point, Marx turns his attention to the weaknesses of the political doctrine of emancipation. He begins with the failure to eliminate religion and prejudice but his goal is ultimately to examine the relationships between the state and civil society, politics and the economy, and emancipation and rights. This is the beginning of Marx's articulation of a theory of social justice and historical rights. The relationship between religion and political emancipation is difficult in Germany, so Marx turns to another empirical example, North America. The latter is a 'country of religiosity' that has attained full political emancipation where there is no established or church religion guiding its political and cultural beliefs. In spite of this, religion continues to play an important role in this society as it maintains a strong balance with the state. Marx continues: 'But since the existence of religion is the existence of a defect, the source of this defect must be sought in the *nature* of the state itself. Religion no longer appears as the basis, but is the *manifestation* of secular narrowness'.[11]

Marx begins the shift away from the Jewish question with its examination of the theological issues and 'religious narrowness' behind Christian orthodoxy and its rejection of Judaism toward this being fundamentally a political problem. He is no longer interested in returning to the theological issues of the Left-Hegelians with their rejection of God and religion. Marx begins by accepting Bauer's conclusion that political emancipation should entail the emancipation of the state from all religions. However, this is not the end of the argument, only its beginning. Bauer's original question now permits Marx entry into a whole new area – the nature of the state itself – as he moves from theology to political theory. The underlying problem was not religion but politics and the inherent contradictions and weaknesses of the liberal state. 'The state can liberate itself from a constraint without man himself being *really* liberated; that a state may be a *free state* without man himself being a *free man*'.[12]

Religion and Jewish oppression are only the symptoms of much deeper social problems – the moral and structural failures of the state and the relevancy of natural rights in a capitalist economy. Religious emancipation takes religious belief out of the public sphere and turns it into a private issue of individual conviction and personal faith. The laws of the state may profess liberation, but the individual may still hold these prejudicial and abhorrent views. Although religion under these new conditions is no longer a public barrier to Jewish emancipation and rights, it only moves religion from the public to the private sphere. This changes its social location, but not its social abhorrence. Prejudice remains; it is just not state endorsed, only conscience inspired. Marx refers to this as a devious transformation that is only 'abstract, narrow and partial'. The problem of religious prejudice and anti-Semitism is not abolished. The values, hatred, and religious beliefs of Christianity have not been altered; they still affect society as a whole with their pernicious and destructive power. Turning the Jewish question from a political to a personal issue only represses and hides the issue behind the locked doors of an individual's mind or a church's walls. With these changes, nothing has been resolved for Marx. By eliminating the state as a sponsor of a particular religion, that is, by becoming a public atheist, religion continues to exercise its destructive force in a transformed way in the private sphere. But Marx has learned something crucial from the failure of Bauer's analysis. The inability to resolve the Jewish question through political emancipation only highlights the inadequacy of the original question and the inherent structural weakness of the state. Providing Jews with civil and legal rights does not emancipate them from prejudice or truly provide them with civil and legal protections; it actually reinforces and strengthens the prejudice. It does not build stronger communities without internal religious fissures and political conflicts. It hides and represses these conflicts from critical review.

And now the argument that Marx really wanted to examine from the beginning of his essay is out in the open for all to see. Jewish exclusion from German politics and private rights, no matter how serious and denigrating, is only an appearance and distraction from the real problem – the relationship between the state and private property, the state and civil society, and the state and natural rights. Keeping individuals from participating in the political process, whether through excluding a group by religious prejudice or by private property qualifications, is a matter of deep concern for Marx. In both cases religious belief and private property are, at least in America, no longer necessary for political participation. But is this the end of the problem or just the beginning of it? By abolishing religion, private property, birth, rank, education, and occupation as necessary for equal citizenship and full participation in popular sovereignty, these potentially disruptive social elements have been displaced to the private sphere of civil society. Now the new question emerges: What is the relationship between these social functions and the state? Religion is simply one of many conflicting elements that affect issues of equality, freedom, and popular sovereignty. 'But the political suppression of private property not only does not abolish private property; it actually presupposes its existence'.[13] Religious prejudice was suppressed by the government, which only made it stronger in the private recesses of individual souls.

The universality of the state and law is created to be above and to resolve social conflicts that may arise from differences of religion, wealth, property, birth, etc. that might inhibit individual freedom, equality, and rights. This is an established part of political theory. But the state does not eliminate these social factors influencing popular sovereignty and natural rights; it only displaces them from the public to the private sphere. This is the inherent contradiction of modern liberalism – it defends natural rights at the political level, but undermines them at the private level where religious and class privileges rule unchecked. Marx is aware of this contradiction when he writes: 'But the state, none the less, allows private property, education, occupation, to *act* after *their* own fashion ... and to manifest their *particular* nature. Far from abolishing these *effective* differences, it only exists so far as they are presupposed'.[14] Marx quotes Hegel's *Philosophy of Right* (1821) to emphasise his point on universality. The state becomes universal when it controls all particular divisive elements in society.

Marx's critique of Bauer's lack of political theory is reaffirmed by the former's recognition that Bauer's view of political emancipation is only a theological emancipation – an emancipation of the mind. That is, the abolition of religion or private property does not eliminate these social forms. Their strength only increases in the private sphere of civil society. Their abolition or emancipation was a complete illusion, which for Marx means that it is simply a political form of theology or false universality. Nothing really changes, whether it is the exclusion of the Jews from political life or the exclusion of the poor from popular sovereignty. The state loses its claim to universality as it functions as the representative of the different social powers of civil society. Hegel's whole theory of the modern state and law of concrete universality has been undermined.

Natural Rights as Ideology and Alienation

The fully developed political state occupies a theological and ideological position in society because it is grounded in a fundamental structural contradiction. Its theological dimension is expressed in the fact that its soaring values and ideals are so removed from the social reality that the state acts as a religious phenomenon. That is, its transcending values of natural rights and hopes for social emancipation are religious because they are human constructs that are essentially not real; they are political illusions created to give comfort and legitimation to the prevailing social institutions. They attempt to give meaning and purpose to the life of the polity, they attempt to guide and protect the disadvantaged and dispossessed, and, finally, they attempt to provide moral natural laws that guide human behaviour. In the end, however, their values are abstract and speculative at the same time that they conceal their ultimate purpose and social function. Just as the state was impotent in the face of anti-Semitism and could not liberate Jews from their religious and political oppression, the state is powerless to enforce natural rights because they are products of false consciousness and social mystification.

Under the most ideal conditions of natural law and a free and just society, the state is supposed to represent the universal interests and common good of its citizens – the species life of the community – and not the base material interests of industry, banking, and commerce. But even under these ideal conditions, the state faces a contradiction between the structural imperative of the polity and civil society which, ironically enough, is the same dilemma faced in religion. Marx refers to this as a 'double existence' between individual consciousness and social reality, between the celestial and the terrestrial. 'He [the individual] lives in a *political community*, where he regards himself as a *communal being*, and in *civil society* where he acts simply as a *private individual*, treats other men as means, degrades himself to the role of a mere means, and becomes the plaything of alien powers'.[15] From Marx's perspective the state replaces and assumes the traditional role of religion in the modern world. It creates a metaphysical realm of political ideals and economic laws above the physical reality, then proclaims them as real and essential. It endows itself with all ethical perfections and social ideals as it claims to be the ultimate arbiter of legal and civil disagreements. It is the true manifestation of natural law and social justice. But, Marx continues to notice that this turns politics into another form of theology since it creates spiritual illusions and metaphysical canons to resolve real economic problems and differences. The world of political harmony and justice only hides from critical review the harsh realities of poverty, inequality, and injustice. 'The political state, in relation to civil society, is just as spiritual as is heaven in relation to earth'.[16] Grace and salvation have been replaced by profits and material happiness as the state glosses over all inconsistencies in the social reality. Liberal political theory, just like Christian theology, is not supposed to reveal the truth about reality or the social system, but rather to conceal it beneath the canonical laws of justice proclaimed by the ecclesiastical lords of the economy. Adjustment, resignation, and belief are the ultimate goals of economic theology.

The social reality of alienation and the degradation of humans to the technical and mechanical means of production and commerce is the reality of civil society. However, since politics with its natural law and natural rights is both a theology and an ideology – it inspires and represses, legitimates and conceals at the same time – Marx rejects the limits of political emancipation.[17] The latter is only a form of illusory psychological emancipation that ultimately results in greater repression and human suffering. Borrowing from Immanuel Kant and Ludwig Feuerbach, he rejects the idea that humans should be treated as means to an end, however noble and ideal, however shallow and unreal the end may be. Political justice has been theoretically articulated as the goal of humanity to replace the misery of capitalism in the same manner that God was created by humans to allay the fear and trembling before human suffering and death.[18] It is just another form of 'unhappy consciousness'.

By emphasising the political emancipation of the Jews, Bauer had missed the real issue at stake. Political emancipation would only free them in the same way that heaven and salvation emancipated Christians; it would be an illusion with no change in reality. Freeing Jews from an oppressive economic system would require a radical transformation of civil society and the state. The state is in reality an artificial construct of civil society with no independent function of its own; its ultimate purpose is to provide theological and ethical legitimation without changing its own structural dynamic of alienation. It also ensures insulation from critical eyes seeking to change the system. 'In the state, on the contrary, where he is regarded as a species-being, man is the imaginary member of an imaginary sovereignty, divested of his real, individual life, and infused with an unreal universality'.[19] In the economic reality of civil society, there are no universal moral principles or natural rights to give validity to the economy, there is no universal sovereignty of the consent of the majority to validate political decisions, and there is no universal human nature or laws of the market to justify the social distribution of produced wealth. Justice, whether human or divine, has validity only to the extent that it rationalises the harsh realities of human existence; liberal justice and political ideals are human constructs and appearances created to make life and society more palatable. Simply to alter the political reality by adjusting or expanding civil laws, but not fundamentally change the religious consciousness and exclusionary practices in everyday life of civil society, alters nothing for the Jewish community. The same is true for the primacy of private property. Political universality of rights, laws, and citizenship are products of a false and distorted consciousness. The political emancipation hoped for by Bauer would only lead to continued political oppression since the reality of civil society – the principles and structures of political economy – would not be recognised or transformed. He never captures the sophistry or appearances of politics, but simply accepts political emancipation as institutionally real. In the process, he never recognises the schisms or contradictions between the state and civil society, the citizen and the bourgeois, or between general values and private interests that split the political community apart. These same structural divisions have important implications for Marx's analysis of the distinctions between the natural rights of man and the natural rights of the citizen in the political declarations of the French Revolution in the late nineteenth century.

Transition of Politics from Pure Ideology to Human Rights and Emancipation

In true Hegelian fashion, Marx complicates the discussion about political emancipation even more when he moves from a consideration of politics as ideology to politics as an ideal. The conversation about Bauer's political theory has evolved from the issue of religious intolerance and racial dogmatism to a focus on the state as a form of distorted consciousness and political ideology, that is, to the state as the centre of the unresolvable contradictions between public citizens within a market economy. Next, Marx's position undergoes a change in the opposite direction as he rethinks the positive side of the state as a set of moral and legal ideals that go beyond its social origins and contradictions. He slowly transcends the illusions and appearances of political theory to an emergence of the state as a set of real political ideals and actual natural rights.

Moving from a critique of the limits of political thought, Marx changes direction in order to develop a new theory of natural rights based on a revision of the potential for a true democratic state. There is a dialectic here between the state as contradiction and ideology caught in a whirlpool of conflicting self-interests and market forces over which it has limited control and the state as the law of nature and rights with its dreams of justice and democracy. It is both at the same time. The key is distinguishing between the actual and the potential and not confusing the two as Bauer had done. The potential state inspires and provides moral guidance for a better society, but the actual state is unable to deal with the Jewish question because political emancipation is an illusion. The real substance of the state lies in the priorities and protection of the economy – this is why political emancipation would have no effect on Jewish civil liberties.

Civil rights only rationalise civil society; they do not broaden human freedom and individual rights.

Not all dreams, however, are political appearances and illusions as we now enter into the early stage of Marx's theory of the rights of species being. Political emancipation does function as a deception since it conceals the essential relationships 'of wealth and poverty, of prosperity and distress' in the economy; on the other hand, it also offers a certain amount of 'great progress' within the established framework of modern capitalist society. Although very limited in scope, it remains a positive heritage that liberalism leaves to the future since it is 'the final form of human emancipation *within* the framework of the prevailing order'.[20] Political emancipation is viewed within liberalism as the highest achievement of human liberation since it provides citizens with individual rights, guarantees, and protections within a constitutional government. From the very beginning of this essay, Marx has been summarising Locke's theory of government and the social contract in his analysis of political emancipation. As already mentioned, the conversation Marx was having with Bauer was, in fact, a dialogue between Marx and Locke. Bauer just provided the opportunity for the conversation. Marx had approached Locke's political theory to reveal its weakness in dealing with the exclusion of Jews from the German state.

Marx now reveals the true nature of religion and the state as expressing the detrimental private interests of civil society rather than the common consciousness of public law. Both religion and the state have lost their moral grounding in natural law and the public conscience. Even under ideal conditions of a perfect government, political emancipation could not eliminate prejudice and hatred; it just repressed them by displacing religion from the public sphere to the private arena. Religion is changed from a public requirement to a private belief. It, along with private property, would no longer be required for citizenship, but both would still play an active and influential role in defining social relationships in civil society and, ultimately, in the state. Although specifically written about religion, the same may be said of the purpose of the state whose true reality is best expressed in the words of Marx: 'It has become the spirit of *civil society*, of the sphere of egoism and of the *bellum omnium contra omnes*. It is no longer the essence of *community* but the essence of *differentiation*. It has become what is was at the *beginning*, an expression of the fact that man is separated from the *community*, from himself and from other men'.[21] Religion and politics have returned humanity back to the barbaric age of the state of nature; they have justified the market economy with its unimaginative and hedonistic materialism and utilitarian self-interest. Prejudice and property rather than natural justice and social ethics are its guiding spirit. Civil society is an alienated land of laws without law. Self-interest, expedience, and a self-adjusting economic mechanism have replaced any moral canon or higher aspiration of species being as its guiding principle. It represents the modern economic man who is 'corrupted, lost to himself, alienated, subjected to the rule of inhuman conditions and elements, by the whole organisation of society'.[22]

As we have seen in Chapter 1, Locke begins his analysis of the grounding of natural rights in natural law by incorporating the spirit of a market economy into the soul of Thomist theology. By so doing, he undermined his own original intentions and created a new justification for the spirit of capitalism by returning to Hobbes's political theory. He softened Hobbes's aggressive leviathan but did not eliminate it from his political theory. It is interesting that Marx in the mid-nineteenth century also saw that the true soul of political emancipation was the 'war of all against all'. Social differences and economic conflicts are the spirit of capitalism hidden from public view by the theological opiate of the political and legal system. At the very time the state seeks to identify itself with the species life of the community, it only fragments its social functions and preconditions ('decomposition of man') into conflicting and isolated parts of the social system. By attempting to eliminate religion and private property which disrupt the moral primacy of the community, by exiling them to civil society, political emancipation has not changed anything. The negative elements are simply moved to another part of society while still exercising their disruptive prejudices and private interests to the disadvantage of the integrity of the whole. The state remains theologically committed to Christianity in the private sphere as it remains committed to a class system based on the disadvantages of private property. Unless the state can be freed from these corrupting social structures, it always remains religious and ideological.

Critique of Liberal Democracy and Contradictions between Economic and Political Rights

The end result of political emancipation for the Jews, according to Bauer, is the ultimate renunciation of both Christianity and Judaism. Marx views this as simply a means by which religion becomes a private experience of the heart but continues to maintain its presence in civil society. The only solution to this dilemma is to move beyond the political boundaries of modern liberalism to a new and radical form of democracy and human emancipation. This also requires a rethinking of the nature of natural rights. And it is exactly this issue of economic and political rights, the rights in civil society and the rights in the polity to which Marx now turns in his essay. The ideal already exists potentially in the civil rights of liberalism. They must be freed from the barbarism and contradictions of the state of civil society, made democratic, and expanded in new and exciting ways that the following chapters will articulate. Bauer had raised the issue of whether Jews can be given both civil liberties and the 'universal rights of man' in political emancipation. He contends that since the Jews have not given up their particular 'privilege of faith' and continue to hold onto their distinctive relationship with God and nature, they cannot acquire the 'rights of man'. According to Bauer, these rights are not innate or inalienable ideas, nor are they given to humans by God or nature. Rather they are the result of political conflict against the social prejudices of birth and wealth. The Jews have not earned them, nor have they surrendered their isolation from the broader political community. Still continuing to argue with Bauer in this essay, Marx now undertakes an examination of these historical and cultural rights. Toward this end, he critical examines the most developed expression of the 'rights of man' from the French *Declaration of the Rights of Man and of the Citizen* of 1791 and 1793.

Marx begins by distinguishing between two distinctive forms of the 'universal rights of man' – the rights of the *bourgeois* and the rights of the *citoyen*. He sees in these documents of the French Revolution the articulation of both economic and political rights, which are a reflection of the underlying structural contradictions within society between civil society and the state. Rights are the moral part of political emancipation. The emancipation of the Jews is a continuous theme in this essay since it is clear that true Jewish emancipation requires an emancipation from religion and from liberalism. Marx sees that the political outcome for the Jew will be the outcome for all Germans. To liberate Abraham means to free the Jews from Locke which, in turn, will be the beginning of a true emancipation of all of humanity. This analysis of the 'rights of man' also offers Marx a more constructive opportunity to develop an alternative, democratic theory of rights with the real possibilities of human emancipation.

It is also important to note that this legal distinction within civil and political rights in the French constitution between 'man' and the 'citizen' is a reflection of the dualism and contradictions within civil society between the character and capabilities of the bourgeois and the citizen found in the writings of Jean-Jacques Rousseau. The bourgeois individual of the market is characterised by a restless and melancholic desire for material acquisition, physical pleasure, technical calculation, self-preservation, power, and vanity as he inhabits an aimless and unfulfilling life of changing appearances and petty isolation, while the citizen of the state is a person of public virtue, moral nobility, courage, and wisdom, who lives a life of harmonious unity, political participation, love of others, and public happiness. Rousseau outlines the history from antiquity to the eighteenth century of the corruption and inner conflict of this divided soul. Where the bourgeois is an inauthentic, envious, and deceptive being who seeks immediate enjoyment and pleasure, the citizen seeks full realisation of his powers and capacities in patriotism, self-creative freedom, and a commitment to the moral community and general will. For the former, liberty and freedom are expressions of the right to act without interference from others and the right to unrestricted accumulation of private property and security; for the latter, on the other hand, liberty and freedom provide the opportunity to engage in public discourse and civil legislation in the state for the common good. That is, for the bourgeois liberty and freedom are functions of indifference and property, while for the citizen liberty and freedom are opportunities for self-realisation, political participation, and 'love of other'. The highest virtues of the citizen are goodness, friendship, and justice.[23] The world presented by Rousseau is bounded by Adam Smith and the self-interested and materialistic individual of the competitive market, on the one hand, and by Aristotle with his focus on public participation and social justice, on the other. Rousseau feels that the citizen has been lost in modern society, so he returns to the antiquity of Sparta and Rome for his examples of the commitment to the community and others. This contradiction in civil society between the bourgeois and the citizen is then incorporated into the legal structure of the French Constitution of 1793, which, in turn, becomes the basis for Marx's critique of liberalism and natural rights. The contradictions of character and capabilities (Rousseau) become institutionalised in the legal contradictions of the constitution and rights, as well as in the social contradictions of the economy and politics (Marx). They become the basis for Marx's critique and dialectic of political alienation in *On the Jewish Question*. As in the case of Rousseau, these contradictions offer Marx the opportunity to envision an ethical critique of rights theory as well as a transcendence to a higher level of human rights prefigured in Rousseau's 'citizen' and the 'rights of the citizen'.

Reflecting the divisions within society between the state and civil society, the natural 'rights of man' found in the *Declaration of the Rights of Man and of the Citizen* (1793) are divided into two distinct kinds – the economic rights of man and the political rights of the citizen. Both are forms of natural and inalienable rights. The economic rights are the traditional Lockean rights (article 2) of equality (article 3), liberty (article 6), security (article 8), and property (article 16).[24] They are the rights of individuals living in a civil society and, therefore, they are expressions of the political alienation of its members since they protect the rights of egoism, separation from the community, and possessive individualism. Marx quotes from the *Declaration* that 'liberty is the power which man has to do everything which does not harm the rights of others'. Resonating as if it were taken directly from Locke's *Second Treatise of Government*, it represents a freedom of individuals to direct their own lives and actions in any way they think appropriate, so long as their actions do not harm others. Quoting also from the political constitutions of Pennsylvania and New Hampshire, Marx stresses that liberty also includes the rights of conscience, freedom of opinion, the privilege of faith, and the freedom of religious observance. He makes a passing remark that these rights of religious freedom are incompatible with the rights of man but does not delay at this moment to further unpack its implications. The point has already been made in the essay. But there is a clear, if unarticulated sense of irony in the sentence, since liberty is being equated in Marx's eyes not with individual freedom of action and belief but with hypocrisy and prejudice. Thus, as in the case of Locke, there are moral limits to human action but they are not set by the will of God. They are defined and legislated by positive law. Marx is critical of these economic rights because of the way in which they define human beings as isolated, fragmented monads. 'Liberty as a right of man is not founded upon the relations between man and man, but rather upon the separation of man from man'.[25] There is no common ground, no sense of unity or broader purpose, no responsibility to the community and to the general welfare of others, and finally, no moral ground of the individual toward a higher political ideal. The inspiration of Hegel's ideal of the unified ethical life and Greek polity resonates within the words of Marx.

The right of property is a utilitarian and egoistic right to enjoy the products of one's work and wealth and to dispose of them freely without a sense of responsibility to others or to the polity. Although there is a distinct prohibition not to harm others, there is also no moral obligation or social responsibility to others either. Any remnants of natural law are gone. As Marx stresses: 'It leads every man to see in other men, not the *realization*, but rather the *limitation* of his own liberty'.[26] The rights to liberty and property do not enjoin human beings to a common cause for the well-being of others and the political community. Rights do not unite individuals together for a common purpose and ideal; rights are the product of civil society and a capitalist economy. They isolate individuals so that everyone is viewed through the market categories of self-interest, competition, natural necessity, and private property. These economic rights are the legal and civil formalisation of the Hobbesian state of fear and violence. They attempt to justify and contain a barbaric sense of political isolation and existential loneliness and despair; the individual is seen as a self-sufficient monad without moral responsibility, obligation to the broader community, or a meaningful life. Happiness is not defined in terms of public virtue, practical reason, political discourse, life of the soul, or eternal salvation. Rather, it is defined in terms of personal success, acquisition of property, and enjoyment of market benefits. In fact, life itself is reduced to physical pleasure and consumer fulfilment. In the next chapter, we will examine Marx's theory of virtue and happiness, thereby providing a more detailed critique of the materialism and hedonism of economic liberalism. Finally, security is the right of protection to one's person, rights, and property. Although quoting from French and American political documents, Marx's analysis of liberty, property, equality, and security follows closely Locke's theory of the civil polity in his examination of natural rights. The ultimate purpose of these rights is the security of property; the maintenance of the laws of civil society and a market economy is the only purpose and meaning for the existence of the state. This reality is reflected in the very nature of natural rights. Rights and property are synonymous terms at this level of political theory, which is why Locke's theory of rights is rejected by Marx as an inadequate defence of human freedom and individual rights.

Marx summarises his critical position when he states that 'none of the supposed rights of man, therefore, go beyond the egoistic man, man as he is, as a member of civil society; that is, an individual separated from the community, withdrawn into himself, wholly preoccupied with his private interest and acting in accordance with his private caprice'.[27] Rights express the lowest threshold of human self-reflection and animal behaviour as they protect the basest of all human desires and instincts. As we saw in the chapter detailing Locke's theory of rights, this is simply a justification for a state of natural war within a civilised legal system. The economic rights of man are the articulation of natural rights without natural or moral principles and laws to guide human action. But, as we have already seen, political emancipation is not only a theology and justification for this perverse definition of humanity and its lack of ultimate dreams; there is also a transcending element within liberalism itself and this is represented in the other form of natural rights – the political rights of the citizen.

Political rights, on the other hand, are an expression of our species or communal being. Echoes of Aristotle's political animal are reverberating throughout these sections of the essay but in an unarticulated manner. These natural rights are rights individuals have as members of the 'political life of the community' which they share with other members of the state for a common purpose. These species rights entail political liberties of the state and civil rights of the individual to participate in that community. The liberal theory of natural rights is divided between the institutions of the state and civil society, between the economic rights of property and person and the political rights of the species being and community; it is an incoherent divide within liberalism between Locke and Rousseau over the nature of rights and the polity. And Marx will side with Rousseau even as he moves beyond him. The economic rights of man allow the individual to be free – free of commitments to the society as a whole or to any obligation to God or human reason. These are the natural rights that Locke found in both the state of nature and civil society that were free of any law of nature binding the individual to moral principles and laws that obligate a moral duty and social responsibility to others. They are the egoistic rights of possessive individuals. Natural law has been replaced by utilitarian positive laws that simply protect this distorted form of individuality of 'private caprice and private interests'.

However, an older form of natural rights still prevails in Marx's treatment of political emancipation as expressed in the ideas of the species being and political rights of community. By maintaining these rights in contrast to the rights of man, Marx has implicitly returned to the older natural law and Scholastic traditions for inspiration and insight. These provide the higher moral aspirations of humanity to realise the common good and a virtuous life of collective care. Marx recognises the irony of the contradictions of liberalism: Just at the moment when the French claim liberty in their declarations of freedom from the monarchy, just at the moment of the realisation of political emancipation, and just when they throw off the burdens and remnants of feudal society, they are thrown back into a new state of nature where egoism and economic war are the rule. Political emancipation and rights are simply tools used to create and enforce the narrow and poisonous rights of man. Politics itself is turned into a means to protect civil society and the economic system. Citizenship is surrendered to the producers and consumers of wealth and is obedient only to economic interests; political rights are simply theological illusions created to hide and maintain the class reality of capitalism. Whereas Locke stressed that the role of the state was to protect property, Marx maintains that its role is to protect the bourgeois rights of man. This is a distinction without a difference.

Marx's Theory of Emancipation and Human Rights

What has been overlooked in the secondary literature is that Marx has spent most of his time arguing against Bauer and Locke about the nature of the bourgeois state in order to show the uselessness of any political emancipation or legislation of citizenship for the Jews. Any freedom in France or Germany would only be an emancipation of the market and capital toward greater productivity and class inequality. Marx's focus is clear. The real purpose behind his critique of Jewish emancipation is to convey the message that natural rights of man and political emancipation are simply too little, too late. 'Political emancipation is a reduction of man, on the one hand to a member of civil society, an *independent* and *egoistic* individual, and on the other hand, to a *citizen*, a moral person'.[28] The Jewish question is a question about the range and effectiveness of natural rights. In the end, they only emancipate humanity into a new form of economic servitude and injustice that does not reflect the 'true and authentic man'. Again referring to the French declarations of 1791 and 1793, Marx restates the point that the purpose of the state is to preserve the rights of man. 'Political life declares itself to be only a *means* whose end is the life of civil society'.[29] For the moment there is no analysis of who or what constitutes the authentic human being, other than a vague reference to moving beyond political emancipation to human emancipation. For the moment, the central question remains: What has become of those political rights which Marx has only mentioned but discarded in his rush to answer the Jewish question?[30] His conclusion is that there is no answer to the Jewish question from within the framework of the present socio-economic system. Rights do not transcend the economy, they only affirm it; rights are not an articulation of a deeper moral law but an affirmation of the law of capital. And when the political rights come into conflict with the rights of man, which are the true nature and purpose of political emancipation, the former are suspended; the political man is not the authentic individual but only an abstract, artificial man. 'Thus man as he really is, is seen only in the form of *egoistic* man, and man in his *true* nature only in the form of the abstract citizen'.[31] Questions still remain: Is there a transcending force within the political rights themselves? Do these rights possess any hope of resolving the Jewish question in the future? And do they point in a direction where rights still play an important role in Marx's thinking?

The radical French *Declaration of the Rights of Man and of the Citizen* (1793) divides the universal human rights (*Menschenrechte*) into the rights of man (*droits de l'homme*) and the rights of the citizen (*droits du citoyen*), creating a divide between private and public rights. The economic rights of bourgeois man for liberty, equality, security, and property may be found in articles 2, 3, 6, 8, and 16 of the declaration, while the political and civil rights of the citizen are expressed in articles 1, 4, 5, 7, 10–15, and 25 – these are the 'political rights of the community' or the universal man (*Staatswesen* or *Gemeinwesen*) to general welfare, legal and civil liberties (*Staatsbürgerrechte*), general will, universal suffrage, and freedom of assembly, speech, thought, and press.[32] The political and civil liberties permit citizens to enjoy '*participation* in the *community* life, in the *political* life of the community, the life of the state'.[33] These are the rights and liberties of the authentic moral person that transcend the narrow class interests that defend the bourgeois and property rights of man (*droits de l'homme*). They permit citizens to hold office and participate in the legislative function of society as full members of society. Although only illusions and ideologies at this stage of political development in America and France, they do contain the earliest possibilities of an authentic existence beyond the limits of capitalism.[34] The contradictions within the French declaration and constitution between private and public rights permit Marx the objective space to criticise the narrow egoism and selfishness of civil society, the alienation of natural rights as expressions of class interests, the limits of the liberal concepts of equality and freedom attached to private property, and the radical potentialities for substantive change. Liberalism contains its own limits and its own possibilities for transcendence (*Aufhebung*). Marx is clear that the failure of the French Revolution rested in the desire to change the nature of the law and rights within the state, but leave unnoticed and unchanged the social relationships within civil society. '[We] observe that the political liberators reduce citizenship, the *political community*, to a mere *means* for preserving these so-called rights of man; and consequently, that the citizen is declared to be the servant of egoistic "man" ... and finally that it is man as a bourgeois and not man as a citizen who is considered the *true and authentic man*'.[35] Full emancipation will only occur with the dissolution of civil society, with the transcendence of the contradictions of liberalism to where the public citizen becomes the authentic person – to where the species being of each member of society participates in the complete economic and political life of society and where there is a harmonious balance between human needs and powers with the ethical community (virtue) and democracy.[36] A primitive theory of political and human rights represents only the beginning of Marx's quest for social justice. In the next chapter, we will examine workplace justice and his ethical theory of virtue, human needs, individual freedom, and economic emancipation.

Natural Rights of Free Press and Universal Suffrage

Finally, mention should be made of a number of brief essays Marx wrote around the time of the Jewish question on his response to debates held within the Prussian legislative Assembly. The essays are all interrelated because they expand our understanding of his theory of legal rights by including issues such as legislative debates on the Prussian state censorship of newspapers, freedom of the press, landed property rights, forest regulations, customary rights of the poor, and civil laws regarding felled or fallen wood gathering and theft. Marx's defence of the freedom of the press is based on his idea that 'freedom is so much the essence of man' inherent in the human will for the development of a self-conscious spirit of the state and universal wisdom of the individual; and a free press is its public expression in print.[37] The press is the means by which individuals communicate with one another. To this extent, 'the essence of the free press is the characterful, rational, moral essence of freedom'.[38] Marx, in turn, characterises press censorship as 'a civilized monster, a perfumed abortion' and 'degrading punishment' that distorts human reason for the technical function of social control over public opinion. Rights, on the other hand, are the theoretical expression of moral norms and the 'unconscious natural law of freedom' that have been given a legal and institutional framework to promote freedom expressed through conscious positive law.[39] Rights are an essential component of human freedom and any attempt to abridge these rights through self-interest is cowardice.[40] 'The right of the individual citizen is a folly if the right of the state is not recognised. If freedom in general is rightful, it goes without saying that a particular form of freedom is the more rightful as freedom has achieved in it a finer and better-developed existence'.[41] Rights and freedom are synonymous terms for the very early Marx.

Throughout his life, he will expand his understanding of *human rights* and human emancipation as he moves from the *political rights* of the citizen (assembly and freedom of speech and thought), to the *economic rights* of communal democracy (equal rights, fair distribution based on human needs, right to organise co-operatives, and worker ownership), to the *social rights* of socialism (education, welfare state, social insurance, and economic infrastructure). Rights are an essential part of social justice grounded not in God, but in moral nature (virtue and needs) and in economic and political democracy (protection and realisation of nature). Rights without civil society are part of a human emancipation that emphasises freedom as creative self-determination in the workplace and democratic participation reminiscent of classical politics.[42] Although rights are important to the early Marx, they represent only a small part of his broader theory of justice. He is more concerned with examining the wider implications of a secular natural law. Although he does not use that phrase, possibly because of its theological and philosophical connotations, his examination of human nature as teleological, rational, purposeful, political, and meaningful represents a continuation of that tradition into modern times.

Notes

1   *Natural Law and Karl Marx*: Ernst Bloch places Marx within the theoretical orbit of natural law theory. See Ernst Bloch, *Natural Law and Human Dignity*, trans. Dennis Schmidt (Cambridge, MA: MIT Press, 1986), pp. 63, 177–8, and 187–8. See also Philip Kain, *Marx and Ethics* (Oxford: Clarendon Press, 1988) who argues that Marx does have a theory of natural law grounded in the essence of humanity, that is, grounded in his ideas of freedom, essence or function of man, species being, creative self-determination, human dignity, and human needs (pp. 29–33). Morality represents the fullest development of human nature and freedom, not as individual licence, but as 'the unhindered development of what is the essence of the thing' (p. 21). According to Kain's interpretation of Marx, the essence of humanity is its morality (p. 32). C.B. Macpherson, in his essay 'The Maximization of Democracy', in *Democratic Theory: Essays in Retrieval* (Oxford: Clarendon Press, 1973), pp. 3–23, places Marx in the tradition of natural law since his ethical theory is grounded in nature – human essence, ethical maximisation of human capacities and powers, species being, praxis, creativity, and human needs. In his essay 'Profits and Surplus Value: Appearance and Reality in Capitalist Production', in *A Critique of Economic Theory*, ed. E.K. Hunt and Jesse Schwartz (Harmondsworth: Penguin, 1972), Alfredo Medio wrote: 'In other words, the theory of *value* would be something like a theory of *just price* whose forerunners were the medieval doctors, the doctrine of natural law, and of course, Adam Smith' (p. 316).

The crucial questions are whether natural rights are grounded in human nature and the state of nature (natural rights theorists), social convention (Protestant radicals), labour (socialists), or the greatest happiness of the largest number (utilitarians); and whether natural law is grounded in reason (Greeks), God (scholastics), scripture, tradition, and reason (natural rights theorists), laws of practical reason (Kant), or the community and nature (socialists). In Locke's theory of natural law, property initially served the common good, health and well-being of the individual and community, economic sufficiency and life of the community, and the merit of individual labour and industry; in the end natural law was sacrificed on the altar of commerce, banking, finance, and wage labour. Thus, there is a central question around which revolve natural rights and natural law: Are life, liberty, and freedom rights necessary to protect property or is property a way to ultimately ensure life, liberty, and freedom? Is private or productive property an end in itself or simply a means to provide for the common good? The former produces a society of possessive individualism, competition, inequality, and servitude, while the latter is oriented toward the community, egalitarianism, and democracy. Do rights protect aristocracy and power or do rights ensure conscience and moral self-determination?

2   For an overview of some of the secondary literature on the Jewish question, see Eugene Kamenka, 'The Baptism of Marx', *The Hibbert Journal*, 56 (October 1957–8): 340–51; Marx Wartofsky, 'Marx on the Jewish Question: A Review', *The Philosophical Forum*, 19 (1961–1962); Shlomo Avineri, 'Marx and Jewish Emancipation', *Journal of the History of Ideas*, 25, 3 (July 1964): 445–50; Emil Fackenheim, *Encounters between Judaism and Modern Philosophy: A Preface to Future Jewish Thought* (New York, NY: Basic Books, 1973); Hal Draper, *Karl Marx's Theory of Revolution*, vol. 1, books I and II (New York, NY: Monthly Review Press, 1977), pp. 109–28 and 591–608; Julius Carlebach, *Karl Marx and the Radical*

Critique of Judaism (London: Routledge and Kegan Paul, 1978); Louis Harap, 'The Meaning of Marx's Essay "On the Jewish Question"', *The Journal of Ethnic Studies*, 7, 1 (Spring 1979): 43–56; Henry Pachter, 'Marx and the Jews', *Dissent* (Fall 1979): 450–67; W.H. Blanchard, 'Karl Marx and the Jewish Question', *Political Psychology*, 5, 3 (1984): 365–74; Joel Schwartz, 'Liberalism and the Jewish Connection: A Study of Spinoza and the Young Marx', *Political Theory* (February 1985): 58–84; Michael Maidan, 'Marx on the Jewish Question: A Meta-Critical Analysis', in *Studies in Soviet Thought*, 33, 1 (January 1987): 27–41; Dennis Fischman, 'The Jewish Question', *Polity*, 21, 4 (1989): 755–9 and *Political Discourse in Exile: Karl Marx and the Jewish Question* (Amherst, MA: University of Massachusetts Press, 1991); Yoav Peled, 'From Theology to Sociology: Bruno Bauer and Karl Marx on the Question of Jewish Emancipation', *History of Political Thought*, 13, 3 (1992): 463–85; and David Leopold, *The Young Karl Marx: German Philosophy, Modern Politics, and Human Flourishing* (2007), ch. 2, pp. 163–80.

3 Louis Dupré in *Marx's Social Critique of Culture* (New Haven, CT: Yale University Press, 1983) writes that Bruno Bauer's solution to the problem of religion in modern society requires its total negation and secularisation. Marx transcends the original question of religion (Judaism) and civil rights and replaces it with the state and civil society. 'Marx claimed that the secular, democratic state is *the* modern version of the religious illusion. It maintains the same relation of *apparent* dominance and *real* subservience to civil society which exists between the religious sphere and the profane world' (p. 25). Religion is replaced by the state as the focus of Marx's attention. The modern state which mystically conceals the underlying social reality of the market economy in civil society plays the same alienating role that was formerly occupied by religion. Freeing citizenship from the shackles of religion and property only reaffirms and reinforces their power in civil society. This is the essence and profound weakness of liberal rights and bourgeois freedom. Everyone is free before the state and alienated and dominated by class and property in civil society – all of which is concealed from reflective critique.

4 Heinrich Rommen, *The Natural Law: A Study in Legal and Social History and Philosophy*, trans. Thomas Hanley (Indianapolis, IN: Liberty Fund, 1998), p. 79. See also Peter Munz, *The Place of Hooker in the History of Thought* (Westport, CT: Greenwood Press, 1971), who in analysing the six legal principles Locke borrows from Hooker concludes with the comment: 'These principles concern only the technique of government; they say nothing as to fundamental principles of political philosophy' (p. 206). Returning to Rommen, he views Locke's moral skepticism and agnosticism, that is found in his technology or positivism of politics, as a looking back to the nominalism of William of Occam and Duns Scotus and a looking forward to legal positivism and the science of law. Modern political theory would eventually undermine a universal natural law and the moral foundations of liberalism, as it would epistemologically prepare the way for Enlightenment science and positivism. Both movements of political theory and science lead to the fragmentation of ethics from law, morals, and economics. Rommen rejects the positivism and relativism of metaphysics, morals, law, and science: 'Positivism signifies the renouncing of all efforts to know the essences of things (nominalism), the repudiation of the metaphysics of hierarchical being and value' (p. 36). Fleeing the Nazi regime, Rommen came to the US in 1938 to teach at a number of Catholic colleges. Given his critique of positivism and concern

over the loss of the natural law tradition in moral philosophy, politics, and science, that is, given his concern at the loss of its deep moral principles to guide human action and civil legislation, Rommen's book stands as a Catholic response to the eclipse of natural reason.

Richard Tawney in *Religion and the Rise of Capitalism: A Historical Study* (New York, NY: Harcourt, Brace and Company, 1926) makes a similar argument about the silence of moral reason in the sixteenth and seventeenth centuries resulting from the separation of religion and economics. There was no longer a commercial morality to judge economic behaviour. In fact, by the time of Adam Smith the law of economics became an expression of divine providence and the law of nature itself (pp. 191–3). Tawney writes: 'There were, no doubt, special conditions to account for its [the Church's] silence ... But the explanation of its attitude is to be sought ... in the prevalence of a temper which accepted the established order of class relations as needing no vindication before any higher tribunal ... It was that the very idea that the Church possessed an independent standard of values, to which social institutions were amenable, had been abandoned' (p. 193). Tawney saw this position of religion as a 'spiritual blindness which made possible the general acquiescence in the horrors of the early factory system ...' (ibid.). Max Horkheimer, a representative of critical theory, will raise a similar issue again in 1948 in his critique of positivism in the social sciences in *Eclipse of Reason* – the loss of a critical, practical science due to the Enlightenment. Social justice becomes something students study in religion or philosophy but not in science – there is no ecological justice or economic justice.

Rommen places Marx squarely in this positivist tradition of materialism and science. He unfortunately fails see that Marx's own critique of empiricism, positivism, and the method of natural science, along with his rejection of liberal natural rights theory, represents a turn toward a secular natural law that would justify his moral critique of industrial capitalism and ethically ground his theory of democratic socialism.

Natural Law of God and Natural Law of Democracy: It is interesting to note that the universal moral principles and foundations of natural law for the Anglican Richard Hooker and John Locke lay in nature, reason, and God, whereas for the later critical humanists Rousseau, Hegel, and Marx the foundations will shift to nature, reason, and politics. To be more specific, Rousseau grounds natural law in the universality of popular sovereignty and the general will, Hegel in the ethical community and rational state, and Marx in the species being and democracy. The common element among these social theorists is that they sought the moral principles that guide human action in the self-determination of citizens within the political community. For Rousseau and Marx in particular, this secularisation and humanisation of natural law is the means by which God is replaced by democracy as a source of truth, reason, and ethics. The natural moral order is now defined by human nature (virtue, praxis, and beneficence), reason (practical reason and public deliberation), and democracy (ideal polity and the values of equality and freedom). Aristotle's ethics and politics have now replaced Aquinas and Hooker as the foundation of democratic principles and institutions. Eugene Kamenka in *The Ethical Foundations of Marxism* (London: Routledge & Kegan Paul, 1972), has argued: 'For Marx, morality and law represented the unflowering of man's essential being *(Wesen)* and an essence, according to Marx, is always truly universal ... The true basis of morality is not individual conduct, but social organisation. On this ground Marx proclaimed the rational society, "the concretization of human freedom"' (pp. 37–8). Earlier in this work, Kamenka had clarified the use of the term 'freedom' with the words: 'For Marx, as for Hegel, freedom meant self-determination in accordance with one's inner constitution ... [and] the logical principle of one's own development' (p. 23). And the ethical community, for Marx, within which this freedom of praxis and work is manifested is democracy; that is, it is through the institutions and values of democracy that economic and political self-determination and essential self-realisation are made real and concrete. It is through social institutions that morality is actualised, and it is through the science of empirical, historical, and deep structures (concepts) that ethics is made relevant. This is the true meaning of the dialectic. See Ernst Cassirer, *The Question of Jean-Jacques Rousseau* (New York, NY: Columbia University Press, 1954), pp. 70–6; Kamenka, *The Ethical Foundations of Marxism*, pp. 23, 28, 30, 32, 34, 37–40, 43, 56, 110–11, and 146–7; Lucio Colletti, *From Rousseau to Lenin: Studies in Ideology and Society*, trans. John Merrington and Judith White (New York, NY: Monthly Review Press, 1972), p. 144; and George Brenkert, *Marx's Ethics of Freedom* (London: Routledge & Kegan Paul, 1983), pp. 87–9, 90–105, and 157–9.

This replacement of God (revelation, scripture, and tradition) by society had already been attempted in the seventeenth century. Locke had already replaced God by organised society – civil society, the social compact, and property. This is what natural law came to mean in his political theory. Tawney in *Religion and the Rise of Capitalism* recognises this turn when he writes: 'The State, first in England, then in France and America, finds its sanction, not in religion, but in nature, in a presumed contract to establish it, in the necessity for mutual protection and the convenience of mutual assistance' (pp. 8, 179, and 280).

5   Karl Marx, *On the Jewish Question*, *Karl Marx: Early Writings*, ed. and trans. T.B. Bottomore (New York, NY: McGraw Hill Book Company, 1964), p. 3; *Karl Marx/Friedrich Engels Werke* (*MEW*), Band 1 (Berlin: Dietz Verlag, 1961), p. 347.
6   Ibid., p. 7; *MEW* 1, p. 350.
7   Ibid., p. 3; *MEW* 1, p. 347.
8   Tawney, *Religion and the Rise of Capitalism*, p. 36. The contemporary debate within Analytical Marxism about the nature of justice in Marx's social thought does not take this range of issues into consideration. It limits the discussion of justice to its juridical and contractual meaning between labour and capital in the workplace outside of ethical and social theory. See Allen Buchanan, *Marx and Justice: The Radical Critique of Liberalism* (Totowa, NJ: Rowman and Littlefield, 1982), pp. 50–85; Brenkert, *Marx's Ethics of Freedom*, pp. 15–21; and Steven Lukes, *Marxism and Morality* (Oxford: Oxford University Press, 1987), pp. 48–70.
9   Tawney, *Religion and the Rise of Capitalism*, p. 5.
10 Marx, *On the Jewish Question*, p. 10; *MEW* 1, p. 352.
11 Ibid., p. 10; *MEW* 1, p. 352.
12 Ibid., pp. 10–11; *MEW* 1, p. 352.
13 Ibid., p. 12; *MEW* 1, p. 354.
14 Ibid.
15 Ibid., p. 13; *MEW* 1, p. 355.
16 Ibid.

17 By reducing Marx's theory of justice to simply the juridical categories of rights and fairness, many scholars have accepted the Enlightenment definition of justice with all its concomitant problems:

(1) Historical Materialism: development of a non-dialectical theory of historical materialism with its mechanical and materialistic treatment of consciousness, law, and culture turning justice into a form of historical determinism and juridical relativism;
(2) Critical Science: does not distinguish between a positivist and instrumental view of science and a critical/dialectical view;
(3) Ethics and Politics: continues the Enlightenment separation of morality (individual) and ethics (politics), as well as science and ethics;
(4) German Idealism and the Ancients: the juridical concept relies on seventeenth- and eighteenth-century political theory and classical economics and undervalues the importance of Kant (critique), Hegel (ethical life and dialectic), and Aristotle (justice);
(5) By reducing legal values and liberal institutions to a specific capitalist mode of production, the dialectic between the universal and particular, ideals and reality, and rights of the citizen and of man is overlooked. Values of justice are mechanically tied to a specific historical moment and cannot reach beyond the present and particular. On the other hand, Marx's theory of the state distinguishes between the role of the state as an ideal which displaces and represses the egoism of civil society, an ideology which hides and distorts the exploitation of capitalist production, and a set of ideals that transcend civil society and lead to political and human emancipation. Marx sees that justice plays multiple and even contradictory roles in society from ideological repression to political and human emancipation;
(6) Because of number 3, justice does not deal with other moral values of self-realisation, human capacities, freedom, and community, and, thus, assumes the Enlightenment bias of liberalism by continuing to separate the individual from the community, morality (*Moralität*) from ethical life (*Sittlichkeit*), ethics from politics (structures and constitutions), and, ultimately, justice from morals.

Buchanan in his work *Marx and Justice* writes: 'Capitalism is condemned not because it is unjust or immoral, or because it does not accord with human nature, but because it fails at the constitutive task of all human societies: it fails to satisfy needs' (p. 29). On this issue, also see Brenkert, *Marx's Ethics of Freedom*, who rejects Buchanan's thesis that values, such as freedom self-actualisation, and community, are not moral values, but are utilitarian 'needs' or materialist wants (n. 32, p. 240). Buchanan follows Tucker and Wood by rejecting the practical and critical role of justice in social revolution (p. 51). Justice, rights, self-consciousness, and freedom are not central to explaining social critique or social change; this is reserved for an analysis of the productive forces and social relations of production (pp. 52–3). Here, too, issues of social justice are kept separate from a critique of political economy and chrematistics. Buchanan does disagree with Tucker and Wood over the issue of distributive justice: He argues that, even by its own standards of equivalency and fairness in the market, the worker's wage agreement is not just. However, this is relatively unimportant since in a truly democratic and socialist society the social coordination of natural resources and production will be 'sufficiently harmonious and bountiful that whatever conflicts remain will not require reliance upon juridical principles prescribing rights to distributive shares' (p. 57). Justice as a civil and legal category is only necessary within a capitalist and class society to adjudicate conflicts and divisions. The need for justice will be irrelevant under socialism. Overcoming the class and power differences in society, dissolving an economy built on exchange value and wage servitude, and satisfying the fundamental wants and physical needs of its citizens, leads to a free community where juridical rights and fairness – justice – no longer apply. Finally, Buchanan uncritically blends together the egoistic 'rights of man' within civil society and the universal 'rights of the citizen' within the state without recognising their differences, especially for a socialist theory of human rights (pp. 60–9). From this perspective all reference to justice is an unnecessary product of a misunderstanding of Marx, who 'has only scorn for those moralizing socialists' (pp. 74 and 81–7). Others who reject a theory of natural or civil rights in Marx include George Brenkert, 'Marx and Human Rights', *Journal of the History of Philosophy* 24, 1 (January 1981): 55–77 and Steven Lukes, 'Can a Marxist Believe in Human Rights?', *Praxis International*, 1 (January 1982): 344 and *Marxism and Morality*, pp. 48 and 70. Brenkert quotes from the *Grundrisse* that the 'exchange of exchange value is the productive, real basis of all *equality* and *freedom*' (p. 70), thereby confirming that the key categories of liberalism and natural rights – equality, freedom, and security – are products of property ownership and rights in a market economy. They are all based on exchange value and capitalist property relationships. 'It is in this sense that bourgeois property is the foundation of human (i.e. bourgeois) rights' (ibid.). Rights protect bourgeois, egoistic, and class interests in civil society (pp. 73–4) and, therefore, cannot be the basis for a critique of capitalism as unjust (p. 75). Brenkert agrees and substitutes for justice the moral categories of an ethic of virtue and human freedom. With the dissolution of exchange value and market relationships in socialism, rights will no longer be necessary; they are historically and structurally tied to a specific set of market and social relationships.

Brenkert also recognises that some of the confusion surrounding Marx's theory of moral values lies in his avoidance of the traditional moral philosophy of Hume, Kant, John Stuart Mill, etc. which emphasises individual will and practical action, while he stressed the ethical social system (pp. 12–13) or the moral values embedded in political and economic structures and social relationships. Brenkert then makes the powerful argument that 'morality is not primarily concerned with rules and principles [Kant], but with the cultivation of certain dispositions or traits of character [Aristotle] ... In this sense, Marx's approach to morality is akin to that of the Greeks for whom the nature of virtue or human excellence was the central question of morality' (pp. 17–18). This is a key point that Brenkert, unfortunately, never develops. He ultimately fails to connect the moral values of virtue, human excellence, freedom, community, self-determination, and self-objectification (labour creativity) to the broader issues of Aristotelian social justice, just as he fails to connect the questions of distributive justice and human needs (nature, wants, and passions) back to the Greek view of reciprocity and need, but instead reduces them to issues of the mode of production and consumption (pp. 42, 60, 99, 150, and 152). By failing to break the hold of a deterministic historical materialism and a too narrow view of liberal justice, Brenkert does not develop his initial insights into the Hegelian distinction between morality and social ethics, or connect human need to his own understanding of moral values. 'Rather, he [Marx] considers capitalism unjust because it does not satisfy human needs within its own productive possibilities and thus violates the principle of distribution according to need' (p. 152). Finally, in his essay 'Marxism and Human Rights', *Daedalus*, 112, 4 (Fall, 1983), Leszek Kołakowski argues that the historicism and relativism of morality for Marx makes it impossible that the concept of justice could become the basis for social criticism (pp. 81–92). Instead, Kołakowski contends that the natural and inevitable tendencies of capitalism would bring about a new society (p. 86). This reading of Marx represents a return to the early positions of 'scientific socialism' of Karl Kautsky and Rudolf Hilferding. See Lukes, *Marxism and Morality*, p. 18. For a summary of the secondary literature on the critics of a deterministic reading of Marx's theory of historical materialism, see Norman Levine, *The Tragic Deception: Marx Contra Engels* (Oxford: Clio Books, 1975), pp. 104–5.

18 On the issue of humans as means and ends, see Immanuel Kant, *Fundamental Principles of the Metaphysic of Morals* and Ludwig Feuerbach, *The Essence of Christianity*, trans. George Eliot (New York, NY: Harper Torchbooks, 1957).

19 Marx, *On the Jewish Question*, pp. 13–14; *MEW* 1, p. 355.

20 Ibid., p. 15; *MEW* 1, p. 356.

21 Ibid.

22 Ibid., p. 20; *MEW* 1, p. 360.

23 This distinction between the bourgeois and the citizen is to be found throughout Rousseau's *Emile*, *First and Second Discourse*, and *The Social Contract*. Karl Löwith, *From Hegel to Nietzsche: The Revolution in Nineteenth-Century Thought*, trans. David Green (Garden City, NY: Doubleday Anchor Books, 1967), pp. 233–7; Arthur Melzer, 'Rousseau and the Problem of Bourgeois Society', *American Political Science Review* 74, 4 (1980): 1018–33; Judith Shklar, *Men and Citizens: A Study of Rousseau's Social Theory* (Cambridge: Cambridge University Press, 1985), pp. 12–32; Pierre Manet, 'Rousseau, Critic of Liberalism', in *An Intellectual History of Liberalism*, trans. Rebecca Balinski (Princeton, NJ: Princeton University Press, 1995), pp. 67–8; Katrin Froese, 'Beyond Liberalism: The Moral Community of Rousseau's Social Contract', *Canadian Journal of Political Science* 34, 3 (September 2001): 579–600; and Joseph Reisert, *Jean-Jacques Rousseau: A Friend of Virtue* (Ithaca, NY: Cornel University Press, 2003), pp. 106–40.

24 Under the 'rights of man' of the *Declaration of the Rights of Man and of the Citizen* of 1793, Marx includes the rights to liberty, security, and property and also from the 1795 *Declaration* he includes the right to equality. Marx lists the right to equality under article 5 but, in fact, it is actually article 3 of both the 1793 and 1795 *Declaration*. The original version of the *Declaration* from 1789 listed life, property, security, and resistance to oppression as the key principles of the natural rights of human beings. Drafts of the first declaration of rights were written by the Marquis de Lafayette with help from Thomas Jefferson; they were aided in their work by the *Virginia Declaration of Rights*, drafted by James Mason in May 1776 and the American *Declaration of Independence*, drafted by Jefferson in July 1776.

25 Marx, *On the Jewish Question*, pp. 24–5; *MEW* 1, p. 364. Colletti, in his work *From Rousseau*

to Lenin, outlines Locke's theory of the state and social contract. He contends that Locke held a view of liberty and rights founded on the indifference and separation of individuals from each other; the formation of civil society, law, and the state creates a formal and legal unity through the social contract which only further promotes this isolation and separation from others (p. 150). From this perspective, liberty is defined as freedom from others, freedom from society, and freedom to dispose of oneself and one's property in a competitive market economy where the central role of the state is to ensure the protection of property and private interests (p. 167).

26 Ibid., p. 25; *MEW* 1, p. 365. This is what Isaiah Berlin will later call in *Four Essays on Freedom* (Oxford: Oxford University Press, 1969) the difference between positive and negative freedom. In a market economy we have negative freedom, since we have the total freedom to do what we want, when we want, where and how we want. In an authoritarian society, the state directs individuals toward a certain social ideal and positive outcome that, although appearing to represent freedom, is its exact opposite. Only the market definition of negative and unrestrained freedom is real. A similar position is held by Milton Friedman in *Capitalism and Freedom* (Chicago, IL: University of Chicago Press, 1974), p. 12. This idea of negative freedom simply equates freedom with the market and assumes the market as the positive dimension of freedom.

27 Marx, *On the Jewish Question*, p. 26; *MEW* 1, p. 366. There are a number of works that dismiss the importance in this essay of the state since it is only an enchanted region concealing the truth of private interests and passions. The key is to get behind the state to civil society and the structures of exploitation and power. See Nancy Schwartz, 'Distinction Between Public and Private Life: Marx on the zoon politikon', *Political Theory*, 7, 2 (May 1979): 245–66. She contends that authors such as Hannah Arendt and Sheldon Wolin dismiss the importance of the political as a distinctive sphere of activity in the early Marx because it hides the real problem of the economy. She argues that they believe that Marx has a thin, illusory notion of politics as representing only class interests and the principles of private property. Schwartz wants to preserve the centrality of the state in Marx as it parallels the political commune in the philosophy of Aristotle. I would take the discussion one step further: Although not examined in any detail in this essay on the Jewish question, Marx does rescue the political from subsumption under civil society by stressing the distinctions between the public and private sphere of rights and the transcendence of rights into human emancipation.

28 Ibid., p. 31; *MEW* 1, p. 370.

29 Ibid., p. 27; *MEW* 1, p. 367.

30 Ziyad Husami, 'Marx on Distributive Justice', *Philosophy & Public Affairs* 8, 1 (Autumn 1978): 267–95 and in *Marx, Justice and History*, ed. Marshall Cohen, Thomas Nagel, and Thomas Scanlon (Princeton, NJ: Princeton University Press, 1980), pp. 42–79; G.A. Cohen, 'Freedom, Justice and Capitalism', *New Left Review*, 126 (March–April 1981), pp. 11–12; and William McBride, 'Rights and the Marxian Tradition', *Praxis International*, 4 (April 1984): 57–74.

31 Marx, *On the Jewish Question*, p. 30; *MEW* 1, p. 370.

32 'Declaration of the Rights of Man and Citizen', in *A Documentary Survey of the French Revolution*, ed. John Hall Stewart (New York, NY: Macmillan Company, 1951), pp. 455–8.

A number of scholars have recognised this distinction between the rights of man and the rights of the citizen as the basis for moving beyond liberalism to a higher stage of human development in socialism. See Sidney Hook, *Revolution, Reform, and Social Justice: Studies in the Theory and Practice of Marxism* (New York, NY: New York University Press, 1975), pp. 80–3 and Amy Bartholomew, 'Should a Marxist Believe in Marx on Rights?', *The Socialist Register* (1990), pp. 248–9.

33 Marx, *On the Jewish Question*, p. 23; MEW 1, p. 362. According to Robert Sweet in *Marx, Morality and the Virtue of Beneficence* (Lanham, MD: University Press of America, 2002), there are two relevant secondary interpretations of Marx's critique of natural rights theory by Stephen Lukes and Allen Buchanan. Lukes in *Marxism and Morality* and Buchanan in *Marx and Justice* reject what they see as Marx's narrow interpretation of Locke's theory of rights and private property as the sole foundation for the French *Declaration* of 1789. They accuse Marx of reducing the individual right of freedom to the right of private property which in their view is a 'narrow and impoverished' view of rights (p. 59). Because Marx does not consider in his analysis of the Jewish question the 'uninterpreted articles' 7, 8, 9, 10, and 11 in the 1789 *Declaration*, they reject Marx's analysis as a form of economic reductionism. They contend that the rights to freedom of opinion and thought, as well as civil and legal rights, were neglected by Marx. By reducing rights to the contradictions of egoism and civil society – private property – Marx has missed important political principles that go beyond the economic rights of civil society. This would be a legitimate criticism of Marx, if that was, in fact, the position he actually held. Lukes and Buchanan fail to distinguish between the 'rights of man' and the 'rights of the citizen' and the philosophical traditions out of which they develop; they also fail to see how Marx's concept of human emancipation expands throughout his writings and how this affects his understanding of the nature of political and human rights.

Sweet responds to both of the above critics of Marx by drawing upon the writings of Shlomo Avineri, *The Social and Political Thought of Karl Marx* (Cambridge: Cambridge University Press, 1968) and Thomas Keyes, 'The Marxian Concept of Property: Individual/Social', in *The Main Debate* (New York, NY: Random House, 1987). He draws the reader's attention to Marx's distinction between the egoistic rights of man and the political rights of the citizen as the basis for reconsidering the whole issue of a theory of natural rights. By recognising that Marx did not totally reject a theory of rights but simply transcended (*Aufhebung*) the Lockean theory, he preserved and incorporated a revised and more critical theory of political rights into his theory of human emancipation (pp. 76–9). Unfortunately, Sweet gets caught up in his debate with Lukes and Buchanan and does not develop the implications of his own insight into these different forms of rights which presupposed differing views of individuality as egoism and species being. Only the rights of the species being will be able to provide a theory of political and human rights for a free and democratic socialism. Sweet moves the discussion in an important direction in his critique of Lukes and Buchanan but falters when he contends that both the rights of man and the rights of the citizen are 'subcategories of human rights' (p. 57). The argument made in this chapter is that only the rights of the citizen can be the basis for human rights in the political sphere since the rights of man only reinforce the liberal and Lockean notions of person and property. In an interesting essay 'The Marxian Critique of Citizenship: For a Rereading of *On the Jewish Question*' in *The South Atlantic Quarterly*, 104, 4 (Fall 2005), Stathis Kouvelakis writes that there is an emancipatory potential lying in the alienated but generic essence (*Gattungswesen*) of human beings that is presupposed by the distinction and 'primordial separation' between the abstract universal rights of the *Declaration of the Rights of Man and of the Citizen* and the idealism (or religion) of the 'community of citizens' (pp. 709–10). Kouvelakis argues that Marx is reticent to explicate the nature of the citizen's universal essence because of his 'fundamentally anti-utopian stance' (p. 710). 'The state claims to dominate, and even transcend, this reality even though the state is in fact dominated by it and condemned to reproduce its constitutive separations' (p. 713). The Jacobin Terror of the French Revolution was a result of this inability to understand the actual relations between politics and civil society. One cannot simply revolutionise the abstract state because that is basically to misunderstand it and its relation to the capitalist economy. Rights, citizenship, and personhood were categories limited to the bourgeois owner of property at a time when the state and principles of political rights of the citizen appeared to transcend civil society. Rights, according to Kouvelakis, are simply political expressions and legitimation of this continued abstraction and separation of the state and economy. To accomplish this de-legitimation and human emancipation requires a revolutionising of the means of production. Although he does not develop the implications of his argument in this essay, he does ask the question as to whether it would be better to abandon the concept of rights or to redefine them (p. 715). There is in this question itself and the distinction between the private rights of civil society and the public rights of the state a whisper of the classical horizons and the universal being of man in political *praxis*, discourse, and participation.

34 Drucilla Cornell, 'Should a Marxist Believe in Rights?', *Praxis International*, 4, 1 (April 1984): 'The classical ideal of political freedom had to do with the freedom to be a full and participating member of the polis ... An essential aspect of Marx's critique of the bourgeois constitution is that the classical understanding of the role of law in the protection of the public realm has been lost. The protection of the political community is no longer conceived as an end in itself' (p. 50). To reconstruct an adequate appreciation of Marx's theory of rights is to recognise that it is part of a broader theory of social justice that also reconnects Marx with the ancients. Cornell draws upon Hannah Arendt to reconnect the ideas of Marx, Hegel, and the ancient Greeks. She then proceeds to connect the discussion about rights to Marx's analysis of freedom, self-determination, and social justice by relying on the writings of Carol Gould, *Marx's Social Ontology: Individuality and Community in Marx's Theory of Social* Reality (Cambridge, MA: University of Massachusetts Press, 1980) and Mihailo Markovic, 'Philosophical Foundations of Human Rights', *Praxis International* 1, 4 (January 1982). This idea that freedom is the essence of Marx's writings is also to be found in Bertell Ollman, *Alienation: Marx's Conception of Man in Capitalist Society* (Cambridge: Cambridge University Press, 1975), pp. 116–20 and István Mészáros, *Marx's Theory of Alienation* (New York, NY: Harper & Row Publishers, 1970), pp. 162–89.

35 Marx, *On the Jewish Question*, p. 26; *MEW* 1, p. 366.

36 It is this balance between the public and private spheres that Nancy Schwartz, in 'Distinction between Public and Private Life', recognises as a defining characteristic of classical Athens (pp. 250–2, 256, and 260).

37 Karl Marx, 'Debates on Freedom of the Press', *Karl Marx/Frederick Engels Collected Works*, vol. 1 (New York, NY: International Publishers, 1976), p. 155; *Karl Marx/Friedrich Engels Werke (MEW)*, Band 1 (Berlin: Dietz Verlag, 1961), p. 51.

38 Ibid., p. 158; *MEW* 1, p. 54. Marx summarises his theory of the right to a free press: 'The free press is the ubiquitous vigilant eye of a people's soul, the embodiment of a people's faith in itself, the eloquent link that connects the individual with the state and the world, the embodied culture that transforms material struggles into intellectual struggles, and idealises their crude material form. It is a people's frank confession to itself, and the redeeming power of confession is well known. It is the spiritual mirror in which a people can see itself, and self-examination is the first condition of wisdom' (pp. 164–5; *MEW* 1, pp. 60–1).

39 Ibid., pp. 158 and 161–2; *MEW* 1, pp. 54 and 57–8.

40 Karl Marx, 'Debates on the Law on Thefts of Wood', Karl *Marx/Frederick Engels Collected Works*, vol. 1 (New York, NY: International Publishers, 1976), pp. 236–7; *Karl Marx/Friedrich Engels Werke (MEW)*, Band 1 (Berlin: Dietz Verlag, 1961), p. 121.

41 Marx, 'Debates on Freedom of the Press', p. 173; *MEW* 1, p. 69.

42 For an overview of the secondary literature on the influence of Aristotle and ancient Greece on Marx's theory of justice, see J.P. Sullivan, ed., *Marxism and the Classics, Arethusa*, 8, 1 (Spring 1975); George E. McCarthy, *Marx and the Ancients: Classical Ethics, Social Justice, and Nineteenth-Century Political Economy* (Savage, MD: Rowman & Littlefield Publishers, 1990), n. 2, pp. 303–4 and *Dreams in Exile: Rediscovering Science and Ethics in Nineteenth-Century Social Theory* (Albany, NY: State University of New York Press, 2009), n. 3, p. 288.

CHAPTER 4

Workplace Justice: Ethics, Virtue, and Human Freedom

As we saw in the previous chapter, Marx approaches the issue of social justice by first developing the outlines of a theory of political rights, political alienation, and the structural contradictions between the polity and civil society in *On the Jewish Question*. In his *Early Economic and Philosophical Manuscripts* of 1844, all the main questions are touched upon again, including natural rights, liberties, freedom, individuality, and human emancipation. In this next stage of his development, he begins to unpack a more comprehensive treatment of the nature of civil society and economic alienation with a focus on the issue of his central moral categories of individual freedom, creativity, work, and human needs. Expanding the definition of the human being beyond the limits established by the liberalism of Hobbes and Locke, he incorporates new traditions that include Kant, Hegel, and the Left Hegelians (Bruno Bauer and Ludwig Feuerbach), German Romantic poets (Friedrich Hölderlin, Heinrich Heine, and Friedrich Schiller), and Greek philosophers (Aristotle and Epicurus). This broadening of his philosophical horizons opens up newer avenues of expressions of social justice than those available during the Enlightenment. With new concepts of individuality and freedom, he poses new questions about the possibilities of human emancipation and participatory democracy. Our understanding of the broadening of the context of his ideas and the traditions he borrows upon helps us to expand the content of his theory of social justice.[1]

The crucial concepts from the previous chapters focused on Locke's theory of the ethical principles and structural limits of natural law and Marx's theory of the emancipatory political rights of the citizen. We will return to the issue of natural rights again when examining the nature of political and economic democracy in later chapters in this work. As we have already seen, the law of nature in the seventeenth century was borrowed from the classical Greek and medieval Thomistic traditions as it found its expression in Locke's ethics of compassion, love, friendship, and justice balanced by his theory of labour, sufficiency, and spoilage as the ethical limits to the accumulation of private property and economic expansion. Both of these latter elements were viewed as detrimental to the pre-political good. Also, this chapter on Marx's early *Paris Manuscripts* will help expand our understanding of his theory of natural law. Of course, Marx does not use the term nor mention the traditions from which it comes, but he does clearly offer a secular nontheistic variation of the natural law tradition as he borrows the ethics and economics of a social theory of labour, sufficiency, and human needs from Aristotle, Hooker, and Locke.

The central ideas in this chapter form the basis for a social ethic of virtue, happiness, beneficence, and the good life. Marx accomplishes this through the examination of the nature of creative work (*praxis*), human needs, and economic alienation; his later writings on democracy form the foundation for his politics and the institutional form for his ethics of a good and virtuous life. By following Hegel's early and later writings, Marx rejoins ethics (moral principles) and politics (social institutions). In this manner he moves beyond Enlightenment liberalism as he returns to a richer philosophical tradition in which ethics involves both the development of the rational character of the individual and the political and economic institutions which nurture that individuality and human potentiality (function of man). Ethics in the classical ideal of Aristotle and the modern political theory of Hegel always involves an embedded social ethics whereby moral principles are incorporated into the social life of the community; they are its moral guiding force and its ethical legal justification. Social justice is the fusion of horizons of ethics and politics into one vision of a participatory democracy in the workplace and polity. This will form the ethical and institutional foundations for Marx's theory of justice. The early writings certainly supplement his analysis of political alienation in *On the Jewish Question* while they expand our understanding of economic alienation and his path to human emancipation. This approach will also widen our appreciation for his ideas of equality and freedom beyond person and property to include subjectivity and happiness, as well as the values of classical ethics and politics.

The driving force of Marx's early philosophical writings is the horizon set by German Idealism with its spirit of human consciousness, freedom, and creativity. Alienation is that social form of modern production that undermines the potentialities of the human spirit through the alienation of the product (private property), process (organisation of production), species being (communal self), community (democracy of others), and nature (physical environment).[2] Although Marx frames alienation as the historical destruction of the human soul resulting from the dehumanising nature of work and production in capitalist society, as well as the distortion of human consciousness and freedom in a liberal polity based on power, class, and property, alienation has much deeper roots in an undermining of a phenomenology of spirit and critical self-consciousness. That is, individuals lose not only their humanity in alienating work, but they also lose their potential to dream – to reason, reflect, and offer alternative historical possibilities for species development.

The mind and the body are reunited in capitalism after the Enlightenment had broken nature apart. But it is a sad reunion since both partake of this universal alienation of the spirit where humans lose their own history of critical reflection in the alienation from the product through the loss of control, equality, and decision-making in producing their own world (Aristotle and Rousseau); from the process through the loss of aesthetic creativity and artisanship (Winckelmann and Schiller); from the self through the loss of freedom, rationality, self-determination, and moral sovereignty (Kant and Hegel); from others through a loss of community, *Sittlichkeit*, democracy, and the ethical community (Torah, Hebrew Prophets, Aristotle, Spinoza, Rousseau, and Hegel); and from nature through the loss of our immediate physical environment and living ecology (Epicurus, L.H. Morgan, J. von Liebig, C. Darwin, and P. Proudhon). We have not only lost our immediate social and physical environments and no longer control our own history or fate, we have also lost the ability to reason and reflect on alienation itself to fully appreciate the meaning of our own lives and histories. There is a strong humanist existential element in Marx's early analysis of work.[3] Alienation steals not only our work but also our reason and self-conscious history of enlightenment. The traditions by which we could rediscover and reclaim our own intellectual and philosophical heritage necessary to give birth to critical reflection from the ancient Hebrews and Greeks, through modern political theory, Romantic poetry and art, and German Idealism have been lost too. And to give this self-consciousness of the tradition a name is to call it a phenomenology of natural law. As a final introductory word, alienation is not just a social critique of capital but a way of articulating the basis for Marx's theory of ethics and politics since it provides the reader with his view of virtue, freedom, and human subjectivity. In the state of nature before political emancipation, Locke's theory of natural rights was circumscribed by moral principles and economic and structural limits; in the state of nature of rampant capitalism before human emancipation, Marx's theory of natural law is bounded by an ethics of virtue and beneficence and the structures of freedom and democracy. In both cases, ethics and economics are closely aligned to produce a truly human world based on the divine creative will of God for Locke or the divine creative will of humanity for Marx.

Alienation and the Virtue of Work and Self-Determination

Alienation is the dehumanised and estranged work conditions of the capitalist mode of production, but it is also the manner in which Marx introduces his view of a historical and social human nature. He begins the essay, 'Alienated Labour', with an appeal to the immediate empirical reality of the prevailing economic system by accepting its major categories of political economy, including private property, division of labour, market, capital (profit), and land (rent). How and why this economic system developed is simply assumed by classical economists but never explained. Marx's goal is to show the relationship between the structures and functions of a capitalist economy and the complex system of alienation among workers. He rejects the method of the political theorists who attempt to explain the rise of capitalism using the primordial state of nature argument which he sees as a set of rationalist assumptions and clever deductions with no ability to inquire into the actual historical origins of capitalism itself. Here he has taken up Hegel's critique of empiricism and the natural rights tradition. He likens economics to theology in that the latter asserts the original state of grace and the Fall as an empirical fact without justification. Marx begins with the existing conditions of work under capitalism: poverty of work, the fragmentation of workers, the devaluation of work into a commodity, and the growing inequality and class divisions created by the new economic system. It is this economic situation which must be first examined and explained.

The first form of alienation (*Entfremdung*) is expressed in the loss of the objects produced in the workplace. Labour is not simply an abstract term used to define a general type of human activity, but is an activity performed within the modern economy of capitalist production. Marx uses the terms 'objectification' (*Vergegenständlichung*) and 'externalisation' (*Entäusserung*) which he borrowed from Hegel, to explain this economic activity. Labour produces objects or commodities which are not owned by the workers themselves. This objectification, or turning labour into an object or commodity, and externalisation, or producing an object outside of the control of the worker, produce commodities for sale in a market economy. However, they also produce a historically specific form of work and worker. It is the latter which interests Marx the most. The result is that the 'object produced by labour, its product, now stands opposed to it as an *alien being*, as a *power independent* of the producer'.[4] Workers live in a world constructed by them over which they have no control; their very beings have been externalised and imprisoned in a foreign economic system. The world produced is one ruled by private property and capitalist production, and ultimately justified by the political and legal system. Labour has no control over any aspect of the product produced by this system because it is owned by the capitalist, not labour. Workers, in turn, become subservient to the object and its mechanical economic laws and social relationships because they have no legal power of disposition over the products of their own labour. This is the bourgeois world of property and person and the limits of equality and freedom.

Marx likens this form of alienation to religion since humans have created a metaphysical universe of sin and punishment, grace and salvation, and ecclesiastical power – all governed by God and natural law – over which humans have no control. He views religion as a destructive concept governed by an alien force which undermines the virtues of humanity for goodness and happiness. 'The more of himself man attributes to God the less he has left in himself. The worker puts his life into the object, and his life then belongs no longer to himself but to the object'.[5] The more compassion, love, justice, and charity humans attribute to God, the less is left to humanity; everything human is devalued because it comes from God, not humanity itself. Every aspect of human life, its goals, values, ideals, and ultimate reality are defined and organised by God; humanity's final goal is religious salvation and metaphysical happiness. There is nothing left for humans to accomplish but to passively serve the external force of a metaphysical principle. Everything human becomes projected onto an external object over which they have no control and that rules their daily lives as an alien power. The most positive elements of humanity are externalised onto a transcendent God or an immanent market. The end result of theology and economics is the same. Humans create a world that is foreign to them, which they do not understand and to which they cannot relate; and, in the end, it steals their humanity and dignity. There is nothing left for humans to do but serve; life itself becomes a form of 'servitude to the object', a form of mechanical idolatry to that which is created by humans themselves.[6] We worship ourselves as a worship of the divine laws of God or the deterministic laws of the marketplace without realising this as a form of idolatrous alienation. In the process of an unconscious self-worship, we lose all that is good and virtuous in humanity – reason, compassion, kindness, wisdom, friendship, citizenship, and justice. These values are 'objectified' onto an 'external' metaphysical and economic system over which we have no control or understanding. In the end, we lose the moral principles of natural law derived from the ancients and filtered through earlier traditions which gave meaning and purpose to human life.

Although Marx is clearly talking about the physical abuse of estranged labour under capitalism, his real concern appears to be for the spiritual implications of this kind of work. The more the worker creates, the poorer he or she becomes due to the increase in power of the profits and capital going to a particular class in society. As the economy grows, poverty and inequality measurably increase. Workers are producing their own poverty since they are always a necessary part of the production process but receive less and less of the material benefits and rewards. Marx recognises that the more wealth a society creates, the more human misery and personal disenchantment result. 'The *devaluation* of the human world increases in direct relation with the *increase in value* of the world of things'.[7] Work creates commodities along with a certain type of work and its corresponding social relations among workers, managers, and owners; it creates commodities and a social system. But the real damage is done to the human soul since as the economy becomes stronger 'the more powerful becomes the world of objects which he creates in face of himself, the poorer he becomes in his inner life, and the less he belongs to himself'.[8] Not only is the body in servitude to this new economic system which it worships as a god, but the spirit and self-consciousness of humanity is severely damaged – its inner self as its essence, being, and potentiality is lost.

Marx is now pushing Hegel's concept of the alienation of consciousness beyond the Enlightenment, Kantian philosophy, and the French Revolution; he places it squarely in the organisation of production and the structures of private property. The worker not only does not own productive property, he no longer owns his own person or the ability to define and create the social world. Marx characterises the transformed person in this society as 'worthless', 'crude and misshapen', 'deformed', 'barbarous', and 'homeless' living in an alien and hostile world.[9] The whole fabric of Locke's defence of natural rights in the state of nature and political society collapses under the weight of Marx's critique of capitalist production. Locke's idea of liberalism is that we own our own bodies, labour, actions, and their products. This is what protects our rights to life, liberty, and equality. But the new mode of production of modern society has resulted in a new social organisation of production which, in the end, forms a society that is anathema to the very values and principles of liberalism itself.

The second form of alienation appears in the process or method of production. The activity of work is powerless and joyless with no sense of identification with the object it produces. No longer is the worker part of a team of apprentices, journeymen, and masters in the neighbourhood workshop and village guild who own their own work area and tools and make all the relevant decisions regarding the quality of their production. Now workers are simply mechanical tools themselves and part of the means of industrial production owned by others. Work is no longer a reflection of human nature and self-determination since the worker 'does not fulfil himself in his work but denies himself, has a feeling of misery rather than well-being, does not develop freely his mental and physical energies but is physically exhausted and mentally debased'.[10] Underlying Marx's critical analysis of the structures of alienation is a recognition of the function and ideal of humanity. Before one can take a critical position on the economy, there must be some perspective on human nature, the 'function of man', or the final cause or telos that directs that criticism; existence can only be judged by essence or final causality. This is central since it offers the perspective by which to make critical judgements about the nature of work, production, and property in nineteenth-century capitalist society. Marx is integrating his empirical analysis of alienation with his ethics to arrive at the beginnings of a critique of political economy and, thereby, expanding the range of issues discussed under the heading of social justice.

Underlying his theory of alienation is a particular understanding of human nature (human need) based on the creativity, spontaneity, and productivity of work as *praxis*; treating humans as ends in themselves; realising the physical and spiritual needs or ultimate ends of humanity; creating a world of beauty, proportion, and elegance; defining humans in political terms of freedom and self-determination; and, finally, providing the space and spirit for a true moral community. Drawing upon a wide range of philosophical, political, and aesthetic traditions, Marx has constructed a modern social concept of the individual that goes well beyond the boundaries set by the positive ideals of natural rights and liberalism. The philosophical strengths of his theory of humanity lie in his incorporation of modern British, French, and German social theory with ancient and medieval natural law principles within an empirical analysis of the actual conditions of industrial production and class formation. This is Marx's real contribution to modern social theory – his fusion of the ideals of the ancients and moderns, natural law and natural rights, ethics and politics, and ethics and science as he moves beyond the limits of Enlightenment science, morality, and politics to a broader appreciation of the potentiality and ideals of humanity.

Production itself is alienating because of its very organisation and design for greater efficiency and productivity at the expense of the human spirit. Labour is divided into the most mechanical and mindless jobs which offer owners greater flexibility and interchangeability of their moveable and segmented parts. With the fragmentation and division of labour, more products are produced faster and cheaper but under conditions of forced labour and industrial servitude. With this modern reorganisation of production in the factory, the workers lose a sense of the whole process of production from the beginning to the end. They are no longer involved in the overall organisation, planning, imagination, or creativity of work and what is produced; they can only concentrate on the mindlessly narrow range of assigned tasks dictated by owners, managers, and supervisors. In the process of production there is a corresponding loss of the meaning and purpose of human labour – of human life itself; workers lose their humanity and their divinity as art and praxis are reduced to wage labour. Marx is appalled by the suffering and powerlessness resulting from capitalist work. Perhaps the most revealing idea in this essay is the line that 'it [work] is not the satisfaction of a need, but only a *means* for satisfying other needs'.[11] The 'other needs' mentioned by Marx are the physical needs or means for the mere continuance of physical life. Work in this context simply satisfies our need for self-preservation. This was the concept upon which Hobbes and Locke built their political theories; Marx turns it on its head so that it is no longer the bedrock of political obligation or natural rights but the basis for economic alienation. Under the alienating and oppressive conditions of modern industrial labour, the satisfaction of true needs as ends in themselves is lost. Marx calls for work that is an end or need in itself. This would involve a kind of work that fulfils workers as real individuals, helps define them as rational beings, and supports their nature as species or communal beings. All this has been suppressed in order to maintain a system of class, profits, and production. Unfortunately from Marx's perspective, Aristotle's 'theory of needs' for moral and intellectual virtues in a moral economy has been supplanted in modern industrial society by Hegel's 'system of needs' in a market economy. The irony in Marx's analysis is that the only refuge of the worker from these conditions of 'homelessness' lies in leisure time away from work in the activities of eating, drinking, and procreation. In the twentieth century even these isolated places of leisure and consumption, which workers had previously used to hide from the monotony and stultification of work, have themselves become homes for the commercialisation and repression of their private lives.[12]

Work as Productive Life and Creative Beauty

The third type of alienation lies in the effects of the economy on the nature of humans as species beings. In the process of production humans are alienated from their own self-identifying activity as communal beings. 'For labour, *life activity, productive life*, now appear to man only as *means* for the satisfaction of a need, the need to maintain his physical existence. Productive life is, however, species life. It is life creating life. In this type of life activity resides the whole character of a species, its species character'.[13] Labour is a means for satisfying the basic human need for physical survival, but, perhaps more importantly, it is also an end in itself as a life activity that defines our existence, creates our values and social institutions, directs our personal fate and individual biography, and forms the history of our species. Labour as praxis is a fundamental need of humanity to create the world we live in according to our own ideals and plans. It is built on the premises of individual freedom, self-determination, and human dignity which are the main characteristics that differentiate the human species from other animals. Marx will argue throughout his life as a historical materialist that human nature is something that evolves throughout time and through different historical social forms that humans themselves create. However, by introducing a historicist element into the discussion he does not thereby undermine the idea that there is in his writings a clear view of human nature that transcends history; historicism is not to be reduced to nihilism. Historicism and human nature are not incompatible terms when dialectically interrelated. Without essence or telos, there is no critique, no purpose, and no existential meaning to human existence; but without existence, there is no actualisation of essence or nature, only endless becoming in a meaningless world. How human essence appears in history can be uncovered through theoretical and empirical research. But underlying its different historical forms is this view that humans are species beings who through their own labour and the social organisation of production create their own universe both theoretically and practically (technologically and ethically). In effect, humans are divine because the world they inhabit, which can be oppressive and mindless, can only be reconstructed along self-conscious designs according to aesthetic drives, human needs, and political ideals. According to Marx, we are what we eat (Feuerbach), but we are also what we create (Kant and Hegel), and it is this creative capacity of humans to form their relationships with themselves, nature, and society that is the main defining element of our species being. 'Free, conscious activity is the species character of human beings'.[14]

There is a dialectic here between essence and existence, between species being and history. Since we create our being, it changes over time reflecting the economic and political systems in which it develops; but there is also a residual element of human nature and human needs in the historical process. We create our world, but we do so socially and historically. The content of that world changes throughout time but the need to create, to form political communities and obligations, to structure the productive process, and to move in a universe of self-consciousness and freedom are all essential elements of our self-understanding as human beings. In the process of creating and legislating our social lives, history becomes an object of our 'self-conscious being' as we create the social institutions of the objective spirit and the moral values of the subjective spirit in ethics and politics. This integration of free, self-conscious creativity in society, this integration of reason and will, spirit and heart, politics and ethics forms the foundation of Marx's theory of natural law and social justice in his early writings. He has simply given Hegel a materialist foundation for self-consciousness and freedom in political economy. Marx continues to stress that the main difference between animals and humans is that the latter produce universally and are driven by more than physical needs; they are driven by a need to self-consciously create themselves. Human beings reproduce themselves practically within nature and a community, and reproduce themselves theoretically as universal values in morals, ethics, and politics – as ends in themselves in a free and democratic community. It is the self-consciousness of these values that defines labour as an activity of species life. The true human need is not for survival but for nature and humanity. 'Animals produce only themselves, while man reproduces the whole of nature'.[15] Humanity produces the environment and human nature; the social ecology and social relationships; and reflective theory as natural science and critical science. All this is accomplished following the aesthetic and moral 'laws of beauty' in which the sensuous and reason, matter and form are integrated into a beautiful work of art.[16]

This notion of the laws of beauty is taken from Friedrich Schiller's *On the Aesthetic Education of Man* (1794), Expanding upon the ideas of subjectivity (consciousness) and human creativity, Schiller has taken Kant's theory of knowledge and representations as a synthesis of the mind (forms of intuition and categories of the understanding) and body (sensuous impressions) in the formation of a coherent object of perception and experience. He developed a theory of aesthetics in which sensuousness and reason are integrated into the objective experience of art. Hegel had added the notions of the phenomenology of spirit, history, and society to show how the Objective Spirit or human self-consciousness articulated in social institutions results in greater freedom. Within the German Idealist tradition, the objects of knowledge evolved from objects of experience, phenomenal self-consciousness and the spirit of culture, and aesthetics and art, to the objects of work. Schiller writes that through art 'Man carries the potentiality for divinity within himself' by creating the world of our own experience.[17] The world is not given but has infinite possible expressions as it is formally sculptured in a reciprocal exchange between the human senses and reason. When the two are reconciled in a harmonious unity, there is an aesthetic unity of beauty 'whose highest ideal is therefore to be sought in the most perfect possible union and equilibrium of reality and form'.[18] Truth and freedom occur when beauty integrates the opposing forces in nature and society to the point where reality is formed by the moral and political ideal. Marx borrows from Schiller's ideal that beauty is the highest manifestation of the dignity, gracefulness, and nobility of humanity as he integrates epistemology, phenomenology, and aesthetics in the earliest writings to create his own theory of work and alienation. The species life of humanity is a form of beauty that creates the world that surrounds us. The passive acceptance of the world through the senses of experience (empiricism), art (sensuous perception), morality (utilitarianism), and science (positivism) disfigures humanity and turns the sovereign into a slave, ends into means.[19]

According to Marx, work, as the integration of nature and consciousness, sensuousness and reason, is an aesthetic experience by which we give form and order to the universe – the unity of nature – as we construct our immediate physical world, but also the moral and social world that gives meaning and coherence to human life. Human beings are inherently sovereign and divine because of this creative power to shape their sensuous and spiritual environment. It is this process of giving form to nature and society which is beautiful. Schiller so elegantly expresses this feeling about the unity of matter and form: 'When both qualities are united, Man will combine the greatest fullness of existence with the utmost self-dependence and freedom, and instead of abandoning himself to the world he will rather draw it into himself with the whole infinity of its phenomena, and subject it to the unity of his reason'.[20] In an alienated economy, work is functionally dismembered and distorted; it loses all meaning as we are unable to construct reality according to the laws of beauty. In the end, we only have an ability to make persons, profits, and property. Work, as art and the true spirit of human creativity, is turned into profit accumulation to maintain class rights and privileges. The ethics of species being is displaced by an ethic of natural rights and possessive individualism, the true materialist view of history.

In a capitalist society, objectification leads to the alienation of work based on private property and the division of labour.[21] However, in a free society, objectification becomes the concrete manifestation of self-determination in the work of the human species. Through physical and intellectual labour we become conscious creators of the concepts, ideas, theories, and methods that reflect the human species at a particular historical moment in time (historical materialism). The theoretical objectifications of the Enlightenment in the natural and social sciences reflect the material foundations of society in a capitalist mode of production. We see in science what we ourselves have placed there from consciousness and society. Concepts are merely the theoretical reflection in consciousness of the economic world; in an ironic, and perhaps perverse way, concepts are the mirror of reality and the mirror of production. The Enlightenment and capitalism are inextricably interlinked.[22] In an alienated economy, self-consciousness and freedom to create – the basis of life for the species being – become impossible because the ideas we have are not consciously chosen, nor is our creative activity self-conscious and free. In this type of economy, workers have lost control over the product and process of production; now workers have lost their essence as a species being. And as a result of this transformation, the worker is alienated from others within the community.

The final social form of alienation is that of the estrangement of the worker from others in the workplace as alienation recreates the class relations of production between the bourgeoisie and the proletariat just as it produces profits and property. (Alienation from nature will be discussed as part of the chapter on ecological justice). It is here that Marx stresses that private property is not the cause of alienation, but its product. The cause lies in the structures of power and privilege of a class system for the organisation of work and the expropriation of surplus and profits. Property stands in the same relationship to alienation as religion does to humanity. Just as property is the result of alienated labour and the social system that underlies it, religion and its gods are the consequence and product of human reason. These causal connections are important in order to appreciate the contradictions of society and the real possibilities of social change. This is especially true in Marx's relations to the socialist Pierre Proudhon. Accepting property as the cause of capitalist production not only misses the historical origins of capitalism, it also has important implications for the reorganisation of the social life of production. Marx is attempting to uncover the structural dynamic within alienation between labour and private property. By viewing property as the cause of alienation, its alleviation would necessitate an increase in wages which he argues would 'be nothing more than a *better remuneration of slaves*, and would not restore, either to the worker or to the work, their human significance and worth'.[23] Proudhon had called for an 'equality of incomes' as the only adequate solution to the problem of alienation within the capitalist mode of production. But, according to Marx, this is a totally inadequate understanding and response to the reality of capitalism. Rights and distribution of property must be understood within a more comprehensive critique of political economy and democracy. Not being able to see the relationship between essence and existence, the logic and structure of capital and its daily empirical appearances, is not to have an adequate theory of the real possibilities for social change.

As in the case of the Jewish question, Marx's solution moves beyond political emancipation and the readjustment of wages – beyond rights and distributive justice. Economic redistribution is not the immediate answer to the problems of the structures of alienation. Alienation is neither a psychological condition of cultural adjustment to, or personal estrangement from, the institutions of modernity; nor is it a question of the just distribution of income and wealth within capitalism. Marx calls for the more radical solution of human emancipation as he moves beyond the simple adjustments of political rights, obligations, and distribution of property incomes. Political solutions to the contradictions between labour and production are merely theological solutions as they leave untouched the reality and theory of political economy. Both political emancipation and political economy, as the practice and theory of capital, conceal the actual forms of structural and organisational alienation in the class relationships of production. Alienation is reduced to the existence of a thing that can be changed with some adjustments and accommodations within the present system. Social relationships become a fetish hidden behind the object of private property and are never critically examined as part of the laws of political economy.

Ethics, Human Needs, and Natural Law

These questions about the alienation of labour lead Marx to a further discussion about the nature of private property in another early essay of the *Economic and Philosophical Manuscripts of 1844*, entitled 'Private Property and Communism'. This early essay on private property and communism begins where the previous essay on alienation left off with a critical analysis of Proudhon's socialism and the latter's suggestion for expanded remuneration and a fair wage in production. Marx contends that Proudhon's call for an equality of wages among workers only equalises alienation as everyone becomes an 'abstract capitalist'. For him, the utopian socialist form of distributive justice is inadequate because it never questions the underlying form of capitalist production or its notions of alienation and production. It does not see that the subjective essence of private property is labour or that its objective manifestation is capital; and it is this very relationship between labour and capital that is problematic. To critically examine the nature of private property requires that alienated labour and capital be seen as irreconcilable contradictory forces in production that are reflected in the structures and classes of society. The fair distribution of property and wages is not the real issue if it leaves intact the actual structures of alienation that created the initial contradictions between labour and capital in the first place. A demand for distributive justice is also inadequate because it does not examine the assumptions of this 'crude communism' and its relations to real human needs. Marx's theory of needs adds another crucial dimension to his early theory of human nature along with his previously discussed investigation into the nature of work and species being. These central categories of work, species being, and human needs are, in turn, intimately connected to the theory of practical reason and natural law of Aristotle and the social ethics of Kant and Hegel.

Marx quickly considers and rejects the political recommendations for the amelioration of the negative effects of private property in the writings of Charles Fourier, Henri de Saint-Simon, and Proudhon. He concludes that by universalising private property, giving all the workers their fair share, property has not been eliminated, but only universalised to all. Workers now become capitalists and thereby engage in their own form of self-exploitation; distributive justice not correctly perceived or understood leads to further alienation. This type of socialism represents only the generalisation and completion of capitalist relations of production that absorbs workers and the community into a 'crude and unreflective communism'.[24] Under these conditions communism becomes the universal form of capitalism. However, nothing has changed the underlying social relations of production and their dehumanising effects of reducing human life to the domination of nature and humanity. Alienation as the destruction of rational human possibilities remains unseen and unexamined.

Property has been universalised while production remains particular, estranged, and foreign: distributive justice in this form of communism is simply radical liberalism. It represents a dissolving of Locke's class structure at the level of distribution and consumption while maintaining it at the level of property and production. Alienating work along with private property has become universal. 'The relation of private property remains the relation of the community to the world of things'.[25] Property relationships in the form of labour and production now permeate all physical and spiritual aspects of human life. The Lockean ideals and rights of person, liberty, health, and survival are all reduced to the market imperatives of property and capital. Rights, distribution, and justice are no longer ethical principles that provide the goals and limits of liberalism or the possibilities of socialism. They are now simply reflections of the primacy of private property. They are liberal values that do not touch the heart of alienated production. Rather, they are subsumed under the internal logic of capitalist production to be revived only as ideological supports and rationalisations of the market economy.

Marx sees that creative work, economic freedom, and self-determination are essential parts of human virtue and the social life of the community; without them humans lose their species being and thus the very essence of humanity itself. Under the alien conditions of capitalism, we live a life of servitude and possessive individualism with its distorted forms of personal liberty, freedom, and justice within industrial production and a market economy. We are no longer sovereign creatures who define our own history, culture, and social institutions but, instead, live in an alien world estranged from the productive features of the good life within the community. Natural rights have been truly universalised but at the expense of natural law. The capitalist has exchanged virtue and freedom for property and liberty, human emancipation and social justice for liberal rights and income redistribution. And this is not a fair exchange.

Marx now makes an interesting comparison of the private property of capital to the private property of marriage as he contrasts capitalist production to bourgeois marriage. Both production and marriage are forms of private property in nineteenth-century society. Marx hypothesises that if the solution to the problems of capitalism is to universalise property, then the solution to the exclusivity and private ownership of women in marriage would be to universalise women within the community – turn women into common property and the universal prostitutes of men. 'One may say that this idea of the *community of women* is the *open secret* of this entirely crude and unreflective communism'.[26] Both property and women in this form of communism would become universally owned. The absurdity of the suggestion by Marx about women is only surpassed by the original absurdity of the political suggestion by the utopian socialists. Neither solution resolves any of the problems of the alienation and oppression of work or women; neither solution understands or deals with the real problems of the body of private property under consideration. Both forms of crude and underdeveloped communism are market solutions applied to their particular areas since both resolve their issues by 'envy and competition', not by critical or reflective thought. The abolition of private property is attained by making everyone an abstract capitalist or universal prostitute, which involves keeping the repressive social system intact without the necessity of changing the alienation of production or its cultural values. This transformation of self-alienation places the individual back beyond human and political emancipation to a place of universal enmity and competition. This perversion of the species being and humanity's relation to nature and women turns the community into a universal capitalist and results in an 'infinite degradation'. Alienation is liberalised and the immediate physical relationship to nature and women is equalised. The solution to the problem is not the universalising of private property but its abolition, in labour and capital, production and consumption, and industry and the market.

The relationship of men to women under capitalism is, for Marx, the barometer by which humanity's relationship to nature is measured. 'The relation of man to woman is the *most natural* relation of human being to human being. It indicates, therefore, how far man's *natural* behaviour has become *human*, and how far his *human* essence has become a *natural* essence for him, how far his *human nature* has become *nature* for him'.[27] Of central importance to Marx is that the relationship of men to women also reflects a change in the nature of human needs. The true intimate bond between two individuals is a fundamental physical and social need and not simply a mechanical pairing for society's reproduction and self-preservation. This human need is destroyed when it is replaced by a social bond based on property and rights. The questions raised by crude communism offer Marx the opportunity to consider the communal ramifications of private property and open a new consideration of the central Aristotelian notion of human needs. What makes us human? What defines us as communal or species beings? And what is our natural essence as living beings? Are humans simply historical and material beings changing with the winds of technology and the economy? Is all human interaction relative to the empirical moment? Is each person a grain of sand blown around by the wind while having no more substantive reason for being other than an accidental fate of nature and existence? Or is there a core set of moral principles that guide us through life providing direction and purpose? The issue of human needs in Marx plays a similar role to Aristotle's ethical and political theory and Aquinas's natural law theory – needs reflect human nature and its underlying moral values. In Aristotle this is manifested in the need for intellectual and moral virtue, the need for family, friendship, and citizenship, and the need for economic (distributive and reciprocal) and political (democracy) justice. Marx summarises this change when he writes: 'It will be seen from this, how, in place of the *wealth* and *poverty* of political economy, we have the *wealthy* man and the plenitude of *human* need'.[28] It is at this point in his analysis of political and economic alienation that the solution lies embedded within human history in the ancient and medieval traditions of nature and need.

Alienation is now replaced by need as the defining characteristic of the species life of humanity. These needs will delineate what is human and social in our species being. Is it the need for self-preservation (Hobbes), the need for natural rights and property (Locke), or the need for the harmony and self-consciousness of the Absolute Spirit (Hegel)? The fundamental driving force of humans, according to Marx, is the need for self-realisation, a purposeful life of meaning, and a sense of community and responsibility with others which begins with the end of private property and human self-degradation.[29] If alienation was the result of the estrangement of individuals from the loss of control over property, the process of production, one's self-conscious activity and life direction, and one's species being and the community, then true human needs would represent a reclamation of these very losses. Alienation is simply the modern incarnation of chrematistic production. Rediscovering and reclaiming spiritual control and direction over property and production, self-identity and self-determination of one's inner life, and emancipation of our species and communal being for the common good and general welfare are the real goals of a critical and democratic socialism. These are the activities of the social being of praxis and the social life – these 'become the *activity* of my being'.[30]

Towards the end of this essay on the human emancipation from private property and alienation, Marx summarises the central elements for his moral theory of human need – the need for individuality, self-consciousness, creative activity, freedom, nobility, companionship, sovereignty, and self-determination are the defining characteristics of the species being.[31] 'A man who lives by the favour of another considers himself a dependent being. But I live completely by another person's favour when I owe to him not only the continuance of my life but also *its creation*; when he is its *source*'.[32] When abstractions become the source of the human essence, whether it is God or private property, we lose our essence to religion and economics – we lose our natural being as creators of our immediate theoretical and practical environment.[33] These characteristics are what make us human and divine, and are what are most abrogated at the moment of alienation. When the spiritual needs of virtue and goodness are replaced by the materialist needs of money and wealth in liberalism, human life no longer has a meaningful and moral purpose. Although Marx reaffirms his atheism at the end of the essay on private property and communism by rejecting the existence of God and reasserting the primacy of the essence of humanity as creators, he does so in a very unusual manner: He reaffirms those ethical principles that lie at the heart of the natural law in the Hebrew, Greek, and Christian traditions, while fighting against the same materialism, utilitarianism, and liberalism that sought, if only unconsciously, to undermine those ancient and medieval traditions. One can only wonder if Marx appreciated the irony underlying his whole social theory?

The concepts of species being and human need are expressions of the essence of humanity or rational human nature that, in turn, provide the ethical foundations for his critique of liberalism and capitalism, as well as the ethical directives for a socialist society. Species being and human need are both forms of a secular natural law. Still relying on Hegelian terminology, Marx refers to the truly free human being as a universal self-consciousness, but now placed within the historical and empirical conditions of modern industrial society. The new ideal is not represented by aesthetic, religious, or philosophical self-consciousness of the cultural Objective Spirit but by a socialist party of artisans who have a new need and end for humanity in the recovery of the species being of individuals in society itself. Marx refers to this new need of friendship as the collective self-awareness within 'the brotherhood of man' (*Brüderlichkeit der Menschen*) and characterises it as the essential reality and highest need of humanity in the workplace.[34]

Marx rejects any division between science and ethics as he characterises the moral values of capitalism as privation, gain, thrift, and sobriety. These values express the unnatural law of economics as the perverse values of egoism and asceticism whose 'principal thesis is the renunciation of life and of human needs ... The less you are, the less you express your life, the more you have, the greater is your alienated life and the greater is the saving of your alienated being'.[35] Throughout these early essays of the *Paris Manuscripts*, alienation is generally described as the displacement of ethics and the disfigurement of virtue and the species life and activity of humanity. It manifests itself in the class organisation of production, labour, and private property, but the real effects of alienation reach deeply into the very spirit and being of the human species. Political economy has always been, as are the other social sciences, a moral science because underlying its objective and neutral disposition has been an underlying metaphysics of money.[36]

Opposed to human needs that express human potentiality and virtue, there are also artificial and egoistic needs of the market that are self-stupefying and utilitarian and that produce only crude dependency and degradation to the machinery of production. This is an alienation of consumption and unhealthy needs that completes the cycle of market reproduction. 'The need for money is, therefore, the real need created by the modern economic system, and the only need which it creates'.[37] It creates a consumer psychology of market appetites and false desires that are 'inhuman, depraved, unnatural, and *imaginary*' that return the individual back to a state of 'bestial savagery' and 'crude barbarism'. But these false needs are reduced to the simple reproduction of labour's physical existence (later he will use the term labour power). There are now no longer authentic needs of praxis or activity for the creation of the possibilities of human life.[38] Marx refers to this form of alienation as a 'pure abstraction from all activity' in which the species being no longer creates the world of objects in consciousness or the self and social life in self-consciousness. Humanity is simply surrendered to the alien forces of labour and production. Human subjectivity, as self-conscious creativity and freedom, that is, as practical activity, is lost and forgotten in a world designed by the laws of economics and machine production. The nature and product of work in capitalism is not part of human nature, but a distortion of it.

Virtue and Late Medieval Thomistic Natural Law

Richard Tawney published an important work in 1926 on the rise of capitalism and the decline of natural law in Europe entitled *Religion and the Rise of Capitalism*. Responding to Max Weber's thesis in *The Protestant Ethic and the Spirit of Capitalism* (1905) that Calvinism with its theological doctrines of faith, asceticism, and predestination was a major cultural underpinning to the historical origins of capitalism, Tawney took a more materialist approach in arguing that the religious and cultural features of modern society developed after and in response to the rise of commercial and industrial capitalism. It was in this work, while outlining the moral theology of medieval Christian economics within natural law theory which was losing its powerful influence in the sixteenth and seventeenth centuries, that Tawney referred to Marx as the 'last of the Schoolmen' or last of the late medieval theologians. This was a clear reference to the fact that Marx stood at the end of a long line of moral philosophers and theologians who developed theories of the value of labour and the economic ethics of natural law.[39]

By characterising Marx as the 'last of the Schoolmen', Tawney was referring to Thomas Aquinas's labour theory of value and the continuity of traditions between Marx and neo-Aristotelian medieval Scholasticism. Tawney argued that Marx was the end of a long tradition of theorists that included the thirteenth-century theologian Thomas Aquinas, the fourteenth-century scholastic Henry of Langenstein, and the sixteenth-century Protestant reformer Martin Luther who made the point that the appropriate and 'reasonable remuneration' of wages for a worker or merchant should be based on their labour and contribution to the common good. 'The medieval theorist condemned as a sin precisely that effort to achieve a continuous and unlimited increase in material wealth which modern societies applaud as a quality, and the vices for which he reserved his most merciless denunciations were the more refined and subtle of the economic virtues'.[40] The Scholastics considered economic speculation, avarice, and exploitation as 'unpardonable sins' as they stressed 'the just price and prohibition of usury'. Usury was condemned because it was living without labour.[41] This natural law became part of ecclesiastical doctrine and cannon law of medieval Christianity. This was their economic ethic and, according to Tawney, Marx must be considered within the theoretical and historical context of this tradition.[42] Tawney recognised the utopian element of medieval economic ethics in the face of the transformation of the market economy, agricultural productivity, and the industrial and financial explosion of the sixteenth century. The dramatic growth of international markets and banking, colonial expansion in the Americas, the imperial state, commercial towns, guild and monopoly organisations, new merchant and joint stock companies, along with the emergence of Antwerp and Lisbon rather than Rome and southern German cities as the centres for international commerce during the period of the Reformation, led to the evolution of Scholastic theology and ethics in both the Roman and Reformed Churches.[43]

Christianity focused on issues of money, interest, business finance, legitimate trade, just price, labour, and the condition of the poor, along with the general moral limits of economic activity, as its ethical and theological response to the rise of the new economic system. However, in spite of this movement of history, Tawney writes: 'Labor – the common lot of mankind – is necessary and honorable; trade is necessary, but perilous to the soul; finance, if not immoral, is at best sordid and at worst disreputable'.[44] Trade and reasonable profits are central to a society which cannot satisfy the classical and medieval need for self-sufficiency; profits based on middle-man commerce are always of a 'dubious propriety' and should always be calculated on the basis of 'labor, skill, and risks'.[45] Tawney continues his analysis with the comment that 'the suspicion of economic motives had been one of the earliest elements in the social teaching of the Church ... In medieval philosophy the ascetic tradition, which condemned all commerce as the sphere of iniquity, was softened by practical necessities, but it was not obliterated'.[46] It supported the material life of the community, but undermined justice and charity; it transformed trade from a means to an end. Because trade and profits also encouraged an extreme individualism of aggressive appetites and inhuman lustful desires, social theologians saw it as both a necessary phenomenon for the survival of society but also likened it to holding a wolf by the ears because it was both 'perilous to the soul and essential to society'. As Tawney outlines the fourteenth-century medieval critique of merchant speculations, the same issues mentioned by Locke are present – moral condemnation of economic activity not based on the positive values of labour, sufficiency (support of family and beneficence), and need (spoilage). Wealth acquisition beyond labour restraints is condemned as a deadly sin of 'avarice, sensuality, and pride'.[47]

In addition to the parasitic merchants, the medieval theologians condemned usury (interest on loans or higher prices of items bought on credit) and organised industry and monopolies. This was a society of peasant farmers and small workshop masters. Tawney briefly outlines Aquinas's labour theory of value through his theory of the just price. Prices in the market were to be determined by the labour contained in the product. The market was not set up to service the interests of economic expediency or impersonal forces of supply and demand, although even in the fourteenth century issues of utility and the market were being considered.[48] The market was limited by a clear articulation of moral principles that constrained market activity and accumulation. Anything beyond the community consensus could be characterised as a moral transgression and was intended to contain extortion and usury.

Usury had been rejected by scripture and by Aristotle since 'it is to live without labour; it is to sell time, which belongs to God, for the advantage of wicked men; it is to rob those who use the money lent ...'.[49] It is contrary to the laws of God, nature, and man and condemned by the Catholic Church in its various ecclesiastical Councils from the twelfth to the early fourteenth century which refused to administer confession, absolution, communion, or even burial services to the usurer. In some cases excommunication was recommended. Naturally, of course, monetary restitution is also required of the moral offender, including those merchants found guilty of unnatural wealth acquisition in the market. If those offended cannot be found, then the interest or profits accrued in these immoral transaction should be given to the poor. Even into the sixteenth century, there were prohibitions against 'usurers, masters who withheld wages, covetous merchants who sell fraudulent wares, covetous landlords who grind their tenants', as well as against anyone who exploited and impoverished their neighbour.[50] This is an ethic of compassion, fairness, and mutual aid to the dispossessed. Over time with the growth of the large towns and power of local principalities and the king, the ecclesiastical courts and canon law began to decline until the major economic advances of the sixteenth and seventeenth century forced a reconsideration of all these issues again.

The purpose here is not to definitively establish specific connections between Marx and Aquinas or the medieval Schoolmen, but rather, to tie the logic and framework of Marx's overall theory of justice in ethics, politics, and economics back to the ancient and medieval traditions of Aristotelian social theory and political economy; this is how he defined his view of economic ethics and social justice.[51] Unlike the modern Enlightenment theories of justice, the breadth and depth of Marx's theory reflect the profound influence of these premodern theories. Unlike the theories of liberalism, utilitarianism, and classical economics with their emphasis on material pleasure, happiness, and property, Marx returned to a more classical tradition for his inspiration and insight. In his view the goal of human life is the good or happiness defined as the self-actualisation of human potentiality (human nature and human needs) in ethics (creative praxis of species being and human virtue) and politics (solidarity and democracy). His turn to Aristotle's theory of justice included issues of character, virtue (*arete*), happiness (*eudaimonia*), human need (*chreia*), knowledge, wisdom (*phronesis*), law, constitutions, economic or particular justice, political or universal justice, best societies, and ideal polity.

For Marx, social justice is a moral and intellectual virtue promoting individual freedom, self-development, and self-realisation of human rationality and creativity in productive, aesthetic, and practical activity (*praxis*) and a social ethics for the general welfare and common good within a political and economic democracy. Justice promotes the creative development of human powers, capacities, and character within an egalitarian and free polity. This definition of social justice integrates Aristotle's theory of virtue, the good life, human needs, and justice with Kant's theory of subjectivity, freedom, creativity, and human dignity and Hegel's attempt to integrate German Idealism and

Greek philosophy within the concrete social institutions of the ethical life of the community.[52]

Notes

1   Drucilla Cornell, in her essay 'Should a Marxist Believe in Rights?', *Praxis International* 1 (April 1984), argues that questions of equality, freedom, self-determination, praxis, species being, and human creativity are fundamental issues of justice (pp. 45–56). Philip Kain in *Marx and Ethics* (Oxford: Clarendon Press, 1988) refers to these same categories as the 'moral good' (p. 21). Although Kain sees Marx as reconciling Aristotle (essence) and Kant (universalisation of the categorical imperative) in his ethical theory of species being, freedom, self-actualisation of human potentiality, and moral obligation (pp. 64 and 71), he later separates these issues of ethics and justice (p. 98). He also contends that Marx's early ethical theory is incompatible with his later historical materialism; ethical theory is abandoned beginning with *The German Ideology* in 1845–6 (pp. 1–6, 103, 106, and 199) as a form of ideology and bourgeois thought. He argues that, according to Marx, issues of the state, law, morals, and rights are ultimately manifestations of class and property interests (pp. 77, 83, 97–8, 111–12, 106, and 125–6). Here Kain is clearly following Jürgen Habermas, Albrecht Wellmer, and Alvin Gouldner, who have also articulated this separation and contradiction between ethics and science within Marx's theory. In the third or dialectical phase of his writings in the *Grundrisse* and *Capital*, Marx returns to integrate ethics back into his social theory by means of a 'transcendence of morality' and the 'full and free development of every individual' (p. 153). However, by focusing on Aristotle's influence in his early period with his questions of human nature, essence, freedom, and creativity, Kain unfortunately misses the broader impact of Aristotle on Marx, especially the importance of the former's theory of ethics (virtue, knowledge, and justice), politics (best constitutions and ideal state), and economics (chrematistics and economics) on Marx's later writings.

On these issues, also see George Brenkert, *Marx's Ethics of Freedom* (London: Routledge & Kegan Paul, 1983), pp. 85–130. Brenkert distinguishes between an ethics and virtue of freedom ('character, disposition, and ways of being') and self-development (praxis) grounded in the mode and form of production (forces and relations of production) and a theory of justice based upon distribution, exchange, and consumption (p. 157). Capitalist production undermines human freedom, but at the same time is not unjust because there is an exchange of equivalents in the purchase and reproduction of labour power. Brenkert fails to see that this distinction between production and distribution, as well as virtue and justice, is a false and arbitrary distinction that conceals the breadth of Aristotle's and Marx's theory of social justice.

Allen Buchanan, working within a critical variation of the Tucker-Wood thesis in *Marx and Justice: The Radical Critique of Liberalism* (Totowa, NJ: Rowman and Littlefield, 1982), argues that justice is a derivative and ideological concept of capitalism (historical materialism) and would be irrelevant as a regulatory idea or institution in a socialist or communist society. He writes that Marx 'never so much as suggests that production will be regulated by principles of justice' (p. 59). Buchanan then proceeds in chapter 4 of his work to examine Marx's critique of civil and political rights of man and of the citizen which he argues had been neglected by Robert Tucker and Allen Wood. His conclusion is that Marx believed that communism will so dismantle the structures of power and conflict that there will be no need for any form of juridical or distributive justice; justice is a defective bourgeois concept reflective of both a 'defective society' and of 'the egoistic, isolated individual'. In a post-capitalist world, justice, as well as the state, would be irrelevant and unnecessary. Buchanan concludes with the comment: 'Hence, he [Marx] must conclude, both the rights of man and the rights of the citizen will have no value and hence no place in communism ...' (pp. 64–5).

For the analytic philosophers, justice reflects the legal, civil, and political rights that compensate and correct for the deficiencies of the capitalist social system; for the ancients and Marx, justice, on the other hand, represents the social institutions, structures, and cultural ideals that further the self-development and self-realisation of the human being. That is, they provide the structural foundations for their social dreams. Justice provides the social, political, and historical form within which ethical principles are made real and relevant – the integration of philosophy and sociology, ethics and politics. The ethical dualism of analytic theorists found in their concept of justice between production and distribution is just a further articulation of the political incoherence within their moral philosophy with its separation of morality and social ethics, ethics and social justice, moral philosophy (virtue, character, and happiness) and political economy (structures, institutions, and history), and the individual and community.

2   István Mészáros, *Marx's Theory of Alienation* (New York, NY: Harper Torchbooks, 1972), pp. 38–9 and 254–5. Mészáros concludes that Marx's analysis of alienation and reification is built on the fundamental ontological or anthropological question of human nature or human essence as it evolves in history. An ahistorical, transcendental view of humanity is just another form of religion or mysticism, but in the historical context human nature provides a 'standard or ideal' by which to judge both the moderns and the ancients. This social critique built upon a theory of human nature is the common core for both Marx and Aristotle. 'Such a question [about human nature] cannot be answered ahistorically without being turned into an irrational mystification of some kind' (p. 39). See also Shlomo Avineri, *The Social and Political Thought of Karl Marx* (Cambridge: Cambridge University Press, 1968) for a discussion of the relationship between alienation and human nature (pp. 86–92 and 104–23). Avineri sees the basis for Marx's social critique grounded in both anthropological assumptions of human nature and the actual transformations occurring within society itself – the future is already contained in the present social organisation of production (pp. 92, 131, 142–3, 149, and 180–1). In a crucial point Avineri writes: 'Political power may be crucial for the realization of potentialities, but it does not create the new structures realized. It perfects existing reality ...' (p. 181). The potentialities of human beings and society, along with the principles of equality, freedom, and rights, already exist in the present society. 'Conditions, Marx says, never give rise to ideas; they just make their realisation possible. The *idea* of communism, after all, is as old as Plato, the medieval monasteries, and Thomas More' (p. 187). The ideals of democratic socialism first appeared in the French Revolution but it will take a radical transformation of civil society to bring

about human rights and the rights of the citizen. See also Louis Dupré, *The Philosophical Foundations of Marxism* (New York, NY: Harcourt, Brace & World, 1966), Bertell Ollman, *Alienation: Marx's Conception of Man in Capitalist Society* (Cambridge: Cambridge University Press, 1975), pp. 75–127, Richard Schmitt, *Alienation and Freedom* (Boulder, CO: Westview Press, 2003), and Rahel Jaeggi, *Alienation*, trans. Frederick Neuhouser and Alan Smith (New York, NY: Columbia University Press, 2014).

3   Erich Fromm, *Marx's Concept of Man* (New York, NY: Frederick Ungar Publishing Company, 1961), pp. 3, 29, 61–3, and 71.

4   Karl Marx, 'Alienated Labour', *Karl Marx: Early Writings*, trans. and ed. T.B. Bottomore (New York, NY: McGraw Hill Book Company, 1964), p. 122; *Karl Marx/Friedrich Engels Werke* (*MEW*), Band 40, Ergänzungsband, Erster Teil (Berlin: Dietz Verlag, 1968), p. 511.

5   Ibid.; *MEW* 40, Ergänzungsband 1, p. 512.

6   Fromm, *Marx's Concept of Man*, p. 44.

7   Marx, 'Alienated Labour', p. 121; *MEW* 40, Ergänzungsband 1, p. 511.

8   Ibid., p. 122; *MEW* 40, Ergänzungsband 1, p. 512.

9   Ibid., pp. 123 and 124; *MEW* 40, Ergänzungsband 1, p. 513. The very adjectives Marx uses to describe the individual in this state of civil society are reminiscent of the barbarism of Hobbes's state of nature.

10 Ibid., p. 125; *MEW* 40, Ergänzungsband 1, p. 514.

11 Ibid.

12 The critique of the expansion of the methods of industrial production into the private social spheres and the inner recesses of the unconscious mind involved a synthesis of Marx and Freud: R.D. Laing, *The Divided Self: The Existential Study in Sanity and Madness* (Baltimore, MD: Penguin Books, 1970); Philip Slater, *The Pursuit of Loneliness: American Culture at the Breaking Point* (Boston, MA: Beacon Press, 1970); Bruce Brown, *Marx, Freud, and the Critique of Everyday Life: Toward a Permanent Cultural Revolution* (New York, NY: Monthly Review Press, 1973); Michael Schneider, *Neurosis and Civilization: A Marxist/Freudian Synthesis*, trans. Michael Roloff (New York, NY: The Seabury Press, 1975); Russell Jacoby, *Social Amnesia: A Critique of Contemporary Psychology from Adler to Laing* (Boston, MA: Beacon Press, 1975); Stuart Ewen, *Captains of Consciousness: Advertising and the Social Roots of the Consumer Culture* (New York, NY: McGraw Hill Book Company, 1977); and Christopher Lasch, *Haven in a Heartless World* (New York, NY: Basic Books, 1979) and *The Culture of Narcissism: American Life in an Age of Diminishing Expectations* (New York, NY: Warner Books, 1979).

13 Marx, 'Alienated Labour', p. 127; *MEW* 40, Ergänzungsband 1, p. 516.

14 Ibid.

15 Ibid., p. 128; *MEW* 40, Ergänzungsband 1, p. 517.

16 Ibid. At this point in his analysis of human creativity Marx makes reference to Friedrich Schiller, *On the Aesthetic Education of Man: In a Series of Letters*, trans. Reginald Snell (New York, NY: Ungar Publishing Company, 1986), p. 110; *Über die ästhetische Erziehung des Menschen* (München: Wilhelm Fink Verlag, 1967), p. 160.

Creativity and the Constitution Theory of Art, Experience, Spirit, and Work: Marx joins together Schiller's ideas of artistic beauty or 'living form', Kant's theory of representations, and Hegel's theory of the Objective Spirit into his own theory of the creative experience of work as the integration of the mind and body and the transcendence of the Cartesian dualism and, in turn, the class dualism of modern capitalism. It is interesting to note that both Hegel's and Schiller's ideas are responses to their perception of the failure of the ideals of the French Revolution and how art or the Absolute Spirit of art, religion, and philosophy could overcome that estrangement and alienation. By integrating matter and form, Schiller saw humanity as actualising its potentiality in our sensuous experience of the world. Beauty is the unity of these experiences into a harmonious whole. And it is this human activity which he characterises as noble and divine (pp. 63–4; *Über die ästhetische Erziehung des Menschen*, p. 113): 'Through Beauty the sensuous man is led to form and to thought; through Beauty the spiritual man is brought back to matter and restored to the world of sense' (p. 87; *Über die ästhetische Erziehung des Menschen*, p. 139). For a more detailed analysis of the importance of Schiller in Marx's theory of labour and praxis, see Philip Kain, *Schiller, Hegel, and Marx: State, Society, and the Aesthetic Ideal of Ancient Greece* (Kingston, Canada: McGill-Queen's University Press, 1982), pp. 13–33 and 83–102.

17 Schiller, *On the Aesthetic Education of Man*, p. 63; *Über die ästhetische Erziehung des Menschen*, 112.
18 Ibid., pp. 81 and 85; *Über die ästhetische Erziehung des Menschen*, pp. 132 and 136.
19 Ibid., pp. 120–1; *Über die ästhetische Erziehung des Menschen*, p. 170. 'From being a slave of Nature, so long as he merely perceives her, Man becomes her lawgiver as soon as she becomes his thought. She who had formerly ruled him only as *force*, now stands as *object* before the judgement of his glance ... Man proves his freedom by his very forming of the formless ... Man is superior to every terror of Nature so long as he knows how to give form to it, and to turn it into his object'. This is the basis for Schiller's claim that humans are superior to the terrors of nature as they inform and transform nature according to the principles of 'pure spontaneity', 'human dignity', 'noble freedom', and 'self-dependence', as they rise from the passive acceptance of what is through the senses – mere life of the world of sense – to contemplation of the truth as 'logical and moral unity' (pp. 120–1; *Über die ästhetische Erziehung des Menschen*, pp. 170–1).
20 Ibid., p. 69; *Über die ästhetische Erziehung des Menschen*, pp. 119–20.
21 For a further discussion of alienation, exploitation, and the social organisation of labour in terms of the division of labour, machinery, and modern industry, see Karl Marx, *Capital: A Critique of Political Economy*, vol. 1: *The Process of Capitalist Production*, ed. Friedrich Engels, trans. Samuel Moore and Edward Aveling (New York, NY: International Publishers, 1968), pp. 336–507; *Karl Marx/Friedrich Engels Werke (MEW)*, Band 23 (Berlin: Dietz Verlag, 1962), pp. 356–530.
22 See the debate between Herbert Marcuse and Jürgen Habermas over the nature of natural science and capitalism in Herbert Marcuse, 'Industrialization and Capitalism in Max Weber', in *Negations: Essays in Critical Theory*, trans. Jeremy Shapiro (Boston, MA: Beacon Press, 1969), pp. 201–26 and 'Ecology and the Critique of Modern Society', *Capitalism Nature Socialism*, 3, 3 (1992): 29–38; and Jürgen Habermas, 'Technology and Science as "Ideology"', in *Toward a Rational Society: Student Protest, Science, and Politics*, trans. Jeremy Shapiro (Boston, MA: Beacon Press, 1971), pp. 81–122.
23 Marx, 'Alienated Labour', p. 132; *MEW* 40, Ergänzungsband 1, pp. 520–1.
24 Karl Marx, 'Private Property and Communism', *Karl Marx: Early Writings*, trans. and ed.

T.B. Bottomore (New York, NY: McGraw Hill Book Company, 1964), p. 153; *MEW* 40, Ergänzungsband 1, p. 534.

25   Ibid.
26   Ibid.
27   Ibid., p. 154; *MEW* 40, Ergänzungsband 1, p. 535.
28   Ibid., p. 164; *MEW* 40, Ergänzungsband 1, p. 544. The concept of human need occupies a central place in the political and economic writings of both Aristotle and Marx. Aristotle stressed in the *Nicomachean Ethic* and the *Politics* the 'need' for a virtuous and good life, happiness, love (*philia*), friendship, citizenship, practical wisdom (*praxis*), economic reciprocity, grace and mutual sharing, self-realisation, belongingness to the community, democratic polity, and social justice. Marx is critical of modern political economy because 'despite its worldly and pleasure-seeking appearance, it is a truly moral science, and the most moral of all sciences. Its principal thesis is the renunciation of life and of human needs' (Karl Marx, 'Needs, Production and Division of Labour', *Karl Marx: Early Writings*, trans. and ed. T.B. Bottomore [New York, NY: McGraw Hill Book Company, 1964], p. 171; *MEW* 40, Ergänzungsband 1, p. 549). The more property displaces public virtue and private character, the less existential meaning there is in human life.
29   Marx, 'Private Property and Communism', p. 165; *MEW* 40, Ergänzungsband 1, p. 544.
30   Ibid.
31   Ibid., pp. 164–78; *MEW 40*, Ergänzungsband 1, pp. 544–55. For a further discussion of these issues, see Ollman who writes: 'Free activity is activity that fulfills such powers and freedom, therefore, is the condition of man whose human powers are thus fulfilled; it passes beyond the absence of restraint to the active unfolding of all his potentialities ... Only in community with others has each individual the means of cultivating his gifts in all directions; only in community, therefore, is personal freedom possible' (*Alienation*, p. 117).
32   Ibid., p. 165; *MEW* 40, Ergänzungsband 1, p. 544.
33   For a more detailed analysis of Marx's theory of abstractions, see Ollman, *Alienation*, pp. 62–3, 131–6, and 145. Ollman juxtaposes the notion of abstraction to the dialectic which examines internal and functional relationships among social institutions and cultural values (pp. 66–71).
34   Ibid., p. 176; *MEW* 40, Ergänzungsband 1, pp. 553–4.
35   Marx, 'Needs, Production and Division of Labour', p. 171; *MEW* 40, Ergänzungsband 1, p. 549.
36   Marx appears to be echoing the thoughts of Aristotle here. In his work *The Politics*, trans. T.A. Sinclair, revised trans. Trevor Saunders (London: Penguin, 1981), Aristotle drew the connection between the market economy (*chrematistike*) and the moral economy (*oikonomike*). The market economy, too, had moral values but they were the converse of the ideals of the Greek polity. Thus the moral values of steadfastness, justice, moderation, courage, honour, reason, and virtue over time in a market economy become the distorted market values of persistence, fair return, cautiousness, risk taking, economic differences, technical calculation, and profit making, respectively (book I, chapter ix, 1257b40, p. 85).
37   Marx, 'Needs, Production and Division of Labour', p. 168; *MEW* 40, Ergänzungsband 1, p. 547.
38   Aristotle, *Nicomachean Ethics*, book I, ch. 7, 1097b20–1099b8, pp. 317–22. This is what Aristotle referred to as the function or telos of man, the virtuous life within the polity.

Although Aristotle defined the activity of friends and citizens within a self-sufficient moral economy and democratic polity, Marx universalises the concept of activity as praxis beyond political participation to include both economic production and democracy.

39 Richard Tawney, *Religion and the Rise of Capitalism* (New York, NY: Harcourt, Brace and Company, 1926), p. 36. See also the central place of freedom and self-determination in Marx's social theory in Carol Gould, *Marx's Social Ontology: Individuality and Community in Marx's Theory of Social Reality* (Cambridge, MA: MIT Press, 1980), pp. 101–28 and Ollman, *Alienation*, pp. 116–20.

40 Tawney, *Religion and the Rise of Capitalism*, pp. 35–6. Recognising that the seventeenth century was a watershed of ideas rejecting an objective and universal standard of natural justice and economic equity, Tawney writes: 'The law of nature had been invoked by medieval writers as a moral restraint upon economic self-interest. By the seventeenth century, a significant revolution had taken place. "Nature" had come to connote, not divine ordinance, but human appetites, and natural rights were invoked by the individualism of the age as a reason why self-interest should be given free play' (pp. 179–80 and 22). Tawney concludes his analysis of the rise of individualism with a crucial observation about the weakness of the medieval Church. He observes that it was unable to provide a social ethic for the Industrial Revolution and modern capitalism because natural law was no longer a relevant factor in the new mechanical economy. Religion, in fact, became the apologist for the new social system. He concluded with the sad observation: 'It was that the very idea that the Church possessed an independent standard of values, to which social institutions were amenable, had been abandoned ... The spiritual blindness which made possible the general acquiescence in the horrors of the early factory system was, not a novelty, but the habit of a century' (p. 193). Throughout the Middle Ages, the Church did not question the oppressive land tenure system of medieval fiefdom, but it did morally condemn individual economic transactions (p. 60). How interesting that it would be Marx who rediscovers this lost tradition. Tawney also rejected Weber's thesis of the protestant ethic with his argument that the dramatic economic changes in the sixteenth century were not caused by the Reformation but by radical changes in the commercial and financial economy. In fact, he contends that the Protestant reformers continued to argue for an economic ethic based on natural law well into the seventeenth century (pp. 84–5).

41 Ibid, p. 43.
42 Ibid., pp. 39–55.
43 Ibid., pp. 36–62, 66–79, and 79–132.
44 Ibid., p. 33. The same is true for Marx. Tawney was an Anglican social theorist who, like John Locke earlier in the seventeenth century, was also influenced by another Anglican theologian and neo-Aristotelian, Richard Hooker. Tawney was appreciative of medieval economic ethics but skeptical of its real effects and accomplishments: 'When all is said, the fact remains that, on the small scale involved, the problem of moralizing economic life was faced and not abandoned. The experiment may have been impracticable ... but it had in it something of the heroic, and to ignore the nobility of the conception is not less absurd that to idealize its practical results' (p. 62).

45 Ibid, p. 34.
46 Ibid.

47 Ibid., pp. 35–6. Wealth was to be used to help support the poor and as far as possible to be held in common; labour was to be used to support the family, not to create profits. Tawney quotes the twelfth-century theologian Gratian, who emphasised helping the poor and retaining land held in common and based on human need in a primitive form of communism (p. 32). Tawney again quotes Gratian, who saw the medieval merchant as being in a similar position to that of the money changers in the temple whom Jesus had cast out. Marx, as a student, had attended the lectures of Friedrich Carl von Savigny, the founder of the Historical School of Jurisprudence, for two terms on jurisprudence at the University of Berlin. He wrote on Gratian. Anders Winroth, in his book *The Making of Gratian's Decretum* (Cambridge: Cambridge University Press, 2004), maintains that Marx was the greatest of Savigny's students (p. 162).

48 Ibid., pp. 40–1.

49 Ibid. p. 43.

50 Ibid., p. 50. Tawney summarised the Church's economic ethic as follows: 'In the early Middle Ages it had stood for the protection of peaceful labour, for the care of the poor, the unfortunate and the oppressed – for the ideal, at least, of social solidarity against the naked force of violence and oppression' (p. 60). Tawney recognises that with the transformation of civil society in the late medieval period and with the weakening of the Church's authority and power, the actual implementation of these policies was limited. Whatever the distance between theory and practice, it did, however, indicate that the medieval Church saw society as a 'spiritual organism, not an economic machine' embraced by the moral principles of natural law (p. 62).

51 Natural law is not a universal moral order given for all times as it was for the ancients and Scholastics, but a 'representation' (*Vorstellung*) or 'concept' (*Begriff*) of social justice that evolves in history and society. Marx thus filters his theory of natural law through the German Idealism of Kant's and Hegel's theory of representations, phenomenology, and social ethics. Following upon his rejection of an objective reality or thing-in-itself, Kant's argument that the objects of perception and thought are constructions of the categories of the understanding (substance and causality) and the intuitions of the mind (time and space) is applied to both cognition and consciousness and to moral precepts by Hegel and Marx. The latter continues this critical method when he maintains that social justice is something that is mediated, expanded, and historically developed through the economic and social relations of production and through cultural self-consciousness.

52 For more on the topic of Marx and the Greeks, see Horst Mewes, David Depew, Steven Smith, Michael DeGolyer, Laurence Baronovitch, Martha Nussbaum, Philip Kain, William James Booth, Richard Miller, Alan Gilbert, Joseph Margolis, and Tom Rockmore in *Marx and Aristotle: Nineteenth-Century German Social Theory and Classical Antiquity*, ed. George E. McCarthy (Savage, MD: Rowman & Littlefield Publishers, 1992).

The Five Traditions of Social Justice in Marx: Ancient Hebrews, Ancient Hellenes, Ancient Hellenists, German Romantics, and German Idealists: Marx is influenced by these five traditions from which he explicitly and implicitly borrows the spirit of his ideas: (1) *Torah and the Hebrew Prophets*: covenant, community, love, righteousness and justice (*sedakah*), compassion and loving kindness (*hesed*), charity (*mishpat*), fairness, moral economy, critique of idolatry, and the restoration of unity (*tikkun olam*) in the Jubilee (fair prices, principle of release of property, right of redemption of property and homes, return of property to original owner, and release from servitude in *Leviticus* 25) and the Sabbath (loans, credit, fallow land, rejection of usury, right of the poor to eat, and release of slaves and debt in *Exodus* 21–23 and *Deuteronomy* 15); (2) *Aristotle and Ancient Greeks*: moral economy, grace, reciprocity, mutual sharing, forms of justice, friendship, citizenship, moral and intellectual virtue, reason as *phronesis* (practical wisdom), love (*philia*), political democracy, economic equality, and the critique of chrematistics and a market economy; (3) *Luke, Acts, and the New Testament*: community, equality, common property, human need, and love; (4) *German Romanticism of Goethe, Schiller, and Winckelmann*: beauty, creativity, art, harmony, simplicity, and integration of mind and body; and (5) *German Idealism of Kant and Hegel*: love, self-realisation, the practical reason of individual freedom and moral autonomy, self-determination and self-legislation, and creativity (subjectivity) and the social ethics of human activity or praxis, political community, human needs, moral economy, and human dignity (ends).

CHAPTER 5

Ecological Justice: Historical Materialism and the Dialectic of Nature and Society

The next element in the analysis of Marx's theory of social justice is his theory of nature and ecological justice. Social justice involves the organisation of individual life and society for the realisation of the highest functions and possibilities of human existence. Justice leads to the fulfilment of the good life characterised by virtue, practical wisdom, beneficence, freedom, self-determination, and citizenship. Its main focus is thus on ethics and virtue, as well as politics and democracy. The ethics of a virtuous life and the politics of the brotherhood of humanity and the ideal state necessitate the construction of the political and economic life of the community for the benefit of self-realisation and human freedom. Besides ethics and politics, there is a third major component in Marx's theory which is the human being's relationship to nature. Although this has been a neglected area within Marxian scholarship until very recently, it remains a central building block toward an ideal and just society. This chapter will examine the primary and secondary literature at the micro and macro level to better understand the relationship among ethics, politics, and nature.[1]

According to John Bellamy Foster, much of the misunderstanding surrounding Marx's theory of nature is the result of a theoretical divide within the Marxist tradition itself between the positivism of Soviet Marxism and the idealism of the Frankfurt School. As a result of these conflicting theoretical perspectives, Marx's dialectic of nature was replaced by a dualism between humanity and nature; his historical materialism by a mechanical and deterministic materialism; the dialectic of nature by a dialectic of society; critical science by positivism; and, finally, his theory of the historical mode and social relations of production by the unquestioned industrialisation and technological developments of capitalism.[2]

To some extent socialism became an issue of the proportionality and redistribution of the social wealth of society and less about the nature of technology and the social organisation of political economy. Some scholars interpreted Marx as rejecting the social organisation and distribution of production of the capitalist system, but accepting the basic principles of Enlightenment science and industrial technology. Without industrial expansion and technological innovation, the material well-being of society cannot be assured. Science and technology were viewed as independent of history and capitalism and, therefore, could be applied in any socialist society with a completely different organisation of production which was no longer tied to the law of value, class system, and wage labour. Marx's ideas about species being as *homo faber* and the evolution of capitalism were also interpreted as technical and instrumental features of modern development.

In this chapter we will rethink Marx's theory of nature in order to re-establish the dialectic between nature and society, nature and capitalism. In order to accomplish this task, it will be necessary to establish the connection between the dialectic and contradictions of the economic system and the dialectic and contradictions of social metabolism and the metabolic rift, that is, the relationship between society (political economy) and the environment. The ultimate goal is to re-establish the link between production and nature, as well as to reconnect the economic and ecological crises at the heart of modern capitalism.[3] A just society would thereby attempt not only to re-establish a harmonious balance between the individual and society, but also between society and nature. This harmony between political economy and nature will provide the foundations for a theory of ecological justice. Just as one can distinguish between Marx's early writings on human nature, alienation, and species being and the later writings on economics and crisis theory, we can distinguish between his early philosophy on the alienation of nature and consciousness and his later theories of technology, social metabolism, and the ecological crises of soil nutrient depletion, deforestation, desertification, climate change, pollution, industrial wastes, overpopulation, etc.[4] Thus Marx's dialectic of nature may be divided into his early anthropological theory of labour and consciousness and his later structural theory of production and crises. In his doctoral dissertation *Difference between the Democritean and Epicurean Philosophy of Nature* (1840–1) and his earlier *Notebooks on Epicurean Philosophy* (1838–40), Marx engaged the theory of nature, materialism, and science of Greek philosophy in the writings of Aristotle, Democritus, and Epicurus.[5] These works had a profound impact on his early philosophical writings on alienation, nature, and economic production.

Nature, science, technology, and industry are socially mediated, defined, and constructed and are various social manifestations of the historical process of alienation within capitalist society.[6] Nature has a number of different meanings in the early writings of Marx: Nature is viewed as an object of perception and consciousness (epistemology), means for the satisfaction of human needs (consumption and material basis for an ethical and virtuous life), external reality, object of beauty and sensuousness (aesthetics), objectification and praxis (production and work), natural reality and social form of production (historical materialism), nature and the law of value and concept of capital (critique of political economy), nature as the unity of the dialectic of history and nature, the unity of humanity and nature (*Naturphilosophie*), and, finally, nature as the physical reality of the environment transformed by social praxis and democratic socialism (ethics and moral ecology). The breadth of his view of nature is very extensive as it encompasses issues of philosophy, art, history, economics, natural philosophy, and moral ecology. Marx's theory of nature is a unique combination of the *Naturphilosophie* of Schelling and Hegel and the *Naturrecht* of Spinoza and Hegel.[7]

Nature is essential for the production of material goods necessary for human survival, as well as central to the creation of social interaction, human identity and self-consciousness, and the realisation of human potentiality. In turn, democratic socialism is essential for a balanced and harmonious relationship between humanity and nature; without true political and economic democracy, nature turns into a commodity to be dominated and exploited, not for human use, but for profit making. A society built upon the foundations of economic alienation and exploitation, class inequality and power, structural chasms and contradictions, and economic crises produces a physical nature which, in turn, will manifest some of these same social and structural deficiencies and abnormalities. It turns nature from an organic, integrated whole and partner in the creation of a free society into a dead and deterministic mechanism. The Enlightenment and modern science end in the domination or inquisition of nature which turns both labour and nature into forms of servitude and false needs for the benefit of a small minority of the population; it ends in economic crises and ecological breakdown. The problems of the two spheres of production and nature are interwoven into a complex web of relationships that can only be resolved by a democratic restructuring of the social relations of production. With the development of capitalism, there is a break in the fundamental laws of nature that guide our relationships to society and nature, species being and nature. Natural moral law was sundered with the rise of liberalism in the seventeenth century, while the natural law of physical nature was broken with the rise of economic expansion and technological innovation in the sixteenth and seventeenth centuries with their construction of false needs, waste of natural resources, and the evolution of possessive individualism based on self-interest, market competition, and private property accumulation. When there is a break between the harmony of production and natural renewal, the use of nature and the replenishment of its resources, and between production and fair distribution, there is a break in the moral economy which binds society and nature together. In the end, this unbridgeable divide in the moral economy leads to a social revolution in the organisation of production, exchange, and distribution and to an ecological crisis with the breakdown of nature.

Alienation of Production, Labour, and Nature

There are a number of scholars who have argued that Marx's views of work, praxis, and species being, historical stages of economic development, and science, productive forces, and modern technology are to be understood within the framework of instrumentalism, determinism, and positivism. We live in a deterministic universe where the laws of nature also apply to the historical and social world. History is predetermined, structural crises and economic breakdowns are inevitable, and human labour is simply the technical activity of a tool maker or producer of material goods. The categories used to describe nature have been shifted to an explanation of the laws of social evolution – all in the name of turning Marx's critical social theory into a predictive and explanatory natural science. Friedrich Engels, in his famous work *Dialectics of Nature* (unpublished 1883), has been accused of providing the intellectual groundwork for the rise of Soviet Marxism and its radical positivism and anti-environmental policies. This not only distorts our understanding of history and the logic of value and capital, it also distorts our relationship to nature. Some have even argued that Marx has no developed theory of nature or any sensitivity to environmental matters. On this subject, Joel Kovel nicely summarises this position in his writings: 'Specifically, there is no language within Marxism beyond a few ambiguous and sketchy beginnings that directly address the ravaging of nature or expresses the care for nature which motivates people – Marxist or not – to become engaged in ecological struggle'.[8]

Some continue this train of thought by insisting that Marx did not have to concern himself with a consideration of environmental issues because with the development of Enlightenment science and industrial technology of the productive forces, material scarcity would be eliminated resulting in an overabundance of natural resources and consumer goods necessary for a good life. Socialism would lead to a post-scarcity society because of the application of science and technology to the problems of production. In fact, these problems are for the most part the result of the social relationships of production – division of labour, specialisation, law of value, class power in the workplace, and profit accumulation – and not the technical and scientific side of the productive forces themselves. This position of technological determinism further argues that technological development controls the changes in the social relations of production; it is technology which determines the inevitability of history and the forms society will take; and, finally, progress is defined by the advances in science and technology. Science and technology are transcendent and neutral factors in the production process since they themselves evolve in history but are fundamentally independent of it.[9] In fact, it is science and technology without the class system that resolve the contradictions of value production, push it beyond the limits of capitalism, and, in the end, produce abundance and happiness for all in a classless society. This position fundamentally creates a dualism between society and nature as it reduces society to the laws of nature. Scientific and technological domination of nature remain unproblematic, which has to be challenged from within Marx's writings.[10]

The position taken in this chapter is that there is a coherent theory of nature and ecology in Marx; just how developed it is in his writings is a matter of open debate. As already noted in the previous chapter on ethics and workplace justice, Marx develops a theory of alienation in his early writings of 1844. There he outlines the nature of capitalist production, the alienation of humanity, and its loss of control over the product (private property), process and social organisation of production (aesthetic creativity), self as a species being (moral sovereignty), and others as community (democracy). Workers are no longer in control of the what, how, where, or why of production. Marx's theory of alienation is important because it provides an avenue of entrance into broader ethical questions about the nature of a virtuous life and the exercise of individual creativity, self-determination, and human freedom. These are issues that develop into his theory of ethics and workplace justice. There is a fifth form of alienation in his study of alienated labour which receives much less attention in the secondary literature and is crucial to the development of a theory of ecological justice – the alienation of nature.

Marx's first encounter with a theory of nature comes in the middle of his early essay, 'Alienated Labour' as part of the *Economic and Philosophical Manuscripts of 1844*. Nature is intimately linked to human nature and species being since it provides the foundation for both human physical survival and human creative praxis; nature is essential to self-preservation and being.[11] Humans are species beings for two reasons: First, the community is made into the 'theoretical and practical object' of human activity, and humans are treated as universal, free beings.[12] Marx's terminology here is very much influenced by the language of Kant and Hegel and does not mesh well with present-day English even under the best of translations. According to Kant, humans are free when they define their own moral actions through the use of practical reason and the universal categorical imperative; Hegel uses his phenomenology of spirit – the history of the objective universal spirit – to trace the development of human self-consciousness and freedom from the ancient Greeks to the French

Revolution. Marx appropriates the philosophical language of German Idealism, but now within a materialist or economic framework for the examination of the alienation of these universal or species aspects of human consciousness and freedom.

As we have seen in the previous chapter, Marx took the position that the community is made into a theoretical and practical object by the mental and physical labour of humans, by their consciousness (ideas) and work (objects), and by their culture and political economy. The community and its universality are expressions of our common heritage and traditions, our collective organisation of work and society, and our cultural principles and moral values that define our species. Community is not given by nature as with animals but is a social and historical construct of human labour. In the process, human activity is universal because it creates the distinctive physical community within the household, neighbourhood, factory, and nation along with its ethical and political ideals. At this point Marx's theory of alienation and human nature is simply being summarised. In this intellectual and material creativity the community itself becomes a universal expression of human individuality and the essence of human nature. We are social and political beings in our practical activities of everyday life in which we express the meaning, purpose, and goals of human existence. We accomplish this by our universal or species activity in which we create the meaning in our lives through self-determination and aesthetic creativity in work; we pursue the purpose of human existence through a life of virtue, political wisdom, friendship, and citizenship; and we fulfill these functions through workplace and political democracy. Thus reading this section of Marx's essay in its broader context of the various forms of alienation more thoroughly discussed in Chapter 4, we can conclude that to make the community his object practically means to form the ethical and political heart of human existence in the moral activity of democratic socialism. To accomplish this theoretically means that the community becomes the universal standard of morality and justice by which we measure the ideals and dreams of humanity.

It is within this context that Marx now introduces the concept of nature. 'Species life, for man as for animals, has its physical basis in the fact that man (like animals) lives from inorganic nature and since man is more universal than an animal so the range of inorganic nature from which he lives is more universal'.[13] The search for Marx's theory of social justice entails a consideration of both ethics (character and virtue) and economics (structure). To this must now be added the reflective consideration of nature and the dialectic between species being (human nature) and external nature. Nature provides the means for the satisfaction of survival just as for other animals, that is, it provides for the physical ground of life. But it also affects the quality and activity of life because it is the basis for the aesthetic creativity and moral sovereignty in work which are the defining characters of our species being. Nature appears to us as the objectification of spiritual and corporeal labour. 'Plants, animals, minerals, air, light, etc. constitute, from the theoretical aspect, a part of human consciousness as objects of natural science and art. They are man's spiritual inorganic nature, his intellectual means of life ...'.[14]

Nature is not an external limit or barrier to human existence, but, rather, is an essential part of human consciousness, culture, and society. Nature is part of their theoretical and ideational expressions (science and culture) as humans create the world they inhabit. Even at this early stage of development of his ideas, Marx has turned the epistemology of Kant and Hegel into a materialist philosophy of nature. The constructionist and idealist view of reality and truth in understanding, experience, and spirit – the world of representations – is replaced by the life activity of human labour. There is no romantic nature pristine and unmediated by human thought and action. It is ultimately the mode of production which defines our interaction with the objective world of knowledge (Kant) and culture and social institutions (Hegel). The concepts by which we organise our worldviews are the product of the interaction and interconnectedness of humanity with nature. But nature is not a mere means to experience and production – an opportunity to create objectivity – but should be viewed as part of the very essence of humanity, part of the productivity of life itself.

Nature, as part of human consciousness, is an essential element in the manner in which nature and consciousness become self-aware. It is the integration of subjectivity and objectivity, now at the level of an initial theory of historical materialism. The forms of intuition and categories of the understanding in time, space, substance, and causality organise nature into a coherent pattern by the transcendental subjectivity in Kant's *Critique of Pure Reason* (1781); it is then reconstructed within history and society in the phenomenology of Hegel. The dialectic of the phenomenology of self-consciousness and spirit presupposes a primary dialectic between the material world and cultural spirit. The natural sciences are the product of this interconnection between nature and consciousness. Nature as food, heating, clothing, and housing for the universal and technical side of human existence is balanced by the theoretical understanding of nature and society in the cultural spirit. Alienation as an economic phenomenon is simply the loss of this connection to nature and, thus, the loss of existential meaning in humanity's life activity as social praxis.[15] As with other aspects of Marx's early writings, his concepts remain very philosophical in language and orientation. Here Marx establishes the ecological balance between humanity and nature; the economic implications of these ideas, especially concerning political economy and the internal contradictions of capitalism and ecology will be discussed in his later works. But in these writings, the initial tone is being set for a balanced social metabolism or material exchange (*Stoffwechsel*) between nature and human consciousness.

Marx makes much of the idea of the universality of humanity – its universal appropriation of nature in practice, its universal categories of subjectivity and consciousness, and the material basis for physical objects, life, and praxis. 'Nature is the inorganic body of man ... man lives from nature means that nature is his body with which he must remain in a continuous interchange in order not to die'.[16] Nature is the external human body and, therefore, initial means for the development of the objective world of thought, imagination, art, science, and morality. Subjectivity gives meaning and purpose to a world only by practical activity within it, including technical, conceptual, theoretical, and moral activity of the pure and practical reason. Work constructs a world of theoretical meaning and practical necessity. The practical or life activity of the species has two connotations in this context: the technical activity of work and the moral activity of the practical reason. Aristotle's classical distinctions between *techne* and *phronesis* are being adjusted by Marx for the modern age as he blends together work and politics, production and citizenship, and labour and morality. At the same time, Marx has synthesised the Kantian distinctions between pure and practical reason, scientific and moral reason. The ideal of citizenship in the modern age has been expanded by industrial production and economic democracy. Work and culture, nature and art, and the physical and spiritual are reconnected in a critical response to the neo-Platonic dualism of Cartesian philosophy and traditional Western science. 'The statement that the physical and mental life of man, and nature, are interdependent means simply that nature is interdependent with itself, for man is part of nature'.[17] The alienation of labour in modern capitalist society results in the alienation of nature from humanity. The two processes are interlinked; political economy and the institutions of work, private property, and social class are part of the problem of the alienation of nature. To overcome the damage of the latter requires a response to the former, not through a reconfiguration of concepts and ideas but through a materialist understanding of history and the economy.[18]

Nature is bound to the species life of the individual which creates the categories of the understanding and the structures of social institutions. In this way, the mind and the body are bound together in a materialist interpretation of history and society. Nature is part of both the species life of practical activity and the production of capital and wage labour. The physical and spiritual life of the community – its self-conscious activity, freedom, self-realisation, and happiness – resides in this complex relationship between nature and production. In his essay 'Alienated Labour', Marx asserts: 'Conscious life activity distinguishes man from the life activity of animals. Only for this reason is he a species being. Or rather, he is only a self-conscious being, i.e. his own life is an object for him, because he is a species being. Only for this reason is his activity free activity'.[19] In the very act of creating the world though labour and production, we help form nature, consciousness, work, and society. Alienation occurs when this human activity and dialectic between nature and species being is interrupted by a social system based on profit, property, and class prosperity. 'The practical construction of an *objective world*, the *manipulation* of inorganic nature, is the confirmation of man as a conscious species being, i.e. a being who treats the species as his own being or himself as a species being'.[20]

Marx in his definition of species life as a 'practical construction of the objective work' has incorporated into his ideal of humanity the richest elements of Western consciousness from the practical activity of the Athenian citizen and theoretical activity of Athenian philosophers, Kantian subjectivity as pure and practical reason, and Hegel's view of the subjective (moral), objective (social), and absolute spirit (harmonising culture) of humanity in his understanding of the relationship between nature and human praxis. For Marx, the world is a construct of human activity, science, and production. Human construction and creativity lie at the heart of Marx's theory of nature. Humans are free when they create their political, philosophical, scientific, and moral worlds universally, that is, when their creations of the objective world are the result of free, self-conscious human need. Creation is an ethical and political imperative that gives coherence and meaning to the world. While animals fashion the world according to their immediate physical needs for survival and must conform to those needs, humans transform nature freely according to the 'standards of every species' and according to 'the laws of beauty'.[21] Marx seems to recognise that humans must be conscious of the living nature as a delicate whole that must be considered when building their own world of objects which, in turn, are constructed according to the laws of beauty from the ancients' respect for balance and harmony of nature.

As we have already seen, the laws of beauty is an idea borrowed from Schiller's *On the Aesthetic Education of Man* and refers to the integration of the material and sensuous worlds and the theoretical and spiritual worlds. The end result is that 'nature appears as *his* work and his reality'.[22] In the alien world of capitalism, the objects of labour in consciousness and empirical reality negatively transform human development and self-consciousness. The world we experience every day both practically and theoretically is a non-human world of a distorted economic system where the laws of objective nature and the natural laws of ethics no longer reflect the free and creative species life of humanity; this is a world of fetishism and idolatry. The natural world, along with the life activity and consciousness of the individual, becomes a mere commodity that is bought and sold in a market economy; humanity and nature are simply means for profit accumulation and have no other value. This process of the alienation of ecology and the dialectic of nature is certainly the beginning of what in Marx's later writings appears as a crisis of the ecology and environmental breakdown.

Dialectic of Nature and the Alienation of Consciousness

In another essay from the early manuscripts, entitled 'Private Property and Communism', Marx re-engages the issue of the intimate relationship between nature and humanity. The defining characteristics of humanity are activity and mind, which produce society as well as being produced by society. This dialectical relationship is the bond that holds society and nature together. Repeating the argument introduced in 'Alienated Labour', Marx maintains that nature is at the foundation of humanity's essential life activity, human experience, and society itself. 'The *natural* existence of man has here become his *human* existence and nature itself has become human for him. Thus *society* is the accomplished union of man with nature, the veritable resurrection of nature, the realized naturalism of man and the realized humanism of nature'.[23] This non-instrumental and non-mechanical relationship between nature and society is central to Marx's theory of critical ecology and environmental justice. The potentialities that lie within physical nature and human nature are only expressed in the non-alienated union of the two realms of nature. Combining these statements on nature with those from his essay on alienation, we can see that in the natural drive for self-preservation – the fundamental need of nature to live – society is formed not for the protections of natural rights to market liberties, private property, or consumer goods, but for the fundamental satisfaction of the human need for society, knowledge, and virtue.

The natural existence or drive for survival ends not in a chrematistic economy of property and profit accumulation, but in a human existence of social praxis. It is in this way that the primordial strangeness, isolation, and violence of nature turn into a human experience as naturalism turns into humanism, as nature becomes human, as nature is reborn with a human face. However, all that changes in an alien environment under capitalism where the chrematistic economy becomes the telos of human and natural existence. In a truly democratic and socialist society there will be an integration of naturalism and humanism, nature and society. The end result will be a *'definitive* resolution of the antagonism between man and nature, and between man and man'.[24] The dualisms and antagonisms that plague class society will be negated when human needs are not seen as physical desires but teleological needs for self-realisation and freedom. Private property in production and consumption represents the social expression of alienation, while the domination of nature is its physical manifestation. One results in the exploitation of humanity, the other the exploitation and alienation of nature.

Humanity expresses itself in the world as an individual member of a species being and as a form of universal consciousness in thought. It is an objective communal being involved in creating the world and an inner, subjective consciousness reflecting on the theoretical implications of that activity in its various cultural forms of art, music, literature, law, etc. Marx summarises this position when he writes: 'He [the individual] exists in reality as the representation and real mind of social existence, and as the sum of human manifestations of life'.[25] As with Kant and Hegel, the real world is a construction of representations and the real mind of social existence, but this occurs now in the context of productive work activities touching objective nature. 'Thought and being are indeed *distinct* but they also form a unity'.[26] In these pages Marx is starting to expresses in abstract language the beginnings of his theory of historical materialism and the relationship between thought and reality, essence and being, culture and the economy. 'Religion, the family, the state, law, morality, science, art, etc. are only *particular* forms of production and come under its general law'.[27] Consciousness, society, and nature are now integrated into the species life of individuals so that they are expressions of each other at different levels of existence, and the alienation of one sphere directly affects the other spheres.

Marx has just examined in this essay the interconnections between nature and society and now turns to a consideration of the relationship between nature, the senses, and consciousness. This section reads like a rewrite of the Kantian critique of scientific reason, but after the discovery of social praxis and historical materialism. The transcendental subjectivity or pure consciousness is replaced by a historical consciousness engaged in the creation of society, nature, and reason. As the social landscape has been radically altered with the imposition of private property and capitalist production, nature, in turn, has been exploited and alienated in the process. The world we see and interpret through the vision of sensuous experience is a world constructed by not only subjectivity but also objectivity in the form of a historical mode of production. '[P]rivate property is only the sensuous expression of the fact that man is at the same time an objective fact for himself and becomes an alien and non-human object for himself'.[28] Enlightenment nature as the world of objective facts is a construct of capitalism. Thus private property is not simply an economic category immortalised as a natural right by John Locke as the basis for human survival and liberty but is something much more profound: It is, as Marx says: the 'sensuous appropriation of the human essence and of human life' or the physical and spiritual world we create through labour in an alienated fashion. It is the world that surrounds us and is the basis for human life but also human life activity. It is the latter which creates the social institutions, culture, natural environment, and the objects of perception. Marx explicitly states that this world is not just for utilitarian enjoyment or the expression of legal rights of possession; it is the objective world constructed by reason within the broader parameters of political economy. Objectivity is a construct of social and historical subjectivity in the material world; epistemology has been integrated with a critical sociology.

The natural world we see, hear, smell, taste, touch, reflect upon, desire, love, etc. is a pre-formed experience that has been mediated by the historical development of the alien production of capital and labour. Thus the world of sensibility, experience, and consciousness is not filtered through the *a priori* categories of the understanding or the cultural forms of the objective and absolute spirit. Rather, we experience alienation in conscious thought and immediate experience because the objective and subjective worlds are the result of social praxis. The objective world is created by labour and reappropriated by sensuous experience. But the world of everyday life is alien because the objective reality in nature and society is a production of alienated labour and the logic of capital. The world appropriated in production, experienced in perception, and utilised in consumption distorts our relation to the objectivity of society and nature. Ontology (world of objective reality), existentialism (world of meaning), and epistemology (world of consciousness) are all framed within capitalism. The social system based on capital production reduces the consumption of products to a crude utilitarianism of 'having' or ownership and the consciousness of ideas to an unreflective consumption of the objects of labour in thought. Production, which was to express the human essence in creative work and precipitate a critical reflection on the ethical meaning of life and the empirical study of the natural laws of physical reality, now has turned the world we inhabit into a mechanical and lifeless machine. Everything is simply a means for the accumulation of dead objects and experience. Perception, art, institutions, and science are the products of this alien world of capital and serve it only as a means to the end of further accumulation of private property. In turn, individuals serve and worship property as their new god, and the stronger the world appears, the weaker the inner soul of individuals who experience it: 'For it is clear ... that the more the worker expends himself in work the more powerful becomes the world of objects which he creates in face of himself, the poorer he becomes in his inner life, and the less he belongs to himself'.[29] Humanity has created a divine realm of natural and cultural laws of nature that rule human relationships with an iron hand, thereby destroying the possibilities inherent in the real productive activities of species life. 'Private property has made us so stupid' because everywhere we turn in our economic and political life, everywhere in our sensations and consciousness of the world, everywhere in our theoretical and cultural reflections, we experience our own alienation at every level of human existence. We are locked in an iron cage with a distorted objective reality that has value only to the extent that it can be experienced and privately used for personal pleasure and consumption.

Natural Science as the Objectification and Social Praxis of Species Being

The end result of such alienation is an 'absolute poverty' of the senses and consciousness because the reality it sees, hears, and acts upon is a production of economic and natural alienation. Modern political economy creates a social system in which the mode of production lies in the hands of those with agricultural property and industrial capital; but it also creates a subjective and theoretical consciousness that is another form of alienation that has to be changed through revolutionary social praxis. This just adds another dimension to Marx's notion of human emancipation from the economic slavery of wage labour, oppressive work, and class inequality. Even experience, thought, and reason must be emancipated for they are pervaded by a distorted objective reality that must be transcended. As in philosophical idealism, the objectivity of the natural world and the subjectivity of consciousness are intimately and dialectically interrelated. Marx has just moved away from idealism to a historical materialism where objectivity has been expanded to include both nature and society. 'The supersession of private property is, therefore, the complete *emancipation* of all the human qualities and senses. It is such an emancipation because these qualities and senses have become *human* from the subjective as well as the objective point of view'.[30] In a socialist society, eyes and ears become human because the natural and social worlds they experience have become the product of human activity and organisation. In a just society, democracy not only affects the decision-making process in economic and political institutions, but the world of nature that we inhabit, produce, and experience. Consciousness, objective ideas, and absolute culture reflect the economic substructure of society as they are the spiritual and theoretical forms of objective social relations. Through human emancipation we relate to the external world no longer bound to utilitarianism, egoism, and the categories of radical individualism, but relate to a world created by the human desire for freedom, self-consciousness, and moral sovereignty. Humans relate to nature out of care and human need. The very concepts by which we organise our perception of the world are no longer abstract fetishisms imposed by an imperative of laws and domination but by a double dialectic between society and nature.

The social values of justice, virtue, goodness, and friendship now become the foundations of human experience and consciousness. We see and think about a world mediated by the values and institutions of human emancipation, not by those of natural rights and the capitalist mastery of nature. This is why the objects we know through experience and science have become human since the organising principle of that world is now social justice. As already mentioned in this work, Marx does not use the term social justice but the term is not inconsistent with his concepts of human senses, social objects, and objective humanity. '[I]t is only when the object becomes a *human* object, or objective *humanity*, that man does not become lost in it'.[31] It is when both objectivity and subjectivity become human or part of a new democratic socialism where individuals regain their humanity and control over the products and process of production that they also regain control over the products and process of consciousness formation. When nature becomes a truly human reality by unalienated human labour – naturalism as humanism – and when humanity realises its natural potential as a social being – humanism as naturalism – then nature and society will no longer be at odds with each other. This is the meaning of his statement: 'Communism as a fully developed naturalism is humanism and as a fully developed humanism is naturalism. It is the *definite* resolution of the antagonism between man and nature, and between man and man'.[32] A revolution in the manner in which society is organised is necessary for a radical rethinking of the nature of modern natural science. This intimate interlinking of production and consciousness, capitalism and Enlightenment science provides the basis for our understanding of the alienation of nature and science. Science, its methods and concepts, are not independent categories reflecting the truth about nature and its laws as objective reality. Rather, they are social manifestations of alienated consciousness that must be historically transcended.[33] Science in the form of the domination and exploitation of nature has become an expression of enlightened alienation.

Science as Objectivity and Alienation

When human beings are no longer egoistic images of competing market forces or commodities to be bought and sold, then science will experience human objects created by species beings in a free society. It is then that 'all *objects* become for him the *objectification* of *himself*. The objects then confirm and realize his individuality, they are *his own* objects, i.e. man himself becomes the object'.[34] The world that humans beings perceive through the physical, spiritual, and practical senses; the world that we experience and know; and the world of science and human reason is a creation of human labour. When the species activity of human labour occurs under capitalism, the world we know is distant and alien, while under socialism these objects of human perception, reason, and labour again become human; they are expressions of the activity of species life. 'It is therefore not only in thought, but through all the senses that man is affirmed in the objective world'.[35] To perceive a world of beauty, the natural and social objects must first be created under the umbrella of a self-conscious freedom within a humanised nature. The beauty of experience, nature, music, and science presuppose the subjectivity of a social being or the humanisation of human labour. Private property and industry destroy sensibility and reflective thought because they create an artificial and dominated world of objects that form the basis of our perception, ideas, and scientific theories. The world becomes humanised only when it is created within a human society, that is, by a post-capitalist production of praxis, sensibility, and thought where industry is turned into a creative and free activity under the democratic control of the free association of producers. Marx summarises his position with the words: 'Thus the objectification of the human essence, both theoretically and practically, is necessary in order to humanize man's essence, and also to create the human senses corresponding to all the wealth of human and natural being'.[36] This is the theoretical beginning of the dialectic of nature and society.

Marx presents a twofold dialectical understanding of nature with his idea of the objectification and humanisation of nature, along with the parallel naturalisation of man. The 'humanisation of nature' takes place as a social praxis with its focus on issues of human creativity in work along with the corresponding sensibility and consciousness of the spirit (phenomenology of consciousness) and nature (labour and production). Labour constructs the natural and social reality that surrounds us in everyday life and experience. At this level of reflection, Marx is joining together the Aristotelian theory of political activity and practical wisdom, Hegel's view of theoretical activity and self-consciousness within history (consciousness, self-consciousness, reason, and spirit), and the labour theory of value of Locke and Ricardo. Politics, phenomenology, and economics are being integrated into a constitution theory of knowledge, a broader theory of human creativity, and a radical philosophy of science and nature. The second part of his dialectic begins with the 'naturalisation of man' as a reflection on human nature and the wealth of human needs. Succinctly put, the dialectic of nature entails the interconnection between the humanisation of nature as labour, sensibility, and consciousness and the naturalisation of humanity with human nature (virtue, ethics, and self-determination) and human needs (realisation of human nature). Marx has created a new dialectic of nature which examines the natural world within a new historical form of materialism.

At the very end of this essay on private property and communism, Marx condenses these questions into that of industry (labour) and psychology (consciousness). The traditional dualisms and antinomies in Western thought between the subject and object, mind and body, individual and society, and nature and human beings can never be resolved by philosophy or theology, but only by the practical activity of social praxis which ultimately entails resolving the dialectic of society (socialism) and the dialectic of nature (science and production). As Marx puts it, they are not simply theoretical questions of knowledge or being, but questions of 'the real problems of life'. Marx states that up to the middle of the nineteenth century, natural science has only been understood in terms of the utilitarian categories of the domination and mastery of nature; nature is simply the naturalisation of industry. Nature is less an expression of the social potentialities of human nature than the concepts and logic of capitalist production and class exploitation. He wonders what natural science would be, if it were an expression of humanity's species being, that is, a reflection of humanity's own real potentiality. Science, as the theoretical form of labour, has been such an intricate part of industrial technology and economic development – alienation – that it, too, requires an emancipation from capitalist industry. This would entail a corresponding humanization (species being) of nature. Wolfdietrich Schmied-Kowarzik in his seminal work *Das dialektische Verhältnis des Menschen zur Natur* (1984) has argued that Marx in these pages is developing a new dialectic of nature that is anti-positivistic and anti-utilitarian. He also recognises that there are clear limits to Marx's approach in these early writings.[37] Natural science has historically always been connected with an instrumental and technical activity compatible with industrial production.[38] As we have already seen, Enlightenment morality, religion, and political theory have been a product of this same underlying economic system. Marx appears to reject science's privileged and theological position in Western thought as somehow methodologically objective and independent of any normative influence that could distort its empirical study of natural reality.

With his materialist theory of science and critical rejection of its utilitarian alienation, Marx locates science within natural and social history as a product of alienated wage labour and capital production. Nature has been transformed into fetishised, mechanical objects and natural, deterministic commodities by the law of value (*Werttheorie*); science is a historical and alienated form of knowledge for the domination and control over nature.[39] Because of the intimate connection between nature and society, on the one hand, and science and society, on the other, changing the social praxis or the economic and social mode of the organisation of production will also require a change in the nature of science itself and make it more human. The categories of intuition and understanding will change accordingly. What becomes of natural science based on a non-alienated economy is open to wide interpretation since Marx leaves the question unexamined: Is it a question of the technical use or exploitive abuse of science or is it a question of the very concepts, ideas, and theories of science itself? Social critique is a dialectical method that points to the future and the ethical demand for social change but leaves both the description and type of new society and future science open for further discussion.

The natural sciences based on sense experience have opened up new worlds of discovery, collected an enormous amount of empirical information about the objective world, and have been technically useful with their quantitative and explanatory laws of nature.[40] But unfortunately, the world that they study is a product of alienated labour and the method of application is instrumental and technological. Natural science studies a physical nature transformed by human intervention and industry. Marx writes that science 'has transformed human life and prepared the emancipation of humanity, even though its immediate effect was to accentuate the dehumanisation of man. *Industry* is the actual historical relationship of nature, and thus of natural science, to man'.[41] Schmied-Kowarzik accepts the fundamental principles of Marx's argument which he reads through Schelling's natural philosophy (*Naturphilosophie*). Humanity both creates the objective world through alienated labour and then reflects upon it in the sciences. Natural science is a form of alienated consciousness because it does not understand nature as a living being in solidarity and alliance with the political community or ethical life of society.[42] Rather science is an alien imposition for the utilitarian and instrumental purpose of controlling what it sees and experiences; science and industry are part of the same mode of production and to change one area requires the transformation of the other. The closest Marx gets to offering any concrete solutions to this problem of modern science besides the complete restructuring of industrial society is the comment: 'Natural science will then abandon its abstract materialist, or rather idealist, orientation, and will become the basis of *human science*'.[43]

Science is abstract because it is not understood concretely as part of a living whole but as something arbitrarily imposed from the outside; it is also not understood historically and materially as part of the development of the industry and technology of industrial capitalism. It is conceived abstractly above all consideration of economic and social influences because it is presumably concerned with the absolute truth and laws of nature. Marx, on the other hand, wants science to be appreciated as part of a dialectic between nature and society and as the product of capitalist wage labour. Science is not a product of the universal and abstract laws of nature, but the product of the laws of value framed by the social forms of production within capitalism. The Enlightenment is a form of alienated labour in both its view of natural rights and politics (Hobbes and Locke) and its view of science (Bacon and Descartes). For science to break with alienated consciousness and sensibility, it must become a human science and be appreciated as part of a more extensive historical and social landscape. Only then will science be perceived as a human or social science. Under the conditions of a socialist society both science and nature change into a dialogue between humanism and naturalism, the natural sciences and social sciences. In a non-alienating society nature becomes human in the study of industry, psychology, and the physical sciences: 'Nature as it develops in human history, in the act of genesis of human society, is the *actual* nature of man'.[44] Nature is understood as a product of a historical mode of production and under capitalism it is the alienated inorganic essence of humanity. Objectification through species labour creates the immediate objects of human experience (knowledge) and action (will). The objects of perception and experience are historical objects created by social praxis. It is at this point in his analysis that Marx takes an interesting and unexpected turn. He remarks that the true foundation of natural science lies in sense experience and human need, consciousness and human nature.

For Hegel, the whole of human history is a preparation for the development of the absolute and objective spirit of self-consciousness and the ethical community (*Sittlichkeit*); this is what Marx refers to as theoretical (culture) and practical (social institutions) activity of the social life force of the individual. Again paralleling Hegel's phenomenology of Spirit, it is consciousness of nature that begins the movement toward self-consciousness within the community. Natural science which experiences a nature created by society turns into a human science of physical laws that represent the symbiotic balance and interdependence of nature and society. Natural science and consciousness of sensuous objectivity are a social experience developed through a relationship with others. Nature is an essential element in the development of human consciousness toward a science of humanity and self-consciousness of history. The reality of nature is social as sense experience and the reality of humanity is natural as human needs. It is at this point in his essay 'Private Property and Communism' that Marx turns away from the issues of wealth and poverty in political economy and turns to the issues of wealth and abundance of human need. A socialist society is not ultimately concerned with the distribution of the economic wealth of society but with the distribution of human needs. The latter are the key elements of natural science because they are issues of the naturalisation of humanity. Science is no longer to be concerned with the abstract laws and domination of nature but with the emancipation and expression of true wealth or social and natural needs. Humans are natural beings because they have natural needs; nature is human because it is the product of the essential needs for theoretical and practical productivity and self-determination. And the greatest of humanity's needs and the greatest form of the social wealth of the community is that of the other person – the species being as it productively creates and self-consciously experiences and transforms the sensuous world of nature within the friendship and bonds of the 'brotherhood of man' – this is a world of grace, reciprocity, and friendship.[45]

Social Metabolism, Contradictions, and Ecological Crises

Marx continues his analysis of the dialectic between nature and society in his later writings in order to form a more comprehensive connection between the critique of political economy and the contradictions of the natural ecology. As he moves beyond the philosophical discourse about social praxis to an empirical and scientific explanation of the internal logic and structural contradictions and fluctuations of capital accumulation tending toward full-blown economic crises and social breakdown, Marx also brings along the dialectic of nature in this development. So in the *Grundrisse* (1858) and *Capital* (1867, first volume), he continues his analysis of nature but in an ecological crisis theory mirroring the economic crisis of production. The dialectic of production will be discussed in more detail in Chapter 8 of this work. Reflecting on the dialectic of nature in the first volume of *Capital*, Marx writes:

> Labour is, in the first place, a process in which both man and Nature participate, and in which man of his own accord starts, regulates, and controls the material reactions [metabolism or *Stoffwechsel*] between himself and Nature. He opposes himself to Nature as one of her own forces, setting in motion arms and legs, head and hands, the natural forces of his body in order to appropriate Nature's productions in a form adapted

to his own wants. By thus acting on the external world and changing it, he at the same time changes his own nature.

> It [the labour process] is the necessary condition for effecting exchange of matter [the metabolic interaction or *Stoffwechsel*] between man and Nature; it is the everlasting Nature-imposed condition of human existence.[46]

What is distinctive about these two passages is that Marx is tying together his early materialism from Epicurus and Lucretius and his philosophy of nature (*Naturphilosophie*) from Kant, Hegel, and Schelling with his more recent fascination with the natural science theories of physiology and chemistry. These studies of metabolism based on the physiology of respiration and the chemistry of living cells and organisms are then expanded to an examination of the total systems of nature and society as an integrated organism, that is, to the broader issues of a theory of social metabolism and historical materialism. In his book *Marx's Ecology*, John Bellamy Foster has detailed Marx's knowledge of and reliance upon the scientific works of Theodor Schwann (cellular metabolism), Justus von Liebig (agricultural and animal chemistry, metabolism, soil and tissue degradation, and the circulation of soil nutrients), Julius Robert Mayer (law of conservation of energy), John Tyndall (absorption spectroscopy, infrared radiation in the earth's atmosphere, ozone, and molecules, greenhouse effect, solar radiation, the effects of fluctuations of water vapour and gases, especially carbon dioxide on climate change, and energetics), and Charles Darwin (biology, natural evolution, and the environment).[47]

The word 'metabolism' was used extensively within the natural sciences, especially cellular biology and chemistry in the 1830s and 1840s, to express material exchanges in the body and between organisms. Marx uses it to explain the relationship between human production and the environment. These works in the mid-nineteenth century in biology and chemistry lead Marx to appreciate the relationship in bio-chemistry and evolutionary biology of the interaction between an organism and its immediate environment. Marx then applies these insights to a systems theory of political economy and natural ecology. As a result, he is the first social theorist to systematically tie economic alienation and exploitation in the process of production to the exploitation and ecological crises of nature. The mechanised deskilling and specialised division of labour based on private property and wage labour result in the estrangement and fragmentation of human life, while production based on the law of value, surplus labour, and class power results in the structural crises of capitalism manifested in the tendential fall in the rate of profit, rising organic composition of capital, the overproduction of capital, underconsumption of material goods, unemployment, and economic crises. The two components of the barriers to capitalist production – class alienation and the dynamic logic of capital – have serious repercussions for nature because of the interdependency between society and nature. Because of the rapid advances in nineteenth-century biology, physiology, chemistry, and physics, especially in areas of cellular and animal metabolism, global warming, and climate change, Marx integrated the dialectic of nature with social metabolism to develop the beginnings of a theory of the universal metabolism of nature and society.[48]

The underlying chrematistic economy with its internal law of self-expanding capital, scientific and technological acceleration, and the rising productivity of labour is the ultimate cause of the rift or break in the social metabolism and harmonious balance of nature, thereby producing an environmental decay and breakdown manifested in the contradiction between production and the natural conditions of production, between town and country, industry and agriculture, and production and the circulation of matter and natural waste which ultimately result in serious environmental problems: ecological degradation, depletion of natural resources, nutrients, and organic matter, soil defertilisation, deforestation, industrial waste from production and consumption, air, water, and sewage pollution with high concentrations of nitrogen, phosphorus, and potassium in large cities, climate change, commodification of nature, toxic contamination, poor health and high mortality of industrial workers and children, environmental degradation of soil, vegetation, and animals, and the failure of matter recycling and agricultural sustainability.[49] These ecological crises are displaced forms of economic crises caused by a specific historical and social form of production of exchange value; they are crises of the conditions of production that turn nature from a living entity with its own natural laws into a dead, mechanical object of manipulation.[50]

Marx reflects on this very point in the *Grundrisse*: 'For the first time nature becomes purely an object for humankind, purely a matter of utility; ceases to be recognised as a power for itself; and the theoretical discovery of its autonomous laws appears merely as a ruse so as to subjugate it under human needs, whether as an object of consumption or as a means of production'.[51] Capitalist society is built on a structural and irreparable rift since production is for two contradictory purposes – production of use values for the satisfaction of basic human needs and the production of exchange value for profit and capital accumulation. Nature, as the basis for production of utilities and value, is also torn asunder by the same two contradictory structural imperatives of capitalism, thus explaining the necessity to consider both nature and society as part of the same social system. This is the dialectic of nature.[52]

With the rise of industrial alienation in both urban factories and rural agriculture, problems begin to develop in nature also. Just as capitalism creates its own contradictions and crises in the history and structures of political economy, it also produces contradictions and chasmic rifts in the metabolism of the environment.[53] The delicate balance between production and reproduction, labour and nature, ruptures due to the inner logic of capital to expand at the cost of environmental concerns. Since nature and industry are so interconnected, a structural problem in one area equally affects the other. Marx develops the implications of this insight in his later writings. In the *Grundrisse* he writes:

> It is not the *unity* of living and active humanity with the natural, inorganic conditions of their metabolic exchange [metabolism] with nature, and hence their appropriation of nature, which requires explanation or is the result of a historic process, but rather, the *separation* between these inorganic conditions of human existence and this active existence, a separation which is completely posited only in the relation of wage labour and capital.[54]

As we have already seen in this chapter, Marx had examined the dialectical connections between nature and society in *The Paris Manuscripts*. Now his attention has turned to the issue of the 'separation' or metabolic ruptures in nature caused by the production of wage labour and capital. The distortions and alienation of the economy have resulted in distortions and rifts within nature; in the end, nature becomes as much a barrier to capital accumulation as the production and value process itself. The social system cannot rationally protect nature or its long-term sustainability since its immediate economic interests require its exploitation and alienation. The driving imperative of a market economy and industrial production is increased productivity that only intensifies the break between nature and industry. Economic expansion and technological developments only exacerbate these social and environmental problems. Both labour and nature are sacrificed on the alter of commodity production.

This 'metabolic rift' in nature or the second contradiction of capital tears asunder the system stability within nature and between nature and society.[55] This rift results in serious ecological problems and the degradation of the natural environment. One manifestation of this environmental decay is the 'exploitation and squandering of the vitality of the soil' which calls into question the very ability of nature to reproduce itself.[56] Referring to the impact of large estates and a rigid class system in agriculture, Marx writes in the third volume of *Capital* (1894): 'It [large landed estates] thereby creates conditions which cause an irreparable break [*einen unheilbaren Riss*] in the coherence of social interchange [social metabolism or *vorgeschriebnen Stoffwechsels*] prescribed by the natural laws of life. As a result the vitality of the soil is squandered, and this prodigality is carried by commerce far beyond the borders of a particular state (Liebig)'.[57] Whether it is a case of the industrial economy 'laying waste and ruining' the natural basis for large-scale agricultural production in a healthy soil environment or exhausting labour as the foundation of political economy, the very structures of production are endangered. This unholy and irreparable tear in the living fabric of nature only intensifies the initial difficulties and contradictions of capital; it makes it that much more difficult, if not impossible, given the logic of capital, to maintain productivity and profits necessary for the stability and legitimacy of the social system.

The logic of value production creates an alienation in labour but also a metabolic or systems rift in nature in the form of nutrient depletion and soil exhaustion.[58] According to Marx, with the concentration and centralisation of capital in urban centres, capitalism destroys the traditional relationship and balance between agriculture and industry, between rural life and the town. By creating concentrated urban centres, complex infrastructure, and overpopulation, it forms real limits or barriers to both agricultural and industrial productivity. Marx views this process of capitalist production and alienation clearly in environmental terms:

> It [urban production] disturbs the circulation of matter between man and the soil, i.e., prevents the return to the soil of its elements consumed by man in the form of food and clothing; it therefore violates the conditions necessary to lasting fertility of the soil. By this action it destroys at the same time the health of the town labourers and the intellectual life of the rural labourer ... In agriculture as in manufacture, the transformation of production under the sway of capital, means, at the same time, the martyrdom of the producer; the instrument of labour becomes the means of enslaving, exploiting, and impoverishing the labourer; the social combination and organisation of labour-processes is turned into an organised mode of crushing out the workman's individual vitality, freedom, and independence ... Moreover all progress in capitalistic agriculture is a progress in the art, not only of robbing the labourer, but of robbing the soil; all progress in increasing the fertility of the soil for a given time, is a progress toward ruining the lasting sources of that fertility.[59]

Modern industry results not only in destroying labour, human creativity, with its corresponding institutions of democracy and social justice, but it also destroys nature, depletes the soil of rich nutrients, undermines the circulation of matter and waste between humanity and the soil, makes it necessary to rapidly industrialise nature with modern technology and synthetic fertilisation, creates serous health problems for the labourers, and prepares the way for an ecological crisis. Cultural waste and human waste accumulate, leaving pollution in all forms. Marx is concerned by the level of sewage pollution in the Thames River, the failure to recycle for agricultural use the essential soil nutrients of potassium, nitrogen, and phosphorus, and the conservation of natural resources. The range and detail of Marx's writings on the natural sciences, agricultural and industrial production, and the environment are fascinating: He mentions the contamination of the Thames with the excretion of four and a half million inhabitants and the expense to clean it up. He also details the waste of both production and consumption and the application of science to re-utilise this matter in various industries, including the manufacture of cotton, wool, grain, silk, flax, shoddy, indigo, coal, gas, iron, wood, leather, etc.[60] Liebig was writing about chemistry and industrial agriculture in *Organic Chemistry in its Application to Agriculture and Physiology* (also referred to as *Agricultural Chemistry*, 1840) in which he examined issues of environmental decay and nutrient depletion in the soil resulting from urban population concentration and the necessity to create fertilisers from the bones of the Napoleonic battlefields and guano (bird excrement) in Peru.[61]

With the concentration of population and capital in urban centres and with its growing needs, nature is despoiled and robbed of its future agricultural productivity. 'Capitalist production, therefore, develops technology, and the combining together of various processes into a social whole, only by sapping the original sources of all wealth – the soil and the labourer'.[62] Capital and value production in industry destroy the spirit of human development and self-consciousness, while at the same time destroying the physical nature underlying the process. Spirit and nature, self-consciousness and physical existence are intimately interlinked in this social metabolism of capitalism. The dialectic of nature and capital have been joined together so that Marx clearly sees that the modern form of industry destroys the social wealth of the community in the productivity of the soil and labour. Capitalism as a social system is antithetical to the needs of all of living nature. And it is not just the fertility of the soil that has changed. Friedrich Engels writes in the *Dialectics of Nature* (1883) that the whole of nature is affected by these industrial transformations. 'But it is precisely the alteration of nature by men, not solely nature as such, which is the most essential and immediate basis for human thought ... The earth's surface, climate, vegetation, fauna, and the human beings themselves have infinitely changed, and all this owing to human activity ...'.[63] All of physical nature is radically transformed by modern industry and technology.

Social Justice and the Natural Laws of Ethics and Ecology

In the end, a new socialist society will be formed through economic and political transformations that will also change humanity's relation with nature. There will be a return to an ecological balance and harmony with nature.[64] Previous societies and their historical modes of production, including capitalism, were only concerned with increasing productivity and accumulation, but not with the effects of production on nature.[65] To respond to the alienation and exploitation of class production and its corresponding alienation of nature due to value production requires a revolution in both the productive forces and social relations of production. Near the end of the third volume of *Capital*, Marx recognises the new relationship between democratic socialism and nature when he writes:

> Freedom in this field can only consist in a socialised man, the associated producers, rationally regulating their interchange [metabolism] with Nature, bringing it under their common control, instead of being ruled by it as by the blind forces of Nature ... Beyond it begins that development of human energy which is an end in itself, the true realm of freedom, which, however, can blossom forth only with this realm of necessity as its basis.[66]

True democracy will also entail a reciprocal social metabolism. This metabolic interchange between nature and society is essential for the realisation of social justice; this balance between ethics of human nature (praxis, self-determination, and freedom) and the natural ecology of physical nature (ecological sustainability) is essential for social justice. Thus issues of nature, the environment, and justice can only be resolved by expanding the questions of social justice to include political, economic, and ecological justice. This is why in his analysis of nature Marx reintroduces the issues of human emancipation, wealth of human beings, and human needs. These issues were the focus of attention in Chapter 4 when discussing the virtuous and good life and workplace justice; the issues of social metabolism and the dialectic of nature, in turn, anticipate the following chapters on political and economic justice.

ECOLOGICAL JUSTICE

Although Marx had begun to create a dialectic of both society and nature inherent in the very structures and contradictions of capitalist production, there have been a number of important recent works which expand the horizons of Marx's ecological theory into the twenty-first century.[67] This is relevant for our examination of Marx because it only enhances our understanding of the range of issues to be discussed in a theory of social justice. In the *Dialectics of Nature* Engels writes:

> Let us not, however, flatter ourselves overmuch on account of our human conquests over nature. For each such conquest takes its revenge on us ... Thus at every step we are reminded that we by no means rule over nature like a conqueror over a foreign people, like someone standing outside nature – but that we, with flesh, blood, and brain, belong to nature, and exist in its midst, and that all our mastery of it consists in the fact that we have the advantage over all other creatures of being able to know and correctly apply its laws ... But the more this happens, the more will men once more not only feel, but also know, themselves to be one with nature.[68]

Engels recognises that the attempt to expand cultivable land from the forests in Mesopotamia, Greece, Asia Minor, and Italy led to the destruction of the forests, water reserves and springs, soil moisture, and agricultural industry; it also resulted in floods during the rainy season. The reintegration of human production and nature will also result in overcoming the contradictions between society and nature, mind and matter, mind and body expressed in the neo-Platonism of medieval Christianity and modern Cartesian science. Engels reminds the reader that to undertake this reintegration of nature and humanity 'requires something more than mere knowledge. It requires a complete revolution in our hitherto existing mode of production and with it of our whole contemporary social order'.[69] Society's relationship to nature must be changed along with the capitalist mode of production. With the domination of nature, the dialectic between nature and society is broken. There needs to be a new framework of interaction between the two. Marx in the third volume of *Capital* has presented these necessary changes in the following passage:

> From the standpoint of a higher economic form of society, private ownership of the globe by single individuals will appear quite as absurd as private ownership of one man by another. Even a whole society, a nation, or even all simultaneously existing societies taken together, are not the owners of the globe. They are simply its possessors, its usufructuaries

[beneficiaries], and like *boni patres familias* [good heads of household], they must hand it down to succeeding generations in an improved condition.[70]

It is not simply a question of rethinking the economic foundations of production as we move toward social justice in nature and society. Marx is returning to Aristotle's theory of the intersection between ethics and physics with his dialectic of nature and society. Just as the *Nicomachean Ethics* was grounded in the teleology of biology and the function and form of physics, just as ethics was grounded in human nature, so, too, for Marx, there is a dialectical metabolism between ethics (Chapter 4) and nature (Chapter 5). Aristotle had grounded ethics broadly in his theory of matter, form, causes, and motion (final end).[71] He placed an emphasis on the central importance of a self-sustaining household economy and polity and their relationship to a living, organic nature reconfirming the intimate bond between natural law and nature. Marx, in turn, develops his critical social theory in terms of physical natural law or the matter, function, and form of nature, that is, in terms of both human nature (ethics, virtue, and reason) and the laws of nature and dialectical theory of metabolism in organic chemistry, evolutionary biology, and physics. Throughout his later writings, especially in the *Grundrisse* and *Capital*, Marx continuously refers to the natural laws of society and nature: the objective laws of capitalist production, economic law of motion of natural history, human nature, and the social ecology.[72] In a letter to Leo Kugelmann on 11 July 1868, Marx writes: 'No natural laws can be done away with. What can change, in changing historical circumstances, is the *form* in which these laws operate'.[73] On the other hand, the laws of capitalist accumulation are historical laws that operated as natural laws within the parameters set by a historically specific form of economic relationship. That is, they are valid for a particular historical moment in time; they are temporary, historical laws created by humans and not universal, theological laws. For Marx, these laws must be changed because externally they are exploitative and oppressive and internally they produce logical and structural contradictions that are irrational and immoral, leading to economic and ecological crises.

There is a distinction between the natural law of capital and the unchanging natural law of physics. Neil Smith argues that the law of gravity as a universal and physical law cannot be destroyed, but the social law of value as a historically specific law can and must be changed. Marx views human nature – human creativity and social praxis – as having many different historical appearances. This is why Hegel's phenomenology as an expression of the history of human self-consciousness is so important to him. But by transforming Hegel's idealism into a historical and critical materialism, Marx rejects various claims to the inevitability and naturalness of history by systematically revealing each historical period and each historical manifestation of human nature as based on contradictory and immoral social institutions and values. These weakness are formally expressed as social and ecological barriers, contradictions, or metabolic rifts that inhibit further economic development of human potentiality. Smith summarises this problem of capital when he states:

> It [capitalism] creates a scarcity of needed resources, impoverishes the quality of those resources not yet devoured, breeds new diseases, develops a nuclear technology that threatens the future of all humanity, pollutes the entire environment that we must consume in order to reproduce, and in the daily work process it threatens the very existence of those who produced the vital social wealth.[74]

The economic dimension of these contradictions will be seen more clearly in Chapter 8 of this work on economic justice.

Both Aristotle and Marx reject the pure idea or universal form of the good in itself since they view the good as something that develops out of practical activity (*praxis*). Moral values are not the product of philosophical or theoretical activity but social action. Humans are by nature political and social beings involved in the creation and sustainability of the household and the community. And both accept the notion that although grounded in nature, the truth about moral virtue and social ethics is ultimately a product of civic participation in democracy and the ethical life of the community. The good life of virtue, excellence, and beneficence either in a democratic polity or democratic socialism is the ultimate goal of human nature and reason since both articulate a potentiality of humanity, but it is through practical activity that the final end is defined and reached. The end of human nature is a potentiality and form that reaches actuality through the social praxis of reason, dialogue, and democratic practice. Marx has pushed the envelope of the constitution theory of truth of German Idealism. Epistemology and phenomenology have been turned into a historical and materialist theory of knowledge and science. The door has been opened to a developed theory of nature but Marx did not walk through. He instead turned his attention in his later life to a critique of political economy and ecological crisis.

Notes

1 *Marx, Nature, and Moral Ecology*: For an examination of Marx's theory of nature and implications for a critical theory of ecology in its broadest sense, see Leszek Kołakowski, 'Karl Marx and the Classical Definition of Truth', in *Marxism and Beyond*, trans. J.Z. Peel (London: Pall Mall Press, 1969), pp. 58–86; István Mészáros, *Marx's Theory of Alienation* (New York, NY: Harper & Row Publishers, 1970), pp. 100–19 and *The Power of Ideology* (New York, NY: Zed Books, 2005), chapter 4, pp. 175–202; Alfred Schmidt, *The Concept of Nature in Marx* (London: NLB, 1973); David-Hillel Ruben, *Marxism and Materialism: A Study in Marxist Theory of Knowledge* (Atlantic Highlands, NJ: Humanities Press, 1979); Wolfgang Methe, *Ökologie und Marxismus* (Hannover: SOAK Verlag, 1981); Patrick Murray, 'The Frankfurt School Critique of Technology', *Philosophy and Technology*, 5 (1982): 223–48; Trent Schroyer, 'Critique of the Instrumental Interest in Nature', *Social Research*, 50, 1 (Spring 1983): 158–84; Wolfdietrich Schmied-Kowarzik, *Das dialektische Verhältnis des Menschen zur Natur. Philosophiegeschichtliche Studien zur Naturproblematik bei Karl Marx* (Freiburg: Verlag Karl Alber, 1984), pp. 61–116, Hans Immler and Schmied-Kowarzik, Hg., *Marx und die Naturfrage. Ein Wissenschaftsstreit* (Hamburg: VSA-Verlag, 1984), and Hans Immler and Wolfdietrich Schmied-Kowarzik, Hg., *Natur und Marxistische Werttheorie* (Kassel: Kasseler Philosophische Schriften, 23, 1986), pp. 25–34; Neil Smith, *Uneven Development: Nature, Capital and the Production of Space* (Oxford: Basil Blackwell, 1984), pp. 1–31; Philip Kain, *Marx and Ethics* (Oxford: Clarendon Press, 1988), pp. 65–6 and 70–1; Lawrence Wilde, *Ethical Marxism and its Radical Critics* (Basingstoke: Macmillan, 1998), pp. 122–41; Paul Burkett, *Marx and Nature: A Red and Green Perspective* (New York, NY: St. Martin's Press, 1999); John Bellamy Foster, *Marx's Ecology: Materialism and Nature* (New York, NY: Monthly Review Press, 2000), pp. 141–77; Jonathan Hughes, *Ecology and Historical Materialism* (Cambridge: Cambridge University Press, 2000); Justin Holt, *Karl Marx's Philosophy of Nature, Action and Society* (Cambridge: Cambridge University Press, 2009); and Jason Moore, *Capitalism in the Web of Life: Ecology and the Accumulation of Capital* (London: Verso, 2015).

Kain writes that 'morality is the perfection of our nature' as a free, rational, and creative species being (p. 66), but he could just as well have written that morality is a perfection of nature itself; nature within a moral economy and democratic socialism would become a moral ecology. For a deeper analysis of the relationship among nature, consciousness, and objectification, the relationship between nature and aesthetics (simplicity, harmony, and balance) in Schiller, Hegel, Feuerbach, and Marx, and the idea that the fullest development of nature and humanity occurs within a democratic polity, see Philip Kain, *Schiller, Hegel, and Marx: State, Society, and the Aesthetic Ideal of Ancient Greece* (Kingston, Canada: McGill-Queen's University Press, 1982), pp. 89–91 and 98–103.

2 Some authors view Marx's technical solution to the economic exploitation and structural crisis of capitalism as dismantling class and expanding production. For a summary of the tradition that Marx is a technological and scientific optimist and determinist without ecological sensitivities and reservations based on his crude positivism, materialism, and mechanical understanding of the productive forces, see K.J. Walker, 'Ecological Limits and Marxian Thought', *Politics* 14, 1 (May 1979): 35–6; Val Routley, 'On Karl Marx as an

Environmental Hero', 3, 3 *Environmental Ethics* (Fall 1981): 242; Herman Daly, *Steady-State Economics* (London: Earthscan, 1992), p. 196; Robyn Eckersley, *Environmentalism and Political Theory* (Albany, NY: State University of New York Press, 1992), p. 80; Victor Ferkiss, *Nature, Technology, and Society: Cultural Roots of the Current Environmental Crisis* (New York, NY: New York University Press, 1993), pp. 109–10; John Bellamy Foster, 'Marx and the Environment', *Monthly Review* 47, 3 (July–August 1995): 108–9; Ted Benton (ed.), *The Greening of Marxism* (New York, NY: Guilford Press, 1996); and Burkett, *Marx and Nature*, pp. vii, 2–7, 12–14, 30–1, 38–47, 99–106, 147–50, 169–70, 176, 182–3, 223–5, and 239–40, 'Was Marx a Promethean?', *Nature, Society, and Thought*, 12, 1 (1999): 7–42, and 'Marx's Vision of Sustainable Human Development', *Monthly Review*, 57, 5 (October 2005): 35 and 59, n. 3. For a further overview of the criticisms of Marx as anti-ecology, see John Bellamy Foster, 'Marx's Theory of Metabolic Rift', *American Journal of Sociology*, 105, 2 (September 1999): 366–405 and *Marx's Ecology*, pp. 9–11 and 169–70; and Maarten de Kadt and Salvatore Engel-Di Mauro, 'Failed Promise', *Capitalism Nature Socialism*, 12, 2 (June 2001): 52–5. Also see John Bellamy Foster, 'The Communist Manifesto and the Environment', *Socialist Register* (1998) for a critical response to the view that Marx is anti-ecology in the works of Ted Benton, Kate Soper, Victor Ferkiss, John Class, Robyn Eckersley, Murray Bookchin, Gary Snyder, and Anthony Giddens (pp. 180–1 and n. 2, 186). Foster, taking the opposing side of the argument, writes about Marx as a serious social ecologist: 'But, paradoxically, capitalism's antagonistic relation to the environment, which lies at the core of our current crisis, was in some ways more apparent to 19th and early 20th century socialists than it is to the majority of today's green thinkers', in 'Marx's Ecology in Historical Perspective', *International Socialism Journal*, 96 (Winter 2002).

Foster divides the critics of a Marxian ecology into two groups: the scientific positivism of Soviet Marxism and the rejection of naturalism, scientism, and positivism of the Western Marxism of Georg Lukács, Karl Korsch, Theodor Adorno, Max Horkheimer, and Antonio Gramsci. In the preface to *Marx and Nature*, Burkett lists the general criticisms of Marx and his approach to nature as follows: (1) Marx rejects the capitalist class relations of production but unreflectively and uncritically uses science, technology, and the productive forces to produce for the common good; (2) he does not emphasise the importance of nature for production; and (3) the contradictions of capital are not affected by nature (p. vii).

3   In his essay, 'Ökonomischer Formwandel und Naturfrage', in *Natur und Marxistische Werttheorie*, Horst Müller contends that Schmied-Kowarzik appreciated that Marx was the first social theorist who anticipated the ecological crisis as a further development of the problem of the alienation of capitalist production (p. 87). Schmied-Kowarzik, in his work *Marx und die Naturfrage*, makes a strong case for exactly this position. Breaking with the traditional dogmatic interpretations of Marx as a 'propagandist for the unlimited development of the industrial productive forces and domination of nature', he writes, 'Marx was the first philosopher and social theorist, who in anticipation of the ecological crisis ... had thought through the problem of the alienation of the capitalist industrial mode of production in relation to living nature in order to lay the foundations for its revolutionary overcoming' (p. 25). Since Schmied-Kowarzik was writing in the early and mid-1980s on Marx's social theory of ecology, he represents an important part of this new mosaic of scholars

discovering a dialectic of nature and critical ecology in his social theory. In 1984, Schmied-Kowarzik first published his major work on Marx and nature in the *Kasseler Philosophische Schriften*, entitled *Das dialektische Verhältnis des Menschen zur Natur*. About the same time, he was engaged in a public discussion of these same issues on Marx and ecological theory with Hans Immler in *Marx und die Naturfrage*. Finally, in 1986 there was a *Kasseler Wissenschaftsstreit* conference which highlighted the earlier writings of both scholars along with a public discussion of these same issues of Marx, critique of political economy, and the ecological crisis; they referred to the issue as *die Naturfrage* (nature question). Schmied-Kowarzik attempts to reintegrate the law of value, surplus labour, and the logic of capital with the degradation of nature caused by economic expansion for private profits. The exploitation of workers and nature are intimately linked in Marx's writings. In turn, by reintegrating political economy and nature, he also reintegrates Marx and Aristotle by recognising that the former's critique of political economy and the logic of capital is also the latter's critique of *chrematistik*. Nature is both a dialectical and a social concept.

4   John Bellamy Foster, 'Marx's Ecology in Historical Perspective', *International Socialism Journal*, 96 (Winter 2002): 3.

5   For an analysis of the Greek philosophy of nature in Marx's dissertation on Democritus and Epicurus and his earlier notebooks on Epicurus, see George McCarthy, *Marx and the Ancients: Classical Ethics, Social Justice, and Nineteenth-Century Political Economy* (Savage, MD: Rowman & Littlefield Publishers, 1990), pp. 19–55 and *Classical Horizons: The Origins of Sociology in Ancient Greece* (Albany, NY: State University of New York Press, 2003), pp. 17–25 and 51–9. See also Cyril Bailey, 'Karl Marx on Greek Atomism', *Classical Quarterly*, 22 (July 1928): 205–6; Henry Mins, 'Marx's Doctoral Dissertation', *Science and Society*, 12, 1 (Winter 1948): 157–69; Rolf Sannwald, *Marx und die Antike*, hrsg. Edgar Salin and V.F. Wagner (Zurich: Polygraphischer Verlag, 1957); *Marxism and the Classics*, *Arethusa*, ed. J.P. Sullivan 8, 1 (Spring 1975); Laurence Baronovitch, 'German Idealism, Greek Materialism, and the Young Marx', *International Philosophical Quarter*, 24, 3 (September 1984): 245–66; Peter Fenves, 'Marx's Doctoral Thesis on Two Greek Atomists and the Post-Kantian Interpretations', *Journal of the History of Ideas*, 47, 3 (July–September 1986): 433–52; Panajotis Kondylis, *Marx und die Griechische Antike. Zwei Studien* (Heidelberg: Manutius Verlag, 1987); G. Teeple, 'The Doctoral Dissertation of Karl Marx', *History of Political Thought*, 11, 1 (1990): 81–118; John Stanley, 'The Marxism of Marx's Doctoral Dissertation', *Journal of the History of Philosophy*, 33, 1 (January 1993): 133–58; and the essays by D.C. Lee, C. Tolman, J.P. Clark, J.B. Foster, H.Y. Jung, and T. Benton in *Karl Marx's Social and Political Thought*, vol. 8: *Nature, Culture, Morals, Ethics*, ed. Bob Jessop and Russell Wheatley (London: Routledge, 1999), pp. 1–69.

6   This position is summarised by Schmied-Kowarzik in *Das dialektische Verhältnis des Menschen zur Natur*, pp. 77–84, which is a product of numerous articles since the end of the 1970s. With the discovery and publication of the early *Paris Manuscripts* in 1932, the 'nature problem', the philosophical foundations of Marxist theory in human nature, and the one-dimensionality of Western reason, was again introduced by Herbert Marcuse and Henri Lefebvre (p. 124). Schmied-Kowarzik stresses the importance of Marx's early writings for the development of the rudimentary foundations of a philosophy of nature

and the later expansion of these ideas in the works of Ernst Bloch (returning to Schelling in *The Problem of Materialism, Its History and Substance*, 1972 and *Experimentum Mundi: Question, Categories of Realization, Praxis*, 1975) and Alfred Sohn-Rethel (returning to Kant in *Intellectual and Manual Labour: A Critique of Epistemology*, 1977) (ibid., pp. 16–17 and 125–9). Schmied-Kowarzik argues that the ecological crisis lies in both the abstract categories of the modern science of domination and the structures of the organisation of production (pp. 12–13). The alienation of nature requires a response to the defective form of reason and production under modern capitalism. Thus, he calls for a critical theory of social praxis that is grounded in Marx but at the same time moves beyond him into an expanded theory of social action. He thus incorporates members of critical theory and the Frankfurt School into his dialectic of nature reintegrating idealism and materialism. The very concept of science is itself an expression of the alienation of nature (p. 15). Schmied-Kowarzik argues that Marx joins Kant and Schelling together in a new and critical philosophy of nature (*Naturphilosophie*) (p. 16).

7   Ibid., pp. 68–9.
8   Joel Kovel, 'Ecological Marxism and Dialectic', *Capitalism Nature Socialism*, 24 (December 1995): 31–50. On the reduction of Marx to a positivist, see the works of Jürgen Habermas, *Knowledge and Human Interest*, trans. Jeremy Shapiro (Boston, MA: Beacon Press, 1971), pp. 43–63; Murray Bookchin, 'Listen Marxists', in *Post-Scarcity Anarchism* (Berkeley, CA: Ramparts Press, 1971), pp. 173–220; Alvin Gouldner, *The Two Marxisms: Contradictions and Anomalies in the Development of Theory* (New York, NY: Oxford University Press, 1980); and Merrit Roe Smith and Leo Marx (eds.), *Does Technology Drive History? The Dilemma of Technological Determinism* (Boston, MA: The MIT Press, 1994). Bookchin writes, in 'Listen Marxists': 'Marxism has ceased to be applicable to our time not because it is too visionary or revolutionary, but because it is not visionary or revolutionary enough' (p. 177). He suggests that, like Hegel, it is time to transcend Marx.
9   This argument of the primacy and independence of industrial technology and the productive forces is a restatement of the relationship between the technical base and the social and cultural superstructure. Rejecting the dualism and primacy argument, István Mészáros, drawing upon the earlier work of Georg Lukács, reaffirms the dialectic between the economy and society, between the productive forces and social relations of production in *Social Structure and Forms of Consciousness: The Dialectic of Structure and History*, vol. 2 (New York, NY: Monthly Review Press, 2011), p. 57. The productive forces are only part of a more comprehensive dialectic or interchange between technology and the social relations of production; together they constitute the historical mode of production. See also Paul Burkett and John Bellamy Foster, 'Metabolism, Energy, and Entropy in Marx's Critique of Political Economy', *American Sociology Association Meetings*, San Francisco, CA (14–17 August 2004), p. 18.
10 Foster, *Marx's Ecology*, pp. 131–40 and 141–77; and Smith, *Uneven Development*, pp. 28–31 and 60–5.
11 Norman Geras, *Marx and Human Nature: Refutation of a Legend* (London: Verso, 1983). This book is a discussion about Marx's theory of human nature based on the sixth thesis of the *Theses on Feuerbach*: 'But the human essence is no abstraction inherent in each single individual. In its reality it is the ensemble of the social relations' found in *Marx and Engels*:

Basic Writings on Politics and Philosophy, ed. Lewis Feuer, (Garden City, NY: Anchor Books, 1959), p. 244; *Karl Marx/Friedrich Engels Werke*, Band 3 (Berlin: Dietz Verlag, 1978), p. 6. That is, there is no transcendental or abstract form or eternal essence defining the nature of humanity. Human nature is defined by our species characteristics of social relations, production, sensuous life, and human praxis. The essence of humanity is historical and social, and framed by the mode of production in each society. In capitalism there is a dialectical and reciprocal relationship between the economic base and the cultural superstructure.

12 Karl Marx, 'Alienated Labour', *Karl Marx: Early Writings*, ed. and trans. T.B. Bottomore (New York, NY: McGraw-Hill Book Company, 1964), p. 126; *Karl Marx/Friedrich Engels Werke*, Band 40, Ergänzungsband, Erster Teil (Berlin: Dietz Verlag, 1968), p. 515.
13 Ibid.
14 Ibid.
15 This blending of existentialism and Marxism in the analysis of alienation and human praxis is a main theme in Erich Fromm, *Marx's Concept of Man* (New York, NY: Frederick Ungar Publishing Company, 1969), pp. 69–83.
16 Marx, 'Alienated Labour', pp. 126–7; *MEW 40*, Ergänzungsband 1, p. 516.
17 Ibid., p. 127; *MEW* 40, Ergänzungsband 1, p. 516.
18 Although Marx is writing in the nineteenth century, even his earliest ideas on the subject of nature and society reveal a strong materialist interpretation of the problem which would in a different historical context have led Marx to seriously question the idealism and spirituality of much of twentieth-century social ecology.
19 Marx, 'Alienated Labour', p. 127; *MEW* 40, Ergänzungsband 1, p. 516.
20 Ibid, pp. 127–8; *MEW* 40, Ergänzungsband 1, pp. 516–17.
21 Ibid., p. 128; *MEW* 40, Ergänzungsband 1, p. 517.
22 Ibid. The early philosophy of alienation and nature is not an unfortunate detour or delay before we get to Marx's more advanced ecological theory, but, as in the case with his later economic theory, it provides the intellectual foundations upon which he develops his more ecological and dialectical theory of nature.
23 Karl Marx, 'Private Property and Communism', *Karl Marx: Early Writings*, ed. and trans. T.B. Bottomore (New York, NY: McGraw-Hill Book Company, 1964), p. 157; *MEW* 40, Ergänzungsband 1, p. 538.
24 Ibid., p. 155; *MEW* 40, Ergänzungsband 1, p. 536.
25 Ibid., p. 158; *MEW 40*, Ergänzungsband 1, p. 539.
26 Ibid.
27 Ibid., p. 156; *MEW 40*, Ergänzungsband 1, p. 537.
28 Ibid., p. 159; *MEW* 40, Ergänzungsband 1, p. 539.
29 Marx, 'Alienated Labour', p. 122; *MEW* 40, Ergänzungsband 1, p. 512.
30 Marx, 'Private Property and Communism', p. 160; *MEW* 40, Ergänzungsband 1, p. 540.
31 Ibid.; *MEW 40*, Ergänzungsband 1, p. 541.
32 Ibid., p. 155; *MEW 40*, Ergänzungsband 1, p. 536.
33 In *The German Ideology* by Karl Marx and Friedrich Engels, parts I and III, ed. and intro. R. Pascal (New York, NY: International Publishers, 1965), there is a critique of Feuerbach's philosophical materialism and his romantic view of nature as they write about the dia-

lectic between science and production: 'He [Feuerbach] does not see how the sensuous world around him is, not a thing given direct from all eternity, ever the same, but the product of industry and of the state of society ... Even this "pure" natural science is provided with an aim, as with its material, only through trade and industry, through the sensuous activity of men' (pp. 35–6; *Karl Marx/Friedrich Engels Werke*, Band 3 [Berlin: Dietz Verlag, 1962], pp. 43–4).

34 Marx, 'Private Property and Communism', p. 161; *MEW* 40, Ergänzungsband 1, p. 541.
35 Ibid.
36 Ibid. p. 162; *MEW* 40, Ergänzungsband 1, p. 542.
37 Schmied-Kowarzik, *Das dialektische Verhältnis des Menschen zur Natur*, pp. 101–16 and 117–29.
38 Marx, *The German Ideology*, p. 36; *MEW* 3, pp. 43–4. Marx and Engels agree with Feuerbach, the Left Hegelian philosopher, that humans are sensuous objects. But they disagree as to the reasons for this insight. For Feuerbach, humans are sensuous because of his general materialist philosophy. Marx and Engels see humans in this way because their industry and production have created a material and natural world of objects of which humans are a part (p. 37; *MEW* 3, p. 44).
39 Marx, 'Private Property and Communism', p. 163; *MEW* 40, Ergänzungsband 1, pp. 542–3.
40 In *The Holy Family or Critique of Critical Critique, Karl Marx/Frederick Engels Collected Works*, vol. 4 (New York, NY: International Publishers, 1975), Marx and Engels define the scientific method based on the rational method and methodological principles outlined by Francis Bacon as grounding itself in sense experience from induction, comparative analysis of the data, observation, and experimentation (p. 128; *Karl Marx/Friedrich Engels Werke*, Band 2 [Berlin: Dietz Verlag, 1962], p. 135).
41 Marx, 'Private Property and Communism', p. 163; *MEW* 40, Ergänzungsband 1, p. 543.
42 Wolfdietrich Schmied-Kowarzik, 'Die Entfremdung der gesellschaftlichen Produktion von der Natur und ihre revolutionäre Überwindung', in *Marx und die Naturfrage*, hrsg. Hans Immler and Wolfdietrich Schmied-Kowarzik (Hamburg: VSA Verlag, 1984), p. 17.
43 Marx, 'Private Property and Communism', pp. 163–4; *MEW* 40, Ergänzungsband 1, p. 543. This line of argument is continued in *The German Ideology* where Marx echoes his idea of human science from the *Paris Manuscripts* when he writes: 'We know only a single science, the science of history. One can look at history from two sides and divide it into the history of nature and the history of man. The two sides are, however, inseparable; the history of nature and the history of men are dependent on each other so long as men exist'. This passage was deleted in the original manuscript but reappears in an endnote in the *Collected Works* of Marx and Engels. Later in the same work, Marx criticises the discipline of history for its emphasis on peripheral issues of the political actions of princes and states, the motivation of religion and politics, and, finally, the movement of the Hegelian self-conscious world spirit. History is a metaphysical undertaking. True materialism and history, on the contrary, should examine the material practice of humans, their production of social life, and the relationship between nature and society (pp. 28–30; *MEW* 3, pp. 37–9). Mészáros in *Marx's Theory of Alienation* emphasises the central point that the dialectic between humanity and nature does not involve 'some misconceived ideal of remodelling philosophy on *natural* science. Indeed he [Marx] sharply criticizes both philosophy and

the natural sciences ... In Marx's view both philosophy and the natural sciences are manifestations of the same estrangement' (p. 101). Both are to be replaced by a human science – historical materialism and critical social theory.

44 Marx, 'Private Property and Communism', p. 164; *MEW* 40, Ergänzungsband 1, p. 543.

45 Karl Marx, 'Needs, Production, and Division of Labour', *Karl Marx: Early Writings*, ed. and trans. T.B. Bottomore (New York, NY: McGraw-Hill Book Company, 1964), p. 176; *MEW* 40, Ergänzungsband 1, p. 554. It is no accident that the next essay in these early manuscripts is 'Needs, Production, and Division of Labour', which continues to examine Marx's theory of human needs in more detail.

46 Marx, *Capital: A Critique of Political Economy*, vol. 1: *The Process of Capitalist Production*, ed. Friedrich Engels, trans. Samuel Moore and Edward Aveling (New York, NY: International Publishers, 1968), pp. 177 and 183–4; *Karl Marx/Friedrich Engels Werke* (*MEW*), Band 23 (Berlin: Dietz Verlag, 1962), pp. 192 and 198.

47 Foster, *Marx's Ecology*, pp. 14 and 155–63. 'The German word "*Stoffwechsel*" directly sets out in its elements the notion of "material exchange" that underlies the notion of a structured process of biological growth and decay captured in the term "metabolism." In his definition of the labour process Marx made the concept of metabolism central to his entire system of analysis by rooting his understanding of the labour process upon it ... Marx utilized the concept of metabolism to describe the human relation to nature through labour ... The concept of metabolism, with its attendant notions of material exchanges and regulatory action, allowed him to express human relations to nature as one that encompassed both "nature-imposed condition" and the capacity of human beings to affect this process' (pp. 157–8). Finally, and perhaps most importantly of all, the concept of metabolism helped Marx connect his early theory of alienation and labour to his later theory of social production and the dialectic of nature and ecology. As Foster recognises, the later Marx used the term social metabolism to describe the general interchange between nature and humanity in praxis, production, circulation of material goods, fulfilment of freedom and human needs, and exchange of equivalents. Foster maintains that the concept of metabolism, used throughout his later writings, provides Marx with the scientific grounding for his earlier ecological theory of labour and nature. See also his 'Marx and the Rift in the Universal Metabolism of Nature', *Monthly Review*, 65, 7 (December 2013): 1–19. In this article, Foster mentions the importance of the philosophical tradition after Marx which emphasised the concept of social metabolism in the writings of Georg Lukács, *History and Class Consciousness* and István Mészáros, *Marx's Theory of Alienation* and *Beyond Capital* (pp. 4–5).

48 Foster, 'Marx and the Rift in the Universal Metabolism of Nature', pp. 9–10. Foster mentions that toward the end of his life, Marx was studying 'shifts in isotherms [the temperature zones of the earth] associated with climate change in earlier geological eras [which] led to the great extinctions in Earth's history' (p. 9).

49 *Marx/Engels Ecological Crisis Theory*: The ecological crisis of Marx and Engels is outlined in their later writings, including:

   – Friedrich Engels, *The Conditions of the Working Class in England in 1844* (Moscow: Progress Publishers, 1973), pp. 60–1, 65, 94–9, 102–3, 112–13, 134–71, and 275; *Karl Marx/*

- *Friedrich Engels Werke* (MEW), Band 2 (Berlin: Dietz Verlag, 1962), pp. 254–5, 258, 287–91, 294–5, 304–5, 324–59 and 454; and the *Dialectics of Nature* (Moscow: Foreign Language Publishing House, 1954), pp. 330, 459–64, 511 and 583–5; *Karl Marx/Friedrich Engels Werke* (MEW), Band 20 (Berlin: Dietz Verlag, 1975), pp. 322–3, 451–5, 499 and 564–6.
- Marx and Engels, *The German Ideology*, pp. 7, 16–20, 30, 34–8, 49–50, 63–4 and 70; *Karl Marx/Friedrich Engels Werke* (MEW), Band 3 (Berlin: Dietz Verlag, 1978), pp. 21, 28–31, 39, 42–5, 54–5, 65–6 and 70–1.
- Karl Marx, *Grundrisse: Foundations of the Critique of Political Economy*, trans. Martin Nicolaus (New York, NY: Vintage Books, 1973), pp. 141–5, 158, 334, 400, 408–10, 471–514, 527–8, 541–2, 611–12, 694–5, 700, 704–9 and 749–50; *Karl Marx/Friedrich Engel Werke* (MEW), Band 42 (Berlin: Dietz Verlag, 1983), pp. 76–80, 91–2, 252–3, 314–15, 322–4, 383–421, 433–4, 447–8, 512–13, 595, 596, 600–5 and 641–3.
- *Capital*, vol. 1, pp. 42–3, 79, 82, 151–2, 177–85, 196, 202, 205, 264–6, 269–70, 352–3, 372–3, 386–8, 397–9, 422–7, 450–1, 468–9, 504–7, 511–22, 564–5, 599, 603–4, 645, 654–63, 673–5, 737, 742–9 and 761–4; *Karl Marx/Friedrich Engels Werke* (MEW), Band 23 (Berlin: Dietz Verlag, 1962), pp. 56–8, 93, 97, 166–7, 192–200, 210, 216–17, 219–20, 279–82, 284–5, 373–4, 392–3, 407–9, 419–21, 444–50, 474–5, 492–3, 527–30, 533–45, 589–90, 612–13, 630–1, 658, 684–93, 701–4, 765, 770–7 and 789–91.
- *Capital: A Critique of Political Economy*, vol. 2: *The Process of Circulation of Capital*, ed. Friedrich Engels (New York, NY: International Publishers, 1975), pp. 122, 141–3, 238–40, 243–5, 259, 356 and 359–60; *Karl Marx/Friedrich Engels Werke* (MEW), Band 24 (Berlin: Dietz Verlag, 1963), pp. 125, 142–5, 241–3, 246–8, 261–2, 356, 359–60.
- *Capital: A Critique of Political Economy*, vol. 3: *The Process of Capitalist Production as a Whole*, ed. Friedrich Engels (New York, NY: International Publishers, 1975), pp. 79, 86, 94, 101–4, 108–21, 194–5, 248–50, 258, 263–4, 484, 514–16, 617–20, 632–5, 645–7, 650–1, 708–10, 733–4, 745–6, 766, 776, 779–81, 785–6, 812–13, and 818–21; *Karl Marx/Friedrich Engels Werke* (MEW), Band 25 (Berlin: Dietz Verlag, 1964), pp. 89, 96–7, 104–5, 110–14, 118–31, 204–5, 258–60, 268–9, 273–4, 501, 530–2, 630–3, 645–8, 658–60, 663–4, 720–2, 736–7, 753–4, 775, 784, 787–9, 793–4, 820–1 and 826–9.
- *Theories of Surplus-Value* (Moscow: Progress Publishers, 1968), pp. 99–101, 269, 422–3, and 515–16; *Karl Marx/Friedrich Engels Werke* (MEW) Band 26, Zweiter Teil (Berlin: Dietz Verlag, 1967), pp. 92–5, 267–8, 424–5 and 516.
- 'Economic Manuscript of 1861–1863, Conclusion', (second draft of *Capital*), in *Collected Works*, vol. 34 (New York, NY: International Publishers, 1994), pp. 32–8 and 57; *Karl Marx/Friedrich Engels Gesamtausgabe* (MEGA), Zweite Abteilung, Band 3 (Berlin: Berlin-Brandenburgische Akademie der Wissenschaften, 1976–1982) and Band 4.1 (1988).

For an overview of Marx's theory of ecology, see Howard Parsons (ed.), *Marx and Engels on Ecology* (Westport, CT: Greenwood Press, 1977).

50 James O'Connor, 'Capitalism, Nature, Socialism: A Theoretical Introduction', *Capitalism Nature Socialism*, 1, 1 (1988): 439 and 'On the Two Contradictions of Capitalism', *Capitalism Nature Socialism*, 2, 3 (1991): 107–9; Burkett, *Marx and Nature*, pp. 87–9, 108–32 and

203–7; and Foster, *Marx's Ecology*, pp. 144–70. Marx emphasises the unsustainable self-expansionary character of capital as a central ingredient in his economic and ecological crisis theory in *Capital*, vol. 1, pp. 151–2; MEW 23, pp. 527–30. For an examination of the ecological crisis in the *Grundrisse*, which integrates Marx's early writings on the philosophy of nature with his later dialectic of nature in *Capital*, see Foster, 'Marx's *Grundrisse* and the Ecological Contradictions of Capitalism', in *Karl Marx's Grundrisse: Foundations of the Critique of Political Economy 150 Years Later*, ed. Marcello Musto (London: Routledge, 2008), pp. 93–106.

51 Marx, *Grundrisse*, p. 410; MEW 42, p. 323.
52 O'Connor, 'Capitalism Nature Socialism', pp. 444–53. It is in this essay that O'Connor introduced the concept of 'the second contradiction of capital', which is an ecological contradiction 'between capitalist production relations and productive forces and conditions of production' (p. 444). See also Burkett, *Marx and Nature* for an analysis of capitalism's contradictions and the accumulation and ecology crises (pp. 175–93) and for an analysis of O'Connor's theory of the 'two contradictions' (pp. 193–7).
53 One of the main causes of the ecological crisis is the relationship between town and country, industry and agriculture. See Marx and Engels, *The German Ideology*, pp. 43–58 (MEW 3, pp. 50–61); *Grundrisse*, pp. 83–111 (MEW 42, pp. 19–45); and *Capital*, vol. 1, pp. 504–7 (MEW 25, 527–30). With the growing antagonisms and disparity between town and country, industry and agriculture, there is a corresponding decline in the ecological balance within nature. For a discussion of the 'metabolic rift' in nature, see Foster, *Marx's Ecology*, pp. 141–77 and Burkett, *Marx and Nature*, pp. 119–25.
54 Marx, *Grundrisse*, p. 489; MEW 42, p. 397.
55 Foster, *Marx's Ecology*, pp. 155–63.
56 Marx, *Capital*, vol. 3, p. 812; MEW 25, p. 820.
57 Ibid., vol. 3, p. 813; MEW 25, p. 821.
58 John Bellamy Foster and Fred Magdoff, 'Liebig, Marx, and the Depletion of Soil Fertility: Relevance for Today's Agriculture', *Monthly Review*, 50, 3 (July–August 1998): 44–60.
59 Marx, *Capital*, vol. 1, pp. 505–6; MEW 23, pp. 528–9.
60 Marx, *Capital*, vol. 3, pp. 101–7; MEW 25, pp. 110–17.
61 Foster, 'Marx and the Rift in the Universal Metabolism of Nature', p. 5 and Foster and Magdoff, 'Liebig, Marx, and the Depletion of Soil Fertility', p. 45. Besides Liebig (*Agricultural Chemistry*, 1840 and *Animal Chemistry*, 1842), Marx was also influenced by other prominent scientists who examined the effects of capitalist agriculture on soil nutrients and sustainability, such as James Anderson, an agronomist and economist (*An Enquiry into the Nature of the Corn Laws*, 1777) who created a theory of rent or premium to explain the charge for the use of agricultural land with greater soil fertility (this theory was later incorporated into the economic theories of Thomas Malthus and David Ricardo) and *A Calm Investigation of the Circumstances That Have Led to the Present Scarcity of Grain in Britain* (1801), an investigation into the possibility of rational and sustainable agriculture; James Johnston, who studied soil depletion in New York State (*Notes on North America, Agricultural, Economical, And Social*, 1851); and the US economist Henry Carey (*Principles of Social Science*, 1858), who studied the distance between town and country as an important factor in the agriculture industry and loss of natural soil fertility and nutrients (pp. 46–50). It

was these agrarian economists and natural scientists who influenced the development of Marx's later theory of critical socialist ecology. See also Burkett, *Marx's Ecology* for an analysis of the importance to Marx of James Anderson (pp. 144–7), Liebig (pp. 148–62), and Charles Darwin and natural history (pp. 178–225). Marx read the 1862 edition of Liebig's *Agricultural Chemistry*, in which the latter wrote in his introduction: 'If we do not succeed in making the farmer better aware of the conditions under which he produces ... wars, emigration, famines, and epidemics will of necessity create the conditions of a new equilibrium which will undermine the welfare of everyone and finally lead to the ruin of agriculture' (cited in Foster, *Marx's Ecology*, p. 154).

62 Marx, *Capital*, vol. 1, pp. 506–7; *MEW* 23, pp. 529–30.
63 Engels, *Dialectics of Nature*, p. 511; *MEW* 20, p. 499.
64 The concept of the domination of nature has become more problematic among Marxist theoreticians who are also interested in a critical social ecology. Neil Smith in *Uneven Development* argues that science is deeply embedded in the mode of production, and a number of secondary interpreters have argued that Marx uncritically takes over Enlightenment science and technology for future socialist production through the workers' control over production and nature. This seems like the parallel argument found in the *Communist Manifesto* of the socialist revolutionary takeover of the modern state for its purposes, a position that Marx later rejects in the *Critique of the Gotha Program* as too superficial an understanding of the role and structure of the state. For him, the state, too, must be changed, leading to a decentralised, federated and anarchist view of the state along the lines of the Paris Commune in his later writing. If the bourgeois state cannot simply be taken over by a socialist government but must be radically transformed, modern science may also have to be transformed. This position has logical justification from his theory of historical materialism. That is, just as there is a difference between a bourgeois and socialist state, is there also a difference between bourgeois and socialist natural science (and productive forces)? Does socialism change the relationship between society and nature, and does it change the conceptual and metaphysical imperatives of science from the domination and alienation of nature? Finally, is there an emancipatory science in Marx or does he only wish to change the social relations of production but leave intact bourgeois science? These questions are implicit in the distinction between 'domination of nature' and 'control over nature': the domination of nature for the production of exchange value and the control of nature for the production of use values for the satisfaction of human needs and for the benefit of future generations. Although Smith does not phrase the issue this way, it is implicit in his discussions at the end of the chapter 'The Production of Nature' (pp. 22 and 60–5). Smith closely examines Alfred Schmidt's work *The Concept of Nature in Marx*, which is critical of Marx's analysis of science and the domination of nature. Schmidt contends that Marx's position is as follows: In a socialist society there will be a '*total automation* of industry, which would change the worker's role more and more into that of the technical "*overseer and regulator*"' (p. 27). In socialism there will be an emancipation from the capitalist social relations and class society of domination but not from the necessity to dominate nature. This will always be a historical necessity in capitalism, as well as in socialism. In this interpretation of Marx by Schmidt, there will be a technical transformation of the use and application of science and the productive forces; there will be a utopian

humanisation and emancipation of nature and society as a result of the unrestrained use of the productive forces (p. 22). Smith rejects Schmidt's interpretation of Marx as being utopian and dualistic (productive forces and the social relations of production). He views Schmidt and the other members of the Frankfurt School, with the exception of Marcuse, as having lost the traditional Marxian emphasis on changing the mode of production and the dialectical interrelationship between the productive forces and class relationships. By stressing a dualism, Schmidt deemphasises revolutionary change and the transformation of the structure and organisation of production; this explains his emphasis on science and technology with their positivistic concepts, theories, and methods. Smith rejects this reading of Marx as technological utopianism since it loses Marx's insights into the dialectic and social metabolism between nature and society, between technology and class, and between use value and exchange value. Smith refers to this as the 'fetishism of nature' and a 'politics of despair' – domination is a universal category impermeable to social change. He believes that Schmidt turned Marx's dialectic into a bourgeois concept of nature and a deterministic view of science that necessitated the continued domination of nature (pp. 27–9). Smith sees a solution to the Frankfurt School impasse by reconnecting the dialectic between the productive forces and social relations of production. Returning to the insights of Martin Jay in *The Dialectical Imagination*, Smith succinctly summarises the central problem of the Frankfurt School's position, which is that the crisis of modern production does not lie in the class structure and logic of capital, but in the domination of nature and the resulting dualism between the productive forces and value relations of production (pp. 29–30). Smith wishes to replace the concept of the domination of nature with a more dialectical concept of the production of nature (pp. 32–65). For an overview of Marx's theory of historical materialism, see Derek Sayer, *The Violence of Abstraction: The Analytical Foundations of Historical Materialism* (Oxford: Oxford University Press, 1987).

65 Engels, 'The Part Played by Labour in the Transition from Ape to Man', *Dialectics of Nature*, pp. 462 and 463–6; *MEW* 20, pp. 454 and 455–7. On the contradiction between capital accumulation and consumer realisation, and economic expansion and natural limits, Burkett in *Marx and Nature* writes: 'The limitless expansionary tendency contained in capital as a social form of wealth contradicts all limiting factors imposed on human production by its natural environment' (p. 88). The 'limitless expansionary tendency' of capital is grounded in the contradiction between production for use value and exchange value; the production of value (abstract labour and surplus value) is the root cause of ecological imbalance. Besides labour, nature also presents a limitation on capital accumulation with two major reasons for the ecological crisis of nature: One is based upon the limited access to and depletion of natural resources of energy and supplies by capital production and the other by the inability to recycle excrements or natural wastes of production (supply) and consumption (demand), leading to the further depletion of natural resources and ecosystems. With limitless demand and production, there are real restraints of limited supply and natural resources. With problems in resource depletion and material recycling, there is a tendency within capitalist production toward ecological crises. Burkett continues: 'In *Capital*, Marx posits that the monetization of wealth and the goal of rapid capital accumulation directly contradict environmentally sound and sustainable farming practices' (pp. 88–9). The life needs of society and nature are contradicted by the logic and structural

imperatives of capital accumulation and the requirements of private property. Burkett summarises his argument by stating that there are two distinct types of environmental crises: (1) crisis of capital accumulation caused by the imbalance between production requirements and access to raw material; and (2) the division between town and country resulting in disturbances in the circulation of matter and waste (pp. 107–8). Finally, he examines the issue of the price and profitability of natural resources that do not have an exchange value produced by surplus labour time. The answer lies in Marx's theory of rent and the monopolisation of nature as private property (pp. 90–8).

66   Marx, *Capital*, vol. 3, p. 820; *MEW* 25, p. 828.
67   *Marxist Ecology After Marx*: Much of the primary and secondary literature favourable to Marx's critical ecology emphasises and rejects the mechanical and deterministic laws of the social relations of production of a historically specific mode of capitalist production in economics and the other social sciences. These laws are based on a universalistic approach to human nature and the laws of society. Lukács stressed the connection between natural science and social science as a process of commodity fetishism and reification. Human relations and the social relations of production were turned into the reified and mechanical categories of natural science further separating nature from society in Marxist theory. Marcuse is one of the first theorists to push this criticism beyond the relations of production to the productive forces themselves, that is, to question the very unarticulated and unconscious assumptions of modern science and technology – the metaphysics and politics that underlie natural science. The analysis of the positivism and mechanical determinism of nature found in Marcuse and Habermas contained a more subtle debate over whether Enlightenment science is built upon *a priori* metaphysical and political ideologies hidden within its epistemology, methodology, and technical application. They were both interested in the public policy implications of these insights about the constitution of nature and science: Herbert Marcuse, 'Industrialization and Capitalism in Max Weber', in *Negations: Essays in Critical Theory*, trans. Jeremy Shapiro (Boston, MA: Beacon Press, 1969), pp. 201–26 and 'Ecology and the Critique of Modern Society', *Capitalism Nature Socialism*, 3, 3 (1992): 29–38, along with the commentaries by Andrew Feenberg, Joel Kovel, Douglas Kellner, and C. Fred Alford; Jürgen Habermas, 'Technology and Science as "Ideology"', *Toward a Rational Society: Student Protest, Science, and Politics*, trans Jeremy Shapiro (Boston, MA: Beacon Press, 1970), 81–122; Georg Lukács, 'Reification and the Consciousness of the Proletariat', *History and Class Consciousness: Studies in Marxist Dialectics*, trans. Rodney Livingstone (Cambridge, MA: MIT Press, 1971), pp. 83–222; William Leiss, *The Domination of Nature* (Boston, MA: Beacon Press, 1974); and C. Fred Alford, *Science and the Revenge of Nature* (Gainesville, FL: University Presses of Florida, 1985). Marx's theory of critical ecology was expanded by O'Connor and Harvey in their discussions about the 'second contradiction of capitalism': James O'Connor, 'Capitalism, Nature, Socialism', pp. 11–38 and *Natural Causes: Essays in Ecological Marxism* (New York, NY: Guilford Press, 1998); David Harvey, *Justice, Nature, and the Geography of Difference* (Oxford: Wiley-Blackwell, 1997), 'Marxism, Metaphors, and Ecological Politics', *Monthly Review* (1 March 1998), and *Seventeen Contradictions and the End of Capitalism* (New York, NY: Oxford University Press, 2014); and Foster, 'Marx and the Rift in the Universal Metabolism of Nature', pp. 11, 18–19, n. 38, 13, and 19, ns. 43, 44 and 45. Smith in *Uneven Development*

sees the issue of science and technology as one of social domination in the productive forces or the social relations of production. He writes: 'While recognizing it [technology] as a social product, even Marcuse tended to dwell on the abstract philosophical necessity of technology for mediating human-natural relations. Domination of nature thereby appeared to spring from this abstract necessity and not from the specific social and historical relations within which technology was produced and used' (pp. 28–9). Smith interprets Marcuse as a German idealist who, in his critique of positivism and economism, turns the dialectic of Marx into a dualism between technology and society while losing all connections to the critique of political economy (p. 29).

68   Engels, *Dialectics of Nature*, pp. 460–4; *MEW* 20, pp. 452–5.
69   Ibid., p. 462; *MEW* 20, p. 454.
70   Marx, *Capital*, vol. 3, p. 776; *MEW* 25, p. 784.
71   T.H. Irwin, 'The Metaphysical and Psychological Basis of Aristotle's Ethics', and David Furley, 'Self-Movers', in *Essays on Aristotle's Ethics*, ed. Amelie Oksenberg Rorty (Berkeley, CA: University of California Press, 1980). See also Jonathan Lear's book on Aristotle, *Aristotle: The Desire to Understand* (Cambridge: Cambridge University Press, 1988), which begins with the *Physics* and *De Anima* and moves from there to the *Nicomachean Ethics*. For an entirely different perspective on the foundations of Aristotle's ethics in everyday received opinions (*endoxa*) rather than empirical observations, see also Martha Nussbaum, 'Aristotle on Human Nature and the Foundations of Ethics', in *World, Mind, and Ethics: Essays on the Philosophy of Bernard Williams*, ed. J.E.G. Altham and Ross Harrison (Cambridge: Cambridge University Press, 1997), pp. 86–131.
72   Marx, *Capital*, vol. 3, pp. 813 and 820; *MEW* 25, pp. 821 and 828. See also Smith, *Uneven Development*, pp. 57–60. For Marx, natural laws are found in ethics, history, society, human nature, and natural science, but it is a nuanced view of nature that is not positivistic or mechanical but dialectical.
73   Smith, *Uneven Development*, p. 57. This letter may be found in the Marx-Engels *Selected Correspondence* (London: 1943), p. 246. For a further analysis of this issue of natural laws in the history of capitalist production, see Smith, *Uneven Development*, pp. 57–60. Smith argues: 'Looking forward in history, only by discovering and identifying natural laws will we actually be able finally to distinguish and reveal the natural laws that underlie human nature' (p. 59).
74   Ibid. For Smith, Marx never developed the full implications of his own critique of the mode of capitalist production and the domination of nature but instead continued to 'cling to the obsolete notion of mastery' (p. 62).

PART 3

Structures of Democracy, Economy, and Social Justice in Marx

∵

CHAPTER 6

Distributive Justice: Justice of Consumption, Economic Redistribution, and Social Reciprocity

Two German socialist parties met at the Gotha Unification Congress in May 1875 to write a joint social and political programme on the questions of the socialist state and distributive justice for the nascent Social Democratic Party (SPD). The two major parties were the Social Democratic Workers' Party (SDAP) with which Marx aligned himself and the General German Workers' Association (ADAV) whose leader was Ferdinand Lassalle.[1] The original draft proposal of this unity programme dealt with issues of human misery, the socialist society, elimination of exploitative wage labour and the capitalist means of production (iron law of wages), social and political inequalities, realisation of the 'brotherhood of all mankind', formation of socialist productive associations, direct democracy and public legislation, progressive income tax, and defence of political and social rights, such as universal suffrage, freedom of the press, secret ballot, and the rights to life, health, sanitation, and free and compulsory education.[2] Although Marx was in general agreement about the political value of the joint declaration of the principles and necessary union between his followers of international or revolutionary socialism and the social democracy or reform socialism of Lassalle, he did pen his political disagreements over specific proposals of the programme. The importance of his work *Critique of the Gotha Program* (1875) is that it gives us insights into the differences between the two schools of thought within German socialism in the nineteenth century, as well as Marx's heated rejection of the social reformism of the state. And, perhaps more importantly, it provides Marx with the opportunity to develop his views of social justice, as he expands his ideas about the state, human emancipation, and human rights. In particular, his attention in this work is directed specifically at the questions of labour, common property, state expenditures, fair distribution, and equal rights.

Just as Aristotle had focused on the nature of Greek constitutions and the distribution of citizenship, honours, public office, and political sovereignty based on birth (monarchy), merit and virtue (aristocracy), and the popular mass of citizens (democratic polity) for the common interest,[3] Marx, too, is concerned with the various forms of just distribution of income and wealth grounded in the values of different political constitutions based on merit (liberalism), contribution (socialism), and human need (communism). Here is another example of Marx responding to the liberal and reformist views of justice but from within the general framework of the classical Greek view of social justice, including distributive, reciprocal, and political justice.[4] Marx responds in these brief marginal notes to the original draft of the *Gotha Program* and to the inadequacies of both liberalism and reform socialism in the writings of John Locke and Lassalle by combining Aristotle's theories of distributive and reciprocal justice, that is, the distribution of the public wealth and the reciprocal grace and fair exchange of private goods to satisfy the social needs of the polis and household (*oikos*). The critical theory of distributive justice may be broken down into two distinct types of justice in Marx's writings: the ideal of distributive justice found in consumption and based upon the ethical principles of the equivalency of exchange or market wages, individual contribution in worker co-operatives, and human need, as well as the parallel economic reality of distributive justice found in the means of production based upon the essence of labour, subsistence wage, labour power, and surplus value.[5]

Labour, Nature, and Society in the *Gotha Program*

Marx begins his analysis with a textual exegesis of the *Gotha Program* itself and then proceeds to deconstruct its meaning and implications for the expansion of his own theory of just distribution. Locke had argued that labour was the ultimate justification of private property in the state of nature and civil polity, while the social democrats contend that 'labour is the source of all wealth and all culture'.[6] Marx is critical of placing so much influence initially on labour as found in liberalism and social democracy because it ignores other central elements in the process of capitalist production, including social structures, social relations or organisation of production, and nature. In fact, he maintains that the statement in the *Gotha Program* attributes 'a *supernatural creative power* to labour'. There is a dual danger in attributing a religious dimension to labour – it abstracts from the historical, class, and institutional complexity of industrial production and the labour market and leads to a false and exclusive emphasis on labour as the key to ethics and distributive justice. Nature, too, is an essential element in the production of social wealth and continues Marx's general interests in nature as the basis for human consciousness, economic productivity, and a stable physical environment. By isolating labour out of the broader context of nature and society, Marx accuses the reform socialists of misunderstanding and continuing to use bourgeois economic categories which only continue to enslave workers. If labour is the only source of use value and material wealth then the rights attributed to it – the right to private property – result in the moral justification of wage slavery since workers have no property, no material conditions of labour, and by definition, no rights. They only have their power to labour but not the rights to ownership. Rights have been subverted and have themselves become just another form of property, adhering not to the person but to the owner of property. Workers do not own their own labour, but are treated as just another material means of production, like nature.

Marx continues to examine the full passage in part I, paragraph 1 of the *Gotha Program*: 'Labour is the source of all wealth and all culture, *and since useful labour is possible only in society and through society, the proceeds of labour belong undiminished, with equal right, to all members of society*'.[7] He proceeds first to criticise the implications behind the use of the term 'society' in this preliminary statement of purpose. He thinks that, in the context of this political platform, the word 'society' was being abused by the Lassallean socialists to mean 'the state'. It is true for Marx that labour is social by necessity since to create wealth and culture it must be undertaken within a social context and organisation; but, just as quickly, Marx maintains that social labour also produces class, inequality, and poverty. This, too, might seem as trite and obvious as the original statement of the *Gotha Program*. But Marx's intent here is to show that when examining the nature of labour there are necessary social and economic preconditions which make labour possible within a capitalist mode of production. Thus, changes to labour would also require changes in the structures of the social system. There is, however, no structural statement in the proposal and, thus, no real chance of a successful transformation to a socialist society. Without understanding the underlying structural elements of production and their functional interconnections, there is no real possibility for transforming society as a whole. There is no way to 'lift this social curse'.

According to Marx, the terms 'undiminished proceeds of labour' and 'equal right' are simply party slogans to inspire the workers, since they have no explanatory or revolutionary value. To transform society is to know the pressure points of where and how to change the system. This criticism is the same type of criticism of religion and moral abstractionism that occupied much of Marx's early manuscripts. Marx reads this passage as a defence of the status quo and the prevailing power of the state. The proceeds of labour belong by equal right to all members of society without the necessity to change the structures of society or the current organisation of the state. Socialism could fit into the prevailing bureaucracy and monarchy of Germany. The Lassalleans want to create an egalitarian society without changing the structures of the state or economy; they want social change, but from within the present conditions of society. The state's only goal is the 'maintenance of the social order' just as the economic conditions of alienation and private property remain unexamined and unquestioned. Marx dismissively concludes this section with the comment: 'One sees that such hollow phrases can be twisted and turned as desired'.[8] He next quotes the second passage about the means of production being the monopoly of the capitalist class with a passing reference to the omission by the Lassalleans of landed property.

It is the third principle of the main programme that is central to the issue of distributive and social justice: 'The emancipation of labour demands the promotion of the instruments of labour to the common property of society and the co-operative regulation of the total labour with a fair distribution of the proceeds of labour'.[9] It is this passage that occupies the majority of Marx's theoretical consideration with its questions of labour emancipation, equality, common ownership of property, co-operative regulation of labour, and fair distribution. His critical reaction to this section enables him to undertake an expansion of his theory of distributive justice. Marx begins his analysis of this principle with an examination of the phrase 'proceeds of labour'. His criticism of Lassalle here is the same as in the previous sections of the programme. The phrase is too abstract and vague, contains no explanatory value, and provides no theoretical guidance in making proposals for social change. It is socialist ideology which stirs the soul but does nothing to enlighten the workers, alter the course of history, or rid themselves of alienated labour. Marx asks if the 'proceeds of labour' refer to the products of production or to their value. He is asking the reformists how they are calculating the concept of labour – as an activity which produces a commodity or object of labour, or as a social relationship that produces use value, surplus value, and the social relations of production. Is labour the recently added value to production, or is it the whole production process itself? Should the issues of distribution and justice focus on the proceeds of labour as questions of consumption or questions of production? The answers to these last questions clearly demarcate the differences between liberalism and socialism. How one defines the proceeds of labour will help define what the concept and role of labour is in modern industrial production and also help delineate how and what is to be distributed fairly among the workers. When this issue is resolved, the opportunity is present to consider the heart of the issue – the nature of fair distribution.

Equality, Fair Distribution, and the Public Expenses of Production

Throughout modern history the question of fair distribution has had many conflicting responses, especially over the issue of the criteria by which it is measured: wealth, status, work, merit, contribution, and need. The fairness of distribution within capitalism is unproblematic since the fair exchange of labour (wages) and distribution of consumer goods (income) is defined within the clear parameters of the legal categories of rights, contracts, markets, and obligations. However, Marx notices that within the various sectarian groups of socialism, there are real differences and disagreements of opinion regarding the nature of fair distribution. We have reached the heart of Marx's concerns about the inadequacies of the *Gotha Program* which provide him the opportunity to develop an expanded theory of distributive justice. To appreciate the full meaning of the phrase 'fair distribution', Marx places it in the broader context of the draft proposal. Thus, fair distribution must be understood in the context of the idea that the instruments of labour are to be the common property of the workers and that the whole of labour and production is to be co-operatively regulated. That which is produced by the new economic system – the undiminished proceeds of labour – is to be distributed equally to all members of society. Again, Marx approaches this question of distribution with the same critical concerns that he expressed initially about the use of the terms labour, nature, and society. These categories are too broad and abstract; they are unconnected with each other and with concrete empirical reality; and they result in more questions about their meaning and implications. They produce nice, meaningless phrases that excite the workers, but they do not really aid in a dialectical understanding of the inner dynamic or structure of the economic system.

The main questions remain unanswered: What are to be distributed, in what manner are they to be distributed, in what proportion, and to whom? Are they to be distributed equally and on the basis of what criteria? Does the term 'equal right' refer to everyone in society or only to those who have worked? There are a number of important theoretical issues about the nature of distributive justice that are not considered in this document. It is obvious that Marx is critical of the ideology of the reform-minded socialists, not just on philosophical grounds. Revolution, for Marx, is contingent upon science, since without it real social change cannot be accomplished; people will not know what is to be changed or how it is to be changed. Simply to feel alienation and exploitation is not enough. Just as social ethics binds moral principles to social institutions to be made real, the self-conscious revolutionary must move beyond the rhetoric of a particular party and society in order to make change relevant, concrete, and long lasting.

Marx turns to the pragmatic concerns of running society with an expanded view of the nature of the co-operative worker associations and the socialist state. Before the proceeds of labour or the 'total social product' can be fairly and evenly distributed, there are three forms of general public expenses that must first be considered since they are absolutely necessary for the effective and just organisation of the economy. These three public sector expenses include the economic (production), social (state and social services), and welfare (poor relief) costs to society which have priority over the immediate issue of distributive justice because they are essential prerequisites for stability, growth, and fairness. Marx breaks down the economic expenses into the means of production (labour and capital) and the means of consumption (consumer goods). The general political and social responsibility for maintaining high levels of the means of production and industry must be insured. There is a social need to replenish the costs of production by replacing used technology, equipment, labour, industry, infrastructure, etc.; planning for the future expansion of production; and providing social insurance against accidents, natural calamities, etc. Before a fair distribution can take place, these expenses must be considered and adequately dealt with. Added to the reproduction of the means of production, other social expenses must also be considered, such as the political costs necessary to maintain the state administration and legal bureaucracy – law, legislature, courts, prisons, and military. Since these costs were mainly a continuation of those expenses of the bourgeois administration for the maintenance of a class society, Marx anticipates that they will decline over time in a socialist society. Another group of social costs include the social services for the 'common satisfaction of needs' with the state payments for schools, health care, parks, and libraries; they will rise dramatically with the progressive values of the new society. Finally, welfare payments must be made to insure a quality of life for those who are poor and unable to work in society. The state, even in diminished form, will continue to play an important and central role in a socialist society as it provides for the maintenance of the state bureaucracy, social services, and social welfare of the community.[10]

When dealing with the issue of distribution and justice, a central concern is the relationship between wealth and income, capital and personal spending, and production and consumption. Marx emphasises the nature of production and industry in society, whereas the Lassalleans place their attention on the products or means of consumption. After the economic, social, and welfare expenditures are considered, there is obviously less of the means of consumption to distribute to the citizens of the political and economic community. As Marx recognises, the 'undiminished proceeds of labour' have become the 'diminished proceeds of labour'.[11] Although there are fewer consumer goods to be distributed, society is in a better position for future development because its economic base and infrastructure, state bureaucracy, education, health, and social services have all been secured and strengthened. With these essential adjustments to the total social product of society, the very idea of the undiminished proceeds of labour is no longer a relevant category for use in considering the range and scope of distributive justice.

Distribution, Fairness, and the Means of Social Consumption

In order to undertake an analysis of distributive justice, Marx dispenses with the abstract and ideological concepts of the *Gotha Program* and turns to a discussion of the stages of development of the principles of just distribution in capitalism (exchange of equivalents), first stage of communism (contribution), and the higher stage of communism (human need).[12] With the coming of a new socialist society, there will be a transitional period in which the standards of rights, distribution, and justice remain the same as in the old capitalist economy. Instead of beginning with a completely new utopian vision of justice based on its own foundations and moral principles, Marx outlines the ideal of fair distribution of socialism as evolving from within the remnants of the old market economy. He characterises the process as a temporary and peaceful transition to socialism. The latter is implanted not through imposing a utopian ideal on virgin territory, but is initiated using the old institutions and cultural values as the basis for the new social system as it '*emerges* from capitalist society'. There is a continuity here between distributive and legal justice since this is the same approach Marx took regarding the issues of rights and emancipation in *On the Jewish Question* (1843).

Since the initial stage of development of the revolutionary society starts with the transformation of capitalism, this provides Marx with the beginnings of his analysis of distributive justice. The capitalist principle of fair distribution is ideally based on the assumption that a day's wages equals the total amount of labour invested in a day's work. Market wages are equal to the quantity of labour time or hours worked, that is, they are equal to the exact amount of labour contribution of the producer minus the common fund for the economic and social expenses mentioned above. The mercantilist assumption underlying this principle of equivalency exchange is that profits accrue to the capitalist during the process of circulation and exchange of goods, not during production itself. In circulation the old axiom holds – buy cheaply in one country, sell dearly in another.[13] Profits are defined as value-added and calculated on the basis of sales revenues minus the production costs or the total price minus the total costs of labour and materials. The value added comes from the increase in price over costs; thus profits come from within the circulation of commodities itself. In the socialist stage of development, the traditional elements of profitability as property and commodity production are negated, so that the reality of circulation matches its ideological ideal; reality is made to conform to the ideal as the price (wage) matches the labour costs within the new co-operative associations of workers. The producer receives a certificate of contribution or voucher of work hours which he/she uses to withdraw from 'the social stock of the means of consumption'.[14] Distribution and consumption are tied to work hours, labour contribution, and a right to equality of treatment; they are no longer connected to the private ownership of production.

Fair distribution under this new social system amounts to the exchange of an equal amount of labour for an equal amount of social or consumer goods. Under these conditions of fairness, equality, and labour within the residual elements of capitalist production, the ideal of an equal exchange of labour for equal and fair wages is realised. Within this transitional first stage of socialist development as it moves to a higher stage of social justice, the liberal exchange of equivalents is retained without the capitalist mode of production or drive for profit accumulation. There is a social surplus but this is used for economic and public expenditures necessary for the replacement and expansion of production and as a fulfilment of the social/welfare needs of the broader society, not as a foundation for class and private wealth. There is no exploitation or abuse of labour, no private ownership of property, capital, or the means of production under these new conditions where the ideal and reality of the exchange of commodities are integrated. Production is for the creation of use value for the benefit of the whole community since the law of value, market exchange, and labour exploitation no longer exist.

> Within the co-operative society based on common ownership of the means of production, the producers do not exchange their products; just as little does the labour employed on the products appear here *at the value* of these products, as a material quality possessed by them, since now, in contrast to capitalist society, individual labour no longer exists in an indirect fashion, but directly as a component part of the total labour.[15]

The means of production and the distribution of the social surplus now belong to the working class which has effectively negated commodity production and the class system.

The old social relations of capitalist production are no longer in existence, while the ideal of capitalist justice is fully realised; the capitalist ideal is present without the capitalist economic and social system. Property is no longer a commodity that can be individually owned; the only things that can be owned are the consumer goods (products of labour) or means of consumption. In the capitalist principle of distributive justice, equal amounts of labour are exchanged for an equal amount of labour which is 'the same principle [that] prevails as in the exchange of commodity equivalents: a given amount of labour in one form is exchanged for an equal amount of labour in another form'.[16] Labour remains the measure and medium of exchange based on the bourgeois principles of equal right and fair distribution. The producer has a right to the proportion of the common stock of consumer goods equal to the amount of labour invested in the production process. The principle guiding this form of society is: 'From each according to his ability, to each according to his contribution'. From Marx's perspective this socialist principle is the same as that of the equivalent exchange of commodities in a market economy. Socialist labour is combined with the idealism of capitalist justice during this period of transition to a better society. This first stage of socialism represents a true meritocracy for the producers, since what one puts into the system, one receives back in benefits. But, at the same time, this marks the limitation of this co-operative society since it still reflects residual aspects of capitalism. Marx emphasises this point when he writes: 'What we have to deal with here is a communist society, not as it has *developed* on its own foundations, but, on the contrary, just as it *emerges* from capitalist society, which is thus in every respect, economically, morally, and intellectually, still stamped with the birthmarks of the old society from whose womb it emerges'.[17] The cultural values of distributive justice still contain elements of the old ideals of capitalist market exchange which will be eliminated in the next stage of development.

As a transitional stage, socialism is grounded in the principles of labour and equal right which Marx argues contain the serious limitation of liberalism. 'The right of the producers is *proportional* to the labour they supply; the equality consists in the fact that the measurement is made with an *equal standard*, labour'.[18] The equality of citizens within a community is only proportional to the amount of labour they contribute to society as a whole. The limits of this standard rest in the idea of labour which is affected by duration and intensity. That is, some producers are physically and intellectually superior to others; some are bigger and stronger, more durable and resistant to physical problems; some are more intelligent and imaginative; while some work harder and longer than others. These differences may not necessarily be the result of moral dedication or passionate desire, but simply the result of physical or mental abilities from birth which influence the productivity of human labour that is outside the control of producers. This introduces an arbitrary division into society that differentiates productive from less productive workers and creates a de facto class system of social inequality based on talent and ability. Since labour time and intensity are the basis for the measurement of the quantity of labour expended, Marx views this as an inadequate foundation for a just and fair distribution of social consumption. In reality, this kind of labour standard results in a distortion of the principle of equal right of labour since it results in 'an unequal right for unequal labour'.[19]

In its application in the real world, equal right acts as the balance between different forms of labour so that there is an equality of production and social consumption – an equality of products and consumer goods. But Marx recognises that what begins as an equality within the exchange of labour ends in an inequality of results due to different labour duration and intensity: Equal right turns into an unequal right. The legal principle is undermined by the economic reality. Although privileges and differences within society remain, they are no longer based on the economic inequality of property ownership, but on the inequality of labour production. Since individuals are unequal in abilities, so, too, must inequality be the defining characteristic of the first stage principle of distribution. At this level of historical development, the ability to work remains the only basis upon which a just distribution may be judged; work itself becomes the final measurement of fair remuneration and reward within socialism.

The individual has been reduced to the barest definition of work which Marx clearly recognises is only a partial vision of human labour that he had in the *Economic and Philosophical Manuscripts of 1844*. There is still a great chasm at this point in social evolution between socialist production (worker co-operatives) and capitalist distribution (contribution of labour). Distribution is no longer based on labour power, wages, and unpaid labour surplus, but rather, on labour time and effort. It is an improvement upon the servitude of wage labour, even in its idealised form, because everyone begins as a equal worker but, unfortunately, this evolves into an inequality of ability and effort in the determination of the final distribution of social consumption. Socialism is certainly an improvement toward the end of fairness and justice since the bourgeois class has been eliminated along with its social organisation of alienated production. But it remains only a transitional stage because it, too, is based on an inequality of labour – not an inequality of profits in production but an inequality of labour contribution. At first consideration an inequality of right to the products of the general fund for social consumption based on the inequality of labour appears justifiable. No longer are class interests and privileges the basis for consumption. However, labour no longer can be the basis for an egalitarian and just society since, in the final analysis, it also produces an inequality of final distribution based on innate physical abilities and not the ethical and social principles of justice.

At this point in his analysis, Marx recognises that among the workers there are differences of social situations – some are married, some have children, and some have more responsibilities and obligations than others. As we have seen, with the nature of socialist labour equal right turns into an unequal right. How can this situation be remedied? Marx's response is that 'to avoid all these defects, right instead of being equal would have to be unequal'.[20] Inequality in a just society cannot be its end product; as counterintuitive as it may sound, inequality must be built into its very beginnings and the structures of the economy itself to reflect the inequality of human need. Since socialism emerged out of capitalism, it contains many of its residual negative effects, such as an inequality of distribution and a one-dimensional understanding of productive labour. The inequality of production resulting in alienation and exploitation of the workers had been fixed by socialism, but the inequality of social consumption still remains an important issue to be considered. Class antagonisms, wealth inequality, division of labour, and the dualism between mental and physical labour have disappeared with the end of capitalism. In turn, the transformed productive forces, along with the co-operative worker associations, have expanded to provide more social goods for society as a whole. Socialism has radically altered the process of production as it changed the economic structure of society to the point where now in a communist society the purpose of human work is to become 'not only a means of life but life's prime want' for the purpose of fulfilling the 'all-round development of the individual'.[21]

During his analysis of the two stages of true socialist development after capitalism, Marx makes an interesting and ambiguous comment about the transformation of legal rights based on his theory of historical materialism and the relationship between the economic base and political/legal institutions or superstructure of society. As the economy evolves from a distribution grounded in exchange of equals, to labour contribution, to human need, Marx writes in a provocative manner: 'Right can never be higher than the economic structure of society and the cultural development conditioned by it'.[22] This is one of those comments so intriguing and yet, so confusing, that it has been at the centre of many debates about whether Marx has or has not a theory of distributive justice. This is not the place to unpack this debate, but suffice it to say that it revolves around the core issue of whether rights as legal principles are specific to a particular socio-economic system and thus not applicable beyond that system. That is, the natural rights tradition from the seventeenth to the nineteenth century was a reflection of the principles and laws that grounded the capitalist system. When that system begins to evolve through the various stages of communism, those legal foundations will no longer be applicable or relevant. Rights are forms of state and property legitimation, not forms of critical inspiration and, thus, are not transferable to a new social system based on other sets of moral principles.

As articulated by Locke, and later by Robert Tucker and Allen Wood, rights are closely aligned with possessive individualism, private property, and a market economy. They are part of a complex network of a political, economic, and cultural system, and cannot be separated from that system. When the economic structure begins to fade or collapse entirely, the theory of rights, equality, freedom, and distribution associated with capitalism will also change and will, in turn, no longer be necessary. From their perspective Marx's theory of socialism and the dismantling of the capitalist mode of production and class structure will also entail a negation of liberal rights and market distribution that provided for its legitimation. Marx recognises that rights can never be higher than the economic structure of society because rights reflect that society in its moral values and legal institutions; this is the heart of his theory of historical materialism. A transformation from capitalism to the higher stages of socialism entails abandoning the legal and cultural vestiges of the outmoded and repressive economic system. Rights, distribution, and consumer justice are categories that are part of the old economy and no longer relevant in a free and democratic society. The converse would also be true. 'Need' could not be the defining characteristic of pre-capitalist and capitalist economies because need-based justice requires an advanced means of production and social infrastructure, the abandonment of a market economy and labour exchange, the creation of common property and surplus public funds, and new modes of production based on socialist ideals and democratic worker co-operatives. This transition period of the first phase of socialism as it emerges from capitalism thus involves the abolition of the liberal state, money, wealth and capital, private property of the means of production, commodity exchange, and the law of value; workers will no longer receive wages but will be given labour certificates that they then use to withdraw consumer goods from the common stock of the workers' means of consumption.[23] Distributive justice based on needs requires a technically advanced, post-scarcity economy and post-liberal participatory democracy. Rights can never be higher or lower than the economic structure of society in which they are embedded.

There is, however, another way to look at Marx's statement that involves seeing a more complex dialectic between historical materialism and cultural idealism, between historical reality and cultural ideals, and between actuality and possibility.[24] This means that rights have a twofold role to play in society.

They act as the foundation stone for the legal justification for personhood and property under capitalism; many of these specific rights will disappear with the rise of socialism. On the other hand, rights also express a higher vision and broader horizon reflecting, not the reality of capital, but the possibilities of human development beyond capital. Therefore, rights may be seen as a legal tool that rationalises the present social system, while at the same time may be understood as an ethical vision of species being in a democratic society. A similar dialectic was expressed in the early work *On the Jewish Question* when Marx distinguished between political emancipation and human emancipation, between the rights of man and the rights of the citizen, and between civil society and the liberal state. Rights play a twofold role in society and are not reducible to one or the other. They are a reflection of both the limits and oppression of the prevailing mode of production, but they also reflect the idealism and dreams of future possibilities. To reduce Marx to holding only one aspect of the dialectic is to fail to appreciate the debate between science (historical materialism) and ethics (virtue, freedom, and self-determination), between the historically defined and the transhistorically ideal, between materialism and idealism. Marx was too sophisticated a theorist to fall into the one-sided trap of Enlightenment moral philosophy and science that was rejected by Hegel. He used the dialectic to present a dialogue between science as historical materialism and ethics as the virtuous life seeking happiness and the good, between what empirically is and what ideally and ethically could and should be. This is the dialogue between Locke and Hume, on one side, and Kant and Hegel on the other. The concept of justice remains a central category for Marx, only now it is transformed into a form of distributive justice based on human need of the communal being for self-determination, friendship, and citizenship. As the capitalist ideal of distributive right as market equivalency is replaced by the initial socialist ideal of contribution and merit, so, too, both are replaced by the higher stage ideal of human rights and human need.

Socialism, Self-Realisation, and Human Need

With the final stage of communism and distributive justice, Marx has returned to the values of his early writings with their emphasis on the self-realisation of the good and virtuous life of the species being through creative self-determination in private and public work. The ultimate goal of this final stage, which Marx refers to as the 'higher stage communism', is to maintain some of the structural and technical advances of capitalism and socialism, while radically altering the moral principles of distribution and consumption to meet its own new ideal: 'From each according to his ability, to each according to his need'.[25] With the coming of communism and the transcendence of socialism, we have also moved beyond the bourgeois ideal of equal right to wage compensation to a higher moral level by returning to the ideals of classical antiquity and Aristotle's theory of human need. As classical antiquity replaces liberalism as the new standard of distributive justice, we have entered a new phase of development beyond the ideals of bourgeois and early socialist justice.[26] Need is not simply the right of physical existence determined by one's contribution to the economy, but the human need for intellectual, spiritual, and social development. Aristotle saw the primary need of citizens as the full development of human capacities in virtue, wisdom, and the state, whereas Marx expands the natural needs to include work creativity, self-realisation, and participation in industrial democracy. In his early writings Marx introduces this classical concept when he writes in the *Paris Manuscripts*:

> It will be seen from this how, in place of the wealth and the poverty of political economy, we have the wealthy man and the plenitude of *human* need. The wealthy man is at the same time one who *needs* a complex of human manifestations of life, and whose own self-realization exists as an inner necessity, a *need* ... The sway of the objective entity within me, the sensuous eruption of my life activity is the passion which here becomes the activity of my being.[27]

The highest need of human beings is the freedom and self-realisation of the human potential for self-determination of species life and social activity. And for both Aristotle and Marx, this means that the highest form of virtue and the highest form of happiness is a life of social justice.[28] This is only possible within an ethical community of others. The essence of humanity lies in its historical self-creation within a moral community. Need is articulated as a productive and creative life in work, self-realisation, self-consciousness, community, and friendship. In the *Paris Manuscripts*, Marx proclaims: 'Man produces when he is *free* from physical need and only truly produces in freedom from such need'.[29] He produces the whole of nature and needs, including his objective reality, species being, history, and self-consciousness. Whatever is and will be are either products of human creativity or human servitude, products of beauty or human misery and degradation. In the essay 'Needs, Production, and Division of Labour', Marx further outlines his theory of human needs which he juxtaposes to the moral ideal of the classical nineteenth-century economists. The ideal of the latter as gain, work, and savings requires 'the renunciation of life and human needs' by the reduction of physical and spiritual needs to a minimum in order to maximise profits and capital accumulation.[30] In his brief response to the *Gotha Program*, Marx does not go into detail about what a theory of human need at this highest stage of social development would mean or how it would affect his understanding of the moral principle and foundation of communist distribution. He simply assumes his own early analysis of these issues while living in Paris.

Readers today must supplement his statements about distributive justice and human needs by placing Marx's words back into the classical tradition of Aristotle's theory of reciprocal justice, friendship, and human need. Only when this is accomplished will we begin to more fully appreciate the core ethical values underlying Marx's theory of distributive justice. These Aristotelian principles embody the social ideals of mutual caring and the reciprocal sharing of household goods among friends and fellow citizens – reciprocal justice – which become the foundation upon which Marx responds to the Lassallean socialists. Reciprocity, according to Aristotle, was based on love, grace, and kindness in proportional exchanges in barter and natural trading between friends and fellow citizens; it was not based on a principle of abstract or arithmetic equality.[31] It was grounded in the ethical principles of mutual generosity and proportional reciprocity for the purpose of maintaining a moral economy based on communal caring and solidarity. This idea of proportionality is extended to Marx's principle of fairness and distribution that is not based on merit, contribution, or abilities. Rather, it is based on individual, family and social needs. The central issue is that remuneration is not a reward for labour and accomplishments, but for the maintenance of the happiness and general welfare of the workplace and political community. The physical needs must first be met before the ethical and spiritual needs can be realised.

In a communist society the social product of labour would first be used to maintain the administrative and economic infrastructure of society along with its social and welfare programmes. Only then would it be distributed to the workers. The ethical principles guiding this distribution would no longer be based on an equal exchange of labour (wages) or the quantitative and equivalent amount of the contribution of labour. Rather, its basis would rest in the common criteria of need that recognises certain physical and social differences due to one's particular standing in society, along with the universal need for freedom, self-realisation, and community. Some social needs would be handled by welfare expenditures, others by additions from the social product as a result of physical problems, ability to work, size of family, distance from social amenities, and availability of health care, day care, transportation costs, education and housing needs, etc. All these different needs by individuals and families would result in a reciprocal distribution of the communal social goods. Some may receive more than others at particular times due to their special needs, but it will not result in an inequality of power, since its purpose is only to reaffirm and respect unique individuality and natural differences within a classless society.[32] The social criteria of need is thus a summary of the characteristics of virtue within a free polity. The community itself would have to decide what the appropriate formula would be to satisfy the specific criteria of social needs. The final result may be an unequal division of the 'common consumption fund'. But distribution would also result in a fair share to each 'which is neither too much nor too little – and this is not one, nor the same for all'; it is the mean between gain and loss and provides the ethical bond that holds the community together.[33] Whatever the specific criteria established by the new society, need produces a relative or proportional equality of benefits whose ultimate goal is to make all individuals equal. No one should be burdened by the hardships of special needs not shared by other members of the community. In the final analysis needs are determined by physical desires and ethical imperatives. Distribution is accorded on the basis of relative needs and also whether the needs are appropriate for society. Using this criteria, the need for liberal rights of equality, liberty, property, and security which are the foundations of Western political constitutions in the eighteenth century are inappropriate expressions of need. For Marx, the concept of need is synonymous with the character, powers, and essence of human beings; in the last analysis, the highest need is for individual self-realisation and virtue within a moral economy (Aristotle), ethical community (Hegel), and participatory democracy (Rousseau).[34] Philip Kain has summarised this position in the following manner:

> Thus, Marx envisions a society in which need directly regulates production. Individuals work not merely as a means to exist, but in order to satisfy and develop needs, that is, to realize their essence. The distribution of products in this society should take the form of direct communal sharing purposely designed to satisfy the needs of others such that a conscious bond is formed.[35]

The ethical principle of human needs defines the manner of distribution of production in a communist society based on the ideal of the self-sufficiency of the family and polity; it also refers to the notion that the purpose of distribution is not just to sustain human life, but its highest form. Need is the underlying foundation of praxis and democracy. There is a naturalistic element in Marx's theory of needs that reconfirms his ideal of human nature and species being from his earlier writings. Distributive justice should be directed in a manner to reinforce the underlying purpose of society, which is to produce the good life characterised by virtue, wisdom, and political participation in the workplace and polity. It enhances and realises the telos of humanity of self-conscious labour activity and communal production which serves the need for freedom and self-realisation. It reinforces political and workplace justice by providing for its material foundations. In order to accomplish this task it must dismantle any form of distribution based on market exchange (wage labour) and commodity production (law of value) which are exploitative and unjust.

The ethical polarity of this new system has been reversed as the old values of materialism, utilitarianism, and natural rights are no longer relevant. The market exchange or labour contribution only resulted in social and individual inequalities detrimental to a democratic society. In this brief letter critical of the proposed *Gotha Program*, Marx did not have time to develop his full argument. He did not expand on the meaning of the term 'needs' which has produced enormous interpretive problems when discussing exactly what he meant. It seems clear that his concept of need reaches back into his earliest writings where he deals with a theory of human need based on virtue, freedom, self-realisation, friendship, and human emancipation.[36] Humans certainly have the physical need for survival, but also the need for self-determination through human labour within the community of a 'brotherhood of man'. Marx is translating the classical tradition for the modern economic era as Aristotle's theory of need is incorporated into the democratic polity and the co-operative worker associations of communism. The nature of these political organisations will be examined in more detail in the next chapter. Distributive justice requires that an entirely new ethical formula be used for the redistribution of the social wealth of society. Distribution is no longer the final goal of society, nor is it simply an issue of juridical principles of rights and law. Discussion about the nature of distribution and justice now entails a comprehensive social and economic theory about the nature of capitalism and socialism. It is not simply a matter of distributing the social wealth of the community, but, instead, involves a consideration of the more profound questions of the nature and end of human existence as a species being.[37] Economics under these changed circumstances again becomes an important, but secondary, consideration to the existential questions of the meaning of species life and its private and public activities in a socialist democracy. Marx is always on the cutting edge of questions about social existentialism.

To concentrate on the rights of the citizen and political emancipation is to misunderstand the nature of civil society, while to focus on fairness, equality, and distribution is equally to misunderstand the nature of the capitalist mode of production. Under these conditions, rights and distribution become forms of religious repression and false consciousness that hide the economic and social reality beneath theological and political ideals. Marx was very critical of political emancipation and the rights of the citizen in *On the Jewish Question*, not because they were invalid ethical norms, but because they conceptually and theoretically repressed the economic reality behind the heaven of abstract ideals; they were not realisable within the existing social system and deflected criticism of that system. Some authors have interpreted this as Marx's rejection of both rights from his early writings and distribution from his later works as important components of social justice. They conclude, therefore, that justice itself is an unimportant category simply reflecting verbal nonsense and abstract moralism. Marx's social theory does not represent a rejection of legal rights and distributive justice. It is only that they are being used not for an expansive self-enlightenment, but inappropriately as an ideology: In the context of natural rights, they conceal civil society and the economic rights of man, on the one hand, and, in the context of fair and equal distribution, they conceal the system of wage labour and the industrial organisation of capital.

With the introduction of the changes of the higher phase of the communist society, the categories used by the Lassalleans such as 'undiminished proceeds of labour', 'equal right', and 'fair distribution', have become outdated and are no longer relevant to a discussion about the socialist party platform and its highest ideals. They may have been relevant for the earlier stages of development of distributive justice and the early stages of transition to a more advanced society when labour was the main moral criterion for distribution. Now, however, they are simply outmoded and irrelevant slogans and dogmas. Labour, exchange, wages, and contribution have been abandoned as the foundation for the principle of distribution. In his famous statement, Marx refers to the capitalist and socialist principles as 'obsolete verbal rubbish'.[38] He is concerned about the advances of the socialist party being overturned by these empty phrases and political platitudes that are theoretically and practically irrelevant in the fight for justice in the future. Marx juxtaposes to these verbal abstractions the social realism which marks his understanding of the nature of the economy in the socialist and communist stages.

Concepts must entail an element of dedication and passion, but that cannot be their only connection to sensuous reality. Ideas must be relevant and reflect the internal dynamics and structure of reality of modern society in order to know how to change it. The wrong, or in this particular case, the false and ideological diagnosis can only lead to lost causes, utopian visions, and failed revolutions. To continue to talk about labour, proceeds, rights, and fair distribution is to be caught in a verbal trap 'of ideological nonsense about right and other trash so common among the democrats and French socialists'.[39] The danger these ideas possess is that they characterise previous historical and philosophical periods in the evolution toward a higher community. A new vocabulary and self-consciousness must replace the old concepts about distributive justice. Although Marx is very critical of the party platform that will unite the two branches of socialism in Germany, he does not appear to reject ideas about rights and justice. His major concern is that these older ideas reflect a previous stage of development and are no longer relevant to an understanding of the present situation. He rejects particular theories of rights and justice. History and social evolution have made these older concepts irrelevant to an understanding of the present, especially since they do not take into consideration the advanced technical means of production. The emphasis so far has been on the distribution of the means of consumption and the total social product of consumer goods. New ideas must be incorporated into this discussion that will reflect the changed class structure and mode of production of the capitalist economy in Germany in 1875.

There is also an interesting symmetry between Marx's *On the Jewish Question* (1843) and his *Critique of the Gotha Program* (1875). Just as the modern liberal state and economic rights are abstract universals that hide the reality of property, wage exchange, and class inequality, so, too, are the political principles of equality, proceeds of labour, and fair distribution forms of mysticism. Both liberal rights and fair distribution are forms of distraction that redirect attention away from the central issues of production and power as they focus on issues of property, wages, and consumption. Abstracted from the empirical structures of industrial production and economic exploitation, they foster a belief in justice as rights and distribution that distorts the ability of individuals to arrive at a self-consciousness about the institutions and culture of modern industrial society. Political emancipation and the rights of the citizen hold the same position as liberal and socialist (Lassallean) justice; they contain an emancipatory potential locked in a repressive and false ideology. They both redirect attention away from the real social and economic problems of society toward expanding rights and adjusting wages for the purpose of incorporating and indoctrinating a larger group of individuals within civil society. Satisfaction can be achieved by broadening the base of citizenship and distribution without changing the nature of the social system as a whole.[40] This is not to say that rights and distribution should be abandoned as crucial elements of a theory of social justice as socialism moves to a higher stage of development. The rights of the citizen protecting public participation, assembly, freedom of speech, etc. should continue to be protected and expanded through human emancipation so as to reach into the economic structures of production. Rights and distribution make sense in an advanced socialist society when that society is also built upon the institutions of virtue, freedom, and industrial democracy. Marx's distinctive gift is to be very critical of certain political ideals while at the same time recognising their immanent possibilities for human liberation; it is all a question of the social and historical context of the ideals themselves.

Marx himself is aware that it was a mistake to concentrate so much attention on the issue of distribution. He writes that 'it was in general a mistake to make a fuss about so-called *distribution* and put the principal stress on it'.[41] But it is not because it will disappear with the fuller development of socialism. At first, his comment may appear a little disconcerting because distribution is central to any consideration of social justice; it is a matter of fairness, equality, and freedom. But a closer look at his comment reveals that there is more to his initial dismissal than at first appears. He is not saying that distribution is unimportant, only that we must have a more comprehensive view of it that goes beyond distribution as a function of circulation or consumption. The concept must also be incorporated into a critical reflection on the organisation and process of production: 'Any distribution whatever of the means of consumption is only a consequence of the distribution of the conditions of production themselves. The latter distribution, however, is a feature of the mode of production itself'.[42] This central idea has unfortunately been misinterpreted as a confirmation of a deterministic or positivistic form of historical materialism, thereby reinforcing the notion that justice is a derived class concept and cannot be used to normatively evaluate or reject capitalism. Quite the contrary. Marx is only reaffirming his view of the relationship between science and ethics. An ethical critique of political economy requires that it be framed within an empirical and historical analysis of the structures of capitalist production and the laws of value and surplus value. To separate distributive justice from a critique of the institutions of political economy is to separate ethics from science and, thus, turn ethics into a political form of utopian mysticism or socialist ideology and turn science into a mechanical reproduction of the natural sciences. This also reconfirms his original insights from *On the Jewish Question* where an understanding of the state (appearances) as unconnected to civil society (essence) results in false consciousness and political religiosity.

Marx expands his theory of distributive justice to incorporate both consumption (social goods) and production (wages), thereby broadening the range of issues to ultimately include a detailed empirical analysis of the capitalist enterprise in order to move beyond the appearances to the reality of capitalist society. Simply redistributing the total social product of industrial production without changing its internal structures of alienation, power, and exploitation is to use justice as a theological weapon against the working class. Nothing within civil society changes even when rights and distribution are expanded; only the cultural and political expression of that society changes. The law of production and value – economic justice – must be addressed before there can be any real change in the human condition of the working class. Any changes which the Lassallean socialists introduce, no matter how provocative the political and ideological language, which do not consider a total reorganisation of the capitalist mode of production, will not produce real lasting or revolutionary change. Marx realises that building upon the cultural superstructure of bourgeois rights and liberal distribution without transforming the capitalist economy itself changes little, if anything, but the outside appearances.[43] Thus the means of distribution or distribution of the total social product is based on the prior distribution of private property and the material conditions of production. It is not labour, wages, or contribution that define liberal distribution; it is the ownership of the property of production which best characterises the alienation from the object, organisation, and process of labour. Those who own the factories and means of production own the disposition of property and the distribution of the social wealth. Workers only own their own labour power or the capacity to exchange their labour in a market exchange. Distribution is a secondary consideration and flows from the class power of productive property. 'If the elements of production are so distributed, then the present day distribution of the means of consumption results automatically'.[44] Marx is aware that a focus on rights and distribution, although important for the protection and sustenance of the working class and the development of self-consciousness, is theoretically secondary to the primacy of the social organisation and relations of production. The first step of socialism is not distribution but the reorganisation of production into common property, true equality, and worker collectives.

Critique of Reformist and Vulgar Socialism – Happiness without Meaning

It is these very issues of the deep structures of society that Marx feels are not the focus of the *Gotha Program*. Although the reform or liberal socialists express a genuine concern for the economic conditions and social problems of workers, they lack a consistent probing and theoretical insight into the underlying causes of the real problems and, by implication, effective solutions. Simply spouting ineffective political clichés or 'obsolete, moral rubbish' will not transform the actual work conditions and structures of oppression. Marx is quite clear at this point in his analysis. The focus by liberal democrats and reform or vulgar socialists on issues of distribution is a form of alienation and profound loss of the classical tradition of justice. This does not mean that distribution should not play an important role in the socialist party platform; it only means that distribution must first be provided an economic and historical context in the mode of production. Distribution remains a central issue for Marx; his criticism is only that there must not be a 'consideration and treatment of distribution as independent of the mode of production'.[45] To connect this insight into the other forms of justice already considered in this work, ethics, rights, and distribution should not be neglected or even rejected as valid components in Marx's theory of social justice. They are not to be abandoned in the march toward revolution; they must instead be considered as part of a comprehensive and dialectical whole reflecting the ideals of the classical Greek tradition. Marx is concerned that a focus on extending rights, broadening equal suffrage, enlarging production, increasing wages, widening citizenship, expanding state functions, and creating a better, more pleasurable and happy life only lessens the chance for real substantive change. It is a simply a retrogression in the face of real structural needs and possibilities. These goals are not ends in themselves but means toward the classical and socialist ideals.

Marx ends his letter criticising the Lassallean reformism of the German Workers' Party by rejecting its theories of class, wages, and the liberal state.[46] Not different from the liberal economists, these state socialists merely want to separate distribution from production. The main effect of this decision is that socialism focuses entirely on the radical redistribution of the social wealth of the community. But this limited menu for social change is no different from that of liberalism. It is simply a matter of the distribution of goods, not a revolution of the mode of production; the debate between liberalism and socialism is only over a disagreement about the extent of redistribution. With an emphasis on a more egalitarian distribution, the social reformers have omitted questions of civil, workplace, ecological, political, and economic justice. They simply want to make life a little better and more comfortable for the working class while leaving intact the economic, technical, and political institutions of social oppression. And this is accomplished by refusing to question the economic structure, the wage system, class system, or the existence of the free state.

In part I, principle 4, Marx undertakes a critical analysis of the wording in the *Gotha Program* of the emancipation of labour by the working class in the face of the reactionary forces of the other economic groups in society. Marx stresses that it is not the 'emancipation of labour' but the emancipation of the working class that is the key issue at stake. The significant question remains: who belongs to the working class? He recognises that the bourgeoisie once was a revolutionary class of its own as it dismantled the medieval economic system based on the manorial fiefdoms, lords, and serfs. But in the nineteenth century, it is false to mechanically juxtapose the bourgeoisie and working class since the artisans, small manufacturers, the lower-middle class, and even the peasants are not simply a reactionary mass of people. The new capitalist system is reframing the old class relationships so that even these groups are becoming more and more revolutionary as industrial production pushes them down into the proletariat. They cannot be dismissed as simply part of the mass of reactionary forces in society and mechanically grouped with the property owners who oppose the working class and revolutionary social change. Marx sees that the emancipation of labour through class struggle will entail and enable a larger arrangement of classes than those viewed by the reformists. Because of their restrictive theory and politics, the reformers limited their understanding of class, and thus, the real possibilities of social change.

Marx is also critical that Lassalle contends that the revolution is possible within the present framework of the national state. Lassalle, in his understanding of the class struggle and the liberal state, is making a fundamental break with the revolutionary socialists and the position they have taken in the *Communist Manifesto* (1848). The first thing that must be accomplished is the organisation of the working class as a coherent and self-conscious class within the modern German state. But its real goal is to move beyond national borders to the international realm since only then is a successful revolution possible. Since the modern state is itself part of an international economic system, keeping the revolution at the national level only dooms it to failure because of the transnational power of the German economy in the world market. While the liberal state is in reality creating an international economic and political system, the reformists are creating their abstract illusions of an 'international brotherhood of peoples' in its struggle against the 'ruling classes and their governments'.[47] Marx fumes at the inability of the reformists to comprehend the actual international function of labour. Again he directs the same criticisms against the reformists who have no clear appreciation of the nature of the international market economy or industrial production. They want to build a revolution based on the power of words rather than the power of the working class. The German Workers' Party is deemed by Marx as inadequate to meet the demands of revolutionary change. Even the bourgeois Free Trade Party is more advanced than the reformers in using the phrase 'the international brotherhood of peoples' to generate solidarity and commitment to its political ideals of an international market economy based on the principles of free trade.[48]

In the second part of the letter, Marx continues his criticism of the reformist position of the *Gotha Program* with an analysis of the nature of the free state and socialist society through 'the abolition of the wage system *together with* the *iron law of wages* – and – exploitation in every form; the elimination of all social and political inequality'.[49] Marx objects to the use of the phrase 'wage system' instead of 'system of wage labour'. What might appear as a politically minor and petty issue over terminology is of vital importance for Marx. This iron law states that over time wages seek their lowest level for the minimum wage necessary to sustain human life. This economic law of subsistence wages is based on the law of population growth developed by Thomas Malthus in *An Essay on the Principle of Population* (1798). Blending Malthus's demographic theory with the notion of market competition of classical economics (Adam Smith and David Ricardo), Lassalle concludes that with the growth of population rates, increase in the supply of labour, and competition among workers for jobs, there is an eternal iron law that worker's wages have an inevitable tendency to decline until subsistence levels are reached. Marx is unclear in this passage but seems to argue that Lassalle has reduced the system of wage labour to the iron law of subsistence wages and, thereby, again reduced production to distribution. He had done this first with the issue of distributive justice and now again with his theory of the iron law of wages. The wage system could be understood as the system of compensation and distribution, and this confusion leads us back to the difference between a critical focus on production or distribution. The abolition of the iron law of wages is, at least for Marx, a false issue. First, the elimination of the system of wage labour and the law of value (wealth) would necessarily entail the elimination of Lassalle's law of wages.

Marx believes that the iron law of wages is the signature issue for the reform Lassalleans. He argues that to abolish wage labour would be to successfully abolish all economic laws of capital. On the other hand, if this minimum wage law is correct, as claimed by the Lassalleans, then the abolition of capitalism would have no effect on this law since it would be applicable to all social systems. Capitalism or socialism would entail a system of economic distribution that, as in the case of Malthusian population growth, would result in greater human misery and poverty for the working class. This law has been used to criticise both capitalism and socialism – capitalism for its creation of poverty and inequality, and socialism for its inability to eliminate poverty and inequality. Since poverty and a subsistence economy are products of the law of nature, then any attempt to alleviate or destroy this law is mistaken. Here again, as in the case of distribution, Marx takes the position that the reformists are unaware of the real economic laws that govern modern capitalism; they are simply following in the footsteps of classical economics.

At this time, Marx briefly compares the law of value (wage labour, labour power, surplus value, and profits) to the law of wages (population growth, poverty, and subsistence wages). At this point in his analysis, he summarises the revolutionary socialists' law of value which will be examined in more detail in Chapter 8 on economic justice. He contends that wages do not reflect the value or price of labour, but the value of labour power. The distinction between labour (use value) and labour power (exchange value) is a distinction between the actual productive activity and the ability or capacity to labour, respectively. The labourer sells his labour power, not his labour. In this distinction between labour and labour power lies the secret to unpaid or surplus labour and profits, and, thus, the secret to the whole bourgeois system of wage labour, economic exploitation, and social and political inequality. Marx concludes with the observation that 'the system of wage labour is a system of slavery', no matter how developed the productive forces or how generous the wage contract remains.[50] The real issues remain those of alienation and exploitation in production, not fairness and equality in distribution. Slavery is not ameliorated by higher levels of compensation in the workplace or 'whether the worker receives better or worse payment'. This focus on wages and remuneration is to mistake 'the appearance for the essence'.[51] In fact, he contends that with the development of technical and productive forces, economic expansion, and rising wages, the system of slavery becomes even more oppressive. Marx ends this part with the cooling comment that this reform proposal is the work of 'criminal levity and lack of conscience' since it may make some slaves more comfortable with higher wages but not change the structure of slavery that underlies it. With a more radical understanding of the law of value along with the dismantling of the system of wage labour, issues of distribution, wages, exploitation, and inequality will disappear.

Nearing the end of his analysis of the proposed draft of the socialist document in part III, Marx continues to argue that the Lassalleans do not have a 'scientific' or historical and dialectical understanding of the class struggle or any concrete proposals toward transforming capitalism.[52] Socialism is not viewed as a product of class consciousness or a revolutionary change in the mode of production. Serious historical analysis of German capitalism is replaced by phrases such as 'the social question' and 'state aid under the democratic control of the toiling people'.[53] In fact, the draft states that the revolution and socialist organisation of labour will occur with the help of state aid in forming the socialist producers' co-operative associations. At this point in his analysis, and with utter incredulity, his contempt for the reform platform of this state socialism can no longer be hidden. The revolution, as understood by the Lassalleans, will be brought about through the state and not through the class consciousness and revolutionary activity of the workers themselves; there will be no creative contribution on the part of labour. Socialism is thus a gift of the state to the needy labouring class. The oppressive organ of the state which has been protecting and legitimating the capitalist social system is now supposed to lead the fight to socialism. No longer to be led by the working class but by the 'toiling people', the radical transformation of society takes place under the aegis of the state. How the state became democratically controlled without changing the capitalist organisation of production is a complete mystery to Marx. So, again, the proletariat, class consciousness, revolution, production, and the dismantling of the liberal state all disappear beneath 'newspaper scribbler's phrases', which have no real bearing on the issues at hand. This is revolution by political platitudes and empty slogans. Marx does not even know what the term 'toiling people' means. He fears that the great mass of people will not have a consciousness of the need for change, nor understand the structural economic problems and underlying causes of human misery, nor will they have an understanding of how to accomplish such change. The dialectical understanding of systems, structures, functions, and crises is missing from their political vocabulary.

Revolution will not be something they accomplish, but something given to them. Everything is to be done through the beneficence of state funding and passed down to the passive people in state-constructed associations for the benefit of everyone; there will be no radical overhauling of the economic and political system since social change will be brought about by working within the present political institutions. The language by which Marx dismisses this proposal is certainly the language of Feuerbach's critique of religion; it is a disbelief in the power of metaphysics and theological irrationality. The creation of real worker co-operatives requires the socialists to undertake a 'revolutionizing [of] the present conditions of production'. Marx juxtaposes state-funded worker associations to revolutionary worker co-operatives. He fears that the reform socialists have no plan, organisation, or critical theory of historical materialism that could lead to a true revolution of capitalism.

Marx has reached part IV in the final section or appendix of the *Gotha Program* with its call for the following changes to the foundation of the state: universal suffrage, secret ballot, freedom of the press, and universal, equal, free, and compulsory education. Along with these changes the proposal calls for changes in the foundation of society that include: an extension of political rights and freedom, a single progressive income tax, unlimited right of free association, normal working day, prohibition of child labour and restrictions on women's labour, protection of the life and health of workmen, sanitation control, state inspection of factory, workshop, and domestic industry, and state regulation of prisons. Marx asks: What is the free state? His response is that the state is not a governmental organisation imposed upon society from above but subordinate and responsive to it. This definition is applicable only to present-day states in Switzerland and the United States, and certainly not in the Prusso-German Empire. And socialist ideals had already been tried in French workers' programmes under Louis Philippe and Louis Napoleon. The socialist party seeks the free state, but does not understand its meaning; in fact, Marx continues, its ideal of the state is 'not even skin-deep'. The party proposals in the unity programme continue to treat the state as an independent unity 'that possesses its own *intellectual, ethical, and libertarian bases*'.[54] This was Marx's first critique of Hegel's theory of the state in his *Philosophy of Right* (1821) now applied to the *Gotha Program*. The liberal state is not an independent institution, but a product of the capitalist mode of production that then reacts back upon the economy as it protects it, enforces its laws, legitimates its institutions, and oppresses those who disagree. The state is a political mechanism of social oppression based on a liberal economy that could not possibly be the basis for revolutionary change.

It is at this point that the real question pertinent to the Unity Congress is finally asked: 'What transformation will the state undergo in communist society? In other words, what social functions will remain in existence that are analogous to present functions of the state?'[55] What will the final stage of communism look like and how different will it be from the present state? He has already raised aspects of these questions throughout his early and later writings, but never so clearly and directly. Will the democratic state protect human rights and distributive justice? Will the state even be necessary in a truly free society unburdened by the irrationality and immorality of the capitalist economic system? Marx's response is immediate and frustrating. He states that the answer to these questions can only be determined 'scientifically' and not through the use of abstract moralisms and political aphorisms using terms such as the 'people' and the 'state'. That is, the answer to the question is not something that can be theoretically predetermined in a utopian manner before the actual transformation occurs. Theory is always bounded by empirical analysis and practical activity and cannot be anticipated beforehand in a positivistic manner using empirical data, explanatory laws, and a predictive science.

The nature of the state will be defined as society moves from capitalism through the various stages of transitional and higher stage communism. During this time, the state will act as the 'revolutionary dictatorship of the proletariat'. Engels would claim in 1891, on the twentieth anniversary of the Paris Commune, that the Commune was the model for this form of workers' government.[56] Marx stops here and does not examine any specific aspect of this new state, saying that the programme does not deal with the revolutionary state or with the revolutionary society. Its goal is simply to outline its basic ethical and economic principles with some immediate strategies for social change. Because of the nature of historical materialism, immanent critique, and the dialectical method, Marx cannot establish clear blueprints for a picture of the future. Institutions, culture, and consciousness are things that evolve within history and cannot be mechanically predetermined beforehand.

Although Marx cannot give a clear view forward other than intermediary steps, he is equally certain that the reform policies contained in the proposed programme 'contain nothing beyond the old democratic litany familiar to all: universal suffrage, direct legislation, popular rights, progressive income tax, a people's militia, etc.'.[57] These are restatements of liberal propaganda and ideology which in Switzerland and the United States have been realised. Both these countries, even with all these political advances, are still based on an oppressive economic system.

Political transformation alone is not enough to transform society into a truly free and open democracy with popular sovereignty. To demand of the German state, as socialist workers had previously demanded of the French state, that it, too, become a democratic republic is absurd and would only result in 'a police-guarded military despotism, embellished with parliamentary forms, alloyed with a feudal admixture, already influenced by the bourgeoisie, and bureaucratically carpentered ...'.[58] All this was to be accomplished using the state law, the police, and the rights of man. In the final analysis, the radical reforms proposed by the Lassallean socialists are the same type of reforms already instituted in the political constitutions of liberal democratic republics. Marx had previously examined in *On the Jewish Question* a similar declaration of principles and political reforms in the French *Declaration* of 1793 with his analysis of the rights of civil society and the rights of political emancipation. Lassallean socialism is no different from the bourgeois liberalism of political emancipation; the democratic republic is no different from the socialist state. Neither has called into question the system of wage labour upon which they rest. The reform socialists in their party platform are asking for political rights that already exist in Western countries. The state of the future already exists today; there is no need to organise for the future, since the future is already the present state of affairs. Exasperated, Marx claims that the proposal of the reform socialists is the same as that of the bourgeois financial reformers in Liverpool, England.

The initial proposal also calls for a firm foundation of the socialist state in universal education, but this, too, will be criticised by Marx. Education in the new socialist society is to be universal, compulsory, and free. Marx, however, objects to the state (or the church) having such enormous power over children's education along with the supervision and evaluation of teachers. It would be dangerous to have the type of teacher and the content of the classroom under the direct control of the present state. He concludes with the stinging comment that 'the whole program, for all its democratic clang, is tainted through and through by the Lassallean sect's servile belief in the state, or, what is no better, by a democratic belief in miracles ...'.[59] With the Lassalleans so closely aligned with the present form of the state, these educational ideals, including the freedom of conscience and freedom of science, are simply the belief in liberal reforms within the oppressive police state of Germany. The appendix of the *Gotha Program* contains issues of the normal working day, restriction of female labour and prohibition of child labour, state supervision of factories, regulation of prison labour, and effective liability law. Marx runs quickly through these items and concludes that they have been poorly thought out and that more consideration should have been given to the nature of different levels of education, health and safety regulation, clarification of the nature of restrictions and exclusion of female and child labour, worker control over state supervision of factories, etc. His comments on the appendix read more like a rushed afterthought than a serious outline of their weakness. Marx concludes his analysis of the principles and proposal of the *Gotha Program* by saying that in their present form they represent state reformism of the capitalist system without serious consideration or transformation of its underlying economic structure.

Notes

1   At the German Unification Congress in 1875 there was an attempt to unify two German socialist parties. One was led by Ferdinand Lassalle (the *Allgemeine Deutsche Arbeiterverein*) and the other was the Eisenach faction, among whom were the followers of Karl Marx (the *Sozialistische Arbeiterpartei Deutschlands*). They eventually came together to form the unified *Sozialdemokratische Arbeiterpartei Deutschlands* or the Social Democratic Party of Germany (1890). The Eisenachers had sent Marx a draft copy of the proposed platform of the unified programme for his comments. His letter, originally entitled 'Marginal Notes to the Programme of the German Workers' Party' and later published by Friedrich Engels as the *Critique of the Gotha Program*, is his response to the unified programme; it is a searing critique of the reform or state socialism of the Lassalleans in particular. In the foreword to this piece, written by Engels, he states quite clearly that this is Marx's first critical statement regarding the economic principles and political strategy of Lassalle. This piece, first published after Marx's death, also offers the most concrete and programmatic details about Marx's view of the socialist revolution, the international proletarian movement, the dictatorship of the proletariat, and the transition from capitalism to communism. The marginal notes were originally sent to Wilhelm Bracke with the expressed request by Marx to pass the letter along to his socialist friends August Geib, Ignaz Auer, August Bebel, and Wilhelm Liebknecht who were members of the Eisenach group. Since the letter was not made public during his lifetime, it did not have an important impact at that time, but did so after its publication in 1891 in the journal *Die Neue Zeit*. It was during that year that his ideas on the *Gotha Program* were incorporated into the principles and public charter of the Erfurt Program of the Social Democratic Party by Eduard Bernstein, August Bebel, and Karl Kautsky. Whereas the *Gotha Program* represen-

ted the split between Marx and Lassalle, the Erfurt Program manifested the split within the Marxist party between the Marxist orthodoxy of Kautsky and social democratic revisionism of Bernstein.

2   Theodore S. Hamerow (ed.), *The Age of Bismarck: Documents and Interpretations* (New York, NY: Harper & Row Publishers, 1973), pp. 230–2.

3   Aristotle, *The Politics*, trans. T.A. Sinclair, revised Trevor J. Saunders (London: Penguin, 1981), 1279a32–1280a6, pp. 190–2. The distortion of these three criteria result in an alternative arrangement of distorted political constitutions: tyranny (birth), oligarchy (wealth), and democracy (poor). In each case, there is no longer a concern for the common welfare of the polity but rather the political rule for the benefit of the one, few, or many. The purpose of the ideal state is to ensure the material foundations of a self-sufficient economy and to promote the values of a good and virtuous life. Thus the deep and intimate connections among the state, economy, and ethics. The same interconnections exist in Marx's approach to social and moral issues. It is not that Marx just borrows some ideas about social justice from Aristotle; a secret to his overall writing lies in the awareness that the underlying substructure of his critical social theory and political economy is Aristotelian. These interconnections among the functional components of society are the basis for his theory of the dialectic and critique of abstractions – the fragmentation of work, along with the fragmentation of consciousness, culture, politics, and economy. The difficulty of interpreting Marx is that his whole life was spent weaving together that which had been torn asunder by the Enlightenment and liberalism, by science and capitalism. To truly understand Marx is to appreciate the fact that he is simply a theoretical artisan trying to repair the fabric of society (virtue and justice), reason (practical wisdom and political deliberation), and ethics (natural law) that had been destroyed by modernity. This was the real moral crime of alienation and the impoverishment of human needs.

4   Aristotle, *Nicomachean Ethics*, trans. W.D. Ross, in *Introduction to Aristotle*, ed. Richard McKeon (New York, NY: The Modern Library, 1947), book V, 1129a–1138b, pp. 397–423.

5   *Forms of Distributive Justice*: The distributive justice of consumption (fair wages and consumer goods) is to be found in Karl Marx, *Critique of the Gotha Program*, *Marx and Engels: Basic Writings on Politics and Philosophy*, trans. Lewis Feuer (Garden City, NY: Anchor Books, 1959), whereas the distributive justice of production (exploitative wages) is to be found in *Contribution to the Critique of Political Economy*, ed. Maurice Dobb (New York, NY: International Publishers, 1970), *Grundrisse: Critique of Political Economy*, trans. Martin Nicolaus (New York, NY: Vintage Books, 1973), and *Capital: A Critique of Political Economy*, vol. 1: *The Process of Capitalist Production*, ed. Friedrich Engels, trans. Samuel Moore and Edward Aveling (New York, NY: International Publishers, 1968); *Karl Marx/Friedrich Engels Werke* (*MEW*), Band 23 (Berlin: Dietz Verlag, 1962).

6   Marx, *Critique of the Gotha Program*, p. 112; *Karl Marx/Friedrich Engels Werke* (*MEW*), Band 19 (Berlin: Dietz Verlag, 1962), p. 15.

7   Ibid., p. 112; *MEW* 19, p. 15.

8   Ibid., p. 114; *MEW* 19, p. 16.

9   Ibid., p. 115; *MEW* 19, p. 18.

10 Kai Nielsen, 'Marx, Engels and Lenin on Justice: The Critique of the Gotha Program',

Studies in Soviet Thought, 32 (1986), disagrees with Marx that a priority for the social administration of these expenses will necessarily result in the expansion of production. He argues that there may be alternative social needs of the community, such as less work and more free time (p. 27). One could anticipate today that with the reality of the ecological crisis, economic expansion may not be a top priority at all. For Marx, the 'total social product' or means of consumption equals the public expenditures or common funds (economic or means of production, social, and welfare costs) plus the social consumption fund (the consumer goods produced by labour). In the first stage of socialism, this is now all common property. See also Karl Korsch, 'Introduction to the Critique of the Gotha Program', in *Marxism and Philosophy*, trans. Fred Halliday (New York, NY: Monthly Review Press, 1970), pp. 145–70.

11   Marx, *Critique of the Gotha Program*, p. 117; *MEW* 19, p. 19.

12   Marx refers to the various stages of economic development from capitalism to the future co-operative society in the following manner: capitalism (labour exchange), dictatorship of the proletariat, first stage of communism (contribution), and higher stage of communism (need). In this chapter, reference will be made to the first and higher stages of communism as the evolutionary path and stages of socialism to avoid any confusion that arises from later theoretical developments after Marx between socialism and communism. The terms socialism and communism will refer to the same historical developments since Marx himself at times used the terms interchangeably.

13   In this theoretical landscape, profits accrue as a result of price adjustments within the circulation of commodities. In the socialist stage of production and circulation, the means of consumption (consumer goods) are equal to the amount of labour employed and distribution is based on the quantity of labour utilised. Equal right represents a fair and equitable balance between equal labour and equal share of products. It should be noted that this is not Marx's position or that of the classical economic theorists Adam Smith or David Ricardo. Marx locates the source of value, surplus value, and profits in the process of production and not exchange or circulation. This is one of the important implications of his labour theory of value which will be examined in more detail in Chapter 8 on economic justice.

14   Marx, *Critique of the Gotha Program*, p. 118; *MEW* 19, p. 20.

15   Ibid., p. 117; *MEW* 19, pp. 19–20.

16   Ibid.; *MEW* 19, p. 20.

17   Ibid.

18   Ibid., p. 118; *MEW* 19, p. 20. This market standard of equality, merit, and contribution at the heart of the exchange relationship between the two commodities of labour and wages is the secret to Marx's immanent critique of capitalism. The ideals of vulgar free trade in simple circulation are compared to reality as the moral values and natural rights of freedom, equality, liberty, and property are seen as contradicted by the actual social relations of production based on the distinctions between labour power and labour, wages and the products of labour. This contradiction between the Eden of innate rights of man and the real structures of commodity production and surplus labour and value undermines the ability of the economic system to legitimate and ultimately reproduce itself. Capitalism is ultimately seen as irrational, exploitative, wasteful, and alienating.

See Marx, *Capital*, vol. 1, p. 176; *MEW* 23, pp. 189–90. Marx, in the fashion of Hegel's logic, undermines capitalism on the basis of capitalism's own ethical and political standards. But there is another side to his social critique and this is grounded in his theory of social justice. The first stage of socialism begins by accepting the principles of equal rights and fair exchange in a market without the capitalist organisation of production and property. These normative values of rights, equality, and fairness are only temporary solutions on the path to a more just social arrangement. They will be replaced in time by the final stage with its principles of human need and self-realisation.

19 Marx, *Critique of the Gotha Program*, p. 119; *MEW* 19, p. 21. Marx recognises that even in the first stage of socialism, equal rights are in reality unequal rights based on the ability and talents of labour. Because of this inherent inequality, contribution cannot be the ultimate foundation of justice. Rousseau had already discussed the different kinds of inequality in his *A Discourse on the Origin of Inequality* (1754), in *The Social Contract and Discourses*, trans. G.D.H. Cole (New York, NY: E.P. Dutton and Company, 1950) where he distinguished between natural or physical inequality of the natural law of pure reason and merit and the moral or political inequality of positive law and social convention (p. 196). Just as it is against the law of nature that children should command adults or an idiot a wise man, it is also against natural reason that there should be massive inequality and poverty (pp. 271–2). Later in *The Social Contract or Principles of Political Right* (1762), Rousseau writes: 'I have already defined civil liberty by equality, we should understand, not that the degrees of power and riches are to be absolutely identical for everybody, but that power shall never be great enough for violence, and shall always be exercised by virtue of rank and law; and that in respect of riches no citizen shall ever be wealthy enough to buy another, and none poor enough to be forced to sell himself' (p. 50). According to Rousseau, distributive justice is a function of the material sustenance of human life for equality, freedom, self-determination, popular sovereignty, and direct democracy; that is, justice lies not in the rights conferred by property, merit, or contribution, but by the fundamental needs of society for freedom and democracy.

20 Marx, *Critique of the Gotha Program*, p. 117; *MEW* 19, p. 21.

21 Ibid.; *MEW* 19, p. 21. These ideals of freedom, self-realisation, and human need reflect the 'real wealth' of the individual and continue to be essential to Marx's social theory in the *Grundrisse*, pp. 287–9; *MEW* 42, pp. 212–15; and *Capital: A Critique of Political Economy*, vol. 3: *The Process of Capitalist Production as a Whole*, ed. Friedrich Engels (New York, NY: International Publishers), p. 820; *Karl Marx/Friedrich Engels Werke* (*MEW*), Band 25 (Berlin: Dietz Verlag, 1964), p. 828.

22 Marx, *Critique of the Gotha Program*, p. 119; *MEW* 19, p. 21.

23 The idea of a labour certificate to be drawn from the common stock of produced goods is an idea developed by the utopian socialist John Gray and continued by Pierre Proudhon. In his *Contribution to the Critique of Political Economy* (1859), Marx criticises Gray for his use of 'certificates of labour' or 'bank notes' as the measure of value or labour because he avoids consideration of the more important issues of labour as a commodity, exchange value, and money. The idea of labour certificates challenges the bourgeois idea of money and exchange but leaves intact the whole question of the capitalist mode of production and social relationships. This type of reform of exchange is only a bourgeois reform which

results in a confusion of 'flagrant absurdities' because the real problems are not examined (pp. 83–6; *MEW* 13, pp. 66–69).

24 This integration of historical materialism and cultural idealism requires that we return to Hegel's concepts of the dialectic (*Dialektik*) and transcendence (*Aufhebung*) to fully appreciate his intentions in this cryptic passage. Historical materialism is not a mechanical or deterministic theory of history which simply places ontological primacy of one aspect of society (economy) at the expense of the other structures and functions or that 'negates' or leaves behind rights without first transforming and incorporating them into the next stage of development in a historical transcendence.

25 Marx, *Critique of the Gotha Program*, p. 119; *MEW* 19, p. 21.

Marx and Aristotle on Human Nature and Human Needs: For a detailed analysis of Aristotle's and Marx's theory of human need, see George E. McCarthy, *Marx and the Ancients: Classical Ethics, Social Justice, and Nineteenth-Century Political Economy* (Savage, MD: Rowman & Littlefield Publishers, 1990), n. 2, pp. 303–4 and *Dreams in Exile: Rediscovering Science and Ethics in Nineteenth-Century Social Theory* (Albany, NY: State University of New York Press, 2009), pp. 27–44, n. 13, p. 272, n. 3, p. 288, n. 13, p. 289 and n. 37, p. 291. See also Norman Levine, *Tragic Deception: Marx Contra Engels* (Oxford: Clio Books, 1975), pp. 1–42; Agnes Heller, *The Theory of Need in Marx* (New York, NY: St. Martin's Press, 1976), pp. 1–42; Patricia Springborg, *The Problem of Human Needs and the Critique of Civilisation* (London: George Allen & Unwin, 1981), pp. 94–117, 'Aristotle and the Problem of Needs', *History of Political Thought*, 5, 3 (Winter 1984): 393–424 and 'Marx, Democracy and the Ancient Polis', *Critical Philosophy* 1, 1 (March 1984): 47–66; Norman Geras, 'The Controversy about Marx and Justice', *Philosophica* 33 (1984): 33–86; Philip Kain, *Marx and Ethics* (Oxford: Clarendon Press, 1988), pp. 25–33 and 51–82; Kate Soper, 'A Theory of Human Need', *New Left Review* 197 (1993): 113–28; Martha Nussbaum, 'Nature, Function, and Capability: Aristotle on Political Distribution', in *Marx and Aristotle: Nineteenth-Century German Social Theory and Classical Antiquity*, ed. George E. McCarthy (Savage, MD: Rowman & Littlefield Publishers, 1992), pp. 175–211, 'Human Functioning and Social Justice: In Defense of Aristotelian Essentialism', *Political Theory*, 20, 2 (May 1992): 202–46, and 'Aristotle, Politics, and Human Capabilities', *Ethics*, 111, 1 (October 2000): 102–40; and Soran Reader, 'Aristotle on Necessities and Needs', *Royal Institute of Philosophy Supplement*, 57 (December 2005): 113–36. And for an analysis of the need for love (*philia*) and friendship in a household (*oikos*) or moral economy, see William James Booth, *Households: On the Moral Architecture of the Economy* (Ithaca, NY: Cornell University Press, 1993), pp. 36–7, 46–7 and 53–5.

26 Some scholars have interpreted this transcendence (*Aufhebung*) of bourgeois legal principles as a determinate rejection of all principles of social justice. A society based on human need is beyond justice and beyond the legal principles of bourgeois rights. See John Rawls, *A Theory of Justice* (Cambridge, MA: Harvard University Press, 1999), p. 112. However, Marx's critique of bourgeois rights should not be interpreted to mean a critique of human rights in general.

27 Karl Marx, 'Private Property and Communism', *Karl Marx: Early Writings*, trans. and ed. T.B. Bottomore (New York, NY: McGraw Hill Book Company, 1964), pp. 164–5; *Karl Marx/ Friedrich Engels Werke* (*MEW*), Band 40, Ergänzungsband 1 (Berlin: Dietz Verlag, 1968), p. 544. In an interesting analysis of human needs, William McBride, in 'Marxism and

Natural Law', *American Journal of Jurisprudence*, 15 (1950), develops the argument that Marx's theory of needs is connected with his theories of 'naturalism' and natural law. In an unusual twist to the traditional view, McBride argues that natural law as viewed by Aristotle, Thomas Aquinas, Marx, Rudolf Stammler, and Leo Strauss has a historical and changing content. He attempts to connect a changeable natural law to a historically defined human nature (human potentialities) (pp. 127–53). Later Norman Levine continues this line of thought in his work *The Tragic Deception* in his analysis of Marx's philosophical anthropology when he writes: 'In the later Marx also, communism was eudaemonistic. Happiness, for Marx, means the freedom to be a total person, that is, freedom to indulge all of our productive power and expressive capacities' (p. 37). This need to be truly human and develop the potential of humanity ties together Marx and Aristotle, as well as species being and natural law.

28 Kain in *Marx and Ethics* affirms the concept of human need as fundamentally an ethical and political category: 'To realize the human essence, for Marx, it is not only necessary to realize and to satisfy the needs of human beings but it is also necessary to develop their powers ... For Marx, as for Aristotle, the human being is exclusively natural and morality is the perfection of our nature. Virtue – the realization of our nature – is something we naturally seek ... We ought to work for the realization of the species in order to realize ourselves' (pp. 57 and 66). The concept of need is intimately connected with that of species being and the moral good – the need for freedom, self-determination, and self-realisation of our essence as humans in our private and public lives. Need as the essence of species being replaces equal market exchange (capitalism) and contribution (socialism) in the later stage of communist development. Kain argues that Marx's theory of needs represents his theory of essence, species being, and human capacities which revives the tradition of Aristotle and Kant (pp. 51–82). See also Charles Taylor, 'Marxism and Empiricism', in *British Analytic Philosophy*, ed. Bernard Williams and Alan Montefiore (London: Prometheus Books, 1966), pp. 244–5; Adam Schaff, *Marxism and the Human Individual*, trans. Olgierd Wojtasiewicz, ed. Robert Cohen (New York, NY: McGraw-Hill Book Company, 1970), pp. 49–102; István Mészáros, *Marx's Theory of Alienation* (New York, NY: Harper Torchbooks, 1972), pp. 162, 167, and 184–5; Carol Gould, *Marx's Social Ontology: Individuality and Community in Marx's Theory of Social Reality* (Cambridge, MA: MIT Press, 1980), pp. 108–9, 130–1, 159, 169–78; and Philip Kain, *Schiller, Hegel, and Marx: State, Society and the Aesthetic Ideal of Ancient Greece* (Kingston, Canada: McGill-Queen's University Press, 1982), pp. 81–113. In Marx's early writings human essence and natural law are characterised by species being, whereas in his later works it is expressed as human need. This change reflects the evolution in his moral philosophy, similar to Aristotle, from an early emphasis on ethics, virtue, and practical action to his later focus on structures, politics, and democracy.

29 Marx, 'Alienated Labour', *Karl Marx: Early Writings*, trans. and ed. T.B. Bottomore (New York, NY: McGraw Hill Book Company, 1964), p. 128; *MEW* 40, Ergänzungsband 1, p. 517.

30 Karl Marx, 'Needs, Production, and Division of Labour', *Karl Marx: Early Writings*, trans. and ed. T.B. Bottomore, p. 171; *MEW* 40, Ergänzungsband 1, p. 549.

31 Patricia Springborg, 'Karl Marx on Democracy, Participation, Voting, and Equality', *Political Theory*, 12, 4 (November 1984): 554, n. 30. Springborg also emphasises Marx's key point

from the *Grundrisse* that in a moral economy individuals meet each other in a natural exchange as human beings having needs and not as commodities of exchange value. This only reaffirms 'their common species being' (*Gattungswesen*) (p. 243; MEW 42, p. 168). It also transforms the economic values of equality and freedom from justifications of the market and exchange value to the political ideals of classical antiquity (pp. 245–9; MEW 42, pp. 169–71). The danger, as seen by Marx, is that the French socialists fail to see this distinction and wish only to realise the values of equality and freedom defined as legal and market categories based on wage labour and market exchange. Equality in distribution, commerce, and exchange value turns into its opposite since it would only result in further oppression and alienation. Instead, Marx calls for an equality in production, as well as distribution. Justice entails the totality of the social system; a revolution of only parts of the system changes nothing except the appearances.

32 Husami, 'Marx on Distributive Justice', p. 46.

33 Aristotle, *Nicomachean Ethics*, book II, chapter 6, 1106a30–2, p. 339, book V, chapter 4, 1132b16–17, p. 407, and book V, chapter 5, 1133a27–8, p. 409. Springborg recognises that there is ambiguity in Aristotle's criterion of needs in her essay 'Aristotle and the Problem of Needs', p. 414. The same point may be made of Marx. These ambiguities are to be worked out within the democratic polity and producers' associations. 'Thus Marx's theory of alienation may be seen as the full elaboration of Aristotle's distinction between *oikonomia*, economic activity geared to communal needs and the production of use-values, and *chrematistike*, money-making in a society governed by *pleonexia* [unlimited accumulation of material possessions and the pursuit of wealth for its own sake] and oriented to the production of exchange-values. The more Marx in his later writings became preoccupied with the process of production, exchange and circulation, the closer his concept of needs approximates that of Aristotle ...' (p. 419).

34 Kain, *Marx and Ethics*, pp. 53–75.

35 Ibid., p. 55.

36 A number of scholars have reduced Marx's theory of 'need' to the satisfaction of basic physical needs and private interests; this crude materialism is a result of interpreting Marx through the classical economics of Smith and the later Hegel (system of needs in civil society from the *Philosophy of Right*), rather than through the ideas of Aristotle. With the dismantling of the capitalist social relations of production, economic expansion, and technological developments under socialism, the ideals of bourgeois justice, juridical rights, and fair distribution will no longer be necessary. Thus the satisfaction of needs has replaced civil and legal rights and the fairness of equivalency and contribution as the measure of a good society. See Allen Buchanan, *Marx and Justice: The Radical Critique of Liberalism* (Totowa, NJ: Rowman and Littlefield Publishers, 1982), pp. 29, 57, and 59 and George Brenkert, *Marx's Ethics of Freedom* (London: Routledge & Kegan Paul, 1983), p. 152. This reductionism and naturalism of human needs to physical properties satisfied by a specific mode of production leads to an inability to rise above the immediate empirical circumstances of the economic life of capital. For a broader understanding of Marx's theory of human needs that provides a profound moral critique of capitalism and is not tied to Enlightenment thought and utilitarianism, one must turn to Aristotle's theory of needs for virtue, justice, freedom, and self-realisation.

37 Nielsen, 'Marx, Engels, and Lenin on Justice', responds to the problem of the relationship between historical materialism and distributive justice, especially when different historical periods are compared and judged: 'But this is not at all a form of relativism but a contextualism which is perfectly compatible with a belief in moral objectivity. What it does appeal to is a recognition that material conditions and the economic organisation of social life strongly condition what we can rightly say is just or unjust ...' (p. 26). This same dilemma of comparing different historical moments and societies applies also in the application of different moral values or theories of justice in the act of normative evaluation. Whether the societies or moral principles are different, the issue of moral objectivity remains. This moral and epistemological issue has not been addressed by Marx.

38 Marx, *Critique of the Gotha Program*, p. 120; *MEW* 19, p. 22. In his analysis of natural rights and economic distribution, Marx applies the same argument: In both cases these ethical norms were being used to conceal the economic base of society so that real social change would be impossible. Without knowing the economic physiology and financial neurology of modern industrial society, attempts to fix structural and functional problems are useless and bound to fail. Worse yet, real revolutionary change turns into reformism and political adaptation to the economic reality. The inadequacies of rights and distribution are more the effects of the system than their underlying cause. Thus the discussions about the nature of rights – natural rights, legal rights, rights of the egoistic man, rights of the communal citizen, political and human emancipation, etc. – and the nature of distribution – proceeds of labour, equal rights, fair distribution, total social product, contribution, etc. – when taken out of historical and structural context become forms of ineffective and useless moralism and abstract ethical condemnation. Marx is always working within the Aristotelian orbit of material, efficient, formal, and final causality in his approach to capitalism as a total social system.

39 Ibid.; *MEW* 19, p. 22.

40 Stathis Kouvelakis, 'The Marxian Critique of Citizenship: For a Rereading of *On the Jewish Question*', trans. Alex Martin, *The South Atlantic Quarterly*, 104, 4 (Fall 2005): 715. There is an issue in the secondary literature about whether legal and distributive justice should be abandoned or redefined. Those who view Marx as necessarily abandoning both issues of rights and distribution take the position that they are remnants of bourgeois liberalism and thus unnecessary in an advanced socialist society. Kouvelakis argues that the 'modern state can very well eliminate the restricted franchise, thereby removing all directly political significance from property, effectively guaranteeing the right to vote to those who do not own property, and yet leave intact even the most concentrated ownership of property, since property is now "merely" a civil difference' (ibid.). There can be an extension of rights within an oppressive economic system without contradiction. Kouvelakis asks whether the rights of man grounded in the right to property in the French *Declaration of the Rights of Man and of the Citizen* could not be redefined and made 'more appropriate'. He responds in the negative because all rights are ultimately reducible to property rights and when there is a conflict between property and political rights, the former always wins out as the political rights 'degenerate into pure formalities' (p. 716). Eventually, political emancipation and the 'existing world order' must be left behind with the transformation of the social relations of production, wage labour, and technical tools of production.

41 Marx, *Critique of the Gotha Program*, p. 120; *MEW* 19, p. 22.
42 Ibid.; *MEW* 19, p. 22. This idea of the intimate connection between distribution and production is also stated in Marx's early writings in *The Poverty of Philosophy* where he writes: 'The mode of exchange of products depends upon the mode of exchange of the productive forces. In general, the form of exchange of production corresponds to the form of production'. Karl Marx, *The Poverty of Philosophy: Answer to the Philosophy of Poverty by M. Proudhon, Karl Marx and Frederick Engels Collected Works* (New York, NY: International Publishers, 1976), vol. 6, p. 143; *Karl Marx/Friedrich Engels Werke (MEW)*, Band 4 (Berlin: Dietz Verlag, 1977), pp. 104–5.
43 This distinction between essence and appearance (noumena and phenomena, spirit and phenomena) is the key part of the argument about rights and distribution in Marx's theory. Focusing on rights and distribution is only another form of alienation because the Lassallean socialists mistake the empirical phenomena for the underlying social reality. If rights can never be higher than the economic structure, then the expansion of rights (or the wider redistribution of wages) will not transform the structure, but only make the chains of the working class more secure and bind labour more closely than ever to capital.
44 Marx, *Critique of the Gotha Program*, p. 120; *MEW* 19, p. 22.
45 Ibid.
46 The German Workers' Party or the *Allgemeiner Deutscher Arbeiterverein* (General German Workers' Association, ADAV) was formed by Lassalle on 23 May 1863.
47 Marx, *Critique of the Gotha Program*, p. 122; *MEW* 19, p. 24.
48 The German free trade or low tariff on customs movement was created by John Prince and influenced by the writings of Smith and Jeremy Bentham. See Ralph Raico, 'John Prince Smith and the German Free-Trade Movement', in *Man, Economy, and Liberty: Essays in Honor of Murray N. Rothbard*, ed. Walter Block and Llewellyn H. Rockwell, Jr. (Auburn, AL: The Ludwig von Mises Institute, 1988), pp. 341–51.
49 Marx, *Critique of the Gotha Program*, p. 123; *MEW* 19, p. 24.
50 Ibid., p. 124; *MEW* 19, p. 26.
51 Ibid.
52 Marx's methodology of historical materialism and dialectical analysis will be examined in more detail in Chapter 8 on economic justice and the critique of chrematistics.
53 Marx, *Critique of the Gotha Program*, p. 125; *MEW* 19, p. 26.
54 Ibid., p. 127; *MEW* 19, p. 28.
55 Ibid.
56 Friedrich Engels, 'Introduction', in Karl Marx, *The Civil War in France: The Paris Commune* (New York, NY: International Publishers, 1972), p. 22; *Karl Marx/Friedrich Engels Werke (MEW)*, Band 22 (Berlin: Dietz Verlag, 1977), p. 199.
57 Marx, *Critique of the Gotha Program*, p. 128; *MEW* 19, p. 29.
58 Ibid.
59 Ibid., p. 130; *MEW* 19, p. 31.

CHAPTER 7

Political Justice: Ethics and the Good Life of Democratic Socialism

Just as the previous chapter traced the development of distributive justice from capitalism through the various stages of communist distribution of social consumption from exchange and contribution to human need, this chapter will trace the development of political emancipation to human emancipation through an analysis of the socialist state of the Paris Commune of 1871.[1] In his writings, Aristotle had used his theory of political or universal justice as a way of integrating his economic or particular theories of restitutive, distributive, and reciprocal justice, as well as his ethics and politics into his ideal state of a democratic polity. In a similar fashion, Marx's analysis of the worker commune will integrate his various forms of social justice into a comprehensive theory of democratic socialism. We will examine the exceptionally broad intellectual range of Marx's theory of political justice and the principles of natural law with a focus on the economic and political institutions that give concrete life to the values and ideals of economic freedom, equality, and democracy in the Paris Commune, the human emancipation of labour, freedom from racial, social, and wage slavery, workplace democracy as the ideal polity, and decentralised workers' councils and producer co-operatives. In addition to these key features, there will also be an examination of the issues of the expropriation of the expropriators and the dissolution of class inequality, private property, and centralised state power, as well as the rise of collective ownership of property, economic self-government, and universal suffrage, recall, and popular sovereignty.

To further justify his theory of political and economic democracy, Marx will also ground his theory of social justice within a history of human emancipation and phenomenology of the modern spirit (*Geist*). This phenomenology involves tracing the development of the self-consciousness of human freedom and political liberalism in Western society from the natural rights of John Locke (property), political rights of Rousseau and the French Revolution of 1789 and 1793 (citizenship and sovereignty), inalienable rights of Thomas Jefferson (foreign oppression), human rights of Abraham Lincoln (racial equality), economic rights of Ferdinand Lassalle (rights of fair distribution), and the economic rights of Karl Marx (democracy). By drawing on these traditions, Marx is integrating the British, American, French, and German traditions of rights and freedom into a comprehensive theory of human rights and social justice. In turn, his work on the Paris Commune, *The Civil War in France*, provides us with his clearest and most concrete statements on the nature of human emancipation and political justice.[2]

Franco-Prussian War and the Formation of the Paris Commune of 1871

In July 1870, France under the leadership of Emperor Napoleon III and the Northern German Confederation under the Prussian leadership of Otto von Bismarck went to war ostensibly over a diplomatic incident. For Prussia and the northern German alliance, it provided the ideal opportunity to create the unified state of Germany by incorporating the southern German states of Bavaria, Württemberg, Hesse, Saxony, and Baden into the new German Empire. The French army was quickly and decisively defeated at the battles of Metz and Sedan. On 2 September, Napoleon, at the head of an 80,000 man French army, was captured at Sedan, effectively ending the government of the Second French Empire. He would comfortably spend the rest of the war as a prisoner in Wilhelmshöhe castle in the city of Kassel. Within days of the surrender, the republican and radical delegates of the French National Assembly led a popular uprising on 4 September, went to the Hôtel de Ville in Paris, and publicly announced the creation of a new provisional republican government called the Government of National Defense. The Paris deputies of the previous government now constituted the new self-appointed republic for Paris and the nation. The Paris Revolution began with the fall of Napoleon's empire and ended with the rise of the Third French Republic. All this occurred with the German army standing before the walls of Paris and ready for a blockade of the city.[3]

The new self-appointed national government was led by Adolphe Thiers with a conservative and monarchist majority in the National Assembly. With the defeat of the French army at Sedan and the French army at Metz under a blockade, the German army began its advance on Paris with little resistance. But Paris was a heavily fortified walled city with a complex maze of external forts to protect the inner city. Two weeks after the Paris Revolution on 18 September, the siege began, and the city was completely surrounded by Prussian troops two days later. With most of the French army either surrounded in Metz or held captive in Germany, the new French government called upon the remote provinces to form new armies to come to the rescue of Paris. While the siege of Paris continued, there were numerous battles in other parts of France at Orléans, Le Mans, Amiens, Bapaume, St. Quentin, and Lisaine. The situation was becoming hopeless as news reached Paris in late October that the French army attempting to relieve the city under the leadership of the president of the new republican government, General Louis Jules Trochu, had been defeated. At just about the same time, Parisian citizens learned that the 160,000 French troops under Marshal Bazaine, surrounded in Metz by the Germans for over two months, had surrendered. With French armies defeated, captured, or in retreat, it was generally recognised that the remaining National Guard units defending Paris were simply not sufficient to resist the German army, especially if there was no hope of rescue on the horizon. But in the face of these enormous setbacks, Paris refused to submit to the invading army, which later earned their citizens a great deal of respect from the Germans, who did not occupy the city even after its surrender.

The French army, exhausted and overwhelmed after a more than four month siege, was finally defeated, ending in the surrender of Paris on 8 January 1871, with a peace armistice signed on 26 January. The outer fortifications were surrendered and the regular army disarmed. What was singularly important at the time, especially for an understanding of later events, was that the National Guard was not disarmed, in order to maintain peace in the city. Paris had been under military siege since 19 September 1870. The blockade, constant attacks, and bombardment of the city by the German army, cold weather, unemployment, and hunger resulting from a lack of food and medicine, caused great physical hardships; people were forced to eat dogs, cats, and rats.[4] But at the same time, this situation also galvanised their political and military opposition to both the Germans and to the newly elected government of Thiers. Because of the unusual circumstances and military defeats, the National Guard, which was a citizen militia, was the most powerful and important military force in Paris at the time. Since they were not part of the regular army, discipline among the guardsmen was lax, military orders were first discussed among the soldiers, and officers were elected by the soldiers themselves. The National Guard units defending the city were organised around the local neighbourhoods, with the working class representing the core of this military organisation. The peace treaty was finally signed in Frankfurt on 10 May 1871, ceding the French territory of Alsace-Lorraine to Germany, which would continue to create tensions between France and Germany up to World War I and beyond.

Since Paris came under attack within months of the start of the war, the city was heavily fortified by the Government of National Defense which created a large, but inexperienced, untrained, and undisciplined, and, it should be added, poorly led force of the working class National Guard.[5] The city was surrounded by high walls with 16 detached forts protecting its outer parameters.

Throughout September and October, the radicals in the government publicly protested the conditions in Paris and the need for more equipment and regular French army troops to defend the city. They also wanted new elections and the formation of a commune. Of course, they were resisted by the few regular army units of the republican government of Thiers. News from the battle front continued to be disturbing as military defeats continued, and there was no relief in sight from the French army.

After the defeat and fall of the French Empire, the national government of France, which was located in Bordeaux during the war, called for immediate parliamentary elections. The provisional government was disbanded and a new National Assembly was elected on 8 February with Thiers chosen soon thereafter as its head; the emperor was deposed in early March, and eventually fled to England. The new national government had a conservative majority from the monarchist party; they represented the Catholic provinces, which had the effect of alienating the more radical republican elements of the Paris population. Things moved quickly after the new national elections; opposition to the Thiers government in Bordeaux spread throughout the working-class districts of northern and eastern Paris in Montmartre and Belleville. Informal groups and political committees were created in each of the 20 administrative districts (*arrondissements*) of Paris calling for local elections in the city and a democratic republic.[6] Since February, with the national government still located in Bordeaux, a parallel government of the National Guard had been formed in Paris, and by the middle of the month five hundred delegates were meeting regularly. One month later, on 18 March, the new national government and the French army, attempting to confirm and solidify the 4 September revolution, sought to disarm the National Guard of its cannons and capture some of its leaders. The attempt failed due to the formation of spontaneous crowds led by women in some cases.[7] The Parisians, under the orders of the Central Committee, which was the main governing body in the Commune, had removed the cannon to Montmartre, Belleville, and La Villette before the Germans briefly entered Paris in order to protect them from confiscation. Now, it was the French government who was attempting to take them away and with them a key military element of the National Guard's ability to defend itself and the city. Two republican army generals who led the attack, Lacomte and Clement Thomas, were killed; they initially ordered the army to fire into the rebellious crowds but were instead executed by their own men.

In his public address to the general council of the International Working Men's Association in 1871, Marx writes that Paris had to be disarmed in order for the new republic to succeed and removing the cannon was only the first step toward total disarmament of the Guard. Twenty years later, in his introduction to this address, Friedrich Engels concurred with Marx's analysis: The propertied classes of the large landowners and capitalists felt threatened by the existence of the Commune with its large working class army.[8] After the failure to remove the artillery of the Guard from Montmartre and Belleville, the regular army, chief government officials, and the police force left Paris for Versailles in complete disarray and confusion, thereby leaving the city in control of the National Guard whose ranks because of the war had swelled to about 320,000 men.[9] The latter immediately proceeded to take over key government offices; a few days earlier, on 15 March, the National Guard had elected a Central Committee located at the Hôtel de Ville to run the city, and on 22 March this Committee declared itself the legitimate government of Paris with elections for the Commune to be held four days later.

The day after the start of the revolution on 18 March was unusually quiet.[10] When power was taken from the national government and with Thiers in a hasty and confused retreat from Paris, there was no central coordination of events in Paris. Things were happening very quickly and spontaneously throughout the city, and government buildings were being occupied but on the basis of many individual decisions in different city districts. There were hopes and exhilaration, but no plans for a new revolutionary government. That would have to evolve over time, if there was time. Everyone was preparing for a military counterattack by Thiers, but it never came, which led some to naively think the revolution was a success and peace was at hand; some even thought that the Thiers government and the Second Republic would simply disappear after its humiliating defeat.[11] The Central Committee met early on the following morning to discuss the next steps to be taken. Some argued for a consolidation of the gains of the previous day and preparation for municipal elections; others thought that the next move should be an attack on Versailles to eliminate a counterattack. The decision was made to secure the recently won rights of the Paris citizen, inform the public of what had happened, and prepare for new elections to validate the communal revolution. Their goal was basically defensive, to protect the provisional government, prepare for the new elections, and encourage other large cities and municipal governments to create their own communes. Some even saw this as the beginning of the 'emancipation of the proletariat'.[12] In a letter to Dr. Kugelmann, Marx despairs that if the citizens of the Commune are defeated it will be because of their own 'good nature'. They should have attacked the republican army in Versailles and ended all conceivable counter-revolutionary possibilities: 'The right moment was missed because of conscientious scruples. They [the Commune] did not want to *start the civil war*, as if that mischievous *abortion* Thiers had not already started the civil war with his attempt to disarm Paris'.[13] In the same letter, Marx criticises the Central Committee for its failure to retain its political power longer to provide continuity and coherence to the revolution.

There was no real awareness of the powerlessness and disarray of the government or the deterioration of the regular army due to the war with Germany. Retreating in confusion, the Thiers government had no immediate plans for a military response because their army was for all practical purposes non-existent. They needed time to rearm and recreate the French army, which occurred with the help of the German army. As soon as it attained political power, the Central Committee, which from the beginning was uncomfortable with its newly found political power and concerned about the legitimacy of its actions and claims, sought to transfer power to the duly elected representatives of the citizens in Paris. On 26 March, the day of the municipal elections, the Central Committee of the National Guard handed over government power and its functions to the newly elected Council of the Paris Commune. There was no ready-made social and political design outlining the concrete programmes of the new government to be immediately initiated. For that matter, there was no real coordinated leadership at all.

As a result of the Franco-Prussian War, the surrender of the French army, the collapse of the French Empire of Emperor Napoleon III, and the creation of a republican National Assembly under Thiers, the citizens of Paris had enough and finally united together to resist the newly created provisional French government to form their own political and economic system on 18 March – the Paris Commune. What began as a war between the French and German monarchies ended as a war between labour and capital. Viewed from Marx's perspective, this new political entity rejected the values and institutions of modern capitalism and its centralised state. Within two months of the French military surrender and within a week of the official signing of the peace treaty, a civil war between the socialist Commune and the republican government of Thiers began. Marx refers to this class conflict and civil war as a 'slaveholders' rebellion'.[14] The Thiers government could not repay French national and municipal debt along with German war reparations of five billion francs, to be paid within five years, without first crushing the Paris Commune and their opposition to the new French republic. The large agricultural and industrial landowners did not want these enormous war expenses to be a burden on their future productivity and profits; nor did they want to pay higher taxes for the foreign adventures of the king and republic if they could be transferred to the working class of Paris.[15] Thiers, in defence of the French Republic, finally attacked Paris at the beginning of April, and throughout early and mid-May there were skirmishes along the periphery of the city. Many soldiers of the Versailles army, who had been captured during the war and later freed by the Germans, were now fighting with the regenerated and resupplied French army against the gravely outnumbered Communards in Paris.

Finally, on 21 May the walls of the city were breached by the forces of Marshal MacMahon, the defences crumbled, and the defenders haphazardly retreated back to their particular neighbourhoods from which they were originally recruited. Street by street, barricade by barricade, the bloody fight continued for one week. Because of the decentralised and independent nature of the National Guard battalions, there was little centralised coordination of the various guard units to resist; and there were few barricades set up in the middle of the city to slow the advance of the invading troops. Summary military courts were created by the regular army which then proceeded to execute captured defenders by firing squad. Realising they were losing, the National Guard started burning a number of public buildings, including the royal Tuileries Palace and the headquarters of the Commune at the Hôtel de Ville. As the regular army continued its march through the city of Paris, the summary executions of the remaining Communards increased. On the evening of 27 May, the last remaining serious resistance of the National Guard was finally overcome at the cemetery of Père-Lachaise on the heights of Belleville; on the following day of the 'bloody week', after eight fierce days of intense fighting, these last scattered remnants of the Commune's heroic stand were executed and buried in the cemetery, and with them all resistance ended.

For 72 days, from 18 March to 28 May 1871, the citizen defenders of Paris withstood the armies of the republic. The French army, assisted by the Germans who turned over to them some key captured Parisian forts, was able to attack the city from unexpected and sparsely defended sides. At the same time they were defending the city, the Communards attempted to construct a new social system based on economic democracy and workers' control over production. And it was this socialist experiment in workers' self-government – this storming of heaven – that Marx praised in his eulogy to the inspiration and courage of the men and women of the Paris Commune. They provided him with the first concrete designs for a truly democratic society.[16]

Dismantling the Old State and Rise of Political Democracy in the Commune

On 18 March 1871, the same day as the failed attempt to disarm the National Guard, the Central Committee of the Paris Commune issued a declaration and began to dismantle in a non-violent manner the centralised republican government and the national hierarchical orders of class and property within the old regimes of the French political system.[17] The Commune held its first meeting on 28 March, two days after the general election, and created ten commissions to run the various functions of the government in Paris. Following closely the military and political events surrounding the Commune, Marx recognised very quickly that some of his earlier ideas about the socialist state contained in the *Communist Manifesto* (1848) were no longer relevant: '[T]he working class cannot simply lay hold of the ready-made state machinery, and wield it for its own purposes'.[18] The state is not an independent and neutral political organisation capable of yielding power for one class and then another; it is not simply an issue of gaining control over the state and then implementing economic and social reforms. Rather, the republican state, utilising its political and legal apparatus, is an oppressive mechanism of social control preserving the class interests of the bourgeois economic system, and this, too, would also have to be restructured. Continuing arguments from *On the Jewish Question* (1843), Marx contends that the role of the French state was to maintain the economic and political power of the propertied class: '[T]he state power assumed more and more the character of the national power of capital over labour, of a public force organised for social enslavement, of an engine of class despotism'.[19] Therefore, with this in mind, the Commune's first actions were to dismantle the various component parts of the French state, including the army, police, bureaucracy, clergy, and the judiciary. Thus an entirely new form of government would have to be constructed that conformed to the socialist ideals of human emancipation and political freedom. These ideas, as we have already seen in the previous chapter, will become central to Marx's later critique of the *Gotha Program* (1875).

To undertake this radical transformation of French society, the centralised state power of the liberal republic would have to be dismantled. Over time there was growing power of the propertied classes over the old feudal system through their expansion of industry, commerce, and finance. And with this growth came imperial wars of national glory and the domestic wars of civil repression as forms of 'class terrorism' used to solidify and justify the newly achieved power of the bourgeoisie. A 'national war engine of capital against labour' was created.[20] Marx summarises this view of the state when he writes:

> Imperialism is, at the same time, the most prostitute and the ultimate form of the state power which nascent middle-class society had commenced to elaborate as a means of its own emancipation from feudalism,

and which full-grown bourgeois society had finally transformed into a means for the enslavement of labour by capital.[21]

According to Marx, this accounts for the wars against Germany and Paris. The state was to be used to destroy all opposition to the new owning class and its prerogatives and values, whether it came from the old royal regimes of the French empire, foreign imperial competition from Berlin, or internal class dissent from the communes of Paris and the provinces.

The old monarchical and republican state was to be dismantled by tearing apart the political organs of class repression of the state. Just as the various aspects of the macro and micro economy were diffused by an alienating division of labour, so, too, was the political sphere. This division of the political into its various functional parts had the effect of fragmenting and repressing consciousness of the oppressive and ideological nature of the liberal political apparatus.[22] Originally this division of labour was effective in dismantling the feudal system and now it was being used to oppress the working class. To counter these developments, the national standing army was replaced by the citizens' militia of the National Guard consisting mainly of workers; the local police force in Paris was stripped of its political power and reduced to being responsible to the people; and the legislative, executive, and judicial branches of government and the whole institutional hierarchy and political division of labour were dismantled and democratised as these positions were filled through elections based on universal suffrage, social responsibility, and citizen recall. The clergy and church, which acted as 'a spiritual force of repression' on behalf of the ruling class, lost their property and political power within society as the clergy became private citizens and church property was confiscated and redistributed. The old state power was to be replaced by an entirely new political system:

> The Commune was formed of the municipal councillors, chosen by universal suffrage in the various wards of the town, responsible, temporary, accessible, and revocable at short terms. The majority of its members were naturally working men, or acknowledged representatives of the working class. The Commune was to be a working, not a parliamentary body, executive and legislative at the same time.[23]

Opposing the idea of the republican separation of powers among the three branches of government, the Commune would combine them into one working body politic. The defining characteristic of this new political system is that it is a participatory and working-class democracy in which the workers themselves take a central role in making all the decisions that affect the everyday lives of its citizens. This new form of democracy represented a major break with the parliamentary republic and bourgeois government of Thiers whose only purpose was to protect and expand private property.

The police were no longer to be agents of the state but to serve as public servants and representatives of the Commune, and, as with all the other branches of the administration, they could be instantly recalled for misdeeds. Government positions were no longer to be used for personal advancement (careerism), or financial enrichment. The wages of all government officials were to be set at those of workman's compensation. The great divide between elected officials and citizens was overcome as officials became more responsible to the local needs of the people who were more actively engaged in the political and economic decision-making within the commune. 'Public functions ceased to be the private property of the tools of the Central Government'.[24] Other social institutions such as education and science were to be freed from the external authority of the state and the church and opened to all. Science was to be freed of all 'class prejudice and governmental force'. Finally, judges were to be made independent of the existing political forces and they, too, would become 'elective, responsible, and revocable'.[25] Authority and control within society were decentralised and shifted to the workers' communes in local municipal districts, rural communities, county hamlets, and to the elected representatives of the National Delegation in Paris. Marx made the analogy that universal suffrage and local democracy now had the same power of self-determination as the 'individual suffrage' of property owners who were able to choose their own workers and managers and who could remove them at will to redress specific problems in the workplace. With the end of the private property of capital and politics, the power and responsibility of universal suffrage rested in the hands of the citizens of the commune.

The Commune is a socialist or working-class government grounded in the ethical principles of 'the self-government of the producers' and 'the economic emancipation of labour'.[26] These political ideals, manifested in the constitution of the Paris Commune, represent an expansion of Marx's earlier understanding of the nature of political rights and human emancipation. His original ethical theory of natural law and social justice is now being made real and concrete in the values and institutions of the Commune itself. With the abolition of class rule, property is expropriated by the co-operative associations or production communes so that the means of production are now transformed into 'the instruments of free labour'. The Paris Commune was seen as the model for the expansion of the communal government to all corners of French society. Local communities in the distant provinces would regulate their activities using this political model; the ideal state was a decentralised, federal polity. The local communes, in turn, would send representatives to the central government or National Delegation in Paris. Since the regular army was to be turned into a workingman's militia and the state bureaucracy was to be dismantled, the size of the state would shrink in proportion. As the political bureaucracy and functions of class repression disappeared, more attention and time were directed at public participation and collective decision-making. The state, judiciary, and police were now to be utilised for the benefit of the working class. Marx writes: 'While the merely repressive organs of the old governmental power were to be amputated, its legitimate functions were to be wrested from an authority usurping pre-eminence over society itself, and restored to the responsible agents of society'.[27]

Citizens are to be educated, informed, and responsible to the broadest concerns of the whole community. Elections are no longer to serve as mechanisms of consecration and investiture of the ruling elite to positions of authority. Nor were elections every three or six years to serve as legitimations for the republic. For Marx, only a communal and democratic form of government in which the people decide the issues would be legitimate. At this point in his analysis, Marx is clearly following the ideas of Jean-Jacques Rousseau in his work, *The Social Contract* (1762). Rousseau, in reflecting about representative or parliamentary government in the eighteenth century, wrote: 'Every law the people has not ratified in person is null and void – is, in fact, not a law. The people of England regards itself as free: but it is grossly mistaken: it is free only during the election of members of parliament. As soon as they are elected, slavery overtakes it, and it is nothing'.[28] Parliamentary elections may validate a particular candidate for office, but elections are themselves not valid forms of government creation since they are not democratic. Rousseau continues to argue that elections, laws, and legislation are valid only when they are expressions of the general will of the citizens assembled to give voice to their communal opinion.

Organisation of Labour and Economic Democracy

Over the years, there have been a number of different interpretations of the true social meaning and implications of the Paris Commune. Although the Paris Commune has at times been mistaken for a recreation of the medieval commune, a federation of small states based on the ideas of Montesquieu and the Girondins, a recreation of the French Revolutionary commune of 1791, and even the repressive Prussian state, Marx holds that it represents a dismantling of republican state power and its redistribution to the working class and local municipal governments. This was accomplished by destroying 'the standing army and state functionalism'. But its real accomplishment was that 'it was essentially a working class government, the produce of the struggle of the producing against the appropriating class, the political form at last discovered under which to work out the economical emancipation of labour'.[29] The project which began in his early philosophical writings on the Jewish question in which he initiated a discussion on the nature of political and human emancipation has now reached its end point.

Marx has integrated his work on ethics and politics in a manner similar to Aristotle's integration of the *Nicomachean Ethics* and the *Politics*. The ethical issues of virtue, freedom, practical wisdom, friendship, citizenship, and social justice have been combined with the empirical and structural analysis of the ideal political constitution and the democratic polity. Human emancipation, which in Marx's early writings was only a vague philosophical and political ideal that evolved out of the limits of the bourgeois revolution in France in the eighteenth century, has now developed into the real emancipation of labour from the capitalist economic system. The ideals of political emancipation have been released from the institutions of 'social slavery' – property interests and class rule. The new commune would upend the old state and with it the old social relations of production. As political emancipation freed the citizen, now the commune or 'the political rule of the producer' would emancipate labour. Labour would now become its own end or human need and would no longer be part of the law of value, commodity exchange, or wage slavery. Labour emancipation would become the fullest expression of human emancipation, and the Commune was the political mechanism toward that final goal.

The Commune introduced a new economic system based on the principles of workers' control and co-operative production. The purpose of this new social arrangement was to lay bare the internal structural contradictions and logical inconsistencies of the political ideals of the old class system.

> [T]he Commune intended to abolish that class property, which makes labour of the many the wealth of the few. It aimed at the expropriation of the expropriators. It wanted to make individual property a truth by transforming the means of production, land and capital, now chiefly the means of enslaving and exploiting labour, into mere instruments of free and associated labour.[30]

This involves a complete transformation of society where means now become the ends, where labour is changed into a self-determining and self-fulfilling activity of the species being and a true reflection of humanity's real freedom and needs. According to Marx, the bourgeois response can usually be anticipated with its ideological fervour, theoretical simplicity, and return to the classical ideals of liberalism which have long since been negated by the historical reality of capital. Claims of individual self-consciousness, freedom, rights, and liberties have long ago been suppressed by the brutality of the economic enslavement of the majority and the intellectual passivity of the few. The contradictions of the social system at the practical and theoretical level can no longer be ignored once the workers have taken control of the means of production for their own purposes. Finally, utilitarianism and materialism can no longer remain the foundations of ethics and politics under co-operative production. The foundation of the Commune is now a democratic polity and self-governing, worker controlled economy. The classical ideals of a democratic polity and Aristotle's ideal state have now merged with the socialist principles of co-operative production into one new coherent historical form which Marx characterises as 'a national production upon a common plan, thus taking it under their own control, and putting an end to the constant anarchy and periodical convulsions which are the fatality of capitalist production'.[31] The same formal ideals of liberalism are attached to the Commune with its goals of individual freedom, liberty, self-realisation, rights, and happiness. It is just that these words have lost their bourgeois content and defence of the private property of money, land, and capital. Marx has transcended the ideals of liberalism by turning back to the classical period.[32]

Marx is clearly aware that Aristotle did not provide ready-made ideals or utopias to be realised; this was part of the latter's theory of *praxis*, *phronesis*, and political deliberation, as well as his critique of Plato's theory of knowledge, forms, and political ideals in the *Republic*. There are no roadmaps that can be used. This would be anathema to the very principles Marx has been articulating throughout his life. He rejects *a priori* application of concepts, principles, and ideals that would leave the Commune powerless to establish its own priorities and goals. Neo-Platonic social theory turns citizens into means toward the realisation of the correct political order in a class society; it is the philosophical correlate of a market economy. In both cases, individuals are simply the means for the realisation of profits or ideal forms. Democracy or self-determination in the workplace and government becomes an impossibility when society moves in a direction determined by the market or utopian form. Members of the Commune

> know that in order to work out their own emancipation, and along with it that higher form to which present society is irresistibly tending by its own economical agencies, they will have to pass through long struggles,

through a series of historic processes, transforming consciousness and men. They have no ideals to realise, but to set free the elements of the new society with which old collapsing bourgeois society itself is pregnant.[33]

The ideals are not superimposed upon reality but immanently evolve as society develops its productive and technological forces to free humanity from hunger and human misery at the same time that it expands its understanding of its own history. Ideals are no longer ideologies or forms of false consciousness that hide reality or promote class production and prejudices for the benefit of the few, but, instead, have become products of democratic self-reflection and collective action.

'Declaration to the French People' and the Social Programmes of the Commune

When fully constituted, the new Commune consisted of 81 members whose political characteristics could be broken down into the following economic categories: eighteen members were from the middle class, 30 came from the professions (journalists, doctors, lawyers, teachers, etc.), and 35 were manual workers or small shop craftsmen (metal workers, carpenters, masons, etc.). Of these 81 members of the Commune or municipal council, about half had been involved in the labour movement through political organisations, trade unions, and workers' associations.[34] Their numbers consisted of followers of Pierre Proudhon, Louis-Auguste Blanqui, the Jacobins, and radical socialists. Immediately after the elections, ten Commissions or ministries were formed to run the various administrative functions of the municipal government – Executive, Finance, Military, Supplies, Education, Foreign Relations, Public Services, Justice, General Security, and Labour and Exchange.[35] Sixty-one members of the Commune were assigned to these ten commissions. The last department of labour and exchange was new and reflected the leftist political leaning of many members of the Commune.[36] The main purposes of this municipal committee were to develop social programmes that would equalise labour and wages based on the principle of equal wages for equal work and to restructure the organisation of production for the benefit of labour. Its goal was neither the nationalisation of factories nor centralisation of the state, but the creation of workers' co-operatives and a decentralised, federal state of interdependent and independent communes across France; its long-term goal was to dismantle the political and economic institutions of capitalism. It was from this Commission run by Leo Frankel, a friend of Karl Marx, along with the Commission of Education headed by Edouard Vaillant, that the more radical programmes of the Paris Commune originated. Two days after the election, the Commune publicly offered its statement of principles to the citizens of Paris. Of the work of these two commissions Stewart Edwards has written:

> The work of these two commissions supported by activity at the local level and a number of specific decrees constitute the socialist work of the Commune, as the term was understood at the time. These were measures that were intended to enable everyone to live with some decency, in a juster society, in which the concentration of capital and property had been broken down by means of the workers' producers' associations.[37]

The Commune initiated its main programmes in the areas of educational reform and workers' industrial co-operatives as it attempted to institute a new form of working-class democratic polity.[38]

There were a number of broad pressing social questions that the Commune quickly responded to, including the economic issues of financial and economic stability, rents, abolition of nightwork in bakeries, unemployment, pensions to unmarried companions and children of killed National Guard soldiers, overdue bills, pawn shops and the system of credit, small loans, interest rates and the poor, restitution of worker's tools and household items taken in loans, workingmen's bank, commercial loans and interest on debt, fines imposed on workers by employers to reduce wages, food distribution within the city during the siege and civil war, and, finally, and most importantly, worker ownership and control of abandoned workshops and factories. The Commune also introduced new republican and socialist reforms focused on education, including the right to free compulsory education, egalitarian public education for both sexes, integrating secular education and participatory democracy, separation of the state and church, removing the church and religion from public education, emphasising education in science and the scientific method, training teachers in physical education, art, and music, stress on women's education, health care, and the building of nurseries, and the creation of a 'new education society' near factories and working-class districts to promote these educational principles of the Commune.

During the brief time of the civil war, the Central Committee was able to issue a number of decrees, including the official proclamation and manifesto of the Paris Commune, 'Declaration to the French People', on 19 April. By mid-April, the men, women, and children of Paris are again surrounded, under siege, and facing bombardment, but this time by their own people and the regular army of the Thiers republic. During these fatal times, the Commune produces a statement of its proletarian principles and purpose in the 'Declaration to the French People'. It announces the inherent rights and absolute autonomy of the Paris Commune and the corresponding rights and decentralised autonomy for all the communes throughout France, thereby rejecting the despotic centralisation of the Thiers republic. It proudly proclaims its republican ideals of liberty, equality, and fraternity as it articulates the reasons for its resistance to the national government and its suffering at the hands of those whom they claim had betrayed France. It emphasises that the communal revolution was a popular uprising, a scientific experiment undertaken for the common good and general welfare to end the oppression and anti-democratic institutions of state bureaucracy, clerical hierarchy, economic monopolies, political privileges, and proletarian slavery. The declaration states that the reasons for the 'movement of March 18th' have not always been made clear, and the propaganda of Versailles has sometimes overwhelmed the Commune's attempt to explain it. They are defending the government which is the only one compatible 'with the rights of the People and with the free, regular development of society'.[39] The claims of the Thiers government are not recognised, and the rights of the Paris Commune are extended to all other communes throughout France, including self-determination and autonomy.

The revolutionary document announces that the universal goal of the Commune is to protect human rights and the full development of human capabilities. It then proceeds to list the particular rights of the citizens: rights to vote on Communal budget and expenses, levy taxes, and organise the local services, government, police, education, and public property; election, control, and revocation of municipal magistrates and officials; absolute right of individual liberty, liberty of conscience, and liberty of work; citizen participation in Communal affairs through free speech, free publication, defence of interests, and public meetings; and the right to urban defence and the National Guard which elects its own leaders and alone defends the social order of the city. The document continues with its list of protected rights to include independence, collective self-determination of the common good by means of administrative and economic reforms, reforms in education, production, exchange, and credit, and, finally, the right to universalise power and property based on communal needs and collective interests. The Commune rejects traditional French unity imposed on the people by the tyranny of the empire, monarchy, and parliamentary government with its centralisation of despotic power. The unity of France should not be determined by the power of the monarchical or bourgeois class elites but by 'the free and spontaneous co-operation of all individual energies with the common object of wellbeing, liberty, and security for all'.[40] The declaration ends with an appeal to all of France to support the Commune's revolution and ideals. This document was a clarion call to all the citizens of Paris to resist the forces of repression of the National Assembly in Versailles. It represented a defence of the Commune's newly found human rights expressed as protecting equal rights and duties, solidarity of the commune, and universal justice. Another document of the time posted earlier during the election of 26 March by the central electoral committee of the 11th Arrondissement of the city summarised the fight for human rights by the Commune as a protection of the political rights to life, freedom, thought, assembly and association, universal suffrage, speech, press, and expression, and elections. (These are the same rights which Marx defended as the 'rights of the citizen' in *On the Jewish Question*). The declaration then went on to clarify its main economic goal: 'The whole system of work should be reorganised. Since the aim of life is the limitless development of our physical, intellectual and moral capacities, property is and must only be the right of each one of us to share (to the extent of his individual contribution) in the collective fruit of labour which is the basis of social wealth'.[41] A new socialist ideal of work is to replace the liberal view of private property and capitalist production.

Marx's defence of the governance system of the Commune begins with his analysis of the dismantling of the structures of the centralised state and the subsequent creation of a constitution based on the 'self-government of the producers'. His observations develop into a penetrating critique of capitalist production as the Commune moves to the emancipation of labour through co-operative production. In line with his anarchist tendencies, the goal is not the nationalisation or centralisation of production, but the formation of independent worker co-operatives. In the new economy of the Commune, worker-run production was to replace capitalist production. To facilitate this transformation, on 16 April the Commission of Labour and Exchange ordered that factories abandoned by their owners could be appropriated by the workers for their use. In fact, ten factories and their equipment were taken over by trade unions and workers' co-operatives.[42] Although the owners had abandoned their factories at the start of the civil war, the Commission had promised appropriate remuneration when they returned to Paris. Control over production would now rest with the workers as the class nature of property would be transformed in a democratic republic. This was the start of social reform although the Paris government never took the next logical and radical step of socialising the means of production and confiscating the large industries for the workers.[43]

Edwards reports that by 14 May, 43 worker co-operatives were created among such groups as state catering-service workers, café waiters, concierges, shoemakers, tailors, and workers in other industries. He concludes that 'although few of these amounted to much, they are indicative of the strong current within the working class towards co-operative production'.[44] The social experiment did not last long enough to develop the possibilities inherent in its nascent institutions. Marx's public statement is an attempt to give voice to these possibilities. Another goal of the Commission was to eliminate the anarchy of production in a competitive market economy. This could be accomplished by a national integration of local co-operatives into a new system of co-operative societies in which production would be regulated for the benefit of the common good. Its purpose, according to Marx, was to end class property 'by transforming the means of production, land and capital, now chiefly the means of enslaving and exploiting labour, into mere instruments of free and associated labour'.[45]

The Commune undertook a number of other measures to ameliorate the negative effects of capitalist production on Parisian society. Wages of those elected to local government positions were set comparable to workers' wages; nightwork of journeymen bakers was abolished; and workplace fines intended to reduce wages were eliminated. Marx is aware that these were relatively modest steps toward economic transformation, but they were at least a beginning. He had hoped that the Commune would confiscate the large financial institutions, great Church estates, and large factories to be redistributed among the workers.

On 3 May 1871, a workers' co-operative armaments factory located at the recently converted war museum at the Louvre in Paris submitted a list of 22 articles outlining the regulation of worker activity in the production plant for the approval by the Commune. These particular statutes help us to understand the broad range of social and economic issues being considered by the factory workers while the city was under direct artillery bombardment and attack from the French army. The workers appropriated the privately owned armament factory and turned it into a workers' co-operative and an example of economic and participatory democracy. Toward that end, the workers will elect (and remove, if necessary) the manager of the factory who will also be a delegate to the Commune, as well as the workshop supervisor or foreman and the charge-hand. They, too, will be responsible for their duties, and revocable upon complaints, to the factory workers. The duties of the foreman are the following: supervise workshop, organise and collect production, keep a time-clock record of hours worked, and insure that workers clock in within fifteen minutes of the opening of the factory. The duties of the charge-hand or head worker are to oversee the immediate work on their machine lathes, provide workers with the information for performing their particular work tasks, and, at the end of the day, provide reports on the work accomplished. Finally, there will be checkers and clerks elected by the workers who maintain quality checks on all the arms produced during the day.

A Management Council will have mandatory meetings every day at the end of the work shift to discuss the nature of production in the factory. It will consist of the manager, supervisor, charge-hand, and worker representatives from each work area within the factory. Half of the worker delegates will be replaced on a weekly basis to ensure general participation by all within the plant. The worker representatives will inform the factory workers of their activities and decisions, as well as bring any suggestions and grievances before the Council. At the same time, the majority of workers may call a special meeting of the Council to discuss issues of their choosing. If a special meeting is not called, the workers as a collective democracy have the right to call a general meeting for their consideration. Finally, the worker representatives on the Council have the right to form a special 'control committee' or natural work group in order to request any information pertinent to the work of the factory, including the financial statements in possession of the manager and supervisor. A recording secretary is elected weekly to inform the workers of the occurrences within the Council that week; their records will be posted weekly and then collected into a workers' archive for future reference. Decisions about the internal needs of the workplace and the addition of new employees will be the final responsibility of the Council. If there is a cutback in production, and thus the amount of labour required, the Council will have the final say in this matter also.

If there are labour problems with a particular worker, the supervisor may bring a complaint to the Management Council, who will make the final decision about future employment; similarly, if there is a need to curtail production, the last hired will be the first fired unless the Council decides that some workers are grossly inefficient and unproductive. The average workday will be ten hours with one hour for lunch. If necessary repairs have to be made, overtime will be decided by the Council using normal rates of pay. The pay scale for the manager and workers is set at the following rates: manager's salary is set at 250 francs a month, shop-foreman's at 210 francs a month, charge-hand wage rate at 70 centimes an hour, and workers' wage rate will be a maximum of 60 centimes an hour. Changes to these articles for the organisation of production are open to consideration at the discretion of the Council and the majority of workers with the agreement of the Director of Artillery Supplies, one of the commissioners who run the Commune.[46] This is a workers' co-operative where management and labour have a natural, non-antagonistic, and dignified relationship with each other; are responsible to each other to fulfill their proper roles in production; and where workers elect the management team of manager and shop foreman.

The labour commission under Frankel permitted workers to appropriate factories that had been abandoned by owners during the Prussian siege of Paris. The trade unions and co-operative associations would now be in control of production. Unfortunately, this transformation to a new system of industrial production did not include all private factories. The old economic order was to be replaced by a new form of workers' democracy and co-operation among the various levels of production. Idle production was to become productive again but under the direct control of labour. The Commune had to deal with serious issues of unemployment and starvation. The older social relations of production of capitalism were to be replaced by a new economic system. The decree of the Commune permitting the formation of co-operative associations was proclaimed on 16 April.

Marx, Lincoln, and the Human Emancipation from Racial and Wage Slavery

All these socialist programmes introduced by the Paris Commune highlight the significant attempts at radical social change within the two and a half month period of its heroic resistance to the bourgeois republic. Marx recognises that 'the great social measure of the Commune was its own working existence. Its special measures could but betoken the tendency of *a government of the people by the people*'.[47] This is an interesting phrase that Marx uses when describing the accomplishments of the Commune. The phrase 'a government of the people by the people' is a line delivered by Abraham Lincoln during another famous funeral oration after the key battle fought around the small town of Gettysburg, Pennsylvania, which turned the tide in another civil war on another continent eight years earlier.[48] The *Gettysburg Address* was an immortal eulogy given by Lincoln on 19 November 1863, four months after the key Northern victory that represented the beginning of the end of the conflict that would culminate in the political emancipation of African Americans by ending the plantation economy and racial slavery in the United States. Marx recognises the central importance of Lincoln's call in 1863 for racial justice in his brief, but eloquent, dedication of the 'Soldiers' National Cemetery' in Gettysburg and combines it with his demand for political and economic justice in the Paris Commune of 1871. The Commune was a social republic or working-class government grounded in the ethical principles of self-government and economic emancipation.[49] The Paris Commune is not an abstract utopian ideal but rather presents us with the social and economic fruition of the history of Western liberalism: the ideal and the real have merged during the French

Civil War as the ideals of liberalism are radicalised and institutionalised in the Commune. 'The political rule of the producer cannot co-exist with the perpetuation of his social slavery'.[50] Economic inequalities, wage slavery, and the structures of class power would be dissolved, ending class rule. It is this that would produce a government of and by the people.[51]

Marx's own eulogy for the Communard in his 'Address of the General Council of the International Working Men's Association on the Civil War in France, 1871' (30 May 1871) is, in fact, a funeral oration for the fallen members of the Paris Commune which afforded him the opportunity to develop his theory of human emancipation that self-consciously continues the tradition of Jefferson, the French Revolution, and Lincoln. The history of human emancipation was a struggle to affirm equality and freedom, political and human rights, and the right to human dignity and emancipation from racial slavery; to this list Marx adds a new form of emancipation – the primacy of natural law and the community to be free from the alienation of work, exploitation of private property, and the slavery of wage labour and capitalist production. Toward this end, the worker associations and production co-operatives create a new form of human emancipation. It also represents the culmination of the fight for human rights and a new form of political and economic democracy expressed as the 'self-government of the producers' and as a 'government of the people by the people'. These ideals are viewed by Marx as part of the evolution of Western thought in the writings of Locke, Rousseau, Jefferson, Lincoln, and Lassalle. By using the phrase from the *Gettysburg Address*, by recognising its historical context and meaning, by appreciating the expansion of equal rights to a broader populace, and by understanding the larger historical tradition and significance of these political and philosophical concepts, Marx, borrowing from Lincoln, has created a new phenomenology of spirit and history of the development of human self-consciousness and socialist emancipation. He sees the Civil War as a continuation of the American Revolution and its values as it ended slavery in America.[52] The fundamental principles of liberty and equality which provided the foundation for the new American nation now, with the American Civil War and the successful battle of Gettysburg, have produced a 'new birth of freedom' for a new group of people – the former slaves.

One year before Gettysburg, another important political document was issued – *The Emancipation Proclamation* (1862) – that also connected the American Civil War to the Revolutionary War in the eighteenth century.[53] Marx sees these two documents as central to understanding the full implications of the Paris Commune. The latter is a continuation of these same struggles for equality and human rights as it attempts to free the French workers from wage slavery and a poverty of mind and body. The Commune again expanded the vision and the range of political emancipation, justice, and the end of slavery. And for Marx, although many of the political and economic ideals of the Commune developed out of the old social system, his imaginative dreams of the Commune were in many instances also a radicalisation of the ideals of the ancient past.

On 22 September 1862, Lincoln had proclaimed the freeing of three million slaves in the Southern states after the victory of Union troops over General Robert E. Lee's army at Antietam Creek in Maryland. Following his success at the second battle of Bull Run, Lee invaded Maryland with the hope of securing a quick victory which did not materialise. After the battle of Antietam, Marx pens an article for the Viennese newspaper *Die Presse* entitled 'On Events in North America' in which he writes that a great strategic victory had occurred for the North on 17 September which has decided the fate of the American Civil War by keeping both Britain and France from recognising the Confederacy and, thereby, keeping them out of the war. Marx writes that even more important than the Maryland campaign was Lincoln's preliminary *Emancipation Proclamation* written five days later on 22 September which he characterises as 'the most important document in American history since the establishment of the Union, tantamount to the tearing up of the old American Constitution'.[54] It is the true realisation of the emancipatory potential of the *Declaration of Independence*. For Marx, the result of the proclamation is that Lincoln will have a revered place in history next to George Washington. He views the Civil War as a fight between the 300,000-person Southern slave oligarchy and the Northern working class. By connecting the eighteenth-century *Declaration of Independence* with the nineteenth-century *Emancipation Proclamation* and *Gettysburg Address*, a new history of the charters of human freedom is being built from Jefferson and Lincoln to Marx which has important implications for the grounding of the historical and moral values of the Paris Commune. Lincoln now explicitly states that the Civil War is about the end of slavery and expansion of bourgeois freedom and rights; he referred to the emancipation of slave labour as 'an act of justice warranted by the Constitution'.[55] With the Commune these rights and freedoms are substantively changing into socialist rights and freedoms.

Lincoln wished to emancipate the slaves by incorporating them as human beings into the Western tradition of rights, freedom, and the pursuit of happiness. By doing so, he both broadened our understanding of human rights, which Marx, in turn, continued to expand to include worker rights and economic self-determination. The spirit of self-consciousness and individual freedom is now concerned no longer with a simple justification of utilitarian property and a market economy, but with a larger tradition of political liberation from medieval feudalism, English imperialism, French monarchism, American slavery, and English industrial capitalism as it evolves in the writings of John Locke, *Second Treatise of Government* (1690), Thomas Jefferson, *Declaration of Independence* (1776), Marquis de Lafayette, *Declaration of the Rights of Man and of the Citizen* (1789), the French Revolution *Declaration of the Rights of Man and of the Citizen* (1793), Abraham Lincoln, *Emancipation Proclamation* (January 1863) and the *Gettysburg Address* (November 1863), the Paris Commune, *Declaration to the French People* (1871), and Ferdinand Lassalle, *The Gotha Program* (1875). These political documents articulate the evolution of liberal self-consciousness that incorporates the American rights to life, liberty, and the pursuit of happiness and the freedom from political bondage and slavery to a foreign power, the French rights of the citizen to political assembly and public participation, the American freedom from racial slavery and bondage to another person, and the French social rights to economic democracy.

In 1863, following the military conflagration initiated by Generals Lee and Meade, Lincoln dedicated the battlefield of Gettysburg as a cemetery in memory to its fallen citizens, just as Pericles had done in ancient Athens after the first year of the Peloponnesian War and just as Marx was doing after the fall of the Commune.[56] It is Marx who sees in Lincoln a necessary stage in the process of human liberation that requires not only political freedom but racial and economic emancipation and social justice.[57] Lincoln builds upon the stated values of Thomas Jefferson's *Declaration of Independence* that there are certain self-evident truths, such that 'all men are created equal, that they are endowed by their Creator with certain unalienable rights, that among these are life, liberty, and the pursuit of happiness'.[58] Lincoln only universalises these rights and makes them applicable to all men. Marx had in his early work *On the Jewish Question* turned to the French *Declaration of the Rights of Man and of the Citizen* as a means to broaden the nature of individual rights beyond their 'natural' moorings in materialism and capitalism. In this essay Marx outlines a more comprehensive view of human rights based on citizenship, practical wisdom, public participation, and economic democracy. The American and French Revolutions produced the key political documents articulating the legal and political rights of humanity within the limits of liberal and bourgeois society. Marx universalised these rights and made them applicable to all members of society so that the memory of the fallen soldiers, the sacrifices of a nation, and the long-time suffering of those in slavery would not be forgotten.

Marx turns the liberal documents of rights into a universal declaration of human rights that includes all workers as well as all citizens. His thought recapitulates the history of modern liberalism as part of the radical transformation of the nature of equality and rights to include the social and economic arena. He expands natural rights and politics beyond the spheres of possessive individualism and the protection of property to include economic rights and human emancipation. In the process, he transforms rights from their materialist foundation in private property and the state of nature to a declaration of the possibilities inherent in the human spirit and democratic community. Socialism represents a radical departure from liberalism, but it is also a synthesis that is part of the broader historical and social fabric that evolved out of the earliest artifacts of liberalism. Human emancipation in the Commune integrates the American, French, and German traditions into a new and more comprehensive definition of individual freedom and democracy. What Marx has accomplished in his praise of the defenders of the Parisian barricades is a reconciliation of the moral principles of the greatest orations and traditions in Western history.

During the American Civil War, Abraham Lincoln recognised that, as a result of the war and the famous battle at Gettysburg, there were new political truths that had become self-evident. In his *Gettysburg Address*, he eloquently stated 'that we here highly resolve that these dead shall not have died in vain, that this nation, under God, shall have a new birth of freedom, and that government of the people, by the people, for the people shall not perish from the earth'.[59] As Marx writes about the Commune and quotes from Lincoln's famous address, he is also reconstituting the tradition behind Lincoln's ideas and at the same time expanding upon his theory of social justice; he places the Commune in illustrious company that broadens human rights to include all people. Marx only wishes to push Lincoln's own ideas and words to their logical conclusion by extending human rights and freedom to all men, including workers within a truly democratic society. Equality and freedom have now become not only political and racial categories but also economic ones that transcend the plantation and capitalist economies. In a letter written to Lincoln by Marx on behalf of the International Workingmen's Association offering congratulations for his second presidential victory in 1864, he clearly connects the fight against slavery and the Confederate gentry as part of a broader struggle between labour and capital – a struggle for freedom and human emancipation.[60]

Marx's oration for the defenders of a workers' democracy on 30 May, two days after the surrender of the Commune, ends with the hope that 'working men's Paris, with its Commune, will be forever celebrated as the glorious harbinger of a new society. Its martyrs are enshrined in the great heart of the working class'.[61] It has been estimated by historians that between 20,000–30,000 Parisians had been killed in the resistance to the French oligarchy during the 'bloody week' of fighting and in the summary military trials and executions.

Marx was under no illusions about the reality of the Paris Commune and its reformist principles and proclamations. The Commune manifested great possibilities but lacked a crucial element for revolutionary success – time. However, it did provide for one brief moment a spark of greater possibilities ahead and a concrete manifestation of the meaning of the spirit of freedom and human emancipation as he articulated in his early *Paris Manuscripts*: 'Communism is the *positive* abolition of *private property*, of *human self-alienation*, and thus the real *appropriation of human* nature through and for man. It is, therefore, the return of man himself as a *social*, i.e. really human, being, a complete and conscious return which assimilates all the wealth of previous development'.[62]

Notes

1 There have been a number of helpful works written on the Paris Commune, including the following: Pierre Vésinier, *History of the Commune*, trans. J.V. Walsh (London: Chapman and Hall, 1872); Prosper Olivier Lissagaray, *History of the Paris Commune of 1871*, trans. Eleanor Marx Aveling (London: Reeves and Turner, 1886); Thomas March, *The History of the Paris Commune of 1871* (London: Swan Sonnenschein, 1896); Edward Mason, *The Paris Commune: An Episode in the History of the Socialist Movement* (New York, NY: Macmillan Company, 1930); Roger Williams, *The French Revolution of 1870–1871* (New York, NY: W.W. Norton and Company, 1969); Frank Jellinek, *The Paris Commune of 1871* (London: Victor Gollancz, 1971); Stewart Edwards, *The Paris Commune 1871* (New York, NY: Quadrangle Books, 1971) and 'Introduction', in *The Communards of Paris, 1871, Documents of Revolution*, ed. Stewart Edwards, trans. Jean McNeil (London: Eyre & Spottiswoode, 1971); Eugene Schulkind (ed.), *The Paris Commune of 1871: The View from the Left* (New York, NY: Grove Press, 1971); John Hicks and Robert Tucker (eds.), *Revolution and Reaction* (Amherst, MA: University of Massachusetts Press, 1973); Timothy McCarthy, *Marx and the Proletariat: A Study in Social Theory* (Westport, CT: Greenwood Press, 1978); Gerhard Haupt and Karin Hausen, *Die Pariser Kommune: Erfolg und Scheitern einer Revolution* (Frankfurt/Main: Campus Verlag, 1979); Robert Tombs, *The Paris Commune* (Cambridge: Cambridge University Press, 1981); Anne-Louise Shapiro, *Housing the Poor of Paris, 1850–1902* (Madison, WI: University of Wisconsin Press, 1985); Michelle Perrot, *Workers on Strike: France, 1871–1890*, trans. Chris Turner (New Haven, CT: Yale University Press, 1987); Roger Gould, *Insurgent Identities: Class, Community, and Protest in Paris from 1848 to the Commune* (Chicago, IL: University of Chicago Books, 1995); Martin Johnson, *The Paradise of Association: Political Culture and Popular Organization in the Paris Commune of 1871* (Ann Arbor, MI: University of Michigan Press, 1996); David Harvey, *Paris, Capital of Modernity* (New York, NY: Routledge, 2003); David Shafer, *The Paris Commune: French Politics, Culture, and Society at the Crossroads of the Revolutionary Tradition and Revolutionary Socialism* (New York, NY: Palgrave Macmillian, 2005); Colette Wilson, *Paris and the Commune, 1871–78: The Politics of Forgetting* (Manchester: Manchester University Press, 2007); Alistair

Horne, *The Fall of Paris: The Siege and the Commune, 1870–1871* (New York, NY: Penguin, 2007); Donny Gluckstein, *The Paris Commune: A Revolution in Democracy* (Chicago, IL: Haymarket Books, 2011); John Merriman, *Massacre: The Life and Death of the Paris Commune* (New York, NY: Basic Books, 2014); and Kristin Ross, *Communal Luxury: The Political Imaginary of the* Paris Commune (London: Verso, 2015).

2   There is a slow evolution of Marx's ideas of human emancipation, social justice, and human rights from *The Paris Manuscripts of 1844* (emancipation from the alienated workplace, nature, senses, and consciousness), *On the Jewish Question* (natural rights and natural law, rights of man: bourgeois or economic rights, and rights of the citizen: political rights of Locke, Rousseau, and the French Revolution), *Paris Commune* (economic democracy, self-government of the producers, and democracy of the people by the people), and the *Critique of the Gotha Program* (equal rights, distributive justice, and human need: Aristotle).

3   Friedrich Engels, 'Introduction', to Karl Marx, *Civil War in France: The Paris Commune* (New York, NY: International Publishers, 1972), p. 13; *Karl Marx/Friedrich Engels Werke* (*MEW*), Band 22 (Berlin: Dietz Verlag, 1963), p. 192. In Marx's analysis of the civil war in France, he blames the eventual destruction of the Commune on two things: class conflict and the counter-revolution of the propertied class of the republican government against the proletariat of the commune exacerbated by the enormous financial debt incurred by Napoleon and Thiers during the war against Germany resulting in a doubling of the national debt and sustaining high municipal debt in large towns and cities. These war expenses had to be paid along with the war reparations and bonds demanded by the German government as part of the agreement of the peace accords. See Karl Marx, 'Address of the General Council of the International Working Men's Association on the Civil War in France, 1871', in *The Civil War in France: The Paris Commune* (New York, NY: International Publishers, 1972), pp. 44–5 (referred to as *The Civil War in France*); *Karl Marx/ Friedrich Engels Werke* (*MEW*), Band 17 (Berlin: Dietz Verlag, 1962), pp. 327–8. According to Marx, 'it was only by the violent overthrow of the (social) republic that the appropriators of wealth could hope to shift on to the shoulders of its producers the cost of a war which they, the appropriators, had themselves originated' (p. 45; *MEW* 17, p. 327). Three paragraphs later, he writes: 'Armed Paris was the only obstacle in the way of the counter-revolutionary conspiracy' (p. 46; *MEW* 17, p. 328).

Edwards, in his *The Communards of Paris, 1871*, argues that there was dissatisfaction among the radicals in Paris from the beginning of the September Revolution because they saw that the new provisional government of National Defense was not willing to fight a difficult war with Germany but sought immediate peace. In turn, the new self-appointed provisional government under Thiers saw Paris as a threat to its power and the social order. The conservatives within the new government wanted immediate elections for a new National Assembly in order to validate their authority, and peace with Germany was therefore necessary to accomplish this end (p. 17). But the city of Paris with its strong working-class districts did not want to surrender to Germany. Thus there was a real disagreement between the provincial conservatives and the radicals of Paris. In fact, Thiers had to conduct the peace negotiations in secret because of the Parisian opposition (p. 18). Edwards argues that it was this 'frustrated patriotism' of Paris and 'dishonorable

peace' with Germany that accounted for much of the antagonism between the National Government and Paris.
Summary of the chronology of the French Civil War:
19 July 1870: the Franco-Prussian War with Germany begins.
4 September: the French Empire of Napoleon III collapses, Paris Revolution occurs, and a provisional Republic is formed.
18 September: the four-month siege of Paris begins.
26 January 1871: armistice with Germany is signed.
8 February: new elections are held and a new National Assembly created.
12 February: first meeting of new National Assembly headed by Thiers meets in Bordeaux.
15 March: National Guard of Paris elects a Central Committee to run city.
18 March: Central Committee takes over the governance of Paris after failed attempt by Thiers to capture the cannons at Montmartre, and the Thiers government retreats to Versailles.
26 March: the Paris Commune is elected.
30 March: the civil war between Versailles and Paris begins and the national army attacks Paris.
2 April: actual fighting starts.
19 April: only official proclamation of the Commune, 'Declaration to the French People'.
9–13 May: the large forts of Issy and Vanves surrounding Paris fall to Thiers' army.
21 May: the walls of Paris are breached and the Versailles army begins march and executions throughout the city.
27 May: last remaining defenders in Paris are defeated at the cemetery of Père-Lachaise on the heights of Belleville.
28 May: total surrender of the Commune and the end of the French civil war.
The civil war between Paris and Versailles lasted from 18 March to 28 May 1871.

4   Horne, *The Fall of Paris*, pp. 220–40.
5   Mason, in *The Paris Commune*, writes that the National Guard officer corps, which lacked professionalism, was self-appointed and amateuristic. Mason, a conservative historian of the civil war, quoting from Louis Rossel, one of the commanders-in-chief of the Communal army who is observing the first contact between the National Guard and regular French army on 1 April, said that two battalions of the guard were 'completely drunk' and other battalions were 'without authority', leaderless, and in a state of complete anarchy (p. 210). Mason's invective was not directed just against the National Guard but also against the Communal Assembly which he characterised as 'a body without a program, without unity of purpose, and without both the capacity and the opportunity to produce either the one or the other … The revolution drifted on following pretty much its own course, carrying the Commune along and molding rather than being molded by it' (p. 186). His main criticism is that the Commune issued many decrees but did not consider military options against Versailles, which at the time had a defeated and dispirited army of about 20,000 troops. Thinking that Paris was morally right and had history on its side, citizens of the Commune incorrectly thought that the Thiers government would collapse on its own (p. 187).
6   Edwards, 'Introduction', in *The Communards of Paris, 1871*, pp. 19–20. See Edwards's more

detailed analysis in his own monograph, *The Paris Commune, 1871*. In this work Edwards outlines the three main political forces in Paris after the revolution of 18 March: there were the district mayors, republican and socialist political clubs, and committees formed throughout the city, including the International Working Men's Association and the Delegation of the Twenty Arrondissements representing the 20 Paris districts formed during the German siege. The mayors, the only constitutional and legal representatives remaining in the city and appointed by the national government, finally relented after one week to permit the Central Committee to hold elections on 26 March for the Commune based on proportional representation which would ultimately favour the working-class districts within the city. Edwards contends in his monograph that this was an intentional plan on the part of some of the mayors to give the Thiers government time to recreate its new army to attack Paris.

7   When the Thiers government initially evacuated Paris on 18 March, it had 22,000 army regulars. The preliminary peace terms with Germany limited the size of the French army to about 30,000 troops. Later, the Thiers government was allowed by the Germans to attack Paris. Bismarck was concerned that a united Versailles and Paris could present a unity government that would not pay its war reparations. Thus, he acted to help Thiers attack Paris. In fact, Bismarck permitted the French army to expand from 30,000 to 80,000 men. In addition, French soldiers captured during the war were permitted to reattach themselves to the regular army, which brought the attacking army up to 130,000 men. On the other side, the National Guard in Paris probably numbered only about 160,000 irregular troops on paper with the actual number around 30,000, according to Roger Williams, who characterised the Parisian army as 'withering away'. See Williams, *The French Revolution of 1870–1871*, p. 136. Williams characterised the Communard army as 'obvious underdogs; poorly armed but resolute human beings confronting an impersonal, battle-hardened military machine' (p. 149). See also Jellinek, *The Paris Commune of 1871*, p. 207; and Mason, *The Paris Commune*, p. 354. The latter sees a very weak National Guard which by the middle of April consisted of about 30,000 troops and at the end had only about 10,000. For Tombs, in *The War Against Paris 1871*, the National Guard had about 20,000 men. The actual casualties of the army were relatively low at 400 killed and 1,100 wounded, with most units spending 'only a day or two engaged in combat' (p. 162).

8   Engels, 'Introduction', *Civil War in France*, p. 14; MEW 22, pp. 192–3.

9   Tombs, *The War Against Paris 1871*, p. 52. Tombs argues that the failure of the French army on 18 March rested with its limited number of troops; their unwillingness to act on the occasion because of their connection to the citizens or because of a 'failure of will'; the unanticipated and spontaneous hostile reaction of the populace to the events of the day; lack of conservative support for the troops resulting from their exodus from the city caused by the German siege; anger at the national government who were viewed by many as traitors because of the surrender; and the radicalisation of the workers within Paris (p. 52). Thiers left Paris in despair with an impotent army and events beyond his control. His first reaction afterwards was extremely cautious – go slowly, set up defensive positions, reestablish order, morale, and discipline within the army, and, at all costs maintain peace, at least for a couple of weeks (pp. 54–70).

10 Ibid. p. 57. Tombs writes that the situation for Thiers in his retreat to Versailles on 18 March

11 Edwards, *The Paris Commune 1871*, pp. 153 and 156.
12 Ibid., p. 156. The official publication of the Central Committee *Journal Officiel* called for the 'proletarians of capital' to begin to take matters into their own hands and use the revolution for the emancipation of the proletariat (pp. 155–6). Edwards mentions that 'the Commune itself in its official pronouncements never reached this level of political class consciousness' (p. 156). Edwards was in basic agreement with Marx that the Central Committee was too concerned with legal legitimacy and elections; they should have been more concerned with Versailles and attacked early the weak forces of the republic. Edwards's analysis of the political situation at Versailles indicates that an attack by the Commune would have been successful since the morale of the French troops was very low. This failure to attack Versailles appears to have been not only a serious, but a fatal mistake by the Commune. By not destroying the remnants of the regular army, they gave it time to regenerate and also gave it time to destroy the other developing communes throughout France (pp. 157–8). Paris did not reach out and coordinate its activities with these regional communes, ultimately resulting in their destruction. Edwards does mention that a probable cause of the fear of attacking the national government was the possible intervention of the German army which still occupied much of northern France. Germany had a strong interest in protecting the Thiers government in order to 'guarantee repayment of the war indemnity' (p. 158). On the issue that the communards represented the 'dictatorship of the proletariat', or working-class democracy, see John Ehrenberg, *The Dictatorship of the Proletariat: Marxism's Theory of Socialist Democracy* (New York, NY: Routledge, 1992), pp. 88–95.
13 Karl Marx, 'Letter to Dr. Kugelmann on the Paris Commune' (12 April 1871), in *Civil War in France: The Paris Commune* (New York, NY: International Publishers, 1972), p. 86; *Karl Marx/Friedrich Engels Werke (MEW)*, Band 33 (Berlin: Dietz Verlag, 1976), p. 205.
14 Marx, *The Civil War in France*, p. 45; *MEW* 17, pp. 327 and 335.
15 Marx recognised quite early on that the war against the Commune was about money and reparations. He maintains that Thiers 'had formulated a civil war against the revolution, to shift on to the peasant's shoulders the chief load of the five milliards of indemnity to be paid to the Prussians' (p. 63; *MEW* 17, pp. 344–5).
16 Marx, 'Letter to Dr. Kugelmann on the Paris Commune' (12 April 1871). In a famous line, Marx writes: 'Compare these Parisians, storming heaven, with the slaves to heaven of the German-Prussian Holy Roman Empire, with its posthumous masquerades reeking of the barracks, the Church, cabbage-*junkerdom* and above all, of the philistine' (p. 86; *MEW* 33, p. 206). This 'storming heaven' by the Communards was Marx's way of poetically expressing the attempt to realise the highest ethical and political values of humanity in the concrete form of the Paris Commune. Ideals were no longer lost in an unhappy consciousness, an abstract moral idealism, or the mysticism of a Christian heaven, but, for the first time, they were made real as citizens fought and died to defend them. It should be noted that at the same time the revolutionary Paris Commune was constituting itself, other communes were being created throughout France in Lyons, Marseilles, Toulouse, Narbonne, St. Etienne, and Le Creusot. But these social experiments in participatory democracy were short-lived as Paris could not unite them into a coherent resistance to

the national government. Just days after the Paris Commune was declared, these cities declared their own revolutionary governments only to falter within days or weeks of their declarations.

17 For a collection of the various documents, announcements, and publications of the Paris Commune, see Schulkind (ed.), *The Paris Commune of 1871* and Edwards (ed.), *The Communards of Paris, 1871*. These edited works provide the principles, proclamations, and programmes of the Paris Commune issued by the Executive Committee of the Commune, Central Committee of the National Guard, Commission of Labour and Exchange, Commission for the Organization of Education, Central Committee of the Twenty Arrondissements, craft trade unions, factory co-operatives, men's and women's popular and revolutionary clubs and committees, republican and socialist vigilance committees, political parties, commune newspapers, election posters, International Workingmen's Association, New Education Society, etc. with special emphasis on worker co-operatives, education, and the functioning of the public services for the city and district governments. These published documents provide the best empirical evidence for the structural mechanism and internal workings of the Paris Commune. See the first public proclamation of the Central Committee of the Twenty Arrondissements (15 September 1870) and its call for communal elections and a democratic republic in Edwards's edited work (pp. 44–7). See also the socialist 'Declaration of Principles' of the Parisian vigilance committees on 20 and 23 February 1871 in Edwards (ed.), *The Communards of Paris, 1871*, pp. 53–4 and the 'Address' demanding free producers' co-operatives from the Central Committee of the Women's Union for the Defense of Paris and for Aid to the Wounded (ibid., pp. 135–6). On 23 March, the International Workingmen's Association Federal Council in Paris outlined its principles for a new commune, including social equality, end to class warfare, respect for the value of labour, reorganisation of the finance and credit industry, labour exchange, and workers' associations, free and secular education, freedom of press, citizenship, expression, and association, and the municipal organisation of police, military, health, statistics, etc.

18 Marx, *Civil War in France*, p. 54; MEW 17, p. 336. Also read the first paragraph of Marx's letter to Dr. Kugelmann on the Paris Commune (12 April 1871) in the *Civil War in France*. Marx suggests that Dr. Kugelmann look at the last chapter of the *Eighteenth Brumaire of Louis Bonaparte* where he clearly remarks that the next revolution in France will require the smashing of the 'bureaucratic-military machine' of the liberal state (p. 86; MEW 33, p. 205).

19 Marx, *Civil War in France*, p. 55; MEW 17, p. 336.

20 Ibid.; MEW 17, p. 336.

21 Ibid., p. 56; MEW 17, p. 338.

22 The political and moral categories in John Locke's *Second Treatise of Government* performed the same role as the mystical concepts of the division of labour and the diffuse political functions of the state. Locke's defence of individual freedom, liberty, and rights proved another mechanism for the diffusing and alienation of consciousness. Natural law and natural rights integrated a wide range of philosophical and theological traditions that made it extremely difficult for the average citizen to think critically outside the recognised framework of Western thought. One form of alienation rested in the political institutions

and the other in its cultural values. In both cases, however, awareness about the nature of the political system was rendered nearly impossible. This is why Marx's social theory has been so valuable; it has taken the natural law tradition outside the realm of political mystification and abstractionism and placed it within the heart of a critical historical science.

23   Marx, *Civil War in France*, p. 57; *MEW* 17, p. 339.
24   Ibid.
25   Ibid., p. 58; *MEW* 17, p. 339.
26   Ibid., pp. 58 and 60; *MEW* 17, pp. 339 and 342. There were a number of other changes within the Commune beyond those already mentioned in this chapter, including organised food distribution and public assistance by creating food and clothing vouchers for redistribution during the Prussian and French sieges, limiting food hoarding, speculation, and high prices for scarce goods, and finding vacant apartments for those who lost their homes in Neuilly as a result of army bombardment in April. There were attempts to suppress prostitution and gambling. The Archbishop of Paris and about one hundred priests were held as hostages. The Archbishop was eventually executed because the Thiers government would not exchange Louis-Auguste Blanqui, the socialist radical, for him. On 16 April, the Commune issued a financial decree which gave debtors three years to pay their debts at no interest. This was in response to the siege and rising unemployment in the city. The Commune was also active against individuals who speculated on the misery of others. The Bank of France and its enormous amount of money were not touched since its funds were used as loans to pay the wages of the National Guard. In the Commune local *mairies* or town halls of the arrondissements became the new heart of employment exchanges. See Edwards (ed.), *The Communards of Paris, 1871*, p. 35 and Williams, *The French Revolution of 1870–1871*, p. 138. Williams mentions that there were many political clubs throughout the city in which social and economic issues were continuously discussed even as the war raged in the streets of Paris. Mason, in his *Paris Commune*, points out that the revolutionary socialists and Blanquists on the Commune wanted the finance committee to seize the bank and its funds in order to pursue the war more aggressively against Versailles (pp. 202–3). This was also Marx's position. The head of the Commission of Finance was Charles Beslay, an unrealistic, utopian Proudhonian socialist who seemed to be more interested in a visionary future than the immediate implications of communal policy. Mason attempted to defend Beslay's policy; the former thought that the real failure of the Commune lay in the failures of the provincial communes (pp. 203–4). Finally, the outstanding loans of the pawnshops amounted to 38 million francs which, the Commune thought, could be liquidated in five years (p. 254). It is interesting to note that the Commune borrowed about 15 million francs from the Bank of France during the siege (p. 204). Mason lists all the social programmes and economic legislation of the Commune from 'the laws on rents, maturities, pawnshops, night work, fines, utilization of abandoned workshops, etc.'. He maintains that the theory guiding the revolution was socialist only 'in the narrow sense of the term' mainly because of the lack of an overall socialist theory or programme, a leaderless Commune always engaged in disagreements and debates, a realistic fear of antagonising the liberal and moderate elements in Paris, and because of the disorganisation caused by the war and siege of the Thiers government (pp. 254–8). The proposals were mainly reform oriented, including the 'Declaration to the French People' (19 April). He concluded by say-

ing that 'one gets the impression that the Commune was leaning over backward in its attempt at moderation' (p. 256). But as the civil war moved into May, the language of the Commune became more revolutionary and socialist and less reformist (p. 260) – by that time it became a clearer struggle between labour and capital, the proletariat and bourgeoisie. For a different political perspective, see Eleanor Marx Aveling's introduction to Lissagaray, *History of the Commune of 1871*, where she writes about the Paris Commune: 'It is time people understood the true meaning of this Revolution; and this can be summed up in a few words. It meant the government of the people by the people. It was the first attempt of the proletariat to govern itself' by seizing government power and abolishing all class rule (pp. vii–viii). Tombs, *The War Against Paris 1871*, takes the position that the underlying cause of the civil war was not the Franco-Prussian War; rather, it was the traditions from 1830 and 1848 behind the Parisian republicans' defence of the rights of workers that pushed Paris toward social revolution (pp. 2–3).

27 Marx, *Civil War in France*, pp. 58–9; *MEW* 17, p. 340.
28 Jean-Jacques Rousseau, *The Social* Contract, in The *Social Contract and Discourses*, trans G.D.H. Cole (New York, NY: E.P. Dutton and Company, 1950), p. 94.
29 Marx, *Civil War in France*, p. 60; *MEW* 17, p. 342.
30 Ibid., p. 61; *MEW* 17, p. 342.
31 Ibid.; *MEW* 17, p. 343.
32 For a contemporary analysis of the historical and institutional foundations of classical democracy, see A.H.M. Jones, *Athenian Democracy* (Baltimore, MD: Johns Hopkins University Press, 1957); Mogens Hansen, *The Athenian Assembly in the Age of Demosthenes* (Oxford: Basil Blackwell, 1987) and *The Athenian Democracy in the Age of Demosthenes: Structures, Principles and Ideology*, trans. J.A. Crook (Oxford: Basil Blackwell, 1991); R.K. Sinclair, *Democracy and Participation in Athens* (Cambridge: Cambridge University Press, 1988); and David Stockton, *The Classical Athenian Democracy* (Oxford: Oxford University Press, 1991). For an analysis of the consciousness, ideology, cultural traditions, and political ideals of classical Athens, see M.I. Finley, *Democracy Ancient and Modern* (New Brunswick, NJ: Rutgers University Press, 1988); Ellen Wood, *Peasant-Citizen and Slave: The Foundations of Athenian Democracy* (London: Verso, 1988); Josiah Ober, *Mass and Elite in Democratic Athens* (Princeton, NJ: Princeton University Press, 1989) and *Political Dissent in Democratic Athens* (Princeton, NJ: Princeton University Press, 1998); Cynthia Farrar, *The Origins of Democratic Thinking: The Invention of Politics in Classical Athens* (Cambridge: Cambridge University Press, 1988); Christian Meier, *The Greek Discovery of Politics*, trans. David McLintock (Cambridge, MA: Harvard University Press, 1990); William James Booth, *Households: On the Moral Architecture of the Economy* (Ithaca, NY: Cornell University Press, 1993); and Jennifer Roberts, *Athens on Trial: The Antidemocratic Tradition in Western Thought* (Princeton, NJ: Princeton University Press, 1994). In his work, Ober examines the implications of the methodological dispute within classical history between empirical positivism and interpretive, historical analysis.
33 Marx, *Civil War in France*, pp. 61–62; *MEW* 17, p. 343.
34 Edwards, 'Introduction', *The Communards of Paris, 1871*, p. 28. Edwards makes an important observation that the traditional proletariat of large industries on the outskirts of Paris was not represented in the Commune (p. 29).

35 Vésinier, *History of the Commune*, pp. 160–78; and Mason, *The Paris Commune*, p. 193.
36 Rogers, *The French Revolution of 1870–1871*, pp. 135–6. Immediately after the elections, on 28 March, the newly elected government met to discuss technical issues of official salaries, loyalty oaths, payment of rents and debts, and the role of the National Guard in the defence of Paris. The following day the Commune formed ten commissions to run the government and various functions of the city. Rogers reports that there was a great deal of mistrust among the different political groupings on the 'reformist' Executive Committee (three generals and four civilians appointed by the Commune) and the increasingly more radical Central Committee of the National Guard which represented 'the claims of the proletariat and revolutionary socialism more than did the Commune itself' (p. 136). The latter did not appear to surrender its military power to the military Commission of the Commune. These dysfunctional disagreements were only exacerbated by the forming of a five-man Committee of Public Safety on 1 May and with it the formation of new commissions and a new Executive Committee consisting of members of the various commissions. 'The midwives of the Revolution could not bear to give up its supervision' (ibid.). Some members of the Commune had hoped that the new Committee of Public Safety could provide the new leadership and a clear direction lacking in the government (Mason, *The Paris Commune*, pp. 193–4 and 199–201). Others feared it would replicate the dictatorship of Robespierre and the French Revolution of the eighteenth century. Rogers maintains that the Commune ceased to exist after the creation of the Committee of Public Safety; many members of the former stopped attending the meetings after 1 May (pp. 143–4). Two days after the publication of the Commune's formal programme, 'Declaration to the French People', Charles Delescluze called for a reorganisation of the Commune on 21 April that would dismantle and reform the Executive Committee and replace it with a new committee consisting of the new members of the various Commissions (Jellinek, *The Paris Commune of 1871*, pp. 224–6). Following some military defeats connected with the fortification system of Paris, the Committee of Public Safety was reorganised about one week later, on 9 May. For a summary of the Commune's social programme and public policies, see Lissagaray, *History of the Commune of 1871*, pp. 217–35; Mason, *The Paris Commune*, pp. 242–78; and Edwards, *The Paris Commune 1871*, pp. 249–76.
37 Edwards, *The Paris Commune 1871*, p. 250.
38 Gould, in his work *Insurgent Identities*, argues that the various French uprisings from the 1830s to 1871 had different origins and causes. The revolutions of 1847–8 were caused by economic hardships and working-class consciousness, while the revolution of 1871 resulted from a general insurrection of Paris citizens against the Prussian army, French state, and conservative rural peasantry. His central thesis is that the Paris Commune was not a working-class revolution against capital (pp. 4–5) but an urban revolution against Prussian imperialism and the centralisation of the modern state. Its goal was local autonomy, militia self-defence, and municipal self-determination. Rejecting Marx's thesis about the origins of the Paris Commune, Gould emphasises that the revolutionaries came from the skilled and semiskilled craft workers dispersed throughout Paris and not the proletarian factory workers. According to the records of the military courts which tried the insurgents after the capture of Paris, the trades that contributed most to the armed uprising were machine builders, stonemasons, painters, roofers, and shoemakers. Gould contends that

these are not the groups usually associated with the socialist labour movement in France in the nineteenth century (p. 172). This disparity between the participants of the working-class movement and the Paris Commune forced him to question whether the Commune was an example of a proletarian revolution. Industrial production grew in the periphery of Paris thus permitting residential communities and neighbourhood loyalties to develop within the city which would play a crucial role in the revolution. Paris was a city of 'residential neighbourhoods' and 'urban villages' (p. 193). Municipal autonomy rather than the right to work and class interests became the clarion call for the resistance. Political geography and the National Guard would play a central role in the formation of collective identities and social networks.

Edwards takes a similar position in his introduction to *The Communards of Paris, 1871*. Edwards writes that 81 citizens of Paris were elected to the Commune of which 35 were manual labourers who were crafts- and tradesmen usually belonging to a small workshop. The proletarian factory workers from the large industries were not well represented or organised at this time (pp. 27–30). On this point, see also Gould, *Insurgent Identities*, p. 166. But Edwards does not draw the same conclusions as Gould. He maintains instead that the Paris Commune was still a working-class movement. He turns his attention to the study of the revolutionary organisations, Commission on Labour and Exchange, Paris clubs, and the popular press in the local municipalities and labour organisations in order to show the continuity between the French labour movement of the 1830s and 1840s and the socialism of the Commune (*The Communards of Paris, 1871*, p. 122). Edwards views the Commune as a working-class revolution whose ideas about co-operative production went back to Louis Blanc's work, *The Organization of Labor* (1839).

Gould briefly outlines the debate between the radical social scientists represented by David Harvey, Manuel Castells, and Henri Lefebvre and contemporary social movement and social network theorists who argue for historical explanations based on independent collective identity in urban settings. This debate centred round the differences between the key concepts of class and community or neighbourhood. Harvey, in his work *Consciousness and the Urban Experience* (Baltimore, MD: Johns Hopkins University Press, 1985), writes from a Marxist perspective that the foundations of the Paris Commune rested upon the structural contradictions of capitalist production and class antagonism (p. 154). See also Henri Lefebvre, *La proclamation de la Commune* (Paris: Gallimard, 1965). On the other hand, Manuel Castells rejects this view and sees the Commune as a municipal revolution with its own distinctive political identity and culture in his *The City and the Grassroots* (Berkeley, CA: University of California Press, 1983), p. 29.

39 Paris Commune, 'Declaration to the French People', in *The Communards of Paris, 1871*, ed. Edwards, p. 81. This was the official programme of the Paris Commune proclaimed on 19 April and was produced by a committee consisting of Louis Charles Delescluze, the Jacobin, and Albert Theisz and Jules Vallès, who were followers of Proudhon. See also Williams, *The French Revolution of 1870–1871*, pp. 139–40.
40 Paris Commune, 'Declaration to the French People', p. 83.
41 Edwards (ed.), 'Statement of Principles', Central Electoral Committee of the 11th Arrondissement of the City of Paris, in *The Communards of Paris, 1871*, p. 72. This document is from the election poster of 26 March.

42   Edwards, *The Paris Commune 1871*, pp. 259–62.
43   Mason, in his *The Paris Commune*, quoted from the Commune's decree of 16 April outlining the functions of the Commission of Labour and Exchange: 'The Commission is charged with the propagation of socialist doctrine. It must be a means for equalizing work and wages. It must also concern itself with the furtherance of French Parisian industry' and international trade. The decree went on to say: 'Whereas a number of workshops have been abandoned by those who directed them, in order to escape their civic obligations, and without consideration of the interests of the labourers …' (p. 245). Meetings were held in the middle of May for labour unions to create a committee to examine the issue of workers' co-operatives. The committee was formed and within a week the French army was inside the walls of Paris. Mason concludes: 'If the Commune had lasted longer, this measure might have led to the expropriation of absentee owners; it was certainly a tentative step in the direction of socialism' (p. 246). But there was just not enough time to effectuate any substantive change.
44   Edwards, 'Introduction', in *The Communards of Paris, 1871*, p. 36.
45   Marx, *Civil War in France*, p. 61; MEW 17, p. 342.
46   Louvre Armaments Factory Co-operative, 'Regulations of a Factory Co-operative', in *The Communards of Paris, 1871*, ed. Edwards, pp. 127–30. The intellectual inspiration for much of the co-operative movement came from the writings of Proudhon and his French followers. At the time, according to Edwards, they were critical of state socialism and favoured a decentralised worker-controlled production. This workers' democracy was also influenced by utopian socialists, the worker co-operative movement, well into the Second Empire and the initial experiments in producers' associations and national workshops initiated by the 1848 revolution. Edwards reports that over 300 meetings were held during the revolution of 1848 by workers to form workers' co-operatives that later became the model for the Paris Commune (Edwards, *The Paris Commune 1871*, p. 260). These worker movements were all based on the same premise that 'it was labour, not capital, that created wealth' (p. 261).
47   Marx, *Civil War in France*, p. 65; MEW 17, p. 347, emphasis added.
48   Robin Blackburn, 'Introduction', in *An Unfinished Revolution: Karl Marx and Abraham Lincoln*, ed. Robin Blackburn (London: Verso, 2011), pp. 1–100 and 'Karl Marx and Abraham Lincoln: A Curious Convergence', *Historical Materialism*, 19, 4 (2011): 145–74; and John Nichols, 'Reading Karl Marx with Abraham Lincoln', *International Socialist Review*, 79 (2011).
49   Marx, *Civil War in France*, pp. 58 and 60; MEW 17, pp. 339 and 342.
50   Ibid., p. 60; MEW 17, p. 342.
51   Ibid., p. 65; MEW 17, p. 347.
52   Donny Schraffenberger, 'Karl Marx and the American Civil War', *International Socialist Review*, 80 (November 2011). Schraffenberger writes regarding Marx's relation to the American Civil War: 'Marx and Engels argued that Lincoln's *Emancipation Proclamation* and the North's arming of Black soldiers transformed the Civil War from a purely constitutional war to preserve the country with slavery intact, into a revolutionary war. They did not characterise the Civil War as a socialist revolutionary war, but they believed that it advanced the cause of all workers, both white and Black, by destroying chattel slavery. The

revolution armed former slaves, destroyed the horrendous institution of slavery without compensation to the slave-owners, and opened the way for a struggle between the working class and the capitalist class. As a result, our next revolution in this country will be a working-class revolution'.

53 For copies of the *Emancipation Proclamation* (preliminary document issued on 22 September 1862 and official document made public on 1 January 1863) and the *Gettysburg Address* (19 November 1863), see Blackburn, *An Unfinished Revolution*, pp. 115–17 and 119, respectively.

54 Karl Marx, 'Comments on the North American Events', *Karl Marx/Frederick Engels Collected Works*, vol. 19 (New York, NY: International Publishers, 1984), p. 250. This article originally appeared in the Viennese paper *Die Presse*, 12 October 1862. See also Kevin Anderson, *Marx at the Margins: On Nationalism, Ethnicity, and Non-Western Societies* (Chicago, IL: University of Chicago Press, 2010), p. 102.

55 Abraham Lincoln, 'Emancipation Proclamation', in *An Unfinished Revolution*, pp. 115–17. It was Lincoln who wanted the Republican Party platform of 1864 to include a constitutional amendment to abolish slavery. The Thirteenth Amendment to the US Constitution ending slavery had been introduced in January 1864.

56 For an analysis of the Paris Commune as the modern realisation of the principles of Athenian democracy and Aristotle's democratic polity, see George E. McCarthy, 'In Praise of Classical Democracy: The Funeral Orations of Pericles and Marx', *Graduate Faculty Philosophy Journal*, Department of Philosophy, New School for Social Research, 27, 2 (November 2006): 205–27.

57 *Marx's Theory of Racial Justice*: This analysis of Lincoln's *Gettysburg Address* and *Emancipation Proclamation* adds another dimension to Marx's theory of social justice – the outlines of a theory of racial justice. This must be added to Aristotle's outline of social justice as a modern addition to it. Marx also took a broad view of the concept of 'race' to include issues of colonialism, imperialism, slavery, racism, US civil war, and economic exploitation in Ireland, India, and Indonesia. For a further analysis of these issues, see Friedrich Engels's analysis of the Irish immigration in the *Conditions of the Working Class in England* (Moscow: Progress Publishers, 1973); Karl Marx and Friedrich Engels, *Ireland and the Irish Question* (New York, NY: International Publishers, 1972); articles published in the *New York Herald Tribune* on colonialism in India and Ireland, especially 'The British Rule in India', in Karl *Marx/Frederick Engels Collected Works*, vol. 12 (New York, NY: International Publishers, 1979), *Marx and Engels on Ireland* (Moscow: Progress Publishers, 1971), Marx *and Engels on Colonialism* (Moscow: Foreign Languages Publishing House, 1972); Iqbal Husain (ed.), *Karl Marx on India* (New Delhi, India: Tulika Books, 2006); and *The Civil War in the United States*, ed. Richard Enmale (New York, NY: International Publishers, 1937).

Some of the important secondary sources on Marx and race include: Ralph Fox, *Marx, Engels, and Lenin on Ireland* (London: Modern Books, 1940); Edward Said, *Orientalism* (New York, NY: Pantheon Books, 1978); Shlomo Avineri (ed.), *Karl Marx on Colonialism and Modernization: His Dispatches and Other Writings on China, India, Mexico, and the Middle East and North Africa* (Garden City, NY: Doubleday and Company, 1969); Dilip Hiro, *Between Marx and Muhammad: The Changing Face of Central Asia* (New York, NY:

HarperCollins, 1995); Cedric Robinson, *Black Marxism: The Making of the Black Radical Tradition* (Chapel Hill, NC: University of North Carolina Press, 2000); Walter Kennedy, *Red Republicans and Lincoln's Marxists: Marxism in the Civil War* (Lincoln, NE: iUniverse, 2007); John Rodden, 'The lever must be applied in Ireland: Marx, Engels, and the Irish Question', *The Review of Politics*, 70, 4 (Fall 2008): 609–40; Anderson, *Marx at the Margins*; Kolja Lindner, 'Marx's Eurocentrism: Post Colonial Studies and Marx Scholarship', *Radical Philosophy* (May–June 2010); Salome Lee, 'Until We Are All Abolitionists: Marx on Slavery, Race, and Class', *The International Marxist Humanist* (October 2011); Blackburn, *An Unfinished Revolution*, pp. 127–215; Schraffenberger, 'Karl Marx and the American Civil War'; Bertell Ollman and Kevin Anderson (eds.), *Karl Marx* (London: Ashgate, 2012); and Eric Foner, 'The Emancipation Proclamation at 150: Abraham Lincoln's Turning Point', *The Guardian* (17 September 2012). There are a number of leftist scholars who have responded to the criticisms of Marx on race by Edward Said, Timothy Wise, and others through a close reading of Marx's writings, including Sumit Sarkar, Irfan Habib, Aijaz Ahmad, Pranav Jani, Neil Lazarus, and August Nimtz.

58   Thomas Jefferson, 'The Declaration of Independence', in *The Encyclopedia of Colonial and Revolutionary America*, ed. John Faragher (New York, NY: Facts on File, 1990), pp. 103–4. See Richard Schlatter, *Private Property: The History of an Idea* (New York, NY: Russell & Russell, 1973), pp. 195–9 and William Scott, *In Pursuit of Happiness: American Conceptions of Property from the Seventeenth to the Twentieth* Century (Bloomington, IN: Indiana University Press, 1977), pp. 24–35 and 41–4.

59   Lincoln, *The Gettysburg Address*, p. 119. Also see the *Emancipation Proclamation*, pp. 115–17, and the *First and Second Inaugural Addresses of Abraham Lincoln*, pp. 105–14 and 121–2, along with the exchange of letters between Marx and Lincoln, pp. 211–14, in *An Unfinished Revolution*, ed. and intro. Robin Blackburn.

60   Karl Marx, 'Address of the International Workingmen's Association to Abraham Lincoln', letters between Marx and Lincoln, in *An Unfinished Revolution*, ed. Blackburn, pp. 211–12. Marx writes: 'The workingmen of Europe feel sure that as the American War of Independence initiated a new era of ascendency for the middle class, so the American antislavery war will do for the working class' (p. 212). In this letter, Marx clearly sees a direct connection between the Civil War in America, the French *Declaration of the Rights of Man and of the Citizen*, and the fight of the labouring poor throughout Europe as part of one continuous struggle. Blackburn emphasises the point that Marx in his letter to Lincoln uses the word 'emancipation' a number of times and ties it to the emancipation from both slavery and wage labour (pp. 56–7).

61   Marx, *The Civil War in France*, pp. 81–2; MEW 17, p. 362. In a more critical vein, Mason, in *The Paris Commune*, writes: 'In its death the revolution was far more robust than it had ever appeared in life' (p. 282). Casualties of the resistance were very high. Records were not kept, so estimates vary but the total number is between 10,000 to 30,000 Parisians killed, most being executed. See Tombs, *The War Against Paris 1871*, p. 191.

62   Karl Marx, 'Private Property and Communism', *Karl Marx: Early Writings*, trans. and ed. T.B. Bottomore (New York, NY: McGraw Hill Book Company, 1964), p. 155; *Karl Marx/Friedrich Engels Werke*, Band 40, Ergänzungsband, Erster Teil (Berlin: Dietz Verlag, 1968), p. 536.

CHAPTER 8

Economic Justice: Ethics, Production, and the Critique of Chrematistics and Political Economy

In this last chapter on Marx's theory of social justice the issue of macroeconomic justice will be investigated. Just as Aristotle, in his analysis of the forms of justice, developed a critique of chrematistics or unnatural wealth acquisition in a market economy, Marx will undertake a similar critique of political economy and the laws of value production and exchange. At first this critique of political economy may not seem to have an immediate relation to issues of justice but, like Aristotle, Marx is interested in examining the empirical structures of alienation and exploitation that would make the good life and best citizens impossible.[1] Economics is not the teleological end of human existence, but it is the necessary and universal prerequisite for happiness, the ethical community, and the democratic polity. Aristotle was suspicious of all forms of market activity and wealth creation that undermined the self-sufficiency and self-sustainability of the democratic polity, distorted its moral and intellectual values in the pursuit of profit, turned friendship and citizenship into monetary interactions, and transformed reason into technical calculation and social justice into the fair price for consumer goods. Questions of individual virtue and perfection (*arete*), practical wisdom (*phronesis*), social beneficence, public happiness (*eudaimonia*), economic reciprocity, and political democracy were displaced by economic calculations and the beginnings of economic self-interest; ethics and politics became subsidiary functions of economics. As we have already seen, Marx's vision of human emancipation and the good life was accompanied by social praxis and human creativity, reciprocal grace and mutual sharing among friends and citizens, self-realisation of virtue and human needs, and political participation in producers' associations and the decentralised government. Capitalist production and exchange are antithetical to the moral values of rational production and the ethical community.

The whole political structure of Aristotle's ideal polity was turned upside down as the good life became the profitable life. Following closely Aristotle's treatment of justice, Marx continues in this theoretical vein in his later writings. It is not economics as a modern positivistic and explanatory science that interests Marx. This would explain his unusual integration of the classical economic theory of Adam Smith, David Ricardo, and Thomas Malthus, the utopian socialism of Henri de Saint-Simon, Charles Fourier, and Robert Owen, the anarchism of Wilhelm Weitling and Pierre-Joseph Proudhon, and the German idealism of Immanuel Kant, Georg Wilhelm Friedrich Hegel, and Friedrich Wilhelm Schelling. The developed economic theory in the *Grundrisse* (1857), *A Contribution to the Critique of Political Economy* (1859), *Theories of Surplus-Value* (1862), and the multi-volumes of *Capital* (1867, 1885, and 1894) was the means of developing Marx's critique of political economy that would supplement his theory of social justice and would show the manifest weaknesses of capitalist production and market exchange – its logical and structural contradictions and its unethical and destructive forms of practical action.[2]

The difference between Marx's early and later writings is not a difference between his philosophy and science or between his social theory and economics. The later writings represent a continuation of his early focus on ethics and politics, and therefore, a continuation of his theory of social justice, into an empirical and historical critique of industrial chrematistics and the completion of his Aristotelian enterprise for the study of the modern polity.[3] This explains his rejection of abstractionism and moralism throughout his writings and especially in the *Critique of the Gotha Program*. Simply moralising or castigating the social system because it does not equate with one's moral values is not a sufficient standard for the scientific analysis of capital. We have seen in previous chapters that Marx rejects the abstract universal rights of nature, economic distribution based on natural abilities and merit, individual liberty expressed in terms of material utility and private property, and justice defined in terms of market categories of possessive individualism and economic materialism. The ultimate telos of humanity is not the acquisition of property and the self-seeking of material pleasure in hoarding and consumption, but the realisation of humanity's potential as species beings in order to create their own history, institutions, and life of virtue, self-determination, and freedom. Toward this end, Marx's analysis of the nature of value, exchange value, abstract labour, surplus labour, primitive accumulation of property, the economic laws of capital accumulation and realisation, and the internal contradictions of capitalism reflects his profound understanding of the real possibilities of human existence and participatory democracy. In the thought of Marx, moral critique has been re-engaged with economics, ethics reunited with science as he creates a new critical and dialectical theory of society and nature.[4]

In the first chapter of his *Politics*, Aristotle began his study of economics and commodities with an analysis of the direct barter of commodities between friends and neighbours (C-C), exchange or trade of necessary commodities in the local market (C-M-C), commerce for money and profits among artisans and merchants (M-C-M'), and the accumulation of capital (M-C-M') and finance (M-

M') by city merchants.[5] Aristotle distinguishes between two types of economy: The *oikonomike* or household or family (*oikos*) economy grounded in the ethical principles of the satisfaction of human needs, self-sufficient community, familial devotion and love (*philia*), and grace, reciprocity, and mutual sharing (*metadosis*) of material goods which will form the basis of his ideal polity (*polis*) and the *chrematistike* or unnatural wealth economy based on market rationality and profit making which will destroy the possibilities of a democratic and free society. This is the distinction between a moral economy of family, friends, and citizens and a market economy of artisans, merchants, and moneylenders. Following Aristotle, Marx begins his analysis of industrial production in a capitalist society with an examination of the cell-form of bourgeois society in the commodity, then proceeds to study the exchange of commodities, circulation of money and commerce, and, finally, capital as private property and production.

As we have seen in Chapter 4, for both social theorists, happiness is defined as a virtuous life of public discourse and political participation within a democratic society; economics is fundamentally a question about the material conditions of human life and the possibilities for a good, happy, and virtuous life – *eudaimonia* of the political animal for Aristotle and social praxis of the species being for Marx.[6] And, finally, for both, market and industrial capitalism based on inequality, class, and property, along with a personality characterised by acquisitiveness, greed, and self-interest, will divide and destroy democracy as it undermines the ethical and political foundations of society. Capitalism destroys democracy and replaces natural law with abstract natural rights and liberal values which conceal the true relationships between the state and civil society. About these issues Richard Miller has insightfully written: 'Marx's theory of alienated labour is, in its more abstract features, largely a description of deprivation that, in Aristotle's view, would deny people a good life ... Marx, like Aristotle, judges societies by the kinds of human lives they create'.[7] Thus for Aristotle and Marx capitalist production and social organisation are contradictory to the ethical and political tenets of social justice.

Marx begins the first volume of *Capital* with the simplest of economic categories – the commodity – then proceeds through the next four chapters detailing the evolution of capitalism from the commodity and market exchange to capital production. His purpose is to begin with the nature of a commodity and develop his analysis into the power structure, social organisation, and social relations of production behind commodity production and the accumulation of private property as capital. As the economy develops from simple commodity exchange to the commercialisation of trade to the accumulation of property, there is an increased social alienation of production. Throughout this first volume, Marx is continuously comparing the institutions of modernity to the lost traditions and lost possibilities of ancient and medieval natural law. Compared to these traditions, capitalism is immoral, unethical, and antidemocratic because it replaces the ethical traditions of ancient Greece with the hedonism, egoism, and materialism of modern liberalism. The result is an empirical and historical study – historical materialism and science – of modern capitalism. Also, seen from the perspective of the structural contradictions and irrational constraints on an economic system based on the law of value, commodity exchange, and capital accumulation, the realisation of natural law of virtue, self-determination, and freedom becomes impossible.[8] Economic justice demands a transformation to an entirely different type of economic system based on the ethics of nature and need.

If volume 1 of *Capital* revolves around Marx's ethical critique of the values of political economy, volume 3 continues the ethical critique but in the area of the systems rationality, efficiency, and the logic of capitalist production. A life of virtue and reason in everyday life, aesthetic creativity in the workplace, friendship and citizenship in economic and political democracy, and mutual love and sharing of natural resources in producers' associations is morally and logically incompatible with the institutions and organisations of production in capitalism. The ethical justification of this position lies in the logic and structure of capital itself. From a consideration of the general ideas of commodity, money, and capital, Marx turns in volume 3 to an examination of the ethical dimension of the actual and concrete structural and historical contradictions (*Widersprüche*) of capitalist production. These contradictions result not simply in economic crises or social problems that can be easily fixed or adjusted once properly understood, but are irreparable rifts and fissures in the ethics and institutions of capitalism itself. The problem lies in logic and not history. By relying on Hegel's phenomenology and logic for the architectonic of his own analysis of capital, Marx is again following Aristotle, making an ethical critique of political economy by arguing that the inner logic and rationality of this economic system is incompatible with the values and principles of a good and virtuous life; chrematistics is incompatible with the ethics and institutions of social justice. The ethics of Aristotle is joined to the method of Hegel. Economics must again become a sub-branch of ethics and politics; it is not an independent social science with its own fetishised hypotheses, scientific predictions, and explanatory laws of social behaviour. This explains the epistemological and methodological difficulties encountered in reading *Capital*. It is a work firmly implanted in the issues of ancient Greek political and economic philosophy while using the Hegelian method of immanent critique, contradictions, and the dialectic. Suffice it to say at this point that the use of Aristotle and Hegel is not arcane. Once the reader is assured that Marx is not attempting to develop a predictive science of the inevitable breakdown of capitalism, but instead is writing a major work on ethics and political economy in order to set the parameters for his theory of social justice, then much of the confusion surrounding his work disappears. Marx's later writings represent an examination of the concept (*Begriff*) and logic (*Logik*) of capital and property in order to confirm his ideas that capitalism is a social system based on irrational contradictions and metabolic rifts and, therefore, incapable of providing the material and economic foundations for self-determination, freedom, and democracy. Economic justice must be founded upon an entirely different social system of producers' associations and workers' communes for a self-government 'of the people, by the people'.

Again, Marx returns to Aristotle to set the stage for his analysis of capital. Aristotle, like Marx, recognised an irreparable divide in his *Politics* between a household and a market economy, use value and exchange value, human needs and material wants, and a democratic polity and a materialist culture. These divisions are taken up by Marx and incorporated into *Capital* as he adds the further economic developments of a liberal polity and industrial production. Now these opposing divides are turned into the logical and class contradictions of socialised production and private accumulation as they manifest themselves in various forms of economic stagnation and laws of capitalist production: (1) concentration and centralisation of capital; (2) changing organic composition of capital; (3) tendential fall in the rate of profit; (4) overproduction of capital; (5) problems of capital accumulation (factory production) and profit realisation (market consumption); and (6) economic disproportionality and dysfunctionality between rational production and class consumption, between the workplace and the market.[9] These opposing forces in society produce crises, poverty, inequality, and class power that are anathema to an egalitarian life of civic virtue (ethics) and public deliberation (democracy).

And, finally, these social divisions are logical and nontranscendable, that is, they are embedded into the very social fabric of capitalism itself and are not amenable to change or amelioration. Marx recognises the implications of this approach to the dialectic of society: 'All these antitheses and contradictions, which are immanent in commodities, assert themselves, and develop their modes of motion, in the antithetical phases of the metamorphosis of a commodity. These modes therefore imply the possibility, and no more than the possibility, of crises'.[10] He readily admits that there are historical and structural countertendencies to the logic of capital, including extending the working day, intensifying exploitation and surplus value, finding new markets, and expanding imperial and colonial policy. These countertendencies may modify these logical conditions for a time, but they can never overcome or negate them. They will always be present in capitalist production, thereby making it impossible to realise the potential of human existence and reason in the modern economy. As Marx so succinctly put it in *Capital*, 'The *real barrier* to capitalist production is *capital* itself'.[11] Every ideal of justice whether of liberalism (immanent critique) or socialism (substantive critique) falters before the law of value and the logic of capital. This story of the difference between a social economy for the production of use values (C-C and C-M-C) and a political economy of exchange values (M-C-M' and M-M'), which is a cautionary tale about the fate and tragedy of modernity, is truly worthy of the talents of an Aeschylus or Sophocles.

Commodities, Exchange, and the Labour Theory of Value

Marx begins *Capital* by unravelling the secrets of the commodity and market exchange. He hopes to reveal deeper and more profound insights into the nature of capitalist circulation, consumption, and production, along with their corresponding contradictions and crises. The commodity itself is an objectification or manifestation of the contradictory imperatives of the social production of use value and exchange value. That is, the production for human need and the production for economic profits push the economy in two different directions that ultimately lead to serious social, political, and economic crises. The commodity is the microcosm and secret to the internal logic and laws of capitalist production. By examining the simplest element of consumption and wealth within the process of production as it is divided between use value (satisfying human needs) and exchange value (accumulation of profits), that is, the nature of the commodity itself, the inner dynamics of the whole social system – the functional and structural interrelations of the social totality – are openly displayed. Marx views the commodity as the window into the workings of modern capitalism. He begins to examine the commodity as having a specific quantity and quality whose initial purpose is to provide a material use-value or utility to the consumer.

Immediately after introducing his subject of analysis, Marx introduces Aristotle's famous distinction between use value and exchange value.[12] Aristotle had discovered the two crucial elements of commodities in their use for immediate consumption and their value for market exchange for other commodities. Referring to Aristotle in *Capital*, Marx writes: 'For two-fold is the use of every object … The one is peculiar to the object as such. The other is not, as a sandal which may be worn, and is also exchangeable. Both are uses of the sandal, for even he who exchanges the sandal for the money or food he is in want of, makes use of the sandal as a sandal. But not in its natural way. For it has not been made for the sake of being exchanged'.[13] The commodity owner has no particular use for it but wishes only to exchange it in the market for another use value. It is this distinction that will then open the discussion into Marx's labour theory of value grounded in the writings of William Petty, John Locke, Adam Smith, and David Ricardo. The original micro-economic focus on the nature of the commodity as the simplest and most immediate (abstract) object of economic analysis soon turns into an examination of labour and the social relationships at the heart of the production of commodities. This, in turn, will lead to a broader and more comprehensive study of the macro-economic laws of value and capital production.

The contradictions and crises that will undermine the production of class wealth and private capital are buried within the dual moments of use value and exchange value for both Aristotle and Marx. The most important characteristic of use value is that it satisfies a particular human need whether physical or mental. On the other hand, the market exchange value of a commodity is more difficult to describe since it changes with the time and place of sale. According to Marx, the price of a commodity first appears as a quantitative relation which is both 'accidental and purely relative, and consequently an intrinsic value, i.e., an exchange value that is inseparably connected with, inherent in commodities …'.[14] The commodity in the marketplace appears to different individuals as both relative and essential, which strikes Marx as contradictory and cannot provide the basis for an understanding of either exchange value or market interactions.

Commodities produced in industrial factories in the modern era have exchange value since they are specifically produced for trade in a market economy for a commodity of equal value and worth measured by money. Money is the form of circulation of exchange value, but it, too, is based on some universal principle that makes each exchange commensurate and each commodity equal. Money is the social mechanism that measures the quantitative relationship of the value of commodities exchanged, thereby making them equal to each other. There must be a universal standard of measurement that allows the market to anticipate prices and function effectively. Exchange value is only the phenomenal form inherent in each commodity that provides it with a standard of measurement. There must be a common substance or essence which makes exchange possible. For Marx, 'The exchange of commodities is evidently an act characterised by a total abstraction from use value … As use values commodities are, above all, of different qualities, but as exchange values they are merely different quantities, and consequently do not contain an atom of use value'.[15] In his reflections on these same issues, Aristotle was unable to arrive at this universal basis for commercial exchange.[16] Marx contends that it was due to the fact that the Athenian market was only in its earliest stage of development and, thus, did not provide Aristotle with a clear insight into its internal workings. But now industrial production and market circulation within capitalism are fully advanced and the question of the universal standard of exchange can be answered, especially with the aid of classical economists.

Attempting to unravel 'the whole mystery of the form of value [which] lies hidden in the elementary form' of the simply commodity exchange (barter) between two owners of linen (weaver) and a coat (tailor), Marx begins with the assumption that twenty yards of linen are equal in value to one coat. Though on the surface they appear to be relatively unexciting and banal, the equivalency and exchange of two commodities will reveal the underlying secrets of the hidden structural relationships of modern capitalism. Toward that end, Marx continues with the central question of what makes the two items commensurate and thus forms the basis for a more developed material exchange in the market? We know from everyday experience that commodities are traded on the basis of some common value-form or substance which Marx also calls the 'money-form' which makes both simple barter exchange and more developed market exchange possible. It does not lie in the specific quality of the productive activities of a weaver and a tailor since they are different types of activities, different divisions of labour, and different expenditures of energy. It must be something more abstract and universal that makes an economic comparison and equation possible. What makes the value (value-form or money-form) underlying the exchange value possible? Commodities as use values are produced by combining matter and labour. This idea of the combination of nature and labour as the source of material wealth is investigated in the chapter on environmental justice. Justice is thus the social manner in which humans relate to both aspects of the process of production of use values or commodities. The application of specific amounts of human labour is the common substance in both types of commodities and productive activities. What began as an object of utility and consumption is now viewed as a social activity. According to Marx, 'we [must] bear in mind that the value of commodities has a purely social reality, and that they acquire this reality only in so far as they are expressions or embodiments of one identical social substance, viz., human labour ...'.[17] What at first appears as a relationship between things or commodities turns out to be a social relationship based on human labour.

The value relation between two commodities, that is, 20 yards of linen = 1 coat, is what facilitates the equation and exchange between two different consumer products. The value of the linen is expressed in terms of the coat; the coat serves as the equivalent and relative value of the linen. Marx has broadened his understanding of this market relationship without actually arriving at the key insight into the nature of commodity exchange itself. Two different commodities can be compared quantitatively in both forms of direct barter and monetary pricing only when they share a common substance. That is, a specific quantity of linen has value expressed in the form of one coat or five marks based on the assumption that a specific magnitude or product has a specific value compared to other items. It should be mentioned in the middle of these reflections on the nature of simple commodity exchange that these considerations are primitive but essential since Marx is setting the foundation for his more developed theory of the social extortion, exploitation, and organisation of industrial production. In his early writings his purpose was to show that the social relations of production undermined the possibility of praxis, virtue, and beneficence; in his later writings his purpose is to show that these same relationships undermine the institutions and structures underlying praxis, virtue, and beneficence. Just as Aristotle wrote the *Politics* to give institutional support for his work on ethics and virtue in the *Nicomachean Ethics*, Marx writes *Capital* to detail the alienation of labour at the structural level of the *Paris Manuscripts*. Patricia Springborg summarises this relationship succinctly: 'Thus Marx's theory of alienation may be seen as a full elaboration of Aristotle's distinction between *oikonomia*, economic activity geared to communal needs and the production of use values, and *chrematistike*, money-making in a society governed by *pleonexia* and oriented to the production of exchange values'.[18] Whether engaged in philosophical and anthropological analysis or economic theory, Marx's writings, as with Aristotle's, reflect different forms of social justice.

The coat is the equivalent form of the linen and thus the measure of its true value only because labour is the value common to both items. They are created by two different types of activities but share a common substance in human labour itself which makes them comparable, exchangeable, and the basis for material wealth. Marx summarises his position in the following passage: 'It is the expression of equivalence between different sorts of commodities that alone brings into relief the specific character of value-creating labour, and this it does by actually reducing the different varieties of labour embodied in the different kinds of commodities to their common quality of human labour in the abstract'.[19] The coat and linen are qualitatively the same because both are the product of human labour power. And the form of value that the linen takes is expressed in terms of the coat. This is an important development in Marx's analysis since the object and the value of the object are not simply material things to be traded but are manifestations of labour and the social relations necessary for the creation of various commodities. And most importantly, the value-form is the quantitative expression of the value of the linen itself. As history develops the value-form of the commodity, that is, its material form or the form and measurement of value in terms of other commodities, it is expressed in a simple form of equivalency (another commodity), a particular form (series of commodities), or a universal form (money). Marx's goal is to show that money as the universal form of value, and thus as the basis for exchange in a market economy, is ultimately a social relation of production. This is the real mystery of the nature of value. Marx is critical of classical economics for not uncovering this mystery: 'He [the bourgeois political economist] has not the least suspicion that the most simple expression of value, such as 20 yds. of linen = 1 coat, already propounds the riddle of the equivalent form for our solution'.[20] It is no longer a simple object or quantitative price used in classical economics but a social relationship based ultimately on property, division of labour, worker's skill, social organisation of production, the means of production of science and technology, and the class system.[21] Marx is aware that, with the depreciation of soil conditions, the labour time necessary for the production of flax doubled, while with the invention of new power looms the labour time necessary for linen is reduced by one-half. This means that the value or congealed labour time in each commodity will be increased or decreased accordingly. And from the nature of value – its logic and laws – lies the answer to the further questions of the nature of the contradictions and crises in capitalist production which Marx will develop in volume three of *Capital*.

Commodities and the exchange of commodities are the result of the labour-time socially necessary for its production. 'But if we abstract from their use value, there remains their Value as defined above. Therefore, the common substance that manifests itself in the exchange-value of commodities, whenever they are exchanged, is their value'.[22] Marx earlier in the previous paragraph describes this labour as 'a mere congelation of homogeneous human labour'. And later adds that the amount of value or labour in each commodity is based on 'the labour time socially necessary for its production'.[23] This means that the standard of measurement and basis for equitable exchange is the labour time necessary to produce a commodity under normal conditions and average skills and intensity of production. The material form of measurement and commensurability can be another commodity (coat), a series of commodities (coat, iron, coffee, etc.), and, finally, a universal commodity (gold) taken to represent all possible exchanges. Commodities are exchangeable because they express equal quantities of labour contained in them. This is what Marx refers to as 'abstract labour'. 'Commodities, therefore, in which equal quantities of labour are embodied, or which can be produced in the same time, have the same value'.[24] He is aware at this point in his analysis that even though there is an equivalency stated between the linen and coat, there is, however, no direct quantitative measurement of value. Value is only relational at this point in his analysis between the linen and coat. There is no abstract and quantitative determination of the value of each separately; they are only measured in terms of the use value and physical form of different commodities. Thus, what at first appearance takes on the different forms of tailoring and weaving, that is, they appear to be quite different types of activities, on closer examination by Marx, they look remarkably similar. The two differing productive activities of human labour produce an equivalent form that now appears as expressions of a common value, abstract human labour, and a social phenomenon. And the analysis of the concepts of equivalent form in commodity exchange will help Marx move toward an analysis of congealed labour, surplus value, profits, and capital formation. These are all forms of abstract labour as they are manifested within a historically specific form of the social relations of production. What begins as an analysis of a simple commodity, the most fundamental principle within capitalist exchange, quickly develops into an analysis of the process of the production of commodities and the exploitation of labour.

It is at this point in the analysis of his labour theory of value that Marx returns to Aristotle for more insight and inspiration. Aristotle had recognised the importance of the elementary and money-form of commodities based on equality and commensurability but never was able to get to the foundation of these categories of equality and measurement. This is Marx's goal at the beginning of *Capital* as he attempts to move beyond Aristotle by considering the elementary or historically primitive form of value of a commodity in the simple equation and exchange between two commodities as the start of a longer analysis of commodity exchange. Two commodities are exchangeable because they have the same value and that value can be expressed quantitatively (20 yards of linen = 1 coat). The value or abstract labour contained in the product is now objectively expressed in the form of exchange value (particular quantity of products). Value underlies exchange value and makes the latter possible; exchange value is only the particular form that value takes in an exchange. This is an important point for Marx since it so different from the position of the mercantilists (F.L.A. Ferrier and Charles Ganilh) and the French classical economist (Frédéric Bastiat). These economists reduce exchange value to price, thereby avoiding the necessity to consider the issue of the value-form of a consumer product as labour and the opposition between use value and exchange value. In the above equation, the linen is a use value while the coat, as the standard of measurement, is an exchange value. This distinction is important since 'the elementary form of value of a commodity is the elementary form in which the contrast contained in that commodity, between use value and value, becomes apparent'.[25] Although this distinction between use value and exchange value remains central to Marx's critique of capitalism, it does not explain the nature of qualitative equality and quantitative proportionality between commodities. In the elementary form of value there is only one other commodity (coat) that is equated with the linen, only one other commodity that expresses the value of linen. In spite of this temporary weakness in the analysis, this line of argument remains important because this is the beginning of the distinction between a society organised around the satisfaction of human needs and use value and a society based on exchange value and market profits. Aristotle used this distinction to outline the differences between oikonomike and chrematistike, between a moral economy and a market economy.

Soon, there is an expanded form of value and many different possible commodities made commensurate and proportional to the linen. Now the linen is equal to a certain amount of tea, coffee, iron, corn, or gold. The elementary value-form has now been expanded to include a large number of other commodities. The nature of exchange has not altered, only the number of commodities potentially involved. 'It is thus, that for the first time, this value shows itself in its true light as a congelation of undifferentiated human labour. For the labour that creates it, now stands expressly revealed, as labour that ranks equally with every other sort of human labour, no matter what its form, whether tailoring, ploughing, mining, etc., no matter, therefore, whether it is realised in coats, corn, iron, or gold'.[26] The social relationship between the linen and coat has now expanded to all commodities being produced in an 'interminable and infinite' series of value and social relationships through human labour. This is crucial, according to Marx, because now the reader is in a position to recognise that it is not exchange or circulation that produces the value and worth of a marketable product. Price and profit are ultimately not defined by the market economy of the utilitarian economists who argued that the key to success is 'buying cheap and selling dear'. The secret to the creation of wealth and power in exchange and production is not to be found in the utility and cleverness of market rationality. Rather, the secret to capitalism lies in the 'metaphysical subtleties and theological niceties' of the commodity as these are manifested in the social relations of production.[27] And just as the simple commodity exchange and its relative value-form (20 yards of linen = 1 coat) has been replaced by the expanded or particular form of value among commodities, and then later by the general form of value (20 yards of linen = a particular amount of tea, coffee, corn, iron, etc.), and, finally, replaced by the money-form of value in which gold becomes the quantitative measure and universal equation of all commodities (2 ounces of gold = a certain amount of tea, coffee, corn, or iron). Linen and then gold becomes the universal equivalent and bodily form of the common standard of measurement. Commodities have become qualitatively equal because they are products of abstract and undifferentiated social labour in weaving, tailoring, agriculture, industry, and mining, and quantitatively equal because there is now a common standard of measurement – labour time. Marx has now reached the point where social labour and labour time are the key categories for understanding the nature and foundation of value and commodity exchange. Over time gold becomes the socially accepted expression of labour and value; money now becomes the final value-form and standard of market measurement. Marx is aware in all these carefully crafted categories of his theory of value that it is human labour that is the ultimate measure of productive worth. 'The general value-form is the reduction of all kinds of actual labour to their common character of being human labour generally, of being the expenditure of human labour-power'.[28] The reader must forgive Marx the exquisite and, at times, excruciating details as he moves from commodity exchange, markets, and prices. His ultimate goal at this point in his analysis is to show that human labour is the real foundation of a market economy, and that labour itself is an ethical principle.

Marx characterises the social labour time necessary to make a particular commodity and to determine the magnitude and equivalency of its value as an 'over-riding law of nature' like the law of gravity. What troubles him is that this economic natural law is generally hidden from view by the mystical veil of the discipline of economics. In fact, the whole nature of common substance, universal equivalency, and labour power is ignored by bourgeois economics which represses the magic and mysteries of production. The question is: Why is this so important for Marx; why did he have to introduce a new section on fetishism after the publication of the first edition of *Capital*? The answer lies in his analysis of surplus value, profits, and economic exploitation. If profits are achieved in the circulation of commodities and not in their production, if value is expressed in terms of price and not labour, if there is a contradiction between exchange value and use value, then the secret of capitalism remains a theological experience hidden from public view. But with the further investigation of commodities and human labour beyond circulation and commerce into the production process itself, and with the unfolding of the distinction between labour and labour power, value and surplus value, the secret of production is revealed and with it the alienation of chrematistic production and the corresponding distortion of social justice that lies at the very heart of a capitalist economy. As long as economics remains at the phenomenal level of commodities, circulation, and commerce – supply and demand – economics remains a mystical theology. Marx is aware that the political economist has developed a labour theory of value but 'has never once asked the question why labour is represented by the value of its product and labour time by the magnitude of that value ... [It] has never succeeded, by means of its analysis of commodities, and, in particular, of their value, in discovering the form under which value becomes exchange value'.[29]

Aristotle and classical economists have been aware of the importance of human labour but have not pushed beyond the surface to ask about the nature of the common substance and universal equivalent as expressions of a historically specific social mode of production of commodities. They did not inquire into the nature of exchange value nor did they see the connection between commodities and the form of value, that is, money or capital; they did not inquire into the historical or social form of value and its specific mode of production. That would demand asking a new set of questions about the nature of labour time, production, and commercial and industrial capital. The role of money in exchange is to make objective and concrete the value of a commodity in terms of the labour time necessary to make it; value equals labour.[30] Marx maintains that neither Smith nor Ricardo accepted the central importance of value and, in fact, saw no real connection between value and commodities; they were interested in the quantity of value (price and profits) but not the form of value in money and capital, nor the analysis of the nature of labour and labour time that underlies commodity production. Their interest lay in the magnitude of labour in exchange or circulation, not the quality of human labour in production. Thus, in the end, they understood neither the nature of commodity exchange, wealth creation, class and inequality structure, the social relations of production, nor the underlying economic exploitation of capitalist production. According to Marx, what is missed by the classical economists is that capitalism by its very nature is a historical and social manifestation of alienation, exploitation, and injustice.

Labour Power, Surplus Value, and the Alienation of Chrematistic Production

The circulation of commodities for the satisfaction of a use value in the oeconomic form of C-M-C is juxtaposed to the circulation of capital to satisfy the desire for chrematistic money and unnatural profits in the form of M-C-M'. As in the nature of the commodity, the process of circulation and its more advanced form of commerce is built around the same opposition between use value and exchange value. The natural circulation of use value is limited by human needs and self-sufficiency, while the circulation of exchange value as capital is unlimited as it encourages individual wants and the rights of private property. It is as money in circulation and commerce that capital makes its first appearance since it can be accumulated and hoarded for future use. Money can be used to facilitate the sale and purchase of commodities for use and personal consumption, but capital begins with a purchase and ends with a sale for a surplus to increase the original amount of exchange value and capital. Money is exchanged for more money and there are no limits to the process; exchange under these circumstances 'has acquired the occult quality of being able to add value to itself'.[31] In this type of economy, there is no higher purpose to exchange than unlimited accumulation of capital and wealth. This is the very essence of an unnatural economy and is an entirely different type of circulation than one founded upon human needs.[32]

In Chapter 5, 'Contradictions in the General Formula of Capital', Marx makes quite explicit what he had been hinting at in the previous chapters: In the process of circulation there is an exchange of value equivalents expressed in terms of monetary price. The form of value changes from commodity to money but the value remains the same because in each commodity there is an equal amount of labour contained therein. The focus of Marx's attention now is on the nature of value as money and capital. The natural law of exchange stipulates that for exchange to take place under normal conditions the two commodities must be equal. Exchange itself does not provide for the increase in value (labour). Marx concludes in his critique of classical economics: 'Hence, we see that behind all attempts to represent the circulation of commodities as a source of surplus value, there lurks a *quid pro quo*, a mixing up of use value and exchange value'.[33]

Etienne Bonnot de Condillac sees trade as an exchange of use value and individual desires, and not as an exchange of value and human labour. There is always an inequality of desires in exchange, thus explaining how profits are produced in circulation and commerce. Certain commodities are worth more to certain people. Those exchanging commodities have no use for the products and do not value them while those wishing to buy have an added incentive because of their wants. Commodities are worth more to those in need. According to Condillac, surplus value and profits arise out of exchange itself. Marx rejects this confusion of use value and exchange value and the misplaced emphasis on the circulation of commodities as the basis for surplus value. Surplus value and its production is the key to Marx's theory of alienation, exploitation, and economic crises. Not to understand the source and nature of surplus value is to misunderstand the complex nature of chrematistics and capitalism, and in turn, to misunderstand the nature of social justice. Marx concludes with the statement: 'If equivalents are exchanged, no surplus value results, and if non-equivalents are exchanged, still no surplus value.

Circulation, or the exchange of commodities, begets no value'.[34] Since the circulation of commodities requires an equivalency between commodities based on abstract and socially necessary labour, there can be no surplus in exchange.

If the source of surplus value, which is the whole purpose of capitalist circulation, does not lie in exchange, where does it lie and how is it created? The answer lies in the purchase of labour power which is the physical capability and capacity to labour and produce a product having a use value. Whereas Locke had emphasised the natural right of the individual to the products of their labour, Marx begins his analysis of production with the right of a person to sell their own labour power. Possessive individualism has been integrated with the reality of the market since workers do not own what they produce (alienation); they own only their ability to sell their labour power in the market. Circulation involves the exchange of different forms or types of values from commodities, money, and capital. But the exchange is just a transfer of value-forms. The mystery of surplus, profits, and capital accumulation lies in the nature of abstract labour in the process of production and the difference between the selling of labour power as exchange value and purchase of labour as a use value. Workers sell their labour power on the market for a wage; in exchange they receive money that will reimburse them for recreating their physical capacity and ability to labour.[35] Labour power is a commodity or exchange value which the worker sells to the owner of the means of production (factory, machinery, raw materials, science and technology, etc.) for a set daily or weekly price.

Equality, rights, and human freedom are bourgeois concepts derived from the nature of private property and a market economy. These natural rights express the concrete relations within the circulation of commodities, including the sale of labour power. However, they do not express the social relations of production that create labour power and surplus labour. In fact, these bourgeois political and moral values, along with classical economics with its focus on circulation and money, only conceal the nature of production and the creation of capital and industrial property. Nor do they express the potentiality of the human species as a social being capable of creating its own institutions and history. Instead, these categories are economically reductive since their collective role is the justification of the self-interested and aggressive economic animal. This relationship presupposes a social division of labour between worker and owner at a certain developed stage of the circulation of commodities. Labour power itself has become its own commodity and exchange value. With the move to a consideration of abstract labour, surplus value, and the organisation of production we have moved beyond the classics of Aristotle and free-market economics.

As with every other commodity sold on the market, the value of labour power is determined by the average labour time necessary for its continued production, that is, for the reproduction of the power and capacity to labour in terms of food, clothing, housing, education, family, etc. 'The value of labour power is the value of the means of subsistence necessary for the maintenance of the labourer'.[36] The classical labour theory of value is integrated with Marx's theory of labour power. To recreate the labour power expended in a day may require only a portion of the day's average social labour. The whole day is not spent by the labourer reproducing their physical qualities and abilities. If that occurred, production would end. Labourers work for a period of time reproducing their labour power ('necessary labour time') and the remaining social labour of the day ('surplus labour time') which is the private property of the owner. The labourer sells his labour power as exchange value and in return receives an equal amount of average labour in the form of subsistence wages. However, at the same time the work contract is formed and the worker sells his labour power, the owner receives in return the worker's full labour as use value; the worker sells the exchange value, while the owner receives the use value of labour. In the difference between the selling of labour power and the purchasing of labour lies surplus value as unpaid labour. This distinction between labour power and labour is just a continuation of the distinction from the first pages of *Capital* between exchange value and use value at the point of production.[37] Marx writes: 'The daily cost of maintaining it [labour power], and its daily expenditure in work, are two totally different things. The former determines the exchange value of the labour power, the latter is its use value'.[38]

The daily cost of maintaining labour power (wages) is different from the surplus use of labour. While a labourer may work only half a day to recover his necessary energies and capabilities in labour power, the rest of the day's work is a surplus belonging to the owner of the factory. All production beyond the consumption and recreation of labour power is surplus, that is, private property or capital. The labour power expended to make tea, corn, iron, etc. produces more value than its own actual worth measured in minimum wages. This is the foundation of the '"eternal laws" of the exchange of commodities' and wage slavery. 'A capitalist pays for a day's labour power at its value; then the right to use that power for a day belongs to him, just as much as the right to use any other commodity, such as a horse that he has hired for the day'.[39] This is the essence of commodity production and surplus value in Marx's expanded labour theory of value. Within this distinction between labour power and labour, one can find the source of the production of surplus value and the continued contradictions of capital founded upon workplace exploitation – what Marx calls 'wage slavery'. These contradictions are reflections of the natural law of capital and in the end will result in the structural and ethical breakdown of the total social system. The workplace is so organised as to minimise the costs of labour power and to maximise the surplus, profits, and capital in a capitalist economy; when there is a balance between the two things everything is fine, but when there is an imbalance, the system generates its own crisis. Marx writes that 'the minimum limit of the value of labour power is determined by the value of the commodities, without the daily supply of which the labourer cannot renew his vital energy, consequently by the value of those means of subsistence that are physically indispensable'.[40]

In one of the more controversial passages in Marx's writings and a passage that has central prominence in the Tucker-Wood thesis, Marx appears to argue in volume 1 of *Capital* that the commodity exchange of labour power and money in the wage contract is just and fair even if the worker eventually produces surplus time, labour, and value for the owner of the means of production. The difference between the initial quick recovery of the price of labour power and the further application of the use value of workers is something that is '... without doubt, a piece of good luck for the buyer, but by no means an injury to the seller'.[41] The worker appears to receive a fair price for his work, while the owner is fortunate to receive the surplus work as an added bonus. The results are sustenance wages for the worker and profits for the owner. But in neither case is anyone disadvantaged because the fundamental principle of simple commodity exchange states that in a market transaction equal value is exchanged for equal value. In the process the worker receives full value for his or her work since market exchange represents an exchange of equivalents in different value-forms of commodity (labour power) and wages. The positive side for the owner of the production process is that he receives the full labour capabilities of the workers beyond the reproduction of labour power. As we have already seen in the Introduction to this work, those who support the Tucker-Wood thesis contend that there is no injustice in the market as everyone is commensurately and fairly reimbursed for the expenditure of their labour power; no one is disadvantaged. Notice should be made of the sentence that immediately follows the above quoted passage: 'Our capitalist foresaw this state of things, and that was the cause of his laughter'. There is a great deal of irony in Marx's tone here. There may be justice in the exchange measured by wages and labour power, but certainly no justice measured by wages and labour.

Justice and rights hinge on whether the emphasis is on labour power or labour, exchange value or use value. As we have seen, Marx had preliminarily accepted the ethical categories of liberalism – freedom, equality, and property – in his analysis of the simple circulation or exchange of commodities in the market in the first two parts of *Capital* on 'Commodities and Money' and

'The Transformation of Money into Capital'. But with part III and the analysis of the production of absolute surplus value, they are no longer applicable. The generation of surplus labour and value lies not in the circulation of commodities, but in both the circulation and the production process. Natural rights have not been violated in the circulation of commodities, but with the creation of surplus value in production based on the distinction between labour as a use value and an exchange value, there is a clear violation of the standards of social justice. The laughter of the capitalist at 'this trick' only confirms this.[42]

In addition to the substantive content of his analysis, there is also the formal structure of his argument. It is true that Marx does not use the term 'justice' when outlining this theory of economic exploitation and wage slavery in the factory, but perhaps more importantly these key chapters are placed within the framework of social justice – that is, they are placed within Aristotle's theory of moral economy, natural law, and economic (particular) and political (universal) justice. Aristotle, whom Marx refers to as the 'greatest thinker of antiquity', is mentioned in six of the chapters of *Capital*: (a) framing Marx's discussion of equality, commensurability, and exchange in Chapter 1; (b) slave labour in classical antiquity and its relation to historical materialism in Chapter 1; (c) the distinction between use value and exchange value in Chapter 2; (d) the nature of barter, trade, and commerce in relation to a natural moral economy (*oikonomia*) and an unnatural market economy (*chrematistike*) in Chapter 4; (e) further discussion of the chrematistic economy in relation to merchants' capital (M-C-M') and bankers' capital (M-M') in Chapter 5; (f) the political and social nature of human beings in co-operative production as distinct from the idea of the tool maker in Chapter 13; and (g) analysis of machinery and possible automation for the intensification and emancipation of human labour in Chapter 15. These references help us expand our understanding of Marx's intentions in this work toward creating a critique of political economy within a more profound appreciation of social justice. There is no need to use the term justice when there are so many key references to Aristotle's theory throughout the work and when his analysis is grounded in Aristotle's theory of moral economy.

Natural Law of Contradictions, Crises, and Capital

Once Marx establishes his labour theory of surplus value, the next step is to investigate the nature of macro- and micro-economic exploitation in a chrematistic economy. This is accomplished in two ways by manipulating the forms of surplus value: Relative surplus value is increased by means of the reduction of necessary labour time and wages through work intensification, whereas absolute surplus value is increased by raising the surplus labour time (profits) by increasing the hours worked. The former is accomplished by technologically increasing labour productivity and the latter by expanding work activity. In both cases the goal is to reduce the total cost of commodities and expand surplus labour by lowering the costs of the production of variable capital or living human labour and constant capital or the means of production of raw materials, technology, machinery, utilities, and factories.[43] With this transformation in Marx's analysis from simple commodity exchange to capital production, there is a transformation from natural rights and liberalism in market exchange to profit maximisation, capital accumulation, and the intensification, degradation, and exploitation of human labour under the 'despotism of capital' in Chapter 10, 'The Working Day'. Human emancipation, economic democracy, and human dignity, creativity, and freedom become impossible under the empirical and historical conditions of wage labour and private property. Marx was also aware that even the ideals of John Locke become impossible under capitalism. This is the final irony of capitalism – even its own liberal values of equality and freedom become impossible under this type of economy system.[44] Marx will finally argue that the structures of capitalist production themselves are incompatible with the underlying logic and laws of capital accumulation.[45]

With the transition of Marx's analysis to the third volume of *Capital* the initial contradictions between use value and exchange value, labour and labour power, and socialised production and private accumulation have deepened into the structural contradictions of the capitalist mode of production. The inner logic of capital and the law of value toward greater productivity and expansion create their own inner barriers and gravediggers that make the economic institutions of capitalism incompatible with its own free market ideals (immanent critique). But Marx's analysis is even more radical. The immanent natural law or structural telos of capitalist development tends toward a progressive fall, economic stagnation, and structural crisis that are incompatible with the ideals of the rationality and efficiency of capital production and accumulation; the destructive end of capital is already prefigured in its beginning as simple commodity exchange with the contradictions between use value and exchange value, that is, a contradiction between an economic system based on human needs (*oikonomike*) and market exchange (*chrematistike*). 'It cannot be otherwise in a mode of production in which the labourer exists to satisfy the needs of self-expansion of existing values, instead of, on the contrary, material wealth existing to satisfy the needs of development on the part of the labourer'.[46] This is not a social or economic problem within the capitalist mode of production, but an inherent structural rift that makes the long-term prospects of the economic system problematic.[47] This represents a fundamental rejection of the laws of supply and demand, competition, market price, and the price and value of production articulated by the classical economists Smith and Ricardo. Marx sees these categories as articulating surface phenomena of market competition and self-interest without digging deeper to the underlying law of value, rate of surplus value, and rate of profit. Smith conflated the different forms of capital and, thus, did not distinguish between constant and variable capital. The result was that he confused the rate of surplus value with the rate of profit and the reduction of value to prices of production.[48]

Inquiring even further, Marx unearths the inherent logical flaw and historical tendency toward the overproduction and destruction of capital which makes the long-term prospects and continued viability of capitalist production highly questionable: rising organic composition of capital, tendential falling rate of profit, intensification of labour exploitation, lengthening of the workday and expansion of labour time and constant capital (means of production), increased productivity of the machinery and technology of constant capital, growing disproportionality of capital development and rising surplus population, economic concentration and centralisation, growing disparity between capital accumulation and profit realisation, and, finally, functional stagnation and systems breakdown.[49] Of course Marx, following Hegel's own systematic method in his *Logic*, is aware that there is dialectic within the mode of production between logic and history, economic natural law and fundamental economic structures, and that these tendencies also encounter counteracting influences that may blunt for a time the necessary development of the logic of capital.[50]

In a competitive market economy based on industrial production and wage labour – the structural imperatives of exchange value – there is a constant desire to expand commodity production, intensify labour exploitation of variable capital, increase the flow of surplus value and unpaid labour, expand constant capital and the means of production, and create the conditions for the further expansion of profits and capital. In the final analysis, 'the degree of exploitation of labour determines the rate of surplus value, and therefore the mass of surplus value for a given total mass of variable capital, and consequently the magnitude of the profit'.[51] This systems imperative of capital production requires continuous adjustment in the organic composition of the total mass of capital, that is, in the adjustments between variable capital or living labour and constant capital or congealed labour which underlie the ebb and flow of supply and demand, sale and purchase of goods at the surface of the market economy. With the growing productivity of labour and the desire to produce more commodities and profits, each capitalist utilises more and more technology and machinery in relation to fewer and fewer workers; the organic proportion between constant and variable capital changes. There is a rapid increase in the constant capital of technology and industry in relation to variable capital of human labour. The first two parts of the third volume of *Capital* are introductory sections to the heart of the work in Chapter 13, 'The Law of the Tendency of the Rate of Profit to Fall' which includes three chapters on the technical natural law itself, historical counteracting influences to attenuate the law, and the contradictions of capital within the law.

It is through changes in the organic composition of capital and the proportion of variable to constant capital in the process of production, assuming, as Marx does, a consistent variable capital of wages, workday, and rate of surplus value, that the rate of profit will vary. The reason for this is that the rate of surplus value is based on the exploitation of living labour, whereas the rate of profit is based on relationship between variable (living labour) and constant capital (labour contained in means of production). As competition, market, and production change to meet the requirements for the intensification of labour exploitation – creation of more surplus value – the composition of capital will also adjust to these changes, thereby creating a universal natural law of production. With gradual changes in the organic composition of capital in the important spheres of production, there is a 'gradual growth of constant capital in relation to variable capital [which] must necessarily lead to a *gradual fall of the general rate of profit*, so long as the rate of surplus value or the intensity of exploitation of labour by capital remain the same'.[52] It is this natural law of value and production at the heart of capitalism which destroys its rational foundations because of the essential and inherent tendency of the system to stagnation, crises, and breakdown at the same time that it destroys its moral legitimation in liberalism and natural rights because of its structural alienation and economic exploitation. The law of value and logic of capital undermine the rationality and ethics of a society based on chrematistic production. Production based on the ethical values of an ancient moral economy, medieval natural law, or Marx's ethical theory of natural law and species being is made impossible by the inner logic and dynamic of a capitalist society.

The changes in the organic composition of capital or the relationship between living labour and accumulated labour in the process of production are driven by the broader requirements of factory production within a competitive market economy with its drive for greater labour exploitation and surplus value (profits). These changes have important implications for both the mass of surplus value and the rate of profit. Surplus value and the rate of profit are the key determining factors in the success or failure of industrial production. They are the driving force of capitalism which, if they decline, will negatively affect the system's economic and financial stability. The measurement of the rate of surplus value is defined as the relationship within variable capital between unpaid labour (s) and necessary labour time or wages (v): s' = s/v. On the other hand, the rate of profit is measured by the ratio between surplus value and the total amount of social surplus in both variable and constant capital: This rate of profit (p') is expressed in the formula: p' = s/C = s/c+v where C is equal to the total capital plus the surplus. Whereas the rate of surplus value is measured in terms of the ratio between surplus value and variable capital, that is, in terms of unpaid and paid labour, the rate of profit is measured by the ratio of surplus value and total capital, that is, in terms of the value of constant and variable capital. Marx begins his analysis of the tendential fall of the rate of profit with a model based on a set of assumptions that the rate of surplus value, the workday, and wages (labour power) remains constant through the process.[53] With a rate of surplus value set at a constant 100 percent, half the workday reproduces the value of variable or living labour set in wages and the second half of the workday is unpaid, surplus labour producing surplus value.

c = 50,   and v = 100,   then p' = 100/150 = 66.66%
c = 100,   and v = 100,   then p' = 100/200 = 50%
c = 200,   and v = 100,   then p' = 100/300 = 33.33%
c = 300,   and v = 100,   then p' = 100/400 = 25%
c = 400,   and v = 100,   then p' = 100/500 = 20%

As the constant capital applied in production moves from 50 to 400, as more and more science, technology, and heavy machinery are introduced into the factory to increase production and profits, the rate of profit over time falls from 66.66% to 20%.[54] As more and more total capital is being utilised, as more and more of the means of production increases, the total cost of production rises at the same time that the mass of value or unpaid labour in both variable and constant capital increases; as the organic composition of capital rises (total unpaid labour as capital) and the disproportionate ratio between variable and constant capital increases, more and more of the means of production will be employed with the same amount of variable labour. The result of these growing industrial expenditures and declining proportion of variable labour required to maintain continuous profits represents a decline in the rate of profits. The logic of capital embedded in modern production and private property for greater profit and greater application of the means of production (constant capital) results in a tendency for the rate of profits to decline. If the exploitation of labour in the factory remains constant, while the material growth of the means of production expands – greater application of the technical means of production to living labour – there will be a decline in the cost of products and ultimately a lower rate of profit. The importance of Marx's insight is that the rate of surplus value and the rate of profit can move in opposite directions; higher labour productivity, higher use of modern technology, higher levels of labour exploitation, lower prices, and a higher mass of surplus value are not incompatible with a decline in the rate of profits. More and more products with less and less labour will be sold on the market. The total mass of surplus and profits produced will rise, but the rate of profit will fall. Although the rate of exploitation and surplus value grows in a capitalist economy, the general costs of production increase and the rate at which profit is accumulated declines, resulting in serious economic crises. This means that although the number of labourers employed in a sphere of production remains the same, the total social capital (unpaid labour in both variable and constant capital) increases; proportionately over time fewer and fewer labourers are employed with more and more raw materials and industrial technology and machinery. The cost of labour decreases while the costs of production increases. Since the rate of profit is calculated on the basis of the surplus value to the total social capital in production, the rate of profit declines at the same time that the mass of both variable and constant capital increases.

Marx's conclusion is that a chrematistic economy based on profit, private property, and unpaid labour is not only unjust, but is also not rational, natural, or self-sustaining. Its breakdown is a logical inevitability and a historical possibility. The countertendencies mentioned above are measures to increase the rate of surplus value and labour exploitation which in Marx's model had remained constant to emphasise clearly this natural law of capital. Marx as the great synthesizer is integrating the classical economics of the ancients and moderns into a coherent theory of economic crisis: This law is ultimately based on the distinction between use value and exchange value (*oikonomike* and *chrematistike*) in Aristotle, the labour theory of value of Locke and Smith, and the law of the decline in the rate of profits articulated by Smith, Ricardo, and John Stuart Mill.

Marx is aware that although this tendency of capital manifests itself historically in the institutions and crises of capitalism, he treats it in the third volume of *Capital* as a conceptual paradigm or law of production; its universality and necessity remain logical features of the social system. Marx's goal was not to predict its breakdown but to anticipate its human exploitation and structural irrationality. He summarises the methodological implications of his position when he writes:

> The progressive tendency of the general rate of profit to fall is, therefore, just *an expression peculiar to the capitalist mode of production* of the

progressive development of the social productivity of labour ... But proceeding from the nature of the capitalist mode of production, it is thereby proved of logical necessity that in this development the general average rate in surplus value must express itself in a falling general rate of profit.[55]

The competitive nature of the market and production forces individual owners continuously to add to the means of production in order to increase productivity and lower the costs of raw materials, labour, capital. This, however, changes the ratio of living labour to labour materialised in constant capital or the means of production; more science, technology, and machinery, that is, materialised labour consumed in production, are set in motion in the production process in relation to existing variable capital. Even if the latter also increases, the gulf between constant and variable labour widens. As a result of increasing rationalisation of the workplace and increasing labour productivity, the relative proportion of workers to constant capital rapidly changes with workers utilising more and more of the means of production. More constant capital is being used by the same or declining amount of living labour, while less and less living labour is incorporated into commodity production.

The proportion of living labour or surplus value must decline as a portion of total capital because less and less of it is necessary to produce consumer goods. By so doing the social system generates its own internal law of capital production which drives the system unknowingly toward a falling rate of profit and eventual crisis because, unlike surplus value, the rate of profit is measured by total capital. The value of unpaid labour, which according to Marx is the only source of surplus value,[56] proportionately declines, even though the mass of surplus labour and value increases. There is a relative decrease in variable capital because of the enormous increase in the centralisation and concentration of constant capital, even though there may be a total increase in both forms of capital. Even with a fall in the rate of profit (relative decline of living labour compared to total capital), there can still be an increase in the absolute mass of both surplus value and profits since they are, in fact, the same. Both the quantity of surplus value and profits arise out of variable capital but appear differently because they are measured against variable capital and total capital, respectively.[57]

With the further concentration of capital, the productiveness of social labour, and relative decline of variable capital, the same amount of variable capital and labour power are employed with ever increasing means of production. As a result of this law of capitalist production, there is a corresponding increase in labour exploitation accompanied by the lengthening of the workday, intensification of labour, or a decline in the value of wages. According to

Marx, these are the natural laws of production: 'Hence, the same laws produce for the social capital a growing absolute mass of profit, and a falling rate of profit'.[58] This relationship between the absolute mass and relative distribution of capital is crucial for an understanding that the mass of profits can increase while their rate of increase declines. Corresponding to the capitalist production process is the capitalist accumulation process and the corresponding increase in the centralisation and concentration of capital in fewer hands which only increases these tendencies. However, this natural law only leads to further contradictions within the economic system with its increased exploitation of labour and the depreciation, underutilisation, overproduction, stagnation, and crisis of capital. There is a point reached where the existing, but tenuous, rate of profit is not sufficient to sustain continued economic development, further commitment of capital expenditures, and the high expectations of profit maximisation.

The various parts of the production system have contradictory elements which have a tendency to pull the system apart and destroy it. Its own internal logic and structure act in a fashion contradictory to its stated political and economic ideals and interests. Following the inner dynamic and natural laws of production and accumulation, Marx argues that the total mass of variable and constant capital, along with the absolute mass of profits, grows. Thus we have a tension between two diametrically opposed economic forces building within the substructure of capitalist production and accumulation. There is also a contradiction between accumulation and realisation, that is, between the enormous accumulation and growth of capital and productive capacity and the limited realisation of production in sales and consumption: Industry and the market are growing, capital is expanding and concentrating, and the mass of surplus labour is increasing, but on the other hand, there are forces at work which are undermining these very technical advances, including the rise of a surplus population, drop in prices of capital and products, too rapid growth of production and an underconsumption of commodities, labour disproportionality, unemployment, and falling wages, growing class conflict among capitalists, a faltering economy, and economic depression. This tension within the circulation and reproduction of capital between production and the accumulation of capital and consumption and the realisation of profits is only a further expression of the essential contradictions of capitalist production between advanced production and profit accumulation.[59] The underlying problems are the overproduction of capital, of the means of production and the over-exploitation of human labour beyond a certain point where neither can reproduce themselves. Accumulation cannot develop further because the economy has reached its own structural limits of production and profits. The economy cannot reproduce itself because profits cannot be made. 'The contradiction of the capitalist mode of production, however, lies precisely in its tendency towards an absolute development of the productive forces, which continually come into conflict with the specific conditions of production in which capital moves, and alone can move'.[60]

Another aspect of the economic crisis and stagnation is the resulting disproportionality of labour, production, and consumption which only tend to deepen the original problem. With the growing social productivity and exploitation of labour and the increasing constant capital, the same quantity of labour is utilised in production. As a result of this accelerated accumulation of capital, there is a disproportionality of labour that manifests itself in an expanding and productive economy with a parallel growing surplus population no longer needed to maintain industry at its increasing levels. Labour's growing productivity creates a growing unemployment and surplus population no longer needed to keep the mass industrial apparatus functioning. As capital continues to increase, labour becomes less and less necessary. There is also a disproportionality created between human needs and the means of subsistence, productivity and human life as a result of overpopulation and underemployment at the same time that there is a progressive growth in the total mass of surplus labour, value, and profits.[61] At the same time as there is an acceleration of efficiency and productivity and an increase in the absolute amount of surplus and profits, there is a corresponding increase in human exploitation and suffering. This is the fullest expression of the contradiction between use value (material production) and exchange value (profit accumulation).

Finally, there is a further imbalance in consumption between accumulation and realisation or the realisation of the sale and profits of commodity production. The irrationality and contradictions of modern capitalism are quite visible to Marx. As production increases through the application of rational technology, science, and machinery, the effects are the opposite of what is expected. Marx is not enjoining the discussion with an analysis of labour alienation at the moment but simply considering the functional rationality of the material tools or means of production. Abstracting from his theory of alienation, the rational means of production, in turn, transform the economic system into a living contradiction between the functional priorities of serving the interests of human needs or profits, community or class, democracy or plutocracy. The growth of industry and technology has produced the economic marvels of modernity at the same time that it has produced wage slavery, a surplus population, and increased human misery, along with an imbalance between expanding production and growing unemployment, production and consumption, accumulation and realisation, and economic production and economic stagnation. As Bertell Ollman has said – this is a tale of two cities.[62]

There is a contradiction between production and reproduction driving the economy as it expands at the expense of human labour. But it is labour, exploited and abused, which must be part of the economy's own reproduction and realisation. The two forces counter each other to such an extent that the original contradictions between capital and labour expressed in the declining rate of profit only intensify. And it is the underlying class foundations of the self-expansion of capital and the resulting declining rate of profit that are the essential causes of these structural contradictions of industrial capital and the inability of the modern industrial economy to form a stable, prosperous, and democratic society. With all these inner contradictions disrupting industrial production, Marx concludes with a stunning comment: 'This process would soon bring about the collapse of capitalist production if it were not for counteracting tendencies which have a continuous decentralizing effect alongside the centripetal one'.[63] The logic of the system directs the economy toward its own collapse but there are empirical and phenomenal realities which can deflect the natural laws of capital from immediately realising themselves. The economy is more resilient than the underlying systems imperatives and can counter its own inner logic. By introducing new machinery and technology into production, capital lowers the cost of production, reduces that part of variable capital that is paid labour, and increases its surplus or unpaid portion. Marx contends that these methods temporarily delay the effects of the declining rate of profit by increasing exploitation and reducing the relative number of workers employed in industry. The result is an economic crisis that produces class inequality, lower employment and a surplus population, lower consumption and capital realisation, and enormous waste in the form of the depreciation and underutilisation of capital and labour. The material capacity and conditions for production are in place to satisfy human needs, but the system stagnates because the rate of profit declines, products cannot be sold, labour is unemployed, and capital production stops. This is the immanent force or telos of capitalism.[64]

With all these internal contradictions to capital production, the final barrier to further production lies in the overproduction of labour. There are limits to the continued exploitation of labour. Reduction of paid labour and wages, increase in working time and labour intensity, and the extraction of surplus labour and value have real structural limits against which crashes the tendential fall in the rate of profit. When these limits are reached, there is nothing more that the economic system can do to extract more surplus and profits, even given the countervailing forces designed to overcome these structural and logical contradictions of capital. These absolute limits to working time and surplus value only exacerbate the continued fall in the rate of profit. At the end of this process, neither the rate of surplus value nor the absolute mass of profits could be increased. The barriers to rational production lie deep within the workings of capital (overproduction of capital and the accumulation problem), labour (limits to exploitation and surplus value), and commodity exchange (overproduction of commodities and the realisation problem). These barriers serve as limits to the ideals of possessive individualism, the rights to private property, and the production of capital and profits. They are limits to production not because there is poverty, physical suffering, and distorted human needs, but because there are immanent limits to property accumulation and profit realisation. The overproduction of capital as the overproduction of productive capacity and the means of production is the result of human greed and arrogance.

Marx throughout his life attempted to develop an ethical critique of capitalism; now he has shown how chrematistic production is contradictory to human reason. But in the end, the real contradiction of capitalism lies not only in economics, but also in ethics. Marx summarises these essential problems of capital as a contradiction within the capitalist mode of production between the productive forces of the technical achievements of capital and the social conditions and organisation of labour. However, the real contradiction is the ethical disparity within a society that has the productive capabilities to alleviate human misery but the moral imperative to achieve surplus value. 'There are not too many necessities of life produced, in proportion to the existing population. Quite the reverse. Too little is produced to decently and humanely satisfy the wants of the great mass'.[65] Production under capitalism is not subservient to the needs of human potentiality and the natural law of compassion, beneficence, and friendship, but rather is obedient to the production of property and profits. This is a distortion of human reason, ethical principles, and the creative potential of species being. It is a world turned upside down, clearly mirroring Aristotle's critique of the values of a chrematistic economy in the *Politics*.[66] This is a utilitarian life of exchange and consumer pleasure, not the good life of virtuous activity, rational deliberation, and political participation within the polis. Justice is sacrificed on the altar of property and commerce, greed and self-interest.

Natural Law of Justice and Natural Law of Value

Capital represents a clash between the ancients and the moderns, natural law and natural rights, social harmony and economic contradictions, and Aristotle and Ricardo. Although the clash manifests itself as a struggle between the bourgeoisie and the proletariat over private property and capital, Marx examines its underlying structures and logic with an emphasis on the law of value and the structural contradictions of the economy. The latter pulls in different directions as it utilises the development of science and technology in the means of production at the same time that it creates its own barriers to production in the social relations of production of a class society. The production of material goods has the distinct purpose of accumulation of class property and private power and not the satisfaction of basic human needs; human freedom is defined in terms of property and rights and not moral autonomy, self-determination, and democracy. As a result of the dysfunctional economic imperatives of the industrial system, the internal logic of capitalism has an inherent tendency to decline and stagnate. Marx could have undertaken a historical and empirical analysis of the specific causes of the economic crises in nineteenth-century England. Instead, he applies the Hegelian dialectical method to classical political economy in order to derive an analysis of capitalism's essential logic, structure, and natural law based on the contradictions implicit in its whole social system. He approaches the topic in this manner because his goal was to uncover the essential logic and structure of the system itself.

The essential question remains: Why would he take this approach and create a new dialectical science of capitalism? His ultimate goal was to frame *Capital* within the broader issues of ethics and justice.[67] Since modern capitalism was founded upon logical contradictions and natural economic laws that made a rational and self-sustaining economy based on human needs impossible, it could not become the basis for building a view of justice based on the principles of human rights and emancipation, ethical community and social praxis, natural environment and self-sustainability, economic redistribution, reciprocity and human need, and workers' democracy and producers' associations. In this broader context of Marx's whole corpus of writings, and in the context of Aristotle's theory of social justice, *Capital* begins to make more sense. Its overall meaning takes shape from its location in the depth of his writings. An economy built on the natural rights of possessive individualism, class inequality, selfishness and personal greed, the abrogation of social responsibility to the community of friends, neighbours, and citizens, and the loss of the human soul and spirit in the natural laws binding citizens together for a common purpose and ideal is unnatural and unjust. Capitalist production produces waste – wasted resources and productive capacity, wasted natural environment, wasted lives in body and spirit, wasted opportunities, and wasted species being potential.[68] According to Marx, in capitalism 'things are produced only so long as they be produced with a profit' to maintain a chrematistic and class economy.[69] The self-expansion of capital and increased productivity are the only legitimate reasons for production. Human life has no higher purpose than the production of surplus value. One can only think that at the moment he was writing this section he was thinking of the history of Western thought and the natural law tradition from the ancient and medieval to the modern times. Capitalism has squandered these traditions and in its place has created a false ideology that reduces the meaning and purpose of human existence to property acquisition and profit accumulation, market competition and chrematistic production. The natural law of love and compassion has been replaced by the natural law of value and commodity production.

Human existence has become existentially meaningless and absurd; labour is just a means for the expansion of constant capital in a society of producers; life is simply a means to increase production and exchange value as the final goals of life itself. Marx's concept of alienation has now been joined to his theory of capital production to complete his theory of social ethics. The theory of value and crisis theory – logic, structure, and contradictions of capital – are more developed variations of Marx's theory of ethics and virtue. The good and virtuous life of rational self-determination and moral autonomy within democracy becomes impossible under capitalist production. Ethics is incompatible with capital; the law of value contradicts ancient natural law; and the very possibility of a society built upon equality, freedom, reason, and justice is an ideological fiction. *Capital* was an attempt to unite the practical reason and moral will of Kant with the phenomenological reason and ethical spirit of Hegel into a comprehensive science (historical materialism and dialectics) and ethics (character and virtue) in order to realise the natural law of the 'brotherhood of humanity' and the potentialities of species being. The result is a critical science in which moral and intellectual virtue and democracy are part of a broad critique of political economy grounded in the contradictions and crises which make justice impossible to realise. Seen from this perspective, volume one (theory of value) and volume three (crisis theory) of *Capital* are fundamentally works in ethics, thereby completing for the modern industrial era the ethical ideals of Aristotle and Hegel.

The absurdity of liberalism and capitalism lies in their inability to form real communities, to nurture human creativity, human dignity, and freedom and to actualise the rational potential of humans for self-determination and self-realisation. The capitalist natural law of value production makes the realisation of the natural law of human nature and human needs impossible. The latter can only be accomplished in an economy based on producers' co-operatives and workers' democracy. Within modern liberalism ethics, freedom, and democracy are words whose content has been replaced by the values of the natural rights to private property, exploitation, and human suffering. Bourgeois liberals replace the natural law of reason and ethics with the natural law of capitalist production and the logic of surplus value. The world has been distorted by a universe of possessive individualism and class democracy – and only the mad cry out for truth. *Capital* applies the method of Hegel in order to return to Aristotle; in the end, *Capital* represents a critique of political economy and its laws of value and the contradictions of production – it is an ethical critique of a distorted economy which undermines human nature and human needs, distorts political rights and human emancipation, represses economic and political democracy, and separates humanity from nature and science. Marx's goal is to create a harmonious world which realises the potential of human self-realisation, freedom, and beneficence and releases nature and technology for human happiness.

The critics of a Marxian theory of justice are certainly correct in arguing that Marx was critical of the use of justice as a form of political moralising. Real social change would only come about by recognising the inherent flaws and rifts in the economic system that make it incompatible with communal, creative, and spiritual human needs. Simply to condemn capitalism because it did not conform to natural law would be unscientific and idealistic. But to combine ethics (natural law and justice) with science (the law of value and the contradictions of capital) would provide the foundations for true revolutionary social change. This also explains the debates about the relationship between the early philosophical Marx and the later scientific Marx. These writings were all part of a comprehensive mapping – closely paralleling Aristotle – of the natural law of justice and value that rationally demanded a new type of social existence. Due to the symmetry between Aristotle's theory of economic (particular) and political (universal) justice and Marx's theory of social justice, one can say that the dreams of the ancients have become the modern vision of the future. Critical theory is an adventurous odyssey to return to our dreams and ideals in order to change our anticipated fate. Dreams and traditions do not represent the fulfilment of our ancient memories, only the beginning of social action toward their concrete realisation; they are not only the memories of our past but the key to our future. Guiding us in the present, constructing our social reality, and transforming our social ideals, they are what make us distinctively human. And it was Marx who summarised in a comprehensive social theory the ancient and medieval traditions and made them relevant for a critique of modern political economy. Although he may not be the last word on the subject of social justice, as the 'last of the Schoolmen' and first of the modern neo-Aristotelian social theorists, Marx is certainly the beginning of any future discussion on the topic.

Notes

1 Richard Miller, 'Marx and Aristotle: A Kind of Consequentialism', *Marx and Aristotle: Nineteenth-Century German Social Theory and Classical Antiquity*, ed. George E. McCarthy (Savage, MD: Rowman & Littlefield Publishers, 1992), p. 277. In the modern age, the relationship between economics (appearances) and politics (essence) are reversed as the full development of human potentiality is reserved only for wealth creation. This is why Marx states in the *Grundrisse* that 'the childish world of antiquity appears on one side as loftier' than modernity. See Karl Marx, *Grundrisse: Foundations of the Critique of Political Economy* (New York, NY: Vintage Books, 1973), p. 488; *Karl Marx/Friedrich Engels Werke* (*MEW*), Band 42 (Berlin: Dietz Verlag, 1983), p. 396. Justice protects the individual through civil and political rights (political and human emancipation), provides the material foundations of community life through distributive justice (human needs), and also nurtures the full development of the human potential of productive species being and participatory citizens (virtue and democracy). Sidney Hook has written: 'When Marx makes explicit the values he regards as central to the life of the free citizen, what is suggested is not Christianity or the fraternity of the Enlightenment but rather the life of the freeman in the Greek *polis* – Aristotle rather than Christ or Rousseau'. Richard Hook, *Revolution, Reform, and Social Justice: Studies in the Theory and Practice of Marxism* (New York, NY: New York University, 1975), p. 83. Fulfilment of the needs for self-realisation, freedom, community, and self-determination requires a balance and harmony within society that demands the elimination of private property. This insight was something that Marx learned early through the writings of Wilhelm Weitling and Moses Hess. For a further analysis of this point, see Norman Levine, *The Tragic Deception: Marx Contra Engels* (Oxford: Clio Books, 1975), pp. 21–5.

2 This integration of science and ethics or the structural analysis of the logic and contradictions of capitalist production and moral criticism, that is, Marx's critical science as the integration of dialectics (contradictions) and critique, is the key to understanding the relationship between the early and later writings of Marx and the synthesis of his critique of alienation and political economy. See Eugene Kamenka's analysis of Marx's 'logico-ethical criticism' in *The Ethical Foundations of Marxism* (London: Routledge & Kegan Paul, 1972), pp. 70–81. Marx wrote four drafts of *Capital*, including the *Grundrisse* (1857–8), *Economic Manuscripts of 1861–1863*, *Economic Manuscripts of 1863–1865*, and *Capital* (1866–80). For a historical and theoretical overview of the second of the four drafts, see Enrique Dussel, *Towards an Unknown Marx: A Commentary on the Manuscripts of 1861–63*, trans. Yolanda Angulo, intro. Fred Mosely (London: Routledge, 2001) and 'The Four Drafts of

Capital: Towards a New Interpretation of the Dialectical Thought of Marx', online, and Fred Mosely, 'Introduction to Dussel: The Four Drafts of *Capital*', *Rethinking Marxism*, 13 (2001). A detailed examination of the first draft is found in Roman Rosdolsky, *The Making of Marx's Capital – Volume One* (London: Pluto Press, 1992).

3   George E. McCarthy, *Dialectics and Decadence: Echoes of Antiquity in Marx and Nietzsche* (Lanham, MD: Rowman & Littlefield Publishers, 1994), p. 34. Summary of Aristotle's critique of chrematistics: 'In book I, chapter 9 of the *Politics*, Aristotle outlines seven reasons why chrematistics is detrimental to the polis. For him chrematistics represents a critique of unlimited property acquisition that (1) undermines the ethical values of the political community; (2) distorts human needs into market wants; (3) turns economics into a technique for the unlimited acquisition of material goods, money making, and profits; (4) transforms household and community economics into an unnatural means of unlimited acquisition; (6) mistakes the perpetuation of the good life and concern for scarcity with a fear of death; and (7) results in the inversion of moral and intellectual virtues into the means for the acquisition of property' (p. 34).

4   *Ethics, Production, Labour Theory of Value, Contradictions, and Exploitation*:
    In his work *Marxism and Ethics* (London: Macmillan, 1969), Eugene Kamenka writes that conflict and contradictions, history and structure, are 'the marks of that inadequacy, one-sidedness, incompleteness which produces a necessary instability'. He concludes this idea by saying: 'Thus "contradictions" (practical and theoretical incoherence, conflict, instability) become for Marx moral criteria. The "contradictions" of capitalism are not mere signs of impending collapse, but also symptoms of its inhumanity, of its (historically conditioned) failure to make the free man, consciously controlling his fate, the basis of the whole system ... Marx, on the other hand, insists that ethical deficiency and logical "contradiction" are necessarily connected' (pp. 12–13). Critique (political economy) and Ethics (morals philosophy) are integrated into a critical social theory. To remove ethics from Marx's historical materialism and economic crisis theory is to abstract, objectify, and alienate his ideas (ibid.).

    Both Hans Immler and Wolfdietrich Schmied-Kowarzik, in their essays in *Natur und Marxistische Werttheorie*, hrsg. Immler and Schmied-Kowarzik (Kassel: Kasseler Philosophische Schriften, 23, 1986), make the clear connection between Marx's critique of political economy and theory of socialism with Aristotle's theories of *Chrematistik* and *Oikonomia*, respectively (pp. 35 and 50). Immler and Schmied-Kowarzik continue their analysis of Marx and Aristotle in *Marx und die Naturfrage. Ein Wissenschaftsstreit um die Kritik der politischen Ökonomie* (Kassel: Kassel University Press, 2011), pp. 163–6, 177–9, 184–9, 193–4, and 200–1. Schmied-Kowarzik views Aristotle's theory of *Oikonomia* as a moral ecology, while he sees Aristotle's *Chrematistik* as the basis for Marx's critique of political economy, value theory, and structural contradictions of the concept of capital (p. 184). *Chrematistik* joins together the *critique* of political economy (Kant), the *contradictory concept and logic* of capital (Hegel), and the theory of *value* (Locke and Ricardo) into an economic crisis theory. When speaking about Marx's theory of socialism, Schmied-Kowarzik refers to it as 'eine solidarische und ökologische Oikonomia', that is, as a communal and ecological economy with direct reference to Aristotle (pp. 16–17).

5   Karl Marx, *Capital: A Critique of Political Economy*, vol. 1: *The Process of Capitalist Pro-*

duction, trans. Samuel Moore and Edward Aveling, ed. Friedrich Engels (New York, NY: International Publishers, 1967), p. 152; *Karl Marx/Friedrich Engels Werke (MEW)*, Band 23 (Berlin: Dietz Verlag, 1962), pp. 167–8.

6 Aristotle, *Nicomachean Ethics*, trans. W.D. Ross, in *Introduction to Aristotle*, ed. Richard McKeon (New York, NY: Modern Library, 1947), book 1, chapter 7, 1098a15, p. 319.

7 Miller, 'Marx and Aristotle', p. 277.

8 Franz Petry, *Der soziale Gehalt der Marxschen Werttheorie* (Hannover: Verlag Willie Hammer, 1984, originally 1915); Ronald Meek, *Studies in the Labour Theory of Value* (New York, NY: International Publishers, 1956); Paul Mattick, *Marx and Keynes: The Limits of the Mixed Economy* (Boston, MA: Extending Horizons Books, 1969); Henryk Grossmann, *Das Akkumulations- und Zusammenbruchs-Gesetz des kapitalistischen Systems* (Frankfurt/Main: Neue Kritik Verlag, 1970, originally 1929); Isaak I. Rubin, *Essays on Marx's Theory of Value*, trans. Milos Samardzija and Fredy Perlman (Detroit, MI: Black & Red, 1972); Alfredo Medio, 'Profits and Surplus-Value: Appearance and Reality in Capitalist Production', in *A Critique of Economic Theory*, ed. E.K. Hunt and Jesse Schwartz (Baltimore, MD: Penguin, 1972), pp. 312–46; Geoffrey Pilling, 'The Law of Value in Ricardo and Marx', *Economy and Society*, 1 (1972): 281–307; Rudi Schmiede, *Grundprobleme der Marxschen Akkumulations- und Krisentheorie* (Frankfurt/Main: Athenäum Verlag, 1973); Hans-Georg Backhaus, 'Materialien zur Rekonstruktion der Marxschen Werttheorie', in *Gesellschaft Beiträge zur Marxschen Theorie 1* (Frankfurt/Main: Suhrkamp, 1974), pp. 16–177; Marc Linder, *Reification and the Consciousness of the Critics of Political Economy: Studies in the Development of Marx's Theory* of Value (Copenhagen: Rhodos International Science and Art Publishers, 1975); George E. McCarthy, *Marx' Critique of Science and Positivism: The Methodological Foundations of Political Economy* (Dordrecht: Kluwer Academic Publishers, 1988); Patrick Murray, 'Marx's "Truly Social" Labour Theory of Value: Part I, Abstract Labour in Marxian Value Theory', *Historical Materialism*, 72, 3 (December 1999): 295–318; and 'Marx's "Truly Social" Labour Theory of Value: Part II, How Is Labour that Is Under the Sway of Capital Actually Abstract', *Historical Materialism*, 7, 1 (2000): 99–136.

9 To this list of the various forms of accumulation crises should be added the information provided in Chapter 5 on environmental justice and the second contradiction of capital in nature. See James O'Connor, 'Capitalism, Nature, Socialism: A Theoretical Introduction', *Capitalism, Nature, Socialism*, 1, 1 (1988): 439 and 'On the Two Contradictions of Capitalism', *Capitalism, Nature, Socialism*, 2, 3 (1991): 107–9.

10 Marx, *Capital*, vol. 1, p. 114; *MEW* 23, p. 128.

11 Karl Marx, *Capital: A Critique of Political Economy*, vol. 3: *The Process of Capitalist Production as a Whole*, ed. Friedrich Engels (New York, NY: International Publishers, 1967), p. 250; *Karl Marx/Friedrich Engels Werke (MEW)*, Band 25 (Berlin: Dietz Verlag, 1964), p. 260.

12 Marx, *Capital*, vol. 1, pp. 36 and 85; *MEW* 23, pp. 50 and 100.

13 Ibid., vol. 1, p. 85; *MEW* 23, p. 100.

14 Ibid., vol. 1, p. 36; *MEW* 23, p. 50.

15 Ibid., vol. 1, pp. 37–8; *MEW* 23, pp. 51–2.

16 It should be noted that Marx's critique of Aristotle may not be adequate to the latter's theory of exchange. Marx is outlining the nature of market exchange in a capitalist society, while Aristotle's theory is based on grace, reciprocity, and mutual sharing among family,

friends, and neighbours within an ancient polity. The basis for exchange in the market among fellow citizens and foreigners rests upon tradition, custom, and law. Aristotle's emphasis is on questions of barter, trade, and non-profit market exchange. He develops his theory of exchange and reciprocal justice to provide the foundations for his ideal community and political governance. Marx's theory of exchange value (use value or objects of utility for others) permits him to introduce the basic features of an alienated economy and economic exploitation. Aristotle seeks to analyse the nature of oikonomic commensurability in the polity based on reciprocity, love, fair price, and economic justice, while Marx examines it based on the chrematistic market, exchange value of commodities, and profits. Thus the two social theorists are after different forms of economic activity with their theories of exchange value. Aristotle develops a theory of value, equality of exchange, and the commensurability within commodity exchange in book 5 of the *Nicomachean Ethics* and book 1 of his *Politics*. Aristotle was aware of the issues of exchange value and commensurability, but did not look into the issue of forms of value and the substance of commensurability and exchange because they were antithetical to his purposes of establishing exchange on the basis of reciprocity and grace. Marx attributed this to the existence in the Athenian polity of slavery, an underdeveloped market economy, and the lack of equality of labour power. However, it just may be that Aristotle was not interested in pursuing an analysis of a chrematistic economy and focused instead on the conditions for a moral economy and economic justice. For more on the connection between Marx and Aristotle in *Capital*, see George E. McCarthy, *Dialectics and Decadence*, pp. 3–65.

17   Marx, *Capital*, vol. 1, p. 47; MEW 23, p. 62.
18   Patricia Springborg, 'Aristotle and the Problem of Needs', *History of Political Thought*, 5, 3 (Winter 1984): 419.
19   Marx, *Capital*, vol. 1, pp. 50–1; MEW 23, p. 65.
20   Ibid., vol. 1, pp. 57–8; MEW 23, p. 72.
21   Mattick, *Marx and Keynes*, pp. 40–50.
22   Marx, *Capital*, vol. 1, p. 38; MEW 23, p. 53.
23   Ibid., vol. 1, p. 39; MEW 23, p. 54.
24   Ibid.
25   Ibid., vol. 1, p. 61; MEW 23, p. 76. The contradictions between use value and exchange value will be at the heart of Marx's analysis of commodities, money, and capital, that is, the circulation of commodities and money, commercial capitalism, and industrial capitalism. And just as commodities are divided into use value and exchange value, labour, too, is divided into useful labour and abstract labour. We will see presently that these distinctions ultimately lead to Marx's theory of economic crises in volume 3 of *Capital*.
26   Marx, *Capital*, vol. 1, p. 63; MEW 23, p. 77.
27   Ibid., vol. 1, p. 71; MEW 23, p. 85. This is the secret of the fetishism of the commodities. What at first appeared as something trivial turns out to be a complex social relationship based on the opposition between use value and exchange value, human needs and market wants, and social production (social relations) and private accumulation (profit). The secret of value, surplus value, and capital lies in the social relations of production and not in market exchange; social production, not circulation, is the key to understanding the mechanics and logic of capitalism.

28 Ibid., vol. 1, p. 67; *MEW* 23, p. 81. Marx characterises this insight into the nature of commodities and exchange as 'an epoch in the history of the development of the human race' (p. 74; *MEW* 23, p. 88). It will turn our attention away from treating commodities, exchange, money, circulation, commerce, industry, and capital as dealing with objects of production rather than social relationships of labour. To turn political economy into a fetish is to treat it as a religion created by humanity but having the status of an objective and distant reality unconnected to our species being and social praxis. The equality of commodities, the universal equivalent in money, and the foundations of economic exchange are all based on the common substance of human labour as a social action which, in turn, creates the specific form of value. Marx says that money is the phenomenal form of value and the material expression of human labour and price: 'The first chief function of money is to supply commodities with the material for the expression of their value' (p. 94; *MEW* 23, p. 109) and 'the circulation of commodities is the starting point of capital' (p. 146; *MEW* 23, p. 161).

29 Ibid., vol. 1, pp. 80–1; *MEW* 23, p. 95. Neither Smith nor Ricardo was interested in the various value-forms of commodities – commodity-form, money-form, and capital-form. Though these classical economists accepted that labour time is the measure of the magnitude and quantity of value, they focused on the examination of the magnitude of the commodity and value. That is, they were not interested in the various manifestations of labour as value in the commodity, money, and capital as various forms of commercial and industrial private property. For a critique of the transhistorical nature of labour and value by Ricardo, classical political economy, and traditional Marxists such as Paul Sweezy, Maurice Dobb, Ronald Meek, and Joan Robinson, see Moishe Postone, *Time, Labor, and Social Domination: A Reinterpretation of Marx's Critical Theory* (Cambridge: Cambridge University Press, 1996), pp. 7–10, 16–17, 27–8, and 43–83. Postone rejects this approach because it takes a transhistorical view of labour and capital that focuses on the problems of social and class relationships within a market economy and on the solutions to these problems through expanded labour, intensified production, increased industrial growth, and economic redistribution. The exploitative social relations are defined in terms of market exchange, class, and private property while the solutions focus on an expansion of the unfettered productive forces. This traditional Marxist approach ignores the historical and social nature of the commodity, value, and the organisation of production. The social relations are defined in terms of exploitation, market exchange, class structure, and property – distribution – and not in terms of value, abstract labour, and surplus value – production. In fact, value is treated as 'a category of distribution' (p. 60). In the end, revolutionary transformation will only change the method of distribution, but not the mode, organisation, and technology of production. Postone rejects this approach because industrial production is not viewed as part of the economic problem; when liberated by socialism, the unfettered mode of value production will be the basis for freedom and continued industrial production (p. 65). Postone wishes to return to Marx's critical analysis of value and exchange value, as well as the dialectic between the productive forces and social relations of production as interconnected elements of capitalism (p. 351).

30 The exchange process is a social construct based on the mutual consent of the producers to respect the rights of each private owner of commodities. This mutual consent to the

rights of private proprietors forms the basis for the social contract and exchange relations of civil society. Thus Marx treats John Locke's theory of natural rights not as an inalienable feature of the state of nature but as a historical moment in the legitimation of capitalist social relations of production and ownership. Freedom is defined only in the limited historical form of the ownership of commodities and the reciprocity of that recognition of ownership and rights (*Capital*, vol. 1, pp. 84–5; *MEW* 23, pp. 99–100). This is a far cry from Aristotle's theory of reciprocity, freedom, and justice.

31   Ibid., vol. 1, p. 154; *MEW* 23, p. 169.

32   Ibid., vol. 1, n. 1, p. 152; *MEW* 23, p. 167. Marx is critical of those who confuse the two forms of circulation: the simple circulation of commodities (C-M-C) and the capitalist circulation of money (M-C-M') which lies at the heart of his and Aristotle's criticism of market capitalism. Barter and simple or retail trade are both necessary for the existence and self-sufficiency of the household and the state. They provide the material and economic foundations of a democratic society. On the other hand, commerce or the art of making money becomes the distinguishing characteristic of the modern economy. It is this form of commercial trade that creates alienation and the destruction of the forms and institutions of social justice. See also Meek, *Studies in the Labour Theory of Value*, pp. 155–6 and Pilling, *The Crisis of Keynesian Economics: A Marxist View* (Totowa, NJ: Barnes & Noble Books, 1986), pp. 68–70.

33   Ibid., vol. 1, p. 159; *MEW* 23, p. 173. Marx does not accept the position of Étienne Bonnot de Condillac, who, in *Le Commerce et le Gouvernement* (1776), rejected the notion that there is an equal exchange of value in an exchange of commodities. He took the position that in the very act of trading, some receive higher and some receive lower value for their products. Profit is made in the act of exchange. The value of a commodity is measured not by human labour but by human wants. In exchange, values are not exchanged; wants and desires are exchanged and these are not equal. Marx uses Condillac as an example of an economist who confuses use value and exchange value.

34   Ibid, vol. 1, p. 163; *MEW* 23, pp. 177–8. To emphasise his main point, Marx writes: 'The creation of surplus value, and therefore the conversion of money into capital, can consequently be explained neither on the assumption that commodities are sold above their value nor that they are bought below their value' (p. 161; *MEW* 23, p. 175). The economist Robert Torrens continues Condillac's position by arguing that effectual demand pushes consumers to pay more for a commodity than it is worth (ibid., vol. 1, pp. 161–2; *MEW* 23, p. 176). Profits arise from the nominal increase in prices by sellers who sell products above their value. But for Marx such an economy cannot sustain itself because profits from this perspective arise only from selling and not producing.

35   Ibid., vol. 1, p. 167; *MEW* 23, p. 181. Marx defines labour power as 'the aggregate of those mental and physical capabilities existing in a human being, which he exercises whenever he produces a use value of any description'.

36   Ibid., vol. 1, p. 171; *MEW* 23, p. 185. See Meek, *Studies in the Labour Theory of Value*, pp. 183–4.

37   In a footnote in Part III, Section 2 of the first volume of *Capital* entitled 'The Production of Surplus Value', Engels introduces another distinction between work and labour. The former involves the production of use value, while the latter involves the creation of exchange value (ibid., vol. 1, n. 1, p. 186). It is here, too, that Marx summarises his theory

of surplus value, writing: 'We know that the value of each commodity is determined by the quantity of labour expended on and materialised in it, by the working-time necessary, under given social conditions for its production' (ibid.; *MEW* 23, p. 201). The total cost of a particular commodity on the market is constituted by the individual labour in each of its component parts. For example, the price of cotton equals the labour time in producing the raw material of the yarn, the spindle as a means of production, and the socially necessary labour time or expenditure of labour power of the spinner. The labour time necessary to produce various products is determined by experience and tradition. There is no increase in value in this process of producing cotton. The surplus value was derived from the original purchase of labour power in the work contract: 'The value of the product is exactly equal to the value of the capital advanced. The value so advanced has not expanded, no surplus value has been created' (p. 190; *MEW* 23, p. 205). The total cost of cotton production is a summary of the various factors of production or a summary of the values of the commodity of cotton, that is, the value of yarn, spindle, and spinning.

38 Ibid., vol. 1, p. 193; *MEW* 23, p. 208.
39 Ibid., vol. 1, p. 185; *MEW* 23, p. 200.
40 Ibid., vol. 1, p. 173; *MEW* 23, p. 187.
41 Ibid., vol. 1, p. 194; *MEW* 23, p. 208. Marx writes that the production of surplus value is 'a process which is entirely confined to the sphere of production' (p. 195; *MEW* 23, p. 209). The second half of the first volume of *Capital* represents a historical introduction to the social form of production of abstract or average labour and surplus value. Their production requires a developed form of production and capital (means of production and labour power) that presupposes the historical conditions of capital: existence of free labour, private property, class, commerce, social labour, specialisation and the division of labour, labour co-operation, exploitation and wage slavery, extraction of surplus value, industry, machinery, and modern technology, division between town and country (industry and agriculture), primitive accumulation and the enclosures, and the modern state (taxes, fiscal policy, banking, debt financing, colonialism, protection of international trade, and the military).
42 *Marx's Theory of Equivalent Exchange and Labour Theory of Value*: Both Robert Tucker, *The Marxian Revolutionary Idea* (New York, NY: W.W. Norton & Company, 1969) and Allen Wood, 'The Marxian Critique of Justice', *Marx, Justice and History: Philosophy & Public Affairs Reader*, ed. M. Cohen (Princeton, NJ: Princeton University Press, 1980): 3–41 and *Karl Marx* (Boston, MA: Routledge & Kegan Paul, 1981) have argued, as we have already seen, that Marx does not have a theory of legal rights or a theory of distributive justice. Tucker and Wood viewed the wage contract as a just distribution within capitalism based on the legal principle of equivalency between the amount of labour provided and the amount of wages offered – this is the basis for a fair exchange: An equal amount of labour time in the form of work is exchanged for an equal amount of labour time in the form of wages. This is the position of Adam Smith. Tucker and Wood contend that this is the only form of justice, parallel to the theory of natural rights, which Marx rejects in his critique of the exploitation and oppression of wage labour in the workplace. Marx, on the other hand, interprets the notion of bourgeois fair wages in volume 1 of *Capital* as a 'trick' or mystification which only appears to be based on the equivalency of labour and wages

but, in fact, is essentially based on the purchase of labour power, and not labour itself. See Henryk Grossmann, 'Marx, Classical Political Economy and the Problem of Dynamics', trans. Peter Burgess, *Capital and Class*, 2 (Summer 1977): 32–55 and 3 (Autumn 1977): 67–99 and Geoff Pilling, 'Marx's Critique of Classical Economics', in *Marx's Capital: Philosophy and Political Economy* (London: Routledge & Kegan Paul, 1980). According to Grossmann, Adam Smith and David Ricardo were aware of the problem in their law of value and equal exchange but could not explain any discrepancies within the limits of their theory. For Marx, an equal exchange of commodities between labour and wages would not permit the accumulation of surplus and profits.

Even by the standards of liberalism, receiving the full value of labour (actual physical work) while only paying for labour power (replenishment of labour capacity) results in a robbery of the working class by the bourgeoisie. Full equivalency within liberal justice would entail a wage system in which workers are paid for both necessary (labour power) and surplus labour (actual labour). Note that this principle of distributive justice as equivalency and fair wage was the position taken by Marx in his analysis of the first stage of socialist development in his *Critique of the Gotha Program* (1875). In this work he distinguishes between equivalent exchange and just distribution as commodity exchange (labour power exploitation) and its ideal form of total labour exchange, respectively. Property and factories would be socialised but the wage contract would remain liberal in the earliest stage of social revolution with the following difference: There would be an equal and fair exchange between wages and the actual labour expended during the workday. The trick of substituting an exchange between wages and labour power or partial labour would be unacceptable. Although he rejects the appearances of liberal justice in the form of rights and distribution, Marx does develop his own modern version of justice based on the principles of natural law and social justice of the ancient Greeks. The Tucker-Wood thesis has reduced justice to the values of liberalism – rights and distribution – and then proceeded to argue that Marx does not have a theory of justice. An implication of their argument is that Marx is not a liberal, does not hold liberal values of rights (Locke) and distribution (Smith), and, therefore, does not have a theory of justice. They have failed to see that both liberalism and socialism have different theories of justice based on the context of different intellectual traditions of natural rights and natural law, possessive individualism and species being, and the self-interested person and the 'moral man'. For a further critique of the Tucker-Wood thesis, see the critical responses of Ziyad Husami, 'Marx on Distributive Justice', *Marx, Justice and History: Philosophy & Public Affairs Reader*, pp. 42–79; Robert Sweet, *Marx, Morality and the Virtue of Beneficence* (Lanham, MD: University Press of America, 2002), pp. 55–102; Nancy Holmstrom, 'Exploitation', *Canadian Journal of Philosophy*, 7, 2, (June 1977): 353–69; and Richard Arneson, 'What's Wrong with Exploitation?', *Ethics* (January 1981): 202–27.

43 *Distinguishing a Theory of Value from a Theory of Price – the Mystification and Ideology of Production*: At the very beginning of the third volume of *Capital* Marx defines the value of a commodity with the formula: $c = c+v+s$ (p. 25; *MEW* 25, p. 34). The amount of surplus value is determined by the surplus labour time over the necessary labour time to reproduce labour power (wages); the amount of profit is determined by the surplus produced by the total amount of capital, that is, the surplus in variable and

constant capital. The production of surplus value is directly influenced by the length of the workday, intensity of labour, and wages; extending the workday, increasing work intensity, or lowering wages increases surplus value. The production of profit is directly influenced by the intensification of the productivity of work affected by the technical means of production.

On the other hand, the classical economists from Smith to Ricardo measured profit by the total cost-price of constant and variable capital, that is, by the costs of the material and labour conditions of production: C = k+s. K is equal to the cost-price or quantity of constant and variable capital. What is missing is the surplus labour contained in variable capital (*Capital*, vol. 3, p. 165; *MEW* 25, p. 175). Here the value or cost of a commodity equals the cost-price of the materials and the conditions of production. Thus C = c+v+s is now translated into C = k+s.

Marx's theory of surplus value and profits is quite different from the classical political economist's view of cost, price, and profits. As Marx says: The commodity value equals the cost price plus surplus value. This distinction is important for Marx because in the final determination of the costs of production to the capitalist and the 'value' of a commodity, the classical economists have defined value in terms of the market prices and not in terms of labour or production. The central importance of the social relations of production and the forced extraction of surplus labour is lost and with it the alienation and exploitation of labour. The economists do not make a distinction between constant and variable capital, nor do they understand the creation of value by labour power, nor do they appreciate the creation of surplus value by unpaid labour. They instead have defined the total costs of production and then added a profit generated by an arbitrary payment over and above these production costs. Thus profit is the result of a surplus price created in circulation reflecting the difference between the cost price of a commodity and its sale price; profit is determined by gains above cost price of labour and materials and not by the distinction between paid and unpaid labour. For Marx a commodity sold at its value on the market makes a profit because part of the cost of a commodity contains surplus value. With a 100 percent rate of surplus value, the true price of a commodity sold would contain ½ cost-price (actual market sale price for the economist) and ½ unpaid, surplus labour (not taken into account by economists); the actual price for the economists is that paid only for the variable capital or labour power and does not contain any surplus labour. They do not recognise the issue of the creation of surplus value in production. 'The cost price of a commodity refers only to the quantity of paid labour contained in it, while its value refers to the paid and unpaid labour contained in it. The price of production [p = kp or price equals cost price plus profit] refers to the sum of the paid labour plus a certain quantity of unpaid labour determined for any particular sphere of production by conditions over which it has no control' (p. 165; *MEW* 25, p. 175).

A commodity may be sold below its value and still make a profit because there is a surplus value hidden in its cost price (p. 37; *MEW* 25, p. 47). The capitalist treats this surplus value as a circulation surplus or a profit added on to the initial production costs or cost price, whereas Marx sees it as embedded in the very nature of a commodity. '[T]he excess value, or the surplus value, realised in the sale of a commodity appears to the capitalist as an excess of its selling price over its value, instead of an excess of its value over its cost price' (p. 38; *MEW* 25, p. 48). Here Marx is very playful with the concept of 'value' to make his main point. In the first part of the sentence, it means 'production cost', while in the second part it refers to 'labour'. Profit then is the excess of the sales price over the cost price. Consumers pay more for various commodities than the total of the various elements in their production costs: profits are equal to the production costs of a product plus an added amount in the sale price. Thomas Malthus and Robert Torrens have argued that profits cannot be created in production but are the result of the circulation and sale of commodities above their costs; these costs of production represent the actual value of commodities.

Viewing profits as arising from market circulation rather than industrial production, that is, as arising from the difference between selling price over cost price, deflects attention away from the true nature of private property as capital – alienation, repression, and exploitation – that is, the structures and social relations of production (see endnote 41). Once the concepts of labour power, surplus labour time, surplus value, capital, and the rates of surplus value and profits are understood in relation to the production process, it is no longer possible to provide an ethical justification or foundation for capitalism. Ethics collapses in the face of capital. Therefore, Marx's *Capital* is not just a crisis theory of economics, but a crisis theory of ethics.

Profit is determined by the costs and expenditure of capital and not by the expenditures of labour. This confusion of capital and labour, price and value (actual costs in labour) lies at the heart of modern economic theory (p. 26; *MEW* 25, p. 34): As Marx expresses it – cost price equals the cost of constant capital and labour, whereas the true value of a commodity is equal to the cost of constant capital, labour, and unpaid surplus labour. Because a central element of the final cost is surplus value, this is not incorporated into the final calculations of the production costs of capital investment in industry. The issues of labour power, surplus labour, labour exploitation, and surplus value are lost (pp. 32 and 42; *MEW* 25, pp. 42 and 52) and with them the foundations of an ethical natural law. Marx concludes that 'the cost price assumes the false appearance of a category of value production itself' (p. 28; *MEW* 25, p. 37). Further on in his analysis he writes: 'The profit, such as it is represented here, is thus the same as surplus value, only in a mystified form that is nonetheless a necessary outgrowth of the capitalist mode of production' (p. 36; *MEW* 25, p. 46). Profit is the surface phenomenon manifesting the underlying value production connecting the social relations of production to the means of production. Labour and value are absorbed (and repressed) into constant capital. Cost is calculated on the basis of elements of consumed capital in the forms of the means of production and subsistence wages. Thus he sees the classical economists as dealing with the surface phenomena or appearances of economic reality and not the deeper mysteries and structures of production and labour. The total cost of production must include the expended constant capital in the value of the wear and tear of consumed technology, machinery, and buildings, the value of labour power absorbed by a commodity, and the surplus value included in each commodity. That is, the true total cost includes the capital consumed in production: $C = c+v+s$. See, *Capital*, vol. 3, pp. 25–40; *MEW* 25, pp. 33–50.

Unpaid, surplus labour is the hidden secret to the mystery of surplus value and the organic composition of capital and is the hidden secret to unlocking the mystery of the

ECONOMIC JUSTICE   351

relationship between the rate of surplus value and the rate of profit, and the tendency of the latter to fall over time. Capital of equal amounts but with different combinations and proportions of variable to constant capital from simple commodity production to the application of advanced technology and machinery in production, that is, capital with different organic compositions, produces unequal profits and rates of profits. Because of technology, there is less labour applied in the creation of each commodity and, thus, less surplus is produced; however, the economy compensates for this by a massive increase in the production of goods, a decline in the costs and prices of commodities, and an increase in the total amount of surplus realised. The rate of profit reaches the objective limits of exploitation, that is, surplus extraction becomes more and more difficult. On the issue of the tendential fall in the rate of profit and its reception by Marx and John Maynard Keynes, see Pilling, *The Crisis of Keynesian Economics*, pp. 78–84. The accumulation and expansion of modern technology and industry is irrational because increased productivity does not result in greater material wealth for the community and access to consumer goods, but, on the contrary, leads to a rise in the organic composition of capital, a corresponding increase in the rate and mass of surplus value, and eventually to economic stagnation. Greater production leads to stagnation and crises because of the social nature of production.

44 Marx, *Capital*, vol. 1, pp. 176, 196 and 356; MEW 23, pp. 189–90, 210 and 377.
45 Religion and capitalism are both mystical illusions that unnaturally govern human activity to the detriment of human freedom. The 'despotism of capital' is the ethical and political result of the 'natural law of capitalist production' (ibid., vol. 1, p. 640; MEW 23, pp. 669–70).
46 Ibid., vol. 1, p. 621; MEW 23, p. 649.
47 Marx refers to the natural or general law of production a number of times in *Capital*, including vol. 1, p. 640; MEW 23, p. 669; and *Capital*, vol. 3, pp. 189, 222, 225, 232, 239, 244, 245 and 250; MEW 25, pp. 199, 232, 235, 242, 249, 254, 255 and 260.
48 Marx, *Capital*, vol. 3, pp. 32, 38–9, 42, 44–7, 153, 157–70 and 173–99; MEW 25, pp. 42, 48, 52, 54–7, 162, 167–80 and 182–209; and the *Grundrisse*, pp. 751–8; MEW 42, pp. 644–50. Marx continues to be critical of the ideology of modern economics: 'The transformation of values into prices of production serves to obscure the basis for determining value itself' (*Capital*, vol. 3, p. 168; MEW 25, pp. 177–8). The origins of both surplus value and profit are lost in the process since the capitalist does not see the complete picture of value creation: '[I]t is natural that the conception of value should elude the capitalist at this juncture, for he does not see the total labour put into the commodity, but only that portion of the total labour for which he has paid in the shape of the means of production, be they living or not, so that his profit appears to him as something outside the immanent value of the commodity' (ibid.; MEW 25, p. 178). The price of production is expressed as a fetishism of production, that is, it is simply the general cost price of production plus an external market surplus (profit). On this issue of the confused relationship between value and price in Smith and Ricardo, see Medio, 'Profits and Surplus-Value', pp. 317–22. With the focus of classical economics on money, circulation, prices, and profits, there is a fetishism of economic categories in which the alienation and exploitation of total social production are lost. Karl Korsch in *Karl Marx* (New York, NY: Russell & Russell, 1963) characterised this distinction between value and price as the distinction between *Wertgesetz* (law of value) and *Wertrechnung* (value calculation of commodity prices) in the first and third volumes

of *Capital* as resulting in 'a catastrophic misunderstanding of Marx's economic theory' which was never developed to calculate the prices of commodities or the 'transformation of the "values" of the commodities into "production prices" by the intermediary concept of an "average rate of profit" ...' (p. 153). The law of value was rather an attempt to develop 'the economic law of motion of modern society' and the 'law of historical development' (p. 154). Value is the concept or essence of capitalism which is not an abstract summary or mechanical universal of individual parts but its historical structure and driving force. There is a parallel here between Hegel's phenomenological analysis of self-consciousness and Marx's theory of commodities, capital, and value. Both theorists were searching for the universal essence (logic) of humanity in history. The world is not constructed of mere things, objects, and prices, but of social relationships based on the organisation and division of labour and private property. And it is these social relationships specific to capitalist production which have the objective expression and appearance of exchange value, but have been transformed by the classical economists into fetishised relationships between things or commodities – prices, wages, property, and profits. These economic categories are only disguised illusions of actual social relationships of production. This point is also emphasised, along with a critique of Ronald Meek's utilitarian theory of value (influenced by Vilfredo Pareto and Eugen Böhm Bawerk), by Pilling in 'The Law of Value in Ricardo and Marx', pp. 283–6.

49 The tendential fall in the rate of profit is articulated in volume 3 of *Capital* but also appears in 1857–8 in the *Grundrisse*, pp. 747–50; *MEW* 42, pp. 639–43; and ten years later in Chapter 25 of the first volume of *Capital* (1867). In a recent book by Amy Wendling, *Marx on Technology and Alienation* (Basingstoke: Palgrave Macmillan, 2009), she contends that Marx's theory of production decline, economic crisis, and breakdown in volume 3 was influenced by the developments in thermodynamics, its second law of entropy, irreversible time and heat flow, and the heat loss of the universe and the steam engine. The universe by losing heat is on 'an irreversible system of decline and destruction'. She likens capitalism to a poorly designed steam engine that to be effective must run at top speed which will likely end in its destruction (pp. 90–2). The end of capitalism is already predicated in its very structures of production based upon value and labour power. Wendling also argues that there is no place for ethics in this system which deteriorates because of its own universal laws of social thermodynamics. 'The laws of thermodynamics will themselves prepare and bring about any necessary social and political transformation, largely as epiphenomena to energy movements' (p. 92). For more on these issues, see Fred Moseley's edited works, including *Marx's Method in Capital: A Reexamination* (Atlantic Highlands, NJ: Humanities Press, 1993), *New Investigations of Marx's Method*, ed. with Martha Campbell (Atlantic Highlands, NJ: Humanities Press, 1997), *Marx's Theory of Money: Modern Appraisals* (Basingstoke: Palgrave Macmillan, 2005), his essay 'Critique of Heinrich: Marx Did Not Abandon the Logical Structure', *Monthly Review* (1 December 2013), and *Marx's Capital and Hegel's Logic: A Reexamination*, ed. with Tony Smith (Leiden: Brill, 2014). See also Duncan Foley, *Understanding Capital: Marx's Economic Theory* (Cambridge, MA: Harvard University Press, 1986) and Michael Roberts and Guglielmo Carchedi, 'A Critique of Heinrich's, "Crisis Theory, the Law of the Tendency of the Profit Rate to Fall, and Marx's Studies in the 1870s"', *Monthly Review* (1 December 2013); and Andrew Kliman, *Reclaiming*

Marx's 'Capital': A Refutation of the Myth of Inconsistency (Lanham, MD: Lexington Books, 2006). The law of the tendential fall in the rate of profit has had a number of critics such as Karl Kautsky, Vladimir Lenin, Nikolai Bukharin, Rosa Luxemburg, Rudolf Hilferding, David Harvey, and Michael Heinrich; on the other hand, the defenders of this law have included Henryk Grossmann, Paul Mattick, Fred Moseley, and Michael Roberts.

50   Marx, *Capital*, vol. 3, pp. 232–40 and 246; *MEW* 25, pp. 242–50 and 256. Another element mentioned by Marx, but not stressed in his social ecology, is the destruction of nature and the depletion of natural resources which affect the economy by increasing the costs of constant capital, lowering the rate of profit, and increasing the possibilities of economic crises. The tendency of the economic system to a decline in the rate of profit and the movement toward economic crisis is counterbalanced by other structural tendencies. These counteracting tendencies include: increasing intensity of exploitation (pp. 232–5; *MEW* 25, pp. 242–5); depression of wages below the value of labour power (p. 235; *MEW* 25, p. 245); relative overpopulation (pp. 236–7; *MEW* 25, pp. 246–7); foreign trade (pp. 237–40; *MEW* 25, pp. 247–50); and increase of stock capital (p. 240; *MEW* 25, p. 250). Forces that counteract the fall in the rate of profit are also the bases for further economic crises: rise in productivity, rise in rate of surplus value, lowering of the costs of constant and variable capital, mass unemployment as labour is replaced by machinery, quickening of labour turnover (p. 143; *MEW* 25, p. 152), material depreciation of constant capital, and economic expansion into new markets (colonialism and militarism). But these countertendencies of capitalism cannot transcend the laws of value production; they may weaken and delay their initial effects but cannot repress them completely since these economic natural laws are logical and structural laws and not merely temporary, historical forms.

Marx's anticipation of the crisis and breakdown of capitalism is based on his critique of the logic and structures of political economy and not on an explanatory/predictive analysis by positivistic science. These two distinct forms of science based on the logic of Hegel and Comte, respectively, have framed the modern debate over the nature of science itself. Marx writes in *The Communist Manifesto* in *Marx and Engels: Basic Writings on Politics and Philosophy*, ed. Lewis Feuer (Garden City, NY: Anchor Books, 1959): 'What the bourgeoisie, therefore, produces above all, is its own gravediggers. Its fall and the victory of the proletariat are equally inevitable' (p. 20); *Karl Marx/Friedrich Engels Werke* (*MEW*), Band 4 (Berlin: Dietz Verlag, 1977), p. 474. Marx uses terms such as necessary and inevitable but their meaning should be understood in the context of Hegel and not Comte, dialectical and historical science, not positivism.

Dialectics was developed out of the implications of Kant's constitution theory of knowledge and morality, that is, objective reality and moral principles and actions are constructs of the human mind. Hegel applied these insights to his study of consciousness, history, society, and cultural development. Marx, in turn, uses dialectics to further articulate at the level of philosophy the interactions among consciousness, work, nature, and society and at the level of political economy the structural features of production, market exchange, distribution, society, and culture. His theory of economic crises, therefore, represents a continued development of the functional and logical contradictions of the structures of capitalist economy and of the contradictions between the ideals (political legitimation) and the structural reality of the social system (ethics and immanent critique). Rather than viewing political economy as a distinct and autonomous reality, Marx was the first social theorist to view society as a totality as he followed the interactions and incompatibilities among its component parts.

Marx discusses his use of the dialectical method in the third volume of *Capital* on pages 43–5, 48, 51, 142–3, 153, 167–70, 189–91, 195, 204, 208–13, 225 and 244–64; *MEW* 25, pp. 53–5, 57–8, 61, 151–2, 162–3, 176–7, 199–201, 205–6, 214, 218–23, 235 and 254–74. Rejecting the economics of the classical economists, Marx writes: 'It would seem, therefore, that here the theory of value is incompatible with the actual process, incompatible with the real phenomena of production, and that for this reason any attempt to understand phenomena should be given up' (p. 153; *MEW* 25, p. 162). His goal is not to explain the surface phenomena of supply and demand, along with price and profit determination of a competitive market economy, but to understand the essential elements (logic and history) of the organisation of production and circulation and their relation to the laws of value and capital. This distinction between essence and appearance is a radicalisation by Hegel of Kant's theory of representations, phenomena, and appearances. Marx incorporates it into his analysis of the production of value and capital within the historical mode of production of capitalism.

Not understanding the relationship between constant and variable capital in the production process, the bourgeois economists are unable to understand either the rate of surplus value or the rate of profit. Variable capital thus should include both wages and surplus value. However, when viewed only from the perspective of costs, the concept of surplus value disappears (p. 147; *MEW* 25, pp. 156–7). Also differences in the quantity of living labour initiated by variable capital affects the organic composition of capital and the different proportions of capital and the different amounts of variable capital, thereby affecting the quantity of surplus labour, value, and profits (p. 149; *MEW* 25, p. 158). As Marx says: 'The sole source of surplus value is living labour' (ibid.; *MEW* 25, p. 158). Later in Chapter 13, 'The Law as Such', Marx writes: '[U]p to the present political economy has been running in circles around the distinction between constant and variable capital, but has never known how to define it accurately; that it has never separated surplus value from profit, and never even considered profit in its pure form ...' (p. 213; *MEW* 25, p. 223). Marx goes on to say that these same economists also have not considered the issue of the organic composition of capital or the general formula of the rate of profit (p. 214; *MEW* 25, p. 224). For a further analysis of Ricardo and Smith, see Karl Marx, 'Ricardo's and Adam Smith's Theory of Cost Price', pp. 161–235; *MEW* 26, Teil 2, pp. 158–234, 'Ricardo's Theory of Surplus Value', pp. 395–417; *MEW* 26, Teil 2, pp. 397–419, and 'Ricardo's Theory of Accumulation and Critique of It', pp. 492–535; *MEW* 26, Teil 2, pp. 492–535 in *Theories of Surplus Value*, Part II (Moscow: Progress Publishers, 1968); *Karl Marx/Friedrich Engels Werke* (*MEW*), Band 26, Teil 2 (Berlin: Dietz Verlag, 1967). See also George E. McCarthy, 'Metaethics and the Critique of Classical Political Economy: Marx and Ricardo', in *Marx and the Ancients: Classical Ethics, Social Justice, and Nineteenth-Century Political Economy* (Savage, MD: Rowman & Littlefield Publishers, 1990), pp. 209–46.

51   Marx, *Capital*, vol. 3, p. 197; *MEW* 25, p. 207.
52   Ibid., vol. 3, p. 212; *MEW* 25, p. 222.
53   For an examination of the relationship between Marx's theory of value and crisis theory,

see Grossmann, *Das Akkumulations- und Zusammenbruche-Gesetz des kapitalistischen Systems*; Meek, *Studies in the Labour Theory of Value*; Mattick, *Marx and Keynes*; Rubin, *Essays on Marx's Theory of Value*; Christoph Deutschmann, *Der linke Keynesianismus* (Frankfurt/Main: Athenäum Verlag, 1973); and Schmiede, *Grundprobleme der Marxistischen Akkumulations- und Krisentheorie*.

54 Marx, *Capital*, vol. 3, p. 211; *MEW* 25, p. 221.
55 Ibid., vol. 3, p. 213; *MEW* 25, p. 223.
56 Ibid, vol. 3, pp. 42, 47, 149 and 171; *MEW* 25, pp. 52, 57, 158–9 and 181. This argument is also developed in the *Grundrisse* where Marx recognises the complicated relationship between surplus value and the means of production. As production expands there is an increasing total amount of surplus and profits created, but there is also a declining rate of exploitation of surplus because the technical factors in production are increasing out of proportion to the use of variable capital. As this process begins, technology replaces labour and makes it more efficient and productive through increased exploitation. But there are technical and human limits to this process of production. Constant capital eventually develops well out of proportion to variable capital which is the only source of surplus value; there are internal structural barriers to the extraction of surplus and, thus, internal structural limits to capital itself. 'Its [Capital's] surplus value rises, but in an ever smaller relation to the development of the productive force. Thus the more developed capital already is, the more surplus labour it has created, the more terribly must it develop the productive force in order to realise itself in only smaller proportion, i.e. to add surplus value ... The self-realisation of capital becomes more difficult to the extent that it has already been realised' (p. 340; *MEW* 42, pp. 258–9). More and more total profit is produced, but with a decline in the rate at which it is acquired. Eventually a barrier to continued production and surplus extraction is reached at which time production is curtailed and stagnation begins. The maximisation of profit and the competition of capital result in a declining rate of profit because of a rise in the organic composition of capital – too much science, technology, and production at the expense of too little labour, surplus value, and employment. The limits of exploitation are approached as the limits to the reduction of necessary labour to bare subsistence are themselves reached; also the amount of living and surplus labour capable of producing profits also begins to be exhausted by the introduction of new technology. This results in the narrowing, intensification, and displacement of work by capital. The means of production undermine social production itself; this is the contradiction of capital and the law of value that reveals itself in volume 3 of *Capital*. The system is irrational, erratic, and immoral. Hiding behind the rationality of Enlightenment science, technology, and industry does not aid in the development of species being. Being a further form of structural and systems alienation, it undermines the potential for social justice.
57 Ibid., vol. 3, pp. 216–18; *MEW* 25, pp. 226–8. Marx provides an example comparing the rates of surplus value and profit in an advanced capitalist economy and an underdeveloped economy. Both begin with a total capital of 100 but because of the stage of each economy, there are different organic compositions of capital. He argues that if the rate of surplus value in the advanced economy is 100% (half the workday is for wages and half for surplus), the constant capital is 80c, and the variable capital is 20v (or 20 labourers).

This formula is stated as: 80c+20v+20s=120. In the developing country the formula is: 20c+80v+40s=140 with a reversal of the ratio of constant to variable capital. Now there are 80 labourers working two-thirds of a day for wages and one-third for capitalist surplus with only a 50% rate of surplus value. Marx concludes that the rate of profit for the developed country is 20%, while the developing country maintains a 40% rate of profit. Capital of the same magnitude, with different proportions of capital, produces different rates of profit. The advanced society produces more surplus and profits, but the rate of profit declines because there has been a 'relative decline of appropriated surplus labour compared to the mass of materialised labour set in motion by living labour – the ratio between variable and constant capital' (p. 216; *MEW* 25, p. 226). This occurs even when the absolute mass of living labour and surplus value is the same or increases. The decline in the rate of profit is due to a relative change in the proportion of the composition of capital, not to an absolute change in the size or mass of labour and surplus (p. 217; *MEW* 25, p. 227). This results in the production of more and more use value and consumer goods, and even a temporary condition of higher wages for the workers and overpopulation. According to Marx, 'profit is only the surplus value calculated in relation to total capital' (ibid.; *MEW* 25, p. 227).

58   Ibid, vol. 3, p. 219; *MEW* 25, p. 229.

59   Ibid., vol. 3, p. 245; *MEW* 25, p. 255. Marx writes: 'But the more productiveness develops, the more it finds itself at variance with the narrow basis on which the conditions of consumption rest'. With the self-expansion of capital and the means of production, there is a corresponding relative decline in labour power and the ability to consume and realise what has been produced. With the over-production of capital, there is an underconsumption of consumer goods. At the same time there is an excess of capital and productive capacity, there is a growing surplus population which is unable to absorb the expanding production of capital. All these internal contradictions are only exacerbating the tendential fall in the rate of profit, since to compensate industry must expand to increase surplus and profits, but this means further increasing the productive forces and expanding the economy which, in turn, only exacerbates the initial set of contradictions (pp. 244–5; *MEW* 25, pp. 254–5). After outlining the contradictions between the surplus value and profit and the rate of surplus value and constant capital, increasing production and intensifying labour exploitation, material wealth and class poverty, over-production of capital and surplus population, etc., Marx concludes this idea with the comment: '[I]t would at the same time intensify the contradictions between the conditions under which this surplus value is produced and under which it is realised' (ibid.; *MEW* 25, p. 255). Marx is aware that the initial conditions for creating surplus and profits also require their realisation in the market and consumption. There is a difference between accumulation (exploitation) and realisation (consumption). As industry, production, and competition expand, concentrate, and centralise, the conditions for distribution and consumption contract; there is a contradiction between Enlightenment reason and class, productive forces and the social relations of production and consumption.

In the twentieth century, John Maynard Keynes, as Ricardo and Smith before him, will only treat the apparent symptoms of the conflict between accumulation and realisation, production and consumption, and production and sale as the basis of his demand-side economics. It is the relative imbalance between these dualisms that characterised twentieth-century economic problems. Keynes thought that through state interventionism and the reestablishment of a balance between these conflicting poles of the economy, harmony could be reestablished. But the essential nature of surplus labour, surplus value, and the rates of surplus value and profit is ignored. Overproduction of commodities represents the effects of the deeper contradictions between labour and capital – the overproduction of capital – that cannot be resolved by state interventionism and subsidisation of the economy: '[A] rift must continually ensue between the limited dimension of consumption under capitalism and a production which forever tends to exceed this immanent barrier. Furthermore, capital consists of commodities, and therefore over-production of capital implies over-production of commodities' (p. 256; MEW 25, p. 267). It is not the lack of effective demand that is the real problem, but the lack of effective capital and profits. The metabolic rift within nature has been joined by the economic rift within capitalist production. The real problem is 'the fact that it is a matter of expanding the value of the capital, not consuming it' (p. 257; MEW 25, p. 268). Production not consumption, capital not sale, value not price, accumulation not realisation – these are the real problems and barriers to the further development of capitalism. The conclusion Marx reaches is summarised as his law and logic of capital: 'Thus, the same development of the social productiveness of labour expresses itself with the progress of capitalist production on the one hand in a tendency of the rate of profit to fall progressively and, on the other, in a progressive growth of the absolute mass of the appropriated surplus value, or profit; so that on the whole a relative decrease of variable capital and profit is accompanied by an absolute increase of both' (p. 223; MEW 25, p. 233).

The overproduction of commodities is simply the phenomenal form or appearance of the overproduction of capital, that is, a problem of value production and capital accumulation within the economy. On this issue, Mattick in *Marx and Keynes* has written: 'Thus, the actual glut on the commodity market must be caused by the fact that labour is not productive enough to satisfy the profit needs of capital accumulation ... Capitalist accumulation is not a realisation problem. It is that too, of course, but the realisation derives from the fact that capitalist production is a value-expansion process' (p. 79). Further on in his analysis, Mattick says: 'The real problem of capitalism is a shortage, not an abundance of surplus value' (p. 82). Economic production for human needs is incompatible with an economic system based on surplus value, chrematistic profit accumulation, and capitalist production. This inherent systems crisis of capitalism is thus a result of the overproduction of constant capital or the means of production – accumulation – within the constraints of definite social relations of production – realisation – based on capital and class resulting in a decline in the rate of profit, underconsumption, unemployment, and potential breakdown of the whole social system.

60   Marx, *Capital*, vol. 3, p. 257; MEW 25, p. 268. Mattick has summarised Marx's argument: 'The overproduction of capital with its declining profitability, lack of investments, overproduction of commodities and growing unemployment, all predicted by Marx, was the undeniable reality and the obvious cause of the political upheavals of the time' (*Marx and Keynes*, p. 26). But Mattick is also aware that Marx's model was not to be used as

a basis of economic prediction. The abstract and logical model anticipates the possibility of a crisis but only empirical research of the actual production process could justify the prediction (pp. 61, 63, 91, 98–9 and 104–8). Thus the 'predictions' are only logical consequences and general historical tendencies. Mattick quotes from the second volume of *Theories of Surplus-Value* to make his point. Marx's economic crisis theory is a theoretical and historical natural law, but not an empirical law. The labour theory of value, social production, and the contradictions between use value and needs (oikonomics) and exchange value and productive capital (chrematistics) form the foundation of Marx's theory of the overproduction of the means of production, declining realisation of surplus value, falling rate of profit (pp. 57–72), and economic crises (pp. 83–95). This methodological approach makes sense only when it is tied to Marx's theory of social justice and ethical natural law, rather than to social science and positivism. This critique of positivism in Marx is also taken up by Pilling in his essay 'The Law of Value in Ricardo and Marx' where he rejects the neo-Marxist positivism, empiricism, and mechanical materialism (predictive science) of Ernst Mandel, Paul Sweezy, and Maurice Dobb (p. 289). According to Pilling, Marx's theory of the falling rate of profits is not an attempt to predict the future since its goal is to develop a general law of logical tendency and historical countertendency (p. 290). The danger here is the methodological and theoretical reduction and return of Marx to Ricardo and the latter's theory of value and exploitation which provided the economic foundations of utopian or Ricardian socialism. Pilling is less interested in questions of the exploitation of the working class and more in questions of the contradictions between accumulation and realisation, production and the social relations of production (p. 301). The issues of labour exploitation (ethics) and structural contradictions (science) are part of the larger picture of social justice and are not antithetical to each other. The critique of Ricardo's positivism is also developed by Franz Petry in *Der soziale Gehalt der Marxschen Werttheorie*, pp. 2–20.

61   Marx, *Capital*, vol. 3, pp. 223–7 and 234–5; MEW 25, 233–7 and 244–5. As Marx states: '[A]s the capitalist mode of production develops, an ever larger quantity of capital is required to employ the same, let alone an increased amount of labour power. Thus, on a capitalist foundation, the increasing productiveness of labour necessarily and permanently creates a seeming over-population of labouring people' (p. 223; MEW 25, p. 233). Under these conditions of a falling rate of profit and over-population, there is an increase in the rate of surplus value because of the intensification of labour exploitation (compare pages 226, 234 and 240; MEW 25, pp. 236, 244 and 250).

62   Bertell Ollman, *Dance of the Dialectic: Steps in Marx's Method* (Urbana, IL: University of Illinois Press, 2003), pp. 1–7.

63   Marx, *Capital*, vol. 3, p. 246; MEW 25, p. 256.

64   *Elements of Marx's Economic Crisis Theory* in *Capital*, volume 3, pp. 142–266; MEW 25, 151–277:

– Rising organic composition of capital between variable and constant capital, pp. 142–54, 212–17 and 263; MEW 25, pp. 151–64, 222–7 and 273.
– Tendential fall in the rate of profit, pp. 154, 172, 211–31 and 239–40; MEW 25, pp. 164, 181, 221–41 and 249–50.

- Increased labour productivity, rate of surplus value, and the limits to exploitation, pp. 45–7, 86–7, 197, 226–31, 234–5, 240, 247, 251–3 and 263–4; *MEW* 25, pp. 55–7, 96–7, 207, 236–41, 244–5, 250, 257, 261–3 and 274–5.
- Concentration and centralisation of capital, pp. 218–19 and 241–66; *MEW* 25, pp. 228–9 and 251–77.
- Disproportionality of labour, production, and consumption, pp. 222–7, 234–5 and 256–8; *MEW* 25, pp. 232–7, 244–5 and 266–8.
- Depreciation, underutilisation, and unemployment of capital, pp. 250–8; *MEW* 25, pp. 260–9.
- Overproduction of capital and the underconsumption of commodities, pp. 245–8, 250–8 and 262–3; *MEW* 25, pp. 255–8, 261–3 and 272–3.
- Contradictions between labour and capital, accumulation and realisation, and production and consumption, pp. 224–5, 245, 249, 257 and 262–6; *MEW* 25, pp. 234–5, 255, 259, 267–8 and 272–7.
- Accumulation crisis, pp. 218–19, 224–5 and 241–6; *MEW* 25, pp. 228–9, 234–5 and 251–6.
- Waste of lives and treating humans as commodities and technical means, pp. 249–50 and 258–9; *MEW* 25, pp. 259–60 and 268–70.
- Surplus population and artificial unemployment, pp. 250–8; *MEW* 25, pp. 261–8.
- Economic stagnation, crisis, and breakdown, pp. 226, 246, 249–50, 254–8; *MEW* 25, pp. 236, 256, 259–60 and 264–8.

A further analysis of the economic crisis theory may be found in the *Grundrisse*, pp. 401–71 and 745–71; *MEW* 42, pp. 315–83 and 637–62; and the *Theories of Surplus-Value*, Part II, pp. 492–535; *MEW* 26, Teil 2, pp. 492–535.

65 Marx, *Capital*, vol. 3, p. 257; *MEW* 25, p. 268. There is a nice summary after this quotation of the wasted potentiality of human life and the creation of inverted and distorted values at the hands of capital (pp. 258–9; *MEW* 25, pp. 268–9).

66 Aristotle, *The Politics*, trans. T.A. Sinclair, revised by Trevor Saunders (London: Penguin, 1981), I, ix, 1257b40–1258b18, p. 85.

67 The method Marx uses in *Capital* is very complex, with a combination of different approaches to the study of commercial and industrial production: historical materialism (structures and functional interrelationships within the social totality), dialectic (laws, logic, and contradictions of capital), and critique (categories and forms of thought, immanent, and substantive critique). Relying heavily on a historical and materialist reinterpretation of the Hegelian dialectic, one can only wonder why Marx uses this general approach at a time when materialism was being replaced by naturalism and the use of the methods of the natural sciences in the social sciences (positivism). Positivism could also get access to the inner dynamic of capital, its laws and logic, and make predictions about future crises and breakdowns in the economic system for revolutionary change. But this question becomes moot once we appreciate that Marx's view of science as dialectical critique is intimately connected to ethics. Both Aristotle and Marx saw economics as a sub-branch of ethics and politics. Thus Marx's analysis of money, capital, and production was an attempt to show that the natural law of capitalism was both irrational and immoral. See McCarthy, *Dialectics and Decadence*, pp. 8–12 and 97–123 and Geoffrey E. Maurice Ste.

Croix who examines the relationship between Aristotle and Marx's methods in *The Class Struggle in the Ancient Greek World* (Ithaca, NY: Cornel University Press, 1989), pp. 74–80.

68 Marx, *Capital*, vol. 3, pp. 85–8, 250–1, 259 and 820; *MEW* 25, pp. 96–8, 260–1, 269–70 and 828.

69 Ibid., vol. 3, pp. 250 and 259; *MEW* 25, pp. 260 and 269.

What the Prophets Saw

We shun them, living exiles, labeled mad,
who see the world turned upside down we shrink
by private ownership of all each hand
imprints, and in our iron cage we think

we're free. The mad behold this human treason
and scream against the death of nature's reason.
But dreams reveal to what were blinded eyes
the truth that Justice holds that never dies.

The Commune, like far Ithaka, contains
ideals we journey towards before we die,
when like gods we break our final chains
to boldly face our own Thermopylae.

Life itself is found in simple joy,
in beauty, love, and art – the spinning earth
in all the random grace that hearts employ
will see a new creation at its birth.

In dreams an ancient wisdom whispers: Heal
our modern madness, help the heavens move,
seek a newer world and make it real,
with hearts the sun and stars unite in love.

— ROYAL RHODES

Bibliography

Abensour, Miguel 2011, *Democracy Against the State: Marx and the Machiavellian Movement*, translated by Max Blechman and Martin Breaugh (Cambridge, UK: Polity Press).
Action, H.B. 1975, 'Introduction', to Hegel's *Natural Law: The Scientific Ways of Treating Natural Law*, translated by T.M. Knox (Philadelphia, PA: University of Pennsylvania Press).
Alford, C. Fred 1985, *Science and the Revenge of Nature* (Gainesville, FL: University Presses of Florida).
Althusser, Louis 2007, *Politics and History: Montesquieu, Rousseau, Marx*, translated by Ben Brewster (London, UK: Verso Publishers).
Anderson, Kevin 2010, *Marx at the Margins: On Nationalism, Ethnicity, and Non-Western Societies* (Chicago, IL: University of Chicago Press).
Aristotle 1947, *Nicomachean Ethics*, in *Introduction to Aristotle*, edited and with an introduction by Richard McKeon, translated by W.D. Ross (New York, NY: Random House).
Aristotle 1981, *The Politics*, translated by T.A. Sinclair, revised by Trevor Saunders (London, UK: Penguin Books).
Arkush, Allan 1991, 'Judaism as Egoism: From Spinoza to Feuerbach and Marx', *Modern Judaism*, 11: 211–23.
Arneson, Richard 1981, 'What's Wrong with Exploitation?', *Ethics*, 91, 2: 202–27.
Aveling, Eleanor Marx 1886, 'Introduction' to Prosper Olivier Lissagaray, *History of the Commune of 1871*, translated by Eleanor Marx Aveling (London, UK: Reeves and Turner).
Avineri, Shlomo 1964, 'Marx and Jewish Emancipation', *Journal of the History of Ideas*, 25, 3: 445–50.
Avineri, Shlomo 1968, *The Social and Political Thought of Karl Marx* (Cambridge, UK: Cambridge University Press).
Avineri, Shlomo 1969 (ed.), *Marx on Colonialism and Modernization: His Dispatches and Other Writings on China, India, Mexico, and the Middle East and North Africa* (Garden City, NY: Doubleday and Company).
Avineri, Shlomo 1972, *Hegel's Theory of the Modern State* (Cambridge, UK: Cambridge University Press).
Avineri, Shlomo 1985, *Moses Hess: Prophet of Communism and Zionism* (New York, NY: New York University Press).
Backhaus, Hans-Georg 1974, 'Materialien zur Rekonstruktion der Marxschen Werttheorie', in *Gesellschaft Beiträge zur Marxschen Theorie 1* (Frankfurt/Main: Suhrkamp).
Bailey, Cyril July 1928, 'Karl Marx on Greek Atomism', *Classical Quarterly*, 22, 3–4: 205–6.

Balibar, Étienne 1998, *Spinoza and Politics*, translated by Peter Snowdon (London, UK: Verso).
Baronovitch, Laurence 1984, 'German Idealism, Greek Materialism, and the Young Marx', *International Philosophical Quarter*, 24, 3: 245–66.
Bartholomew, Amy 1990, 'Should a Marxist Believe in Marx on Rights?', *The Socialist Register*, 26: 244–64.
Benton, Ted 1996 (ed.), *The Greening of Marxism* (New York, NY: Guilford Press).
Berlin, Isaiah 1969, *Four Essays on Freedom* (Oxford, UK: Oxford University Press).
Bindoff, S.T. 1966, *Tudor England* (Baltimore: MD: Penguin Books).
Blackburn, Robin 2011, 'Introduction', in *An Unfinished Revolution: Karl Marx and Abraham Lincoln*, edited by Robin Blackburn (London, UK: Verso Books).
Blackburn, Robin 2011, 'Karl Marx and Abraham Lincoln: A Curious Convergence', *Historical Materialism*, 19, 4: 145–74.
Blanchard, W.H. 1984, 'Karl Marx and the Jewish Question', *Political Psychology*, 5, 3: 365–74.
Bloch, Ernst 1986, *Natural Law and Human Dignity*, translated by Dennis Schmidt (Cambridge, MA: MIT Press).
Bloehbaum, Helmut 1988, *Strukturen moderner Dialektik. Am Beispiel Naturzustand und Herr- und Knecht-Verhältnis bei Rousseau, Hegel und Marx* (Frankfurt/Main: Peter Lang).
Bookchin, Murray 1971, 'Listen Marxists', in *Post-Scarcity Anarchism* (Berkeley, CA: Ramparts Press).
Booth, William James 1993, *Households: On the Moral Architecture of the Economy* (Ithaca, NY: Cornell University Press).
Brenkert, George 1981, 'Marx and Human Rights', *Journal of the History of Philosophy*, 24, 1: 55–77.
Brenkert, George 1983, *Marx's Ethics of Freedom* (London: Routledge & Kegan Paul).
Brett, Annabel 1997, *Liberty, Right and Nature: Individual Rights in Later Scholastic Thought* (Cambridge, UK: Cambridge University Press).
Brown, Bruce 1973, *Marx, Freud, and the Critique of Everyday Life: Toward a Permanent Cultural Revolution* (New York, NY: Monthly Review Press).
Buchanan, Allen 1982, *Marx and Justice: The Radical Critique of Liberalism* (Totowa, NJ: Rowman and Littlefield).
Bull, George 1932, 'What Did Locke Borrow from Hooker?', *Thought: A Journal of Philosophy*, 7, 1: 122–35.
Burkett, Paul 1999, *Marx and Nature: A Red and Green Perspective* (New York, NY: St. Martin's Press).
Burkett, Paul 1999, 'Was Marx a Promethean?', *Nature, Society, and Thought*, 12, 1: 7–42
Burkett, Paul and John B. Foster 2004, 'Metabolism, Energy, and Entropy in Marx's Cri-

tique of Political Economy', *American Sociology Association Meetings*, San Francisco, CA, Aug. 14–17 and 2006, *Theory and Society*, 35, 1: 109–53.

Burkett, Paul 2005, 'Marx's Vision of Sustainable Human Development', *Monthly Review*, 57, 5: 34–62.

Butler, E.M. 1935, *The Tyranny of Greece over Germany* (Cambridge, UK: Cambridge University Press).

Campbell, Sally 2012, *Rousseau and the Paradox of Alienation* (Lanham, MD: Lexington Books).

Campos, Andre 2012, *Spinoza's Revolutions in Natural Law* (London, UK: Palgrave Macmillan).

Carlebach, Julius 1978, *Karl Marx and the Radical Critique of Judaism* (London, UK: Routledge and Kegan Paul).

Cassirer, Ernst 1954, *The Question of Jean-Jacques Rousseau*, edited and translated by Peter Gay (New York, NY: Columbia University Press).

Castells, Manuel 1983, *The City and the Grassroots* (Berkeley, CA: University of California Press).

Chernilo, Daniel 2013, *The Natural Law Foundations of Modern Social Theory: A Quest for Universalism* (Cambridge, UK: Cambridge University Press).

Cohen, G.A. 1981, 'Freedom, Justice and Capitalism', *New Left Review*, I, 126: 3–16.

Cohen, Marshall, Thomas Nagel, and Thomas Scanlon (eds.) 1980, *Marx, Justice and History* (Princeton, NJ: Princeton University Press).

Colletti, Lucio 1972, *From Rousseau to Lenin: Studies in Ideology and Society*, translated by John Merrington and Judith White (New York, NY: Monthly Review Press).

Commers, Ronald 1984, 'Marx's Concept of Justice and the Two Traditions in European Political Thought', *Philosophica*, 33: 107–29.

Cornell, Drucilla April 1984, 'Should a Marxist Believe in Rights', *Praxis International*, 4, 1: 45–56.

Deutschmann, Christoph 1973, *Der linke Keynesianismus* (Frankfurt/Main: Athenäum Verlag).

Dooley, Peter 2005, *The Labor Theory of Value* (London, UK: Routledge).

Draper, Hal 1977, *Karl Marx's Theory of Revolution*, vol. 1, books I and II (New York, NY: Monthly Review Press).

Dunn, John 1969, *The Political Thought of John Locke* (Cambridge, UK: Cambridge University Press).

Dupré, Louis 1966, *The Philosophical Foundations of Marxism* (New York, NY: Harcourt, Brace & World).

Dupré, Louis 1983, *Marx's Social Critique of Culture* (New Haven, CT: Yale University Press).

Durkheim, Emile 1975, *Montesquieu and Rousseau: Forerunners of Sociology*, translated by Ralph Manheim (Ann Arbor, MI: Ann Arbor Paperback).

Dussel, Enrique 2001, 'The Four Drafts of *Capital*: Towards a New Interpretation of the Dialectical Thought of Marx', *Rethinking Marxism*, 13, 1: 10–26.

Dussel, Enrique 2001, *Towards an Unknown Marx: A Commentary on the Manuscripts of 1861–63*, translated by Yolanda Angulo, introduction by Fred Mosley (London, UK: Routledge).

Eckersley, Robyn 1992, *Environmentalism and Political Theory* (Albany, NY: State University of New York Press).

Edwards, Stewart 1971, 'Introduction', in *The Communards of Paris, 1871*, documents of revolution, edited by Stewart Edwards, translated by Jean McNeil (London, UK: Eyre & Spottiswoode).

Edwards, Stewart 1971, *The Paris Commune 1871* (New York, NY: Quadrangle Books).

Ehrenberg, John 1992, *The Dictatorship of the Proletariat: Marxism's Theory of Socialist Democracy* (New York, NY: Routledge).

Ellenburg, Stephen 1976, *Rousseau's Political Philosophy: An Interpretation from Within* (Ithaca, NY: Cornell University Press).

Engels, Friedrich 1954, *Dialectics of Nature* (Moscow: Foreign Language Publishing House).

Engels, Friedrich 1972, 'Introduction', to Karl Marx, *Civil War in France: The Paris Commune* (New York, NY: International Publishers).

Engels, Friedrich 1973, *Conditions of the Working Class in England* (Moscow: Progress Publishers).

Enmale, Richard (ed.) 1937, *The Civil War in the United States* (New York, NY: International Publishers).

Ewen, Stuart 1977, *Captains of Consciousness: Advertising and the Social Roots of the Consumer Culture* (New York, NY: McGraw Hill Book Company).

Fackenheim, Emil 1973, *Encounters between Judaism and Modern Philosophy: A Preface to Future Jewish Thought* (New York, NY: Basic Books).

Farrar, Cynthia 1988, *The Origins of Democratic Thinking: The Invention of Politics in Classical Athens* (Cambridge, UK: Cambridge University Press).

Fenves, Peter 1986, 'Marx's Doctoral Thesis on Two Greek Atomists and the Post-Kantian Interpretations', *Journal of the History of Ideas*, 47, 3: 433–52.

Ferkiss, Victor 1993, *Nature, Technology, and Society: Cultural Roots of the Current Environmental Crisis* (New York, NY: New York University Press).

Ferrarin, Alfredo 2001, *Hegel and Aristotle* (Cambridge, UK: Cambridge University Press).

Fetscher, Irving 1962, 'Rousseau's Concepts of Freedom in the Light of his Philosophy of History', in *Liberty*, edited by Carl Friedrich (Piscataway, NJ: Transaction Publishers).

Fetscher, Irving 1975, *Rousseaus politische Philosophie: Zur Geschichte des demokratischen Freiheitsbegriffs* (Frankfurt/Main: Suhrkamp).

Feuer, Lewis (ed.) 1959, *Marx & Engels: Basic Writings on Politics and Philosophy* (Garden City, NY: Anchor Books).
Feuerbach, Ludwig 1957. *The Essence of Christianity*, translated by George Eliot (New York, NY: Harper Torchbooks).
Finley, M.I. 1988, *Democracy Ancient and Modern* (New Brunswick, NJ: Rutgers University Press).
Fischer, Norman 1981, 'Marx's Early Concept of Democracy and the Ethical Bases of Socialism', in *Marxism and the Good Society*, edited by John Burke, Lawrence Crocker, and Lyman Legters (Cambridge, UK: Cambridge University Press).
Fischman, Dennis 1989, 'The Jewish Question', *Polity*, 21, 4: 755–75.
Fischman, Dennis 1991, *Political Discourse in Exile: Karl Marx and the Jewish Question* (Amherst, MA: University of Massachusetts Press).
Foley, Duncan 1986, *Understanding Capital: Marx's Economic Theory* (Cambridge, MA: Harvard University Press).
Foner, Eric 2012, 'The Emancipation Proclamation at 150: Abraham Lincoln's Turning Point', *The Guardian*, Sept. 17: Online.
Foster, John Bellamy 1995, 'Marx and the Environment', *Monthly Review*, 47, 3: 108–23.
Foster, John Bellamy 1998, 'The Communist Manifesto and the Environment', *The Socialist Register*, 34: 169–89.
Foster, John Bellamy and Fred Magdoff 1998, 'Liebig, Marx, and the Depletion of Soil Fertility: Relevance for Today's Agriculture', *Monthly Review*, 50, 3: 32–45.
Foster, John Bellamy 1999, 'Marx's Theory of Metabolic Rift', *American Journal of Sociology*, 105, 2: 366–405.
Foster, John Bellamy 2000, *Marx's Ecology: Materialism and Nature* (New York, NY: Monthly Review Press).
Foster, John Bellamy 2002, 'Marx's Ecology in Historical Perspective', *International Socialism Journal*, 96.
Foster, John Bellamy 2008, 'Marx's *Grundrisse* and the Ecological Contradictions of Capitalism', in *Karl Marx's Grundrisse: Foundations of the Critique of Political Economy 150 Years Later*, edited by Marcello Musto (London, UK: Routledge).
Foster, John Bellamy 2013, 'Marx and the Rift in the Universal Metabolism of Nature', *Monthly Review*, 65, 7: 11–45.
Fox, Ralph 1940, *Marx, Engels, and Lenin on Ireland* (London, UK: Modern Books).
Friedman, Milton 1974, *Capitalism and Freedom* (Chicago, IL: University of Chicago Press).
Froese, Katrin 2001, 'Beyond Liberalism: The Moral Community of Rousseau's Social Contract', *Canadian Journal of Political Science*, 34, 3: 579–600.
Fromm, Erich 1961, *Marx's Concept of Man* (New York, NY: Frederick Ungar Publishing Company).

Furley, David 1980, 'Self-Movers', in *Essays on Aristotle's Ethics*, edited by Amelie Oksenberg Rorty (Berkeley, CA: University of California Press).

Furton, Edward 1999, 'Richard Hooker as Source of the Founding Principles of American Natural Law', in *The Failure of Modernism: The Cartesian Legacy and Contemporary Pluralism*, edited by Brendan Sweetman (American Maritain Association Publication and distributed by the Catholic University of America Press, Washington, D.C.).

Garrett, Aaron December 2003, 'Was Spinoza a Natural Lawyer?', *Cardozo Law Review*, 25, 2: 627–41.

Garza, Abel, Jr. 1990–91, 'Hegel's Critique of Liberalism and Natural Law: Reconstructing Ethical Life', *Law and Philosophy*, 9: 371–98.

Geraint Parry 1978, *John Locke* (London, UK: Allen and Unwin).

Geras, Norman 1983, *Marx and Human Nature: Refutation of a Legend* (London, UK: Verso Books).

Geras, Norman 1985, 'The Controversy about Marx and Justice', *New Left Review*, I, 150: 47–85.

Geras, Norman 1992, 'Bringing Marx to Justice: An Addendum and Rejoinder', *New Left Review*, I, 195: 37–69.

Germino, Dante 1979, *Machiavelli to Marx: Modern Western Political Thought* (Chicago, IL: Chicago University Press).

Gluckstein, Donny 2011, *The Paris Commune: A Revolution in Democracy* (Chicago, IL: Haymarket Books).

Goodwin, Robert 1987, 'John Locke', in *A History of Political Philosophy*, edited by Leo Strauss and Joseph Cropsey (Chicago, IL: University of Chicago Press).

Gould, Carol 1980, *Marx's Social Ontology: Individuality and Community in Marx's Theory of Social Reality* (Cambridge, MA: University of Massachusetts Press).

Gould, Roger 1995, *Insurgent Identities: Class, Community, and Protest in Paris from 1848 to the Commune* (Chicago, IL: University of Chicago Books).

Gouldner, Alvin 1980, *The Two Marxisms: Contradictions and Anomalies in the Development of Theory* (New York, NY: Oxford University Press).

Gray, J. Glenn 1941, *Hegel's Hellenic Ideal: The Mystical Element in Hegel's Early Theological Writings* (New York, NY: King's Crown Press).

Grossmann, Henryk 1970, *Das Akkumulations- und Zusammenbruchs-Gesetz des kapitalistischen Systems* (Frankfurt/Main: Neue Kritik Verlag, 1970).

Grossmann, Henryk 1977, 'Marx, Classical Political Economy and the Problem of Dynamics, Part 1', translated by Peter Burgess, *Capital and Class*, 2: 32–55.

Grossmann, Henryk 1977, 'Marx, Classical Political Economy and the Problem of Dynamics, Part 2', translated by Peter Burgess, *Capital and Class*, 3: 67–99.

Habermas, Jürgen 1971, *Knowledge and Human Interest*, translated by Jeremy Shapiro (Boston, MA: Beacon Press).

Habermas, Jürgen 1971, 'Technology and Science as "Ideology"', in *Toward a Rational Society: Student Protest, Science, and Politics*, translated by Jeremy Shapiro (Boston, MA: Beacon Press).

Habermas, Jürgen 1973, *Theory and Practice*, translated by John Viertel (Boston, MA: Beacon Press).

Hamerow, Theodore S. (ed.) 1973, *The Age of Bismarck: Documents and Interpretations* (New York, NY: Harper & Row Publishers).

Hansen, Mogens 1987, *The Athenian Assembly in the Age of Demosthenes* (Oxford, UK: Basil Blackwell).

Hansen, Mogens 1991, *The Athenian Democracy in the Age of Demosthenes: Structures, Principles and Ideology*, translated by J.A. Crook (Oxford, UK: Basil Blackwell).

Harap, Louis 1979, 'The Meaning of Marx's Essay "On the Jewish Question"', *The Journal of Ethnic Studies*, 7, 1: 43–56.

Harvey, David 1985, *Consciousness and the Urban Experience* (Baltimore, MD: Johns Hopkins University Press).

Harvey, David 1997, *Justice, Nature, and the Geography of Difference* (Oxford, UK: Wiley-Blackwell).

Harvey, David 1998, 'Marxism, Metaphors, and Ecological Politics', *Monthly Review*, 49, 11: 17–31.

Harvey, David 2003, *Paris, Capital of Modernity* (New York, NY: Routledge).

Harvey, David 2014, *Seventeen Contradictions and the End of Capitalism* (New York, NY: Oxford University Press).

Haupt, Gerhard and Karin Hausen 1979, *Die Pariser Kommune: Erfolg und Scheitern einer Revolution* (Frankfurt/Main: Campus Verlag).

Hegel, Georg Friedrich 1932, *Jenenser Realphilosophie. Vorlesungen von 1803/04*, edited by Johannes Hoffmeister (Leipzig: Felix Meiner Verlag).

Hegel, Georg Friedrich 1961, 'The Positivity of the Christian Religion', in *On Christianity: Early Theological Writings*, translated by T.M. Knox (New York, NY: Harper Torchbooks).

Hegel, Georg Friedrich 1961, 'The Spirit of Christianity and its Fate', in *On Christianity: Early Theological Writings*, translated by T.M. Knox (New York, NY: Harper Torchbooks).

Hegel, Georg Friedrich 1967, *System der Sittlichkeit*, edited by Georg Lasson (Hamburg: Felix Meiner Verlag).

Hegel, Georg Friedrich 1967, *Philosophy of Right*, translated by T.M. Knox (London, UK: Oxford University Press, 1967).

Hegel, Georg Friedrich 1970, *Die Grundlinien der Philosophie des Rechts oder Naturrecht und Staatswissenschaft im Grundrisse*, Werke 7 (Frankfurt/Main: Suhrkamp Verlag).

Hegel, Georg Friedrich 1970, 'Über die wissenschaftlichen Behandlungsarten des Naturrechts, seine Stelle in der praktischen Philosophie und sein Verhältnis zu den positiven Rechtswissenschaften', *Jenaer Schriften 1801–1807*, Werke 2 (Frankfurt/Main: Suhrkamp Taschenbuch Verlag).

Hegel, Georg Friedrich 1971, 'Die Positivität der christlichen Religion', in *Frühe Schriften*, Werke 1 (Frankfurt/Main: Suhrkamp Taschenbuch Verlag).

Hegel, Georg Friedrich 1971, 'Der Geist des Christentums und sein Schicksal', in *Frühe Schriften*, Werke 1 (Frankfurt/Main: Suhrkamp Taschenbuch Verlag).

Hegel, Georg Friedrich 1979, *System of Ethical Life*, in *System of Ethical Life (1802–03) and First Philosophy of Spirit (1803–04)* (New York, NY: State University of New York Press).

Hegel, Georg Friedrich 1987, *Hegel on Economics and Freedom*, edited by William Maker (Macon, GA: Mercer University Press).

Held, David 2006, *Models of Democracy* (Stanford, CA: Stanford University Press).

Heller, Agnes 1976, *The Theory of Need in Marx* (New York, NY: St. Martin's Press).

Heller, Agnes 1987, *Beyond Justice* (Oxford, UK: Basil Blackwell).

Herman, Daly 1992, *Steady-State Economics* (London, UK: Earthscan).

Hicks, John and Robert Tucker (eds.) 1973, *Revolution and Reaction* (Amherst, MA: University of Massachusetts Press).

Hinchman, Lewis 1984, *Hegel's Critique of the Enlightenment* (Tampa, FL: University Presses of Florida).

Hiro, Dilip 1995, *Between Marx and Muhammad: The Changing Face of Central Asia* (New York, NY: HarperCollins Publishing).

Hobbes, Thomas 1977, *Leviathan: Or the Matter, Forme and Power of a Commonwealth Ecclesiasticall and Civil*, edited by Michael Oakeshott, introduction by Richard Peters (New York, NY: Collier Books).

Holland, Eugene Fall 1998, 'Spinoza and Marx', *Cultural Logic*, 2, 1: Online.

Holmstrom, Nancy June 1977, 'Exploitation', *Canadian Journal of Philosophy*, 7, 2: 353–69.

Holt, Justin 2009, *Karl Marx's Philosophy of Nature, Action and Society* (Cambridge, UK: Cambridge University Press).

Honneth, Axel 1995, *The Struggle for Recognition – The Moral Grammar of Social Conflicts*, translated by Joel Anderson (Cambridge, MA: Polity Press).

Hook, Sidney 1975, *Revolution, Reform, and Social Justice: Studies in the Theory and Practice of Marxism* (New York, NY: New York University Press).

Hooker, Richard 1845, *Of the Laws of Ecclesiastical Polity*, in *The Works of that Learned and Judicious Devine, Mr. Richard Hooker* (Oxford, UK: Oxford University Press).

Horne, Alistair 2007, *The Fall of Paris: The Siege and the Commune, 1870–1871* (New York, NY: Penguin Books).

Hughes, Jonathan 2000, *Ecology and Historical Materialism* (Cambridge, UK: Cambridge University Press).

Hume, David 1961, *An Inquiry Concerning Human Understanding*, in *The Empiricists* (Garden City, NY: Dolphin Books).
Hundert, Edward 1972, 'The Making of Homo Faber: John Locke Between Ideology and History', *Journal of the History of Ideas*, 33, 1: 3–22.
Hundert, Edward 1977, 'Market Society and Meaning in Locke's Political Philosophy', *Journal of the History of Philosophy*, 15: 33–44.
Husain, Iqbal (ed.) 2006, *Karl Marx on India* (New Delhi, India: Tulika Books).
Husami, Ziyad 1978, 'Marx on Distributive Justice', *Philosophy & Public Affairs*, 8, 1: 27–64.
Husami, Ziyad 1980, 'Marx on Distributive Justice', *Marx, Justice and History*, edited by Marshall Cohen, Thomas Nagel, and Thomas Scanlon (Princeton, NJ: Princeton University Press).
Immler, Hans and Schmied-Kowarzik (eds.) 1984, *Marx und die Naturfrage. Ein Wissenschaftsstreit um die Kritik der politischen Ökonomie* (Hamburg: VSA Verlag).
Immler, Hans 1986, *Natur und Marxistische Werttheorie* (Kassel: Kasseler Philosophische Schriften, 23).
Inwood, M. 1984, 'Hegel, Plato and Greek Sittlichkeit', in *The State and Civil Society: Studies in Hegel's Political Philosophy*, edited by Z.A. Pelczynski (Cambridge, UK: Cambridge University Press).
Irwin, T.H. 1980, 'The Metaphysical and Psychological Basis of Aristotle's Ethics', in *Essays on Aristotle's Ethics*, edited by Amelie Oksenberg Rorty (Berkeley, CA: University of California Press).
Jacoby, Russell 1975, *Social Amnesia: A Critique of Contemporary Psychology from Adler to Laing* (Boston, MA: Beacon Press).
Jaeggi, Rahel 2014, *Alienation*, translated by Frederick Neuhouser and Alan Smith (New York, NY: Columbia University Press).
Jay, Martin 1971, *The Dialectical Imagination: A History of the Frankfurt School and the Institute of Social Research 1923–1950* (Boston, MA: Little, Brown and Company).
Jefferson, Thomas 1990, 'The Declaration of Independence', in *The Encyclopedia of Colonial and Revolutionary America*, edited by John Faragher (New York, NY: Facts on File).
Jellinek, Frank 1971, *The Paris Commune of 1871* (London, UK: Victor Gollancz).
Jessop, Bob and Russell Wheatley (eds.) 1999, *Karl Marx's Social and Political Thought*, vol. 8: *Nature, Culture, Morals, Ethics* (London, UK: Routledge).
Johnson, Martin 1996, *The Paradise of Association: Political Culture and Popular Organization in the Paris Commune of 1871* (Ann Arbor, MI: University of Michigan Press).
Jones, A.H.M. 1957, *Athenian Democracy* (Baltimore, MD: Johns Hopkins University Press).
Kadt, Maarten de, and Salvatore Engel-Di Mauro 2001, 'Failed Promise', *Capitalism Nature Socialism*, 12, 2: 50–6.

Kain, Philip 1982, *Schiller, Hegel, and Marx: State, Society and the Aesthetic Ideal of Ancient Greece* (Kingston, Canada: McGill-Queen's University Press).
Kain, Philip 1988, *Marx and Ethics* (Oxford, UK: Clarendon Press).
Kamenka, Eugene 1957–58, 'The Baptism of Marx', *The Hibbert Journal*, 56: 340–51.
Kamenka, Eugene 1972, *The Ethical Foundations of Marxism* (London, UK: Routledge & Kegan Paul).
Kant, Immanuel 1949, *Fundamental Principles of the Metaphysic of Morals*, translated by Thomas Abbott (Indianapolis, IN: Bobbs-Merrill Company).
Kant, Immanuel 1968, *Grundlegung zur Metaphysik der Sitten, Kants Werke*, Band IV (Berlin: Walter de Gruyter & Company).
Kauder, Emil 1953, 'The Retarded Acceptance of the Marginal Utility Theory', *Quarterly Journal of Economic*, 67: 564–75.
Kaufmann, Walter 1976, 'The Hegel Myth and its Method', in *Hegel: A Collection of Critical Essays*, edited by Alasdair MacIntyre (Notre Dame, IN: University of Notre Dame Press).
Kelly, George 1978, *Hegel's Retreat from Eleusis: Studies in Political Thought* (Princeton, NJ: Princeton University Press).
Kelly, George 1978, *Idealism, Politics and History: Sources of Hegelian Thought* (Cambridge, UK: Cambridge University Press).
Kennedy, Walter 2007, *Red Republicans and Lincoln's Marxists: Marxism in the Civil War* (Lincoln, NE: iUniverse).
Keyes, Thomas 1987, 'The Marxian Concept of Property: Individual/Social', in *The Main Debate* (New York, NY: Random House).
Kliman, Andrew 2006, *Reclaiming Marx's 'Capital': A Refutation of the Myth of Inconsistency* (Lanham, MD: Lexington Books).
Kofler, Leo 1972, *Geschichte und Dialektik* (Darmstadt: Luchterhand Verlag).
Kolakowski, Leszek 1969, 'Karl Marx and the Classical Definition of Truth', in *Marxism and Beyond*, translated by J.Z. Peel (London, UK: Pall Mall Press).
Kolakowski, Leszek 1983, 'Marxism and Human Rights', *Daedalus*, 112, 4: 81–92.
Kondylis, Panajotis 1987, *Marx und die Griechische Antike. Zwei Studien* (Heidelberg: Manutius Verlag).
Korsch, Karl 1963, *Karl Marx* (New York, NY: Russell & Russell).
Korsch, Karl 1970, 'Introduction to the Critique of the Gotha Programme', in *Marxism and Philosophy*, translated by Fred Halliday (New York, NY: Monthly Review Press).
Kouvelakis, Stathis 2005, 'The Marxian Critique of Citizenship: For a Rereading of *On the Jewish Question*', translated by Alex Martin, *The South Atlantic Quarterly*, 104, 4: 707–21.
Kovel, Joel 1995, 'Ecological Marxism and Dialectic', *Capitalism Nature Socialism*, 24: 31–50.

Krancberg, Sigmund 1982, 'Karl Marx and Democracy', *Studies in Soviet Thought*, 24, 2: 23–35.
Laing, R.D. 1970, *The Divided Self: The Existential Study in Sanity and Madness* (Baltimore, MD: Penguin Books).
Lasch, Christopher 1977, *Haven in a Heartless World* (New York, NY: Basic Books).
Lasch, Christopher 1979, *The Culture of Narcissism: American Life in an Age of Diminishing Expectations* (New York, NY: Warner Books).
Lear, Jonathan 1988, *Aristotle: The Desire to Understand* (Cambridge, UK: Cambridge University Press).
Lee, Salome 2011, 'Until We Are All Abolitionists: Marx on Slavery, Race, and Class', *The International Marxist Humanist*, Oct. 22: Online.
Lefebvre, Henri 1965, *La proclamation de la Commune* (Paris: Gallimard).
Leiss, William 1974, *The Domination of Nature* (Boston, MA: Beacon Press).
Lemos, Ramon 1977, *Rousseau's Political Philosophy: An Exposition and Interpretation* (Atlanta, GA: University of Georgia Press).
Leopold, David 2007, *The Young Karl Marx: German Philosophy, Modern Politics, and Human Flourishing* (Cambridge, MA: Cambridge University Press).
Levine, Andrew 1993, *The General Will: Rousseau, Marx, and Communism* (Cambridge, MA: Cambridge University Press).
Levine, Norman 1975, *The Tragic Deception: Marx Contra Engels* (Oxford, UK: Clio Books).
Lincoln, Abraham 2011, 'Emancipation Proclamation', in *An Unfinished Revolution: Karl Marx and Abraham Lincoln*, edited by Robin Blackburn (London, UK: Verso Books).
Lincoln, Abraham 2011, 'First and Second Inaugural Addresses of Abraham Lincoln', in *An Unfinished Revolution: Karl Marx and Abraham Lincoln*, edited by Robin Blackburn (London, UK: Verso Books).
Lincoln, Abraham 2011, 'Gettysburg Address', in *An Unfinished Revolution: Karl Marx and Abraham Lincoln*, edited by Robin Blackburn (London, UK: Verso Books).
Linder, Marc 1975, *Reification and the Consciousness of the Critics of Political Economy: Studies in the Development of Marx's Theory* of Value (Copenhagen, DK: Rhodos International Science and Art Publishers).
Lindner, Kolja 2010, 'Marx's Eurocentrism: Post Colonial Studies and Marx Scholarship', *Radical Philosophy*, 161: 27–41.
Lissagaray, Prosper Olivier 1886, *History of the Paris Commune of 1871*, translated by Eleanor Marx Aveling (London, UK: Reeves and Turner).
Locke, John 1955, *The Second Treatise of Government*, edited and with an introduction by Thomas Peardon (Indianapolis, IN: The Liberal Arts Press).
Locke, John 1988, *Essays on the Law of Nature*, edited by W. Von Leyden (Oxford, UK: Clarendon Press).

Löwith, Karl 1967, *From Hegel to Nietzsche: The Revolution in Nineteenth-Century Thought*, translated by David Green (Garden City, NY: Doubleday Anchor Books).

Lucchese, Filippo Del 2009, *Conflict, Power, and Multitude in Machiavelli and Spinoza* (London, UK: Continuum Books).

Lukács, Georg 1971, *History and Class Consciousness: Studies in Marxist Dialectics*, translated by Rodney Livingstone (Cambridge, MA: MIT Press).

Lukács, Georg 1976, *The Young Hegel: Studies in the Relation Between Dialectics and Economics*, translated by Rodney Livingstone (Cambridge, MA: MIT Press).

Lukács, Georg 2011, *Social Structure and Forms of Consciousness: The Dialectic of Structure and History*, vol. 2 (New York, NY: Monthly Review Press).

Lukes, Steven 1982, 'Can a Marxist Believe in Human Rights?', *Praxis International*, 1, 4: 334–45.

Lukes, Steven 1987, *Marxism and Morality* (Oxford, UK: Oxford University Press).

Lynd, Staunton 1969, *Intellectual Origins of American Radicalism* (New York, NY: Vintage Books).

MacIntyre, Alasdair 1971, *A Short History of Ethics: A History of Moral Philosophy from the Homeric Age to the Twentieth Century* (New York, NY: Macmillan Company).

MacIntyre, Alasdair 1981, *After Virtue: A Study in Moral Theory* (Notre Dame, IN: University of Notre Dame Press).

Macpherson, C.B. 1970, *The Political Theory of Possessive Individualism: Hobbes to Locke* (London, UK: Oxford University Press).

Macpherson, C.B. 1973, 'The Maximization of Democracy', in *Democratic Theory: Essays in Retrieval* (Oxford, UK: Clarendon Press).

Maidan, Michael 1987, 'Marx on the Jewish Question: A Meta-Critical Analysis', *Studies in Soviet Thought*, 33, 1: 27–41.

Manet, Pierre 1995, 'Rousseau, Critic of Liberalism', in *An Intellectual History of Liberalism*, translated by Rebecca Balinski (Princeton, NJ: Princeton University Press).

March, Thomas 1896, *The History of the Paris Commune of 1871* (London, UK: Swan Sonnenschein).

Marcuse, Herbert 1960, *Reason and Revolution: Hegel and the Rise of Social Theory* (Boston, MA: Beacon Press).

Marcuse, Herbert 1969, 'Industrialization and Capitalism in Max Weber', *Negations: Essays in Critical Theory*, translated by Jeremy Shapiro (Boston, MA: Beacon Press).

Marcuse, Herbert 1992, 'Ecology and the Critique of Modern Society', *Capitalism Nature Socialism*, 3, 3: 29–38.

Markovic, Mihailo 1981, 'Philosophical Foundations of Human Rights', *Praxis International*, 1, 4: 386–400.

Marx, Karl and Friedrich Engels 1956–90, *Karl Marx/Friedrich Engels Werke* (*MEW*), Bände 1–43 (Berlin: Dietz Verlag).

Marx, Karl 1959, *Critique of the Gotha Program*, in *Marx & Engels: Basic Writings on Politics and Philosophy*, translated by Lewis Feuer (Garden City, NY: Anchor Books).

Marx, Karl 1959, *Marx & Engels: Basic Writings on Politics and Philosophy*, edited by Lewis Feuer (Garden City, NY: Anchor Books).

Marx, Karl 1964, *Karl Marx: Early Writings*, edited and translated by T.B. Bottomore (New York, NY: McGraw-Hill Book Company).

Marx, Karl 1964, *Economic and Philosophic Manuscripts of 1844*, in *Karl Marx: Early Writings*, edited and translated by T.B. Bottomore (New York, NY: McGraw Hill Book Company).

Marx, Karl 1964, *On the Jewish Question*, in *Karl Marx: Early Writings*, edited and translated by T.B. Bottomore (New York, NY: McGraw Hill Book Company).

Marx, Karl and Friedrich Engels 1965, *The German Ideology*, parts I and III, edited and with an introduction by R. Pascal (New York, NY: International Publishers).

Marx, Karl 1967, *Capital: A Critique of Political Economy*, vol. 1: *The Process of Capitalist Production*, edited by Friedrich Engels, translated by Samuel Moore and Edward Aveling (New York, NY: International Publishers).

Marx, Karl 1968, 'Ricardo's and Adam Smith's Theory of Cost Price', 'Ricardo's Theory of Surplus Value', and 'Ricardo's Theory of Accumulation and Critique of It', *Theories of Surplus Value*, Part II (Moscow: Progress Publishers).

Marx, Karl 1968, *Theories of Surplus Value* (Moscow: Progress Publishers).

Marx, Karl 1970, *A Contribution to the Critique of Political Economy*, edited by Maurice Dobb (New York, NY: International Publishers).

Marx, Karl 1970, 'Preface', *A Contribution to the Critique of Political Economy*, edited by Maurice Dobb (New York, NY: International Publishers).

Marx, Karl 1971, *Marx and Engels on Ireland* (Moscow: Progress Publishers).

Marx, Karl and Friedrich Engels 1972, *Ireland and the Irish Question* (New York, NY: International Publishers).

Marx, Karl 1972, 'Address of the General Council of the International Working Men's Association on the Civil War in France, 1871', in *The Civil War in France: The Paris Commune* (New York, NY: International Publishers).

Marx, Karl 1972, 'Letter to Dr. Kugelmann on the Paris Commune' (April 12, 1871), in *Civil War in France: The Paris Commune* (New York, NY: International Publishers).

Marx, Karl 1972, *Marx and Engels on Colonialism* (Moscow: Foreign Languages Publishing House).

Marx, Karl 1973, *Grundrisse: Foundations of the Critique of Political Economy*, translated by Martin Nicolaus (New York, NY: Vintage Books).

Marx, Karl 1975, *A Contribution to the Critique of Hegel's Philosophy of Law*, *Karl Marx/Frederick Engels Collected Works*, vol. 3 (New York, NY: International Publishers).

Marx, Karl 1975, *Capital: A Critique of Political Economy*, vol. 2: *The Process of Circulation of Capital*, edited by Friedrich Engels (New York, NY: International Publishers).

Marx, Karl 1975, *Capital: A Critique of Political Economy*, vol. 3: *The Process of Capitalist Production as a Whole*, edited by Friedrich Engels (New York, NY: International Publishers).

Marx, Karl and Friedrich Engels 1975, *The Holy Family or Critique of Critical Critique, Karl Marx/Frederick Engels Collected Works*, vol. 4 (New York, NY: International Publishers).

Marx, Karl 1975–2005, *Karl Marx/Frederick Engels Collected Works*, volumes 1–50 (New York, NY: International Publishers).

Marx, Karl 1976, *The Poverty of Philosophy: Answer to the Philosophy of Poverty by M. Proudhon, Karl Marx/Frederick Engels Collected Works*, vol. 6 (New York, NY: International Publishers).

Marx, Karl 1976, 'Debates on Freedom of the Press', *Karl Marx/Frederick Engels Collected Works*, vol. 1 (New York, NY: International Publishers).

Marx, Karl 1976, 'Debates on the Law on Thefts of Wood', Karl *Marx/Frederick Engels Collected Works*, vol. 1 (New York, NY: International Publishers).

Marx, Karl 1979, 'The British Rule in India', in *New York Herald Tribune, Karl Marx/Frederick Engels Collected Works*, vol. 12 (New York, NY: International Publishers).

Marx, Karl 1984, 'Comments on the North American Events', *Karl Marx/Frederick Engels Collected Works*, vol. 19 (New York, NY: International Publishers).

Marx, Karl 1994, 'Economic Manuscript of 1861–1863, Conclusion' (second draft of *Capital*), *Karl Marx/Frederick Engels Collected Works*, vol. 34 (New York, NY: International Publishers).

Marx, Karl 2011, 'Address of the International Workingmen's Association to Abraham Lincoln', letters between Marx and Lincoln, in *An Unfinished Revolution: Karl Marx and Abraham Lincoln*, edited by Robin Blackburn (London, UK: Verso Books).

Mason, Edward 1930, *The Paris Commune: An Episode in the History of the Socialist Movement* (New York, NY: Macmillan Company).

Mattick, Paul 1969, *Marx and Keynes: The Limits of the Mixed Economy* (Boston, MA: Extending Horizons Books).

Mayer, Thomas 1994, *Analytical Marxism* (Thousand Oaks, CA: Sage Publications).

McBride, William 1970, 'Marxism and Natural Law', *American Journal of Jurisprudence*, 15: 127–53.

McBride, William 1984, 'Rights and the Marxian Tradition', *Praxis International*, 4: 57–74.

McCarthy, George E. 1988, *Marx' Critique of Science and Positivism: The Methodological Foundations of Political Economy* (Dordrecht, NL: Kluwer Academic Publishers).

McCarthy, George E. 1990, *Marx and the Ancients: Classical Ethics, Social Justice, and Nineteenth-Century Political Economy* (Savage, MD: Rowman & Littlefield Publishers).

McCarthy, George E. (ed.) 1992, *Marx and Aristotle: Nineteenth Century German Social Theory and Classical Antiquity* (Savage, MD: Rowman and Littlefield Publishers).

McCarthy, George E. 1994, *Dialectics and Decadence: Echoes of Antiquity in Marx and Nietzsche* (Lanham, MD: Rowman & Littlefield Publishers).

McCarthy, George E. 2003, *Classical Horizons: The Origins of Sociology in Ancient Greece* (Albany, NY: State University of New York Press).

McCarthy, George E. 2006, 'In Praise of Classical Democracy: The Funeral Orations of Pericles and Marx', *Graduate Faculty Philosophy Journal*, Department of Philosophy, New School for Social Research, 27, 2: 205–27.

McCarthy, George E. 2009, *Dreams in Exile: Rediscovering Science and Ethics in Nineteenth-Century Social Theory* (Albany, NY: State University Press).

McCarthy, George E. 2015, 'Last of the Schoolmen: Natural Law and Social Justice in Karl Marx', in *Constructing Marxist Ethics*, edited by Michael Thompson (Leiden, NL: Brill Publishers).

McCarthy, Timothy 1978, *Marx and the Proletariat: A Study in Social Theory* (Westport, CT: Greenwood Press).

Medio, Alfred 1972, 'Profits and Surplus Value: Appearance and Reality in Capitalist Production', in *A Critique of Economic Theory*, edited by E.K. Hunt and Jesse Schwartz (Baltimore, MD: Penguin Books).

Meek, Ronald 1956, *Studies in the Labour Theory of Value* (New York, NY: International Publishers).

Meier, Christian 1990, *The Greek Discovery of Politics*, translated by David McLintock (Cambridge, MA: Harvard University Press).

Melzer, Arthur 1980, 'Rousseau and the Problem of Bourgeois Society', *American Political Science Review*, 74, 4: 1018–33.

Merriman, John 2014, *Massacre: The Life and Death of the Paris Commune* (New York, NY: Basic Books).

Mészáros, István 1970, *Marx's Theory of Alienation* (New York, NY: Harper & Row Publishers).

Mészáros, István 2005, *The Power of Ideology* (New York, NY: Zed Books).

Methe, Wolfgang 1981, *Ökologie und Marxismus* (Hannover: SOAK Verlag).

Miller, Richard 1992, 'Marx and Aristotle: A Kind of Consequentialism', in *Marx and Aristotle: Nineteenth-Century German Social Theory and Classical Antiquity*, edited by George E. McCarthy (Savage, MD: Rowman & Littlefield Publishers).

Mins, Henry 1948, 'Marx's Doctoral Dissertation', *Science and Society*, 12, 1: 157–69.

Montag, Warren 1999, *Bodies, Masses, Power: Spinoza and His Contemporaries* (London, UK: Verso).

Moore, Jason 2015, *Capitalism in the Web of Life: Ecology and the Accumulation of Capital* (London, UK: Verso).

Moreau, Pierre-François 1978, *Marx und Spinoza* (Hamburg: VSA Verlag).

Moseley, Fred (ed.) 1993, *Marx's Method in Capital: A Reexamination* (Atlantic Highlands, NJ: Humanities Press).

Moseley, Fred and Martha Campbell (eds.) 1997, *New Investigations of Marx's Method* (Atlantic Highlands, NJ: Humanities Press).

Moseley, Fred 2001, 'Introduction to Dussel: The Four Drafts of *Capital*', *Rethinking Marxism*, 13, 3: 1–9.

Moseley, Fred (ed.) 2005, *Marx's Theory of Money: Modern Appraisals* (Houndmills, Basingstoke, UK: Palgrave Macmillan).

Moseley, Fred 2013, 'Critique of Heinrich: Marx Did Not Abandon the Logical Structure', *Monthly Review*, Dec. 1: Online.

Moseley, Fred and Tony Smith (eds.) 2014, *Marx's Capital and Hegel's Logic: A Reexamination* (Leiden, NL: Brill Publishers).

Müller, Horst 1986, 'Ökonomischer Formwandel und Naturfrage', in *Natur und Marxistische Werttheorie*, edited by Hans Immler and Schmied-Kowarzik (Kassel: Kasseler Philosophische Schriften, 23).

Munz, Peter 1971, *The Place of Hooker in the History of Thought* (Westport, CT: Greenwood Press).

Murray, Patrick 1982, 'The Frankfurt School Critique of Technology', *Philosophy & Technology*, 5: 223–48.

Murray, Patrick 1988, *Marx's Theory of Scientific Knowledge* (Atlantic Highlands, NJ: Humanities Press International).

Murray, Patrick 1999, 'Marx's "Truly Social" Labor Theory of Value: Part I, Abstract Labour in Marxian Value Theory', *Historical Materialism*, 72, 3: 295–318.

Murray, Patrick 2000, 'Marx's "Truly Social" Labour Theory of Value: Part II, How Is Labour that Is Under the Sway of Capital Actually Abstract', *Historical Materialism*, 7, 1: 99–136.

Negri, Antonio 2000, *The Savage Anomaly: The Power of Spinoza's Metaphysics and Politics*, translated by Michael Hardt (Minneapolis, MN: University of Minnesota Press),

Neidleman, Jason Andrew 2000, *The General Will is Citizenship: Inquiries into French Political Thought* (Lanham, MD: Rowman & Littlefield Publishers).

Nichols, John 2011, 'Reading Karl Marx with Abraham Lincoln', *International Socialist Review*, 79: Online.

Nielsen, Kai 1981, 'Introduction', in *Marx and Morality*, edited by Kai Nielsen and Steven Patten, *Canadian Journal of Philosophy*, supplementary volume 7 (Guelph, Ontario: Canadian Association for Publishing in Philosophy).

Nielsen, Kai 1986, 'Marx, Engels and Lenin on Justice: The Critique of the Gotha Program', *Studies in Soviet Thought*, 32, 1: 23–63.

Nielsen, Kai 1988, 'Marx on Justice: The Tucker-Wood Thesis Revisited', *The University of Toronto Law Journal*, 38, 1: 28–63.

Nielsen, Kai 1989, 'Marx on Justice: The Tucker-Wood Thesis Revisited', *in Marxism and the Moral Point of View: Morality, Ideology, and Historical Materialism* (Boulder, CO.: Westview Press).

Nussbaum, Martha 1990, 'Aristotelian Social Democracy', in *Liberalism and the Good Life*, edited by R. Bruce Douglas, Gerald Mara, and Henry Richardson (New York, NY: Routledge).

Nussbaum, Martha 1992, 'Human Functioning and Social Justice: In Defense of Aristotelian Essentialism', *Political Theory*, 20, 2: 202–46.

Nussbaum, Martha 1992, 'Nature, Function, and Capability: Aristotle on Political Distribution', in *Marx and Aristotle: Nineteenth-Century German Social Theory and Classical Antiquity*, edited by George E. McCarthy (Savage, MD: Rowman & Littlefield Publishers).

Nussbaum, Martha 1997, 'Aristotle on Human Nature and the Foundations of Ethics', in *World, Mind, and Ethics: Essays on the Philosophy of Bernard Williams*, edited by J.E.J. Altham and Ross Harrison (Cambridge, UK: Cambridge University Press).

Nussbaum, Martha 2000, 'Aristotle, Politics, and Human Capabilities', *Ethics*, 111, 1: 102–40.

O'Connor, James 1988, 'Capitalism, Nature, Socialism: A Theoretical Introduction', *Capitalism Nature Socialism*, 1, 1: 11–38.

O'Connor, James 1991, 'On the Two Contradictions of Capitalism', *Capitalism Nature Socialism*, 2, 3: 107–9.

O'Connor, James 1998, *Natural Causes: Essays in Ecological Marxism* (New York, NY: Guilford Press).

Oakley, Francis 1997, 'Locke, Natural Law and God-again', *History of Political Thought*, 18, 4: 624–51.

Ober, Josiah 1989, *Mass and Elite in Democratic Athens* (Princeton, NJ: Princeton University Press).

Ober, Josiah 1998, *Political Dissent in Democratic Athens* (Princeton, NJ: Princeton University Press).

Ollman, Bertell 1975, *Alienation: Marx's Conception of Man in Capitalist Society* (Cambridge, UK: University of Cambridge Press).

Ollman, Bertell 2003, *Dance of the Dialectic: Steps in Marx's Method* (Urbana, IL: University of Illinois Press).

Ollman, Bertell and Kevin Anderson (eds.) 2012, *Karl Marx* (London, UK: Asgate Publishing House).

Pachter, Henry 1979, 'Marx and the Jews', *Dissent Magazine*, Fall: 450–67.

Pangle, Thomas, L. 1988, *The Spirit of Modern Republicanism: The Moral Vision of the American Founders and the Philosophy of Locke* (Chicago, IL: The University of Chicago Press).

Parsons, Howard (ed.) 1977, *Marx and Engels on Ecology* (Westport, CT: Greenwood Press).

Peffer, R.G. 1990, *Marxism, Morality, and Social Justice* (Princeton, NJ: Princeton University Press).

Pelczynski, Z.A. 1984, 'Political Community and Individual Freedom in Hegel's Philosophy of State', in *The State and Civil Society: Studies in Hegel's Political Philosophy*, edited by Z.A. Pelczynski (Cambridge, UK: Cambridge University Press).

Peled, Yoav 1992, 'From Theology to Sociology: Bruno Bauer and Karl Marx on the Question of Jewish Emancipation', *History of Political Thought*, 13, 3: 463–85.

Pendlebury, Gary 2005, *Action and Ethics in Aristotle and Hegel: Escaping the Malign Influences of Kant* (Farnham, UK: Ashgate Publishing Company).

Perrot, Michelle 1987, *Workers on Strike: France, 1871–1890*, translated by Chris Turner (New Haven, CT: Yale University Press).

Petry, Franz 1984, *Der soziale Gehalt der Marxschen Werttheorie* (Hannover: Verlag Willie Hammer).

Pilling, Geoffrey 1972, 'The Law of Value in Ricardo and Marx', *Economy and Society*, 1: 281–307.

Pilling, Geoffrey 1980, 'Marx's Critique of Classical Economics', in *Marx's Capital: Philosophy and Political Economy* (London, UK: Routledge & Kegan Paul).

Pilling, Geoffrey 1986, *The Crisis of Keynesian Economics: A Marxist View* (Totowa, NJ: Barnes & Noble Books).

Pirenne, Henri 1937, *Economic and Social History of Medieval Europe*, translated by I.E. Clegg (New York, NY: Harvest Book).

Pirenne, Henri 1956, *Medieval Cities: Their Origins and the Revival of Trade*, translated by Frank Halsey (Garden City, NY: Doubleday Anchor Books).

Plant, Raymond 1983, *Hegel, An Introduction* (London, UK: Basil Blackwell).

Popper, Karl 1971, *The Open Society and its Enemies*, vol. 2: *The High Tide of Prophecy: Hegel, Marx, and the Aftermath* (Princeton, NJ: Princeton University Press).

Postone, Moishe 1996, *Time, Labor, and Social Domination: A Reinterpretation of Marx's Critical Theory* (Cambridge, UK: Cambridge University Press).

Raico, Ralph 1988, 'John Prince Smith and the German Free-Trade Movement', in *Man, Economy, and Liberty: Essays in Honor of Murray N. Rothbard*, edited by Walter Block and Llewellyn H. Rockwell, Jr. (Auburn, AL: The Ludwig von Mises Institute).

Rashid, Haroon 2002, 'Making Sense of Marxian Concept of Justice', *Indian Philosophical Journal*, 29, 4: 445–69.

Rawls, John 1999, *A Theory of Justice* (Cambridge, MA: Harvard University Press).

Reader, Soran December 2005, 'Aristotle on Necessities and Needs', *Royal Institute of Philosophy Supplement*, 57: 113–36.

Reisert, Joseph 2003, *Jean-Jacques Rousseau: A Friend of Virtue* (Ithaca, NY: Cornel University Press).

Riedel, Manfred 1984, *Between Tradition and Revolution: The Hegelian Transformation of Political Philosophy*, translated by Walter Wright (Cambridge, UK: Cambridge University Press).

Ritter, Joachim 1984, *Hegel and the French Revolution: Essays on the Philosophy of Right*, translated by Richard Dien Winfield (Cambridge, MA: MIT Press).

Roberts, Jennifer 1994, *Athens on Trial: The Antidemocratic Tradition in Western Thought* (Princeton, NJ: Princeton University Press).

Roberts, Michael and Guglielmo Carchedi 2013, 'A Critique of Heinrich's, "Crisis Theory, the Law of the Tendency of the Profit Rate to Fall, and Marx's Studies in the 1870s"', *Monthly Review*, Dec. 1: Online.

Robinson, Cedric 2000, *Black Marxism: The Making of the Black Radical Tradition* (Chapel Hill, NC: University of North Carolina Press).

Rodden, John 2008, 'The lever must be applied in Ireland: Marx, Engels, and the Irish Question', *The Review of Politics*, 70, 4: 609–40.

Rommen, Heinrich 1998, *The Natural Law: A Study in Legal and Social History and Philosophy*, translated by Thomas Hanley (Indianapolis, IN: Liberty Fund).

Rosdolsky, Roman 1992, *The Making of Marx's Capital – Volume One* (London, UK: Pluto Press).

Rosenthal, Alexander 2008, *Crown under Law: Richard Hooker, John Locke, and the Ascent of Modern Constitutionalism* (Lanham, MD: Lexington Books).

Ross, Kristin 2015, *Communal Luxury: The Political Imaginary of the Paris Commune* (London, UK: Verso Books).

Rotenstreich, Nathan 1949, 'Between Rousseau and Marx', *Philosophy and Phenomenological Research*, 9, 4: 717–19.

Rousseau, Jean Jacques 1950, *A Discourse on the Origin of Inequality* (1754), in *The Social Contract and Discourses*, translated by G.D.H. Cole (New York, NY: E.P. Dutton and Company).

Rousseau, Jean Jacques 1950, *The Social Contract or Principles of Political Right*, in *The Social Contract and Discourses*, translated and with an introduction by G.D.H. Cole (New York, NY: E.P. Dutton and Company).

Routley, Val 1981, 'On Karl Marx as an Environmental Hero', *Environmental Ethics*, 3, 3: 237–44.

Rubel, Maximilien 1962, 'Notes on Marx's Conception of Democracy', *New Politics*, 1, 2: 83–85.

Ruben, David-Hillel 1979, *Marxism and Materialism: A Study in Marxist Theory of Knowledge* (Atlantic Highlands, NJ: Humanities Press).

Rubin, Isaak I. 1972, *Essays on Marx's Theory of Value*, translated by Milos Samardzija and Fredy Perlman (Detroit, MI: Black & Red).

Ryan, Alan 1965, 'Locke and the Dictatorship of the Bourgeoisie', *Political Studies*, 13, 2: 219–30.

Said, Edward 1978, *Orientalism* (New York, NY: Pantheon Books).

Sannwald, Rolf 1957, *Marx und die Antike*, edited by Edgar Salin and V.F. Wagner (Zurich: Polygraphischer Verlag).

Sayer, Derek 1987, *The Violence of Abstraction: The Analytical Foundations of Historical Materialism* (Oxford, UK: Oxford University Press).
Schaff, Adam 1970, *Marxism and the Human Individual*, translated by Olgierd Wojtasiewicz, edited by Robert Cohen (New York, NY: McGraw-Hill Book Company).
Schiller, Friedrich 1967, *Über die ästhetische Erziehung des Menschen* (München: Wilhelm Fink Verlag).
Schiller, Friedrich 1986, *On the Aesthetic Education of Man: In a Series of Letters*, translated by Reginald Snell (New York, NY: Ungar Publishing Company).
Schlatter, Richard 1973, *Private Property: The History of an Idea* (New York, NY: Russell & Russell).
Schlosberg, David 2007, *Defining Environmental Justice* (Oxford, UK: Oxford University Press).
Schmidt, Alfred 1973, *The Concept of Nature in Marx* (London: NLB).
Schmiede, Rudi 1973, *Grundprobleme der Marxschen Akkumulations- und Krisentheorie* (Frankfurt/Main: Athenäum Verlag).
Schmied-Kowarzik, Wolfdietrich 1984, *Das dialektische Verhältnis des Menschen zur Natur. Philosophiegeschichtliche Studien zur Naturproblematik bei Karl Marx* (Freiburg: Verlag Karl Alber).
Schmied-Kowarzik, Wolfdietrich 1984, 'Die Entfremdung der gesellschaftlichen Produktion von der Natur und ihre revolutionäre Überwindung', in *Marx und die Naturfrage*, edited by Hans Immler and Wolfdietrich Schmied-Kowarzik (Hamburg: VSA Verlag).
Schmitt, Richard 2003, *Alienation and Freedom* (Boulder, CO: Westview Press).
Schneider, Michael 1975, *Neurosis and Civilization: A Marxist/Freudian Synthesis*, translated by Michael Roloff (New York, NY: The Seabury Press).
Schrader, Fred 1985, *Substanz und Begriff: Zur Spinoza-Rezeption Marxens* (Leiden, NL: Brill Publishers).
Schraffenberger, Donny 2011, 'Karl Marx and the American Civil War', *International Socialist Review*, 80: Online.
Schroyer, Trent 1983, 'Critique of the Instrumental Interest in Nature', *Social Research*, 50, 1: 158–84.
Schulkind, Eugene (ed.) 1971, *The Paris Commune of 1871: The View from the Left* (New York, NY: Grove Press).
Schwartz, Joel 1985, 'Liberalism and the Jewish Connection: A Study of Spinoza and the Young Marx', *Political Theory*, 13, 1: 58–84.
Schwartz, Nancy 1979, 'Distinction Between Public and Private Life: Marx on the zoon politikon', *Political Theory*, 7, 2: 245–66.
Scott, William 1977, *In Pursuit of Happiness: American Conceptions of Property from the Seventeenth to the Twentieth Century* (Bloomington, IN: Indiana University Press).
Shafer, David 2005, *The Paris Commune: French Politics, Culture, and Society at the*

Crossroads of the Revolutionary Tradition and Revolutionary Socialism (New York, NY: Palgrave Macmillian Press).

Shapiro, Anne-Louise 1985, *Housing the Poor of Paris, 1850–1902* (Madison, WI: University of Wisconsin Press).

Sharp, Hasana 2011, *Spinoza and the Politics of Renaturalization* (Chicago, IL: University of Chicago Press).

Shklar, Judith 1971, 'Hegel's Phenomenology: An Elegy for Hellas', in *Hegel's Political Philosophy: Problems and Perspectives*, edited by Z.A. Pelczynski (Cambridge, UK: Cambridge University Press).

Shklar, Judith 1978, *Freedom and Independence: A Study of the Political Ideas of Hegel's 'Phenomenology of Mind'* (Cambridge, UK: Cambridge University Press).

Shklar, Judith 1988, *Men and Citizens: A Study of Rousseau's Social Theory* (Cambridge, UK: Cambridge University Press).

Sinclair, R.K. 1988, *Democracy and Participation in Athens* (Cambridge, UK: Cambridge University Press).

Skinner, Quentin 1978, *The Foundations of Modern Political Thought*, vol. 2 (Cambridge, UK: Cambridge University Press).

Slater, Philip 1970, *The Pursuit of Loneliness: American Culture at the Breaking Point* (Boston, MA: Beacon Press).

Smith, Merrit Roe and Leo Marx (eds.) 1994, *Does Technology Drive History? The Dilemma of Technological Determinism* (Boston, MA: The MIT Press).

Smith, Neil 1984, *Uneven Development: Nature, Capital and the Production of Space* (Oxford, UK: Basil Blackwell).

Smith, Steven B. 1989, *Hegel's Critique of Liberalism: Rights in Context* (Chicago, IL: University of Chicago Press).

Smith, Steven B. 1989, 'Hegel and the French Revolution: An Epitaph for Republicanism', *Social Research*, 56, 1: 233–61.

Smith, Steven B. 1994, 'Spinoza's Democratic Turn: Chapter 16 of the Theologico-Political Treatise', *The Review of Metaphysics*, 48, 2: 359–88.

Sohn-Rethel, Alfred 1978, *Intellectual and Manual Labour: A Critique of Epistemology* (Atlantic Highlands, NJ: Humanities Press).

Solomon, Robert 1983, *In the Spirit of Hegel: A Study of G.W.F. Hegel's 'Phenomenology of Spirit'* (New York, NY: Oxford University Press).

Soper, Kate 1993, 'A Theory of Human Need', *New Left Review*, 197: 113–28.

Spinoza, Benedict 1998, *Theological-Political Treatise*, translated by Samuel Shirley (Indianapolis, IN: Hackett Publishing Company).

Springborg, Patricia 1981, *The Problem of Human Needs and the Critique of Civilization* (London, UK: George Allen & Unwin).

Springborg, Patricia 1984, 'Aristotle and the Problem of Needs', *History of Political Thought*, 5, 3: 393–424.

Springborg, Patricia 1984, 'Karl Marx on Democracy, Participation, Voting, and Equality', *Political Theory*, 12, 4: 537–56.
Springborg, Patricia 1984, 'Marx, Democracy and the Ancient Polis', *Critical Philosophy*, 1, 1: 47–66.
Stanley, John 1993, 'The Marxism of Marx's Doctoral Dissertation', *Journal of the History of Philosophy*, 33, 1: 133–58.
Ste. Croix, Geoffrey E. Maurice 1989, *The Class Struggle in the Ancient Greek World* (Ithaca, NY: Cornel University Press).
Stewart, John Hall (ed.) 1951, *A Documentary Survey of the French Revolution* (New York, NY: Macmillan Company).
Stockton, David 1991, *The Classical Athenian Democracy* (Oxford, UK: Oxford University Press).
Strauss, Leo 1965, *Natural Right and History* (Chicago, IL: University of Chicago Press).
Sullivan, J.P. (ed.) 1975, *Marxism and the Classics*, Arethusa, 8, 1.
Sweet, Robert 2002, *Marx, Morality and the Virtue of Beneficence* (Lanham, MD: University Press of America).
Swenson, James 2000, *On Jean-Jacques Rousseau: Considered as One of the First Authors of the Revolution* (Stanford, CA: Stanford University Press).
Tawney, Richard 1926, *Religion and the Rise of Capitalism: A Historical Study* (New York, NY: Harcourt, Brace and Company).
Taylor, Charles 1966, 'Marxism and Empiricism', in *British Analytic Philosophy*, edited by Bernard Williams and Alan Montefiore (London, UK: Prometheus Books).
Taylor, Charles 1979, *Hegel and Modern Society* (Cambridge, UK: Cambridge University Press).
Teeple, G. 1990, 'The Doctoral Dissertation of Karl Marx', *History of Political Thought*, 11, 1: 81–118.
Thompson, Michael (ed.) 2015, *Constructing Marxist Ethics: Critique, Normativity, Praxis* (Leiden, NL: Brill Publishers).
Tierney, Brian 1997, *The Idea of Natural Rights: Studies on Natural Rights, Natural Law and Church Law 1150–1625* (Atlanta, GA: Scholar's Press).
Tombs, Robert 1981, *The Paris Commune* (Cambridge, UK: Cambridge University Press).
Tucker, Robert 1961, *Philosophy and Myth in Karl Marx* (Cambridge, UK: Cambridge University Press).
Tucker, Robert 1969, *The Marxian Revolutionary Idea* (New York, NY: W.W. Norton and Company).
Tully, James 1980, *A Discourse on Property: John Locke and his Adversaries* (Cambridge, UK: Cambridge University Press).
Vésinier, Pierre 1872, *History of the Commune*, translated by J.V. Walsh (London, UK: Chapman and Hall).

Volpe, Galvan dela 1979, *Rousseau and Marx*, translated by John Fraser (Atlantic Highlands, NJ: Humanities Press).
Walker, K.J. 1979, 'Ecological Limits and Marxian Thought', *Politics*, 14, 1: 29–46.
Walsh, W.H. 1969, *Hegelian Ethics* (New York, NY: St. Martin's Press).
Ward, Lee 2011, 'Benedict Spinoza on the Naturalness of Democracy', *Canadian Political Science Review*, 5, 1: 55–73.
Wartofsky, Marx 1961–62, 'Marx on the Jewish Question: A Review', *The Philosophical Forum*, 19, 83: Online.
Weber, Max 1966, *The City*, edited and translated by Don Martindale and Gertrud Neuwirth (New York, NY: The Free Press).
Weinreb, Lloyd 1987, *Natural Law and Justice* (Cambridge, MA: Harvard University Press).
Wendling, Amy 2009, *Marx on Technology and Alienation* (Houndmills, Basingstoke, UK: Palgrave Macmillan).
Wilde, Lawrence 1998, *Ethical Marxism and its Radical Critics* (Houndmills, Basingstoke, UK: Macmillan Press).
Williams, Roger 1969, *The French Revolution of 1870–1871* (New York, NY: W.W. Norton and Company).
Wilson, Colette 2007, *Paris and the Commune, 1871–78: The Politics of Forgetting* (Manchester, UK: Manchester University Press).
Winroth, Anders 2004, *The Making of Gratian's Decretum* (Cambridge, UK: Cambridge University Press).
Wood, Allen 1979, 'Marx on Right and Justice: A Reply to Husami', *Philosophy and Public Affairs*, 8, 3: 267–95.
Wood, Allen 1980, 'The Marxian Critique of Justice', in *Marx, Justice, and History*, edited by Marshall Cohen, Thomas Nagel, and Thomas Scanlon (Princeton, NJ: Princeton University Press).
Wood, Allen 1981, *Karl Marx* (London, UK: Routledge and Kegan Paul).
Wood, Ellen 1988, *Peasant-Citizen and Slave: The Foundations of Athenian Democracy* (London, UK: Verso).
Yolton, John 1991, 'Locke on the Law of Nature', in *John Locke: Critical Assessments*, edited by Richard Aschraft (New York, NY: Routledge).
Young, Gary, 'Doing Marx Justice', in *Marx and Morality*, edited by Kai Nielsen and Steven Patten, *Canadian Journal of Philosophy*, supplementary volume 7 (Guelph, Ontario: Canadian Association for Publishing in Philosophy, 1981).
Zuckert, Michael 1994, *Natural Rights and the New Republicanism* (Princeton, NJ: Princeton University Press).
Zuckert, Michael 2002, *Launching Liberalism: On Lockean Political Philosophy* (Lawrence, KS: University of Kansas Press).

Index

abstractionism   122, 302, 310
abstract labor   230, 310, 318–19, 324, 343–45
abstract rights   74, 84, 91–92, 97, 105, 108, 120, 123, 125–26
abundance   6, 196, 210, 357
accumulation   42–43, 182, 203, 216, 228, 328, 334–35, 338, 348, 351, 354, 356–59, 375
aesthetics   172, 193, 220
agriculture   34, 41, 102, 212–15, 228–29, 321, 347, 367
alienated labour   166, 174–75, 186–87, 196, 200–201, 203, 208–9, 224, 238, 268, 311
alienation   4–6, 95–96, 164–70, 172–80, 185–89, 193, 195–202, 204–7, 213–14, 220–21, 223–26, 254–55, 268–69, 321–24, 349–51
Althusser, Louis   125, 363
American Civil War   292–93, 306, 308
ancient Hebrews   35, 165, 190
antiquity   5, 20, 77, 96, 100–101, 145, 341–42, 377
Arendt, Hannah   159, 161
Aristotle   7–10, 18–23, 55–58, 72–73, 101–2, 111–14, 120–22, 162–65, 188–89, 264, 267–69, 309–17, 319–20, 338–44
Aristotle's ethics   59, 65, 154, 232, 368
Athenian democracy   303, 307
Avineri, Shlomo   12, 112, 119, 124–25, 160, 185, 363

Bacon, Francis   209, 225
banking   21, 45–48, 61, 139, 152, 181, 347
barbarism   53, 91–92, 144, 186
Bauer, Bruno   130–36, 138, 140–44, 148, 153, 163
beauty   10, 80, 94, 169, 172–73, 186–87, 191, 193, 200, 206, 248, 361
Bentham, Jeremy   69, 82, 271
Bernstein, Eduard   263–64
Bookchin, Murray   221, 223
bourgeoisie   62, 90, 174, 256, 262, 279, 303, 348, 353
Buchanan, Allen   6, 12, 155–57, 160, 184–85, 269
Burkett, Paul   220–21, 228–31

Calvinism   31, 60, 180
capacities   12, 17, 82–83, 145, 183, 226, 255, 259, 298, 324–25
capital   2, 111, 165–67, 174–77, 203, 212–20, 226–32, 246–47, 279–81, 283–84, 310–14, 317–19, 321–60
capitalism   2–7, 12–14, 16–18, 154–59, 165–67, 179–80, 192–94, 211–16, 245–47, 263–66, 310–13, 320–23, 336–40, 342–45, 350–54
Cassirer, Ernst   16, 155
chrematistics (*chrematistike*)   11, 19, 21–22, 122, 156, 184, 191, 271, 309, 312, 323, 339, 342, 358
Christianity   32, 72–73, 76–80, 95, 100, 111–13, 120, 130–32, 135, 137, 143, 158, 181
citizenship   18–19, 21–22, 65–66, 132–33, 140, 142, 148, 150, 161, 188, 191–92, 197, 199, 270, 272
civil society   30–36, 50, 52–55, 58–62, 67–68, 81–82, 88–90, 98–107, 120–24, 134, 136–51, 153, 155–57, 159–61, 251–54
classical democracy   10, 106, 110, 121, 303, 307
commodities   2–3, 10, 14, 166, 168, 201, 206, 243, 265–66, 269, 310–26, 328–29, 344–52, 357, 359
Communards   278, 292, 296–98, 300–303, 305–6
crisis theory   21, 193, 339, 350, 352, 354

Darwin, Charles   165, 211, 229
Declaration of Independence   65–66, 293–94
Declaration of the Rights of Man and of the Citizen   2, 130, 144–45, 149, 158, 161, 270, 294, 308
'Declaration to the French People' (Paris Commune)   285–87, 294, 298, 302, 304–5
democratic socialism   19–20, 22, 154, 160, 178, 185, 194, 197, 216, 219–20, 272
Democritus   193, 222
dialectic of nature   192, 201, 207, 210, 212, 215–16, 222, 226, 228
dictatorship   62, 263, 265, 304
disproportionality of labor   335, 359
distributive justice   6, 8, 10, 15, 21–23, 62, 64, 174–76, 235–37, 239–41, 243, 245–55, 261, 263–67, 269–71

INDEX

Duns Scotus   56–57, 69, 153
Dupré, Louis   87, 117, 124, 153
Dussel, Enrique   341–42

ecological justice   192–93, 195–97, 199, 201, 203, 205, 207, 209, 211, 213, 215–17, 219, 221, 223, 225
economic democracy   22, 109, 112, 163, 183, 194, 199, 272, 278, 282, 292, 294, 297, 328
economic justice   8–9, 11, 19, 29, 154, 216, 219, 255–56, 258, 265, 271, 291, 309–59
economists   228, 319, 346, 349, 354
    agrarian   229
    classical   166, 316, 322, 345, 349–50, 352, 354
    liberal   256
Emancipation Proclamation   294, 307–8
empiricism   4, 69, 73, 81–85, 88–89, 114–15, 117, 119, 121, 123–24, 126, 154, 166, 172, 358
Engels, Friedrich   3, 5, 11–12, 15, 217, 223, 225–30, 232, 261, 263–64, 306–8
Enlightenment   9, 16, 20, 73–74, 77, 81, 85, 95–96, 113, 115, 119, 163, 165, 168, 173
Epicurus   163, 165, 193, 211, 222
equal rights   15, 81, 131, 151, 235, 237, 239, 252, 266, 270, 292, 297
ethical community   9–10, 72, 89, 91, 93–99, 101–2, 104–6, 109–12, 120, 122, 125–26, 154–55, 248, 250, 309
ethical life   33, 73–74, 79–81, 88–91, 94–98, 100–102, 104–8, 115, 117–18, 120–21, 123, 126, 156
exchange value   10, 14, 157, 230–31, 266, 269, 310, 313–16, 319–29, 332, 335, 339, 344–46, 352, 358
expropriation   174, 272, 283, 306

family   51, 57, 89, 92, 98–101, 106–8, 116, 118, 121, 123, 126, 178, 182, 249–50, 311
fetishism   201, 321, 344, 351
Feuerbach, Ludwig   125, 171, 220, 223, 225
Fichte, Gottfried   80, 114
Filmer, Robert   31, 63, 70
Foster, John Bellamy   192, 211, 220–23, 228
Fourier, Charles   14, 175, 310
French Revolution   19–20, 95, 116, 122, 141, 144, 185, 187, 292, 294, 296–97, 299, 304–5

friendship   8–10, 20–22, 32, 37—38, 42, 55, 145, 163, 167, 178–79, 188, 191, 197, 205, 210, 247–49, 251, 267, 283, 309, 312, 337
Fromm, Erich   19, 64, 186, 224, 367

German Idealism   13, 22, 156, 164–65, 183, 190, 219, 222, 310
good life   220–21, 33, 65, 69, 94, 119, 164, 176, 183, 192, 195, 216, 219, 250, 272, 309, 311, 337, 342
Gotha Program   1, 3, 11, 14–15, 235–37, 241, 249, 251, 253, 255–57, 260–61, 263–67, 270–71, 294, 297
Greek polity   50, 76, 81, 83, 90, 105, 117, 119, 188
Grossmann, Henryk   343, 348, 353
Grotius, Hugo   57, 59–61, 65, 69

Habermas, Jürgen   71, 114, 184, 187, 223, 231
Hegel, Georg Friedrich Wilhelm   5, 19–20, 72–91, 93–126, 154–56, 163–66, 170–72, 194, 196, 198, 353–54
Heidegger, Martin   68
Heller, Agnes   20, 267
historical materialism   1–2, 4, 6–7, 11–18, 156, 158, 192, 202, 229–30, 245–47, 260–61, 267, 270–71, 342–43
Hobbes, Thomas   27–30, 34–35, 38–39, 46, 51, 53, 57–60, 67–69, 82, 143
Hölderlin, Friedrich   114, 163
Honneth, Axel   13, 112
Hooker, Richard   27–28, 31–35, 38–39, 46, 48, 53, 55, 57–60, 67, 69, 72, 153–54, 164, 167, 189
Horkheimer, Max   154, 221
households   8, 46, 60, 197, 218–19, 236, 267, 303, 311, 313, 342, 346
human creativity   9, 16, 88, 112, 126, 172–73, 184, 206–7, 215, 218, 248, 309, 339
human dignity   1, 8, 22, 32, 39, 152, 170, 183, 191, 292, 308, 339
human emancipation   4, 14–15, 22, 55, 109, 130, 133–35, 142–44, 149, 151, 156, 159, 160–65, 174, 176, 178, 204, 205, 216, 235, 247, 251, 253, 270, 272–3, 279, 281, 283, 291–92, 295–96, 297, 309, 328, 340–41
human nature   19–20, 57–58, 81–85, 109–11, 113, 151–52, 168–69, 171–72, 177–78, 183–85, 196–97, 207, 218–19, 222–24, 231–32

ideology   11, 14, 18, 134, 138, 140–41, 155–56, 184, 187, 303, 348, 351, 365, 369
industrial production   168–69, 176, 207, 213, 215, 253–54, 257, 305, 311, 313, 316–17, 329–30, 336, 345, 350
industry   2, 6, 47–48, 52, 206–9, 212–15, 225, 228–29, 240, 330, 334–36, 345, 347, 350–51, 355–56

Jacobins   19, 285, 305
Jefferson, Thomas   58, 65–66, 158, 292–93, 308
Jewish Question   108–9, 130–37, 141, 145, 149–50, 152–53, 155, 158–61, 163–64, 252–54, 279
Judaism   125, 130, 132, 135–36, 143, 153

Kant, Immanuel   19–20, 73–75, 77, 79–80, 84–88, 110, 113–23, 125–26, 156–57, 196, 198, 223, 339, 342
Kantian   79, 95, 98, 100, 116, 119–20, 199
Kautsky, Karl   158, 263–64
Korsch, Karl   221, 265
Kovel, Joel   195, 223, 231

labour power   2–3, 236, 244, 255, 258–59, 265, 321–22, 324–26, 328, 331, 333, 344, 346–50, 356, 358
Lassalle, Ferdinand   235–36, 238, 257–58, 263–64, 271, 292, 294
legal justice   8, 15, 18, 28, 129, 143–61, 241
liberalism   17–18, 30, 53–55, 70–75, 79–85, 87–91, 95–97, 107–9, 113–17, 119–21, 144–45, 155–58, 168–69, 179, 235–36
Lincoln, Abraham   272, 291–95, 306–8
Locke, John   10, 27–51, 57, 59–61, 70, 73, 154, 189, 203, 236, 272
Lukács, Georg   112, 117, 221, 223, 226, 231

Machiavelli, Nicholas   120, 125
MacIntyre, Alasdair   20, 70, 112, 116–17, 120, 372
MacPherson, C.B.   41, 49, 60–64, 68, 70, 152
Marcuse, Herbert   117, 120, 222, 230–32
market economy   18–19, 22, 27–28, 30, 46, 48–50, 53, 72, 98–99, 101–2, 141–43, 176, 188, 246, 320–21
Marx, Karl   1–23, 105–12, 122–27, 129–71, 173–81, 183–90, 195–233, 235–41, 243–72, 277–84, 291–97, 300–303, 306–60
Marxism   11, 14–15, 116–17, 124, 154–55, 157–58, 160, 220–24, 267–68
materialism   2, 6, 73, 78, 147, 154, 220, 223, 247, 251, 284, 294, 359, 367
Mattick, Paul   343, 344, 353, 355, 357–58
metabolic rift   193, 213, 219, 221, 228, 313, 357
Mészáros, István   19, 161, 185, 220, 223, 226, 268
monarchy   19, 21, 91, 104–5, 123, 148, 235, 237, 287
Montesquieu, Charles-Louis de Secondat   77, 113, 117, 123, 125, 282
moral economy (*oikonomike*)   8, 19, 22, 46, 80, 188, 311, 320, 328, 332

Napoleon, Louis   215, 260, 273, 297–98
natural law   7–11, 27–38, 42–43, 45–46, 48–78, 84–89, 91–94, 104–5, 108–18, 125–26, 129–30, 151–55, 179–81, 268, 336–40
natural rights   18, 29–31, 33–43, 45–47, 49–57, 59–77, 80–81, 89–90, 105–6, 108–12, 129–30, 132–41, 147–50, 168–70
Naturphilosophie   194, 208, 211, 223
needs, theory of   101, 121, 170, 175, 250, 268–69
Nussbaum, Martha   13, 18, 190, 232, 267

Objective Spirit   16, 19–20, 75, 95–97, 98, 102, 171–72, 179, 186
Of the Laws of Ecclesiastical Polity   27, 31, 57–58
Ollman, Bertell   19, 161, 186, 308, 336, 358
organic composition of capital   5, 313, 329–31, 350–51, 354–55, 358
overproduction of capital   11, 213, 313, 334, 347, 357

Paine, Thomas   65–67
Phenomenology of Spirit   73, 95–96, 100, 111, 114, 119–20, 164, 172, 196
phronesis (practical wisdom)   19, 21–22, 71, 110, 183, 191, 199, 284, 309
Plato   5, 16, 32, 67, 89, 113, 185
political emancipation   18, 22, 54, 130–50, 165, 174, 177, 247, 251–53, 262, 270, 283, 291, 293
political economy   13, 15–16, 21, 174–75, 192–

INDEX

94, 210–11, 213–14, 222–23, 227–28, 264, 309–10, 312–14, 339–43, 353–54
political justice   8–9, 19, 20–21, 65, 129, 236, 272–73, 275, 277, 279, 281–307
positive laws   38, 43, 47, 52, 64, 66, 69–70, 74, 82, 118, 146, 148, 266
practical reason   19–21, 32–33, 73, 84–89, 91, 94, 96–97, 99, 115–21, 123, 126, 152, 154, 196, 199–200
private property   35–37, 40–47, 51, 53–56, 60–61, 65–67, 107–8, 137–38, 142–43, 159–60, 173–80, 201–4, 236–38, 281, 324–25
producers' associations   268, 286, 309, 311–12, 338
productive forces   3, 156, 195, 216, 220–21, 223, 228–32, 259, 271, 335, 337, 345, 355–56
Proudhon, Pierre-Joseph   174–75, 271, 305–6
Pufendorf, Samuel   59–61, 70

reciprocal justice   21–22, 102, 236, 249, 272, 344
reciprocity   9–10, 18–19, 22, 60, 78, 101–02, 121, 157, 188, 191, 210, 249, 309, 311, 338, 343–44, 346
revolution   2, 6, 95, 112–13, 117, 120, 158–60, 256–57, 259–60, 276–77, 296–308
Ricardo, David   206, 322, 329, 332, 338, 342–43, 345, 349, 351–52, 354, 356, 358
rights of man (economic rights)   4, 108, 134, 145, 148, 252, 262, 270
rights of the citizen (political rights)   15, 54, 108, 134, 141, 145, 147, 157, 160–61, 163, 247, 251–53, 287–88, 294, 297
Rousseau, Jean-Jacques   19, 108–10, 113, 122, 124–25, 145, 148, 154–55, 158, 165, 266, 282
Rubin, Isaak   343, 355

Saint-Simon, Henri de   14, 175, 310
Schiller, Friedrich   114, 163, 165, 172–73, 186–87, 191, 200, 220, 268
Schmidt, Alfred   229–30
Schmied-Kowarzik, Wolfdietrich   207–8, 220–23, 225, 342
scholastics   70, 76, 113, 152, 181, 190
self-determination   16–19, 76–79, 104, 109–11, 122–23, 126, 154–55, 165, 168–70, 178–79, 191–92, 196–97, 247–48, 312–13, 338–39

self-realisation   1, 4, 8–12, 22, 72, 78, 110–12, 116, 122, 145, 155–56, 178, 183, 185, 188, 191–92, 199, 247–51, 266–69, 284, 309, 341, 355
Sittlichkeit (ethical life of the community)   8, 22, 66, 73, 79, 81, 89, 91, 111, 114, 117–20, 122, 156, 165, 209
slavery   4, 36, 78–79, 132, 259, 282, 292–95, 306–8, 344
Smith, Adam   101, 114, 116–17, 122, 145, 152, 154, 229–30, 232, 258, 269, 271, 309, 315, 329, 332, 345, 348–49, 351, 354, 356
social contract   28, 30, 48, 53, 59, 74, 84, 108, 124, 142, 158–59, 266, 282, 303
social justice   7, 9–11, 18–20, 108–12, 129–30, 160–64, 183–85, 190, 215–18, 252–54, 266–67, 272–73, 309–11, 327, 340–41
social labour   237, 321, 325, 333, 347
social life   79, 119, 164, 174, 176, 178, 180, 225, 270
social metabolism   193, 210–12, 214–16, 199, 216, 226, 230
social order   16, 30, 71, 74, 77, 217, 238, 287, 297
social organisation   54, 154, 168, 171, 185, 187, 192, 196, 244, 255, 311, 318
social praxis   10, 18, 99, 112, 194, 201–4, 206–10, 218–19, 223, 309, 311, 338, 345
social problems   137, 255, 312
social product   232, 249
  total   240–41, 253–55, 265, 270
social production   226, 314, 344, 351, 355, 358
social reality   6, 17, 65, 106, 121, 139–40, 161, 189, 206, 252, 268, 316, 340
social relations of production   4, 15, 11, 156, 176, 190, 192, 194, 216, 223, 229–32, 238, 265, 269–70, 291, 311, 317, 319, 320, 322, 324, 338, 348–50
species being   10, 170–71, 178, 196, 204, 206, 310
Spence, Thomas   66
Spinoza, Benedict   70, 75, 106, 108–9, 125, 153, 165, 194
spoilage   37–38, 42, 45, 47–48, 53, 60–61, 163, 182
state of nature   27–36, 38–48, 50–52, 57, 59–64, 67–68, 74, 81–84, 104–5, 112, 142, 148, 152, 165, 168

Strauss, Leo   47, 59, 61, 62, 67–68, 70
surplus value   14–16, 230, 236, 238, 313, 319, 321–25, 327, 329–33, 337, 340, 344–51, 354–58
Sweezy, Paul   345, 358

tendential fall in the rate of profit   11, 211, 313, 351–53, 358
Thiers, Adolphe   274–77, 281, 297–300
Tucker, Robert   1–3, 6, 11–16, 185, 246, 296, 347
Tucker-Wood thesis   1–2, 7, 11–14, 16, 18, 22, 326, 348

underconsumption   212, 334, 356–57, 359
utilitarianism   2, 69, 119, 173, 179, 183, 205, 251, 269, 284
utility   29, 78, 85, 102, 121, 182, 212, 314, 316, 320, 328, 344
use value   238, 242, 259, 314–16, 318–27, 335, 344, 346, 356, 358

value production   21, 196, 214–16, 309, 340, 345, 350, 353, 357
violence   19, 27, 30, 33, 49, 59–60, 62, 67–68, 146, 190, 201, 230, 266
virtue   9, 20, 32–33, 65, 77–78, 90–93, 111, 116, 118, 121, 167, 188, 192–93, 216, 247, 311–12, 337

wage labour   10, 46, 53–54, 152, 169, 193, 199, 204, 213, 244, 251–52, 258–59, 262, 269–70, 328–29
wage slavery   237, 272, 283, 291–92, 325, 327, 335, 347
Washington, George   58, 293
Weber, Max   63, 113, 187, 231
Wood, Allen   1, 11–12, 15, 185, 246, 347
worker co-operatives   236, 244, 288, 301
workplace justice   8, 10, 18, 150, 163–90, 196, 216, 251

Young, Gary   1, 7, 12

740
(740) 427-5849

Office Manager
(740) 427-8835
(740) 427-5809

Dept. of Sociology
KENYON COLL

Treahorn House
105 W. Brooklyn St.
Room 202
OHIO 43022
GAMBIER